The Assembly of The Lord

28.16

The Assembly of The Lord

Politics and Religion in the Westminster Assembly
and the 'Grand Debate'

by

ROBERT S. PAUL

T. & T. CLARK
36 GEORGE STREET
EDINBURGH

13411

Typeset by John Swain and Son (Glasgow) Ltd.
Printed and bound by Billings, Worcestershire
for
T. & T. CLARK LTD., EDINBURGH

0 567 09341 7

FIRST PRINTED . . . 1985

Contents

ACKNOWLEDGMENT

Quotations from the Minutes of the Sessions of the Assembly of Divines at Westminster, 1643–1652, are taken from the transcript of the original manuscript made by E. Maunde Thompson in 1868 and held by the Library of New College, University of Edinburgh.

PREFACE

"Forth from the war emerging, a book I have made, The words of my book nothing, the drift everything."

Walt Whitman

A preface, I suspect, should attempt to do only three things – first, offer the author's excuse for writing the book; secondly, provide some reason why anyone should read it; and thirdly, acknowledge those without whose help the work would never have been finished.

The reason for the book goes back a long way. In a sense it continues my interest in the relation of politics and religion that had intrigued me when writing *The Lord Protector*, and this interest was re-kindled when I was asked by a denominational publisher over twenty years ago to edit a new edition of *An Apologeticall Narration*. I was immediately struck by the lack of any recent treatment of 'the Grand Debate', or indeed of any thorough study of the Westminster Assembly. This book is simply a response to the pious hope I expressed then that before too long "a fuller account of that very significant event may appear." Since then a few studies of the Assembly have been published, but none of them in my view quite meets the need. As a result I began this piece of research which, despite frequent interruptions for other writing obligations, was to last for over two decades and has become almost an obsession for the last ten years. So much for the author, who could probably pile up excuses, but whose basic plea must be that having felt the need, he could not remain satisfied until it was addressed.

As for the prospective reader, Walt Whitman's exuberant words apply here, for it is urged that if we are to understand the reason for the three hundred years of church history that emerged from the Westminster Assembly and the Grand Debate, we must look beyond the debates themselves to the social and political context of that time: the words are nothing, 'the drift everything.' The book is written simply to help the reader understand that drift.

That leaves me simply with the pleasurable task of acknowledging those who have contributed to this work over the years. First the support I have received from institutions I have served, the Hartford Seminary Foundation and later Pittsburgh

ix

Theological Seminary, for some of the work was begun and carried forward on Sabbatical leaves that they generously granted. A special word of gratitude, however, is due to the institution I serve at present, Austin Presbyterian Theological Seminary, and to its President, Dr. Jack M. Maxwell, for support that goes far beyond the bounds of professional obligation.

During the years I have received help from many different libraries in chasing obscure references and discovering the resources in seventeenth century literature; the British Library, the Humanities Research Center of the University of Texas at Austin, and Dr. Williams's Library in London all rendered invaluable assistance. My thanks are also due to Miss Owen of the Sion College Library in London, to Calvin Klemt, the Librarian of the Stitt Library at Austin, to Mrs. Shadlock, of the Plume Library in Maldon, Essex, who put the resources of that fascinating little library at my disposal during my bibliographic forays into England, and to Dikran Hadidian, formerly Librarian of the Case Memorial Library in Hartford but now of the Barbour Library in Pittsburgh. He has contributed so much beyond the call of duty and the claims of friendship. Dr. Kenneth Peters helped with the preparation of the indexes.

There are two others without whose loyalty and painstaking work this undertaking could not have been completed. Dorothy (Mrs. John) Andrews, my secretary at Austin, wrestled with seventeenth century spelling and punctuation and with my own English idioms to produce the miracle of a legible typescript. My profound gratitude goes to her, and to my wife, Eunice, who often acted as an unpaid research assistant, and supported me in so many ways in some of the more tedious aspects of the research. I hope the end will justify the means.

Robert S. Paul
Austin, Texas
Lent, 1983.

INTRODUCTION

I

A biography of the historian, Lord Macaulay, stimulated a reviewer to remark that it is difficult to write an exciting book about a sedentary life. It is, I suspect, even more difficult to write an exciting book about a sedentary event, and few events would appear to be more essentially sedentary than a conclave of seventeenth century clergymen debating theology.

What provides the Westminster Assembly with its excitement, at least for this writer, is not only its importance in church history, but more particularly the place it occupies in the English Civil War and its influence, through that significant segment of national history, on the forms of society that emerged among the Anglo-Saxon peoples. If a respected modern historian of the American religious scene can affirm that in the 1960s "the great Puritan epoch in America's spiritual history was drawing to a painful and tumultuous close",[1] that may be taken as testimony to the importance and longevity of the principles that had been forged in the world of the Westminster Assembly, a world in which that Assembly may have been the most characteristic single event.

However, partly because England's experiment with a Puritan Commonwealth was eclipsed by return to the traditional monarchy in 1660, and partly because the accession of the 'Merry Monarch' caused the theological mood of the 1640s to be supplanted by a fashionable pose of pragmatic scepticism, the work of the Assembly has been relegated to the dustier volumes and normally uncut pages of church history, or left to the researches of those looking for antiquated ammunition with which to continue obsolete battles of denominational polemics. That is unfortunate.

Certainly it is an important event in church history, and this is

---

[1] Sydney E. Ahlstrom, *A Religious History of the American People*, (New Haven, Yale University Press, 1972) p. 968.

1

the field in which it has had its most obvious impact. Even if the Westminster Assembly of Divines is remembered today solely for the Confession of Faith it produced, the influence of that document alone extends far beyond the Presbyterian churches that have become its primary inheritors.[2] These ecclesiastical results have not been negligible, and to them we must add the direct influence that the Westminster Standards exercized for over three hundred years on Scottish Presbyterianism and its ecclesiastical progeny throughout the world.[3]

Yet this undeniable doctrinal influence with its confessional ramifications may obscure the significance of the Assembly within English history. The Westminster Assembly was an *English* event, and although we discover the fine hand of the Scottish commissioners constantly at work during its sessions, the Church of Scotland had no immediate responsibility for the Assembly's work: it was born in an English context to meet the needs of the Church of England. Even more to the point, the doctrinal restatement of Calvinism, for which it is primarily known today, was not the primary reason for the Assembly's call nor its most immediate concern.

The immediate concern of the Westminster divines was to reform the Church and to provide a theologically viable and ecclesiastically workable system of church government to take the place of the established order swept away by Parliament. Polity and the doctrine of the Church (i.e. ecclesiology) were at the centre of its work; but within the context of seventeenth century thought, it was inevitable that the new ordering of the

---

[2] In its time it was recognized as the finest statement of Calvinistic doctrine that had yet been produced, and its influence is to be seen in the extent to which other Confessions of Faith used it, e.g., the Savoy Declaration of English Congregationalists in 1658, the Boston Declaration of New England Congregationalists of 1680, reaffirmed at Saybrook in 1708. (See Williston Walker, *The Creeds and Platforms of Congregationalism* (New York, 1893; new edition, Boston, The Pilgrim Press, 1960) pp. 354–402, 439 [cf. editor's note], 502). The influence is also seen in the Baptist Confessions, specifically in the London Confession of 1644, the Confession of 1677, and the Philadelphia Confession of 1742. See W. L. Lumpkin, *Baptist Confessions of Faith*, (Chicago, Judson Press, 1959,) pp. 144–171, 235–96. Writing of the Philadelphia Confession Winthrop S. Hudson has observed, "*The Philadelphia Confession of Faith* was simply the *London Confession* of the English Particular Baptists. The *London Confession* represented a slight modification of the *Savoy Declaration* of the English Congregationalists; and this, in turn, was a slightly altered reproduction of the *Westminster Confession of Faith*." Winthrop S. Hudson (ed.) *Baptist Concepts of the Church*. (Chicago, Judson Press, 1959,) p. 21, cf. p. 30. See also the editor's note in *Documents of the Christian Church*, edited by Henry Bettenson, (London, O.U.P., 1943 edn.,) p. 351.

[3] Conservative Presbyterians in all the denominations that carry that name still hold the Westminster Confession to be the norm by which doctrinal orthodoxy is to be measured.

Church[4] would also point to the ordering of a new society in England. Given the presuppositions and the prejudices of the 1640s and 50s, it could be assumed that the Church would be a national Church. It can also be assumed that its form and character carried implications for the structure of society, although this may not have been altogether clear to the members of Parliament. The integral relationship of Church and State had certainly been clear to James I in 1604.[5]

By the time the Civil War broke out in 1642, Parliament had shown that it did not want the form of prelacy represented by Archbishop Laud, but there was as yet no unanimity on what should take its place. Although the Roman Catholic answer was excluded by reason of England's Protestant prejudices, and the established episcopal form appeared to be excluded by reason of Parliament's Puritan leanings, there was still widespread and immense uncertainty about the form that the Church should take;[6] certainly there was enough to add spice and drama to the debates in the Assembly.

Meanwhile, the need to ordain new ministers made a decision on the form of the national Church an urgent priority, and although the re-statement of Calvinistic doctrine may have been an inevitable outcome of the process given the time, place, and personnel of that particular assembly, it was still secondary to the task of proposing to Parliament the form of a national Church upon which the social discipline of the whole nation would be established. But as the social implications of the ecclesiological issue gradually emerged, it became clear that the Assembly's debates would become linked to the political groups in Parliament. Therefore as the debates progress we notice a political

---

[4] We have restricted the capitalization of the word 'Church' to those instances in which the Church in general is intended, to specific titles (e.g., the Church of England), or in the doctrine of the Church (as a synonym for ecclesiology.) In all other uses, (e.g. with indefinite articles, as synonym for 'denomination,' or as a building, etc.) lower case is used.

[5] Cf. *infra* p. 16 and *ibid.* n. 10.

[6] As I pointed out in a different place, this is illustrated by Oliver Cromwell, who admitted in 1641 that although he was more convinced than ever about the irregularity of bishops, he was by no means certain what form the Church should take. He remarked to two of his colleagues in the House of Commons, Sir Philip Warwick and Sir Thomas Chichely, "I can tell you, Sirs, what I would not have; tho' I cannot what I would." Sir Philip Warwick, *Memoirs of the Reign of Charles I*, 1701, p. 177. Cf. Robert S. Paul, *The Lord Protector*, (London, Lutterworth Press, 1955.) pp. 50–55.

The point was made earlier by William Shaw, and has been reaffirmed by Michael R. Watts in his recent study, *The Dissenters: From the Reformation to the French Revolution*, (Oxford, Clarendon Press, 1978) p. 86. Cf. William A. Shaw, *A History of the English Church during the Civil Wars and under the Commonwealth, 1640–1660*, (London, Longmans, Green & Co., 1900, 2 vols.) I. 5–7.

under-current that is linked to the parliamentary power-struggle, and even related to the success or failure of the armies in the field.

II

The call of the Westminster Assembly was set within the complexities of the peculiar ecclesiastical situation that came from the English Reformation. Although it would be too much to expect the present writer to review the chequered history and changes of political fortune that governed the shape of the Church in England from the time of Henry VIII to the accession of the Stuarts, we must note that Puritanism in its various forms[7] arose in a situation that was peculiar to England and from the legacy of the way in which England had become a Protestant country.

One of the singularities of that situation was that it forced ecclesiology into the forefront of interest among those English people who were seriously engaged in the religious issues of the time,[8] and the early reliance of the established episcopal order on the authority of the Crown, practically forced opponents of these Tudor settlements to stress alternatives to this authority and to develop their own alternative ecclesiologies. Roman Catholics could be expected to emphasize the Western tradition as it came to a focus in the Petrine succession, while Protestants of the stricter sort turned to the scriptures and in their clash with the

---

[7] The terms 'Puritan' and 'Puritanism' suffer from considerable ambiguity. They are sometimes used in the more general and inclusive sense to denote the general movement of all those Protestants in England who were opposed to the Elizabethan and Stuart settlement of the Church of England and who wanted to reform the Church in strict conformity to the New Testament pattern.

More precisely the terms distinguish those who wished to accomplish this reform while remaining within the established Church from the 'Separatists' who left the Church of England to form their own 'gathered churches.'

In the early history of the American colonies the Puritans were the non-separating founders of the Massachusetts Bay Colony in contrast to the semi-Separatist leaders of the Plymouth Colony. Cf. Perry Miller, *Orthodoxy In Massachusetts, 1630-1650,* (Boston, Beacon Press, [1933] 1959,) chapters I–V; for the ambiguities of the word 'Puritan' see Robert S. Paul, 'The Accidence and the Essence of Puritan Piety', *Austin Seminary Bulletin* [Faculty Edition], XCIII, No. 8 (May 1978) pp. 7–11. Because of the ambiguity of the ways in which these terms are used, the precise sense can only be inferred from the passage in which they appear.

[8] The relationship of ecclesiology to the English Reformation, and its significance to the history of Britain and its colonies during the Tudor and Stuart period, is dealt with at greater length in my article, ' "A Way to Wyn them": Ecclesiology and Religion in the English Reformation,' in *Reformatio Perennis* [essays in Honor of Ford Lewis Battles], edited by Brian A. Gerrish (Pittsburgh, Pickwick Press, 1980.)

royal laws tended to use the Bible more and more as a book of divine law: the legalism that demanded obedience to Tudor and Stuart laws almost inevitably produced biblical literalism (legalism) in reaction.

Furthermore we must recognize that all kinds of Puritans believed that if Christians were simply to take the plain, literal meaning of the scriptures without ecclesiastical pressure and without prejudice, a single form of the Church would stand clear. What Perry Miller wrote of the Separatists was equally true for all those who embraced the Puritan stance, that "since those [biblical] rules were held to be explicit and all-sufficient, and were to be administered only by God's chosen people, there would be complete unanimity."[9] It should be equally clear that this expected consensus did not happen, and that there was no universally accepted meaning to the disputed passages of scripture. The radical movement soon began to divide – not only as Puritans who wished to reform the Church from within and Separatists who sought a Reformation "without tarying for anie",[10] but further as Presbyterians, Congregationalists and Baptists who differed in their understanding of church polity. When we add to this picture the Catholics who continued to be faithful to their papal allegiance, and the more thoroughgoing exploration of Anglican ecclesiology in the writings of Richard Hooker and the Caroline divines, we begin to realize that English history from the death of Edward VI (1553) to the Restoration in 1660 could very well be represented as one long struggle about ecclesiology, a struggle in which it would be clear to the people of that time, if not to us, that control of the Church and control of the State could not be separated. In that story, the call of the Westminster Assembly plays a very significant part.

III

Secular historians properly remind us that the classic struggle of the English people with their Stuart kings was complex. It may be questioned whether it can be regarded simply as a struggle that engaged the common people of England against the Crown; it was essentially a middle class struggle and one in which the leadership came from the representatives of that class of

---

[9] *Orthodoxy in Massachusetts*, p. 58, cf. p. 64.

[10] From the title of the Separatist, Robert Browne's book, *A Treatise of Reformation without tarying for anie, and of the wickednesse of those Preachers which will not reforme till the Magistrate commaunde or compell them*. (Middleburg, 1582).

Englishman in Parliament.[11] Furthermore, it involved the political confrontation between absolute monarchy and constitutional government, the social struggle of the aspiring classes for a place in the sun against the vested interests of landed aristocracy and royal power, the appearance of new urban proletariats facing the prejudices of rural conservatism, and the economic problems of unattached labourers coming out of feudalism into a new commercial society. Within this general mix – a part of it, but subordinate – historians recognize the contribution of those whom Burke called 'the dissidence of dissent, and the Protestantism of the Protestant religion' in their opposition to the ritual and theology of the Laudian church.

I question whether this reading of the history leads us to a true understanding of the significance of the Puritan movement. There is a great deal of difference between the seventeenth century Puritan and his twentieth century interpreter, for what the interpreter may consider secondary the Puritan himself regarded as primary, even although he may have hidden from himself the material motives that would assume primary importance in later times. A. S. P. Woodhouse pointed out that "the Puritan turned to the theological aspects of a question as naturally as the modern man turns to the economic."[12] If we discount the primacy that the Puritan himself gave to this theological motivation and concentrate upon what happened in commerce, or at the barricades or in the councils of politicians, then we will

---

[11] Lawrence Stone has a valuable discussion of the debate among historians on this point in *The Causes of the English Revolution, 1529–1642*, (London, Routledge & Kegan Paul, 1972.) Chapter 2 of that book on 'The Social Origins of the English Revolution' is particularly valuable, but whether we end by thinking of the English Civil War as being caused primarily by the rise of the gentry (R. H. Tawney) or as the work of the yeoman class (H. R. Trevor-Roper), or as due to the decline of the House of Lords and the rise of the House of Commons (J. H. Hexter), it seems fairly clear that the struggle against the Stuarts drew its major support from those sections of society that we would call 'middle class.'

Of course, Eduard Bernstein took the normal Marxist line in representing the English Revolution as essentially 'bourgeois', but we may accept that description without giving it all the freight that Marxist ideology would put upon it. Eduard Bernstein, *Cromwell and Communism*, (1895; New York, Schocken Books, 1930).

An immense literature on the social sources of the English Civil War has grown up and may be traced within such journals as *The Economic History Review*, *The Journal of Economic History*, and in the more general historical journals. For more readily available discussions of the social aspects, see Christopher Hill, *Puritanism and Revolution*, (London, Secker & Warberg, 1958,) and chapter 9 in *The Century of Revolution*, 1603–1714, (1961; New York, W. W. Norton & Co., 1966,); and Chapter 7 in Michael Walzer's *The Revolution of the Saints: a Study in the Origins of Radical Politics*, (1965; New York, Atheneum, 1968.)

[12] A. S. P. Woodhouse, *Puritanism and Liberty*, (London, J. M. Dent & Sons, 1938), Introduction p. 39.

naturally regard the Westminster Assembly of Divines as an event that is almost irrelevant to the history of the English Civil War – a quaint curiosity belonging to a time when people happened to quote the Bible as frequently (if more perceptively) than a modern person cites the editorial of a favourite news magazine or television commentator, simply as the idiom of the age. The theological cast of the seventeenth century debates might be dismissed as meaningless, if it were not that the theological terms "in which the Puritan insists that the argument shall be carried on, are real to him, and of first-rate historical importance because they are the terms in which he views his world. Ignore the terms, or misunderstand them, and the Puritan mind has eluded you."[13]

That expresses the point clearly, for when we have properly acknowledged that opportunists, cynics and sycophants in any age will use its fashionable language without necessarily sharing its convictions, the theological and biblical form of the debate represented both the idiom and the convictions of men like Oliver Cromwell, Henry Vane, Thomas Fairfax, John Winthrop and John Cotton. These people were putting their stamp on the identity of the English-speaking peoples, and if they put theology at the centre of their action, it cannot be ignored in our interpretation of that time; and equally, we ought not to dismiss too quickly the forum where that theology was given its most explicit expression, the Westminster Assembly.

IV

If secular historians tend to under-estimate the importance of the Church and its theology in this period, Church historians are equally capable of ignoring the purely secular standards of action that the churches adopted to achieve their ends. Representatives of all the polities in the century-long struggle between the death of Edward VI and the Restoration pursued their objectives by political means, and often by force. Whether one considers the methods used by Mary I (and later by James II) to re-establish Roman Catholicism, the power plays and persecutions promoted by Elizabeth I and the Stuarts to set the Anglican bishops in the saddle, or the political and military means employed by Presbyterians and Congregationalists to gain their ends, there was little to choose ethically between them. And if the Anglican prelates in the long run were more successful than the others, it

---

[13] *Ibid.*

was not because the others were any less ready to use the political arts or the force at their disposal, but only because in the outcome the bishops proved to be rather more adept and ruthless (which may be the same thing) in their use.

In their theology all churches claimed that they stood for truth against error and for the gospel of Jesus Christ against anything else, but few people in that century recognized any inconsistency between this profession of faith and the way the churches acted towards each other. For it is as obvious as it may seem to us incredible that in the period of our study people were able to accept the injunctions of the New Testament in their personal relationships and yet were also able to imprison, enslave, torture and even burn others in the name of that gospel with absolute sincerity. That represents a medieval mind-set, which had been in the Church since the time of Constantine.

There is no need to suggest that because the means used by the churches were secular their religious expressions must have been hypocritical. The real problem with church history is not that Christians were consciously hypocritical – that sin has been active for a long time, and it is at least understandable – but that they acted as they did with every evidence of being sincere: these were good people according to their lights.[14]

This is an issue that we can no longer evade by finding excuses for our own Confession and damning all the rest. We will pass over the ecumenical issue of mutual penitence, and simply observe that the time for honesty about confessional history is overdue: ecclesiastical power in this world was, more often than not, won by this-worldly means despite the theology used to justify the actions.

V

The Westminster Assembly of Divines was called specifically to formulate an alternative to an episcopal polity that had always been suspect in Puritan eyes for its similarity to the Roman

---

[14] My quarrel with secular interpreters is that in dismissing the theological language as a cover for unavowed motives, they ignore the real issue. It is the *sincerity* of Christians who act unchristianly that constitutes the main problem: it is the action of the Inquisitor who absolutely believes he is obeying the will of Christ in sending heretics to the fire, or of Zwingli allowing Anabaptists to be drowned, or of Cromwell passionately believing that he was wreaking the vengeance of God on the Irish at Drogheda. It must be obvious that believing as they did about the reality of heaven and hell, they would not have acted in that way if they had not been able to reconcile their actions with their understanding of the gospel. They have historical integrity, but the problem of church history is that of recognizing the suffering and injustice that was often caused by that integrity, i.e., by a sincerely held but terribly misunderstood gospel.

hierarchy, a system of prelacy that had become discredited and obnoxious because of the heavy-handedness of Archbishop William Laud.[15] Under the terms of the Solemn League and Covenant with the Scots, the Assembly was charged with formulating and establishing a new form of church government on the basis of the scriptural evidence alone: the authority of the Bible was invoked over the claims of either church tradition or royal prerogative.

Protestants in general and Puritans in particular held the somewhat naive and overly-simplistic view that if the Bible could be approached with faith and sincerity, a single, unified view of the Church would emerge on which all honest Christians could agree. The event proved them wrong, and during the course of the Assembly we witness not only the division between Presbyterians and Independents (Congregationalists), but also disputes between these zealous exponents of a *jus divinum* and Erastians who argued that the form of the Church should be left in the hands of the civil government and its officers.

With Presbyterians appealing for assistance from the Reformed churches of Europe, Independents calling for the support of their Congregational friends in New England, and the Scottish Commissioners involving themselves in every phase of the struggle, we see not only the ramifications of the ecclesiastical struggle, but also something of the political stakes involved for the control of society. Furthermore, when we set the debates in the Assembly alongside the political manoeuvrings that accompanied its high theology and the military manoeuvrings on the battlefields and in the camps, we have a most significant illustration of the integral relationship between religion and politics within the Puritan mind. For a people who have often been accused of being too concerned with an other-worldly faith, these Puritans seem to have had their feet very firmly planted on the ground, if not in the mud of this life.

---

[15] Caroline Hibbard's book, *Charles I and the Popish Plot*, (Chapel Hill, University of North Carolina Press, 1983), has appeared too recently for our present work to have benefitted from its detailed research. However, it shows conclusively that although historians have often discounted John Pym's accusation of a popish plot, there were, in the plotting associated with the court of Henrietta Maria, solid reasons for English Protestants to entertain such fears. This underlines the importance of the ecclesiological issue, at least in its ecclesiastical implications, as a major reason for the Civil War.

Part I

Context, Call and Covenant

CHAPTER 1

THE NATIONAL CONTEXT

I

The Medieval Ideal and the Authority Issue

In the medieval world people enjoyed a harmony of life that brought the sacred and the secular together in a way that Western man has never quite forgotten. J. B. Priestley observed that in that age, the Western mind "found a home in it and was for a little time at peace with itself, related and integrated as it has never been since", but he also pointed out that Western man has never entirely left those unifying ideals behind, and is nostalgically haunted by them "like some half-remembered dream."[1]

If that is still in any sense true of our twentieth century, it was even more true for people who lived in the sixteenth and seventeenth centuries, for although the Renaissance and the Reformation had begun to bring a new world into being, there were not many prepared to recognize that the change would be permanent or that the earlier stable society was giving place to an entirely new order. The religious wars 1530–1648 were fought on the assumption that the unity of Christendom would be re-established, and it took that amount of bloodshed to convince people that the unity of the Church had been irrevocably broken. The religious settlement reached at Westphalia in 1648 simply endorsed the decision accepted tentatively at Augsburg in 1555, which in turn merely echoed the interim agreement of the Diet of Spiers in 1526 – each ruler would be free to decide on the religious settlement of his own territory. It was not until after Westphalia that Europe began to realize that the dream of Imper-

---

[1] J. B. Priestley, *Literature and Western Man*, (New York, Harper & Bros., 1960,) p. 5.

ial unity had gone for ever, and that with it had gone the dream of religious unity; furthermore, that Providence was not going to take a hand in re-establishing it by granting outright victory to Catholic or Protestant. It might take many more years before this idea percolated into the consciousness of many, but from this time we discern the unmistakable shape of a new and secular world struggling to be born.

In the British Isles, which inevitably suffer the time-lag affecting new ideas that have to cross the water, recognition of the new order took a few years longer. The old order certainly received a decisive blow when Charles I's head fell from the block, but it did not receive its *coup de grace* until the death of Oliver Cromwell or even until the 'Glorious Revolution' of 1688. During the Civil War and Interregnum the old order and the new may have been locked in a struggle to the death both within institutions and within the minds of people, but it was often not a conscious struggle and it was one in which the elements of both the old and the new could become strangely confused. Radical groups like the Levellers may have been precursors of much that has become commonplace in the politics of later times, and in them, we notice "a marked transfer of interest from religion to the world",[2] but this secular interest more often than not sprang from an essentially religious centre and they saw nothing inconsistent in employing the theological armory of the time.[3] The old became the springboard of the new: John Lilburne used biblical ideas to express his radical political principles not because he was a cynic about religion, but because these were the concepts that were natural for him to use out of an inherited world-view that was still largely medieval.[4]

One of the most important parts of that medieval inheritance was the belief that political and cultural unity in society could be guaranteed only in relationship to a single form of the Church. The Reformation may have already destroyed the international unity of Christendom, but for most people, this simply meant

---

[2] A. S. P. Woodhouse, *Puritanism and Liberty*, [p. 56.]

[3] Eduard Bernstein regarded the Levellers as the precursors of 19th century Communism, and disparaged their use of the Bible. Cf. *Cromwell and Communism*, especially chapters VI–XII. For a less biased approach see, W. Schenk, *The Concern for Social Justice in the Puritan Revolution*, (London, Longmans, Green and Co., 1948.)

[4] The reality of John Lilburne's religion and its influence upon his social theory is clear in his writings. See the account he gives of his religious experience in 1638 while being publicly whipped for printing books against the Laudian church, *A Worke of the Beast* (1638); cf. Schenk, *The Concern for Social Justice*, pp. 25ff.

that the vaguely experienced unity of the 'Holy Roman Empire' had been exchanged for a much more immediate, a much more easily recognized unity within the nation. True, this too would pass or take a different form, perhaps more rapidly than the new political actors were able to realize, but during the sixteenth and early seventeenth centuries, this national unity of Church and State was the new form in which the old unity of Christendom re-asserted itself. If a few Republicans, Levellers and other radicals found themselves moving in new and dangerous directions, the enthusiasm which greeted the Restoration in 1660, the popularity of the subsequent laws against dissent, and the national support for the seven bishops in 1688 shows that the ideal of a national unity centring in the traditional form of Church and State continued to have a very vigorous life in the public sentiments and popular prejudices of the English people. Perhaps the success of the peculiarly national form of the Reformation in England was due to its solid rootage in the ideals and order of the earlier medieval world.

The continuation of the medieval idea of unity between the Church and the State made it unthinkable for people in the first half of the seventeenth century to make a clear distinction between their religion and their politics. These two spheres of activity were in the process of becoming separated, but the separation had not yet happened. Seventeenth century Puritanism is neither to be dismissed as "a resurgence of medieval thought" nor as simply "a harbinger of the modern world:"[5] both the old ideals and the new insights live together in that century and in the Puritan movement. As Perry Miller has reminded us with regard to those who settled Massachusetts Bay, Puritans did not initially want to change the medieval unity between Church and State.[6] Still less did English Puritans want to change the fundamental shape of society: the immediate objective of the more radical Puritans was to change the *pattern* of the Church, but not its relationship to the State.[7]

This change in the Church's pattern was proposed not because the Puritans wanted any fundamentally different ordering of society but because they had accepted the authority of the scrip-

[5] Woodhouse, *Puritanism and Liberty*, Introduction, [p. 39].

[6] *Orthodoxy In Massachusetts, 1630–1650*.

[7] It is even questionable how radical the changes were that the majority of English 'Puritans' wished to introduce to the Church. Cf. R. T. Kendall, *Calvin and English Calvinism to 1649*, (Oxford, O.U.P., 1979,) pp. 5f, 53f.

tures in place of the medieval authority of the pope.[8] If the institutions that exercised authority in the Church (or society) were to be changed, it was not because Puritans wanted something new, but because, in their view God wanted something different. This followed from the radically different source of divine authority which they accepted in the scriptural pattern. On the authority of the Bible and its primacy in determining the shape of the Church they could not shift, while in all other things, even in the way they interpreted biblical faith, they might remain just as much medievalists as the rest of their contemporaries. It did not matter to them that the 'papal' authority was now exercised in England by an English monarch – they sought a change in the *source* of authority that could not rest content until the national form of the Church clearly conformed to the pattern of the Church in the New Testament. On the other hand, although they had adopted this distinctive biblical stance, Puritans did not cease to be conservative, seventeenth century English people sharing with their countrymen many of the uncertainties of a people moving from feudalism into something very different, and sharing too the invincible prejudice of believing that in most things the old ways were still best.

But, although the ecclesiastical reformers were not prepared to recognize how radically changes in the Church would affect the society in which it was set, they were introducing a revolutionary yeast that would change the world in which they lived. Given the prevailing belief in a social and religious unity, James I was right in asserting the integral relationship between church and society when, on the second day of the Hampton Court Conference, 1603/4,[9] he delivered the aphorism 'No Bishop, no King.'[10]

---

[8] This was seen clearly by Leonard J. Trinterud, 'The Origins of Puritanism', *Church History*, XX, No. 1 (1951), p. 38. Obviously, in writing of this problem of Authority, we are referring to something far more fundamental than the 'chain of command' by which ecclesiastical authority is normally exercised in the institutional church, although a hierarchy that regards itself as final authority on theological matters may represent one aspect of it. The 'authority' with which we are concerned here relates to what we have described elsewhere as "the problem of establishing the basic authority on which any Christian proclamation can be made whether in word or form:" i.e., the fundamental authority on which a Church establishes its claim to be *the* Church, which defines its purpose, structure and worship. For more extended discussion see Robert S. Paul, *The Church in Search of Its Self*, (Grand Rapids, Wm. B. Eerdmans, 1972,) pp. 36, 37–60.

[9] The conference took place in January 1604. But because the date of the year in the 17th century was not changed until March 25th, to avoid confusion, all dates from this period in England falling between January 1st and March 25th will appear according to this example, '1603/4.'

[10] James I was so convinced about the close relationship between ecclesiastical and civil government, that he reiterated his statement to the bishops later that day, "but if

For obvious reasons, Puritans long denied that connection. During the debate on the 'Root and Branch Petition' (February 9th, 1640/1), Oliver Cromwell vigorously protested against Sir John Strangways's statement that a parity in the church would produce a parity in the commonwealth,[11] but that simply illustrates how little Puritans understood where their theological insights about the Church would lead them in relation to society. Within movements that were in the forefront of reform, we have to recognize the conservative temper of people who clung tenaciously to their traditional prejudices. This caused lawyers to promote far-reaching constitutional changes by urging a return to pre-Conquest Anglo-Saxon institutions,[12] just as it caused Puritans themselves to agitate for a new form of the Church by restoring the New Testament pattern: the conservative world-view into which they were born prevented them from discerning the social implications of their theological insights. It would take the pressure of events and the trauma of civil war to make those implications clearer.

Anglicans differed from their Puritan contemporaries not because they were necessarily more conservative politically or more feudal socially, but because in moving from authority vested in the pope, they centred on authority vested in the reigning monarch; and since the monarch was no less a product of medieval attitudes than they were themselves, the results were likely to be conservative. The Anglican answer to the authority question at first sight appeared to be much simpler and less threatening than that of the Puritans, although all the seventeenth century answers became ambiguous and complex.

The break with Rome had been carried through by royal fiat, and this meant *de facto* that the authority of the pope had been exchanged for the authority of the English crown. Anglican ecclesiology became more complex because the episcopal churchmen's apologetic obviously could not remain at that theologically unsophisticated level. Initially, the royal supremacy was undergirded by an appeal to the authority that the New Testament

---

once you were out, and they in place, I knowe what would become of my *Supremacie. No Bishop, no King*, as before I sayd." William Barlow, *The Svmme and Svbstance of the Conference, which, it pleased his Excellent maiestie to haue with the Lords, Bishops, and other of his Clergie . . . at Hampton Court.* January 14, 1603. London, 1604, p. 82, cf. *ibid.* p. 36.

[11] *The Journal of Sir Simonds D'Ewes*, edited by Wallace Notestein, (New Haven, 1923,) p. 340.

[12] Cf. Christopher Hill, *Puritanism and Revolution*, chapter 3, 'The Norman Yoke.'

seems to allow the civil magistrate,[13] and then by an appeal to historical precedent and to the authority over the Church that had been assumed by the Emperor Constantine.

The circumstances in which England became a Protestant country have to be taken into account, for whereas in continental Europe the power of the prince was used to enforce what the Reformers believed was the scriptural pattern of the Church, in England the authority of scripture was used in the first place by the English Reformers to justify the King's traditional view of what the Church should be. This could very easily develop into an ecclesiology based on the Divine Right of Kings, as it was popularly expressed in this piece of cavalier doggerel:

> Yet know that *Kings* are *Gods* on Earth;
> And those that pull them down,
> Shall find it is no less than Death
> To tamper with a Crown....
>
> Now, when the *King* of *Kings* was born,
> And did *salvation* bring,
> They strive to crucify in scorn
> His *Vice-Roy*, and their King.[14]

At the same time, a simplistic appeal to the authority of the crown was no permanent basis on which to build ecclesiology. More and more people were beginning to read the Bible, and it was clear from any simple reading of the New Testament that the Church in apostolic times stood in marked contrast to the elaborate ritual and structure of the Church of England under the Tudors and Stuarts. Intelligent prelates such as Whitgift and Bancroft recognized that reforms were due, and that discipline in the national Church needed to be tightened.[15] Theological justification for the Church of England became more complex and more subtle because conformist churchmen began to realize that they would have to broaden the basis on which their church

---

[13] E.g., Matthew 22:15–22 (Cf. Mark 12:13–17, Luke 20:19–26) Romans 13:1–7, 1 Peter 2:11–17. It is worth noting that the Puritans seem to have been somewhat embarrassed by these passages – at least this is suggested by their almost absolute failure to comment on them. Apart from a brief passage in Samuel Rutherford's *Lex, Rex* commenting on Romans 13, and in spite of the voluminous exegesis on almost every other part of scripture, Puritans seem to have been extremely reluctant to tackle the texts dealing with the civil magistrate.

[14] *Sir John Berkenhead reviv'd, or a Satyr against the late Rebellion,* (1681). The verses seem to have been penned *ca.* 1648, but revised and perhaps expanded for later publication. We have kept the italics of the original.

[15] Cf. Phyllis Doyle, 'Church and State and the *Jure Divino* theory of Episcopacy in the English Church', *The Church Quarterly Review,* 109 (1929–30), pp. 239–61.

rested: the monarch's will alone was not sufficient, and some-how, what Anglicans claimed about the form and worship of the Church had to be brought into relationship with the scriptures and the Church's tradition. Even the earliest major apologists for the Elizabethan settlement, John Jewell, Bishop of Salisbury,[16] and the scholarly Richard Hooker,[17] present a much more comprehensive and sophisticated argument for their church than a simple appeal to the will of the crown as God's vice-regent.

It has been pointed out that after the death of Elizabeth I, two discrete bases for the form of the Church of England seem to have appeared – first, there were those who "elaborated a theory of royal supremacy based on divine right which acceded to the king control over every department of the state with a primary duty to maintain true religion", but very soon we find a group of theologians emerging which "maintained that episcopacy was established *jure divino* and did not owe its authority to any man-made institution whatsoever."[18] During the course of the seventeenth century struggle these two *jure divino* positions seem to have become fused into a single Anglican position, and pointed to the civil and ecclesiastical leadership of a unified English society.[19]

The Divine Right of Kings could not of itself provide a sufficiently solid basis for maintaining the form of the Church of England under the Tudors and Stuarts,[20] and in the course of the long debate with the Puritans *jure divino* episcopacy became the theological heart of Anglican ecclesiology. This was bound to come into headlong collision with *jure divino* Puritan ecclesiologies based on a more or less literal appeal to the New Testament pattern of the Church, because it represented a different primary authority for structuring the Church's doctrine, order and worship. Was that basic authority to be found in the divinely inspired scriptures (as puritans affirmed), or in the

---

[16] Jewell's *Apologia Ecclesiae Anglicanae* appeared in 1562, and was written to justify the Elizabethan settlement against Roman Catholic claims. Lady Bacon's translation was published in 1564 as *An Apologie or answere of the Churche of Englande.*

[17] The first four books of Hooker's *The Laws of Ecclesiastical Polity* appeared in 1592. Books 5–7 did not appear until 1648–62, (long after the author's death in 1600,) and there is some suspicion that they were modified or expanded to meet the later situation in which the Caroline divines found themselves.

[18] Phyllis Doyle, *op. cit.,* pp. 244–5.

[19] The relationship between these two *jure divino* positions was clearly stated by Charles I at the time of the negotiations at Uxbridge in 1645; cf. *infra* p. 22, note 30.

[20] The idea of the Divine Right of Kings may very well be interpreted as the Divine Right of the civil magistrate. If that is pressed to justify control of the Church by *any* civil ruler, it would become little more than a theological justification for Erastianism.

divinely-guided ecclesiastical tradition (the papal answer), or in some essential relationship between the two (which now appeared to be the answer of the Stuart divines)? The conflict was bound to be bitter, because in the seventeenth century there was no room for mutual recognition or compromise on what Christians were to regard as their basic authority.

It was to be expected that as this issue became clearer, the positions would become polarized and there would be less and less possibility of comprehension within a single national Church. It is also worth noting that just as the Puritans had tended to become more literal in their interpretation of the scriptures as the debate with Elizabeth's bishops had become sharper, so the episcopal appeal to apostolic succession became more legalistic as the issue was fairly joined under the Stuarts. We must refrain from commenting on the soundness of the various claims to *jus divinum*, but we shall see that the exclusivism that appeared in the rival doctrines of the Church – contrary to the way they represented each other in their polemics – did not arise like the Miltonic figure of Sin by springing ready-armed from Satan's mind,[21] but rather tended to germinate, nurture itself and flourish in the struggle for supremacy between the ecclesiologies. It was the bitterness of the contest itself that produced the intransigence.

The claim to *jure divino* episcopacy provides a good example. It is not to be found in the writings of John Jewell or Richard Hooker, but is has been suggested that it had its beginnings in a sermon preached by Richard Bancroft at St. Paul's Cross in February, 1588/9 and then appeared in a book that Thomas Bilson published in 1593.[22] Although the claim to *jus divinum* was implicit rather than explicit, Bancroft's Puritan contemporaries regarded the implication of his words as clearly pointing in this direction.[23] Indeed, we may surmise that the appearance of these incipient theories of divine right episcopacy at that time may have been inspired, at least in part, by the bishops' recognition

---

[21] *Paradise Lost*, Bk. II, lines 752–761.

[22] *A Compendious Discourse prouing Episcopacy to be of diuine institution*. Thomas Bilson (1547–1616) had been appointed Bishop of Worcester in 1596, and translated to Winchester the following year.

[23] "Bancroft's sermon at St. Paul's Cross on 9th February 1588–89 on the text 'Try The Spirits' is often regarded as the first advance to the view that episcopacy is of divine institution. But it is not easy to find much in his actual words." J. W. Hunkin, *Episcopal Ordination and Confirmation in relation to Inter-communion & Reunion*, (Cambridge, W. Heffer & Sons, 1929,) pp. 20f. John Strype seems to have confused Bancroft's sermon with one preached by John Bridges (later Bishop of Oxford,) and this view may have

that the Queen was no longer likely to marry and produce a direct heir to the throne. The succession was therefore likely to pass to the presbyterially-educated James VI of Scotland, whose ecclesiastical preferences remained unknown to the English prelates, but no less feared for that. The theological and political justification of episcopacy would be on very shaky grounds if in the last analysis it rested on a theory of Divine Right of Kings alone.

However, the real development of the theory of *jure divino* episcopacy seems to have taken place during the first half of the seventeenth century,[24] beginning during the primacy of Richard Bancroft and gathering strength during the next few decades in sermons by William Barlow[25] and George Downame (or Downham),[26] and in books by George Carlton[27] and Lancelot Andrewes.[28] It provided an almost certain route to a bishopric, and by the outbreak of the Civil War it had developed sufficiently so that it could be stated with admirable clarity by William Laud at his trial in 1644.[29] It was also affirmed by Charles I during the

---

become popularized through the writings of Strype's younger contemporary, Daniel Neal. At the same time one has to agree with Cargill Thompson when he argues that Bancroft's sermon signified a decisive change in episcopal apologetic by ignoring the argument of earlier episcopal apologists that church government is a 'thing indifferent' and by its frank defence of episcopacy on historical grounds. It is also clear that from this time *jure divino* episcopacy began to be explicit, and was (as Cargill Thompson points out) specifically advanced by Adrian Saravia, the Dutch convert to the Anglican position, in his *De Diversis Ministorum Evangelii Gradibus*. W. D. J. Cargill Thompson, 'A Reconstruction of Richard Bancroft's Paul's Cross Sermon of 9 February 1588/9', *Journal of Ecclesiastical History*, XX, No. 2 (October 1969), pp. 253–266; for Saravia's work see Willem Nijenhuis, *Adrianus Saravia (c.1532–1613.)* (Leiden, E. J. Brill, 1980.) From our perspective, the important thing about Bancroft's sermon is not whether it was the first expression of divine right episcopacy, but that it was delivered so close to the time when that view began to appear, and was later regarded as a significant step in that direction.

[24] It should also be noted that Thomas Bilson, Bishop of Winchester, and Richard Bancroft, Bishop of London, had argued for the divine appointment of episcopacy at the Hampton Court Conference. Cf. Barlow, *The Summe and Substance*, pp. 35–6.

[25] Barlow had been appointed Bishop of Rochester in 1605 and translated to the more lucrative see of Lincoln in 1608.

[26] Later appointed Bishop of Derry in 1616.

[27] Later appointed Bishop of Llandaff in 1618, and translated to the see of Chichester in 1619. He was one of the Church of England representatives at the Synod of Dort.

[28] Bishop of Chichester in 1605, then translated to Ely 1609 and to the still more prestigious see of Winchester in 1619.

[29] Part of William Laud's tragedy was that his sincere desire to promote better relationships with Rome inevitably drove a wedge between his position and all other Protestants, domestic and foreign. At his trial in 1644, he declared: " 'tis through her [Rome] that the Bishops of the Church of England, who have the Honour to be capable of deriving their calling from St. Peter, must deduce their Succession. She is therefore a true Church, though not an orthodox One." Daniel Neal, *The History of the Puritans* (1732–6), III, 227f. Laud also admitted that he held with Jerome, "No Bishop, no Church; and that none but a Bishop can ordain, except in Causes of inevitable Necessity." *Ibid.* p. 228.

abortive negotiations at Newcastle in 1646,[30] but during the extensive debate with the King at the time of those negotiations, Alexander Henderson made the comment "that the Divine Right [of Episcopacy] was not pleaded till of late by some few."[31]

The exclusive *jure divino* view of episcopacy therefore seems to have arisen out of the debate with the Puritans and to have become more intense during the civil war. We have to agree with the statement that "from this period of strife, touched themselves by the fire of religious zeal which was animating the ranks of their opponents, the prelates slowly and tentatively evolved their reply and offered their solution to the problem of their ambiguous position: they postulated the *jure divino* theory of episcopacy."[32] By the time of the Barebones Parliament in 1653,

---

[30] During the unsuccessful negotiations between Charles and the representatives of Parliament at Uxbridge in 1645, the King had declared: "I can't yield to the Change of Government by Bishops, not only because I fully concur with the most general Opinion of Christians in all Ages, in Episcopacy's being the best Government, but likewise I hold my self particularly bound by the Oath I took at my Coronation not to alter the Government of this Church from what I found it." He then went on to state the essential relationship between episcopacy and monarchy in England's unified Anglican state: "as it is the King's Duty to protect the Church, so the Church is reciprocally bound to assist the King in the Maintenance of his just Authority." *Ibid*. p. 254.

Commenting on the debate between Charles and Henderson at Newcastle later, Neal observed, "One may learn from this Controversy, some of the Principles in which King Charles I was instructed; as

(1) The Divine Right of Diocesan Episcopacy.

(2) The uninterrupted Succession of Bishops, rightly ordained, from the Time of the Apostles; upon which the whole Validity of the Administration of the Christian Sacraments depends.

(3) The Necessity of a Judge of Controversies, which his Majesty lodges with the Fathers of the Christian Church, and by that means leaves little or no room for private Judgment.

(4) The Independency of the Church upon the State.

(5) That no Reformation of Religion is lawful but that which arises from the Prince or Legislature; and this only in Cases of Necessity, when a general Council cannot be obtained.

(6) That the Multitude or common People may not in any Case take upon them to Reform the Negligence of Princes. Neither,

(7) May they take up Arms against him, even for Self-Defence, in cases of extream Necessity." *Ibid*. p. 347.

[31] *Ibid*., p. 341. Cf. the whole debate, *ibid*., pp. 337–47. The comparative newness of the *jure divino* view of episcopacy also appears to be suggested by Richard Baxter. Early in his life he had been forced to make a thorough study of the ecclesiastical issues dividing the Church. He pointed out that even those who had made large claims for their ecclesiology had done so on the basis of laws granted by the civil magistrate, "except some few of the higher stiffer sort, who pleaded as the Papists, for somewhat more, which yet they could not themselves tell what to make of." *Reliquiae Baxterianae*, edited by Matthew Sylvester, (London, 1696,) I. ii. 139f, (§2).

[32] Phyllis Doyle, *Op. cit.* pp. 240f.

this was recognised as the basic view of episcopacy to which all Puritans were opposed.[33]

However, this exclusiveness was true not only for episcopacy. In seventeenth century England any view of the Church could justify its position theologically only by virtually making a *jure divino* claim: the exclusive aspect of the ecclesiologies arises out of crucial differences about where the primary authority for Christian faith was located. The course of events, and the assumed relationship between the Church and society, made this ecclesiological debate more intense, and during the Civil War, the divisions in the Church were exacerbated as the prizes and penalties for success or failure became more obvious: England was like a crucible in which the ecclesiastical elements became more distinct and separated as the heat increased.

II

The English Pressure-Pot

This struggle which focused in the theological problem of authority introduced the pressure into the English pressure-pot, because it brought what was happening in society into relationship to the individual's eternal destiny: for Puritans, membership in the true Church was essential to salvation.[34] It is therefore of central importance if we are to understand the relationship between religion and politics in the Westminster Assembly. But in this seventeenth century context there were several reasons why religion and politics would become embroiled together.

First, continuation of the medieval conviction about the essential unity of Church and State forced the theologians and the politicians to take note of each other. Although Puritans like Cromwell might protest that the restructuring they were proposing for the Church implied no similar restructuring of society,

---

[33] At the opening of the Nominated ('Barebones') Parliament, July 4th, 1653, Cromwell declared: "I speak not – I thank God it is far from my heart – for a Ministry deriving itself from the Papacy, and pretending to that which is so much insisted on, 'succession.' The true succession is through the Spirit, given in that measure that the Spirit is given, and that is a right succession." Wilbur Cortez Abbott, *Writings and Speeches of Oliver Cromwell*, (Cambridge, Mass., Harvard University Press, 1937–47, 4 vols.,) III, p. 63; *The Letters and Speeches of Oliver Cromwell with elucidations by Thomas Carlyle*, edited by Mrs. S. C. Lomas, (London, Methuen & Co., 1904, 3 vols.) II. 294f. [Hereafter this is referred to as Lomas–Carlyle.]

[34] Note the title of John von Rohr's article on the ecclesiology of Henry Jacob, '*Extra ecclesiam nulla salus:* An Early Congregational Version', *Church History*, XXXVI, No. 2, (June 1967).

people of that time would be almost unconsciously drawn to look for such a parallel. Individuals might be drawn into the conflict between Charles and his Parliament primarily for political or for religious reasons, but it would not be long before concern for the issues in one area would involve them in the other.[35] However separate the Puritans tried to keep the issue of church polity and the form of civil government – at least during the early days while they were maintaining the fiction that they were fighting 'for King and Parliament' – their own deepest convictions would cause many to look from reform in the Church to reform in the State. After all, the constant prayer of the Church had been that God's Kingdom should come and his will be done 'on earth as it is in heaven', and there were many among them who were expecting that Kingdom to come without too much delay.[36]

The Assembly took place during the bitterest civil war of English history, at the time when the religious convictions and social conventions of the Ages of Faith were confronting ideas that were to bring in an Age of Reason. However ponderous the arguments in the Assembly, however protracted its debates, the divines at Westminster, no less than their lay colleagues in both Parliament and the Army, began to realize that they were standing at a climacteric in history. They may have arrived very reluctantly at the conclusion that they were taking part in a revolution, but once they had reached that conclusion, their most fundamental convictions would have persuaded them that it must be God's revolution. The historical realist may find in the Puritans' attitude a mixture of medieval prejudice, Reformation biblicism, political pragmatism and the dim lines of a secularism that they could neither recognize nor acknowledge. Looked at more positively we see that the Puritan movement produced a distinctive amalgam of religious intensity, theological conviction and political activism;[37] and it may be that this amalgam itself was the key to the future.

---

[35] Many years later Cromwell declared: "for religion was not the thing at first contested for, but God brought it to that issue at last, and gave it unto us by way of redundancy, and at last it proved to be that which was most dear to us. And wherein consisted this, more than in obtaining that liberty from the tyranny of the Bishops to all species of Protestants, to worship God according to their own light and consciences? For want of which many of our brethren forsook their native countries to seek their bread from strangers, and to live in howling wildernesses; and for which also many that remained here were imprisoned, and otherwise abused, and made the scorn of the nation." Speech to the 2nd Protectorate Parliament, 22nd January, 1654/5, Abbott, *Writings and Speeches of O.C.*, III. 586, Lomas–Carlyle, II. 417.

[36] For the extensive literature on Puritan eschatology, cf. *infra* pp. 29f., note 54.

[37] From the death of Cromwell in 1658 to the Great Ejectment in 1662 the Puritans fell from the pinnacle of power to enforced nonconformity, and very soon they fell under the

This suggests it may be pointless to try to determine whether religion or secular motivations should have priority in interpreting this seventeenth century struggle – to decide whether the new independence of Tudor and Stuart Parliaments, the ambitions of the middle classes, and the brash commercialism of a newly-landed Protestant gentry are responsible for the rise of Puritanism, or whether Puritan faith is to be regarded as the prime cause of the new secularity.[38]

There is probably no way of determining that kind of priority, any more than there is any way of reaching a final conclusion on Max Weber's thesis about the relationship of the Protestant ethic to the rise of capitalism,[39] although we recognize that there is plenty of evidence to support a historical connection. Richard Baxter observed that most of the nobility and landed gentry together with the poorest people went to the side of the King during the Civil War, while the main support of Parliament was to be found among tradesmen, freeholders and 'the middle sort of Men', and he went on to make a comment that Max Weber would certainly have appreciated: "If you ask the Reasons of this Difference, ask also, why in France it is not commonly the Nobility nor the Beggars, but the Merchants and middle sort of Men, that were Protestants."[40] We recognize a connection between the Protestant ethic and the rise of modern capitalism, although we cannot determine accurately which was cause and which was effect, and it seems wiser simply to note their interrelatedness and mutual influence.

---

persecuting policy of the Restoration parliaments and began to disintegrate into a number of religiously proscribed and politically impotent sects. The writings of John Bunyan while he was a prisoner in Bedford gaol have been cited as evidence of the 'other worldliness' of Puritanism. This is obviously a very incomplete reading of the Puritan movement, for if Bunyan became the most widely-known writer after 1660, it should be remembered that John Milton was the most representative writer before that; and it was the Milton not of *Paradise Lost*, but of the political pamphlets – the *Areopagitica*, the *Tenure of Kings and Magistrates* and *Defensio secunda pro populo anglicano*.

[38] Conrad Russell has reminded us that there was nothing in the parliamentary history of the Tudors and early Stuarts that made the Civil War happen *inevitably* when it did. Cf. Conrad Russell, 'Parliamentary History in Perspective', *History*, 41 (1976), pp. 1–27.

[39] Max Weber's *Die protestantische Ethik und der Geist des Kapitalismus* first appeared in 1904–5 [English translation by Talcott Parsons, *The Protestant Ethic and the Spirit of Capitalism*, 1958] and it immediately became the centre of a debate which is still lively. Cf. R. H. Tawney's *Religion and the Rise of Capitalism* (1926) and a summary of the debate in Robert W. Green (ed.), *Protestantism and Capitalism: The Weber Thesis and its Critics*, (Boston, D. C. Heath & Co., 1959.) Weber applied his insights more specifically to the Protestant sects in America in 'The Protestant Sects and the Spirit of Capitalism', in *From Max Weber* (translated and edited by H. H. Gerth and C. Wright Mills, New York, O.U.P., 1946.)

[40] *Reliquiae Baxterianae*, I. i. p. 30, (§49).

25

Mention of Weber's thesis, however, prompts the suggestion that the nineteenth and twentieth centuries' preoccupation with economics may have shunted the study of Protestantism's relationship to the modern world into too narrow a siding.[41] Certainly it appears to have been related to the rise of capitalism as we know it, but if the new ethic assisted the rise of a secularized bourgeoisie were there not other aspects of the Protestant stance that stimulated the modern form of political revolution?[42] If the new attitudes helped to produce nineteenth century capitalism, did they not also help to promote science, professionalism and philanthropy? Historical causes of such ideological consequence rarely limit their effects to the singular.

This simply reinforces the contention that there is no way of determining absolutely cause and effect in the historical interplay between secular and religious motives in the seventeenth century, for to the person of that time, life was a unity that ought not to be too neatly separated into the secular and the sacred. Economic changes might give rise to new social ambitions and these in turn demand theological justification, or alternatively new theological insights might stimulate people to branch out into fresh avenues of social and economic development, but in the period of this study it seems that the secular and religious motives were mutually influential and inter-related.

Secondly, the Civil War simply intensified an ecclesiastical/ political struggle that had already shown its face in the reign of Elizabeth.[43] The shifts of fortune suffered by the Puritans during

---

[41] My dissatisfaction with the scope of the debate on Weber's thesis was suggested in 'Weber and Calvinism: the Effects of a "Calling"', *The Canadian Journal of Theology*, Vol. XI (1965), No. 1, pp. 25–41, and in 'The Accidence and the Essence of Puritan Piety', *Austin Seminary Bulletin* [Faculty Edition] XCIII, No. 8, (May 1978).

[42] In her book *On Revolution* (New York, Viking Press, 1963), Hannah Arendt pointed out that revolution in the modern sense as we know it did not arrive on the scene until the Renaissance (Machiavelli). I suggest that it is more properly linked with the whole movement of the Renaissance/Reformation, since the Reformation provided the religious (ideological) justification for overthrowing the older systems of authority without which 'revolution' in our modern understanding would not be possible. If this is valid, then the Great Rebellion (or Puritan Revolution) of seventeenth century England presents the first example in modern times. See also Michael Walzer, *The Revolution of the Saints*, Christopher Hill, *Puritanism and Revolution* and *The Century of Revolution*, 1603–1714, and Lawrence Stone's 'The English Revolution' in *Preconditions of Revolution in Modern Europe*, edited by Robert Forster and Jack P. Green, (Baltimore, John Hopkins Press, 1970.)

[43] Without attempting an exhaustive bibliography of Puritanism during the Elizabethan period, reference may be made to some of the works that have become standard in the field: M. M. Knappen, *Tudor Puritanism* (Chicago, University of Chicago Press, 1939), William Haller, *The Rise of Puritanism* (New York, Columbia University Press, 1938), Patrick Collinson, *The Elizabethan Puritan Movement* (Berkeley, University

this early period shows them using all their ingenuity to avoid complete extinction and to guarantee the continuation of at least a faithful remnant that could eventually win success. So when the Puritan faction failed by a single vote to get reforms regarding vestments through the Convocation of 1563, the leaders had no compunction in·turning directly to Parliament. Indeed the two Admonitions that were offered to Parliament in 1572 seem to have been formulated as much with a view to winning popular support in the constituencies as to influence the members of Parliament themselves.[44] Add to this the creation of a secret Presbytery in and around London, the publication of satirical and provocative pamphlets,[45] the publicity value of 'plain style' preaching within the congregations in town and country, and we see the extent to which even in Elizabeth's reign the struggle had already involved the Puritans in tactics that were implicitly political. This is even further illustrated by those who were later to be known as Independents or Congregationalists,[46] until they managed to secure a haven for their ideas in Massachusetts.[47] It is axiomatic that every ecclesiastical party seeking power acted politically.[48]

---

of California, Press, 1967), and Sir John Neale's studies of *Elizabeth I and her Parliaments* (New York, St. Martin's Press, 1958).

[44] Cf. the Introduction to W. H. Frere and C. E. Douglas (eds.) *Puritan Manifestoes*, (London, S.P.C.K., 1954,) D. J. McGinn, *The Admonition Controversy*, (New Brunswick, N. J., Rutgers Univ. Press, 1949.)

[45] Cf. the activities of such Puritan supporters as John Day, John Field, Thomas Wilcox, Robert Waldegrave and John Canne, or the influence of the anonymous Martin Marprelate tracts.

[46] Despite their rejection of the name 'Independent', it will perhaps assist the reader if we normally employ that term for the 'Congregationalists' of England at the time of the Assembly, and use the word 'Congregational' usually for those who had embraced 'the New England way', although they essentially belong to the same movement. For the evidence on these terms, see my article, 'The Word "Congregational": A Historical Footnote', *The Hartford Quarterly*, IV. No. 1 (Fall 1963), pp. 59–64.

[47] See the note in my Introduction to *An Apologeticall Narration*, (Philadelphia, U.C.C. Press, 1963,) pp. 57f., note 1. To the instances cited there we should add the attempt after 1625 to buy up feoffs for appointing Puritans to Church of England livings, which was crushed by William Laud in 1632–3. Cf. I. M. Calder, *Activities of the Puritan Faction of the Church of England, 1625–33*, (London, S.P.C.K., 1957.) On similar attempts to influence opinion by setting up Puritan 'lectureships', see Paul S. Seaver, *The Puritan Lectureships: the Politics of Religious Dissent, 1560–1662*, (Stanford, Stanford Univ. Press, 1970;) and for Laud's actions against the Puritans in the Netherlands, see Raymond Phineas Stearns, *Congregationalism in the Dutch Netherlands: the Rise and Fall of the English Congregational Classis*, (Chicago, American Soc. of Church Hist., 1940,) and Keith L. Sprunger, 'Archbishop Laud's Campaign Against Puritanism at the Hague', *Church History*, 44, No. 3 (Sept. 1975), pp. 308–20.

[48] The Roman Catholics were the first to be driven to the point of desperation. Excluded from the Elizabethan Settlement, they had hoped for a reversal of their fortunes when James, son of Mary Queen of Scots, came to the English throne. His decision to

Thirdly, the Civil War accentuated the polarities and accelerated the pace of the ecclesiastical debate. The division between the Puritans and the supporters of the episcopate began under Elizabeth and gathered some momentum in the months that led up to the outbreak of civil war, but the differences between the majority of Puritans who remained in England and the bishops does not appear to have been as sharp as it had been during the latter half of Elizabeth's reign or after the outbreak of the Civil War. The opposition of the Puritans to the bishops was certainly shared and pushed even further by Separatists outside the national Church, but throughout James I's reign the Church of England's dominant theology was Calvinist.[49] This stance had been reinforced by its representation at the Synod of Dort, and when war broke out in 1642 many supporters of episcopacy – certainly those invited to sit in the Assembly – were thoroughgoing Calvinists on most points save that of church order.[50]

During the earlier Stuart period, Puritanism was a diffuse movement within the Church of England which may have held generally to the principle of reforming the Church more strictly to the biblical pattern but which included a variety of ecclesiastical opinions from opting for a moderate episcopacy to a demand for presbyterianism or congregationalism. The débâcle of the Hampton Court Conference and James I's policy had cooled the enthusiasm of some and caused others to take a lower profile, but

---

maintain the Anglican episcopacy left them bitterly disappointed, and with two healthy sons to succeed him, Catholicism had little hope of regaining power. Two years after his accession a desperate band of young Catholics tried to secure by insurrection and the Gunpowder Plot (1605) what now seemed impossible for them to gain by means of the succession.

[49] For example, Samuel Ward, later to be one of the English representatives at Dort, had been a convinced Puritan during his early years at Cambridge, but he managed to conform sufficiently to become Master of Sidney Sussex College and Lady Margaret Professor of Divinity. Although later in life he supported the royal cause, he never gave up his Calvinism. Cf. *The Lord Protector*, pp. 29–33, and M. M. Knappen, (ed.) *Two Puritan Diaries*, (Chicago, Am. Soc. of Church Hist., 1933.) See also R. T. Kendall's *Calvin and English Calvinism to 1649*, especially chapter 6.

[50] The earlier Church of England theologians, for example, had a distinctly Reformed soteriology in contrast to the later Caroline divines. Cf. C. Fitzsimons Allison, *The Rise of Moralism*, (New York, Seabury Press, 1966.) An older book that traced the influence of Calvinism on English theology is Charles Davis Cremeans, *The Reception of Calvinistic Thought in England*, (Urbana, University of Illinois Press, 1949.) Recently R. T. Kendall has argued that Theodore Beza and the Heidelberg theologians, Ursinus, Olevianus and Zanchius, may have played a very important role in the way Calvinism was interpreted by William Perkins and his followers. Cf. *Calvin and English Calvinism to 1649*, pp. 55ff.; also Basil Hall, 'The Calvin Legend' and 'Calvin against the Calvinists' in *John Calvin* (edited by Basil Hall; Abingdon, Berks., Sutton Courtenay Press, 1966,) pp. 1–37.

it had by no means forced all Puritans from the Church or all Episcopal sympathizers from Puritanism.[51]

The outbreak of the Civil War changed this. It forced not only people but issues out into the open, and many of those who had counted themselves to be generally sympathetic to Puritan reforms now had to inform themselves more precisely about the ecclesiological issues.[52] Furthermore, in the actual course of the war latent social differences added serious questions about the way in which the war was being conducted.[53] Ideas that had been lying dormant and half formed were pushed into the open to be clarified and developed under the pressure of events and eschatological expectations of the end of the age.[54]

---

[51] This is one of the places where J. R. DeWitt's detailed study of ecclesiology in the Westminster Assembly is open to serious question. He assumed that the Elizabethan Puritan movement continued unabated during the first four decades of the 17th century. There is no proof of such a steady persistence of presbyterian ideas in England, whereas there is clear proof that (1) during James I's reign and throughout the primacy of Archbishop Laud, the extremer Puritans were under constant pressure and in process of being harried 'out of the land'; that (2) at the outbreak of hostilities there were many Puritans who were undecided about ecclesiastical government, or favoured moderate episcopacy. Because of this lacuna, DeWitt does not recognize the strength of the moderates among the Puritans, or recognize that a considerable number of Puritans would have preferred some continuation of the episcopacy if it could have been purged of its prelatical pretensions. Cf. J. R. DeWitt, *Jus Divinum: The Westminster Assembly and the Divine Right of Church Government*, (Kampen, J. H. Kok N.V., 1969.) In contrast, Michael Watts speaks of "the near extinction of English Presbyterianism between 1590 and 1640"; *The Dissenters*, p. 56, cf. *ibid.* p. 60.

[52] In February 1641 Cromwell wrote an interesting letter to a Mr. Willingham asking to have a copy of the reasons that the Scots presented for enforcing religious uniformity. It is an indication that some of those taking active part in opposition to Charles were having to inform themselves on the new issues in religion, and in a hurry! Cf. *The Lord Protector*, p. 51, Abbott, *Writings and Speeches of O.C.*, I, p. 125, Lomas–Carlyle, I, p. 96.

[53] See 'Religion, Politics and War' in my Introduction to *An Apologeticall Narration* (1963) pp. 67–80.

[54] An immense literature has grown up on the relationship of the Puritan movement to eschatology and apocalypticism. Although we may agree that the eschatological element may be over-emphasized (cf. Iain H. Murray, *The Puritan Hope*, London, Banner of Truth, 1971, p. xxiii) yet there was an unmistakable expectation of 'the End' that runs through the Puritan writers of the period, especially among the Independents and those to the left of them politically and ecclesiastically. But it was by no means absent among others including the 'Presbyterians'. Cf. Peter Smith's sermon preached before Parliament, May 29, 1644. In addition to the general works on Puritanism and the Civil War cited previously, see John F. Wilson, *Pulpit in Parliament: Puritanism during the English Civil Wars, 1640–1648*, (Princeton, N. J., Princeton U.P., 1969,) and also his unpublished Th.D. thesis, *Studies in Puritan Millenarianism under the Early Stuarts*, (Union Theol. Sem., New York, 1962;) Erling Jorstad, *The Politics of Doomsday*, (New York, Abingdon, 1970;) Peter Toon (ed.), *Puritans, the Millenium and the Future of Israel: Puritan Eschatology 1600 to 1660*, (Cambridge, James Clarke & Co., 1970;) John I. Morgans, 'The National and International Aspects of Puritan Eschatology,' Unpublished Ph.D. dissertation, (The Hartford Sem. Foundation, 1969;) Bryan W. Ball, *The Great Expectation: Eschatological Thoughts in English Protestantism [Studies in the Hist. of*

Even the major parties that appeared in the Assembly did not remain fixed in their policies but changed with the changing circumstances of the war. Daniel Neal noted a clear development among those who later supported Presbyterianism. When the Assembly was called, all the divines with the exception of the Scottish Commissioners and the ministers of the French churches had been ordained under the episcopal system and were graduates of English universities.[55] He also remarked that although the Scots were strictly for the abolition of episcopacy, the English divines were by no means as certain in their ecclesiological position, and if anything favoured a moderate (i.e. biblical) episcopacy.[56] Indeed, commenting on an earlier skirmish between Charles and his Parliament, Neal observed:

> This was a nice and curious Affair; for the Friends of the Parliament, who were agreed in the Cause of civil Liberty, were far from being of one Mind in Points of Church Discipline; the major Part were for Episcopacy, and desired no more than to secure the Constitution, and reform a few Exorbitances of the Bishops; some were *Erastians*, and would be content with any Form of Government the Magistrate should appoint; the *real Presbyterians*, who were for an entire Change of the Hierarchy upon the Foot of *divine Right*, were as yet but few, and could carry nothing in the House...[57]

Christian Thought, No. 12], (Leiden, Brill, 1975;) also the following articles, Alfred Cohen, 'Two Roads to the Puritan Millenium: William Erbury and Vavasour Powell', *Church History*, Vol. XXXII, (1964,) and the 'Comment' by John F. Wilson in the same issue; Robert Gordon Clause, 'The Influence of Henry Alsted on English Millenarian Thought in the Seventeenth Century', *Church History*, Vol. XXXIII, (1964,) and an earlier article by Alan Simpson, 'Saints in Arms: English Puritanism as Political Utopianism', *Church History*, Vol. XXIII, No. 2, (1954.) Other aspects of the subject, such as the Fifth Monarchy movement, have a very considerable literature of their own.

[55] *The History of the Puritans*, III, 61.

[56] The ambivalence of the English 'Presbyterians' in the Assembly is now generally recognized. Cf. Ethyn Williams Kirby, 'The English Presbyterians in the Westminster Assembly,' *Church History*, XXXIII, No. 4 (December 1964); Jack Bartlett Rogers *Scripture in the Westminster Confession*, (Grand Rapids, William B. Eerdmans, 1967,) p. 124. However, it should be noted that this is not accepted by those who traditionally regard the majority as fully convinced Presbyterians; e.g., J. R. DeWitt charged Kirby with having missed the point because to the Puritans of the 1640s "a non-prelatical polity meant presbytery, the government according to the word of God." J. R. DeWitt, *Jus Divinum: The Westminster Assembly and the Divine Right of Church Government*, p. 31, note 75. But I think De-Witt missed the point because he assumed that 'non-prelatical' is the same as 'non-episcopal' and there is plenty of evidence to show that for many Puritans it was not. He also assumed that the Puritan movement remained virtually unchanged from the time of Cartwright in the 1570s to the call of the Assembly in 1643. Apart from the unique longevity of such veterans as John Dod (1549?–1645), and Laurence Chad[d]erton (1536? 1640), the Puritanism of the 1640s represented a wholly different constituency from the Elizabethan variety.

[57] Neal, *op.cit*. III, 5. The preference of the majority of opponents to Laud's policies for a moderate form of episcopacy is insistently stated by Richard Baxter, who may have

Yet within a few years the main body of Puritans, and probably a majority of Parliament's supporters, were ready to embrace the Scottish system and to establish presbyterian uniformity throughout the nation.[58]

The small body of Independents also shifted their position under the wartime pressures. In some ways the Independents entered the Assembly with a much more precisely formulated ecclesiology than the other English Puritans at Westminster,[59] and they had had the opportunity of experimenting with their views on the Church while they had been in exile in Holland. Although they could not claim the prestige of a national establishment such as the Scottish kirk, their colleagues were setting out to rectify that in Massachusetts,[60] and it is clear that they looked to the New England divines to provide them with evidence that their system could work within the framework of an official establishment. There is no reason to think that when they entered the Assembly the Independents would have been any more reluctant to see Congregationalism established in England than their colleagues had been to establish it in America, or for that matter than the Scots were to have Presbyterianism established.

The circumstances of the war did not allow them to remain at this point. Increasingly they discovered themselves to be a minority fighting a rear-guard action, first to prevent, then to modify, and finally to postpone the establishment of full presbyterian uniformity; and in this struggle they discovered allies among the very sects that would have been vigorously excluded from New England. Liberty of conscience, which had no place among the pre-war prejudices of New England Congregationalists, within a few years became the main plank in their platform within the Assembly and in their representations to Parliament.

It is not suggested that such shifts were hypocritical, but rather that they should be seen in light of the changing situation

---

been the authority behind Neal's account. Writing of those who opposed the Laudian reforms, Baxter claimed that "almost all these were comfortable Ministers". *Rel. Baxt.* I. i. p. 34 (§50); cf. *ibid.* I. ii. p. 146 (§23), p. 411 (§364), III. p. 41 (§91).

[58] The indications of this shift are seen throughout the Grand Debate, beginning with the events described in chapter 8, and especially *infra* pp. 222ff.

[59] E.g., in the writings of William Ames, Paul Baynes, William Bradshaw and Henry Jacob.

[60] John Phillips seems to have been the only member of the Assembly who had served in Massachusetts, but he does not appear to have taken much active part in the debates and was not used much by the Independents. It is intriguing to ponder the reason. Cf. the discussion of this in my Introduction to *An Apologeticall Narration* (1963 edn.), p. 110 and notes, also *infra* pp. 125ff.

imposed by the conditions of civil war. As the exponents of rival views of the Church were forced to review their positions, they drew insights from their theology that would have remained latent (as they did in New England) if the wartime pressures had not been there. Woodhouse was surely right when he said, "partly through force of circumstance, but partly through a logical development of their own basic doctrines, the Independents became the party of toleration."[61] During the course of the war Puritans discovered implications for church and society that carried them far beyond where they had been when the fighting began.

They were brought to their new positions rapidly. The nations of Britain with those on the mainland of Europe were undoubtedly hastening down the road to a secular world, but because the temper of the time and the preoccupation of seventeenth century England were theological, the issue focused in the question of theological authority. For that reason the debates on the Church would be crucial for the Puritans, because they would put the scriptural appeal to its primary test. The basic question at that time was not whether Parliament and the Assembly could produce a new and *different* sort of society and church, but whether they could restore a convincing semblance of the ancient unity of church and society, and in such a way that could convince people of its authority. All Puritans assumed that it could and would be done, and for that reason even the emerging constitutional and social problems would be debated largely in terms of Puritan theology and arrayed with their own panoply of scriptural references.

But it should be seen that if the scriptural authority was to be the final arbiter, the question of consensus was crucial; and when such a consensus evaded them, the debates were likely to become bitter.

III

Natural Allies: Unnatural Friends

The British people comprise at least four distinct nationalities,[62] but in this period it is the relationship of England and Scotland that holds the centre of the stage.

---

[61] *Puritanism and Liberty*, Introduction [p. 16]. Woodhouse's comment may be cited in support of my own view against Perry Miller at this point. Perry Miller did not recognize how far toleration may have been implicit within Congregational ecclesiology. Cf. *Orthodoxy in Mass.* pp. 270ff., *An Apologeticall Narration* (1963), pp. 52f, note 26.

[62] The English, the Scots, the Welsh and the Irish; but even the Cornish and the Manx have from time to time expressed national aspirations.

Friendship and cooperation between England and the northern kingdom had been of very recent growth. The new relationship was entirely due to quirks of history that brought a Scottish king to the English throne and to circumstances which caused both countries to become Protestant at much the same time, and hence it arose from their need of mutual political support. Before the Reformation the Scots had usually found France a more congenial ally, while the English, insofar as they thought of their northern neighbours at all, considered them in terms of potential conquest and subjugation. True, the Tudors had tried to deflect any threat from Scotland when Henry VII had given his daughter, Margaret, in marriage to James IV of Scotland, but this had not changed Scotland's national prejudices and soon it was again fully in the French orbit with the marriage of James V to Mary of Guise in 1542 – an alliance that was further strengthened by the marriage of their young daughter, Mary (Queen of Scots), to the French Dauphin. By the end of the reign of Mary I in England, Mary Queen of Scots was about to ascend the throne of France as the wife of Francis II, while her mother, Mary of Guise, was her Regent in Scotland: Scotland seemed to be firmly set in the French alliance.

This situation was dramatically changed by England's return to the Protestant camp in the accession of Elizabeth I, the daughter of Anne Boleyn, by the rapid spread of Protestant sentiment in Scotland, and by the sudden deaths of Francis II of France and Mary of Guise which induced Mary Queen of Scots to return to her native land. These changes also meant that there could be a natural alliance between Elizabeth and the reforming party in Scotland to defend their common interests against the Catholic and pro-French policy of the Scots Queen, for, as long as Elizabeth remained without legitimate issue, Mary Queen of Scots was her legitimate heir through her grandmother, Margaret of England.

Under the leadership of the redoubtable John Knox, the Protestants in Scotland proved to be too strongly entrenched to be upset by Mary Queen of Scots, although she reinforced her claim on the English throne by marrying Henry Stuart, Lord Darnley, a claimant to that throne in his own right.[63] After several years and a few extramarital escapades Mary found herself defeated by her Protestant subjects at Carberry Hill (1567) and was forced to

---

[63] After the death of James IV of Scotland, his widow, Margaret, had married the Earl of Angus. The daughter of that marriage, also named Margaret, married Matthew Stewart (or Stuart), Earl of Lennox, and Henry Stuart, Lord Darnley, was their son.

flee for protection to her rival, Elizabeth. With the circumstances that led to her trial and execution for complicity in three separate plots against Elizabeth's life, we are not concerned, but our attention is turned to her infant son, James VI, who assumed the Scottish throne after his mother had been deposed, and who would also be heir to the throne of England on the death of his mother. He came to the English throne in 1603 as James I and the first of the Stuart sovereigns. From this time on, it seemed, both politics and religion would unite the two countries in their allegiance to a single royal family.

The story did not develop that simply. If there were strong religious reasons for the new alliance between England and Scotland, there were some equally powerful reasons that could lead to mutual suspicion, for while John Knox, like the personification of an Old Testament prophet, would carry his country into a form of the Church wholly patterned after the Genevan model, Elizabeth would be equally intent on the Church of England becoming a *via media* so that her Catholic subjects would be encouraged to accept her supremacy in Church and State: personal preferences, prejudices and policy all conspired to send Elizabeth in one ecclesiastical direction and John Knox in another.

The roots of these new suspicions went back to Mary I's reign. They centered in the tensions that had developed within the congregation of English exiles in the German town of Frankfort on the Main in the years 1554–5. The dispute which disrupted that congregation was on the form of the Church and its worship, but behind that there was the question of what was to be accepted as the ultimate authority for deciding these matters, the Bible or English law. On the one side there were those who argued that now they were out of England they could explore more freely the biblical form of the Church and its worship, while the opposing party insisted that because they were English, they were bound as loyal subjects of the English Crown to maintain the form of the Church and the Prayer Book as it had been authorized under Edward VI. The leaders of this 'Prayer Book' party would eventually become some of the most important leaders in the Elizabethan Church,[64] but it was unfortunate that Knox, the

---

[64] No less than six future bishops and two future Archbishops of the Elizabethan Church appear in the troubles at Frankfort and took part in the dispute with Knox: Edmund Grindall (Archbishop of York, 1570–75, Archbishop of Canterbury, 1576–83); Edwin Sandys (Archbishop of York, 1576–88); Richard Cox (first of Norwich and then of Ely,) Robert Horne of Winchester, John Jewell of Salisbury, John Parkhurst of Norwich,

personification of the Reformation to most Scotsmen, had been the leader of the reforming party at Frankfort and that because of the efforts of these English divines he had been expelled from Frankfort: he had had the opportunity of seeing as much as he wanted to see both of the Prayer Book and of the men in whose hands Elizabeth would place church affairs.[65] This unfortunate occasion for distrust was exacerbated in 1558 by Knox's diatribe against the female (and largely Catholic) domination of European politics, his *First Blast against the Monstrous Regiment* [*i.e.* Rulership] *of Women*.[66] It had been almost immediately suppressed by the authorities at Geneva, where Knox was minister of the English Church, but the damage was done and its impact came just as Elizabeth was about to ascend the throne. Even Knox admitted that the *Blast* had "blowne from me all my friends in England."[67] Elizabeth was too good a statesman [statesperson?] to allow Knox's ill-timed outburst to affect her political alliance with the Scots, but she never forgave Knox, and it was clear that England and Scotland were by no means set on the same ecclesiastical course.

The accession of James to the English throne in 1603 offered a good deal of hope from the Scottish side that the differences in polity and practice between the two national churches would be

---

James Pilkington of Durham, and John Scory, who had been a bishop under Edward VI (first of Rochester and then of Chichester) and became Bishop of Hereford under Elizabeth.

[65] The full account of this episode appeared in *A Brieff Discours off the Troubles Begonne at Franckford*, (London, 1575.) This is usually attributed to William Whittingham, a partisan of Knox and later Dean of Durham, but Patrick Collinson has argued that the work was published by John Field and a group of London Puritan propagandists, Cf. 'The Authorship of *A Brieff Discours off the Troubles Begonne at Franckford*', in *The Journal of Ecclesiastical History*, IX. No. 2 (October 1958,) pp. 188–208. See also John Knox's brief account of the events that led to his expulsion from Frankfort in his *History of the Reformation in Scotland*, (New York, Philosophical Library, 1950, 2 vols.) I. 110, or in a more recent edition of *A Brieff Discours*, edited by Edward Arber, (London, Elliott Stock, 1908); cf. *ibid.* pp. 24–69.

[66] Catherine de Medici was the most powerful person in France after the death of her husband, Henry II, in 1559 and her son, Francis II, in 1560; Mary I had been Queen in England and carried through the persecution of Protestants that has earned her the title 'Bloody Mary' in history; Mary Queen of Scots was more French than Scots, and during her absence the government of Scotland was under the control of her French mother, Mary of Guise. However, Knox should have been more prudent, for whatever happened in England was likely to bring a Queen to the throne. Even after Elizabeth, the lines of succession led through Margaret and Mary, the daughters of Henry VII – the former leading to Mary Queen of Scots and Arabella Stuart, and the latter to Katherine Grey.

[67] Letter to Mrs. Anna Lock, in *The Works of John Knox*, edited by David Laing, (Edinburgh, The Woodrow Soc., 1846–64,) VI. 14. Both Calvin and Beza condemned Knox's imprudence, and after Elizabeth came to the throne, John Aylmer, who had been a Protestant exile and later became Bishop of London (1577), wrote a reply to Knox's book, *An Harborowe for Faithful and Trewe Subjects* (1559).

settled in favour of the more Reformed pattern. James Stuart was a native-born Scot who had signed the National Covenant and expressed himself publicly as less than enthusiastic about episcopacy, and he had been instructed in theology by the best theologians Scottish Calvinism could produce.

But the Elizabethan bishops had laid the ground work well for the change of dynasty. As soon as the Queen died, or possibly sooner,

> the Archbishop [Whitgift], in his own Name, and of al the Bishops and Clergy, sent Dr. *Nevyl*, the Dean of his Church of *Canterbury*, into *Scotland*, to his Majesty, to give him the Assurance of their unfeigned Duty and Loyalty: and to know what Commands he had for them to observe concerning Ecclesiastical Causes: recommending also the Church of *England* to his Favour and Protection. To which Message he gave a very gracious Answer, and that he would uphold the Government of the late Queen, as she left it. Which, when the Dean returned, and gave the Archbishop an Account of, gave him great Comfort and Satisfaction. For indeed he and some of the Bishops, particularly the Bishop of *London* [Bancroft], feared much, that when this King came to reign in this Realm, he would favour the *New Disciplin*, and make Alterations in the Ecclesiastical Government and Liturgy: and this had made them speak sometimes uneasily of the *Scotch Mist*. [68]

The alacrity with which James changed his position[69] to support the bishops suggests that there may well have been a secret understanding between James and the Anglican prelates. His position as a foreigner in England was not all that strong, his mother had been executed there for High Treason, and he was in need of all the help he could muster to win the throne peacefully and to establish himself in the southern kingdom. Added to this, he had a most exalted view of kingship and found the hierarchical order in the English Church much to his liking. The deference accorded to his royal person by the bishops was in marked contrast to the scant respect he received from the Scottish preachers. Given the circumstances, it was not hard for the new king or his bishops to realize that it was in their mutual interest to remain close.

At the Hampton Court Conference of 1603/4, called ostensibly

---

[68] John Strype, *The Life and Acts of the Most Reverend Father in God, John Whitgift*, (London, 1718,) pp. 559f.

[69] James had recently told the General Assembly that he approved the Church of Scotland and "disclaimed all intention of making any further alteration in its government." W. M. Hetherington, *History of the Church of Scotland*, (New York, Robert Carter, 1845,) p. 118.

to discuss reforms proposed by the Puritans, James put the matter very succinctly in the aphorism, to which we have already alluded.[70] He also made his distaste for Scottish Presbyterians and their English Puritan supporters evident throughout the conference,[71] and left no doubt that the episcopal order in the Church of England was on a firmer base than ever.

The conference, however, did not merely frustrate any Scottish hopes of seeing a presbyterian order in England. Within a short time the Scots had reason to fear for the independence of their Kirk, for James showed full confidence in English prelates such as Richard Bancroft,[72] and he was clearly determined to export the English form of church government and the Prayer Book to his native land.[73] Presbyterian leaders were imprisoned and others sent into exile for their opposition, and James made it unequivocally clear that the unification of the two kingdoms would take place not under the Scottish but under the English system.[74] The irony of the Scots' situation was that their fears were entirely due to a native-born Scots king, although they found it easier to think that his apostasy was due to his English flatterers.

When Charles I succeeded to the two thrones in 1625, he eventually added the injuries of war to the insult of William Laud's episcopal reforms in Scotland. The Church of Scotland continued to squirm under that episcopacy which James had re-introduced in 1610, and after William Laud became Archbishop of Canterbury in 1633, Charles, with the Archbishop's

---

[70] *Supra* p. 16, note 10.

[71] In a private session with the prelates on the first day James declared that "howsoeuer he liued among *Puritans*, and was kept, for the most part, as a Ward vnder them, yet, since hee was of the age of his Sonne, 10 years old, he euer disliked their opinions; as the Sauiour of the world said, *Though he liued among them, he was not of them.*" Barlow, *The Summe and Substance of the Conference . . .*, p. 20. During the course of the conference he made several critical comments about the Scottish Presbyterians, particularly in his reply to Dr. Reynolds, "thinking that they aymed at a *Scottish Presbytery,* which saith hee, as well agreeth with a Monarchy, as God, and the Diuell. Then *Iack* and *Tom,* and *Will,* and *Dick,* shall meete, and at their pleasures censure me, and my Councell, and all our proceedings." *Ibid.* p. 79.

[72] James appointed Bancroft Archbishop of Canterbury after the death of Whitgift in 1604.

[73] See Robert Baillie's *An Historical Vindication of the Government of the Church of Scotland,* (London, 1646.)

[74] *Ibid.* Baillie stressed the close relationship of the Scots with English Calvinists in Elizabeth's reign and the later encroachments of the English prelates. He also recorded the sufferings of the Scottish ministers. Andrew Melvill was imprisoned several times and eventually found himself in the Tower, while after the abortive attempt to hold a General Assembly in 1605, fourteen ministers were put in prison. Later others were imprisoned, summoned to London (!), or banished.

advice, forced Scotland to suffer the imposition of ecclesiastical canons (1636) and liturgical Prayer Book worship (1637) entirely *à la mode anglaise*. Indeed, it was clear that Charles was giving the English primate a free hand in Scottish affairs, and Laud took full advantage of his powers by imposing a Prayer Book that Scottish Calvinists could only regard as a further step towards Rome. Despite the overwhelming opposition of most Scots and the ominous renewal of the National Covenant in 1638, Charles, with encouragement from Laud and his more hot-headed courtiers, had the military naïveté and political gall to invade his native land at the head of an English army (March 1638/9); and after this exercise in arrogant futility he listened to such advisers as the Earl of Strafford who persuaded him to repeat the fiasco a year later.[75] His army was again ignominiously defeated and the Scots occupied Newcastle. By this time both the Scots and the English parliamentary leaders realized that "the liberties of both Nations were at stake" and that they would have to make common cause against the arbitrary encroachments in Church and State.[76]

This rehearsal of the Stuart Kings' relationship to Scotland is necessary background to the Civil War, and specifically to the story of the Westminster Assembly, because it reveals the underlying causes for Scots' suspicion of English churchmen, and explains the attitude with which their Commissioners entered Westminster. Furthermore, it has been pointed out that the difference in national attitudes was in part due to the difference of national history; "in Scotland, the very name 'bishop' had become odious from the fraudulent and unscrupulous measures employed to introduce the order", whereas in England "it had been from the beginning associated with reformation, and sanctified by martyrdom."[77]

Up to the outbreak of the English Civil War the Scots had a right to consider themselves the nation aggrieved, and for this reason we must give full value to the importance they placed in the 1640s on bringing about a permanent ecclesiastical change in England. If James had not gained the English throne it would have been impossible for the Stuarts to subvert the Kirk. The military support that Charles had received from England for his

---

[75] Neal, *History of the Puritans*, II. 339.

[76] Cf. the correspondence between some English and Scottish peers at this time, Neal, *Hist. of the Puritans*, II. 340.

[77] Thomas M'Crie, *Annals of English Presbytery*, (London, James Nisbet, 1872,) p. 113.

forays into Scotland was meagre and ineffectual enough, but his army had been almost entirely English, officered by English courtiers, advised and encouraged by English peers and prelates, and subsidized (not very willingly, it is true) by English money. Moreover, the whole enterprise was undertaken to impose a specifically English form of church government and worship on the Scottish people against their Reformed conscience. National pride as well as ecclesiastical prejudice would be much more likely to explain the recent troubles as the machinations of foreign prelates who had duped Scotland's King, than as the Stuart King's own determination to use the new power base in London as a means of bringing the Scottish Kirk to heel.

In light of this the Scottish ministers resolved to launch an ecclesiastical counter-attack as soon as conditions permitted, because only when the two nations confessed a common Reformed faith would the Scottish Kirk feel safe. As a result of the Scots' occupation of Newcastle in 1640, some of their leading ministers went as chaplains to the nation's Commissioners in London, and not only were the ministers chosen with great care, but they were given specific assignments directed to the eventual goal of winning England for Presbytery. The Scots were nothing if not systematic in launching an offensive, whether in the closets of diplomacy or on the field of battle.

On November 5th, 1640, Robert Baillie wrote to his wife from Newcastle:

> Yesternight the Committee sent for me, and told me of their desyre I should goe to London with the Commissioners. I made sundrie difficulties, which partlie they answered, and partlie took to their consideration till this day. At our Presbytrie, after sermon, both our noblemen and ministers in one voyce thought meet, that not onelie Mr. A. Hendersoun, bot also Mr. R. Blair, Mr. George Gillespie, and I, should all three, for diverse ends, goe to London: Mr. Robert Blair to satisfie the mynds of manie in England, who loves the way of New England better than that of Presbytries used in our Church; I, for the convinceing of that praevalent faction, against which I have wryten; Mr. Gillespie, for the crying doune of the English Ceremonies, for which he hes wryten; and all foure to preach by turnes to our Commissioners in their houses, which is the custome of diverse noblemen at Court, and wes our practise all the tyme of the conference at Rippon.[78]

This suggests that the Scots were very well-informed about the

---

[78] *Letters and Journals of Mr. Robert Baillie*, edited by David Laing, (Edinburgh, Robert Ogle, 1841–2,) I. 268–9.

developing situation in English church affairs, and that each minister had been chosen with a view to the specific contribution he could make to the Scottish strategy. Even at this early date, before the outbreak of the Civil War itself, the Scots obviously had clear ideas about an ecclesiastical counter-offensive. The expedition to London provided an admirable opportunity to study the situation in England, and to prepare the ground for their own plans; and it is clear from the letters that Baillie sent back to Scotland that he and his colleagues took full advantage of their visit to the English capital.[79]

The English Puritans were Calvinists and could therefore be relied upon as allies, but there had been some variant voices heard among them that the orthodox Presbyterians in Scotland would have preferred to see suppressed, and even the Scots' most loyal supporters in Church and Parliament in England suffered the disadvantage of being English. Any future agreement between the two nations (*e.g.* the Solemn League and Covenant) would have to contain an explicit engagement that the Church of England would be brought into the closest conformity with the Reformed Church of Scotland. This would be Scotland's best guarantee for its own independence.[80] If this policy were successful, it would mean not only that the Kirk would never again have to suffer the indignity of English interference, but it would also turn the tables dramatically on what Scotland had regarded as a period of particularly obnoxious Englishness.

IV

'Old England is Lost'

From the English side, the situation naturally looked somewhat different. The first fifty years of the Reformation in Scotland convinced a majority of that nation that the cause of Scottish nationalism was also that of a Reformed Presbyterian Church, but the effect of the first hundred years of the Reformation in England identified an increasing number of the English people as conservative (if none too pious) supporters of the episcopal order 'by law established'.

The interaction of the two nations during the turbulent years of the seventeenth century was to contribute to differences in religious tastes; but not everything is to be explained in those terms, and we must agree with Thomas M'Crie that the reason why England travelled by such a different route from that of her

---

[79] *Infra* pp. 42f., 59 n. 19. Baillie's *Letters and Journals*, I. 268–355.
[80] Cf. *Infra* pp. 94–97.

northern neighbour is in large part to be sought in the earlier religious history and make-up of the English people. When we look at the century that separated the death of Mary (1558) from the Restoration (1660) we find an interesting clue that may have had a good deal to do with the different paths taken by the Church of England and the Church of Scotland, and which may have contributed significantly to the mutual suspicions that would muddy the relationship of the two countries. This is to be found in the make-up of the English people itself, for there are good grounds for suggesting that while in Scotland Knox and his colleagues had been able to enlist the public's enthusiastic support for their extensive reforms, the English public remained essentially conservative in its ecclesiastical preferences.

Elsewhere I have tried to show that at the end of Mary's reign the great majority of English people, if not Roman Catholic by conviction, had been certainly Catholic in sentiment, but that by the time Charles II came to the throne the majority of his subjects was prepared to acquiesce in, if not to welcome, membership in a Church of England governed by bishops and worshipping according to the Book of Common Prayer.[81] The trend to a genuine *via media* had been begun by Elizabeth, for it had been in accordance with Elizabeth's religious preferences and entirely to her political advantage to stress those ecclesiastical and liturgical aspects of her religious settlement which stood best chance of winning over the great mass of conservative opinion. This represented the majority which had overturned the Protestant changes of Edward VI, maintained Queen Mary in power, and dutifully accepted the return to Rome. From the time of the controversy about vestments in 1566, Elizabeth and her ecclesiastical advisers had stressed conformity to those *visible* aspects of piety in government and worship that would minimize the differences in practice between the national Church of England and the Church of earlier times.

The 'protestantism' of the national Church was perhaps visible primarily at those points that invoked the Englishman's patriotism: Pius V's Bull of Excommunication against the Queen, for example, had been an embarrassment to many of Elizabeth's Catholic subjects, just as Mary's unfortunate alliance with Philip II of Spain had been. But there were many other reasons that emphasized the need for national unity, which would begin to push the patriotic Englishman, for all his conservative prefer-

---

[81] This is discussed at greater length in ' "A Way to Wyn them": Ecclesiology and Religion in the English Reformation,' in *Reformatio Perennis*.

ences in religion, in the direction of the national church: the attempted invasion of England by the Spanish Armada in 1588, the Catholic Mary Queen of Scots' repeated involvement in plots against Elizabeth's life (leading to Mary's execution in 1587), the rumours about the Spanish Inquisition, and the stirring accounts of the Dutch nation's stubborn fight for its independence. By the time James I came to the throne in 1603 the 'Black Legend' was well on its way to becoming a national prejudice.[82]

The first two Stuart kings deliberately pursued the ecclesiastical policy of *via media* best suited for winning subjects with Catholic leanings into the national Church. They were helped by events no less than Elizabeth had been: patriotic Englishmen were shocked by the Gunpowder Plot in 1605, outraged by the Thirty Years War in 1618 and the sufferings of James I's son-in-law, the Elector Palatine, humiliated by the insults – actual or imagined – suffered by the young Prince Charles and the Duke of Buckingham in the romantic attempt to woo a Spanish Princess, and finally – close to the outbreak of civil war – horrified by accounts in 1641 of the general slaughter of Protestants in Ireland.[83] The significance of these events is that whereas they caused the comparatively small number of English Puritans to reflect grimly that they had been right all along, they tended to draw the large number of Catholic Englishmen to identify themselves more closely with the national Church.

This process of assimilation must have been well advanced by the outbreak of the Civil War in 1642, and if we are right in suggesting that England's official churchmanship had considerable investment in the determination to withstand foreign interference, then it may help to explain why the Scots were as unsuccessful in winning the English people to their Presbyterianism as the English were at imposing their Prayer Book and episcopacy upon the Scots.

Robert Baillie may have had a glimmering of this in 1641 during his first visit to London. The Scots Commissioners were in the English capital at the time of the early agitation against the bishops, and Alexander Henderson raised a furore by very unwisely deciding to voice publicly his own opposition to the whole episcopal system. Baillie admitted in his report to Scotland

---

[82] Cf. William S. Maltby, *The Black Legend in England: the development of Anti-Spanish Sentiment*, (Durham, N. Carolina, Duke University Press, 1971.)

[83] The reports of the Irish massacre varied between the comparatively conservative estimate of Lord Clarendon (40–50,000 victims) to the 200,000 Lucy Hutchinson and Richard Baxter believed to have been killed. Cf. Robert S. Paul, *The Lord Protector*, p. 52 and notes.

that "diverse of our true friends did think us too rash, and though they loved not the Bishops, yet, for the honor of their nation, they would keep them up rather than that we strangers should pull them down."[84] There were many Englishmen during the life of the Westminster Assembly who would have agreed with Samuel Johnson's complaint a century later, "Sir, it is not so much to be lamented that Old England is Lost, as that the Scotch have found it."

V

Practical Urgency: the Need for Ministers

The concept of Christendom gave the Church responsibility for education, and a nation-wide system of pastoral care. Every baptized subject was under spiritual care, at least in theory, through a network of dioceses and parishes in which bishops and priests had responsibility of providing the nurture and consolation of the Church for every soul. This had been particularly important within the medieval church where salvation had been seen largely in terms of the individual's incorporation into the sacramental system, but despite the break with Rome it seems that the traditional attitudes were still ingrained in the English people.[85]

Civil war totally disrupted the parochial system. The situation was complicated by the ecclesiological dispute and by the awkward fact that many ministers found themselves in parts of the country where they became politically *personae non gratae*. So in places controlled by royalists those of Puritan sympathies were plundered and ejected from their livings, while in areas controlled by the parliamentary forces those who followed the Prayer Book were similarly sequestered. This produced a serious shortage of ministers especially where Parliament was still able to govern, because the Puritans also insisted on getting rid of

---

[84] To the Presbytery at Irvine, March 15th, 1640/1, *Letters and Journals*, I. 306.

[85] James I at the Hampton Court Conference had pointed to the more traditional and sacramental approach that survived in England. Assuring the bishops "That hee also maintained the necessitie of Baptisme", he went on to observe that they might think it strange "that I, who now think you in *England* giue too much to *Baptism*, did 14 moneths ago in *Scotland*, argue with my Diuines there, for ascribing too little to this holy Sacrament. Insomuch that a pert Minister asked me, if I thought Baptism so necessary, that if it were omitted, the child should be dammed? I answered him no: but if you, being called to baptize the child, though priuately, should refuse to come, I think you shall be damned." *The Summe and Substance*, pp. 16, 17. This suggests that English churchmen tended to be more conservative on Baptism than the Reformed Scots, or even than James I.

clergymen and schoolmasters whose lives were no ornament to the professions. In November 1640 Parliament established the Grand Committee for Religion to enquire into "the scandalous immoralities of the clergy", but as the fighting progressed the commissioners found it hard to distinguish between those who were guilty of scandalous conduct and those who were politically sympathetic to the King. These sequestrations aggravated a serious shortage of ministers already made grave enough by the virtual exclusion of graduates from Oxford, Charles's wartime capital. But the biggest cause of the problem was the continuing uncertainty about a regular form of ordination. Episcopal ordination had been excluded, or at least had been made temporarily suspect by Parliament's action against the English prelates, but until a decision was taken on what was to replace the traditional system no graduate from any university could be regularly ordained.

To some extent the shortage could be eased by putting into the vacant livings ministers who had been in prison or exile for their Puritan beliefs. "Those Clergymen who had been silenced and imprisoned by Archbishop *Laud* were set at liberty and encouraged; some who had fled to *Holland* and *New-England* on account of Non-Conformity returned home, and were preferr'd to considerable Lectures in the City, or to the Livings of those who were sequester'd"[86] A Committee for Plundered Ministers was formed to support and relocate those who had suffered or were beginning to suffer in the Puritan cause, collections were taken for them at the monthly fasts, and steps taken to provide for them on a more permanent basis. In addition we read that "Parliament entertained and promoted several *Scots* Divines, and yet after all, they wanted a Supply for several vacant Benefices, which obliged them to admit some unlearned Persons, and Pluralists, not of Choice, but of Necessity, for when Things were more settled the Assembly of Divines declared against both."[87]

The real problem was to know how to ordain the young divinity students from Cambridge who presented themselves for the ministry. It is clear from Richard Baxter's picture of the clergy during his boyhood that ever since the formal break with Rome, England had experienced problems in getting ministers of the 'godly and learned' sort desired by Puritans;[88] and this was

---

[86] Neal, *History of the Puritans*, III. 40f.
[87] *Ibid.* p. 41.
[88] *Reliquiae Baxterianae*, I. i. pp. 1ff. (§1).

to lay both urgency and an administrative burden on the members of the Assembly, for soon after the Assembly opened, Parliament passed an Ordinance declaring that its Commissioners "should not nominate any Persons to vacant Benefices, but such as should be examined and approved by the Assembly of Divines then sitting at *Westminster*."[89] The sooner the Assembly resolved the matter of ordination, the sooner it would be able to relinquish that kind of administrative chore.

The situation presented the divines with a double problem. They had to meet the immediate needs of the parishes and to employ the prospective ministers from the university; but beyond this they had to develop a total ecclesiology with its own authenticated procedure of ordination to take the place of the prelatical system, an ecclesiology that must be demonstrably based on the scriptures. The practical need for ministers meant that the divines of the Assembly were forced to produce an alternative form of church government, since the bishops were naturally unwilling to ordain any but those who were committed to their own cause. With the bishops siding with the King, the Assembly was also under pressure from the political alliance with the Scots, because the Scots already had a system of church government that was maintained as theologically and biblically viable by Reformed churches throughout the rest of Europe. This, together with the urgent need for ministers, clearly became a major factor in persuading those Englishmen of Puritan sympathies, hitherto luke-warm to the Scottish system, to move in the direction of Presbyterianism, and eventually to give that system their support.

VI

From Divine Right to Pluralism

J. N. Figgis, who wrote the classic study on the Divine Right of Kings, claimed that this theory of government should be considered simply as one of the rival forms in which the seventeenth century expressed the *jus divinum*.[90] It represented a basis of authority that appeared to salvage the traditional form of society and essential rightness of the *status quo*, to set the traditional and hierarchical order of things on a firmer basis and, by introducing national modifications, to strengthen the control of those who held political power.

---

[89] July 27th, 1643, Neal, *Hist. of the Puritans*, III. 41f.
[90] *The Divine Right of Kings*, (Cambridge, C.U.P., 1914,) pp. 267ff.

The Stuarts' Puritan subjects were no less medievalists than their sovereigns in the claim to an absolute *jure divino* authority on which to build, but their priorities were different because the 'given' element in their theological position was different. For them, the issue was not that of evolving an authoritative doctrine to justify the traditional view of church and society in England, but it was that of developing the implications for church and society from the divine authority that had been given in the Bible. They were left with the problem of how the words of scripture were to be interpreted, but most of them assumed that there would be no disagreement if the words of scripture were allowed to carry their simple, literal meaning.

At the same time, the most immediate experiment in Reformed national churchmanship had been already carried out in Scotland, and the Scottish Kirk enjoyed prestige among English Puritans not only by reason of its stubborn resistance to Laud, but also because it was generally in agreement with the practice of Reformed churches throughout the rest of Europe. But *was* the Scottish system so fully and unambiguously the pattern enjoined in the New Testament?[91] In his farewell sermon to the Pilgrims at Leyden, the Separatist pastor, John Robinson, had lamented the reluctance of Protestants to see any further than the insights of their original reformers, and had frankly declared that "though they were shining lights in their Times, yet God had not revealed his whole will to them."[92] By the time of the outbreak of the Civil War in 1642, even newer and more radical conceptions of the Church claiming scriptural authority were beginning to appear, from the relatively conservative Congregationalism practiced in New England to the different forms of Separatism and the Baptist movement.

As we have suggested, there is no reason to suppose that the greater number of Puritans had arrived at any fixed opinions on church polity by the outbreak of the Civil War, and there is a good deal to suggest that most of the leaders expected a modified form of episcopacy to be set up.[93] But they were faced with a crisis in Authority: they were forced by royal and episcopal claims to choose between the authority that these claims rep-

---

[91] Cf. Janet G. MacGregor, *The Scottish Presbyterian Polity: A Study of its Origins in the Sixteenth Century*, (Edinburgh, Oliver & Boyd, 1926,) especially pp. 132f.

[92] The substance of his sermon was set down many years later by Edward Winslow in *Hypocrisie Unmasked* (1646), pp. 97f. It is to be found also in W. H. Burgess, *John Robinson*, (London, Williams & Norgate, 1920,) pp. 239–41.

[93] Cf. *infra* pp. 105ff.

resented and that of the Bible, on which alone, they believed, the Reformation faith was based. Certainly the alternatives may not have been as absolute or exclusive as the seventeenth century thought them to be, but within the context of that time there could be little doubt that they would be debated and fought for as mutually exclusive: toleration of such radically different positions was not a live option, and at that time the answer to England's ecclesiastical dilemma could be sought only in a single national Church to take the place of the order that had been discarded.

One material factor that would cause the members of the Assembly to move more rapidly towards the Scots was the increasing number of sects that began to make their appearance. To tolerate groups such as Ranters, Seekers, Antinomians and Socinians was unthinkable for the majority of serious people in the seventeenth century: it would have destroyed forever the medieval dream of unity for which the greater part of the population yearned. The strength of medieval society had been in its certainty, and we must understand the theological debates of the period as an attempt to establish an undisputed authority offering the same kind of certainty for their own time.

The Reformed churches of Europe claimed that Presbyterianism was based solely on the scriptures, although the form may have had as much to do with the élitist character of Calvin's Geneva and the feudalism of Knox's Scotland as it had to the New Testament insights of the Reformers; but within the European Reformed community there already seemed to be a *consensus fidelium* about the biblical form of the Church, and this must have appeared as strong supporting evidence for Presbyterian claims. Looking across the Channel to churches in the war-devastated Palatinate, to those of the Huguenots of France, or to those of the Netherlands, an English Puritan might very well reflect that if one was looking for *consensus fidelium* who had any better right to be regarded as *fideles*?

Politics was interwoven into the struggle at several points – first, and most obviously, because of the essential relationship between Church and State. Whichever form of the Church was finally adopted, it would have to be endorsed, maintained and protected by civil government. What the Puritans and the supporters of Parliament did not realize, or perhaps were not ready to recognize, was that a change in theological authority – from that of a general Christian tradition guaranteed by the 'divine right' of the monarch to that of the scripture alone – would produce not only a different ecclesiastical pattern but also would point to a different form of society.[94] They certainly did not recognize or admit that it would carry implications that would cut at the roots of the class distinction between peers and commoners; for the time would come when there would be all too much point in the cavalier's gibe at the members of the House of Lords who had opposed the King:

> The *Lower* is the *Upper-House*,
> And hath been so seven years:
> Your *Votes* they value not a *Lowse*
> Ye *Antichristian Peers.*

> My Lords, of *Gotham*, not of *Greece*,
> Your *wisdoms* I shall sing;
> And sell you all for *pence apiece*,
> If you reject your *King.*[95]

Few people would have been ready to concede at the beginning of the war that aristocratic or oligarchic interpretations of scripture regarding Church and society would finally give way to the more democratic and populist interpretations that were unconsciously being advanced by the sects, although it is clear that the radical ecclesiologies in the army soon began to foster radical ideas about society as a whole.[96]

Politics would also intervene in the work of the Assembly at a very practical level. There were honest differences of opinion in

---

[94] This is illustrated by the fiction that Parliament was fighting 'For King and Parliament'. However, Baxter notes that as soon as the fighting started, a change soon became apparent among the troops: in 1644, "when the Lord *Fairfax* should have marched with his Army, he would not (as common Fame saith) take his Commission, because it ran as all others before, [*for the Defence of the King's Person*]: for it was intimated that this was but Hypocrisie, to profess to defend the King when they marcht to fight against him; and that Bullets could not distinguish between his Person and another Man's; and therefore this Clause must be left out". *Reliquiae Baxterianae*, I. i. p. 49 (§71).

[95] *Sir John Berkenhead Reviv'd*, pp. 26, 27.

[96] Note Baxter's first encounter with the Levellers in the parliamentary army: "But there was yet a more dangerous Party than all these among them, (only in Major *Bethel's* Troop of our Regiment) who took the direct Jesuitical way: They first most vehemently declaimed against the Doctrine of Election, and for the power of Free-will, and all other Points which are controverted between the Jesuits and Dominicans, the Arminians and Calvinists. Then they as fiercely cried down our present Translation of the Scriptures, and debased their Authority, though they did not deny them to be Divine: And they cried down all our Ministry, Episcopal, Presbyterian and Independent; and all our Churches: And they vilified most all our ordinary Worship; especially singing of *Psalms*, and constant Family Worship: They allowed of no argument from Scripture but what was brought in its express words: They were vehement against both the King, and all Government but Popular; and against Magistrates medling in Matters of Religion . . . These were the same Men that afterward were called Levellers." *Rel. Baxterianae*, I. i. pp. 53–4 (§77).

interpreting scripture, but because practical decisions had to be made, those decisions could be made effective only by political means. No form of truth can be proved ultimately by a majority vote, even if we regard the majority voters as 'saints' or as 'princes of the Church'; but because choices have to be made and decisions have to be translated into laws, there is no other way of accomplishing practical objectives than by acting politically. Short of achieving the ideal consensus, for which there was then no patience and too little time, the only way to resolve the issue in the Assembly was to debate it, agitate for it, lobby for it, and ultimately vote on it.

Nevertheless, a consensus on the meaning of scripture was the Puritans' hope if not almost an article of faith. It was clearly the Assembly's primary task, and perhaps nothing argues more for the basic sincerity of these men than the time spent in trying to achieve it. The centrality of ecclesiology in the seventeeth century is seen in the novelty that as the first two major political parties emerged, they took the names of the rival ecclesiologies that were being debated in the Assembly – Presbyterians and Independents. This is unique in English history, and it underscores the place occupied by ecclesiology at the time when parliamentary government was taking its own distinctive shape.

In a sense the secular future was foreshadowed more clearly by the party that was most insistent on its claims to Divine Right, and it is no accident that Oliver Cromwell – a man in whom the sacred and the secular seem so curiously mixed, but who laid down some basic principles of secular government – was known as 'the great Independent'.[97] The Independents always found

---

[97] Note Cromwell's protest to the Scots Major–General Crawford for dismissing one of his Lieutenant–Colonels for being an Anabaptist: "Sir, the state in choosing men to serve them, takes no notice of their opinions, if they be willing faithfully to serve them, that satisfies." 10th March, 1643/4, Abbott, *Writings and Speeches of O.C.*, I. 278, Lomas–Carlyle, I. 171.

In *The Lord Protector* I argued that Independency represented not only Cromwell's political affiliation but also the ecclesiastical position he reached. Recently this has been challenged by Michael Watts, (following G. F. Nuttall,) who argues that there is no evidence that Cromwell ever carried out his intention to form a 'gathered church' out of his cavalry troop as reported by Baxter, "nor is there any evidence apart, from Baxter's solitary and inconclusive reference, that Cromwell himself ever joined a gathered church." *The Dissenters*, p. 107; cf. *The Lord Protector*, pp. 67f., *Rel. Baxt.* I. 51 (§74) and more explicitly in the Index of that work *ad loc.*

With due respect to the critics, they have brushed aside the supporting evidence – the two occasions when Cromwell almost emigrated, the nature of the Army Debates, Cromwell's readiness to accept criticism (i.e., church discipline) from his fellow soldiers, the style of his Protectorate at its beginning, and his preference in chaplains. A commitment to Independency would also be consistent with the ecclesiastical settlement of the Protectorate, and gathering a troop of soldiers into a gathered church was little different

themselves out-voted in the Assembly, sometimes out-manoeuvred in Parliament, but never out-fought on the field of battle, and this was because under the umbrella of political Independency they attracted into the army those who stood to lose most by the imposition of religious uniformity of any sort.[98] The radicals in the army may not have agreed about the form of the Church, and the Army debates were to show that they did not agree about the shape of society,[99] but they had been forced to make common cause first in opposition to Archbishop Laud and his priests, and then by discovering that 'New Presbyter is but old Priest writ large.'

As a result of this *marriage de convenance* the Independents moved naturally first to the hope of accommodation, next to the plea for toleration, then to the principle of Liberty of Conscience, and hence eventually to a more inclusive doctrine of the Church. Their colleagues in New England might retain the mentality of the 1630s, and in colonies virtually untouched by war might still suppress those who opposed their theocracy, but this was not a viable option for the Independents in England during the 1640s: they were forced to join with Baptists, Separatists, Antinomians and any others prepared to fight for freedom of worship, and they found themselves having to take political leadership in that struggle. In making this change of front they began to discover unsuspected breadth within their own ecclesiology.

It was on the radical side of this Puritan debate that we find a democraticization of society beginning: the doctrine of election could become spiritual élitism as the Puritans originally held it,

---

from the experiment that Thomas Goodwin conducted along those lines with his students at Magdalen College, Oxford. There is a rumour that John Owen tried the same at Christ Church but in Owen we face precisely the same problem that my critics recognize in Cromwell. As one of Owen's biographers has remarked, "Since Owen was as much committed to the ideal of the Congregational way as to the necessity of preaching the Gospel, it is somewhat surprizing to find a curious lack of information about his church membership whilst he was in Oxford." Peter Toon, *God's Statesman: the Life and Work of John Owen*, (Exeter, Paternoster Press, 1971,) p. 57.

If there is such a paucity of evidence for Owen's church membership in Christ Church, I fail to see why we should expect much explicit evidence to have survived about Cromwell's churchmanship during the time he was in the army. And that is the crucial time, for we are all agreed that unless he had been willing to establish a single form of the Church, membership of a particular church would have been inappropriate during the Protectorate. I therefore urge that if the evidence for Cromwell's church affiliation may still be regarded as inconclusive, it at least points in one direction.

[98] The ambiguous relationship of religious Independents and the 'political Independents' has been a matter of some debate. It was raised again by Michael R. Watts in *The Dissenters*, pp. 108f. Cf. *infra* Appendix V.

[99] Cf. Woodhouse, *Puritanism and Liberty.*

but at a different level it at least proclaimed that God's grace had nothing to do with gentle birth, social class, wealth, nationality or even (ultimately) sex.[100] By cooperating politically with other sects, and by fighting side by side with them in the same regiments, the Independents learned to respect other Christians' faith and biblical integrity. People whose views of the Church started out as extremely narrow began to recognize that other churches might also be true churches, and hence to concede that there might be several legitimate ways of interpreting the scripture which all professed to revere. Ultimately, therefore, this pointed to a society in which none would be persecuted because of religious conviction, a society in which all serious interpretations of scripture would learn mutual respect. It is no accident that in this seventeeth century debate we discern the first tentative moves towards an ecclesiology that had room for plural forms of the Church.[101]

---

[100] They were, of course, men of their time, and therefore assumed male superiority, but there were some significant moves in a more liberal direction. The Quakers seem to have been the first to have admitted women preachers, but we also find women beginning to play a significant role among Baptists and Independents. Cf. the writings of the Independent, Katherine Chidley.

[101] The principle of Liberty of Conscience had, of course, been expressed in *The Bloudy Tenent* of Roger Williams, which he had written on his return to England, but it was given ecclesiastical expression in Cromwell's religious settlement, and in Article XXX of the Savoy Declaration's (1658) Platform of Polity, which reads somewhat quaintly: "Churches gathered and walking according to the minde of Christ, judging other Churches (though less pure) to be true Churches, may receive unto occasional communion with them, such Members of those Churches as are credibly testified to be godly, and to live without offence." This recognition of other churches ('though less pure'!) is a shift from the earlier exclusivism towards an ecclesiology that recognized plural forms. For the earlier view see John von Rohr, 'Extra ecclesiam nulla salus: An early Congregational Version', *Church History*, XXXVI, No. 2 (June 1967); for Cromwell's ecclesiastical settlement see Paul, *The Lord Protector*, pp. 324–333; and for the text of the Savoy Declaration of 1658, see Williston Walker, *The Creeds and Platforms of Congregationalism*, pp. 354–408, and especially p. 408.

It is ironic that William Laud expressed a very similar inclusiveness with respect to the Church of Rome at the time of his trial. Cf. *supra* p. 21, note 29.

CHAPTER 2

THE CALL OF THE ASSEMBLY

I

First Political Intrusion: Removal of the Bishops

A new stage in the ecclesiological dispute about Divine Right and a new polarity among English churchmen entered the situation when the Convocation of 1640 passed the *Et Caetera* oath. This took place in the early days of Richard Baxter's ministry when he was acting as assistant to William Madstard, the Puritan Minister of Bridgenorth, Shropshire.

> Whilst I here exercised the first Labours of my Ministry, two several Assaults did threaten my Expulsion: The one was a new Oath, which was made by the Convocation, commonly called *The Et caetera Oath:* For it was to swear us all, *That we would never Consent to the Alteration of the present Government of the Church, by Archbishops, Bishops, Deans, Arch-deacons,* &c. This cast the Ministers throughout *England* into a Division, and new Disputes. Some would take the Oath, and some would not.
>
> Those that were for it, said, That Episcopacy was *Jure Divino*, and also settled by a Law, and therefore if the Sovereign Power required it, we might well swear that we would never consent to alter it; and the King's Approbation of these Canons made them sufficiently obligatory unto us.
>
> Those who were *against* it, said, 1. That Episcopacy was either *contra jus Divinum*, or at best not *Jure Divino*, and therefore mutable when the King and Parliament pleased.[1]

---

[1] *Reliquiae Baxterianae*, I. i. p. 15 (§22). In the second paragraph of this quotation there is a clear example of the way in which *jure divino* episcopacy and the Divine Right of Kings were brought together in the Anglican royalist position. Shaw recognized the significance of Richard Baxter's testimony: William Shaw, *A History of the English Church*, I. pp. 6f.

Baxter went on to list four other reasons why most of the ministers in his area were against the oath, and this situation led him to make a far deeper study of the episcopal claims than he had undertaken hitherto. He came to a conclusion that was typical of moderate Puritan opinion in England, that "though I found not sufficient Evidence to prove all kind of Episcopacy unlawful, yet I was much satisfied that the *English* Diocesan frame, was guilty of the Corruption of Churches and Ministry, and of the ruine of the true Church Discipline, and substituting an heterogeneal thing in its stead."[2] As a result, Baxter admitted, the Oath "was a chief means to alienate me, and many others" from episcopal government, making division where there had previously been relative peace, and causing many who had been 'quiet Conformists' to speak out more bitterly and "to honour the Nonconformists more than they had done".[3]

It is also clear that behind the *Et Caetera* Oath there was a claim to *jure divino* episcopacy. Radical Puritans would not accept that claim because they denied any basis for it in the New Testament, but a claim to divine right episcopacy would also raise questions for Puritans who were less doctrinaire, since it would force them to review the scriptural evidence. And once that process began, as Baxter himself illustrated, moderate churchmen were likely to reach some uncomfortable conclusions.

The political potential of this ecclesiastical dispute was not lost on the politicians at Westminster. Baxter admitted that many Members of Parliament were more concerned at first with the constitutional and legal encroachments of the royal prerogative than with purifying the Church, but they quickly began to realize that ecclesiastical and constitutional issues were all of a piece:

> so accordingly the Parliament consisted of two sorts of Men, who by the Conjunction of these Causes were united in their Votes and Endeavours for a Reformation: One Party made no great matter of these Alterations in the Church; but they said, That if Parliaments were once down, and our Propriety gone, and Arbitrary Government set up, and Law subjected to the Prince's Will, we were then all

---

[2] *Rel. Baxt.*, I. i. p. 16 (§22). Baxter admitted that although he had been born into a Puritan family, until about the age of twenty he had never questioned the Conformist position; "Till this time I was satisfied in the Matter of Conformity: Whilst I was young I had never been acquainted with any that were against it, or that questioned it. I had joyned with the Common-Prayer with as hearty fervency as afterward I did with other Prayers! As long as I had no Prejudice against it, I had no stop in my Devotions from any of its Imperfections." *Ibid.* p. 13 (§17).

[3] *Ibid.* p. 16 (§§22, 23.)

Slaves, and this they made a thing intolerable; for the remedying of which, they said, every true *English* Man could think no price to[o] dear: These the People called *Good Commonwealth's Men*. The other sort were the more Religious Men, who were also sensible of all these things, but were much more sensible of the Interest of Religion; and these most inveyed against the Innovations in the Church, the bowing to Altars, the Book for Sports on Sundays, the Casting out of Ministers, the troubling of the People by the High-Commission Court, the Pilloring and Cutting off Mens Ears, (Mr. *Burtons*, Mr. *Prins*, and Dr. *Bastwicks*) for speaking against the Bishops, the putting down Lectures, the Afternoon Sermons and Expositions on the Lord's Days, with such other things, which they thought of greater weight than Ship money. But because these later agreed with the former in the Vindication of the Peoples Propriety and Liberties, the former did the easilier concur with them against the Proceedings of the Bishops and High Commission Court.[4]

Is this alliance between the 'Good Commonwealth's Men' and the 'Religious Men' simply to be dismissed as a political *quid pro quo?* If the continuation of medieval ideas about the unity of religion and society is true for the early seventeenth century, probably it is not. That Englishmen began to push for constitutional liberties in the face of a despotic threat will not be found remarkable – it has been the constant theme of the Whig historians who first opened up the century to systematic study – but I suggest that historians have accepted too casually the curious fact that the political reformers and constitutionalists not only entered into alliance with the Puritans but even found Puritanism a congenial movement with which to be allied. Whatever secular ideas may have been lying beneath the surface of these events, within the context of that century the Parliamentarians *needed* an alternative theological rationale for their reforms, and it is significant that the 'Religious Men' agreed wholeheartedly with the civil reformers on 'the Vindication of the Peoples Propriety and Liberties'.

We see an illustration of the interrelationship between the reform movement in both Church and State when on November 7th, 1640, John Pym launched an attack on the Stuart administration that was to send the Earl of Strafford to the block and England down the path to civil war. Pym himself was no puritanical bigot: he claimed that "I am, and ever was, and so will Die, a faithful son of the Protestant Religion, without having the least relation in my belief to those gross Errors of *Anabaptism*,

---

[4] *Ibid.* p. 18 (§27).

Brownism, and the like", and protested his faithfulness to "the Orthodox Doctrine of the Church of England", even although he had sought "a Reformation of some gross abuses crept into the Government by the Cunning and Perverseness of the Bishops and their Substitutes".[5] So Pym's first object of attack against Charles I's policy was the Laudian church, levelled in the general charge of a popish plot, "a design to alter the kingdom both *in religion and government.* This is the highest of treason, this blows up by piecemeal and almost goeth through [to] their ends".[6]

It was the *total* society, Church *and* State, that Pym claimed was being subverted, but in his survey of the situation even he gave pride of place to the subversion of the Church. The Laudian party was accused of trying to return England to the Roman allegiance through misuse of the ecclesiastical courts, by its suppression of the most promising clergy, by tying ecclesiastical preferment to its own supporters, and by conducting correspondence with papal agents in order to undermine the Protestant establishment.

Certainly the most obvious issues involving the royal prerogative were constitutional and secular, but in a century when personal destiny in heaven or hell was not doubted, the religious aspects of the struggle were not to be cast lightly aside; and the probability that return to Rome would also demand the return of church and monastic lands, threatened a lot of pockets. This provided a powerful inducement for even the most secular Members of Parliament to look with sympathy on the Puritan cause.[7]

The pulpiteers and pamphleteers were no less influential and possibly no more responsible in their attack on the status quo than the minions of mass media have been in later times, and nowhere was their influence greater than in London. There seems to have been an extremely active and well-organized group of Puritan ministers in London that became adept in using public opinion to bring pressure on Parliament.[8] The mood of London's

---

[5] John Rushworth, *Historical Collections,* (1680, etc.,) VI. 377. The whole of Pym's vindication of his actions is printed by Rushworth, *ibid.* pp. 376–8.

[6] Document 54 in J. P. Kenyon (Ed.), *The Stuart Constitution, 1603–1688: Documents and Commentary,* (London, C.U.P., 1966,) p. 204. My italics.

[7] We do not doubt that the threat of the former church lands being returned to ecclesiastical control was an extremely powerful motive for England's new landowners to support Protestantism; but once Protestantism was embraced, the concern of the individual for his or her own salvation would take pre-eminence over all other considerations. In light of eternal destiny, all other motives would appear secondary.

[8] After October, 1643, Sion College seems to have become the centre of Puritan, and later Presbyterian, influence in London. Cf. *infra* pp.78 n. 18, 118f.

inhabitants may be judged in that by December 11th, 1640, the 'Root and Branch Petition' had the support of 15,000 citizens in and around the city. The petition demanded that episcopacy, "with all its dependencies, roots and branches, may be abolished, and that all the laws in their behalf made void, and [that] the government according to God's Word may be rightly placed among us".[9] Obviously, this carried the threat of a much more radical revision of church structure than the comparatively modest removal of the Bishops from the House of Lords and the reduction of their juridical function: it could imply an alternative form of church government on the basis of strict New Testament restorationism.

The petition is significant for another reason, for it shows how exclusive *jure divino* views of the Church arose in reaction to each other: the view implicit within the paper was itself a reaction to the *jure divino* claims that had been advanced only recently by the supporters of episcopacy. The petition asserted,

> That whereas the government of archbishops and lord bishops, deans and archdeacons, etc., with their courts and ministrations in them, have proved prejudicial and very dangerous both to the Church and Commonwealth, *they themselves having formerly held, that they have their jurisdiction or authority of human authority, till of these later times, being further pressed about the unlawfulness, that they have claimed their calling immediately from the Lord Jesus Christ*, which is against the Laws of this kingdom, and derogatory to his Majesty and his state royal.[10]

Whatever we may feel about the ingenuousness of the petitioners' concern about Charles and his 'state royal', there could be no more explicit statement of how *jure divino* claims about the ordering of the Church tended to produce counter *jure divino* claims on the other side. A great deal that happened in the English Church from the time of the Reformation through the period of the Restoration becomes much clearer when we recognize the development and interplay of these rival 'divine right' views of the Church, and the alternative claims to theological authority on which those ecclesiologies were based.

The original claim of the English royal Establishment had been based on the Divine Right of Kings and backed by English Law, and this caused radical reformers increasingly to appeal to the divine law in the literal words of scripture. But this meant

---

[9] Kenyon, *The Stuart Constitution* [Doc. 49], p. 172, cf. pp. 171–5.
[10] *Ibid.* p. 171. My italics.

that the resulting *jure divino* overtones of Puritan ecclesiology caused both the crown and the bishops to assert even more strongly their own claims to *jus divinum*; and this in turn inevitably forced the Puritans to protest their claims in the divine right that was exclusively scriptural. There is good evidence to show that within the context of English church history the exclusive 'divine right' views of the Church arose in direct reaction to each other: the ecclesiastical legalism of the Anglican bishops stimulated the biblical literalism of the Puritans, and *vice versa*.

Furthermore, the Stuart kings' reliance on the Divine Right of Kings as justification for their own absolute authority reveals an implicit belief that the Crown's exercise of civil power and sovereignty was similarly grounded in the Law of God.[11] If Parliament was to justify its own final authority in the state, it had to find similar justification and if these claims were a little slower in developing it was probably because the Bible seemed to know more of Kings and Princes than it did of parliaments; and yet from the time of the Elizabethan Settlement there had been a very close relationship between Parliament's new self-conscious awareness and Puritanism's view of the Church.[12] This may have contributed to the appearance of the Erastian party in the Assembly,[13] but the support given by the parliamentary politicians to the Puritan cause suggests that they may have been hoping for an alternative to the Divine Right of Kings to develop out of Puritan theology.

The impeachment of Strafford initiated by Pym on November 25th 1640, was the signal for the Long Parliament's all-out attack against Stuart administration on both the civil and ecclesiastical fronts. We are not primarily concerned with the constitutional and economic matters at issue between Charles and Parliament,

---

[11] Cf. *supra* pp. 16–23.

[12] I repeat here a note that I wrote many years ago on this: "It has not been sufficiently realized that to some extent the ecclesiastical settlement of Elizabeth implied a form of Presbyterianism. By the Act of Uniformity (I Eliz. Cap. II) every Englishman was to be *(ipso facto)* a member of the Church of England. It meant that, as far as the State was concerned, England was a country consisting only of Christians, and the House of Commons was therefore an elected body representing not only the civil interests of the English people, but also the laity of the *Church* in England. This was an accidental result of uniformity, but when the House of Commons claimed the right to discuss religion it became a kind of national General Assembly. To *control* national religion, however, the Commons would have first to abolish the bishops, and secondly, to maintain uniformity (since only by so doing could they claim to represent the Church). Hence Presbyterianism and parliamentary supremacy were allied causes." *The Lord Protector*, p. 54, note 2.

[13] Cf. *infra* pp. 127ff.

except as they may bear on the criticism of Laud's ecclesiastical policy and as they illustrate the interrelationship of secular and theological issues at that time. However, in January 1640/1 several committees were set up by the House of Commons to deal with specific abuses of power by the King's government, and of the sixteen items listed, the first dealt with Laud's policies and the ninth with abuses in the ecclesiastical courts of Star Chamber and High Commission. The grand Committee on Religion[14] was the first of five such committees to be set up to consider broad strategy. Laud was sent to the Tower, and others who had acted in line with Laud's repressive policy (*e.g.* Bishop Matthew Wren of Ely) were also prosecuted,[15] while in a short time the courts of Star Chamber and High Commission were abolished. The significance of all this activity was that by this time civil and religious issues had become equally important in the eyes of Charles's opponents.

Meanwhile, public support continued to be stirred up by fear of a popish plot to subvert the nation,[16] and one commentator has observed that by the time of the House of Commons' Protestation on May 3rd, 1641, the King's opponents had "swallowed their own propaganda; they believed that there was indeed a Catholic plot".[17] Very soon their worst fears seemed to be confirmed by Charles's futile attempt to crush the Scots by arresting their leaders in Edinburgh,[18] and by the horrifying rumours of the massacre of the English Protestants in Ireland by the Irish Catholics. Reports on the Irish uprising varied between Lord Clarendon's later modest estimate of between 40–50,000 Protestant victims, and the 200,000 Lucy Hutchinson and Richard Baxter thought were murdered. Few events of the time had a more onimous legacy than that.

It was during the year 1641 that we hear the first suggestion

---

[14] Not to be confused with 'The Grand Committee', which would be established later to administer the terms of the alliance with Scotland.

[15] Cf. the list of clergymen proceeded against by the Long Parliament in Shaw's *A History of the English Church*, Appendix II, II. 295ff.

[16] Baxter indicates that the London mob was used to pressure the Members of Parliament. He writes of those who "stirr'd up the Apprentices to joyn with them in Petitions, and to go in great numbers to *Westminster* to present them: And as they went they met with some of the Bishops in their Coaches going to the House; and (as is usual with the passionate and indiscreet when they are in great Companies) they too much forgot Civility, and cried out, *No Bishops*". Later Baxter added that "some Members of the House did cherish these Disorders; and because that the Subjects have liberty to Petition, therefore they made use of this their Liberty in a disorderly way". *Reliquiae Baxterianae* I. i. pp. 26–7 (§§40, 41).

[17] J. P. Kenyon's comment, *op. cit.* p. 193. But cf. Hibbard, *op. cit.*

[18] The Earl of Argyle and the Duke of Hamilton.

that the problem of the Church's future could best be tackled by calling a national synod of responsible and respected divines, and, significantly, it first appeared in a petition presented to Parliament by the London ministers.[19] It won sufficient support from Parliament to be taken up and included in the Grand Remonstrance that was handed to the King on December 1st, 1641. Those who framed the Grand Remonstrance, after developing at considerable length the reasons for believing that England was being drawn from its Protestant allegiance, went on to suggest:

> And the better to effect the intended reformation, we desire there may be a general synod of the most grave, pious, learned and judicious divines of this island, assisted with some from foreign parts professing the same religion with us, who may consider of all things necessary for the peace and good government of the Church, and represent the results of their consultations unto the Parliament, to be there allowed of and confirmed, and receive the stamp of authority, thereby to find passage and obedience throughout the kingdom.[20]

The proposal seems to have gained momentum during the latter part of 1641, and if the strong endorsement of Sir Edward Dering is anything to judge by, it gained the support of moderate churchmen as the best way of halting the anarchy into which the Church seemed to be falling. Although Dering supported the Puritan Ministers during the early stages of the struggle, he was no extremist – he was strongly in favour of a moderate epis-copacy, supporting the idea of 'bishops in presbytery', and opposed some of the more doctrinaire attempts to reverse Laud's policies. He even had good things to say about the Archbishop, and was particularly appreciative of the unifying features of the reforms that Laud had introduced into the Church. Indeed, Dering was opposed to Members of Parliament meddling in theological matters outside their competence, and on November 6th, 1641, he had been ready with a speech that was extremely critical of the ecclesiastical changes that Parliament had voted earlier. Although that speech was never delivered, he questioned the wisdom of prohibiting such mildly pious practices as bowing at the name of Jesus; "let us be wary of it".

---

[19] Cf. Neal, *History of the Puritans*, III. 51. At the same time, it is worth noting that the Scottish Commissioners had been in London (*supra* p. 39f.) after the Treaty of Newcastle, from November 1640. Robert Baillie had been there from November 1640–June 1641, (*Letters and Journals*, I. 268–355,) and therefore the petition of the London ministers may have received some stimulus from north of the border. It is clear from Baillie's letters that he and his colleagues were actively engaged with Puritans in London.

[20] Item 185. Cf. *The Stuart Constitution* [Doc. 64, pp. 228–40] p. 238.

THE ASSEMBLY OF THE LORD

Dering was certainly no Puritan radical, but it was in that speech and with regard to such innocent ceremonies that he suggested that such points could very well be referred to a National Synod, for, he contended, "one we must have, or else we shall break our Religion into a thousand pieces."[21] A few weeks later he delivered himself even more strongly to similar effect. "We are poysoned," he declared, "in many points of doctrine: And I know no Antidote, no *Recipe* for cure but one: a well chosen & well temper'd *National* Synod, and God's blessing thereon: this may cure us: without this (in my poor opinion) England is like to turn into a great *Amsterdam*. And unless this Councell be very speedy, the disease will be above the cure."[22]

This is a significant reflection of the public mood that led to the call of the Westminster Assembly. From Dering's remarks we may judge that the growing popularity of convening such a synod was as much due to conservative fears about England's loss of religious unity as it was to radical plans to change the structure of the Church, and Dering's approval suggests that it had the support of moderate opinion. Above all, we note the sense of urgency: for "unless this Councell be very speedy, the disease will be above the cure."

As far as the relationship between Charles I and his Parliament was concerned, the disease was already well above the cure. From the end of 1641 when Sir Edward Dering was penning aborted speeches and pondering grave thoughts on religion, events slid rapidly and inexorably to August 22nd, 1642, when Charles raised his standard at Nottingham and the Civil War began. The centre of the public stage during those intervening months was inevitably taken by the political manoeuvring of the contesting parties as they attempted to define their lines of defence, tried to raise armies and the money to fund them, and endeavoured to present their case in the best possible light to everyone at home and abroad.

At the same time, even under these practical pressures Parliament did not ignore religion, and since events have a way of generating their own momentum we may witness the beginnings of the shift that was to change a major body of English Puritans from the kind of people represented by Sir Edward Dering in 1641 into Presbyterian supporters by 1645.

---

[21] *A Collection of Speeches made by Sir Edward Dering Knight and Baronet, in matter of Religion*, (London, 1642,) p. 40. [The pagination of this pamphlet is somewhat eccentric.]

[22] November 20th, 1641; *ibid.* p. 63f.

On May 3rd, 1641, the House of Commons had issued its Protestation in which every Member promised under solemn oath "to maintain and defend, as far as lawfully I may, with my life, power and estate, the true reformed religion, expressed in the doctrine of the Church of England, against all Popery and Popish innovation within this realm",[23] but ten days later it was found necessary to clarify what had been meant by the words "true reformed religion, expressed in the doctrine of the Church of England", and so that there should be no possibility of misinterpretation, it was explicitly stated "that the said words are not to be extended to the maintaining of any form of worship, discipline, or government; nor any of the rites or ceremonies of the said Church of England."[24] At that stage of the dispute the House of Commons seems to have a far clearer idea of what it did *not* want in the Church than of what it wanted to see established.[25]

The House of Lords was more conservative in religious matters than the House of Commons, but by early in 1642 it went along with the exclusion of the bishops from Parliament. Perhaps this simply foreshadowed their exclusion from civil power – probably as far as the moderates wanted to go – but it certainly cleared the way for a review of the Church's order and restructuring according to another pattern. However, despite the trend, the question of the Church of England's future structure was not yet foreclosed. The situation dramatically changed in a way that the Derings of Parliament were powerless to prevent during the almost disastrous early period of Parliament's war with Charles – and because of circumstances that forced the English Parliament to call for help from Scotland.

II

First Moves for an Assembly

The intention of calling a national synod to review the worship and structure of the Church of England was in the forefront of Parliament's mind during the early days of the Civil War when the hope of many had been for a negotiated peace. The Nineteen

---

[23] Document 60, *The Stuart Constitution* (pp. 222f.), p. 223.

[24] 13th May, 1641, Doc. 70, *ibid.* p. 258.

[25] Commenting on the attitudes of a few months earlier, William Shaw observed that in November 1640, "the general frame of mind in the country, as in the Parliament, was negative, not positive – destructive, not constructive." Shaw, *History of the English Church*, I. 7.

Propositions, published on June 1st, 1642, were intended to prevent Charles from receiving help from Catholics either at home or abroad, and several of the provisions therefore dealt with religious issues. On the more positive side, the eighth proposition specifically suggested:

> That your Majesty would be pleased to consent, that such a reformation be made of the Church government and liturgy, as both Houses of Parliament shall advise; *wherein they intend to have consultations with divines, as is expressed in their declaration to that purpose;* and that your Majesty will contribute your best assistance to them, for the raising of a sufficient maintenance for preaching ministers throughout the kingdom; and that your Majesty will be pleased to give your consent to laws for the taking away of innovations and superstitions, and of pluralities, and against scandalous ministers.[26]

Charles rejected the Propositions, as might have been expected, but there are several points of interest in this proposal from the parliamentary side. First we note that the idea of calling a consultative body of divines was of sufficient importance to be included; secondly, we note that the actual church order had not yet been decided, and although the sentiment is anti-Laudian in the sense of opposing plural livings and 'scandalous ministers', there is no suggestion that Parliament was committed to any other church order. The third matter of interest was to be of considerable significance in governing the Westminster Assembly when it met – Parliament's determination that the work of the theologians should be strictly under parliamentary control.[27]

Meanwhile on September 30th, 1642, we find John Pym in a conference between the two houses of parliament suggesting that a unified system of church government should be established throughout all the kingdoms of the British Isles, and that an assembly of divines should be called that would include representatives from other countries committed to the Reformed faith.[28] Pym's proposal at least envisaged close conference and cooperation with the Church of Scotland.

After the outbreak of open warfare in the autumn of 1642, fighting continued in a somewhat confused way through the middle of 1643 with the military advantage resting generally with

---

[26] Doc. 67, *ibid.* (pp. 244–7) p. 246. My italics.

[27] S. R. Gardiner pointed out Parliament would always "refuse to surrender the control over the clergy by the laity which had been the most abiding result of the Tudor rule". *History of the Great Civil War, 1642–1649* (London, Longmans, Green & Co., 1886–91; 4 volume edn., 1893,) I. 228.

[28] *Journals of the House of Commons,* (1743) II. 789; [hereafter cited as *C.J.*].

the royalist forces.[29] Early in 1643 there had been a further attempt to reach a negotiated settlement when the parliamentary commissioners submitted new terms to Charles at Oxford.[30] They were largely a re-hash of propositions that had been rejected earlier. The parliamentary terms demanded that the King should give his Assent to specific Bills prepared by Parliament, including one "for consultation to be had with godly, religious and Learned Divines", and required "That your Majesty will be pleased to promise to pass such other good Bills for settling of Church Government, as upon Consultation with the Assembly of the said Divines shall be resolved upon by both Houses of Parliament, and by them presented to your Majesty."[31] By March 1643 the calling of such an Assembly had become a fixed part of the Long Parliament's policy for reform.

The Treaty of Oxford failed, again as we might have expected, but Parliament was pressured by the Puritan clergy to go ahead with the project of calling the Assembly. Dr. Cornelius Burgess, who had been for a long time associated with Sion College, acting as 'Head of the Puritan Clergy', made representations to Parliament on the subject,[32] "but the Houses were unwilling to take this Step without the King, till they were reduced to the Necessity of calling in the *Scots*, who insisted that *there should be an Uniformity of Doctrine and Discipline between the two Nations*".[33] It was this that eventually induced Parliament to convene the Assembly on the authority of a parliamentary Ordinance,[34] and Neal's comment recognizes, what must be conceded, that the Scots alliance was the most important single factor in bringing the Westminster Assembly into existence. On the other hand, there is evidence that an assembly of divines had featured in Parliament's plans for the reformation of the Church for over a year.

However, we must not read into this intention more than it implied. The conservative nationalism of the English must be taken into account, for it was one thing to want reform or even to plan reform for the Church of England, but something entirely

---

[29] In many quarters the parliamentary cause was regarded as hopeless. Cf. Gardiner, *History of the Great Civil War*, I, *passim*, but especially chapter 8; cf. *ibid.*, pp. 200f.

[30] Rushworth, *Historical Collections*, VI. 164–262, cf. Neal, *Hist. of the Puritans*, III. 9f.

[31] Rushworth, *Historical Collections*. VI. 166.

[32] Neal, *Hist. of the Puritans*, III. 51. Burgess had been one of the original 'Assistants' at Sion College in 1631. Cf. E. H. Pierce, *Sion College and Library*, (Cambridge, C.U.P., 1913,) pp. 36f.

[33] Neal, *Hist. of the Puritans*, III. 51.

[34] Rushworth, *Historical Collections*, VI. 337–9.

different to endorse changes to the extent permitted in the Church of Scotland. We have already seen that even among Englishmen of Puritan sympathies there were many who had no clear idea what should replace the episcopal system and some who were doubtful how far they should go even in that direction.

This is illustrated in the attitude of the House of Lords. In the Spring 1643 the Lords appointed a committee of divines to consider the various 'innovations' that had been introduced to the Church, and if this committee is evidence that the Lords realized they would have to show good faith in this regard before any help could be expected from the Scots, it may also indicate that they hoped to keep ecclesiastical changes within reasonable bounds and even to retain some continuity with English tradition.

The committee consisted of ten bishops and twenty- peers, under the chairmanship of John Williams, Archbishop of York who had known something of Laud's disapproval for his sympathy to Puritan opinions.[35] The Lords went on to name other noted divines for advice and consultation – James Ussher, Archbishop of Armagh; John Prideaux, who was later to become Bishop of Worcester; John Hacket, later Bishop of Litchfield; Samuel Ward, the Lady Margaret Professor of Divinity at Cambridge; and William Twisse of Newbury, who was to become the Prolocutor of the Westminster Assembly. All of these may be counted as moderate Puritan representatives of the Church of England – orthodox Calvinists, sympathetic to many Puritan reforms, but preferring a moderate form of episcopal oversight for the Church. Most of the men named were invited to sit in the Westminster Assembly later that year,[36] although only Dr. Twisse participated. Other clergymen of the same stamp were added to those whom the House of Lords' committee called in for consultation.[37]

The committee of the House of Lords was in conference with these respected divines for six days during which time the

[35] Cf. Thomas Fuller, *The Church History of Britain . . . until the Year MDCXLVIII*, (1655: London, William Tegg, 3rd edn, 1868, 3 vols.) III. 388f, 437–44, 452–4.

[36] Ussher, Hacket, Ward and Twisse. Baxter erroneously says that Prideaux was invited to the Assembly. *Rel. Baxterianae*, I. i. p. 73 (§117).

[37] Robert Sanderson (later Bishop of Lincoln), Ralph Brownrigg (later Bishop of Exeter), Richard Holdsworth (Master of Emmanuel College, Cambridge), Daniel Featley, Cornelius Burgess, John White, Stephen Marshall, Edmund Calamy and Thomas Hill. All of these were invited to the Assembly, although Sanderson, Brownrigg and Holdsworth did not sit, and Featley was soon excluded for his correspondence with the royalists. Burgess, White, Marshall, Calamy and Hill later became staunch leaders of the Presbyterian party in the Assembly, but there is no reason to suggest that they were all committed to the Scots' system at this stage.

Laudian measures were brought under critical review, but although the committee continued until the middle of May, "it broke up without concluding anything".[38] Its ineffectiveness may have been less due to any lack of sincerity as to the fact that the time for moderation had passed and that effective power was now in the hands of more purposeful leadership in the Commons.[39] Although this committee foreshadowed the later work of the Assembly, it was clear by this time that if Parliament was going to win the support of the Scots, it would have to be prepared for much more radical changes in the Church than were likely to be proposed by a committee of the House of Lords in which bishops still held seats.

III
The Scottish Alliance and the Call of the Assembly

The military assistance of the Scots was crucial for Parliament. The Earl of Newcastle's army had made most of the north of England secure for the King, leaving Lord Fairfax and his son, Sir Thomas Fairfax, surrounded in the city of York, and eventually leading to their defeat at Adwalton Moor early in June 1643. The capital was kept on edge by the discovery of continual plots against Parliament,[40] the treachery of Sir John Hotham and his son sending a particular tremor of fear through the city. In 1643 the situation was grim and Parliament needed help.

The Scots had seen themselves in the role of mediators between Charles and the English Parliament, but their overtures had been rejected by the King,[41] and there had been considerable fear in Scotland that Scottish royalists might persuade the Scottish Council either to declare for the King or at least to remain

---

[38] A. F. Mitchell, *The Westminster Assembly*, (London, James Nisbet, 1883,) p. 100. Cf. *ibid.* pp. 97ff, also the recommendations put forward by this committee in Shaw's *A History of the English Church*, II. 287ff.

[39] Cf. my comments on the growing tension between the Lords and Commons in the Introduction to *An Apologeticall Narration* (1963), pp. 74f.

[40] Rushworth, *Historical Collections*, VI. pp. 275f., 295f., 322–30, 798–804.

[41] Cf. Baillie's letter to William Spang, February 18th, 1643, *Letters and Journals*, II. 60. The Scots had appointed 'Commissioners for conserving the peace between both Kingdoms' for negotiating a settlement between Charles and his Parliament. After several months (Sept.–Nov. 1642) they managed to get a safe-conduct from Charles to go to Oxford, and they arrived in February 1642/3 with a petition from the Scottish General Assembly. From the papers that passed between them and the King, however, it is clear that although everyone was in favour of religious uniformity, (a) the nature of that uniformity was a major stumbling-block between the Scots and Charles, and (b) that Charles denied their authority to negotiate between him and the English Parliament. The Scots Commissioners left Oxford in April 1643 when the King refused them permission to proceed to London to treat with Parliament. Cf. Rushworth, *Historical Collections*, VI. 397–406; for the Petition of the General Assembly and Charles's response, cf. *ibid.* pp. 406–410, 459–62.

neutral. While the military situation for the parliamentary forces in England was worsening, many in the Scottish nation were beginning to reflect on what would happen to their Church if everything went the King's way. "We conceave," wrote Robert Baillie, "through the burning of our neighbours houses in England and Ireland, and the great reek that begins to smoak in our own, dangers cannot be small", but he went on to observe that although he had considerable fear about the Scots nobility and some of the gentry, "the ministrie, burrowes, and most of the gentry stands fast".[42] The sympathy of the Scots was rapidly turning to the English Parliament. This was in part due to the cool welcome their commissioners had received in Oxford and to the lack of any assurance from the King, but perhaps most of all by the discovery of the Earl of Antrim's design to invade Scotland in the King's interest from Ireland.

At the beginning of the fighting in July 1642, the Scottish General Assembly meeting at St. Andrews had received intimation through Scottish Commissioners in England that the English Parliament wished to prevent the spread of the Civil War and intended to call an Assembly of divines to settle the matter of religion.[43] The Scots had also received a letter from some London ministers indicating their desire to see Reformed churchmanship established in England and a form of church government uniform with that of the Scottish Church.[44] The General Assembly's reply had left no doubt on the place this matter occupied in Scottish policy, or what would be necessary to win their support.[45] The General Assembly stated bluntly that "The Lord hath now some Controversie with *England*, which will not be removed, till first and before all the Worship of His Name, and the Government of His House be settled according to His own Will."[46] The Scots pointed out that they had for a long time sought a uniform system of worship and church order throughout the two nations and had made unsuccessful representations to that effect even in Elizabeth's reign, and that now they were prepared to renew these overtures "for beginning the work of Reformation; for," they went on to ask, "what hope can there be of Unity in Religion, of one Confession of Faith, one Form of Worship, and one Catechism, till there be first one Form of Ecclesiastical Government; yea, what hope can the Kingdom and

---

[42] Baillie, *Letters and Journals*, II. 60.
[43] Rushworth, *Historical Collections*, VI. 387.
[44] Cf. Baillie, *Letters and Journals*, I. p. xlviii.
[45] Rushworth, *Historical Collections*, VI. 387–90.
[46] *Ibid.* p. 388.

Kirk of *Scotland* have of a firm and durable Peace, till Prelacy, which hath been the main cause of their Miseries and Troubles first and last, be pluck'd up Root and Branch, as a Plant which *GOD* hath not planted, and from which no better Fruit can be expected, than such sour Grapes, as this day set on edge the Kingdom of *England*."[47]

The Uniformity that the Scots envisaged was set out in the clearest terms, and with the strongest affirmation of Presbyterian divine right:

> The Prelatical Hierarchy being put out of the way, the work will be easie, without forcing any Conscience, to settle in *England* the Government of the Reformed Kirks by Assemblies; For although the Reformed Kirks do hold, without doubting their Kirk-Officers and Kirk-Government, by Assemblies higher and lower in their strong and beautiful Subordination, to be *Jure divino* and perpetual; yet Prelacy, as it differeth from the Office of a Pastor, is almost universally acknowledged by the Prelates themselves, and their adherents, to be an human Ordinance, introduced by human Reason, and settled by human Law and Custom, for supposed conveniency; which therefore, by human Authority, without wronging any Man's Conscience, may be altered and abolished . . ."[48]

The English had been left in no doubt even in 1642 where the ecclesiastical issue stood in the political objectives of the Scots, or what a political and military alliance would mean to the Church of England if necessity forced the English to ask the Scots for help.

In 1643, a year later, that necessity was on the English Parliament. Baillie wrote to his relative, William Spang, who was a minister in Holland, describing how the members of the General Assembly had waited almost in vain for the arrival of Commissioners from the Parliament at Westminster. He suspected that the delay had been in part due to the preoccupation with plots and treachery in the English capital but he also noted that "The House of Lords was said to be opposite to the Commons conclu-

---

[47] *Ibid.* p. 389.

[48] *Ibid.* p. 390. Obviously it was not true at that time to suggest that all English prelates regarded their government as merely 'a human Ordinance, introduced by human Reason, etc.' But perhaps the Scots divines looked for their evidence closer to home, for William Prynne reported that in the recantation of Patrick Adamson, Archbishop of St. Andrews (at the Synod of Fife in 1591), the Scots prelate had declared, "That the office of a Diocesan bishop hath no authority at all to support it in the Word of God, [and] that it is onely founded on the politicke device of men." 'Matthew White' [William Prynne] *Newes from Ipswich*, (Ipswich, 1636).

sion of craveing our help."[49] The Lords professed concern that if Parliament brought in the Scots, it would give Charles an excuse to bring Catholic Irish and other foreign troops into England.

In a postscript to the same letter, however, Baillie announced the arrival of a Mr. Corbet from London as an envoy to the National Convention and to the General Assembly.[50] "He shewed to both, his message was to excuse the delay of their Commissioners coming, because of their business in discovering plotts; also to show their calling of an Assembly *at our desyre*, to which they craved some of our Divines to be sent, for whom they had a strong ship in readyness."[51] If this suggests where the real pressure for an Assembly of divines originated, it also suggests that the actual call of the Assembly had been stimulated by Parliament's need to win the Scots to its support.

Baillie went on to say that Robert Meldrum was to be sent on a brief trip to London, presumably to find out what the alliance would mean in practical terms, and Baillie informed his correspondents that "It is thought, that one of Meldrum's instructions is to know what wee may expect from them anent uniformitie of Church Government", and he commented significantly that the Scottish Estates would not take any decision until Meldrum returned.[52] Furthermore, the English Parliament had suggested that among their Commissioners they would be sending two English ministers, Stephen Marshall and Philip Nye, and Baillie added a comment to Spang that might prove ominous for the future. "Mr. Marshall," he wrote, "will be most welcome, bot if Mr. Nye, the head of the independents, be his fellow, we cannot take it weell."[53] It can hardly be regarded as any accident that Baillie had been occupying himself academically with writing a full-length book against the errors of Brownism:[54] when the Scots arrived in England, they would be well prepared.

This evidence suggests that although the idea of calling an assembly of divines had been popular in English parliamentary circles for some time, it was the deteriorating military situation and the imperative need for Scottish assistance that caused the Westminster Assembly to be called in the summer of 1643. Time seemed to be running out for the Rebellion,[55] and if the price the

---

[49] July 26th, 1643, *Letters and Journals*, II. 79f.
[50] Probably Miles Corbet, M. P. for Yarmouth and later one of the regicides.
[51] *Letters and Journals*, II. 80. Italics mine.
[52] *Ibid.* p. 81.
[53] To Spang, July 26th, 1643, *ibid.*
[54] To Spang, June 2nd, July 26th, *ibid.* pp. 71, 76.
[55] Richard Baxter described the situation as follows: "When the Earl of *Newcastle* had

Scots demanded for their help was proof that the English Parliament was serious about the reform of the Church, they should have it.

An Ordinance dated June 12th, 1643, calling the Assembly, had been pushed through both houses of Parliament.[56] The mandate of the divines was very carefully defined: "such a government shall be settled in the Church as may be most agreeable to God's Holy Word, and most apt to procure and preserve the peace of the Church at home, and nearer agreement with the Church of Scotland, and other reformed churches abroad . . . and for the vindicating and clearing of the doctrine of the Church of England from all false calumnies and aspersions"; the members were to "give their advice and counsel therein to both or either of the said Houses when and as often as they shall be thereunto required." To this end, the members were

> to confer and treat among themselves of such matters and things concerning the liturgy, discipline and government of the Church of England, or the vindicating and clearing of the doctrine of the same from all false aspersions and misconstructions as shall be proposed unto them by both or either of the said Houses of Parliament, and no other, and to deliver their opinions and advices of or touching the matters aforesaid, as shall be most agreeable to the Word of God, to both or either of the said Houses from time to time, in such a manner and sort as by both or either of the said Houses of Parliament shall be required; and the same not to divulge by printing, writing or otherwise without the consent of both or either House of Parliament.

Parliament was determined to prevent any future clerical monopoly and to keep control of the Church firmly in its own hands. This emphasis was reiterated time and time again during the course of the Assembly, and if there was any doubt remaining as to the status of the divines, it was explicitly laid down that nothing in the Ordinance was to be construed as giving the members of the Assembly right to "assume to exercise, any

---

over-powred the Lord *Fairfax* in the North, and the Queen had brought over many Papists Soldiers from beyond Sea, and formed an Army under General *King* a *Scot*, and the King had another great Army with himself under the Command of the Earl of *Forth*, another old *Scottish* General; so that they had three great Field Armies, besides the Lord *Goring's* in the West, and all the Country Parties, the Parliament were glad to desire Assistance from the *Scots* . . ." *Reliquiae Baxteriannae*, I. i. p. 48. (§70).

[56] Doc. 74, *The Stuart Constitution*, pp. 261–3; Rushworth, *Historical Collections*, VI. 337–9, Neal, *History of the Puritans*, III. 52–61. The quotations used here are from the modernized version in *The Stuart Constitution*. For the steps leading to the Ordinance, cf. *C.J.* III. 83, 93, 119; *Journals of the House of Lords*, (1742) VI. 81, 84–5, 107–10. [Hereafter cited as *L.J.*]

jurisdiction, power or authority ecclesiastical whatsoever, or any other power than is herein particularly expressed". Parliament held the reins.

At the same time we should note that the efforts of the Assembly were to be directed to produce a form of church government that would be 'most agreeable to the Word of God' and for 'nearer agreement with the Church of Scotland, and other reformed churches abroad'. These were the foci around which the Solemn League and Covenant, and many of the future debates in the Assembly, would revolve. Certainly Parliament may have been no more than tipping its hat to the Scots at this point, and it left undefined what constituted agreement with the Word of God, or what would happen if such agreement proved to be in conflict with reformed positions or incompatible with 'the peace of the Church at home'; but because the scriptures were the one indisputable authority, this was recognized as the primary basis for all the Assembly's future debates.

This meant not only that the Assembly's work would centre in exegesis, but also that as the arguments became more intense, the use of scripture would tend to become more legalistic and literal. Since *jure divino* ecclesiologies would face each other in the Assembly, the tendency to use scripture more legalistically and literally would be inevitable: the terms of the Assembly's appointment would push the positions more firmly in a restorationist direction. It also meant that Parliament's Erastian supporters would ultimately have to justify their position upon the same scriptural base.

This Ordinance also laid down the rules that enabled the Assembly to get under way. It was to begin its work at 9 a.m. on July 1st in the Henry VII Chapel at Westminster, its rates of remuneration for attendance were established, and a Fast Day appointed to pray for its success. Dr. William Twisse was named its Prolocutor,[57] thirty Members of Parliament were named as

---

[57] William Twisse was a Puritan of moderate leanings, and had probably been appointed Prolocutor for that reason. Robert Baillie astutely discerned the political motivation behind the selection of Twisse. "The Proloqutor at the beginning and end hes a short prayer," he wrote to Spang. "The man, as the world knows, is very learned in the questions he hes studied, and very good, beloved of all; and highlie esteemed; but merelie bookish, and not much, as it seems, acquaint with conceived prayer, [and] among the unfittest of all the company for any action; so after the prayer he sitts mute. It was the canny convoyance of these who guides most matters for their own interest to plant such a man of purpose in the chaire." December 7th, 1643, *Letters and Journals*. II. 108. Twisse was in favour of a reformed episcopate, and from this he seems to have been more at home with the Prayer Book than with extempore prayer. By the time he died in July 1646, a very different type of man was needed in the chair – a convinced Presbyterian who had won the respect of the Independents – Charles Herle.

'Lay-Assessors', and one hundred and thirty divines were named to its membership, any forty of which would constitute a quorum. Accordingly, on Saturday, July 1st, 1643, the Westminster Assembly met for the first time in Henry VII's Chapel and in the company of both Houses of Parliament listened to a sermon by the newly appointed Prolocutor, Dr. William Twisse. Then the Assembly adjourned until Thursday, July 6th, to begin work which, if we dare not call it more serious and hesitate to call it more laborious, was certainly more directly relevant to its future programme.

CHAPTER 3

THE ARTICLES AND THE COVENANT

I

For Pedants only: a Note on Sources

Before proceeding we should slow down the pace even further to say something about the sources of our knowledge about the debates in the Assembly. Perhaps we could waive this little exercize if so much confessional capital had not been built on the results of the Assembly in former years, or if the source material did not present the scholar with such a set of intriguing problems. However, the reader who wishes to move to the action had better be warned to proceed directly to the next section of this chapter.

None of the original records of the Assembly is entirely comprehensive, without ambiguity, or wholly without problems. And by a curious quirk of history there has been little incentive until recently to follow up or build upon the meticulous scholarship of the remarkable nineteenth century scholars who salvaged the Puritan period in general and the Westminster Assembly in particular from the prejudices beneath which these events had remained largely hidden.

The problems centre in the so-called 'Minutes' of the Westminster Assembly. The three folio volumes of manuscript 'Minutes' undoubtedly offer the fullest record of the debates that we have,[1] but they do not begin until the 45th session (August 4th, 1643,) and there are huge gaps where the account is either completely missing or the pages left blank to be filled in at some later date. Indeed, these manuscript 'Minutes' are something of a misnomer, since they appear to be little more than the hasty

---

[1] 'Minutes of the Sessions of the Assembly of Divines, from August 4th, 1643, to March 25th, 1652', 3 volumes folio Ms. These are held in Dr. Williams's Library, Gordon Square, London, and are now available in microfilm. [Hereafter this is cited as 'Ms.']

notes of a scribe, probably written in preparation for a fuller account to appear at some later date. The speeches are often cryptic to the point of being almost meaningless, there are frustrating gaps in the text where the scribe had possibly intended to insert summaries of the speeches to be obtained from the notes of the speakers themselves, and the whole is written in an execrable seventeenth century hand of extraordinary abstruseness and complexity. A. F. Mitchell, who collaborated with John Struthers to transcribe, edit and publish the third (and most easily read) volume of the Minutes in 1874,[2] echoed the comment of an earlier historian when he observed that with the exception of the second part of volume III, the manuscript Minutes "are written in a peculiarly hurried and indistinct hand, hardly more easy to be deciphered at times . . . than the shorthand occasionally employed by the scribe."[3]

Recently a transcript of the Minutes made by E. Maunde Thompson at the end of last century was unearthed in the Library of the Church of Scotland.[4] It seems that this transcript was not in final form for publication, but it immeasurably facilitates the use of the Minutes and may persuade scholars to be less intimidated by the Ms. scribe's daunting script.[5] Clearly the Minutes are the primary source for debates in the Assembly, particularly for the period of the 'Grand Debate' on church polity, but because they are incomplete, they must be supplemented by the other eye-witness accounts.

---

[2] Alexander Mitchell and John Struthers (eds.), *Minutes of the Sessions of the Westminster Assembly of Divines, while engaged in writing their Directory for Church Government, Confession of Faith, and Catechisms, (November 1644 to March 1649)* . . ., (Edinburgh, William Blackwood & Sons, 1874,) [This is cited later as 'Minutes III'.]

[3] *Ibid.* p. viii. For additional comments on the interpretation of the Minutes see Appendix IV.

[4] The transcript [cited later as 'TMs.'] is at New College, Edinburgh, and is now available in microfilm. J. R. DeWitt seems to have been the first modern scholar to use it extensively in his book, *Jus Divinum* (1969).

The transcript was not published earlier probably because the transcriber was still intending to work on it. Variant readings with the Ms. are possible, and the transcript should therefore be compared with the original manuscript.

[5] One can hardly speak too highly of scholars such as E. Maunde Thompson and John Struthers, who must have spent an inordinate amount of time in wrestling with the handwriting of that seventeenth century scribe. I first saw the original Minutes at Dr. Williams's Library over twenty-five years ago, and later work on the microfilm of these volumes has simply reinforced my suspicion that the illegibility of this text has been a main reason why there has been virtually no major history of the Assembly since A. F. Mitchell's work, a hundred years ago. The twentieth century has seen a distinct lessening of confessional incentives for re-hashing the issue of church polity – the major subject in the earlier debates – and scholars may have felt much as Macaulay felt about the appearance of a ponderous work of history in his own day, it is unfair "to demand from us so large a portion of so short an existence."

The most important of these for the debates of 1643 and 1644 is the admirably concise and lucid account that appears in John Lightfoot's *Journals*[6], but this is a personal record and although Lightfoot often includes material not to be found in the Minutes, he omits a great deal of material that was of no particular interest to himself.[7] George Gillespie's *Notes* are also valuable, although he did not begin his record until the beginning of the debate on Presbytery in February 1643/4,[8] but these too were written for the writer's own personal use and do not pretend to be complete. Similarly, Gillespie's fellow-Scottish Commissioner, Robert Baillie, offers invaluable insights in the course of his *Letters and Journals*, but his letters were sporadic and written largely to keep his correspondents informed about the general course of the struggle in England.

So the problem presented by the source material of the Westminster Assembly is compounded by the incomplete and sometime fragmentary or enigmatic notes that comprise the 'Minutes', and by the difficulty of reconciling several highly individual accounts that do not claim to be comprehensive in scope or impartial in their judgments.

II

The Work Begins: the XXXIX Articles

The Assembly swung ponderously into action. After Dr. Twisse's opening sermon it adjourned for nearly a week, and this may suggest that there was some uncertainty about its proper course of action. Parliament had called it into being, but as yet the civil authorities at Westminster had given no indication of the scope or extent of the Assembly's work. Were the divines to recommend emendations and relatively minor changes in the Church of England as it was then constituted, or were they to press for a comprehensive restoration of the New Testament

---

[6] John Lightfoot, *The Journal of the Proceedings of the Assembly of Divines, from January 1st, 1643, to December 31, 1644.* [Actually from July 1st, 1643, to December 31st, 1644,] Volume XIII of *The Whole Works of the Rev. John Lightfoot, D.D.*, edited by John Rogers Pitman, (London, J. F. Dove, 1824.)

[7] E.g. there are occasions when the Minutes show Lightfoot to have been active in the debate, but which are omitted in his own record. He gives us no account, for example, of the debates on October 4th and 9th, 1643, although he was present, while his summary of the work on October 5th, simply begins with Sir John Clotworthy's intervention and omits the lengthy debate on procedures. Cf. Lightfoot's *Journal*, p. 16, and TMs. I. 169ff. 180, (Ms. I. f.95b et seq., f.91.)

[8] George Gillespie, *Notes of the Debates and Proceedings of the Assembly of Divines and other Commissioners at Westminster. February 1644 to January 1645*, edited by David Meek, (Edinburgh, Robert Ogle and Oliver & Boyd, 1846.)

pattern of the Church? Since the traditional functions of episcopacy had been suspended, England had had no properly constituted church order for almost a year,[9] and if the country was not to descend rapidly into religious chaos, it was imperative for church order and discipline to be established.

At the same time there was no clear consensus within Parliament or among Puritans generally that *everything* in the traditional form of the Church and its worship should be swept away, and even the Ordinance calling for the Assembly had shown some uneasiness and ambiguity.[10] Read in one way the document sounds radical, but read in another way it sounds hesitant. In one sentence it looks forward to settling church government 'most agreeable to the Word of God', but in another it speaks of 'vindicating and clearing the doctrine of the Church of England from all false calumnies and aspersions'; and if in one passage it envisages bringing the English Church into 'nearer agreement with the Church of Scotland', this did not necessarily imply full identity, for it also insists that the changes should be of the kind 'most apt to procure and preserve the peace of the Church at home'. That does not sound like an unequivocal break with the nation's ecclesiastical tradition. Parliament faced a real dilemma in the midst of all the other problems of fighting a civil war – it was determined to assert its own control over the national form of religion, but it had reached no agreement on what that should be and it could not undertake to do the job for which the Assembly had been called into existence: only the most rabid Erastians in Parliament would dare to take on the theologians in the field of their own expertise.[11]

However, although Parliament may have hesitated to provide theological directives to the Assembly, it was more than willing to give specific instructions about practical procedures. When the members of the Assembly arrived on Thursday July 6th for their first regular session, they found that the Houses had sent down some precise instructions to govern the deliberations in line with parliamentary practice:

1. That Two Assessors be joined to the Prolocutor, to supply his Place, in case of Absence, or Infirmity.

---

[9] Cf. W. M. Hetherington, *History of the Westminster Assembly of Divines* (1843; 1868, New York, Robert Carter & Bros.,) p. 86.

[10] Fuller indicates that a good deal of sympathy for the bishops persisted in the House of Lords; *Church History of Britain*, III. 495.

[11] John Selden, the learned Member of Parliament (M.P.) for Oxford University in the Long Parliament, did this throughout the Assembly's debates, but he was an exception.

2. Two Scribes to be appointed, to set down all Proceedings; and these to be Divines, who are not Members of the Assembly; viz. Mr. *Henry Roberry* [Roborough], and Mr. *Adonian Byfeild* [Adoniram Byfield].

3. Every Member, at his first Entrance into the Assembly, shall make a serious and solemn Protestation, not to maintain any thing but what he believes to be the Truth and to embrace Truth in Sincerity, when discovered unto him.

4. No Resolution to be given upon any Question on the same Day wherein it is first propounded.

5. What any Man undertakes to prove as necessary, he shall make good out of the Scriptures.

6. No Man to proceed in any Dispute, after the Prolocutor hath enjoined him Silence, unless the Assembly desire he may go on.

7. No Man to be denied to enter his Dissent from the Assembly, and his Reasons for it, in any Point, after it hath first been debated in the Assembly; and thence, if the dissenting Party desire it, to be sent to the Houses of Parliament by the Assembly (not by any particular Man, or Men, in a private Way) when either House shall require it.

8. All things agreed on, and prepared for the Parliament to be openly read and allowed in the Assembly; and then offered as the Judgment of the Assembly, if the major Part assent; provided that the Opinion of any Persons dissenting, and the reasons urged for it, be annexed thereunto, (if the Dissenters require it) together with the Solutions (if any were) given in the Assembly to these Reasons.[12]

In these instructions we note the two recurring points to which we have already alluded – Parliament's determination to maintain control over religion, and the scriptural authority to which the reformed Church of England would look for its basis, and by which not only the Church but also the rebellion would be justified.

The real work of the Assembly still hung fire. Friday, July 7th had been designated a Fast Day to ask for God's blessing on the work that was about to begin, and again the members were joined by both Houses of Parliament, to hear Oliver Bowles preach in the morning on 'Zeale for God's House', in which he exhorted his hearers that for want of regularly constituted church government the land was in danger of falling from tyranny into anarchy. In the afternoon Matthew Newcomen preached, reminding them of

---

[12] *C.J.* III. 157. These instructions had been drafted in the House of Lords, and there had originally been nine, but the Commons rejected the fifth of the Lords' provisions, probably because they thought it was unnecessary. It had laid down that no long speeches should be permitted, "that Matters may not be carried by impertinent Flourishes; but by all Debates to be by Way of Argument, soberly and gravely managed."*L.J.* VI. 114. The list of rules as approved by the Commons also appears in Lightfoot, *Journal,* pp. 3f.

the ministers' role as 'Jerusalems Watch-Men, the Lord's Remembrancers'.[13]

It is perhaps worth noting, if only to get a sense of seventeenth century priorities, that during the three months that separated the beginning of the Assembly to October 6th when its members took the Covenant, no less than five occasions were taken out for religious offices of one sort or another in addition to the regular Sundays and monthly Fast Days; and this was by no means exceptional in view of the Assembly's later habits.[14] In 1645 Robert Baillie remarked wearily,

> The contstant practise here, on the least appearance of any publick danger, is to flee both to publick and private fasting. Truely the godly here are a praying people, and the Parliament is very ready to further this disposition. If the godly there have the like care, and if the magistrate be alyke industrious, to crave the assistance of gracious people's fasting and praying, I know not; only it is my wishe that God would make clear, what the cause may be that so long he deserts us.[15]

Baillie's frustration seems to be with a higher authority than Parliament – he did not know whether the parts of the country controlled by Charles were blessed with similar regard for piety, but he wished God would make haste to reveal why all the display of Puritan piety had produced so little result!

Perhaps these public demonstrations of piety should not be taken altogether at their face value: society *was* moving toward secularism, even although politicians might still find it expedient to cover their motives under the forms of traditional religion. It can be shown that there was an extremely intimate relationship between preachers and politicians during this period, and Pym

---

[13] Cf. John F. Wilson, *Pulpit in Parliament*, p. 71.

[14] In a Publick Letter written two years after the beginning of the Assembly, on July 1st, 1645, Baillie protested against these delays: "The Assemblie hes been forced to adjourne on fyve diverse occasions of fastings and thanksgiving lately, every one whereof took from us almost two dayes." *Letters and Journals*, II. 291. Some time later Baillie wrote, "We have many diversions, many dayes of fasts and thanksgivings, with the dayes preceeding them for preparation to them." These exercises, he claimed, together with the administrative chores of "provyding ministers for all vacant churches, even to remote shyres, their tryall and mission . . . takes up almost every day too much of our time." Public Letter, February, 1646, *ibid.* p. 349.

[15] Publick Letter, August 10th, 1645, *ibid.* p. 305. Could this tendency to proliferate the formal occasions for worship in church, which (if Baillie is to be trusted) the English Puritans seem to have had in contrast to the Scots, be another indication that the English were still closer emotionally to the older piety of medieval Catholicism, with its tradition of continual monastery offices?

seems to have manipulated the Fast sermons in a particularly adroit manner during the critical months of 1643.[16]

Meanwhile, on Saturday July 8th, the day after the Fast, the members of the Assembly, 'both Lords and Commons, as well as divines', took an oath to maintain only what they believed to be true in doctrine, and that which they believed would redound to God's glory and the good order and discipline of the Church.[17] During the same session they nominated John White of Dorchester and Cornelius Burgess of Watford 'Assessors'[18] to assist the Prolocutor in presiding at the sessions, and organized themselves into three standing committees.[19] These committees would give preliminary consideration to the matters under discussion by the Assembly, and prepare the propositions to be debated in the plenary sessions. It is possible that some general rules of procedure were adopted, although it has been accurately pointed out that the rules listed by Neal in his account of the start of the Assembly's work represent provisions that that body adopted in course of many months.[20] In any case, this appears to have been the members' first day of constructive work.

In line with the spirit of the original Ordinance calling the Assembly, which charged it with the task of "vindicating and clearing of the doctrine of the Church of England from all false calumnies and aspersions", Parliament directed the Assembly to review the XXXIX Articles of the Church, and this was the work to which the newly-formed committees addressed themselves when they met for the first regular session on Monday, July 10th. The First Committee undertook consideration of the 1st, 2nd, 3rd and 4th Articles, the Second Committee dealt with the 5th,

---

[16] Cf. H. Trevor–Roper"s chapter, 'The Fast Sermons of the Long Parliament', in *The Crisis of the Seventeenth Century*, (New York, 1968,) especially pp. 310ff.

[17] "I, A.B., do seriously and solemnly protest, in the presence of Almighty God, that in this Assembly, whereof I am a member, I will not maintain any thing in matters of doctrine, but what I think in my conscience to be truth; or in point of discipline, but what I shall conceive to conduce most to the glory of God, and the good and peace of his church." Lightfoot's *Journal*, p. 4.

[18] In addition, Cornelius Burgess had had a long association with Sion College. He would become President of that institution in 1647. Cf. the manuscript records of the college: *The Sion College Court-Register from May 3rd, 1631 to April 24th, 1716*, pp. 1, 92, 102.

[19] See Appendix I, pp. 555f.

[20] This is one of the places where Neal was obviously inaccurate. As Wayne Spear pointed out, the rules were passed during the course of several months' work; Wayne Spear, 'Covenanted Uniformity in Religion: the Influence of the Scottish Commissioners on the Ecclesiology of the Westminster Assembly,' (unpublished Ph.D. dissertation submitted to the University of Pittsburgh, 1976,) p. 53 note, cf. Daniel Neal, *History of the Puritans*, III, 63f.

6th, and 7th Articles, while the Third Committee was allocated the 8th, 9th, and 10th Articles.[21]

This was a relatively modest and even conservative assignment, and it appears that the parliamentary leaders were reluctant at this time to let the divines loose on any more radical revision of the Church's worship and structure. Since all the divines, even a known episcopalian like Daniel Featley, were orthodox Calvinists, a review of the Articles of Religion was a fairly safe way of beginning and not likely to reveal any serious rift. One suspects that it may have been a useful device for preventing the divines from getting into the more controversial matter of church government, while Parliament waited on events of more immediate concern.

One of the problems in writing of the Westminster Assembly is the paucity of scholarly work on its methods and procedures.[22] We would like to know much more than we do about how matters were managed before they arrived on the floor of the Assembly. However, Robert Baillie left us with a remarkably vivid description of the Assembly in plenary session when he joined it later in 1643. This is by far the most complete account we have from any eye-witness, and it is so lively and clear that we have transcribed it in full in an appendix.[23] But even Baillie does not tell us how the various matters of concern were selected, or by what system the day-to-day agenda was prepared, and reading through the Minutes or the daily journals of men like Lightfoot or Gillespie, the subjects for debate often appear to arise more or less at random.

---

[21] Lightfoot, *Journal*, p. 5.

A recent work to appear on these earlier debates is Robert M. Norris's unpublished thesis on 'The Thirty-Nine Articles at the Westminster Assembly' (for the Ph.D. degree in the University of St. Andrews, 1977.) Using the Ms. Minutes and E. Maunde Thompson's transcript, Dr. Norris has attempted his own reconstruction of the debates on the XXXIX Articles.

[22] The most thorough treatment to date of the committee structures and procedures is in Wayne Spear's dissertation, 'Covenanted Uniformity in Religion,' pp. 52ff.

Of the published works on the Westminster Assembly, some of the best in this respect are extremely old. However much one deplores W. H. Hetherington's bias, his *History of the Westminster Assembly of Divines* does try to tell us the sequence in which things happened, and the same is true for A. F. Mitchell's *The Westminster Assembly*. But it is not true for the books that have appeared in this century. Benjamin Warfield's *The Westminster Assembly and its Work* (New York, O.U.P., 1931,) for example, devotes only a few pages to such practical matters, and then proceeds directly to the author's major interest in the doctrinal documents that came from its debates. S. W. Carruthers' *The Everyday Work of the Assembly* (Philadelphia, Presbyterian Historical Societies, 1943,) while offering us a great deal of fascinating detail, is silent at this point.

[23] From Baillie's letter to Spang, December 7th, 1643, *Letters and Journals*, II. 107–9; Appendix II.

That was not so. Part of the key to understanding the method by which the Assembly worked is in recognizing the function of the three committees, which were allocated work for preliminary discussion and were then responsible for drafting the propositions that would reach the Assembly in plenary session. A. F. Mitchell says that this committee structure may have been a conscious attempt to conform to the method adopted by the Synod of Dort in 1618.[24] Samuel Ward had been the only one of the British representatives at Dort to be invited to the Assembly, but he never took his seat at Westminster. However, in view of Dort being the most important recent synod of the Reformed churches, and one in which the Church of England had participated, it is plausible. Indeed, when the matter of church government was first broached, Thomas Bayly ('the English Bayly') specifically made the proposal that they should proceed 'as at Dort' with every committee handling the same subjects.[25] The first Committee met in Henry VII's Chapel with Dr. Burgess as its convenor, the second in the Lower House of Convocation with Dr. Stanton as its convenor,[26] while the third Committee assembled in the Jerusalem Chamber (where eventually the Assembly removed itself).[27]

Unfortunately we still do not know in detail how subjects were selected or apportioned out to the various committees, except where there were specific directives. Later, when the Scottish Commissioners arrived with their program for Covenanted uniformity, the 'Grand Committee', originally appointed to confer with them, assumed some responsibility for making this program effective,[28] but even after it was appointed it does not seem to have taken that responsibility for some time. In the earlier stages of the Assembly's life the weekly schedule seems to have been determined by the standing committees, probably working in close association with the officers of the Assembly and a few leaders of the majority party. We do not know. We do

---

[24] *The Westminster Assembly*, p. 142.

[25] 17th October, 1643, TMs. I. 222 (Ms. I., f. 112.) The procedure whatever its antecedents was carried, although John White 'the lawyer' voted against it, Lightfoot, *Journal*, p. 21.

[26] It is now, apparently, St. John's and St. Andrew's Chapel, on the north side of the Abbey. Cf. Mitchell, *The Westminster Assembly*, p. 143. Although Dr. Stanton often reported for this Committee, Thomas Young delivered its report on Oct. 19th, 1643; cf. TMs I. 231 (Ms. I., f. 116b.)

[27] Lightfoot's statement that Gibbon [or Guibon] chaired the third committee is probably in error, since Dr. Temple regularly reported for that committee in the Assembly: cf. Wayne Spear, 'Covenanted Uniformity in Religion,' p. 63; cf. Lightfoot's *Journal*, pp. 5, 26.

[28] Cf. *infra* pp. 242ff.

know from Baillie that each standing committee was open to all members of the Assembly, and therefore the allocation of subjects was perhaps not as important as it would otherwise have been. Writing of this committee structure, Baillie said

> Ordinarlie there will be present above three-score of their divines. These are divided in three Committees; in one whereof every man is a member. No man is excluded who pleases to come in any of the three. Every Committee, as the Parliament gives order to wryte to take any purpose to consideration, takes a portion, and in their afternoon meeting prepares matters for the Assemblie, setts doune their minde in distinct propositions, backs their propositions with texts of Scripture.[29]

The emphasis on proof texts inevitably pointed the Assembly in a restorationist and even a biblicist direction, but it was insisted on from the very beginning.

After the long session on July 8th, the Assembly adjourned as a plenary body until the following Wednesday (12th) to allow the Committees time to prepare work for its consideration. When these reports arrived before the whole body it was at once agreed that to clarify the XXXIX Articles and to define their proper meaning, proof texts should be added, and this policy was followed throughout the Assembly's work.

Most of those who write on the Westminster Assembly do so in order to provide an historical context for the Westminster Confession and the Catechisms. For this reason with Daniel Neal they tend to think that it is not necessary to trouble the reader with the debates on the XXXIX Articles[30] and hurry on to the Assembly's more productive work. After all, the solemn discussions of the first ten weeks were summarily aborted with the signing of the Solemn League and Covenant and the arrival of the Scots Commissioners, and if the major interest is in what the Assembly produced, there is little excuse to spend much time on debates that led nowhere.

Our own primary interest is somewhat different. It is not so much in the Assembly's later theological statements, as on what preceded them and on how the ecclesiological debate related to the wider political and military struggle convulsing the British

---

[29] *Letters and Journals*, II. 108.
[30] *History of the Puritans*, III. 68. However, Neal did include a very interesting comparison between the XXXIX Articles and the Assembly's revision; *ibid.* pp. 555–63. A. F. Mitchell was an exception to the general tendency of writers to ignore the earlier debates on the XXXIX Articles; cf. *The Westminster Assembly*, pp. 146–57, also Robert M. Norris, 'The Thirty-Nine Articles at the Westminster Assembly', pp. 1–158 (Analysis) and pp. 159–385 (the debates).

Isles. From this perspective the first ten weeks may be significant not because they produced anything that lasted, but precisely because they produced nothing. The political and military situation was extremely dangerous, and the alliance of the Scots hung in the balance. The importance of the debates in the Assembly may have been because the politicians could count on them being not only abortive but innocuous. There is no doubt that these sessions were very seriously argued,[31] but as soon as the Scots arrived safely in England the earlier debates were not likely to have any influence on the future form of the Church. Meanwhile since the Assembly was packed with convinced Calvinists, the subject matter was not likely to cause any major strain. The whole exercise was probably a colossal waste of time, but in 1643 few would have dared suggest that, and many would have considered such a suggestion close to blasphemy.

Indeed the religious situation of the country provided a very plausible excuse for debating the Church of England's doctrinal standards, for challenging the errors that had infiltrated through the Arminian opinions of Laudian divines, and for refuting the Pelagianism that Calvinists discovered under the covers of every Prayer Book. On the other side there were the equally horrendous heresies among the sectarians. "As the Assembly were for strengthening the Doctrines of the Church against *Arminianism*," wrote Neal, "they were equally solicitous to guard against the opposite Extream of *Antinomianism*."[32]

At this point Daniel Neal may have placed his finger on a matter of considerable importance for the later history of the Assembly's work, and curiously it is also related to what was happening in New England. Perry Miller pointed out that the orthodox Calvinists of New England found themselves beset theologically by the errors of both Arminianism and Antinomianism, for in the former human ethical response seemed to be in control of God's grace, while the latter hinted that the Elect are so possessed by the Holy Spirit that they could ignore the ethical demands of the Law.[33] Orthodox Calvinism tried to steer a clear path between the opposite dangers, and Miller showed that this

---

[31] There is no complete record of these debates since the Minutes start at Session 49 (Sept. 8th, 1643), but the Ms. Minutes are the most complete account we have. The debate on the XXXIX Articles covers Vol. 1, ff. 1–106 in the Ms (TMs. I. pp. 1–210.) and it continued until October 12, 1643, when the Assembly was peremptorily ordered by the Houses of Parliament to address itself to church order and government.

[32] *History of the Puritans*, III. 68.

[33] Perry Miller, *The New England Mind: the Seventeenth Century*, (Cambridge, Mass., Harvard University Press, 1954,) pp. 365–371.

underscores the significance of the Covenant (or Federal) theology embraced by New England Congregationalism.[34]

However, the Independents in the Assembly were a minority,
and in the eyes of their fellow members they had to establish their
orthodoxy. These early debates show that for the majority within
the Assembly the threat to national uniformity posed by the
proliferating Sectarians was to be feared little less than that posed
by the King, and much more to be feared than the Scots. The
leaders of that Puritan majority in the Assembly were particularly exercized about the spread of Antinomian ideas in the
nation's capital.[35] Early in the Minutes (September 13) Thomas
Gataker exclaimed "that worke doth require expedition [;] when
diseases are desperate [there must be] noe delay of phisicke [and]
this is as desperate as any sprung up in late days". As a result
Gataker, Calamy, Seaman, Goodwin, Cheynell, Palmer, Herle,
Featley and Temple were appointed as a study committee "to
compare the opinions of the Antinominans with the word of God,
and with the Articles of Religion . . . and make report to this
Assembly".[36] The Assembly feared that if these opinions were
not soon suppressed, there would be no hope of re-establishing a
unified form of national religion, which, up to that point in time,
had been the only way of settling religion that England had ever
known.

Moreover, several of the Arminians in the city who were
openly propagating their views, such as John Goodwin, the Vicar
of St. Stephen's, Coleman Street, were closely associated with
the Independent party. It was simply not possible for the Independent leaders in England to establish and maintain the kind of
theological uniformity that Cotton and Winthrop were able to
impose in New England. Although Independent theologians like
Thomas Goodwin and Jeremiah Burroughes were at pains to
maintain their orthodoxy, the members of the Assembly had
grave doubts about other members of that group and suspicions
that they were openly fomenting Antinomianism in the city.

---

[34] Miller argued that their emphasis on the Covenant of grace was in line with the
general move in society from the feudal emphasis on status to the new emphasis on
contract; *ibid.* p. 399. Since God of his free grace had entered into covenant with his
people, there was a place for the ethical response of the Elect as they tried to fulfil the
human side of that covenant, but without making any unwarranted claims for human
goodness. In this way orthodox Calvinists, to their own satisfaction, bridged the gap
between Law and Grace. *Ibid.* pp. 365–462.

[35] Cf. the strong views against Antinomianism aired by Dr. Temple on September
20th, 1643; TMs. I. 142 (Ms. I, f. 71.b.)

[36] TMs. I. 107 (Ms. I, f. 54.) Words or punctuation placed in square brackets [ ] are
added to assist the meaning of the quotations.

The matter seems to have burst into flames on October 9th when Herbert Palmer, one of the most highly respected members of the Puritan majority in the Assembly, "Informed [the Assembly] that Mr. Simpson incouraged the Antinomians [,] and [had] confessed that we ought not to confesse our sins",[37] while Peter Sterry,[38] after a long and somewhat obscure speech in the Assembly, was very pointedly asked to explain himself.[39] Dr. Thomas Temple was probably voicing the suspicions of the majority when he commented that "much of this discourse intrenches on those opinions now abroad in the city", although the Prolocutor, William Twisse seems to have taken a more conciliatory position: Sterry's argument seemed strange to Twisse only "in the close confounding of Justification and sanctification".[40] However, it is not surprising that the next day Herbert Palmer, Cornelius Burgess, Thomas Gataker and Thomas Temple, four of the most respected leaders in the Assembly, were appointed as a committee to prepare a statement "fit to represent to the H. of Co, for the quickening of their proceedings against the Antinomians".[41]

During the months that followed the Independents were increasingly sensitive to this reproach, and in tracing the movement of the Puritan majority from its relatively moderate views on church government to the enthusiastic endorsement of the presbyterian system, it is of great importance to recognize the fear of sectarian heterodoxy. We must also recognize the total inability of most Puritans to understand religious pluralism, and the determination of the majority in the Assembly to maintain uniformity of belief and worship in the form of a national church.

The Assembly worked on the XXXIX Articles for ten weeks, providing the members ample opportunity to hone the sharper points of their theology.[42] One of the major issues discussed at

---

[37] TMs. I. 178 (Ms. I, f. 90.)

[38] Sterry gained a reputation for obscurity. Sir Benjamin Rudyard said that his preaching was "too high for this world, and too low for the other", and Baxter, noting the affinity of Sterry's views for those of Sir Henry Vane made the acid comment that *"Vanity and Sterility* were never more happily conjoined." [*Rel. Baxt.* I. 75 (§119.)] However, he made ample amends after he read Sterry's posthumous book, *A Discourse of the Freedom of the Will* (1675); cf. Baxter's *Catholick Theologie* (1675) Pt. II. 107. Sterry had formerly been chaplain to the Independent peer, Lord Brooke, and was later chaplain to Oliver Cromwell at Whitehall.

[39] TMs. I. 185–7 (Ms. I, f. 93.b et seq.) Cf. *infra* pp. 187ff.

[40] TMs. I. 187 (Ms. I, f. 94.b.)

[41] TMs. I. 188 (Ms. I, f. 95.) The word 'quickening' was struck through in the text, but seems to be appropriate in the sense of the passage.

[42] Cf. A. F. Mitchell, *The Westminster Assembly*, pp. 146–57.

this time was the Article on Justification (Article XI). Dr. Twisse, Thomas Gataker and Richard Vines argued learnedly that only the passive obedience and sufferings of Christ were imputed to the believer, while Dr. Daniel Featley argued just as strongly (and apparently more persuasively) that both Christ's passive obedience and his active obedience to the Law were to be imputed to the believer. This was the view that prevailed in the Assembly, and it was in line with the position taken by Archbishop Ussher in drafting the Irish Articles. One thing is evident, although Daniel Featley was more or less openly an episcopalian, he was no less a Calvinist in doctrine than the rest of the Assembly.[43]

By the time the work was halted, the Assembly had concluded its consideration of the first fifteen of the Articles; but there were interruptions. The summer had gone very badly for the parliamentary armies – in June the Fairfaxes had been defeated in the north,[44] while in the west Sir William Waller had suffered defeat at Roundaway Down.[45] Parliament's Puritan supporters naturally saw these events as God's judgment against those aspects of Church and society that still remained unreformed and therefore unredeemed. When the news of Waller's defeat reached London the London ministers and divines of the Assembly presented a petition to Parliament calling for a special day of Humiliation, listing the sins of the nation that demanded reformation.[46] Parliament accepted the petition and set aside Friday, July 21st, for those solemn exercises, with Thomas Hill, William Spurstow and Richard Vines of the Assembly deputed as preachers.[47]

The Parliament's cause was in deep straits. A few months later Baillie wrote to William Spang, "For the present the Parliament syde is running down the brae. They would never, in earnest, call for help, till they were irrecoverable; now when all is desperate, they cry aloud for our help."[48] In the same letter he told his

---

[43] Daniel Featley delivered no less than five major speeches in the Assembly, which were published posthumously. He was still active in the debates of the Assembly on September 20th, 1643; Cf. TMs. I. 141 (Ms. I, f. 71.)

[44] Adwalton Moor. Baillie had written in July: "Alwayes the report of Fairfax's defeat hes been a spurr at last to that Parliament, much as is thought against the stomakes of manie, to send message on message to us of their Commissioners dispatch, my Lord Gray of Wark from the Lords, and two from the Commons. They are expected dailie." To Spang, 26th July, 1603, *Letters and Journals*, II. 81.

[45] 13th July, 1643. Cf. Appendix III.

[46] Cf. Neal, *Hist. of the Puritans*, III. 65–7.

[47] Wilson, *Pulpit in Parliament*, pp. 241, 260. Neal muddled this with the Fast sermons for July 7th; Neal, *op. cit.* p. 67.

[48] Letter, 22nd September, 1643, *Letters and Journals*, II. 83.

correspondent how the Scots had waited daily through the first week of August for the arrival of English Commissioners empowered to negotiate the terms of alliance. They had waited with growing frustration and impatience, "bot on Munday, the seventh, after we were ashamed with waiting, at last they landed at Leith".[49] The preliminaries for the Solemn League and Covenant had begun.

These events may offer some explanation why the Assembly had been given the unexceptional task of revising the XXXIX Articles as its first assignment. On the one hand the Scots had made it unequivocally clear that the reformation of the English Church was an unconditional requirement for their help, and that they regarded the call of the Assembly as an earnest of England's good faith. On the other hand, it could be extremely dangerous for relationships between the two nations if the members of the Assembly had simply taken the bit between their teeth and started on a wholesale reform of the Church of England's structure and worship before the Scottish Commissioners had arrived to take a hand. Radical reform of the Church with Scots' support was one thing, but radical reform without the Scots' consent and participation might jeopardize the alliance before it had properly begun. We recall that Robert Baillie at the end of July had said that Robert Meldrum had been sent to London to learn "what wee may expect of them anent uniformitie of Church Government".[50] If that was the condition of alliance, participation of the Scots in the Assembly was imperative.

This, I suggest, is the reason why the weeks between the call of the Assembly and the arrival of the Scots Commissioners appear so indecisive and hesitant – as if the Assembly had been deliberately turned down a blind alley. The parliamentary leaders knew that the Scottish Estates and the General Assembly were due to meet at the beginning of August, and that everything would depend on what the English Commissioners could win from the Scots at that time. What the Westminster divines could do for the Church, and how that would be accomplished, would very largely depend on the English Commissioners' negotiations in Scotland. If we take into account the time and dangers involved in travelling three hundred miles north in the middle of a civil war, and the preparations that would have to be made for that hazardous undertaking, we can see that the political moves were initiated very near the time when the Assembly was holding its

---

[49] *Ibid*, p. 88.
[50] Cf. *supra* p. 68. *Op. cit.*, II. 81.

first meeting. A Fabian strategy in the Assembly had been called for, and in a conference packed with Calvinist theologians, a review of the XXXIX Articles of Religion could be guaranteed to provide several months of involved but safe debate.

III

Second Political Intrusion: the Solemn League and Covenant

In May 1643 Charles I published a last appeal to the Scots, a desperate attempt to prevent them from allying themselves with the English Parliament, playing on their fear of the sectaries who were appearing in England.[51] He claimed that his kingdom had been invaded by Brownist, Anabaptist and Independent sectaries, "who in truth are the principal Authors and sole Fomenters of this unnatural War",[52] and warning the Scots that although his opponents in England "seem to desire an *Uniformity* of Church-Government with Our Kingdom of *Scotland,* [they] do no more intend, and are so far from allowing the Church-Government by Law established there (or indeed any Church-Government whatsoever) as they are from consenting to the *Episcopal*".[53]

The King may have been partially right in that, at least in respect to the men joining Cromwell's troops, but the appeal fell on deaf ears. The Scots might have their own suspicions about the intentions of some of their English friends, but they had no doubt whatsoever on what the Church of Scotland could expect from the King backed by a triumphant prelacy. When the General Assembly published its *Reasons* for assisting the English Parliament, it rehearsed the numerous occasions since the Reformation when events had clearly shown that the interests of Protestants in both countries had dictated close alliance:

> we and they sail in one Bottom, dwell in one House, are Members of one Body, that according to their own Principles, if either of the two Nations, or Kirks, be ruinated the other cannot long subsist . . . for we have the same Friends and Foes, the same Cause, and must run the same hazard, and many years experience hath taught us, what influence Popery and Prelacy in *England* may have upon *Scotland*; for from thence came the Prelates, the Ceremonies, the Book of Common Prayers, Service Book, and upon our refusal the bloody

---

[51] At the General Assembly held at Edinburgh, 1643, an Act had been passed on August 9th to search "for all books tending to Separation", and particularly for those "brought to this Countrey from beyond seas". Alexander Peterkin (ed.), *Records of the Kirk of Scotland* (Edinburgh, John Sutherland, 1838,) I. 346f.

[52] Rushworth, *Historical Collections*, VI. 464.

[53] *Ibid.* p. 466.

Sword came from thence; therefore we are to take *England's* conditions to Heart, as a common Cause, to put forth our helping Hand, if
we tender Religion, Laws, and Liberties.[54]

Charles might make a good case, but now the chickens hatched
by his previous policy in Scotland were coming home to roost.
And besides that, in their negotiations with the English politicians, the Scots knew that they were in a position virtually to
dictate their own terms.

The Commissioners appointed by Parliament for the negotiations were the Earl of Rutland and Lord Gray of Wark[55] from
the Lords, Sir William Armyn, Sir Henry Vane, the younger,
Thomas Hatcher and Henry Darley from the Commons, and
Stephen Marshall and Philip Nye from the Assembly of Divines.
Once they arrived in Scotland, there was some hard bargaining
but the work proceeded with considerable expedition. Robert
Baillie, who was in the negotiations from the Scottish side,
informs us that "the English were for a civill League, we for a
religious Covenant", and it is evident that at the point where the
negotiations began in earnest, there were, as Baillie puts it, "hard
enough debates". It also seems clear that the draft of the Covenant to be signed was presented to the English by the Scots, when
once the principle of a Covenant had been accepted:

> When they were brought to us in this, and Mr. Hendersone had
> given them a draught of a Covenant, we were not like to agree on the
> frame; they were, more nor we could assent to, for keeping of a doore
> open in England to Independencie. Against this we were peremptor.
> At last some two or three in private accorded to that draught, which
> in all our three committees, from our States, our Assemblie, and the
> Parliament of England, did unanimouslie assent to.[56]

From there it went to the Scottish General Assembly and carried
unanimously, and hence to the Scottish Estates where it passed
"with the same cordial unanimitie".

The document was then sent down to England. It received
some minor modifications that raised the ire of the Scots until
they realized that the modified text seemed to help their cause
better than the original;[57] but while the Covenant was being
considered the royalists in and around London seem to have
stimulated a riot and public outcry for immediate peace which
had begun innocently enough when a large crowd of women had

---

[54] *Ibid.* pp. 472–3.
[55] Lord Gray did not go to Scotland, pleading infirmity. He was gaoled briefly in the
Tower for Contempt. Cf. *ibid.* pp. 466, 467.
[56] To Spang, September 22nd, 1643, Baillie, *Letters and Journals*, II. 90.
[57] To the same, Nov. 17th, 1643, *ibid.* p. 102.

presented a petition for peace to the Houses at Westminster.[58] Meanwhile the Solemn League and Covenant was passed by Parliament after some face-saving delay by the Lords.[59]

The aforesaid Model of a Covenant sent out of *Scotland*, being presented to the Two Houses of Parliament in *England, Aug.* 28. was by them, after some small alterations, consented unto; and by an Order of the Commons, dated *Sept.* 21. 1643. printed and published; and on the next day it was appointed to be taken publickly in St. *Margaret's* Church at *Westminster*, by the House of Commons, and the Assembly of Divines. And *Philip Nye* (who was then returned from *Scotland*) was ordered to make an Exhortation, Mr. *John White* to pray before, and Dr. *George* [Gouge] after, the Exhortation; and *Alexander Henderson*, as one of the Commissioners from the Assembly of the Kirk of *Scotland*, made also a speech. The manner of taking it was thus: The Covenant was read, and then notice was given, That each Person should immediately by Swearing thereunto, Worship the great Name of God, and testifie so much outwardly, by lifting up their Hands; and then they went up into the Chancel, and there subscribed their Names in a Roll of Parchment, in which this Covenant was fairly written.[60]

C. V. Wedgwood claims with some justification that the choice of Philip Nye to preach on this occasion was significant. "He had already given offence in Edinburgh by a sermon of strong independent colour. Now at Westminster, he emphasised that the goal they had set before them was the purification of religious worship according to no national model, but by 'whatsoever the Word shall discover.'"[61] We should certainly not read too much into the selection of Nye for this honour, since Stephen Marshall was still in Scotland and Nye had been the only other ordained minister to accompany the delegation to Scotland,[62] but it must

---

[58] Rushworth, *Historical Collections*, VI. 357–8.

[59] To Spang, Nov. 17th, 1643, *Letters and Journals*, II. 102. For the text of the Solemn League and Covenant: *Historical Collections*, VI. 478f.; J. P. Kenyon (ed.), *The Stuart Constitution*, Document 75; S. R. Gardiner (ed.), *Constitutional Documents of the Puritan Revolution*, (Oxford, Clarendon Press, 1905,) pp. 267ff.

[60] *Historical Collections*, VI. 475. Rushworth's account is somewhat ambiguous and may give the impression that the Covenant was signed on the 22nd. It was actually signed on Monday, September 25th; cf. Lightfoot, *Journal*, p. 15.

[61] C. V. Wedgwood, *The King's War*, (New York, Macmillan, 1959,) p. 258.

[62] This was pointed out by J. R. DeWitt, who thought that "the significance of the choice is certainly overrated". He cites Robert Baillie to show that Nye's offence in Scotland "was thus exactly the opposite of that suggested by Miss Wedgwood." Cf. *Jus Divinum*, pp. 54f. and note 174.

I am confused by DeWitt's conclusion. Baillie, after criticizing Nye's 'clamorous' voice, his failure to preach about 'the common bussinesse', and his use of sermon notes, went on to say, "All his sermon was on the common head of a spiritual life, wherein he ran out, above all our understandings, upon a knowledge of God as God, without the scripture, without grace, without Christ." *Letters and Journals*, II. 97. When we bear in

have irked the Scots. The English Parliament was either curiously insensitive to Scottish feeling about Nye, or it was giving notice that whatever changes were to be introduced into the Church of England would have to be clearly substantiated by the Word of God: Vane and his colleagues had not insisted on that phrase being included in the Solemn League and Covenant for nothing, and at this date the outcome of the Assembly's work was not to be regarded as a foregone conclusion.

Rushworth, having described the way the Covenant was introduced to Westminster, went on to say that before it was offered to the general population the Assembly of Divines was instructed to prepare an Exhortation to go with it "for Satisfying of such Scruples as may arise in taking it".[63] And there were those who had scruples.

Baillie, who had not yet arrived in England to take his seat as a Commissioner of Scotland in the Assembly, said that during its passage through the Assembly of Divines, "onlie Dr. Burgess did doubt for one night",[64] but Baxter suggests that the opposition was much more extensive than that, and Baxter's words suggest that moderate episcopacy was still widely represented at Westminster.

The Synod stumbled at some things in it, and especially at the word [*Prelacy.*] Dr. *Burges* the Prolocutor,[65] Mr. *Gataker*, and abundance more declared their Judgments to be for Episcopacy, even for the ancient moderate Episcopacy, in which one stated President with his Presbytery, governed every Church; though not for the *English* Diocesan frame, in which one Bishop, without his Presbytery, did by a Lay-Chancellour's Court, govern all the Presbyters and Churches of a Diocess, being many hundreds; and that in a Secular manner by abundance of upstart Secular Officers, unknown to the Primitive Church. Hereupon grew some Debate in the Assembly; some being against every Degree of Bishops (especially the *Scottish*

---

mind the Independents' emphasis upon a church of 'visible saints' and on experimental religion, (and with due allowance for Baillie's animus,) there is probably good ground for thinking that Nye's exegesis must have struck its Scottish hearers as having a 'strong independent colour.' [Incidentally, DeWitt's citation of Miss Wedgwood's book (note 175) should be corrected to '*The King's War*, p. 258.']

[63] Dated Feb. 9th, 1644. For the text see *Hist. Collections*, VI. 475–7; also for the text of the Solemn League and Covenant and the members of the Commons who signed on August 25th, cf. *ibid*. 478–81.

[64] *Letters and Journals*, II. 99.

[65] Cornelius Burgess was not the Prolocutor, but one of the two Assessors. Baxter was not a member of the Assembly and cannot be expected to be too accurate on details. He may have magnified the opposition on the part of those who were in favour of a New Testament episcopacy, since this is the view he favoured himself. On the other hand, he is usually reliable, and Lightfoot indicates that the debate on the issue was heavy and at times acrimonious. Cf. *Journal*, pp. 10–12.

Divines), and others being for a moderate Episcopacy. But these *English* Divines would not Subscribe the Covenant, till there were an alteration suited to their Judgments: and so a Parenthesis was yielded to, as describing that sort of Prelacy which they opposed, *viz*. [*That is, Church Government by Archbishops, Bishops, Deans and Chapters, Arch-deacons, and all other Ecclesiastical Officers depending on that Hierarchy.*] All which conjoyned are mentioned as the Description of that Form of Church Government which they meant by *Prelacy*, as not extending to the ancient Episcopacy.[66]

This point was made explicit when Thomas Coleman preached at the time the House of Lords took the Covenant on September 29th. He "gave it them with this publick Explication, *That by Prelacy we mean not all Episcopacy, but only the form which is here described*",[67] and we can discern precisely the same concern to downplay Scottish Presbyterianism and to insist that all options were open to the Assembly, in the sermons which the popular preacher, Thomas Case, delivered when he urged the Covenant on London congregations.[68] Case had declared that "we are bound no more to conform to Scotland, than Scotland to us", and he had said that all forms of episcopacy were by no means excluded from consideration[69]; but De Witt brushes this aside with the extraordinary claim that Thomas Case was able to make that kind of promise because he was "a Presbyterian":

> Of course he would say that he and his brethren were willing to establish a kind of prelacy were this revealed in the Word. However unthinkable in practice, he was committed to such a point of view in theory. That was part of what it meant to be a Puritan. And Alexander Henderson would have agreed with him.[70]

Certainly Thomas Case was a Puritan, and possibly he was personally committed to the Presbyterian system, but we cannot assume that from these sermons. More importantly, De Witt does not appear to recognize how significant it was that at this time Thomas Case found it politic to make this kind of promise in public.

---

[66] *Reliquiae Baxterianae*, I.i. pp. 48–9, (§70).

[67] *Ibid.* p. 49. Cf. J. F. Wilson, *Pulpit in Parliament*, p. 242.

[68] Thomas Case, *The Quarrell of the Covenant, with the Pacification of the Quarrell, Delivered in Three Sermons on Levit. 26.25 and Jere. 50.5*. Thomas Case (1598–1682) had been curate to Richard Herrick in Norfolk and then joined Herrick in Manchester, but an advantageous marriage brought him some attention, and in 1641 he had removed to London where he had become a popular preacher. He became a very convinced Presbyterian and was one of the divines responsible for bringing Charles II back to England in 1660.

[69] *Ibid.* p. 44, cf. DeWitt, *Jus Divinum*, p. 57.

[70] *Jus Divinum*, p. 57.

What do these sermons tell us about the state of public opinion in the city? In the second of the sermons,[71] Case gives us a clear indication of the kind of criticisms of the Solemn League and Covenant that were circulating among ordinary people. It was objected, he said, that the Covenant was as likely to divide as to unite them, because the English seemed bound "to receive the *Law* of *Reformation* from *Scotland*, and other *Churches*, and not from the *lips* of the great *Prophet* of the Churches"; and also because in swearing to maintain religion as it had been already reformed in Scotland, first, "most shall swear they know not what; and secondly, we swear to conform our selves here in *England* to their Government and Discipline in Scotland, which is presbyteriall, and for ought we know as much *tyrannicall*, and more *Antichristian* then that of Prelacy, which we swear to exptirpate".[72]

What Thomas Case said in answer to those objections is even more illuminating, for he made no attempt to justify the Scottish system but only to stress the centrality of the clause on which the English Commissioners had insisted in Scotland:

First, We do not sware to *observe* the Discipline, but to *preserve* it: I may preserve that, which in point of conscience I cannot observe, or at least, sware to preserve.

Secondly, We sware to *preserve* it, not in opposition to any *other forme of* Government that may be found *agreeable* to the *Word*, but in opposition against *a common Enemy*, which is a clause of so wide a latitude and easie a digestion, as the tenderest conscience need not kick at it.

Thirdly, Neither in the *preservation of their Government; &c* nor in the *Reformation of ours*, do we sware to *any thing of mans;* but to what shall be found to be the *minde of Christ*, witnesse that Clause, According to the Word of God. . . .

Fourthly . . . we are not yet called to sware the *Observation* of any kinde of Government, that is, or shall be presented to us, but to *endeavour* the Reformation of Religion in *Doctrine, Worship, Discipline,* and *Government, According to the Word of God.*

In the faithfull and impartiall and search and pursuite whereof, if *Scotland* or any of the Reformed Churches can hold us forth any clearer light then our own, we receive it not as *our Rule*, but as such *help* to *expound* our Rule. . . .

So that still, it is not the *voyce* of the *Churches*, but of *Christ* in the *Churches* that we covenant to listen to, in this pursuite, that is to say, That we will *follow them, as they follow Christ*. . . .[73]

---

[71] Preached at St. Mary Magdalen, Milk Street, Saturday evening, Sept. 30th, 1643.

[72] *The Quarrell of the Covenant*, pp. 40f.

[73] *Ibid.* pp. 42f. The italics of the original may retain something of the preacher's emphasis.

Therefore, he went on to say, "by this Covenant *we* are bound no more to conform to *Scotland*, then *Scotland* to us: The *Astipulation* being mutuall, and this Astipulation binding us not so much *one* to *another*, as *both* of us to the *Word*".[74]

Undoubtedly the preacher had made as good an argument as possible to convince his English hearers that the Assembly was not bound to Scottish Presbyterianism by the terms of the Covenant, but the way in which this was presented is itself a fairly clear indication that the leaders at Westminster were well aware that conservative Puritan sentiment in the country was uneasy, and that public opinion was, at this stage, not prepared for ecclesiastical changes that would move too far from the traditional pattern. It is also clear that the leadership was extremely sensitive to a latent national suspicion of any system imposed on England by the Scots.

According to John Lightfoot's eye-witness account of the Assembly, Cornelius Burgess was joined in his opposition to the Covenant by William Price, but what is more remarkable about the whole incident is the extravagant way in which Lightfoot and others in the Assembly reacted to this opposition to the Covenant.[75] According to the original rules for the Assembly laid down by Parliament, members had the right to dissent, and Burgess was voicing a legitimate concern. Perhaps the violence of the reaction, better than any other evidence we could bring, illustrates the desperate straits into which the parliamentary cause had fallen, and the crucial importance at that time of the alliance with Scotland.

It was the petition that Cornelius Burgess and William Price addressed to the House of Commons that raised most ire among their colleagues at Westminster. After that, Lightfoot's language about Burgess became even more blistering. He called him "a wretch", and said that Burgess deserved to be "branded to all posterity, who seeks for some devilish ends, either of his own or others, or both, to hinder so great a good of the two nations."[76] We notice the extreme sensitivity of Lightfoot and presumably

---

[74] *Ibid.* p. 44.

[75] The debate leading to the amendments to the Covenant occurred before the Assembly handed its approval to the House of Commons on August 30th. It was then that Burgess had claimed liberty of conscience for entering his dissent. Lightfoot observed that "This was judged, and that justly, to be intolerable impudency, that the great affairs of two dying kingdoms, should be thought fit by him to stay and wait upon his captiousness." *Journal*, p. 11.

[76] *Ibid.* p. 12. We should note that there is more than a hint that there was some hidden plot in Burgess's actions, and that is not surprizing because Parliament was only just recovering from the embarrassment and shock of the Waller plot. The party had been

his colleagues in the Assembly for anything that seemed to threaten the safety of the cause, and perhaps in view of the dangers they faced in 1643, that is understandable enough.

William Price seems to have made his submission on September 2nd, "but not so the doctor"[77] who held out for a few days longer. The scribe in the Minutes obviously intended to add more later under Price's name, for under September 8th the name appears followed by a blank space, as if the notes of a speech were to be added. But also under that day's entry Dr. William Gouge presented a statement from Cornelius Burgess to the Assembly, "That he is sorry for the unadvisednesse of his proceedings in his late petition although noe way guilty of any designe against the kingdome or our brethren of Scotland 'or'[78] to asperse the Assembly [,] and desires them not to hold him guilty of what he hath not done noe more then he doth not Justify all that he hath done".[79] Later in the same session Dr. Smith brought an additional message from Cornelius Burgess offering "to give any satisfaction that he should be commanded to 'give to the Assembly by the house of Commons' though it were upon his knees".[80]

However, Dr. Burgess's apology was not accepted immediately.[81] It was conceded by one of his protagonists in the Assembly, Thomas Temple, that "his crime is not dissenting . . . but in his petitioning".[82] Burgess was apparently reinstated on September 20th.[83] The incident simply underscores the tremendous importance of the Scottish alliance for the parliamentary cause, and the weight placed upon unanimous acceptance of the Solemn League and Covenant by its supporters.

Matthew Sylvester, editor of Baxter's *Reliquiae*, called it the

---

forced to recognize that there were those within their own ranks at Westminster who were playing the King's game. This accusation was made openly in the Assembly on September 1st by Mr. De la March, who "told plainly, 'that he held it for the most dangerous plot and design, since the Parliament sat;' " and, Lightfoot added, "I believe few of the Assembly took it for any other than a design." (*Ibid.*)

[77] *Ibid.* p. 13.

[78] Words placed in single inverted commas in the transcript were interlined in the manuscript Minutes.

[79] TMs. I. 51, (Ms. I, f.26.)

[80] TMs. I. 56, (Ms. I, f.28.b.)

[81] It is interesting to notice the people who, even during the time of his disfavour, were working on behalf of Cornelius Burgess. For example a few days after Burgess had given his apology cited above (Sept. 13th), Palmer (seconded by Temple) offered "a motion concerning Dr. Burgis, that some way may be thought upon how he may be restored to us againe", and Palmer, Temple and Vines were deputed to work on "a forme of what is fit to present to the house in behalfe of Dr. Burgis". [Session 54] TMs. I. 97 (Ms. I, f.49.)

[82] *Ibid.*

[83] Lightfoot, *Journal*, p. 15.

Scotch Covenant[84] and Scotsmen called it the English Covenant.[85] And that difference in the way it was seen on either side of
the Cheviots may hint at the difference of fortune the Solemn
League and Covenant would suffer in the two countries: for the
Scots it was a Covenant to hold the English, and for the English it
was a Covenant that had been imposed on them by the Scots. A
later enthusiastic heir to Scottish Presbyterianism would see in
Scotland's activity surrounding the Solemn League and Covenant "an act of high chivalry, to call it by no more sacred name, for
them to cast their lot at this time with Parliament".[86] Robert
Baillie too could sound fairly unctuous when rhapsodizing on
Scotland's high-mindedness, but in less guarded letters to his
friend, William Spang, he seems more realistic about the affair.
Commenting upon the almost unanimous way in which the
Solemn League and Covenant received public support in Scotland, he admitted there were some powerful practical arguments
to keep the population in line:

> For the matter, the authoritie of a Generall Assembly and Con-
> vention of Estate was great; the penalties sett down in print
> before the Covenant, and read with it, were great; the chief aime of
> it was for the propagation of our Church discipline to England
> and Ireland; the great good and honour of our nation; also the Parlia-
> ment's advantage of Gloucester and Newbury,[87] bot most of all the

---

[84] Cf. *Reliquiae Baxterianae*, index, *ad loc.*

[85] Robert Baillie, *Letters and Journals*, II. 95.

[86] Benjamin B. Warfield, *The Westminster Assembly and its Work*, p. 23. A more recent
writer, Wayne Spear, also protests that this Covenant should not be dismissed as "the
product of Scottish shrewdness". He points out that the Scots achieved less than they had
hoped in the Form of Government, and that their fidelity to the Westminster Standards
despite this setback argues their good faith. Cf. 'Covenanted Uniformity in Religion,'
pp. 346–50.

The argument, however, does not quite get rid of the suspicion that "the Scots took
advantage of the desperate need that England had for military assistance". We would
point out that it was the Scots who insisted on a religious 'covenant', (when the English
would have been satisfied with a 'civil League',) who insisted on the specific ecclesiastical
terms of Article I, and who remembered the first and second Bishops' wars. Furthermore, they knew that they had the English over a barrel.

[87] Charles I had been besieging Gloucester while the negotiations had been going on in
Scotland. The city had been gallantly defended by Col. Edward Massey, and relieved by
September 8th by the Earl of Essex with an army raised in London. Charles then pulled
off to block Essex's return, but Essex managed to break through at the first battle of
Newbury, 18th September. The seriousness of the situation from the parliamentary side
may be judged from the following: "But the Royalists were scarcely less encouraged.
Charles had raised the siege [Gloucester] only to seek more favorable ground to fight
Essex. Barnstaple and Bideford had been taken; the Parliamentary admiral Warwick had
been beaten off in his attempt to relieve Exeter by sea; and though Plymouth, Lyme and
Dartmouth still held out for Parliament, Bristol and Exeter had been lost, and it remained
only to block Essex's way back to London to bring the cause of Parliament to the ground
before Scotch aid arrived." W. C. Abbott, *The Writings and Speeches of O.C.*, I. 257.

Irish cessation,[88] made the mindes of our people embrace the means of safetie . . .[89]

There was nothing in the Solemn League and Covenant with which any patriotic Scot of presbyterian sympathies could not wholeheartedly agree.

On the other hand, for England the Solemn League and Covenant could not help becoming a symbol of an alliance that the country had been pressured into by force of circumstances. As Baillie observed, "Wee know the best of the English have verie ill will to employ our aid, and the smallest hopes they got of subsisting by themselves, [makes them less fond] of us",[90] and he went on to voice the suspicion that the delay in raising the money needed for enlisting the Scots army was due to "the underhand dealing of some yet in their Parliament, who hes no will, that by our coming in, that business should be ended, lest their regime should too soon end."[91] Alexander Henderson was equally realistic about English feeling, for we read, "Mr. Hendersone's hopes are not great of their conformitie to us, before our armie be in England."[92]

The key to the Solemn League and Covenant, as I have pointed out elsewhere,[93] is in the first Article of the document. This was the reason for Scotland's whip hand over the Church of England, the cause of the debates between the Independents and the Presbyterians in the Assembly, and perhaps the fundamental reason why the presbyterian system was unable to win the support of the English population. That article promised:

> That we shall sincerely, really and constantly, through the grace of God, endeavour in our several places and callings, the preservation of the reformed religion in the Church of Scotland, in doctrine, worship, discipline and government, against our common enemies; the reformation of religion in the kingdoms of England and Ireland, according to the Word of God and the example of the best reformed churches; and we shall endeavour to bring the churches of God in the three kingdoms to the nearest conjunction and uniformity in religion, confessing of faith, form of church government, directory

---

[88] On September 15th a truce for a year's cessation of hostilities between the English and the Irish Catholic forces in Ireland raised fears that not only English troops from the army in Ireland would be brought in to assist Charles, but that Irish Catholics would be brought in to England or Scotland. Cf. Gardiner, *The Great Civil War*, I. 224f.

[89] *Letters and Journals*, II. 102–3.

[90] *Ibid.* p. 103.

[91] *Ibid.* p. 104.

[92] *Ibid.*

[93] Cf. Chapter 3 in the Introduction to *An Apologeticall Narration* (1963), 'Religion, Politics and War', especially pp. 70–73.

for worship, and catechising, that we and our posterity after us may, as brethren, live in faith and love, and the Lord may delight to dwell in the midst of us.[94]

The distinction between the *preservation* of the reformed religion in the Church of Scotland and the churches in England and Ireland that are yet to be *reformed*, is too obvious to need comment; and in case any doubt should remain as to what was intended, it goes on to speak explicitly of the closest possible uniformity of religion in all aspects of faith, church government and practice between the three national churches, and in conformity to the examples of 'the best reformed churches' abroad. The Scots had it all wrapped up.

There was not much that the English Commissioners could do to safeguard England's freedom of action regarding the future shape of the Church in England, but as much as could be accomplished was engineered by Sir Henry Vane, the younger. Baillie had described Vane as "one of the gravest and ablest of that nation" and said that he and Stephen Marshall were "the drawers of all their writes".[95] Vane won credit for whatever modifications were introduced to the original text of the Scots: he was able to get the word 'League' introduced as part of the title,

> and in the first Article he inserted that general Phrase, of Reforming *according to the Word of God*; by which the *English* thought themselves secure from the Inroads of Presbytery; but the *Scots* relied upon the next Words, *And according to the Practice of the best Reformed Churches*; in which they were confident their Discipline must be included. . . . Thus the wise Men on both Sides endeavoured to out-wit each other in wording the Articles.[96]

It is somewhat strange that despite his manoeuvring, Sir Henry Vane seems to have gained the confidence of the Scots. Many months later, when the issue between the Presbyterians and the Independents in the Assembly had been fairly joined, Baillie confidently affirmed that "Sir Harie Vane, whatever be his judgment, yet less nor more, does not owne them [the Independents], and gives them no encouragement".[97] To Baillie he became one of the English politicians "whom we trusted most", so that he was aghast when he had to report in a Public Letter that Sir Henry Vane, "our most intime friend" was joining with

---

[94] J. P. Kenyon (ed.), *The Stuart Constitution*, p. 264.
[95] *Letters and Journals*, II. 89.
[96] Neal, *Hist. of the Puritans*, III. 71f. The quotations between asterisks (* *) have been italicized for the sake of clarity; they are capitalized in the original.
[97] Public Letter, 2nd April, 1644, *Letters and Journals*, II. 146.

others to secure toleration for the sects.[98] Yet Vane in 1636 at the precocious age of twenty-three had been elected Governor of the Massachusetts Bay Colony during a particularly turbulent period in the life of the infant colony, and although on that occasion he had led the opposition to the more repressive aspects of the New England theocracy, he shared its Congregational enthusiasm. However the Scots interpreted the phrase 'according to the Word of God', he certainly thought that it would guarantee something very different from what they had in mind. The Independents claimed that their whole system of church government was based upon the New Testament practice:

> This being our condition, we were cast upon a farther necessity of enquiring into and viewing the *light part*, the positive part of *Church-worship* and Government; And to that end to search out what were the first Apostolique directions, pattern and examples of those Primitive Churches recorded in the New Testament, as that sacred pillar of fire to guide us. And in this enquirie, we lookt upon the word of Christ as impartially, and unprejudicedly, as men made of flesh and blood are like to doe in any juncture of time that may fall out; the places we went to, the condition we were in, the company we went forth with, affording no temptation to byas us any way, but leaving us as freely to be guided by that light and touch Gods Spirit should by the Word vouchsafe our consciences, as the Needle toucht with the Load-stone is in the Compasse.[99]

Certainly when the proviso was inserted that the reformation of the Church should be 'according to the Word of God', "even the Scottish ministers could hardly find any valid reason for refusing to accept this".[100]

But perhaps the Independents were not the only ones who could make this kind of claim. John Row, one of John Knox's colleagues in helping to produce the Book of Discipline of 1560, said of himself and his friends that "they took not their example from any kirk in the world – no, not from Geneva, but drew their plan from sacred Scripture".[101] This may explain why the Scots

---

[98] Public Letter, October 1644, *ibid.* p. 231; cf. the letter for D. D[ickson], September 16th, in which Baillie complained, "Our greatest friends, Sir Henry Vane and the Solicitor, are the main procurers of all this . . . ." *Ibid.* p. 230.

[99] *An Apologeticall Narration*, 1643/4, p. 3.

[100] From my Introduction to *An Apologeticall Narration* (1963 edn), p. 72.

[101] John Anderson, *Chronicles of the Kirk*, (Edinburgh, T. & T. Clark, 1849,) p. 210. Janet MacGregor has shown that although the Scots firmly believed their system of church government to be wholly derived from scripture, it had actually developed from a relatively simple form in which "there is no evidence of a distinctively Presbyterian Church organization" to its final form, and that in that development it had incorporated several external influences from Hesse, from Geneva, from the foreign congregations in England during Edward VI's reign, and from France. *The Scottish Presbyterian Polity*, pp. 132–137.

were so ready to include that phrase in the Covenant – they had complete confidence that their own system could be proved by the scriptures. The Independents in the Assembly might discover that it was a good deal more difficult to persuade the members that biblical authority unequivocally endorsed Congregationalism, than it had been to persuade themselves.

But for the moment everything was amity. What John Lightfoot called 'the Scots' Covenant' was approved by the Assembly and presented to the House of Commons on August 30th, then Alexander Henderson and the vanguard of the Scottish Commissioners[102] were received by the Assembly about two weeks later (fortunate timing!) while the Assembly was listening to its final congratulatory speeches on the Covenant.[103] It was appropriate that Dr. Twisse, "at the desire of the Assembly, gave thanks to God, for the sweet concurrence of us in the covenant"[104] in their presence, and doubtless the Scots were duly impressed.[105]

After the Scottish Commissioners' official entry to the Assembly on September 15th, the next two weeks of the Assembly's time was largely taken up with matters concerning the Covenant and with other public events. On the 25th a solemn service was held at St. Margaret's, Westminster, at which the Covenant was taken and subscribed by Members of the House of Commons and the Assembly;[106] the 28th September was given up to congratulating the Lord General, the Earl of Essex, on his safe and

---

[102] Rev. George Gillespie of Edinburgh, with John, Lord Maitland (later, after the death of his father in 1645, Earl of Lauderdale; and, after the Restoration, Duke of Lauderdale). Robert Baillie and Samuel Rutherford were received by the Assembly on Nov. 20th, 1643; cf. Lightfoot, *Journal*, p. 56. Warriston was admitted on 1st February 1643/4.

[103] Dr. Gouge voiced some scruples but to no effect, and "Dr. Burgess came in, and made a speech, and shewed that he was satisfied with the covenant, and had expressed so much to the House, and they had received satisfaction." *Ibid.* p. 15.

[104] *Ibid.*

[105] They must have been impressed. Robert Baillie was still in Scotland, but the account of the Assembly's 'consent and cheerfulness' had obviously reached him when he wrote to Spang on Sept. 22nd. Cf. *Letters and Journals*, II. 99.

[106] The Puritans were gluttons for punishment in church. Lightfoot says that after the Assembly received notice on Monday, 25th August that the House of Commons was already seated in St. Margaret's church, "we went after them. And after a psalm by Mr. *Wilson*, picking several verses, to suit the present occasion, out of several psalms, Mr. *White* prayed near upon an hour. Then he came down out of the pulpit, and Mr. *Nye* went up, and made an exhortation of another hour long. After he had done, Mr. *Henderson*, out of the seat where he sat, did the like; and all tended to forward the covenant. Then Mr. *Nye* being in the pulpit still, read the covenant; and at every clause of it, the House of Commons, and we of the Assembly lift up our hands, and gave our consent thereby to it, and then went all into the chancel, and subscribed our hands: and afterward we had a prayer by Dr. *Gouge*, and another psalm by Mr. *Wilson*, and departed into the Assembly again; and after prayer, adjourned till Thursday morning, because of the fast." Lightfoot, *Journal*, p. 15.

successful return from the relief of Gloucester and the first battle of Newbury; the 6th October was employed in a public reception with speeches in the Guildhall relating to the Scottish alliance.

But on October 12th, while the members were debating the sixteenth of the XXXIX Articles, there was an Order from both Houses of Parliament that the Assembly "do forthwith confer and treat among themselves, of such a discipline and government, as may be most agreeable to God's holy word, and most apt to procure and preserve the peace of the church at home, and nearer agreement with the church of Scotland and other reformed churches abroad, to be settled in this church instead and place of the present church-government by archbishops, bishops, their chancellors, commissaries, deans, deans and chapters, archdeacons, and other ecclesiastical officers, depending upon the hierarchy, which is resolved to be taken away."[107] The Assembly was also instructed to consider the form of worship to be used in the reformed Church of England "and to deliver their opinions and advices of and touching the same to both or either House of Parliament with all convenient speed they can".[108] It will be noted that although this action of Parliament obviously required the Assembly to take a much broader review of church and government and worship, the Order still reflected the words used in the original Ordinance by which the Assembly had been set up.

But the die was cast; from this point on the Westminster Divines, like some of their more radical brethren before them, were "cast upon a farther necessity of enquiring into and viewing . . . the positive part of *Church-worship* and government",[109] and the issue, as to which ecclesiology, if any, could be regarded as *jure divino*, was bound to be joined.

---

[107] Lightfoot, *Journal*, p. 17.
[108] *Ibid.* pp. 17–18.
[109] *An Apologeticall Narration*, p. 3.

CHAPTER 4

DESCRIPTIVE INTERLUDE: THE PARTIES

I

Polities and Politics

This is a convenient point at which to interrupt the action before it has properly started in order to describe the parties that were beginning to evolve.[1]

Part of the problem with the terms 'Puritan' and 'Puritanism' is that one cannot often be sure how they are being used;[2] but using the terms in what I would regard as their basic form, to denote non-separating English Calvinists in the sixteenth and seventeenth centuries, the Westminster Assembly was broadly representative of the whole Puritan movement, and the parties that appeared within it were the parties that had evolved within Puritanism up to that time. The situation would soon change, for with the exclusion of Daniel Featley the Episcopal position would be no longer openly supported in the Assembly. Indeed, one of the interesting aspects of the period, secondary to our subject but primary for the ecumenical history of the Church, is the obvious hardening of ecclesiastical lines to the point where Puritanism was virtually squeezed out of the Anglican Church, and sympathy for episcopacy was similarly squeezed out of the Puritan movement.

However, that absolute polarity had not yet been reached, and at this comparatively early stage of the Civil War there seems to

---

[1] This chapter necessarily uses material previously covered to some extent in my Introduction to *An Apologeticall Narration* (1963).

[2] Cf. *supra* p. 4, note 7. The four most common uses of the terms are: (1) as inclusive terms to imply the whole Protestant protest to the ecclesiastical policies of Elizabeth I and the Stuarts, (2) to describe non-separating, biblically-centered critics of the established order and worship in the Church of England, predominantly Calvinists, (3) in American usage the terms are used to distinguish between the non-separating Congregationalists of the Massachusetts Bay Colony and the semi-Separatist Pilgrims of the Plymouth Colony, (4) as pejorative terms to describe people of strict morals or of a very narrow-minded code – often used without much reference to the actual habits of the seventeenth century Puritans.

have been considerable latent support for the episcopal concept among Puritans. Although most of the acknowledged episcopalians who had been invited to join the Assembly absented themselves in deference to the King's expressed opposition, they had at least been invited. Perhaps, as some Presbyterian protagonists maintain, this showed "the wish of the Parliament to act with fairness and impartiality" and its determination that "the whole subject might be fully discussed",[3] but we must point out that Parliament's apparent impartiality was strictly limited to those who were known to be Calvinists and who acknowledged the scriptural basis of theology.

It was the scriptural basis that unified all forms of Puritanism and provided the common ground on which differences of worship and polity could be argued with some hope of reaching agreement. There was already a great deal of agreement among Puritans, and if episcopalians among them differed in defending some features of the traditional order and worship of the Church of England, at least they did so on strict biblical grounds. Even the Erastians, who were the most pragmatic of all in the Assembly, defended their views by careful exegesis. However, the early disappearance of advocates for episcopacy in the Assembly and the predominantly political character of Erastianism, meant that the debates in the Assembly on the doctrine of the Church were concentrated in issues between Presbyterianism and the Independents.

Those issues are bound to emerge more clearly as we consider the actual debates of the Assembly. At the moment it is sufficient to note that the chief matters in dispute were restricted to a relatively small theological area regarding the form of the Church. Both Presbyterians and Congregationalists claimed that they were restoring the New Testament pattern of the Church, and both concentrated on a pattern of ministry in which local churches were under the control of Pastors with Elders and Deacons.[4] Both exponents of 'the Congregational Way' and Pres-

---

[3] W. M. Hetherington, *History of the Westminster Assembly of Divines*, p. 93.

[4] In exegeting Ephesians 4:11ff., the Reformers seem to have agreed that the 'apostles, prophets and evangelists' represent extraordinary offices that were peculiar to the church in the apostolic age, and most Puritans seem to have followed them. It may be noted that although Calvin came close to this view of ministry, he did leave open the possibility that God might raise up apostolic offices in other ages as the need demanded. Cf. *Institutes*, IV. iii. 4–9. However, only outside Europe, where Puritans faced the problem of an unconverted people totally ignorant of the gospel, as with the Indians in New England, was the need of an 'evangelist' clearly recognized. This is seen in John Norton's reply to the questions posed by the Dutch theologian. Appollonius. Cf. Norton's *Responsio* (1648), translated by Douglas Horton as *The Answer*, (Cambridge, Mass., The Belknap Press, 1958), chapter VII, pp. 108–113.

byterians put local discipline in the hands of Pastors (as both ruling and teaching ministers) in association with Ruling Elders. However, Independents held that church discipline was the responsibility of the whole membership of the local congregation under the leadership of its Eldership, on the basis – as John Cotton described it – that "Church government is not an authority but a ministry",[5] or – as Richard Baxter interpreted their disciplinary principle – *"A Worshiping Church and a Governed Church is and must be all one."*[6] Presbyterian discipline, on the other hand, was structurally as hierarchical as episcopacy, except it exchanged the hierarchy of individual clergy for that of church courts composed of ministers and elders. These were arranged in ascending order of power, from the authoritative court of the local congregation (the session) to that of local groups of churches (Classis or Presbytery), Provincial Synods and the General Assembly of the whole nation.

The Independents held that the highest authority for the Church on earth is that of the local church under the leadership of its ministers, although wider groups of churches might meet together (Associations, Synods) to give advice and council. In their view, a covenanted church could not be excommunicated because its authority came directly from Christ, although it was always possible for wider bodies of churches to withdraw communion from a congregation considered to be persisting in error. The major issues in the Assembly during this period were concentrated on the need for 'Doctors' and (surprizingly) for Ruling Elders,[7] on the rights of the local congregation vis à vis presbyteries and 'higher' courts, and on the right of church courts to excommunicate. The question of toleration was a political issue, and it was only later, when it became clear that presbyterian uniformity would prevail in the Assembly, that Independents took up the right to dissent.

In the context of the seventeenth century struggle these issues were not remote matters of theology. The political parallels could not be ignored, because there was a close relationship between what Puritans sought to do in the Church and what Parliamentarians were beginning to do in society, and from the beginning the parties in the Assembly had their political allies in parties that were emerging in Parliament. When the Long Parliament began,

---

[5] In the Foreword he wrote to Norton's *Responsio, ibid.* 15.

[6] *Reliquiae Baxterianae,* I. ii. 143 (§13).

[7] This was surprising since both the Scots Presbyterians and the Independents in the Assembly were agreed on the office of Ruling Elder. Cf. *An Apologeticall Narration,* p. 8.

a majority of the Lords and probably a majority of the Commons were looking for comparatively modest changes in church and state, hoping for a structure in both that could combine their 'restorationist' appeal to the primitive society of pre-Norman England and to the New Testament Church with a decent respect for traditional structures. During the Civil War this went by the board, and the participants found themselves forced to align themselves more precisely.

The parties among the divines became no longer simply representative of rival polities in the Church, but the ecclesiastical wings of wider movements that made their appeal to, and formulated their policies for, a total program in church and state. Historians have always had to wrestle with the confusion caused by the ecclesiastical and political aspects of the terms 'Independent' and 'Presbyterian' during the Civil War, but perhaps the problem arises from our own reluctance as moderns to recognize any integral relationship between church and society.

It is important to realize that there was as yet a great deal of fluidity within the parties. During the early stages of the struggle individuals were still finding their own position, and they sometimes had to shift their allegiances to meet the challenge of political and military events in situations that were often violent and never static. This ideological imprecision was particularly noticeable within the right wing of the Puritan movement, i.e., among those who began by preferring a moderate form of episcopacy but who found themselves more and more siding with the Presbyterian party.[8] Some of those who began with this right-wing stance in the Parliamentary cause found that their position was no longer tenable on that side of the struggle, or at least it was not tenable in those terms. They then had the option of either transferring their loyalty to the King, as some did, or of linking their fortunes with the Presbyterians or Independents.[9] Since the Presbyterian party was committed to national uniformity in

---

[8] This appears to be admitted by Thomas Fuller, for in describing the parties in the Assembly, he speaks of "Such who for their judgments favoured the presbyterian discipline, *or in process of time were brought over to embrace it;*" *Church History of Britain*, III. 503; my italics [His account needs some correction, however, for Mr. Carter, the younger, and Joseph Caryl appear to have been more aligned with the Independents than with the Presbyterians; *ibid.*]

[9] The personal problem is illustrated in the career of Sir Edward Dering. As we have seen, he was an advocate of moderate episcopacy, yet he had proposed the first reading of the Root and Branch Bill (27th May, 1641), and later called for an Assembly of Divines. He moved to the Anglican royalist side in the debate on the Grand Remonstrance, and his opposition to the ecclesiastical policy of Parliament caused him first to be briefly imprisoned in the Tower, and then impeached. He escaped, and by the outbreak of war

religion and to a negotiated peace with Charles as the best way of salvaging something of the traditional social order, it is not difficult to see why many appear to have moved in that direction.

II

Puritan Episcopalians

The Solemn League and Covenant had put an abrupt end to the discussion of the XXXIX Articles, and with the expulsion and imprisonment of Dr. Daniel Featley for corresponding with Archbishop Ussher and the royalists at Oxford,[10] no open advocate of episcopacy was left in the Assembly. Therefore a discussion of 'Puritan Episcopalians' would appear to be pointless.

The reason for pursuing it is because one suspects that there were far more Calvinists who supported a moderate form of episcopacy at the beginning of the war than have usually been credited to that position, and although many, perhaps a majority, sympathized with the King, it is not to be assumed that there had been no solid support for this position in the Assembly at the beginning. It was a Calvinist Assembly, and the very fact that so many failed to attend[11] may indicate the strength of what we have called 'Puritan episcopacy' among the clergy at large. But the furore about the opposition of Burgess and his friends regarding the exclusion of episcopacy in the Covenant, and the specific change that the Assembly made in the text, suggests that by no

---

had taken a commission in the King's forces, but he soon became equally disillusioned with the royalist cause. He resigned his commission in 1643, and was the first to accept Parliament's offer of amnesty (Jan. 1643/4) on the basis of the Covenant. For his Humble Petition to Parliament, cf. Rushworth, *Historical Collections*, VI. 383f.

[10] On Oct. 30th, 1643, his intercepted letter to Archbishop Ussher at Oxford was read to the House of Commons. His livings were sequestered on October 23rd.

[11] One hundred and twenty divines had been called to the Assembly, and of these, twenty-eight failed to attend.

The greater number of these did so because of the King's prohibition, and they therefore had episcopal sympathies. The number included Ralph Brownrigg, Bishop of Exeter (who sent an apology); James Ussher, Archbishop of Armagh; Henry Hutton, Prebendary of Carlisle; William Nicholson, Archdeacon of Brechnoch; Henry Hammond, Canon of Christ Church, Oxford; Samuel Ward, Lady Margaret Professor at Cambridge; George Morley, later to be Bishop of Winchester; Robert Sanderson, later Bishop of Lincoln; John Hacket, later Bishop of Litchfield; and John Erle, who was later successively Bishop of Worcester and Salisbury. We should also note that Thomas Westfield, Bishop of Bristol, attended the first session of the Assembly, and that Edward Reynolds became Bishop of Norwich after the Restoration, while Richard Herrick conformed. A comparison of the later careers of the twelve 'Puritans' who were appointed to fill Headships in Cambridge colleges as a result of the Earl of Manchester's Visitation of the University, shows that four of them conformed at the Restoration. Neal, *Hist. of the Puritans*, III. 117f.

means all those who remained in the Assembly could yet be counted as Presbyterians.

Some Puritans had come to the conclusion that the evidence for bishops in the New Testament could not be ignored. This had been fairly and impartially set down by scholars who could never be accused of Laudian prejudices,[12] and among these studies the work of Dr. James Ussher, Archbishop of Armagh carried considerable weight, since he was regarded as perhaps the leading British biblical scholar of the time and highly regarded in Calvinist circles. Richard Baxter whose reputation among the Puritans grew throughout this Civil War period, and who was to be one of their leaders after the Restoration against all the pressures to conform, was completely committed to Ussher's view of primitive, New Testament episcopacy.[13] Even during his early ministry and under the emotional pressures stimulated by the *Et Caetera* Oath, although he became sufficiently convinced against the English Diocesan Order, he admitted. "I found not sufficient Evidence to prove all kind of Episcopacy unlawful",[14] and this apparently remained his firm conviction throughout life. In the passages of his autobiography that relate to his ecumenical studies and set out the *pros* and *cons* for the various ecclesiastical polities, he wrote:

> The Episcopal Party seemed to have reason on their side in this, that in the Primitive Church there were some Apostles, Evangelists, and others, who were general unfixed Officers of the Church, not tyed to any particular Charge; and had some Superiority (some of them) over-fixed Bishops or Pastors! And though the extraordinary Parts of the Apostles Office ceased, with them, I saw no proof of the Cessation of any *ordinary* part of their Office, such as Church Government is confessed to be. All the doubt that I saw in this was, Whether the Apostles themselves were constituted Governours of other Pastors, or only over-ruled them by the Eminency of their Gifts and Priviledge of Infallibility. For it seemed to me unmeet to affirm without proof, that Christ setled a Form of Government in his Church, to endure only for one Age, and changed it for a New one when that Age was ended.

---

[12] *The Origin of Bishops and Metropolitanes briefly laide downe, by Martin Bucer; sometime professor of Divinity in the Vniversity of Cambridge; John Rainoldes; late Professor of Divinity in the Vniversity of Oxford; James Vssher; sometime Professor of Divinity in the Vniversity of Dublin . . .,* Oxford, 1641. See also James Ussher's *The Judgment of Doctor Rainoldes touching the Originall of Episcopacy More largely confirmed out of Antiquity,* London, 1641.

[13] *Reliquiae Baxterianae* I. ii. 206 (§§61–4). Cf. *supra* pp. 52f.

[14] *Ibid.* I. i. p. 16 (§22).

And as to *fixed Bishops* of particular Churches that were Superiours in degree to Presbyters, though I saw nothing at all in Scripture for them, which was any whit cogent, yet I saw that the Reception of them in all the Churches was so *timely* (even in the days of one of the Apostles in some Churches), and so general, that I thought it a most improbable thing, that if it had been contrary to the Apostles mind, we should never read that they themselves, or any one of their Disciples that conversed with them, no nor any Christian or Heretick in the World, should once speak or write a word against it, till long after it was generally setled in the C[h]urches. This therefore I resolved never to oppose.[15]

The passage has been quoted at length because it suggests that the Puritan Episcopalian, Richard Baxter, who after 1660 was an acknowledged leader among English 'Presbyterians', approached the scriptures in the same matter-of-fact, literal way as any other Puritan, and with the same presupposition of Presbyterians, Congregationalists or Baptists at that time, namely, that the problem of church government could be solved very simply by re-establishing the polity of the apostles. Baxter, who supported Parliament, and Ussher, who supported the King, both believed that the New Testament church was basically episcopal in structure, but that it was essentially a *pastoral* episcopacy. Reform of the Church of England would mean supplanting the prestigious diocesan prelacy by bishops who were much more evangelically motivated, pastorally oriented and local in their authority.

This view of episcopacy was to be found both among royalists and among parliamentarians, and there are indications that it continued to live *sub rosa* in the thinking of many who remained in the Assembly, although many of these later became supporters of Presbyterian order. Baxter also discussed this view of episcopacy in a passage where he reported the debate between parliamentary divines and the King's ecclesiastical advisers (who included Ussher) during the Isle of Wight negotiations in 1647; and in his criticism of the arguments put forward from the parliamentary side – "though Persons whom I highly honoured" – he said that they did not take the course most likely to heal the breach between 'these distracted Churches' for "instead of disputing against all Episcopacy, they should have changed Diocesan Prelacy into such an Episcopacy as the Conscience of the King might have admitted, and as was agreeable to that

---

[15] *Ibid.* I. ii. 140 (§3).

which the Church had in the two or three first Ages". Then he went on to observe:

> I confess, Mr. *Vines* wrote to me as their excuse in this and other Matters of the Assembly, that the Parliament tied them up from treating or disputing of any thing at all, but what they appointed or proposed to them: But I think plain dealing with such Leaders had been best, and to have told them *this is our Judgment,* and in the matters of God and his Church we will serve you according to our Judgement or not at all.[16]

However, Baxter admitted that "if they were not of one Mind among themselves, this could not be expected"; but it suggests that there was still some sympathy for the primitive episcopacy among Dr. Vines and his colleagues which had been obscured by political considerations.

Apart from any question of New Testament justification, such a simplified form of church government appeared to be the most pragmatic solution of England's ecclesiastical problem. It had been constantly pushed by Ussher against the Laudian views popular at the court of Charles I, although it was not until the King reached desperate straits in 1647 in the Isle of Wight that he was ready to listen, and it was the view that Baxter tried unsuccessfully to get accepted as the basis of a reconciliation after the Restoration. These two represent a view of church government that spanned distinctions between royalists and parliamentarians.

The failure to achieve concord is a testimony to the perversity of human nature, for commenting on Charles's debates with the Puritans Ussher remarked that, "as *he* would not when *others* would, so *others* would not when *he* would", and this led to Baxter's wistful comment, "and thus the true moderate healing terms are always rejected by them that stand on the higher Ground, though accepted by them that are lower and cannot have what they will: From whence it is easy to perceive, whether Prosperity or Adversity, the Highest, or the Lowest, be ordinarily the greater Hinderer of the Churches Unity and Peace".[17]

In a situation of increasing polarity, this was the basic reason why New Testament episcopacy was brushed aside. During the early stages of the struggle when many Puritans would have been more than willing to accept it, Charles was riding high with a Laudian *jure divino* view of episcopacy backed by a Divine Right

---

[16] *Ibid.* I. i. p. 62. (§93).
[17] *Ibid.*

view of his own sovereign authority; but when the King had been reduced to the point of conceding it, Westminster was riding high with a *jure divino* view of Presbyterianism, and there were popular forces in both Parliament and the Army that were well on the way to asserting the Divine Right of the people. The chance of reconciliation was frustrated because of conceptions of theological authority which maintained that the Holy Spirit speaks through only one channel, and which therefore refused to listen to any alternative claims.

The significance of the ecclesiastical views represented by Ussher and Baxter for our study is not in the practical ecumenical possibilities they offered – that could not of itself be a ruling principle in any theology, and least of all in the theologies of the seventeenth century – but it was in the biblical base. For Ussher, no less than for any of the divines of the Westminster Assembly, the Bible was the primary theological authority,[18] and it was on that basis that he advocated episcopacy. The office of bishop was undoubtedly a recognized office in the New Testament,[19] and if the New Testament principle of pastoral servanthood is coupled to this concept of ministry, then a totally different conception of the office of bishop emerges from that of the powerful and wealthy prelates who sat, by right of royal law and ecclesiastical tradition, among England's peers. The basic criticism of the Church that had been revealed through popular access to the Bible, was then as now in the contrast between what the Church had become and its apostolistic simplicity: it was a credibility gap. If Ussher's and Baxter's view of episcopacy had prevailed, the theological basis for church order would have shifted from one that rested primarily on royal authority and ecclesiastical tradition, to one that would have been based on the scriptures without ignoring the Church's tradition.

We should not give too much weight to this position, because it had remarkably little influence on either side of the Civil War, but the significance of Baxter's testimony is not in the rightness or wrongness of the position he espoused, but because he regarded it as representative of the position taken by the greater number of Puritan ministers. In Baxter's survey of the various ecclesiastical positions to be found in England during the Inter-

---

[18] Ussher dated the history of the world on the assumption that the Bible presents us with objective, scientific facts because it had been divinely revealed. Cf. his *Annals of the Old and New Testament*, London, 1658.

[19] E.g. Acts 20:28, Philippians 1:1, I Timothy 3:1–7, Titus 1:6ff. In I Peter 2:25 the word *'episcopos'* refers to Christ, but it should be noted that it is essentially joined with the pastoral office.

regnum, and of the support for his ecumenical efforts, he declared:

> But the greatest Advantage which I found for Concord and Pacification, was among a great number of Ministers and People who had addicted themselves to no Sect or Party at all; though the Vulgar called them by the Name of *Presbyterians;* And the truth is, as far as I could discover, this was the Case of the greatest number of the godly Ministers and People throughout *England.* For though Presbytery generally took in *Scotland,* yet it was but a stranger here".[20]

In the same passage Baxter went on to say that "though most of the Ministers (then) in *England* saw nothing in the Presbyterian way of *practice,* which they could not cheerfully concur in, yet it was but few that had resolved on their *Principles:* And", he continued, "when I came to try it, I found that most (that ever I could meet with) were against the *Jus Divinum* of Lay Elders, and for the moderate Primitive Episcopacy, and for a narrow Congregational or Parochial Extent of ordinary Churches, and for an accommodation of all Parties, in order to Concord, as well as my self."[21] Baxter's testimony gains some support from two incidents that took place at the beginning and the end of the revolutionary period. The first is from a somewhat unlikely source, for after the Scots Commissioners visited London in 1640, they published a pamphlet specifically attacking this view of limited episcopacy, and this seems to present a tangible clue of the direction from which they expected their own views to encounter their most serious challenge in England.[22] The second event is recorded by Baxter himself: very soon after the Restoration, the Presbyterian ministers who had been responsible for Charles II's recall, presented Ussher's form of church government to the King as the most hopeful way of reconciling their churchmanship with episcopacy and of their remaining within the Church of England.[23] This suggests that the concept of 'primitive episcopacy', far from being dead or even moribund during the years of the Interregnum, had simply remained a dormant but live option in the minds of many English 'Presbyterians'.

---

[20] *Reliquiae Baxterianae* I, ii. p. 146 (§23).

[21] *Ibid.* See also *Ibid.* I. i. p. 33 (§49) III. p. 41 (§91).

[22] *The Unlawfulness and Danger of Limited Prelacie or Perpetuall Precidencie in the Church,* (London? 1641.) This is usually attributed to Alexander Henderson, although the British Library listing suggests it was by either Henderson or Blair, and the Library of Congress offers Blair or Baillie. They were all present in London at the time. Cf. *supra* pp. 39f.

[23] *Rel. Baxt.* II, 231–241 (§§91–99).

III

The Presbyterians

The passage in Baxter is important for a proper understanding of the 'Presbyterians' in the Assembly and throughout the parishes, for it adds considerable weight to the Ethyn Williams Kirby thesis, to which we have referred earlier.[24]

By the time the Westminster Assembly had finished its work, those who were regarded as Presbyterians in the Assembly and in Parliament were able to carry through a complete program for presbyterianizing the Church of England in church order, liturgy, catechizing and discipline. The numerical preponderance of this presbyterian sentiment emerged rapidly during the early debates of 1644 in the Assembly, and from that time its adherents fought tenaciously to ensure that the Presbyterian system was established. This indisputable majority support in the Assembly led some historians to assume that already by the outbreak of the Civil War there was a powerful party within the Church of England that supported well-defined Presbyterian ecclesiology with clear-cut ecclesiastical objectives.

Closer attention to the evidence raises serious doubts about that conclusion. Certainly there was a considerable body of Puritan opinion in England at the outbreak of war which looked back at the 'Old Non-conformists' of Elizabeth's reign with respect if not with reverence, and in the remarkable careers of such men as 'Decalogue Dod' of Fawsley, Northants,[25] and Laurence Chaderton,[26] there were men to remind Puritans of those heroic days when the establishment of the 'holy discipline of the Church out of the Word of God' had seemed within their grasp.[27] It is also evident that there were ministers in and around London who were even then committed to a form of church government very close to that of the Scots. As soon as Puritan

---

[24] *Supra* p. 30 n. 56. In view of Baxter's insistence on this point and the weight of his testimony, we are surprised that Ethyn Williams Kirby apparently did not use *Reliquiae Baxterianae*.

[25] John Dod (1549?–1645) had received his nickname from the exposition of the Ten Commandments he published in 1604.

[26] Laurence Chad[d]erton (1536?–1640) had been Master of Emmanuel College, Cambridge, from its foundation in 1584 to 1622, and had been preacher at St. Clements, Cambridge for fifty years. He had been present at the Hampton Court Conference in 1604.

[27] See the works of William Travers on church discipline; M. M. Knappen, *Tudor Puritanism*, p. 285, Patrick Collinson, *The Elizabethan Puritan Movement*, pp. 107f; also William Fulke's *A Brief and Plain Declaration Concerning . . . Reformation of the Church of England* (1572) in Leonard J. Trinterud (ed.), *Elizabethan Puritanism* [Library of Protestant Thought], (New York, Oxford University Press, 1971,) pp. 239ff.

opinion began to swing in that direction, there would be every reason for the trend to be reinforced by the memory of this older Elizabethan presbyterian tradition, but at the time the Assembly began its work we are not convinced that the great mass of Puritan opinion was already Presbyterian, or that there was any evidence of widespread Presbyterian sentiment within the Church at large. Baxter is insistent on this point, for in describing the situation at the outbreak of hostilities, he declared, "The truth is *Presbytery* was not then known in *England*, except among a few studious Scholars, nor well by them",[28] and it was "the moderate Conformists and Episcopal Protestants" together with a few Independents who had first raised the opposition to Charles.[29] Indeed, the possibility of church government being recast did not arise until Parliament began to move against prelatical episcopacy in 1640, and it seems that the first moves for reform in England were carried through under the cloud-cover provided by Charles's military failure against the Scots.[30]

We have to consider the situation of the English Puritan clergy during the decade or so before the outbreak of the Civil War. Long gone were the enthusiastic days of Elizabeth's reign when men like Thomas Cartwright and John Field had plotted and planned the establishment of reformed church discipline under the noses of the bishops and when their Book of Discipline had been used in secret side by side with the Book of Common Prayer. Those who had felt keenly enough about such matters had either been suppressed and doomed to a life of penury and obscurity, or else they had been forced to exercise their talents abroad. The rest conformed.

It was the more intractable Puritans who had gone into exile.[31] There had been some who had gone abroad and who had decided Presbyterian views, such as John Forbes of Delft and John Paget of Amsterdam, but Forbes had died in 1634 and Paget was dead

---

[28] *Rel. Baxt.* III, p. 41 (§91).

[29] Since Baxter's autobiography was published much later and posthumously it is difficult to see why he should have insisted on this unless he was trying to set the record straight.

[30] Robert Baillie had been a witness to this while he was a chaplain to the Scottish Commissioners in London. "Nothing frayes all here so much as our quick agreeing with the King, and the disbanding of our armie thereupon. Under God, they all every where professe that they are aughtin [i.e., owing, in debt] to that armie their religion, liberties, parliaments, and all they have." To the Presbytery of Irvine, December 2nd, 1640, *Letters and Journals*, I. 275.

[31] Exile in the Netherlands represented only a 'comparative' security. Archbishop Laud had shown that he had a very long arm that was well able to reach into Europe to frustrate the plans of those who dissented from his policies. Cf. *supra* p. 27 note 47.

in 1640 and there is no evidence that those who thought like them had left the country in large numbers or that they had returned to take part in the war. The other exiles in Holland, such as Paul Baynes, Robert Parker, William Bradshaw, William Ames and Henry Jacob had adopted even more radical positions, and they had been forced to develop their views in the relative security and obscurity of a foreign land. At the same time they exercized a powerful influence on a younger generation of exiles – John Cotton, John Davenport, Thomas Hooker, Hugh Peter and the Apologists – who were to be the leading exponents of the Congregational Way in New England and of Independency in the Assembly.

For the rest it appears that while most Puritan preachers in England firmly adhered to Calvinist doctrine and Puritan morality, they swallowed their preferences in the matter of church order, continued in their livings, and postponed the reformation of the Church of England *sine die*.[32] Forty years of Stuart rule without hope of a change in government policy and backed by the ruthless surveillance of men like Bancroft and Laud, did not leave much room for alternative parties to develop and manoeuvre in England. The Courts of Star Chamber and High Commission very effectively stifled opposition before it became more than vocal, and although they left a growing mass of Puritan resentment, it was not until almost the outbreak of war itself that parties felt free to organize .

This underlines the importance of the Scottish Kirk for English Puritans. By the time the Civil War broke out there were undoubtedly many English Puritans who were looking for extensive reforms in the Church of England – not perhaps with any clear ideas or unanimity about what the changes should be, except an aversion to prelacy and Laud's innovations – but they had to look abroad for their examples, and the nearest example of a Church that had tried to organize itself on biblical lines was obviously to be found in Scotland. But there is nothing to suggest that many were committed to Presbyterianism in detail, or that many even knew what the Scottish system would imply for the Church of England.[33]

---

[32] However, there is no reason to suppose that the liturgical non-compliance of Puritans completely disappeared. Cf. Ogbu U. Kalu, 'Bishops and Puritans in Early Jacobean England: A Perspective on Methodology,' *Church History*, Vol. 45, No. 4 (December 1976), pp. 469–489.

[33] In February 1640/1 we find Oliver Cromwell writing to a bookseller to send him "the reasons of the Scots to enforce their desire of Uniformity in Religion, expressed in their 8th Article", Abbott, *Writings and Speeches of O.C.*, I. 125, Lomas–Carlyle, I. 96 (III), *The Lord Protector*, p. 51.

Apart from those who were to become the major exponents of Independency, few Puritans up to that point had been prepared to go into exile for their beliefs, or to risk Archbishop Laud's enmity by openly experimenting along ecclesiological lines. They might look back approvingly to the works of Cartwright and other Puritan writers of the Elizabethan period, but in England during the first four decades of the seventeenth century, one looks in vain for any books advocating Presbyterianism: no books had been written from this standpoint since Cartwright's ill-fated literary marathon with Whitgift, and although there was no dearth of literary output among the Puritans on doctrinal matters during this period, the only books in the field of ecclesiology came from the pens of those who represented the more radical position of the Independents, and they were written from exile.

This should put the Solemn League and Covenant and the alliance with Scotland into perspective: it forced the English Puritans to face the ecclesiastical implications of the covenant with Scotland, and the political and military implications if that alliance were to be frustrated. Daniel Neal, writing less than a century from the event,[34] said of the early days of the Assembly that "the *English* Divines would have been content with revising and explaining the Thirty-nine Articles of the Church of *England*, but the *Scots* insisted on a system of their own".[35] Earlier in his book Neal said that by the time the Solemn League and Covenant was agreed by the Assembly, the Episcopal clergy (i.e. those who were *openly* for the episcopal system) had left it, but he added the intriguing comment that "all who remained were for taking down the main Pillars of the Hierarchy, before they had agreed what Sort of Building to erect in its room", and he went on to suggest that this mass of uncommitted Puritan opinion moved very rapidly into Presbyterianism because of the situation which had produced the Scots alliance:

> The Majority at first intended only the Reducing Episcopacy to the Standard of the first or second Age, but for the Sake of the *Scots* Alliance, they were prevailed with to lay aside the Name and Function of Bishops, and attempt the Establishing a Presbyterial Form upon the Ruins of all others, which at length they advanced into *Jus*

---

[34] Neal lived from 1678–1743, and wrote *The History of the Puritans between* 1732–8. He is sometimes inaccurate in matters of detail, but was still close enough to a living tradition to be treated with respect on the movements within seventeenth century Puritanism.

[35] *History of the Puritans*, III. 378.

Divinum, or *Divine Institution,* derived expressly from Christ and his Apostles.[36]

Neal's comments reinforce the impression we get from Richard Baxter that the Presbyterians were by no means unified and organized in the early days of the Civil War. His words suggest a decided movement *into* Presbyterianism on the part of many Puritans in the Assembly which is at variance with the impression we have often been given that by outbreak of war most Puritans were already Presbyterians and were simply waiting for the opportunity to put their carefully worked-out program into effect.

The reason for this shift may have had less to do with any wide-spread preference for the Presbyterian system itself, as it had to do with a growing conviction that it represented the only church order that could prevent the country from sliding religiously into chaos; it had already proved its capacity to unify the Scottish nation. The groundwork for such a movement had already been well prepared by the Scots, and as the need for an ecclesiastical settlement in war-ravaged England became more urgent, a majority in the Assembly soon became convinced not only that the Scottish system was the best practical solution for England's ecclesiastical dilemma, but that it had been divinely chosen to fill that role. To have maintained anything else would seem to be flying in the face of Providence.

Writing of the Presbyterian movement in the Elizabethan church, Patrick Collinson commented that "evidently, the presbyterian movement derived its energy not so much from intellectual originality as from the pressures under which such extreme positions came to be occupied."[37] Much the same can perhaps be said of the Presbyterians' growth and development during the early years of the war, except that the pressures were different. Instead of a struggle against the bishops, there were the dangers of the war itself, the threat of social disintegration in the burgeoning sects, and the peril of a long drawn-out division in the Assembly while the fate of the nation hung in balance. In light of

---

[36] *Ibid.* p. 139.

[37] *The Elizabethan Puritan Movement,* p. 113. In one sense the strength of the movement was precisely in that it claimed no originality. All Puritans believed that the true form of the Church is not devised by natural genius but given to us by Jesus Christ: they sought simply to restore the New Testament pattern of organization and worship. That was their strength. Any claim to originality in ecclesiology automatically disqualified itself from serious consideration. Such 'originality' as they had – which they would have regarded as insight that came from faith – was in their willingness to exchange the authority of ecclesiastical tradition for the authority of the scriptures.

the calamities of 1643 and the pledge accepted in the Solemn League and Covenant, these things would be powerful arguments in support of the Scottish Kirk.

At the same time there were those who did not need to shift their ground because they came to the Assembly as committed Presbyterians with a clear-cut policy and concrete goals. The Commissioners of the Church of Scotland were obviously in this position, and we do get hints that there may have been a group of London Ministers in and around London with whom the Scots had been collaborating for some time, and whom they may have already won to their cause.[38] Obviously it was within these groups and in their close association that the leadership and direction of the Assembly arose.

1. *The Scottish Commissioners*

The Leaders in the Church of Scotland were already prepared against the time when their own ecclesiastical system might be introduced into the Church of England.[39] Their policy had been stated implicitly in the first Article of the Solemn League and Covenant – complete religious uniformity throughout the nations of the British Isles on the basis of their own system of church government – 'in religion, confessing of faith, form of government, directory for worship, and catechising'. When the Commissioners had entered the Westminster Assembly they had been invited to become full members, but they declined, preferring to maintain an independent status as Commissioners of their own national Church in London to negotiate with all effective branches of English government.[40] However, they were encouraged to participate fully in the debates, and they were active throughout the course of the Assembly, within its committees, and in the caucusing that took place behind the scenes. George Gillespie was their most active spokesman in the Assembly, although Alexander Henderson and Samuel Rutherford also took part on occasion. Robert Baillie did not speak in the Assembly itself, but he was fully occupied in every other aspect of the work. Moreover, the Scots had the advantage of direct contact

---

[38] Cf. the correspondence between 'some Ministers in England' and the General Assemblies at Edinburgh (1641) and St. Andrews (1642). It was from these same ministers that the General Assembly became apprised of the appearance of Independency in England (12th July, 1641), and in the following year the ministers' letter referred to 'dissenting brethren' (22nd July, 1642). Both letters had been sent from London. Alexander Peterkin (ed.), *Records of the Kirk of Scotland*, I. 295f, 329.

[39] Cf. *supra* pp. 40ff., 67ff.

[40] Baillie to William Spang, 7th December, 1643, *Letters and Journals*, II. 110.

with political leaders through the important Committee of Both Kingdoms where the overall strategy of the parliamentary cause was formulated, and maintained a close relationship with Presbyterian leaders in both Houses of Parliament.

2. *The London Ministers*

The picture is far less clear at the beginning of the Assembly when we try to identify committed Presbyterians among the English Puritans, and yet there are signs that such a group had probably been active in London for several years. Part of the problem is that we cannot assume that all the Puritans who agitated against the Bishops and could not otherwise be identified as Separatists or Independents were ready to be counted as Presbyterians. That seems to have been a mistake made earlier by Robert Baillie. He had been in London from November 1640 to June 1641, officially as one of the chaplains accompanying the Scottish Commissioners after the Treaty of Newcastle, but actually to assess the English ecclesiastical situation and promote the interests of the Scottish Church.[41] Commenting on the contacts he and his friends had with members of Parliament such as Viscount Say and Lord Brook, he said:

> Sey and Brook in the Higher House, and these alone, and some leading men in the Lower, were suspected, by their inclination to the Separatists, would divide from the Presbyterians, and so weaken the partie opposed to bishops; bot so farr as yet can be perceaved, that partie inclineable to separation will not be considerable; and whatever it be, these and the rest who are for the Scotts Discipline, do amicablie conspyre in one, to overthrow the Bishops and Ceremonies, hoping when these *rudera* are put away, that they shall weell agree to build a new house, when the ground is weell sweeped.[42]

This could be read as if all those Puritans who were not Separatists were Presbyterians and 'for the Scotts Discipline', and we have seen from other testimonies that this was by no means true. The attack on the abuses of the prelatical system, on the King's two principal advisers (Strafford and Laud), and the agitation leading up to the Grand Remonstrance united many Puritans whose ideas on church government were not yet defined. Baillie mentioned William Twisse, for example, as one of the ministers who was becoming active in the agitation,[43] and we know that

---

[41] See Baillie's letter to his wife, quoted *supra* p. 39: November 18th, 1640, *Letters and Journals*, I. 268–9.

[42] To the Presbytery of Irvine, *Ibid*. I. 275.

[43] To the Presbytery of Irvine, February 28th, 1640/1, *Ibid*. I. 303.

Dr. Twisse was extremely ambivalent on church government and worship. At another point, writing of this agitation, Baillie made the revealing comment, "Doctor Burgesse commonlie is their mouth; we did suspect him as too much Episcopall, and wished he had not been of the number; bot he hes such a hand among the ministrie, and others, that it is not thought meet to decairt him; yea, he hes caryed himself so bravelie, that we doe repent of our suspicions."[44]

Cornelius Burgess did not easily relinquish his preference for moderate episcopacy, as his opposition to the Solemn League and Covenant indicated. Also since 1631 he had been one of the Assistants of Sion College, and this college would become the focal point of London Presbyterianism during the course of the Assembly, and eventually the home of the Provincial Synod of London.

In view of the prestigious place that Sion College was later to occupy in the activities of the Presbyterian ministers of London, it would be plausible to look there for the early leadership of the Presbyterians. Even that, however, is not too sure, because when Baillie and his fellow Scots were fulfilling their first stint in the English capital in 1641, Sion College was by no means committed to Presbyterian polity as it later became. Baillie recorded at the time that "One Ward, in a Latine lecture in Sion College, at our first comeing, had railed at us as rebells", although he added that "upon our complaint he was suspended, and yesterday made his publick recantation in the Church."[45] It is clear that the battle for Sion College had not yet been won decisively for Puritanism, let alone for the Presbyterians.

However, it appears to have been won for Puritanism by the time the Assembly opened, for we read that in April, 1643, John Sedgwick, the Rector of St. Alphage, London Wall, had attacked the way in which the Governor and Assistants [Fellows] were elected, criticized the custom of hearing sermons in Latin (as required by the Trust,) and proposed that none who had been sequestered by Parliament should have any future part in elections for officers.[46] By October of the same year, the President and two of the Assistants had left the city, and a new election became necessary in which three convinced Puritans were put into the places of the incumbents – Andrew Janaway of All

---

[44] *Ibid.* pp. 302f.
[45] To the same, December 28th, 1640, *ibid.* 288.
[46] Cf. E. H. Pierce, *Sion College and Library*, pp. 109ff.

Hallows was elected President, and Edmund Calamy and Henry Roborough Assistants.[47]

Certainly these men could soon be identified as Presbyterians, but the problem we face in trying to identify the Presbyterian leadership is the problem of Puritanism itself: it was not until the fighting broke out, the Scottish alliance concluded, and the Assembly got down to hard cases that Puritans were forced to be more precise about what they wanted in church government.

Perhaps the best way to discover the early Presbyterians is to start with the 'Smectymnuans' – Stephen Marshall, Edmund Calamy, Thomas Young, Matthew Newcomen and William Spurstow – who had attacked Bishop Hall's claims for a Divine Right episcopacy in 1641.[48] These men were all very active on the Presbyterian side of the debates in the Assembly, and during the course of those debates they were joined by Charles Herle, who succeeded Twisse as Prolocutor in 1646.

They were *later* joined by Cornelius Burgess and John White, the Assessors, and by others such as Edmund Stanton, Herbert Palmer, John Arrowsmith, William Gouge, Joshua Hoyle, Thomas Gataker, Anthony Tuckney, Edward Reynolds, Richard Vines, Lazarus Seaman and Jeremiah Whitaker. They all became acknowledged 'Presbyterians', but it is extremely doubtful how far these men supported the 'Scotts Discipline' at the beginning, for as we have seen, many of them seem to have hankered after a moderate episcopacy. We could perhaps with more justification include Erastians such as Dr. John Lightfoot and Thomas Coleman, for although they fought tenaciously against granting *jus divinum* to any polity they staunchly sup-

---

[47] *Ibid.* Edmund Calamy was a member of the Assembly, and Henry Roborough became one of the two Scribes. Andrew Janaway was not involved with the Assembly, but he may well have been the 'Janeway' whom Richard Baxter identifies as an active Nonconformist minister in London after the Restoration, and as "a Man of extraordinary devotedness to God, and zeal for the good of souls, and of great humility, and holiness of Life, and an excellent Preacher." *Rel. Baxt.* III, p. 95 (§205); cf. *ibid.* III, pp. 2, 19.

[48] Cf. *An Humble Remonstrance to the High Court of Parliament, by a dutifull Sonne of the Church,* (London, 1640,) and *An Answer to a Booke Entitled, An Humble Remonstrance, In which, The Originall of Liturgy/Episcopacy is discussed And Queres propounded concerning both,* by Smectymnvvs, (London, 1641). This unleashed a typical seventeenth century pamphlet war, producing: *A Defence of the Humble Remonstrance Against the frivolous and false exceptions of Smectymnvvs,* By the Author of the said Humble Remonstrance (1641); *A Vindication of the Answer to the Humble Remonstrance from the Unjust Imputation of Frivolousnesse and Falshood,* by the same Smectymnvvs (n.d.); *A Short Answer to the Tedious Vindication of Smectymnvvs,* by the Author of the Humble Remonstrance, etc. (1641). This by no means exhausts the list, for in 1642 a work appeared entitled, *A Modest Confutation of the Slanderous Libell Entitled Animadversions vpon the Remonstrants Defence against Smectymnuus,* while John Milton entered the lists in *An Apology for Smectymnuus with the Reason of Church-Government.*

ported the Presbyterian position as most agreeable to Parliament and most likely to meet the needs of the nation.

The impression we get is that although Presbyterianism was fairly rapidly assumed by the majority in the Assembly, that had not been the position of many at first. Their ideas were clarified under the pressures of that time and the pressures of debate, so that by the time the work of the Assembly had been completed, the Presbyterian party included some of the best minds among the English Puritan ministers. So Baillie, when he was asked in 1645 by the Earl of Loudon to suggest the names of ministers who might be recommended as personal chaplains to the King, wrote:

> Of our nation, besyde Mr. Blair, I wish no other but one at most, my worthy brother Mr. Gillespie. Off the English, the ablest Herle, Marshall, Vines, Burgess or Palmer; but I believe Newcomen, Ward, Ashe, Perne, Seaman, Whitaker, Calamy, would give alse good satisfaction.[49]

Neal reminds us that Presbyterianism had some powerful patrons in both houses of Parliament, and although the parliamentary members did not often intrude themselves into the debates of the Assembly, their influence was constantly present. The political objectives of the Presbyterian party in Parliament must not be forgotten if we are to understand the significance of what was happening ecclesiastically at Westminster.

There was a confluence of interests in the political objectives of the Scots and those of the Presbyterian supporters in Parliament, particularly in their determination to bring about a negotiated settlement with Charles I on the basis of the Covenant. In their public attitude to the King, the Scots seem to have entered England 'more in sorrow than in anger': Charles was, after all, a Scotsman born and a Stuart. They entered the struggle against him, first to ensure that no future English prelate would threaten the Scottish Kirk, and secondly, to make doubly sure by tying the Church of England as closely as possible to presbyterian uniformity. The Scots would fight for a treaty of peace with their King if it could guarantee the liberties endangered by Laud and Strafford, and for the rest their system of church government promised to maintain unity of church and state in a traditional

---

[49] 25th December, 1645, *Letters and Journals*, II. 414f. Although the names of Ashe, Perne and Ward do not appear among the names we listed earlier, they were all members of the Assembly – Simeon Ashe filled the place of a member who died before the Assembly sat, Andreas Perne of Northants was a member, and John Ward of Ipswich joined the Assembly after the death of Henry Painter of Exeter.

social order; and apart from some preference for the name and order of bishops among the Edward Derings of this world, that was precisely what the English conservatives of the parliamentary party wanted.

As the war progressed, there were soon other reasons why this conservative policy became linked to the Presbyterian party. Sir Thomas Fairfax's sectarian New Model Army under the charismatic leadership of its Lieutenant-General, Cromwell, became the darling of the Independent party, and its incredible success, in contrast to the reluctance of Parliament's aristocratic and inept generals to pursue Charles to absolute victory, threatened any chance of a gentlemanly negotiated peace with the King.[50] Radical voices from the invincible army began to suggest changes in Church and State that went far beyond the original causes of the struggle. Presbyterianism in Scotland was no friend to this kind of revolution, and the Scots army could therefore be relied upon to support a policy of treating with Charles and of opposing toleration of the sects.

The Presbyterian party gained support from all those influences on the parliamentary side which wanted to prevent the changes from going too far. It drew those who dreamed again of a unified society in Church and State – a majority of the peers remaining at Westminster,[51] the older and largely discredited generals who feared for their commands, the commercial leaders in the city of London who feared for their trade, and many Members of the House of Commons who were horrified at the proliferation of sects and scared of the political fire-brands among Cromwell's too-successful troops. This was the political context in which the struggle of the Assembly took place, and once it is taken into account some of the bitterness that entered into the theologizing will be explained: the stakes were very high.

IV

The Independents

Much of what might be said about the Independents could already be inferred from the discussion of Presbyterianism, and we have already discussed them at length elsewhere.[52] At the

---

[50] Cf. Chapter III, 'Religion, Politics and War' in my Introduction to *An Apologeticall Narration* (1963).

[51] Cf. Baillie's letter quoted *supra*, p. 117. Viscount Sey and Lord Brooke were Independents. Lord Brooke had written an attack on episcopacy; cf. his book, *A Discourse opening the Natvre of that Episcopacie which is exercised in England*, (London, 1641.) He lost his life in a military skirmish in April, 1643.

[52] The whole Introduction to *An Apologeticall Narration* (1963).

present time we must content ourselves simply with accenting the political reality within which the Independent party arose, and which forced Independent churchmen to move from a position that had been at least sympathetic to uniformity, to an enthusiastic support of religious toleration.[53]

Using Ernst Troeltsch's 'church' and 'sect' typology[54] to illustrate the essential differences between the Presbyterians and the sects during the English Civil War, A. S. P. Woodhouse went on to observe that "the problem is the Centre Party, the Independents, who increasingly dominate the situation in and after 1647. They occupy . . . the whole interval between the Right, where the Puritan church-type is dominant, and the Left, where the Puritan sect-type is no less supreme. No fact is more prominent than the existence of the two types side by side, or than their mutual influence particularly in the Centre Party, where indeed they merge."[55]

If this poses a problem for the modern historian, it was an existential problem for the Independents themselves, particularly during the early days of the Assembly when they were emerging as a distinct party in English affairs. In terms of theology and even of church practice the Independents of the Assembly and their colleagues in New England stood very close to the Presbyterians. Their social preferences were decidedly 'church-type' even if their theology was 'sect-type' and for all their unwillingness to call on secular authority – an unwillingness reinforced by their experiments in church discipline in the Netherlands – they were equally reluctant to favour universal toleration; those "who are for a Congregational way", observed one of the most respected of the Dissenting Brethren, "doe not hold absolute liberty for all religions", although he went on to

---

[53] When Baillie had met the returning exiles for the first time, he had been impressed: "All the English ministers of Holland, who are for New-England way, are now here: how strong their party will be here, it is diverselie reported; they are all in good termes with us: Our only considerable difference will be about the jurisdiction of Synods and Presbyteries. As for Brownists, and Separatists of many kynds, here they mislyke them weell near as much as we: of these there is no considerable partie . . . . all of them are learned, discreet, and zealous men, weell seen in cases of conscience. It were all the pities in the world that wee and they should differ in anie thing". To the Presbytery of Irvine, March 15th, 1640/1, *Letters and Journals*, I. 311.

[54] *The Social Teaching of the Christian Churches*, (translation by Olive Wyon of the 1911 *Die Soziallehren der christlichen Kirchen und Gruppen*), New York, Macmillan, 1931, I. 379–81. Troeltsch's typology in relationship to ecclesiology is discussed more fully in *The Church in Search of Its Self*, pp. 18–36.

[55] *Puritanism and Liberty*, Introduction, p. 36.

emphasize that the only reasonable and Christian way to counteract heresy and schism was by spiritual persuasion.[56]

The New Englanders, standing where the Independents stood before exile in the Netherlands, had no such scruples. In a letter of advice deploring the divisions of his native countrymen, 'the Simple Cobbler of Aggawam' stated flatly, "I dare averre, that God doth no where in his word tolerate Christian States, to give Toleration to such adversaries of his Truth,[57] if they have power in their hands to suppresse them", and he went on to declare "He that is willing to tolerate any unsound Opinion that his own may also be tolerated, though never so sound, will for a need hand God's Bible in the Devils girdle".[58]

The comment was shrewd, for this was precisely the position in which the English Independents found themselves through the pressures of war. It is at the same time embarrassing evidence that the New England Congregationalists retained the religious prejudices of the England from which they had emigrated in the 1630s.[59]

But despite their initial distaste for religious toleration, and despite, too, what must have been a very real reluctance to appear in the Assembly as allies of sectarians, the Independents found no other course open to them. Presbyterian uniformity presented no less of a threat to their church system than Episcopacy had before it, and because of the intransigence of the Scots and their English sympathizers, the Independent party became a focus for all the dissidents in Church and State who had nothing to lose and liberty to gain by winning the war decisively and

---

[56] Jeremiah Burroughes, *Irenicum, to the Lovers of Truth and Peace*, London, 1646, p. 41.

[57] I.e. 'Familists, Antinomians, Anabaptists and other Enthusiasts'. 'Theodore de la Guard', [Nathaniel Ward] *The Simple Cobbler of Aggavvam in America. Willing to mend his Native Country, lamentably tattered, both in the upper-Leather and the sole, with all the honest stitches he can take*, (London, 1647,) p. 3. Nathaniel Ward (1578–1652) was a graduate of Emmanuel College, Cambridge, who had served as chaplain to the English merchants at Elbing, Germany (1620–24), and after returning to England had been deprived by Laud for nonconformity. He emigrated to Massachusetts in 1634 and served briefly as minister of Agawam (Ipswich), and in 1638 was appointed to draw up the legal code for New England. He returned to England in 1646, and in 1648 became the incumbent at Shenfield. He was in England when *The Simple Cobbler* appeared, but we can see how such views would be an embarrassment to the Independents of the Assembly.

[58] *Ibid.* p. 8.

[59] Writing to his cousin, Spang, Robert Baillie could with justice expostulate that there was "in all New England, no libertie of living for a Presbyterian". April 19th, 1644, *Letters and Journals*, II. 168. Cf. also the early chapters in Alexander Blaikie, *A History of Presbyterianism in New England*, (Boston, Alexander Moore, 1881.) The widening gap between the English Independents and the New England Congregationalists at this point is also treated in the first three chapters of the Introduction to *An Apologeticall Narration* (1963).

outright. For two things soon became clear – first, that the despised sectarian congregations were the most reliable source for those 'men of spirit'[60] who could withstand the King's military gentlemen: from them Cromwell recruited the "russet-coated captain that knows what he fights for, and loves what he knows".[61] Secondly, without an all-out victory in which toleration would be the primary condition of settlement, the Independents had no more hope of gaining liberty for themselves than the wildest sectary among Fleetwood's troopers,[62] or the most misguided heretic listed by Ephraim Pagit.[63] A negotiated peace with the King might hold out reasonable hope that Presbyterians and Episcopalians could be accommodated within a system of moderate or modified episcopacy, but there would be no room for anyone else. Hence, however disgusted the New Englanders might be, the English Independents were forced by the circumstances of the war to become the leading protagonists of toleration.

The Independents or 'Dissenting Brethren' of the Assembly were led by the five Apologists who produced *An Apologeticall Narration* early in 1644 – Thomas Goodwin, Philip Nye, William Bridge, Sidrach Simpson and Jeremiah Burroughes.[64] Also in publishing their Reasons against Presbyterian uniformity they were joined by William Greenhill and William Carter, and were then sometimes referred to as the 'septemvirs'. Also in the history of the Assembly, during the attempts of the Committee of Accommodation to bring the Independents into the Presbyterian Establishment, John Durie, the pioneer of ecumenism, was named with the Apologists to represent their point of view,[65] but

---

[60] After the battle of Edgehill at the beginning of the war, Cromwell had told John Hampton that the parliamentary armies would never be able to equal the courage and ability of the royalists until they were able to enlist such men. He recalled the incident many years later in a speech, April, 1657; Abbott, *Writings and Speeches of O. C.*, IV. 471.

[61] Letter to the Deputy Lieutenants of Suffolk, 29th Aug., 1643; *ibid.* I. 256.

[62] Fleetwood was a leader of the Fifth Monarchy sect.

[63] Ephraim Pagit (c. 1575–1647) was a royalist Anglican minister who retired to Deptford, Kent, soon after the outbreak of the Civil War. He wrote *Heresiographie, Or a Description of the Heretickes and Sectaries Sprang up in these latter times*, which appeared in 1645 and reached 23 editions in its first year.

[64] For the problem of dating the appearance of this pamphlet, cf. infra pp. 206–9, 218–31 *passim*; and for biographical information regarding the Apologists, see Chapter IV of my introduction to An Apologeticall Narration (1963 edition). Gustafsson's *The Five Dissenting Brethren* does not give much biographical information. He offers more information about their stay in Holland, since his own interest was in the possible connection between the Apologists, the Dutch Remonstrants and the Italian, Jacob Acontius; Berndt Gustafsson, *The Five Dissenting Brethren: A Study on the Dutch Background of their Independentism*, (Lund, C.W.K. Gleerup, 1955.)

[65] Neal, *Hist. of the Puritans*, III. 304.

his appointment was obviously due more to his ecumenical expertise than to any commitment to Independency as such.[66]

Other members of the Assembly with Independent leanings probably included Joseph Caryl, Peter Sterry,[67] John Green, Anthony Burgess and John Phillips. Phillips was the only member of the Assembly, as far as we know, to have had any experience in New England, but none of this group appears to have taken a very prominent or regular part in the Assembly's proceedings. This raises the significant point touched on in discussing *An Apologeticall Narration* – the remarkable absence of men in the Assembly with a first-hand knowledge of New England among the Independent leadership.[68] We know that John Cotton, Thomas Hooker and John Davenport had been invited to the Assembly, and the signatories to that letter indicate that in 1642 there had been serious interest in the New England experiment;[69] but while Cotton and Davenport had been ready

---

[66] John Durie [Dury], 1596–1680, was a Scot who had been minister in Elbing, West Prussia. His father had been minister to the Scots church in Leyden. Durie spent a life-time trying to bring the divided churches of Europe together but without success. His single-minded commitment to the ecumenical cause was not understood in the seventeenth-century, and particularly by his fellow Scots like Robert Baillie, who regarded Durie's ecumenical efforts with deep suspicion. Baillie was particularly suspicious of any attempts by Durie to bring about conciliation with the bishops, and on hearing that Durie had been appointed to the Assembly, he wrote to Spang, "His letter to the Synod I heard with no great regard, for it favoured of somewhat. If he pleased to come over to Oxford, he may resolve to be taken, while he lives, by us all here for a malignant; and if he should come to us with the least tincture of Episcopacie, or liturgick learning, he would not be welcome to any I know. As you love the man, persuade him to stay at this time where he is: he cannot be so well or honourablie imployed any where I know." 19th April, 1644, *Letters and Journals*, II. 166. Durie wrote *An Apistolary Discourse* (London, 1644) on the possibility of either including Independency within the Presbyterian system or allowing toleration outside, and he dedicated it to Thomas Goodwin, Philip Nye, and Durie's associate in ecumenical activity, Samuel Hartlib.

[67] One of the finest expressions of Toleration as a Christian principle is to be found in Sterry's Preface to *A Discourse of the Freedom of the Will*, published posthumously in 1675.

[68] Cf. *An Apologeticall Narration* (1963 edn.), Introduction pp. 110–112.

[69] The letter is printed in Thomas Hutchinson, *The History of the Colony and Province of Massachusetts-Bay*, (Edited by Lawrence Shaw Mayo, Cambridge, Mass., Harvard University Press, 1936, 3 vols.) I. 100f. note.

The letter was signed by 5 peers and 34 commoners. Of the peers, Viscount Say and Sele, Lord Brook and Lord Wharton are known to have been political Independents, and of the 34 commoners 21 can be identified as belonging to the political Independent party. This suggests that those in Parliament who supported the more radical political objectives, were also interested in having ecclesiastical Independency well represented at Westminster. For the identification of political Independents see George Yule, *The Independents in the English Civil War*, (Cambridge, Cambridge University Press, 1958) Appendix A, pp. 83–130.

A further small fact about the signatories of this letter, however, is the omission of Sir Henry Vane's name from the list. That could have a very simple explanation, but on the other hand, in view of his experience at the hands of the New England theocracy in 1635-6, it may be suggestive.

enough to make the journey, Hooker thought it would be a waste of time, and eventually the New England divines were dissuaded from returning to England by negative reports from Hugh Peter and Thomas Weld.[70] As a former historian has pointed out, "had the churches of New-England appeared there by their representatives, or any of the principal divines appeared as members of the Assembly, greater exception might have been taken to their building after a model of their own framing."[71]

This raises the interesting question why men like Hugh Peter and Thomas Weld were not invited to the Assembly, or at least why they did not share the confidence of the parliamentary leaders of the Independent party. The reason, I suggest, has to be seen in the rising importance of the toleration issue for the Independent party.[72] The outspokenness of Hugh Peter, on this issue, might be not only an embarrassment but also a threat to the work of the Independents in the Assembly, for in New England he had openly rebuked Sir Henry Vane for the young Governor's attempt to intervene on behalf of the Antinomian faction in Massachusetts. But in 1643 Sir Henry Vane was one of the most powerful men in Parliament and, whether the Scots recognized it or not, fully committed to the principle of toleration. Hugh Peter's earlier interference had been in defence of religious uniformity and *against* toleration, and one can only conclude that "it was not only the memory of Hugh Peter's effrontery which was the issue, but his support of the religious uniformity which the New England clergy were enforcing, for on this same occasion he had referred very openly to the divisions he had experienced among the churches while he had been in the Netherlands. If the former would still rankle with Vane, the latter might well frighten Nye and his colleagues."[73]

Thomas Weld became equally suspect. He had returned to England in 1641 with Hugh Peter and William Hibbins as agents of the Massachusetts Bay Colony,[74] and had at once been caught up in English affairs on the Puritan side. In 1643 he co-authored with Hugh Peter *New England's First Fruits*, and then had been prevailed upon by Presbyterians to issue, with notes and addi-

[70] James Kendall Hosmer (ed.), *Winthrop's Journal 'History of New England, 1630–1649'*, (New York, Barnes & Noble [1808] 1953, 2 Volumes,) II. 71–2. [This work is hereafter cited as Winthrop's *Journal*.]

[71] Thomas Hutchinson, *The History of . . . Massachusetts-Bay*, I. 101.

[72] Cf. *An Apologeticall Narration* (1963 edn.), Introduction pp. 110–112.

[73] Introduction to *An Apologeticall Narration* (1963), p. 111; cf. Winthrop's *Journal*, I. 204.

[74] *Ibid.* II. 25, 25, 31f., 70.

tions, John Winthrop's account of the Antinomian dispute in New England, which revealed the repressive aspects of the Puritan theocracy.[75] Weld in part was able to undo the unfortunate impression that this work caused by publishing *A Brief Narration of the Practices of the Churches in New England* in 1645, but enough damage had been done to indicate why his testimony would not have been any help to the Independents in the Assembly.

Nye and his colleagues obviously recognized the growing difference between the practices of the New England churches and the exigencies of their own situation in England, and therefore, to counteract any ill-effects of the transatlantic experience, they seem to have emphasized the success of their own ecclesiastical experiments in the Netherlands.[76]

They had engaged in the work of the Assembly as advocates of the 'Congregational Way', but as the political pressures increased, and as their own future became more and more linked to the success of Cromwell's troopers, the principle of toleration assumed new importance. They could not ignore the lesson that was obvious within the *de facto* pluralism of the New Model Army, nor could they fail to see that their hope of survival lay in the success of that army.

V

The Erastians

At the end of his brief survey of the Erastian party, Neal says that its leaders in the Assembly were the divines, Dr. John Lightfoot and Thomas Coleman, and the lawyers, John Selden and Bulstrode Whitelocke – who also had the advantage of being able to represent this point of view in Parliament[77] where they

---

[75] *Short Story of the Rise, Reign, and Ruin of the Antinomians, and Libertines that Infected the Churches of New England*, (London, 1644). Cf. the note of J. K. Hosmer, the editor of *Winthrop's Journal*, I. 242f. Robert Baillie certainly knew of the book and promised to send William Spang a copy: cf. Letter 15th August, 1645, *Letters and Journals*, II. 311.

[76] On the other hand I cannot accept the wedge that Gustafsson tried to drive between the Apologists and the rest of those following the 'Congregational Way.' It makes more sense to see their position on toleration developing in reaction to the situation they faced, than from the tenuous relationships he traced with the Arminian Remonstrants of Holland. Goodwin and his colleagues would not have lasted a day in the Assembly if there had been any taint of Arminius in their theology, and such a connection would hardly have escaped the attention of Presbyterian polemics. Cf. Gustafsson, *The Five Dissenting Brethren*, chapter 2.

[77] Selden was M.P. for Oxford University, and Whitelocke was M.P. for Marlow.

were joined by "*Oliver St. John,* Esq; Sir *Thomas Widdrington, John Crew,* Esq; Sir *John Hipstey*, and others of the greatest names".[78]

This indicates the first of our problems in trying to write with any precision about the Erastians, for most of these men supported the establishment of Presbyterianism, and Oliver St. John, married to Cromwell's cousin,[79] had leanings towards the Independents. The Erastians do not represent a specific ecclesiastical polity but a position that might relate itself to any polity. They denied that *jus divinum* could be applied to any form of the Church. Erastians might align themselves on a pragmatic basis with any views about the Church: they adhered not to a distinct polity, but to a conviction about the Church's relation to the civil authorities.

A further issue that makes for imprecision is the question discussed by J. N. Figgis on how far the views of Thomas Erastus, the sixteenth century Swiss physician who gave his name to the movement, are to be regarded as 'Erastian'.[80] Figgis states that Erastus's main object "was not to magnify the State, nor to enslave the Church, but to secure the liberty of the subject"[81] particularly against the threat of ecclesiastical dictatorship. He shows that Erastus came to his position in the existential situation of the Palatinate and the city of Heidelburg, that had become a place of refuge for the persecuted of several religious persuasions during the latter half of the sixteenth century under the benevolent patronage of a tolerant Lutheran prince, the Elector Otto Henry. The problem arose after the Elector died in 1559 and was succeeded by a Calvinist, Frederick III. The new Elector had come under the influence of Calvinist refugees who entertained the dream of establishing reformed discipline in Heidelburg as had been established in Geneva.[82]

---

[78] *History of the Puritans,* III. 140.

[79] He married two of Cromwell's relatives successively; Joanna Altham, the daughter of Cromwell's cousin, Lady Mashman, by her first husband, and then a daughter of Oliver's uncle, Henry Cromwell.

[80] 'Erastus and Erastianism', in *The Divine Right of Kings*, pp. 293–342.

[81] *Ibid.* p. 335.

[82] Thomas Erastus (1524–83) had been born Thomas Lüber in Baden, Switzerland, and was eventually appointed to the Chair of Medicine at the University of Heidelburg in the Palatinate. In 1558 he became Rector of the University (for the first time), but he also began to interest himself in the question of the Church when, in 1563, the stricter reforming party managed to get the reformed discipline imposed on the basis of the Heidelburg Catechism. The discipline became even stricter after the Elector Frederick's marriage in 1569 to the widow of the Netherlands noble, Bredenrode, and when a scandal broke out on the Trinitarian issue, involving some of Erastus's associates, Erastus found himself excommunicated (1574–6). Eventually on the death of Frederick there was a

Erastus came to the conclusion that the powers claimed for the office of ruling Elder and the power of excommunication were unwarrented in scripture. The matter came to a head when in 1568 an English Puritan, George Wither, who had gone to Heidelburg to avoid the Vestiarian Controversy, submitted a doctoral thesis in which he maintained the full *jure divino* view of the Church and its discipline, claiming the Church's divine right to excommunicate anybody from the prince down. Erastus prepared theses against this position, and circulated them to other reformers including Beza, who countered with a firm but courteous affirmation of the Church's right to discipline.[83] Apparently Erastus sent a response to Beza's objections, his *Confirmatio*, but this was never answered from Geneva, and this later became a matter of great concern to the Rev. Robert Baillie.[84]

The way in which Erastus's Ms. was published may help to explain why the issues he raised received particular attention in England. In 1589 both his original Theses and his reply to Beza's response seem to have been published in London through the instrumentality of the man who married his widow,[85] and there is good evidence that the work was known to English scholars. Erastus himself had not explicitly made the state supreme in ecclesiastical matters, but he had exempted the prince from church discipline and "asserted that in a State of one religion all that was needed for the enforcement of piety and morality could and ought to be done by the magistrate". Figgis's comment appears just when he says:

> Erastianism is not rightly named, if we mean by it the explicit tenets of Erastus. . . . Erastus did not mean to do more than assert that all coercive authority is vested in the State. But he added to this the prevailing notion that the State must support one religion and tolerate no other. It was then not many steps to the theory of Hobbes that the State could support any religion it pleased out of motives of State policy and with no regard to truth.[86]

Figgis shows cogently that it was the exclusive principle of the state acting in relationship to a single church, essentially a

---

reversion to Lutheran control and Erastus resigned his Chair and retired to Basel. As Figgis remarks, "had he been an Erastian in the ordinary sense, he would not have done this." *Ibid.* p. 309.

[83] *Tractatus pius et moderatus de Excommunicatione.*

[84] Cf. his letters to Spang in the summer of 1645, *Letters and Journals*, II. 277, 311.

[85] *Explicatio gravissimae questionis, utrum Excommunicatio, quatenus Religionem intelligentes et amplexantes, a Sacramentarum usu propter admissum facinus arcet; mandato nitatur Divino, an excogitata sit ab hominibus;* cf. Figgis, *The Divine Right of Kings*, pp. 309f.

[86] *The Divine Right of Kings*, pp. 338f.

medieval legacy, that caused the problem;[87] for given that concept, with the assumption that it was based on divine law, there was little option between placing ultimate responsibility in the hands of either a divinely ordained church or of a divinely chosen civil magistrate.

So there are problems with 'Erastianism' as it appeared in the seventeenth century English context, for a great deal depends on how the reader understands the major thrust of the Erastian party. If one concentrates simply on the insistence that the authority of the clergy should be restricted to spiritual and persuasive power, there were many Puritans who would have agreed with that. It comes close to Cotton's statement that "Church government is not an authority but a ministry", or to the thought of Jeremiah Burroughes when he asserted "that the onely way the Church hath to keep downe errors or heresies is spirituall; as for other means they are extrinsicall to the Church".[88] Baxter made the point explicit when he said that "the generality of each Party indeed owned this Doctrine", and went on to declare, "I could speak with no sober, Judicious Prelatist, Presbyterian, or Independent, but confessed that no Secular or Forcing Power, belongeth to any Pastors of the Church as such; and unless the Magistrates authorized them as his Officers, they could not touch mens Bodies or Estates, but the Conscience alone." He made the point doubly clear, when in criticizing the Erastians for wrongly charging other Christians with a claim of coercive power or of trying to create an *imperium in imperio,* he continued, "whereas all temperate Christians (at least except Papists) confess that the Church hath no Power of *Force,* but only to manage God's Word unto Mens Consciences".[89] Erastianism in the sense Erastus originally held it was close to the position of many English Puritans.

On the other hand, the Erastianism that was manifested in the Westminster Assembly and in the English Parliament went con-

---

[87] *Ibid.* pp. 338ff.

[88] *Irenicum,* p. 42. However, Burroughes did concede considerable power in such cases to the civil magistrate, for "as for subjection to the Magistrate if he pleases to interpose, to that both they [those in error] and we must yeeld".*Ibid.* Earlier in his book he wrote: "We may give this account, Lord we have found in thy word that once thou didst make use of the power of the Magistrates in matters of Religion; and in the New Testament there was nothing revealed to forbid their power in them; nay Lord thou toldst us there, that thou hadst appointed them for our own good: and to be a terrour to evill works in generall; from thence we gathered that in yielding to their power, it was thy will we should make use of those generall rules in Scripture we found before the times of the Gospel, and of the light of nature." *Ibid.* p. 27.

[89] *Reliquiae Baxterianae,* I. ii. pp. 140, 141, (§§2, 11).

siderably beyond this, both on the negative side (as Baxter notes) in denying ministers the authority proper to their *spiritual* office in the Church,[90] and on the positive side by asserting the outright control of the Church by the state. "The most of the House of Commons", complained Robert Baillie, "are downright Erastians: they are lyke to create us more woe than all the sectaries of England",[91] and in a later missive to David Dickson, he fumed, "The Pope and the King were never more earnest for the headship of the Church than the pluralitie of this Parliament."[92] Strong words, but that was the issue, and Baillie's terms were certainly no stronger than those the politicians could have used regarding the claims of 'divine right' Presbytery.

Erastian sentiment in Assembly and Parliament was firmly determined to block any attempt to establish the new form of the Church on a *jure divino* basis, and this opposition was reflected in all the areas that affected the Church's discipline. Beyond that, the Erastians were not deeply concerned about the form of churchmanship the Assembly might recommend, although they shared the Puritan prejudice against diocesan prelacy. William Prynne might strongly support Presbyterianism and Oliver St. John might lean towards Independency, but whatever view of the Church the Erastian preferred, the preference would be on political and pragmatic grounds. It was essentially a 'low church' as distinct from a 'high church' approach to ecclesiology, and that is why we are faced with the seeming contradictions of a Parliament approving the Solemn League and Covenant in 1643, urging the Assembly to make haste with its recommendations in 1644, sanctioning Presbyterian order in 1646, and then persistently blocking all attempts to place that establishment on a *jure divino* basis or to set up any effective ecclesiastical discipline.

But the seventeenth century imposed its own conditions of thought, and it is doubtful whether the politicians could have avoided the *jure divino* view of the Church without, at least tacitly advancing a *jure divino* view of the state: a 'low' doctrine of the Church could be maintained only by a 'high' doctrine of Parliament's authority. In the relations between Parliament and the Assembly the issue was ultimately whether the state or the Church would control the shape of English society, and this was the confrontation that emerged in the struggle with the Erastians in the Assembly after the main questions of ecclesiology had

---

[90] *Ibid*. 141.
[91] To Spang, April 25th, 1645, *Letters and Journals*, II. 265.
[92] March 17th, 1645/6, *ibid*. 360.

apparently been settled. "The most part of the House of Commons," wrote Baillie in 1645, "especiallie the lawyers, whereof they are many, and divers of them very able men, are either half or whole Erastians, believing in no Church-government to be of divine right, bot all to be a humane constitution, depending on the will of the magistrates." He then went on to describe the kind of stand-off that Parliament and the Assembly reached on the basic issue of church discipline.[93]

In one sense this represented an impasse since it set the Assembly and the houses of Parliament absolutely against each other; but in a deeper sense that impression is false because Parliament had all the power and the Assembly had been explicitly restricted to making recommendations to Parliament. From the first, in the very terms of the Assembly's appointment, Parliament had laid down the Erastian basis on which the plan for the future of the Church would be discussed, presented and established; and although the Members of Parliament themselves may not have fully understood it, behind these actions there was the *jure divino* claim of the people and their representatives.

---

[93] Public Letter, *ibid*. II. 307.

Part II

Preface to Polemic

CHAPTER 5

THE DEBATE BEGINS:
SEPTEMBER TO DECEMBER, 1643

I

"At last . . . Church Government"

On September 15th, 1643, the first three Commissioners from Scotland, Lord Maitland and the two ministers, Alexander Henderson and George Gillespie were received into the Assembly,[1] and on the 21st the members of the Assembly were given permission to transfer themselves from the Henry VII Chapel to the Jerusalem Chamber where there might be some chance of keeping warm during the oncoming winter. They were to hold their first session in the new meeting place on Monday, October 2nd,[2] but for almost two weeks the Assembly's time was taken up largely with public events.[3]

Lightfoot tells us that on Thursday, October 5th, Sir John Clotworthy came from the House of Commons to ask that the Assembly would stand adjourned and depute some of its members to meet in committee the following afternoon in the Guildhall "to countenance a business concerning the Scottish affairs."[4] This cryptic statement is carried a little further by the Minutes with the note that the Scottish treaty referred "as much to the religion as the safety of the kingdom",[5] so that although the Assembly continued to meet and concerned itself particularly with the suspected Antinomianism of one of the Independent members, Peter Sterry, a change of direction might be expected.

---

[1] Lightfoot, *Journal*, p. 14. TMs. I. 115–117, (Ms. I., ff. 58–9.)

[2] A. F. Mitchell, *The Westminster Assembly*, p. 486 n. 1.

[3] A solemn service had been held in St. Margaret's Westminster on September 25th, when the Covenant had been taken and subscribed by the members of the Assembly and the House of Commons; the 28th was given up to congratulating the Lord General, the Earl of Essex, on his safe return from the first battle of Newbury (September 20th); Oct. 6th was employed in a public reception in the Guildhall with congratulatory speeches relating to the Scottish alliance.

[4] Lightfoot, *Journal*, p. 16. Edmund Calamy, Obadiah Sedgewick and Jeremiah Burroughes were appointed.

[5] TMs. I. 176–7 (Ms. I., ff. 89, 89b.)

It came on Thursday, 12th October, while they were debating Article 16 of the Thirty-Nine Articles. An order was received from both Houses of Parliament that the Assembly "do forthwith confer and treat among themselves, of such a discipline and government as may be most agreeable to God's holy word, and most apt to procure and preserve the peace of the church at home, and nearer agreement with the church of Scotland and other reformed churches abroad, to be settled in this church instead of the place of the present church-government by archbishops, bishops, their chancellors, commissaries, deans, deans and chapters, and other ecclesiastical officers, depending upon the hierarchy, which is resolved to be taken away."[6] The Assembly was instructed to concern itself with the form of worship for the reformed Church of England, "and to deliver their opinions and advice touching the same to both or either House of Parliament with all the convenient speed they can."[7]

The die was cast. While he was awaiting his own passage to England, Robert Baillie wrote a letter to William Spang in which he exclaimed, "At last the Assemblie of Divines have permission to fall on the question of Church Government. What here they will doe, we cannot say"; but he added a comment, which showed that the Scots had no illusions how far acceptance of the Presbyterian system by the English was tied to the military alliance.[8] Nevertheless, by the terms of the Solemn League and Covenant the nature of the Church would receive the kind of biblical critique that all Puritans demanded. Negative criticisms of the Church of England's structure were no longer sufficient, and the members of the Assembly were themselves going to be "cast upon a farther necessity of enquiring into and viewing . . . the positive part of *Church-worship* and government."[9] The issue was bound to be joined.[10]

---

[6] Lightfoot, *Journal*, p. 17. Cf. TMs. I. 210 (Ms. I., f. 106.)

[7] Lightfoot, *Journal*, p. 17f.

[8] 17th November, 1643, *Letters and Journals*, II. 104.

[9] *An Apologeticall Narration* (1643/4), p. 3.

[10] It was not only the alliance with Scotland that pushed the parliamentary leaders in this direction. We must not forget the chaos developing in the parishes, and the need for a regular system of ordination to supply the demand for ministers. The practical need for an acceptable and established means of ordaining new candidates for the ministry had become an urgent problem, and it explains Parliament's insistent demand that the Assembly should provide a Directory to take the place of the Book of Common Prayer. It also explains the impatience of those within the Assembly who would be prepared to accept the Presbyterian system as a practical alternative to the episcopal form as long as it could be shown to have a reasonable basis in scripture. National unity was, at this stage, an absolute priority for most Puritans, and particularly for those Puritans who valued their membership in a *national* church. It was soon clear that no system of government in

1. *Debate on the 'Scriptural Rule'*

After a Fast Day to inaugurate this new phase of its work,[11] the Assembly entered upon a very important debate on October 17th.[12] The members had been given their orders by Parliament, and they now had to decide on their method of getting to grips with the task before them. It was soon agreed that they must first deal with the government of the Church. But battle lines had begun to appear. William Price, Thomas Coleman, and John Lightfoot, who had Erastian sympathies, argued that since the Assembly had been charged with judging all matters by the Bible, they ought first to examine whether such a clear rule could in fact be found in scripture. Other members such as Lazarus Seaman and Samuel De la Place, of the French Church in London, were horrified, and the latter roundly declared that to call this into question was "a blemish on Christ."[13]

But the Erastians' call for this debate was strongly supported by the Independents, not indeed because the Independents shared their scepticism about an explicit scriptural rule, but because they felt that unless the Assembly's members were agreed about this, the determination of specific orders in the Church was bound to suffer. As Thomas Goodwin said, "those that thinke examples doe not bind [,] they will easily object that those [biblical orders] doe not bind, & if you [then] bring rules [from scripture] it will be said that those are but for that time [.] So that first agree upon the rule & how this rule binds . . . my conscience is setled that ther is a rule."[14]

Lightfoot and his friends were more willing to take up that

---

the Church would be acceptable to the Scots that suggested the slightest approval of episcopacy or the name 'bishop' – even the moderate, biblically-grounded episcopacy held by Archbishop Ussher. Cf. Baillie's comments on this kind of 'caulked Episcopacie' in his letter to the Presbytery at Irvine, December 28th, 1640, *Letters and Journals*, I. 287.

The Presbyterian system appeared to be the only viable alternative and once that became clear in the Assembly, there would not be much patience for any who impeded its progress. Just as the delays caused by Dr. Burgess's opposition to the Covenant threatened the security of the country, so the later scruples of the Dissenting Brethren would appear to be deliberately prolonging the dangers of religious uncertainty.

[11] October 16th, 1643; Lightfoot, *Journal*, p. 19. Prayer was offered by Cornelius Burgess, Thomas Goodwin and Edmund Stanton, while Herbert Palmer and Jeremiah Whitaker were the preachers; TMs. I, 212 (Ms. I., f. 107.)

[12] Lightfoot, *Journal*, pp. 20ff. TMs. I. 213–224 (Ms. I., ff. 107b–113.)

[13] TMs. I. 214 (Ms. I., f. 108.)

[14] TMs. I. 215 (Ms. I., f. 108b) For interpreting the Minutes see Appendix IV. We must remember that most of the Minutes were written in note form. In quoting from them we have retained the original spelling and punctuation as far as possible, although the punctuation is almost non-existent. However, the linear form often helps us in determining the end of one sentence and the beginning of a new one. Material in [ ] has sometimes been added to assist the reader in understanding the sense of the passage.

challenge, but it was brushed aside as liable to make "too sudden a trial of the differences in opinion that are like to shew among us."[15] The last thing the parliamentary leaders wanted at the very beginning of the Assembly's serious work was to force a trial of strength between their own Erastian assumptions and the *jure divino* views favoured by the Scots and many of the theologians. John White – probably the Member of Parliament[16] – thought the issue of the scriptural rule should be dealt with "later when it arises", while Thomas Gataker and William Gouge seemed to think that the debate would have "too large an extent." Therefore the majority accepted the suggestion that they should waive the matter and debate the question of church officers.

Positions that would divide the Assembly began to appear – Independents and strict Presbyterians with their own but mutually exclusive appeals to a scriptural rule, Erastians who questioned any absolute scriptural rule, and the Puritan majority that perhaps at this stage wanted simply to handle matters with tact and expedition so that a national form of the Church could be maintained.

2. Program and Procedures

We have already called attention to the paucity of reliable material on the detail of the Assembly's procedures and program.[17] Subjects appear in the record without much warning, and for the few days following their introduction the debate was often fast and furious. Then the issue would be dropped as suddenly as it appeared, only to be revived later. Occasionally the reasons behind this seemingly erratic course were political, but the confusion for the modern reader is in part due to the way the work was presented.

Some overlapping was inevitable in the work of the three standing committees because the Assembly voted that "every committee should have the same work."[18]

However, although the account is sometimes confusing, we can trace a general pattern in the work. After Parliament

---

[15] Lightfoot, *Journal*, p. 20.

[16] Not to be confused with Revd. John White of Dorchester who was also a member of the Assembly and one of the two Assessors.

[17] Cf. *supra* pp. 80f.

[18] Lightfoot, *Journal*, pp. 20f. We get an indication of the method in a remark by Lightfoot. He had been grumbling because the debate had been long "yet concluded nothing upon it" and he had even proposed "that we might hasten the material things that tend to settlement, and let these speculations alone till leisure", (December 14th, 1643, *ibid*. p. 83,) but on December 18th, 1643, he complained, "This morning we wanted work, for none of the committees brought in any thing". (*Ibid*. p. 84.)

instructed the divines to formulate a new ecclesiastical system, the Assembly began its consideration of church government, and it was occupied on and off with this most controversial subject for the next two years. Presbyterian government in a somewhat modified form was eventually voted by Parliament in January 1646.

In 1644 work was also begun on the Directory, particularly those parts that impinged on ordination. The ordination question was concluded on October 3rd, 1644, and the main part of the Directory of Worship on November 12th of that year,[19] but the controversial question of excommunication became a major topic of debate which lasted until March 10th, 1644/5.[20] That really covers the period of 'the Grand Debate' and the Assembly's major work in ecclesiology, although the Assembly's struggle with the Erastianism of the English Parliament was yet to take place and was never resolved. For the rest, it is one of the oddities of history that the work for which the Assembly is best known and in many places still revered did not get under way until, in the eyes of many of its contemporaries, the major reason for its existence was finished.[21]

We are in the first instance concerned with the history of the Assembly up to the end of the year 1644, for this is the period in which the principal issues between Presbyterian and Congregationalist took clear form. It may be too much to declare with an earlier historian of the Assembly that "the debates of the Assembly may be said to have almost terminated with the close of 1644",[22] but it is certainly true that by the end of that year all the major issues between the rival polities had been thoroughly exposed.

II

The Debate on Church Officers

The debate on the officers of the Church was perhaps not expected to produce any open breach in the ranks of the divines,

---

[19] *Ibid.* pp. 314, 326f.

[20] Minutes III, pp. 1–69, *passim.*

[21] A committee was selected to commence work on the Confession of Faith in October 1644, but nothing effective was done on it until May the following year. It was eventually submitted to Parliament on December 4th, 1646, and the Scriptural references added in April, 1647. Concurrently with this work on the Confession, the Catechisms were discussed.The Larger Catechism was submitted to Parliament on 15th October, 1647, the Shorter Catechism went up to the Houses on 25th–26th November, 1647, and the proof texts for both were presented on April 14th, 1648. Cf. Minutes III, 484, 492, 511.

[22] W. M. Hetherington, *History of the Westminster Assembly*, p. 211.

since the forms of ministry were generally agreed. But there are different ways of approaching scripture as well as differences in interpreting it. For example, Thomas Young presented the report of the Second Committee, which had broached the question of the officers of the Church by starting with the offices of Christ. "In inquiring after the officers belonging to the church of the New Testament, we first find that Christ, who is Priest, Prophet, King, and head of the church, hath fulness of power, and containeth all the other offices by way of eminency in himself"; and then they specified "the names of the church-officers that Christ beareth in Scripture", Apostle, Pastor, Bishop, Teacher, and Minister (Diakonos).[23] On the other hand, Dr. Temple reported that the Third Committee had begun by posing four questions: 1. What officers are mentioned in the New Testament? 2. Which of these officers were to be regarded as temporary and which were permanent? 3. What names were common to different officers, and what names were restricted to a single office? and 4. What was the specific function of the standing officers in the apostolic church?[24]

It was eventually agreed that the New Testament recognized apostles, prophets, evangelists, pastors, teachers, bishops, elders, deacons and widows as officers of the Church, but a good deal would depend on how the issue was approached in establishing the form of the new church order. Although there was no necessary contradiction in the approaches taken by Committee Two and Committee Three, one can see that a different style of ministry might develop out of a view of the Church that concentrated primarily on the 'priesthood' of Christ in contrast to one that started simply from the offices mentioned in the Pauline epistles.

Cornelius Burgess had made his apologies[25] and was now back into the Assembly's favour, and as one of the Assembly's Assessors, he very quickly became one of its leaders. There are significant hints that some of these divines, despite their Calvinist theology and later voting record, had only very recently begun to re-consider their adherence to episcopacy. Thomas Bayly – the 'English Bayly' – admitted as much.[26]

---

[23] Lightfoot, *Journal*, pp. 22f. The names of those reporting are not given in Lightfoot, but appear in the Minutes; TMs. I. 231 (Ms. I., f., 116b.)

[24] Lightfoot, *Journal*, p. 23.

[25] After presenting a report on the way in which the Committee on Antinomianism had been received by the House of Commons, he went on to make a speech that is tantalizingly ambiguous. TMs. I. 231–2, Ms. I., f. 117.)

[26] November 30, 1643; Lightfoot, *Journal*, p. 67. Cf. *infra* pp. 168f.

Others had probably not reached that point. For all the revolutionary character of the enterprize in which they were engaged, there is a noticeable strain of conservatism that runs through the debates; but the hints of latent affection for the old order were subtle. Wayne Spear pointed out that while they were debating the pastoral office Dr. Gouge's seemingly innocuous suggestion to regard the public reading of scripture as a distinct ecclesiastical function,[27] went back to the Admonition Controversy of the 1570s and to the classic debate between Whitgift and Cartwright.[28] Gouge's proposal really endorsed Whitgift's side in that dispute, and it received considerable support among the members. Dr. Temple, Charles Herle, Dr. Burgess, Lazarus Seaman, Henry Wilkinson sen., Theophilus Bathurst, John Gibbon, Herbert Palmer, Edmund Calamy and John White all seem to have spoken unequivocably in favour of public reading as a distinct ecclesiastical function, against Stephen Marshall, who declared "The reading of the word in public is not an ecclesiastical office."[29] As Spear observes, "the majority of the Assembly held a high view of reading," and notes that "Dr. Temple probably held the highest view of reading, for he repeated in substance the dictum of Whitgift that 'reading is preaching.'"[30]

That debate had arisen from a consideration of the proper functions of the pastoral office, but we must remember the traditional threefold order of the English Church, bishops, priests and deacons. Spear again makes a shrewd observation regarding the debate on the office of the 'deacon'[31] when he points out that some of the participants seem to have held views closer to the traditional order than to the Reformed pattern.[32] For example, Richard Vines and Brocket (or Peter) Smith appeared to echo the traditional view of the deacon as a grade within the ministry. Vines argued on December 15th that the seven mentioned in Acts 6 were essentially the same office as the deacons in Timothy and Titus. He agreed that while *diakonia* could represent the general office of ministry, in the function of

---

[27] Lightfoot, *Journal*, pp. 36–40. The debate is more fully recorded in the Minutes; TMs. 1.300–323 (Ms. I, ff. 154–165b.)

[28] 'Covenanted Uniformity in Religion,' pp. 150ff.

[29] Lightfoot, *Journal*, p. 37, cf. TMs. 1. 302 (Ms. I., f. 155.) Marshall had been supported by other members, including some of the Independents.

[30] 'Covenanted Uniformity in Religion,' p. 153. Cf. Lightfoot, *Journal*, p. 36 (November 2nd, 1643,) and the Minutes as cited in the notes above.

[31] The debate on the office of Deacon began on 15th December, 1643, but there is a gap in the Minutes after December 20th; TMs. I. 541–73 (Ms. I., ff. 275–291.)

[32] *Op. cit.* p. 195.

'serving tables' "they are to be tryed ther[e], here they are to have hands imposed[;] they have gifts set out ther[e], great gifts, her[e] is an experimentall tryall".[33] It is difficult to avoid the conclusion that in Richard Vine's view the diaconate was preparatory to full pastoral ministry, a distinct grade within ministerial order.

A few days later (December 22nd) Dr. Smith defended a similar view. He argued that the deacons were required to have special gifts, and in respect of ordination they were to be approved, set apart and chosen, examined, and given the imposition of hands with a blessing.[34] All this very clearly in his mind represented a distinct grade of ministry in preparation for eventual priesthood; it suggests the deacon in the old order rather than the deacon of continental Reformed practice.

Then there was a crucial debate on the ruling elder, to which we must refer later, in which the Scots were clearly defensive in presenting this feature of their church government about which the large number of English divines knew nothing and about which they were obviously sceptical.[35] Perhaps the strangest part of that debate, however, was that in their defence of the ruling elder as scriptural, the Scots and the convinced English Presbyterians were supported by the Independents, against most of the remaining members of the Assembly.[36]

When the clues from the debates of the closing months of 1643 are added, we have to question how far many of the English divines who later voted consistently for the Scots proposals could yet be regarded as 'Presbyterians' in the sense that Robert Baillie and his colleagues understood the term. By the end of the year there may have been some signs of movement in this direction, but the veneer of Presbyterianism was very thin.

III

Church Officers: the shadow of things to come

What happened later becomes much more understandable when we recognize that the conservative majority was deter-

---

[33] TMs. I. 543 (Ms. I., f. 276.)

[34] For this period we must depend on Lightfoot, *Journal*, p. 90.

[35] The debate was touched upon in Dr. Stanton's report of the Second Committee on November 8th, and the Assembly returned to it on the 22nd. The Minutes do not seem to mention Stanton's report on Nov. 8th but they note the second report of the First Committee. It appears first in the Minutes on Nov. 22nd. It remained on the agenda, with some interruptions, until December 14th, but apparently without any firm decision. Lightfoot, *Journal*, pp. 43, 60–83. TMs. I. 416–540 (Ms. Minutes I., ff. 212–274.)

[36] *Infra.* pp. 163ff.

mined to maintain the national form of the Church of England, and was becoming increasingly scared of sects and 'gathered churches' that rivalled the regular parish ministry. For those reasons the Puritan majority became more suspicious of the Independents than they were of the Scots. However, although the Independents and the Scottish Commissioners knew they represented rival views of the Church, we gain the impression that during these months neither was anxious to hasten the breach. The Scots probably realized that time was on their side.

During the last few months of 1643 a cleavage clearly began to develop between the small group of Independents and the Puritan majority in the Assembly, but the things that reveal the growth of that tension were often incidental to the matters of immediate concern in the debates. That is where we must direct our enquiry, and we see the pattern emerging almost parenthetically to the great debates on the Officers of the Church during the closing months of 1643.

1. *Who can ordain?*

For example, it appeared in the issue of what interim steps could be taken to provide for ordination in the existing chaos. It was raised by Cornelius Burgess on October 20th in his report to the Assembly on the problem of Antinomianism – itself a sufficient cause for conservative Puritans to fear for the Church's health and orthodoxy. Burgess thought the matter was exacerbated by the need for properly qualified ministers. How could they provide ecclesiastically for regular ordination and induction, when properly educated young men were ready to be introduced to the parishes? The bishops were no longer available even if they had been acceptable. This was the single most urgent ecclesiastical problem faced by the parliamentary government; we read that Burgess himself proposed that "there might be a certain settlement in these things, by the progress of our works":[37] get a regular form of the Church established and the problem of sectarian religion would be easily handled.

In Lightfoot's all too brief summary of the debate that followed we read that "Mr. *Young* moved that young men might exercise their ministry till this settlement without orders conferred upon them: which Mr. *Seaman* backed. But Dr. *Gouge*, Mr. *Gattaker*, Mr. *Palmer*, did very earnestly and very soundly

---

[37] Lightfoot, *Journal*, p. 24.

oppose it."[38] The division of opinion here was between those who were prepared for properly qualified candidates to be admitted to preaching charges *pro tem.* without ordination until the Assembly had determined the scriptural pattern, and those who regarded a *rite* of ordination as absolutely necessary, even if it had to be by means of an *ad hoc* 'presbytery'.

In the fuller if often cryptic account in the Minutes,[39] we find that although the first view was certainly represented by Thomas Young and Lazarus Seaman, who may be counted as convinced Presbyterians at this date, they were joined only by Thomas Wilson[40] and the Independents, and in the ensuing debate it was the Independents who represented that position most persistently.

So Philip Nye wondered by what authority an *ad hoc* 'presbytery' would act, and William Bridge, citing John Knox in his support, urged that properly qualified candidates should be allowed to preach for the present without ordination, although he added "I speake not of administering the sacraments." Thomas Goodwin said that he disputed whether ordination was a matter of such consequence that it could properly precede a call, and he went on to ask whether it was "absolutely necessary to the essential of a mans being a minister". He argued that if holding ministers to episcopal ordination was to be considered a sin, then it would be equally sinful to ordain according to any procedure not determined as biblical; lay members of Parliament who spoke in the Assembly were exercizing "a prophesying & preaching" function, and Goodwin implied that the work of young men sent down to the parishes could be regarded in the same way.[41]

This was a minority opinion, and it is clear that ranged against it were the majority of the members, who believed that the 'imposition of hands' in ordination was an absolute necessity for any ministry. "I cannot see any ground in scripture", declared Herbert Palmer, "that any man should take upon him to be designed to exercise for constant preaching without solemn ordination", while William Price – the one who had opposed the Covenant with Cornelius Burgess – warned that "we shall doe preaching a great deale of dishonour if we hould that preaching may be without imposition of hands." John Ley, in response to

---

[38] *Ibid.*

[39] TMs. I. 232–8 (Ms. I., ff. 117–120.)

[40] Wilson declared, "concerning preaching we must not deferre teaching of the word till ordination come [.] I doe not thinke that men perish for want of sacraments [,] but they perish for want of knowledge". *Ibid.* p. 238 (Ms. I., f. 120.)

[41] *Ibid.*

Nye's doubts about an *ad hoc* presbytery, stated that "extraordinary cases require extraordinary courses" – an argument which could apply equally well to permitting suitably qualified men to occupy pulpits on a temporary basis without ordination.

The problem of the sacraments was of grave importance to the majority, and some of the members like Francis Taylor and John Jackson reminded their colleagues of the parlous conditions in the country at large. Taylor particularly mentioned the number of children that remained unbaptized, and he urged them to "thinke of some way of ordination by presbyters."[42] In response Arthur Sallaway [or Humphrey Salloway?] reminded them that a bill was already before Parliament to put the power of ordination in the hands of special commissioners, and it had been declared in the House that "ordination was Jure divino to all ministers".[43]

This did not end the debate,[44] but it should be seen that the issue – despite John De la March's assurance that French Reformed churches were careful not to permit anyone to preach who had not been first ordained[45] – was not primarily one that set Presbyterians against Independents. It was between the larger number of members in the Assembly who were not prepared to allow unordained persons to perform any ministerial office, even on a temporary basis and however otherwise qualified the individual might be, and those who were prepared to allow unordained but otherwise qualified individuals to fulfill ministerial functions on a provisional basis. Evidently, in order to meet the urgent need for ministers, the majority was less concerned about who would officiate at the rite of ordination than that it should be duly accompanied by the laying on of hands. And two other things are clear in the debate – first that the Independents were joined by a few men whom we can already identify as Presbyterians, Young, Seaman and Wilson; but secondly, we should note that although the views of the minority should not be

---

[42] This did not necessarily imply 'Presbyterianism', but simply ordination by those who were already preaching presbyters within the Church.

[43] It is not clear from the Minutes whether this was Arthur Sallaway, the divine, or Humphrey Salloway, the Member of Parliament.

[44] Herbert Palmer probably had an eye to the foreign churches in London when he reminded his colleagues that the Church of England recognized the ordination of the Reformed churches in Europe. *Ibid.* p. 236 (Ms. I., f. 119.) Norman Sykes has shown that at this period in the English church, the ordination of Reformed churches was generally regarded as acceptable, and re-ordination within the Church of England was not required; *Old Priest and New Presbyter: Episcopacy and Presbyterianism since the Reformation with special relation to the Churches of England and Scotland.* (Cambridge, Cambridge University Press, 1956), especially Chaper IV.

[45] TMs. I. 237 (Ms. I., f. 119b.) John De la March was a minister of the French church in London.

interpreted as an attack on ordination as such, that appears to be the way they were heard; and in that, it was clearly the Independents whose views would be received with most suspicion.

2. *The 'Power of the Keys'*

Another issue quickly surfaced in 'the power of the keys'.[46] Fairly late in the debate on Friday October 27th, John Lightfoot had argued against the proposal of the First Committee that within the proof texts offered the power of the keys had been given immediately by Christ to the apostles.[47] There was little indication at that point what was to follow, because Lightfoot had been opposed by Thomas Coleman (who usually shared his Erastian views,) by Lazarus Seaman, the convinced Presbyterian, and by one of the leading Independents, Thomas Goodwin.[48] That seemed to offer a fairly wide spread of opinion for the debate.

The engagement on the following Monday (30th) began peacefully enough with show of general agreement. Jeremiah Burroughes declared that "this proposition may be granted by all without any further debating", and William Bridge said that although "ther be great disputes concerning keyes yet we shall not much differ as concerning the matter". Seaman then moved that they should take "that propounded for granted" and "let it be soe resolved", and Thomas Gataker said "I conceive we need not inquire any further". All seemed to be sweetness and light.[49]

The situation changed because of a longish speech by Charles Herle, who was clearly a Presbyterian but who shared some of the Independents' theological concerns and remained close to them personally.[50] He thought that the issue should be explored thoroughly before the Assembly moved on to other things, first

---

[46] The 'power of the keys' was an issue that had become particularly acute between Protestants and Catholics since the Reformation, and centred in the different ways of interpreting the promise to Peter: "And I will give unto thee the keys of the kingdom of heaven: and whatsoever thou shalt bind on earth shall be bound in heaven: and whatsoever thou shalt lose on earth shall be loosed in heaven." (Matt. 16:19.)

In the Bible 'keys' were sometimes used as symbols of power and authority (cf. Isaiah 22:22,) and in the theology of the Westminster Assembly they were the symbols of ecclesiastical authority, of the right to exercise church discipline and ultimately to excommunicate the impenitent.

[47] Lightfoot, *Journal*, p. 30. The texts were Matt. 16:19, John 20:23, I Tim. 1:20, III John 9, 10, II Cor. 10:6, and 13:10.

[48] *Ibid.*

[49] TMs. I. 257–8, (Ms. I., ff. 129b–130.)

[50] Cf. Infra p. 151f., 223, 228f.

because "it is very questionable whether the keys were given to the apostles or the church", and secondly, because "the promises are given to the church throughout."[51] At once some important differences began to emerge, with the conservative majority insisting that the power of the keys was given to the apostles as *apostles*, and not simply as believers. Behind this debate one senses there was a very strong and traditional concern for maintaining the distinction between clerical and lay persons and for reaffirming ministerial authority, against the Independents' insistence that ecclesiastical power should be corporately in the hands of the whole congregation.

So the Independent, William Carter, asked what it was that made Peter the 'Rock'? and to that rhetorical question he answered:

> what makes him to be a stone? Christ tells it was his
> confession. now saith Christ I will tell thee something[:]
> this confession is that for which I call thee peter.
> Our confession makes us all peters[.]
> in church feowship[52] we have to doe only with one
> another as confessours[.[53]]

We can almost hear Dr. Joshua Hoyle's incredulous protest that if every believer could be said to have the power of the keys, "then weomen and children have the power of the keyes"![54]

William Bridge thought they should waive Matthew 16 as a proof text, since "It does not relate to Peter as *apostle*", but the debate concentrated on Matthew 16:19. In what sense was the power of the keys given to Peter on that occasion, since strictly he was not yet an 'apostle'? Seaman admitted that Matthew 16:19 could not properly be ignored in proving their case, but now, Seaman said, they were hard put to it since the 'brethren' were questioning whether the power was given to Peter and his colleagues as apostles or as confessors. For himself he affirmed that it was given to them as apostles, first "as church officers, that must needs be the genus", and that this power could not have been granted simply because of faith because "faith is not of publique cognisance". Furthermore it could not have been granted by virtue of a public profession of faith since they were not yet in a church state, nor as members of a particular congre-

---

[51] Lightfoot, *Journal*, p. 31.
[52] *Sic.* Read as 'fellowship'.
[53] TMs. I. 261f. (Ms. I., f. 131b *et seq.*) In quoting from the Minutes, I have transcribed 'Xst' as 'Christ', and 'yt' as 'that'.
[54] *Ibid.* 262, (Ms. I., f. 132.)

gation, "for ther was noe such thing then in being", nor as a "member of the church ecumenicall for then . . . the use of the keyes belong to generall counsells."[55]

Bridge thought that women and children were excepted, but George Walker said that this invalidated his argument, and Lightfoot held that "the keyes were given to none but Peter". Then Dr. Thomas Temple made a lengthy speech maintaining that the power was given to the apostles as apostles. His major argument was that they had been called directly by our Lord himself, and their specific responsibilities – preaching the Word, teaching, remission of sins and church governance – showed that "the holy ghost makes them overseers & not the community of the faithfull". He also maintained that since apostleship was a specific ministry given to the Church (Ephesians 4:11), God "did not give that power to all": ministerial power is a stewardship and "the steward [of a family] doth not receive the keyes from the family but from the master of the family".[56]

Thomas Gataker spoke to the same effect. He invited them to compare the promise and the performance of the promise: the promise had been made to Peter, and presumably the performance of that promise was left with the apostles in the Church. So, he argued,

> titles given to apostels called shepherds [i.e.] pastors
> be[cause] the master of the sheepe doth give
> power to him [Peter] to looke over the flocke for the
> good thereof[;] doth it therfore follow that he hath
> received his power from the sheepe[?][57]

The Independents' suggestion that the power of the keys belonged to the whole church received a very decided reaction from the conservatives in the Assembly, and between the lines we may discern their fears for the traditional authority and status of the ministry.

Sidrach Simpson mentioned the biblical studies of Gerard,[58] who had interpreted the message in Matthew to apply to the Church throughout history, but this suggestion was brushed aside by Cornelius Burgess on grounds that "we are not to looke [to] what Gerrard hath affirmed but never proved". Burgess was

---

[55] *Ibid*. 263–4, (Ms. I., ff. 132–133.) Seaman too pointed out that if the power was granted to members, women and children would have to share that right.

[56] *Ibid*. 264f. (Ms. I., f. 133–135b.)

[57] *Ibid*. p. 266, (Ms. I., f. 134.)

[58] *Ibid*. Simpson was probably referring to the work of John Gerard (1582–1638), professor at Jena, who had published a Harmony of the Gospels at Geneva in 1640.

joined by Seaman (several times), Reynolds, Calamy, Gouge, Marshall, Smith, White and Palmer, while on the Independent side the cudgels were taken up by Philip Nye and Thomas Goodwin. Seaman, indeed, warned the Assembly that what was being argued on the other side would assist Libertines and Socinians,[59] while Calamy thought it tended towards Anabaptism.[60] There was no surer way of arousing the fears of that particular company than by introducing the spectre of the sects. What had appeared to begin in agreement, seemed to open up a wider chasm the longer the debate continued.[61]

Goodwin said "we grant the key is put for power but not for apostolicall power, especially if ther be a power of the keyes besides apostolicall". The Independents were unwilling to concede that the power of the keys was given to Peter by virtue of his apostleship, especially if it were conceived that this apostolical power could be similarly passed on to other officers. Edmund Calamy then asked Goodwin to consider "whether this promise was made to peter as a church officer", and if so, what kind; and Goodwin replied:

> this was the first promise that ever
> Christ uttered that he would build a church and the
> first expression that he would give the power of
> the keyes out of himselfe, & be[cause] peter
> made the first confession[.]

Then, apparently in response to the questions raised by Calamy, he added:

> I believe it falls under both [:1,] he is representative
> of all power whatsoever [:2, that is] the first grand
> charter of the gospell which is afterwards
> to be branched out as Christ hath placed it[.][62]

The debate had begun so innocuously, but the Minutes are even clearer than Lightfoot that a sharp division had appeared between the Independents and the majority, in which the issue was the authority and status of the clergy. Lightfoot informs us that in reply to Sidrach Simpson, Lazarus Seaman had declared "that the apostles used the keys authoritatively, as a master of the house or the steward doth; but the church them ministerially, as

---

[59] *Ibid.* p. 267, (Ms. I., f. 134b.)
[60] *Ibid.* p. 268, (Ms. I., f. 13.)
[61] *Ibid.* p. 266–72, (Ms. I., ff. 134–137.)
[62] *Ibid.* 271, (Ms. I., f. 136b.)

the meaner servant doth."[63] It is interesting that Seaman applied the authoritative (or 'magisterial') image to those who were the first ministers of the Church.

The issues were becoming clearer. Near the end of this debate on the 30th, Sir Arthur Haselrig, a leader of the Presbyterian party in the Commons, observed, "You are now upon the foundation of all . . . give them time[,] you will loose nothing by it".[64] It was as if he had said, 'Give them time, and they will dig a hole and bury themselves!'

The verbal struggle became, if anything, even more intense on October 31st, with Simpson and Goodwin carrying the major responsibility for the Independents,[65] and a small army of speakers on the other side.[66] Perhaps the most significant statements for our purpose were made by Thomas Goodwin, who set out to answer the charges that had been thrown on the previous day.

What interests us in Goodwin's words is not so much his detailed theological argument as his reaction to the way in which the Independents' position had been attacked. He admitted that although in the early church women were forbidden to speak publicly,[67] "unto weomen ther is a sprinkling of those keys[:] they have some hand upon it" since they shared in every believer's duty to admonish an erring member privately. To Calamy's charge that Anabaptism was implied by the suggestion that the power of the keys arose directly out of Peter's confession, Goodwin insisted that "in a church state none ought to have it [i.e. the keys] but believers & 'visible as the church is' especially in the ministry".[68] They should consider what power properly belongs to the people and what power properly belongs to pastors:

Authority properly is Authority where it is put out electively into the hands of some few[;]

---

[63] Lightfoot, *Journal*, p. 32. As we have noted previously, the Independents regarded all government in the Church as essentially 'ministerial'; cf. *supra* pp. 103, 130.

[64] TMs. I. 272 (Ms. I., f. 137.)

[65] Philip Nye and William Carter entered the discussion later, but William Bridge later claimed that he had been absent because of illness.

[66] The leadership in that cause seems to have been taken by Charles Herle and Lazarus Seaman. Calamy, Hoyle, Walker, and Lightfoot all made identifiable contributions in addition to Seaman and Herle. Gouge, Palmer, Temple, and Marshall, who had indicated th ir position on the previous day, also contributed and although we do not absolutely know what was said by others, (Gibson, Ley, Whitaker, and White,) they did not normally side with the Independents.

[67] I Timothy 2:12.

[68] TMs. I. 277, (Ms. I., f. 139b.) In common with the editor of the Transcript, phrases interlined in the Ms. have been placed in single inverted commas [e.g., 'visible as the church is'.]

the same that is power in many is authority in few!
as in democraticall government the power is in the people
the charge of an officer is an act of authority[,] it
is the power of the keyes . . .
When Christ chose 12 this is an act of power[;] why not
soe when done by the people?[69]

Charles Herle admitted that in an admonitory way a layman
can be said to 'bind and loose', but he denied that this implied
anything regarding the status of women in the church:

. . . for whereas he said that
weomen may have some use of the keyes [, which is] true taken[70]
it in this lardge sence[,] but when you come to the
keyes of discipline in 20 Joh[n]: they have noe peice of the
keyes[71]

Although he clearly differed from the Independents, he recognized the force of their argument and he came to their defence
against the charge that by linking the keys to Peter's confession
they ran the risk of Anabaptism, Socinianism and Libertinism;
"the danger is", he said, "we persue this place too farre". He
pointed out that although Brownists and Separatists had said that
Peter received this authority "in the right of the faithful", many
of the fathers and schoolmen had interpreted it in the same way
without implying anarchy. He suggested that "we should carry it
soe as that the officers doe represent the church", and he thought
one of the arguments offered on the previous day had been
unanswerable:

if the power [is] not first in the church then the
officers cannot represent the church[;]
otherwise how [w]ill any of those rules that the officers shall
make bind the church[?]
the consent of the members [is] not necessary further
than the election of the officers[.]
if we setle government upon such a popular way
that will be anabaptisme[;]
[but] the consent of the people in election of officers [is]
absolutely necessary . . ."[72]

Charles Herle's position is interesting. He was clearly a con-

---

[69] *Ibid.* pp. 277–8, (Ms. I., ff. 139b–140.)

[70] The notes read better if this is read as " 'taking' it in this lardge sense".

[71] *Ibid.* pp. 280–1. (Ms. I., ff. 141–141b.) The relative value of the Minutes and
Lightfoot's account in this debate is seen in that the latter has no account of Herle's
speech but concentrates on Lightfoot's own contribution, which occupies a very minor
place in the Minutes; cf. Lightfoot's *Journal*, pp. 32–3.

[72] TMs. I. 281, (Ms. I., f. 141b.)

vinced Presbyterian, for his little book, *The Independency on Scriptures of the Independency of Churches* had either already appeared, or was about to appear;[73] but he was genuinely prepared to make the scriptural evidence the final authority in church government, and he seems to have been honestly concerned that the views of the majority should not be railroaded through without the Independents getting a fair hearing. His position certainly differed from the Independents in some respects, but in them he recognized the Reformed position which accepted the scriptures alone as the authority for church government:[74] it was Charles Herle who in a relatively short time would license the Independents' controversial *An Apologeticall Narration*.

Lazarus Seaman was of a different temper. He declared that he had not heard any new arguments presented, and "not one argument used about this but [was] used by Robinson", i.e. John Robinson, the pastor of the Pilgrim fathers, who had been regarded as a Brownist.[75] Against Goodwin he urged that "the church did never intervene to conferre any authority upon the apostels", and although the notes on his speech are incomplete, the implication is that if the power of the keys was given to Peter in virtue of his status as an apostle, then it could be assumed that church governance was vested not in the church but in its officers.

---

[73] *The Independency on Scriptures of the Independency of Churches. Wherein The Question of Independency of Church-Government is temperately, first, Stated; secondly, Argued; thirdly, Cleerd from Objections; and fourthly, Appeald in, to the judgements of such as stand for it*, by Master Herle, a Lancashire Minister, (London, 1643.) He was arguing for the independence of the Church within the State.

[74] "However, for the difference betweene us and our brethren that are for Independency, 'tis nothing so great as you seemed to conceive it, we doe but (with Abraham and Lot) take severall wayes, we are as (Abraham speakes) brethren still, and (as they were) ready to rescue each other on all occasions against the common enemy; our difference 'tis such as doth at most but ruffle a little the fringe, not any way rend the Garment of Christ, 'tis so farre from being a fundamentall, that 'tis scarce a materiall one, nay not so much as the forme, 'tis but the better or worse way for the exercise of the same forme of discipline that is in question." *Op. cit.* preface. In this preface Herle also went on to give fair and accurate statement of the difference in discipline held by Independents with regard to the function and authority of synods, and their emphasis on the local congregation in excommunication and ordination.

[75] There are grounds for thinking that John Robinson had modified his Separatist position somewhat in the direction taken by Henry Jacob and the Independents. Cf. under 'Jacob' and 'Robinson' in Champlin Burrage, *The Early English Dissenters, 1550–1641* (Cambridge, Cambridge University Press, 1912, 2 vols.) particularly I. chapter xii. I agree with Michael Watts that Burrage went too far in suggesting that Robinson relinquished Separatism (cf. *The Dissenters*, pp. 54f.), but there are grounds for thinking that Robinson modified his earlier Separatist views. See my article, 'Henry Jacob and Seventeenth-Century Puritanism', *The Hartford Quarterly*, VII, No. 3 (Spring, 1967), pp. 95f, 104–113.

Goodwin intervened at that point to protest against Seaman's attempt to sabotage the Independents' position by associating them with separatism:

> for that of brownisme, [it was] said we brought the
> same arguments that Robinson doth[.]
> I chalenge liberty to speake in this case[.]
> I desire it humbly but chalenge it as a liberty[.]
> I thinke the apostells had not their power
> from the church [and that]
> not only the apostells but ordinary officers
> have a power over the church [-]
> wch is all one differing thing from brownisme[.]
> they are the ministers of Christ acting his power[.]
> [We represent] *a middle way betwixt that called brownisme and
> that that it may be hath too much countenance* . . .[76]

This shows that the Independents of the Assembly were close to the Presbyterianism of Charles Herle, but the importance of the speech is that Goodwin's words forecast not only the sense but almost the words in which he would express those views in *An Apologeticall Narration*.

There is one slight but significant difference, for if the words italicized above are compared with the relevant passage in the Independent pamphlet we can see that they did not yet specify the system of church government to be contrasted with Brownism as Presbyterianism: it is simply described as that which "it may be hath too much countenance." And at this stage, this may have been seen by them more as a clerical authority typical of the previous government of the Church of England rather than as 'Presbyterianism'. That lay in the near future, but was not yet altogether clear.

However, it was increasingly clear that the majority in the Assembly would close its ranks against anything that seemed to threaten the authority and status of the clergy. The text in question, Matthew 16:19 was added to the scriptural proofs of the proposition that the power of the keys, church governance, had been given by our Lord directly to the apostles, and the rest

---

[76] TMs. I. 284, (Ms. I., f. 143.) My italics. Cf. the following: "And wee did then, and die here publiquely professe, we beleeve the truth to lie and consist in a *middle way* betwixt that which is falsely charged on us. *Brownisme;* and that which is the contention of these times, the *authoritative Presbyteriall Government* in all the subordinations and proceedings of it." *An Apologeticall Narration*, p. 24. The italics here belong to the original text.

of October 31st was given over to the fairly easy passage of additional proof texts.[77]

3. *The Purity of the Church*

A further issue arose on November 10th in a similarly innocent fashion out of rules for appointing ministers to sequestered livings.[78] One of the questions that the committee proposed should be put to prospective incumbents was whether they were prepared to fulfil the duties of a minister by preaching and administering the sacraments. Stephen Marshall – perhaps with his son-in-law's strict views in mind – thought this should be made more precise to cover the minister who arrived in a parish without knowing "whether he shall find some that are not fit to receive the sacraments of the Lord's supper";[79] but Philip Nye was concerned about a minister who might for that cause be excluded because he had conscientious scruples regarding worship and the administration of the sacraments.[80] Nye had extremely rigorous views on this matter, as we know from Richard Baxter's account of the situation he found in Acton:[81] the Independents believed that the Lord's Supper was to be restricted to 'visible saints',[82] whereas the practice of the Church of England had been to offer the sacrament to all who were not otherwise excluded by ecclesiastical censure.

Dr. Temple voiced the legitimate fear of the conservatives

---

[77] William Bridge tried unsuccessfully to get the matter reopened on Nov. 1st on the grounds that he had been unwell the previous day, TMs. I. 288 (Ms. I., f. 145.) Cf. Lightfoot, *Journal*, pp. 33f.

[78] TMs. I. 345f., (Ms. I., ff. 176b *et seq*.), Lightfoot, *Journal*, pp. 47f.

[79] Lightfoot, *Journal*, p. 48; cf. TMs. I. 346, (Ms. I., f. 177.) Marshall's daughter had married Philip Nye.

[80] *Ibid*. 345, (Ms. I., f. 176b.)

[81] Nye was appointed to the parish in Acton after Daniel Featley had been expelled from the Assembly and sequestered from that living, but after the Restoration Baxter found himself in Acton where a congregation began to gather around him in 1663. In a letter to John Owen (dated February 16th, 1668/9) Baxter described the situation in Acton, where Nye had ministered together with a fellow Independent, named Elford. Baxter did not imply any criticism of Nye's personal qualities, for he described Nye and Elford as "two of the worthiest Persons of your way . . . whose ability and Piety were beyond all question", but the number admitted to the Lord's Supper had been so few "that the rest were partly by this course (and other reasons) distasted, and their dislike increased, and partly neglected and left to themselves: That of rich Families, (Mr. *Rous*, Major *Skippous*, Collonel *Sely*, and Mr. *Humphreys*) were admitted while the rest were refused or neglected". *Rel. Baxt*. III. 67–8 (§143).

[82] Cf. Geoffrey F. Nuttall, *Visible Saints: the Congregational Way, 1640–1660*, (Oxford, Basil Blackwell, 1957), particularly pp. 131ff; and for the New England expression of the same churchmanship, Edmund S. Morgan, *Visible Saints: the History of a Puritan Idea*, (Ithaca, N.Y., Cornell University Press, 1963), particularly chapters 1 and 2.

that by allowing such fastidious emphasis on purity, "you put it under the power of every particular man to put a whole parish from the sacrament",[83] and Calamy pointed out that the intention of the committee had been to exclude the over-scrupulous practices of Anabaptists and Separatists. Nye retorted by asking why should they be specifically excluded rather than others, such as Socinians. He was apparently called to order![84]

The notes of this debate in the Minutes are fragmentary, but out of the exchange there seems to have developed a full-scale debate on how far the Church of England could be regarded as a true Church.[85] We can imagine the fears this issue raised for conservative Puritans who had been conforming members of the Church of England to that point. Palmer stated "it will be noe advantage at all to me [to discuss this] since it is granted that it is a thing [that] may be acknowledged" presumably without debate, while Cornelius Burgess declared "I am sorry it should be opposed to any of our brethren to have this question put", since it would bolster the claims of many who had been sequestered that the Assembly did not represent the Church of England. Dr. William Gouge reminded them that "we that are antient ministers doe know that many have separated upon this ground that we are not a true church".

Nye said that all he asked for was a certain freedom, and he wished people would not make such heavy weather of it – "without casting such heavy words as to say[']I am grieved[';] we meete with such words often and frequently" – but he did not know of anyone who had been put into a living who had yet troubled the peace of the Church, and all he asked was freedom to act according to conscience. On the other hand, William Bridge drew back a little; it was not whether the Church of England was a true church, but whether this question was to be asked of those who were to be admitted to livings, and he thought it should be waived. "For my owne opinion", he said, "I thinke that ther are true churches & parochiall churches in England[,] many & many hundred".[86]

So the debate continued, and as Lightfoot observed "very

[83] TMs. I. 346, (Ms. I., f. 177.)

[84] *Ibid.* 347, (Ms. I., f. 177b.)

[85] Monday 13th November. Philip Nye began the debate, and following his name is apparently a summary of what he said: "the Joyning of those 2 together church & ministry"; but as in so many other crucial cases, the Minutes then frustrate us by apparently leaving the rest of the page blank for a fuller account of Nye's speech to be added later. *Ibid.* 351, (Ms. I., f. 179b.)

[86] *Ibid.* 351f., (Ms. I., ff. 180, 180b.)

many spoke to it."[87] It touched upon the distinction between the visible and the invisible Church, and it skirted the problem of a national Church. Throughout one can sense that while the Independents were not prepared categorically to deny that the Church of England was a true church, for they had deplored Separatism in all their public utterances, they were probably not willing to recognize all the parishes as true churches and all the members as 'saints'. Without knowing it, they shared views that would be held by later Pietists who strove to establish *ecclesiolae in ecclesia* ('little churches within the church',) in the attempt to restrict the sacraments to 'visible saints.'

To the majority that looked like covert separatism. William Price declared "I thinke that man unworthy to have any dignity of remaine in the church that shall disclaime it to be a true church",[88] and Matthew Newcomen, one of the Smectymnuans, pointed out that the issue was not whether particular parishes could be counted as true churches, but whether the whole national Church could be regarded as a token of the Church Universal. He then provided a definition of the Church of England:

> the church of England is that part of the church
> visible professing the faith in this place . . .
> That church that professeth such a faith and
> practises such a worship [so] as everyone that
> sincerely imbraces & performes that faith &
> worship is certainly saved[,] is a true church[.][89]

Sidrach Simpson agreed: "take the church in this sence [and] noe man will deny it", but he pointedly reminded the members of the Assembly that they had been prevented earlier from discussing whether or not there is a scriptural rule for the Church, and he implied that it would be unfair "to keepe a man out of a living for that wch you have not declared to be Jure divino".[90]

The defence of the proposed rule Calamy declared, "I conceive this is a fit question to be put to keep out totall separatists from sequestered livings";[91] but from the rough notes and Nye's response it appears that Nye took considerable umbrage at some of the things that were said: "it is", he said, "a great discouradg-

---

[87] Lightfoot, *Journal*, p. 49.
[88] TMs. I. 355, (Ms. I., f. 181b.)
[89] *Ibid.*
[90] *Ibid.* I. 356, (Ms. I., f. 182.)
[91] *Ibid.*

ment when men cannot speake without such reproofes".[92] Nye still had scruples, and John Ley, who seems to have carried considerable weight in the First Committee, bluntly stated, "we did purposely put the words in that latitude that ther may be no scrupling".[93]

That was not the end of the debate, although it might as well have been, for the positions were becoming increasingly clear – the Independents with their own scripturally worked-out ecclesiology and a doctrinaire insistence that the Church should be visibly holy, and the majority equally determined to maintain the rights of the clergy and the national and catholic character of the Church. So far the division had not become an issue between Presbyterianism and Independency, because at no point in the debates had matters of difference between those two polities been discussed: the issue was one between those who were looking for radical change, and those who wanted at all costs to prevent or modify it.

As the debate continued Dr. Burgess said that he was "sorry this businesse doth hould you soe long", since it was only the discussion of a rule,[94] and John White may have tried to moderate by observing that "it is not denyed by any that the name church doth signify a company of faithfull in a larger circuite than one congregation", and that "true doth not signify perfect". Jeremiah Burroughes reacted by observing that the reason why there had been such a lengthy debate was because there were "such different sences put upon the word church", and he demanded, "let it be shown wher the church is taken for severall distinct congregations". But later he claimed, "it may not be said we deny the church of England to be a true church[;] we grant it", and he explained his understanding of this as meaning first that the association of parishes in England could be understood as a 'church', and that there were people in that number who would "certainly be saved".[95]

Philip Nye, who had started all the argument, observed "It is one thing to say the church of England is a transient way & another in . . ." – then the Minutes are again defective, and we are left to guess at Nye's meaning,[96] but he went on to say "I

---

[92] *Ibid.* 357, (Ms. I., f. 182b.)

[93] *Ibid.*

[94] *Ibid.* I. 358, (Ms. I., f. 183.)

[95] *Ibid.* I. 359–60, (Ms. I., ff. 183b, 184.)

[96] Perhaps the thrust of Nye's remarks was to point out that there is considerable difference between the Church as it was in the present state of flux, and the Church as it ought to be in a more permanent form.

looked upon the church of England to be Integralis pars ecclesia[e] catholicke".[97]

The Rules under discussion were passed as we could expect, and thirteen additional rules were passed without further debate.[98] The majority made its position even firmer by adding a clause to the first set of rules "That if he [the candidate] answer negatively to any of these, he shall not be admitted, but be dismissed". Oddly enough, the only person to vote against that was not an Independent, but Richard Herrick [or Heyrick], who had taken only a very minor part in the debate and was usually one of the majority.[99]

At the close of that same day's debate (November 13th) a committee was appointed, which among other things was to report to Parliament regarding "the multitudes of churches 'gathered' in the 'city &' countrys & disorders therupon, & concerning the speedy providing for the comfortable subsistence of the ministry by quickening the businesse & other dutyes concerning ecclesiasticall dues".[100] These were two of the majority's basic concerns – to curb the proliferation of separatist congregations, and to ensure a proper competence for a regular ministry.

IV

Church Officers: The 'Doctor'

In all these disputes nothing had been heard from the Scots Commissioners, and since they had graced the Assembly with their presence only once or twice,[101] we may assume that nothing yet had appeared on the Assembly's agenda that touched sensitive areas of their church government. However, as the divines prepared to debate 'Teachers' and 'Elders' in the Church, the Scots felt their church order to be vitally involved.

On Tuesday, November 14th, the day following the debate on the Rules governing appointments to sequestered livings, the Scots, through the Grand Committee,[102] submitted an extensive

---

[97] An integral part of the catholic church. *Ibid.* I, 360, (Ms. I., f. 184.)

[98] Lightfoot, *Journal*, pp. 49f.

[99] *Ibid.* p. 49.

[100] TMs. I. 361, (Ms. I., f. 184b.)

[101] On November 14th, after the Scots report had been received, Cornelius Burgess mentioned that the Scots had been "among us once and twice", *Ibid.* I. 367, (Ms. I., f. 187b,) and when Henderson made his first speech later in the next session (Nov. 15th), he said "We have not any of us spoken a word before"; *ibid.* 380, (Ms. I., f. 194.)

[102] This Committee had been ordered by the Houses of Parliament and the order sent to the Assembly on October 26th, 1643. The Committee which had treated with the Scots

paper setting out four essential points that they expected to be the basis of ministry in any new church settlement for England.[103] Lightfoot records that before the Assembly's committee report was debated, Stephen Marshall

> brought in a report from the committee of the Scots, and of the Houses, and of the Assembly, importing the desire of the Scots' Commissioners, which they had imparted to that committee, viz,
>
> 1. That they are very willing and ready to submit to the judgment of the Scriptures, yet they cannot but remember, how eminent and excellent testimonies have been given of the reformation in Scotland . . .
>
> 2. That there are these four permanent officers in the church; pastors, teachers, ruling elders, and deacon: this their church hath ever retained; and their teachers are readers in the universities; but wish some were added to catechize.
>
> 3. The church not to be governed by one man, nor by the multitude; but by pastors, teachers, and ruling-elders; nor hath one church authority over another.
>
> 4. Four sorts of assemblies among them, church sessions, or particular eldershires, classes of presbyters, provincial synods, national assemblies.
>
> The report being read, which was very long, Dr. *Burgess* moved, that Mr. *Marshal* would relate whether the committee had examined, by Scripture, that part of it which concerns church-officers.
>
> To which Mr. *Marshal* answered, that the committee had not debated them all, but had referred it to the Assembly.[104]

The English divines were not to be hurried, and the Scots paper had been received practically without comment. The members of the Assembly then turned to the subject brought in by their own First Committee regarding the office of Teacher.

The scriptural basis for the office of doctor or teacher was accepted without demur, but it was the second part of the

---

Commissioners was to join with a committee from the Assembly "to meet and treat with the Divines from Scotland, concerning a form of church government, directory of worship, confession of faith, and form of catechism." Lightfoot, *Journal*, p. 27. The Grand Committee became a permanent part of the administrative structure as liaison between the Scots, Parliament and the Assembly. Cf. *infra* pp. 243ff.

[103] *Ibid.* p. 51. The Minutes simply report that a paper was received from the Scots Commissioners, but provide no details. Cf. TMs. I. 362, 367, (Ms. I., ff. 185, 187b.) The Scots paper was presented because the Assembly was about to debate the proposition that the "scriptures hold forth the name of doctor and teacher, as well as of pastor."

[104] Lightfoot, *Journal*, pp. 50–51. The Minutes are not as full as we would wish at this point. They do not set down the details of the First Committee's report; cf. TMs. I. 362, (Ms. I., f. 185.)

proposal that sharpened the differences between the Independents and the majority. In this part of the proposition the committee had stated that "The doctor is not an ordinary and distinct office from a pastor, in every particular congregation,"[105] which was different from the Independents' having both a pastor and a doctor (or teacher) appointed to each congregation.[106]

The Independents were very much a minority, but they received support from a few other members of the Assembly on this occasion,[107] and there were those who appear to have been in a genuine quandary on the issue.[108] The debate lasted a week (Nov. 14th–21st) and seems to have maintained a high level of integrity,[109] although it is clear that there was a hard core of conservative opinion in the Assembly that was not prepared to see the Pastor and the Teacher as distinct offices.[110] We detect more than a slight note of sarcasm in one of Dr. Joshua Hoyle's replies to Thomas Goodwin. The Independent, in explanation of his position, had argued that we all have different gifts, some having a greater ability in influencing the understanding and

---

[105] Lightfoot, *Journal,* p. 51.

[106] For example, in 1632 William Ames left his chair at the University of Franeker to become the Teacher of the congregation in Rotterdam of which Hugh Peter had been the pastor. Apparently the possibility of founding a new school in that city had also been mooted. Cf. Keith L. Sprunger, *The Learned Doctor William Ames,* (Urbana, University of Illinois Press, 1972,) pp. 92, 199f. However this must have been a comparatively late development in Independent ecclesiology, for the office does not appear as a distinct office in Ames's *Marrow of Sacred Divinity* (1638); cf. *ibid.,* 1642 edn., chapters xxxiii and xxxiv. The Teacher does, however, appear as a distinct office in John Cotton's *The Way of the Churches of Christ in New-England* (London, 1645) pp. 10–13.

[107] Lightfoot shows us that in the debate on November 14th, Thomas Hodges, William Bridge and Thomas Goodwin denied Stephen Marshall's proposition that pastor and teacher were the same office. They were joined by George Walker, William Carter, Jr., Sidrach Simpson and later Phillips. Cf. Lightfoot, *Journal,* pp. 51f., TMs. I. 362–72, (Ms. I., ff. 185–195b.)

[108] Lazarus Seaman had wanted to know what the other committees had to report on this subject, and in later speech had complained "we may soon bring ourselves into a mist". TMs. I. 363, 364, (Ms. I., ff. 185b, 186.) John Ley also said "I feare we shall lap up all in cloudy conclusions", and hoped they were close to agreement. *Ibid.* 376, 368, (Ms. I., ff. 192, 188.) De la March informed them that in French practice, although "the pastor & doctor are for substance one & the same, yet by the pràctise of reformed churches we find them to be distinct officers & that one may doe what the other cannot". On the other hand, he went on to say that one man could do both, so his contribution was inconclusive. *Ibid.* 368f, (Ms. I., ff. 188 *et seq.*) Vines also seems to have been undecided.

[109] *Ibid.* 362–415, (Ms. I., ff. 185–122b,) Lightfoot, *Journal* pp. 51–60.

[110] In the first few days of debate the conservatives used the great weight of academic eminence they had within their ranks. At least six men who held the prestigious Doctor of Divinity degree took part on that side of the argument – Burgess, Hoyle, Gouge, Smith, Stanton, and later Temple. They were supported by Calamy, Marshall, White, Raynor, Gataker, Price and Hill. Herle also seems to have leaned to this position, and the majority was joined later by Palmer, Gibson and Bathurst. This does not exhaust the list of those who participated in the week's debate, but indicates the extent of participation during the first few days.

others in influencing the will and affections. Hoyle had immediately retorted that if we argued in that way we might appoint more officers in the church than God had provided – some to teach Old Testament, some the New Testament, and some because they had special qualities such as Barnabas's gift of consolation![111] Perhaps the epitome of the conservative position that Hoyle and his colleagues represented was offered by Henry Wilkinson, senior, when he suggested that the matter should be resolved by looking at their present practice – to which Richard Vines, who appears to have been undecided on this issue, said "I move that the disquisition may begin a priori & not looke a posteriori".[112]

On the whole the debate maintained a high level. Robert Baillie and Samuel Rutherford joined the Assembly as Commissioners for the Church of Scotland while it was at its height,[113] and in a letter to William Spang Baillie indicated his initial respect for the Independents as "men full, as it seems yet, of grace and modestie."[114] It was a tribute that he would eventually drastically revise, but it was his expressed opinion before the ecclesiological battles embittered his attitude.

We must remember that in this debate the Independents' position was not so very different from that of the Scots Presbyterians. The Scots really took a position midway between that of the Independents and those English divines who were trying to salvage something of traditional English church order. The Scottish proposals recognized a distinction between pastor and teacher, used the latter office for the theological teaching faculty in universities, and would have welcomed the addition of others to that office for catechizing. The complete identity of the pastoral and teaching offices with no distinction, which was argued by many of the Englishmen, might very well seem to the Scots to be too much like reversion to the earlier style of a single parish priest. On the other hand, Henderson and his colleagues were well aware that the Reformed Churches in Europe would be watching what was happening at Westminster, and they certainly did not want their system to be confused with Independency. The situation called for very careful management.

When Cornelius Burgess, acting as prolocutor, invited the Scots' contribution on November 14th, Henderson at first kept

---

[111] TMs. I. 365, (Ms. I., f. 186b.) Cf. Acts 4:36.

[112] *Ibid.* 369, (Ms. I., f. 188b.) Vines continued by saying that they should "begin at the word of God".

[113] They were received by the Assembly on November 20th; Lightfoot, *Journal*, p. 56.

[114] December 7th, 1643, *Letters and Journals*, II. 111.

his remarks to generalities, reminding the members of the goal of uniformity, warning them that the eyes of the world were upon them, and complimenting them on their deliberations.[115] A little later he said that in "the practice of [the] church of Scotland ther is not a difference betweene pastor & teacher, yet their doctrine seems to import another thing".[116] This was, of course, an extremely politic statement, which appeared to side with the majority at the practical level, even while admitting that the Church of Scotland's doctrine seemed different. He maintained this practical emphasis, because later he suggested that they should judge what was necessary in each church. This would be "better than to descend to metaphysicall questions about distinctions".[117] Several days and many speeches later he wondered "if ther could be any meanes to prevent further debate",[118] and before that day was finished (Nov. 20th), Henderson and his fellow-Commissioner, George Gillespie were pleading for agreement and accommodation between the different opinions.[119]

It is clear from Baillie's letters that the Scots Commissioners were extremely active behind the scenes. Baillie reported, "Mr. Hendersone travelled betwixt them, and drew on a committee for accommodation; in the whilk [i.e., which] we agreed unanimouslie upon some six propositions,[120] wherein", the Scotsman observed with some satisfaction, "the absolute necessitie of a Doctor in everie congregation, and his divine institution, in formall termes, was eschewed; yet where two Ministers can be had in one congregation, the one is allowed according to

---

[115] TMs. I. 380, (Ms. I., f. 194.)

[116] *Ibid.* 381, (Ms. I., f. 194b.)

[117] *Ibid.* 382, (Ms. I., f. 195.)

[118] *Ibid.* 409, (Ms. I., f. 208b.)

[119] *Ibid.* 411, (Ms. I., f. 209b.)

[120] The committee reported on November 21st, and brought in the following proposals regarding the pastor/teacher issue:

"1. That there be different gifts, and different exercises, according to the difference of those gifts in the ministers.

2. Those different gifts may be in and exercised by one and the same minister.

3. Where there be several ministers in the same congregation, they may be designed to several employments.

4. He that doth more excel in exposition, doctrine, and convincing them in application, and accordingly employed therein, may be called a teacher or doctor.

5. A teacher or doctor is of excellent use in schools or universities.

6. Where there is but one minister in a particular congregation, he is to perform, so far as he is able, the whole work of the ministry."

Lightfoot, *Journal*, p. 58.

his gift, to applie himself most to teacheing, and the other to exhortation, according to Scripture."[121]

The Scots Commissioners had good reason to feel satisfied, for in this first foray into the debate they had obtained all they wanted. Not only had they managed to steer the Assembly between the Scylla of Independency and the Charybdis of the old priesthood in a reformed guise, but the vote had decisively gone their way and must have seemed an excellent augury for the future.

V

Church Officers: the Ruling Elder

The major test was in the debate immediately to follow, on November 22nd. As the Assembly moved to discuss the issue of the 'Ruling Elder' it was touching upon something that the Scots regarded as integral to their system, although to most of the English except the Independents it was a novelty. The English divines were not prepared simply to accept Scottish assurances of its value.

Very early in the debate Alexander Henderson spoke on the subject. He said "it is noe marvell ther be some debate concerning the disputing of this question be[cause] it is more materiall than anything you have been about yet". There was relatively little to debate about in the office of pastors and teachers, but "this is a new poynt of reformation", and he admitted that the "B[isho]ps called it Genevating".[122] He then reminded the Assembly, in tones that were to become familiar to the members, of the good example and singular good fortune of the Church in Scotland: "that, however it [the office of ruling elder] be somewhat strange in England, yet it hath been in the reformed churches, even before Geneva, and that it had been very prosperous to the church of Scotland.[123]

---

[121] Baillie, *Letters and Journals*, II. 110.

[122] TMs. I, 418, (Ms. I., f. 213.), 22nd November, 1643.

[123] Lightfoot, *Journal*, p. 60. Before we dismiss Henderson's remarks as overly nationalistic, we should consider the interesting evidence that Richard Baxter came across regarding the value of ruling elders to the Scottish Church.

"The last Week I had with me an honest *Scotchman*, and one of my *Acton* Neighbours, and I asked him how their Nation came to be so unanimous in the approbation of Godliness without any Sect. And he told me that usually they had twelve Elders in a Parish, and every one took their Division and observed the manners of the People, and if any Family prayed not, &c. They admonished them, and told the Pastor; and that the Pastor then went to them (though many Miles off) and taught them to Pray, and led them

163

The visitors from Scotland expected a tough debate, and in that they were not disappointed.[124] Baillie admitted that they expected no more difficult struggle on almost any other subject,[125] and because they were prepared for the opposition most of the Scottish divines took a prominent part in the dispute: Henderson, Rutherford and Gillespie entered the fray with a will. Baillie, still a relative novice to the proceedings, was obviously impressed with the display of erudition and debating skills.[126]

After his account of the way in which the pastor/teacher issue had been resolved he continued:

> The next poynt, whereon yet we stick, is reuling Elders. Many a verie brave dispute have we had upon them these ten dayes. I professe my marvelling at the great learning, quickness, and eloquence, together with the great courtesie and discretion in speaking, of these men. Sundrie of the ablest were flat against institution of any such officer by divine right, such as Dr. Smith, Dr. Temple, Mr. Gataker, Mr. Vines, Mr. Price, Mr. Hall, and manie moe, *beside the Independents, who trulie spake much and exceedinglie well.* The most of the synod was in our opinion, and reasoned bravelie for it; such as Mr. Seaman, Mr. Walker, Mr. Marshall, Mr. Newcomen, Mr. Young, Mr. Calamy. Sundrie times Mr. Hendersone, Mr. Rutherford, Mr. Gillespie, all three, spoke exceeding well. When all were tired, it came to the question. There was no doubt but we would have carried it by far most voices; yet because the opposites were men verie considerable, above all gracious and learned little Palmer, we agreed upon a committee to satisfie, if it were possible, the dissenters. For this end we meet today; and I hope, ere all be done, we shall agree. All of them were ever willing to admit Elders in a prudentiall way; but this to us seemed a most

---

in it, and set them upon other means as we teach Children to read: And that once a Week they had a meeting of the Elders, to consult about the good of the Parish . . . This, and more, the *Scotchman* averred to me." *Rel. Baxt.* III. 67 (§143). It is clear from this evidence that the eldership became an essential part of the Scottish church discipline, and it is also clear that it was regarded by the Scots as one of a major reasons for the unity of the Church of Scotland in the seventeenth century.

[124] It lasted from November 22nd to December 14th without being finally resolved. Cf. TMs. I. 416–540, (Ms. I., ff. 212–274b,) Lightfoot, *Journal*, pp. 60–83.

[125] To William Spang, 7th December, 1643, *Letters and Journals* II. 110f. The passage is quoted below.

[126] Baillie later admitted that he never addressed the Assembly cf. Letter to Spang, 26th January 1646/7, *Letters and Journals*, III, 3. Once, he says, he spoke against "Goodwin's new notions"; but this seems to have been in a sub-committee of the Assembly that was deputed to meet with the Scots for the preparation of the Directory of Worship. At this time worship had not been considered by the Assembly in plenary. Cf. Letters to Scotland, n.d. and 1st January, 1643/4, *ibid.* II. 117, 123.

dangerous and unhappie way, and therefore was peremptorlie rejected.[127] We trust to carie at last with the contentment of sundrie once opposite, and silence of all, their [*i.e.* ruling Elders'] divyne and scripturall institution. This is a poynt of high consequence; and upon no other we expect so great difficultie, except alone on Independencie; wherewith we purpose not to medle in haste, till it please God to advance our armie, which we expect will much assist our arguments.[128]

Whether it was his own distrust of Independency or simply a rare but unfortunate ambiguity in his writing, the passage above could be read as if the Independents were to be numbered among those who denied the scriptural institution of ruling elders.[129] That was not the case. The proponents for the Ruling Elder as a distinct form of the eldership were the Scottish Commissioners, together with several whom we can already recognize as English Presbyterians,[130] *and* the Independents.[131] These were ranged against the rest of the English divines, the Puritan 'conservatives'. Baillie, in the letter we have just quoted, was firmly convinced that if the matter had been pushed to a vote, the Scots and their allies would have carried the day, and possibly he was right, but it would have been an extremely close vote, and would

---

[127] The Scottish Commissioners had been invited to become regular members of the Assembly, but had declined, preferring to maintain their independent status as accredited envoys of their own nation and church. They were therefore in a position of power in being able to determine what would be acceptable terms in fulfilling the Solemn League and Covenant. *Letters and Journals*, II. 110.

[128] *Ibid.* 110–111. Despite the ominous sound of Baillie's last sentence, he meant no more than that he and his colleagues were more likely to get their way in the Assembly once the Scottish army had given some evidence that it meant business. For the significance of the sentence in asterisks, *. . .*, see the following footnote.

[129] The evidence of Lightfoot and of the Minutes is that the Independents sided with the Scots on the Ruling Elder. A. F. Mitchell said that somehow Baillie's punctuation went awry. Commenting on the sentence that follows the words "and many moe", he wrote, "Then follows a clause which I can reconcile with the facts of the case as disclosed in the MS. minutes of the Assembly only by taking it away from the sentence going before and prefixing it with the sentence which follows. 'Besides the Independents, who truly spake much and exceedingly well, the most of the Synod were in our opinion . . .' " Mitchell, *The. Westminster Assembly*, p. 187. This is also DeWitt's view; *Jus Divinum*, pp. 81f.

[130] Particularly the 'Smectymnuans'. Cf. *supra*, pp 119f.

[131] Ruling Elders belonged to Independent ecclesiology. This is explicitly stated in *An Apologeticall Narration*: "For *officers* and publique Rulers in the Church, we set up no other but the very same which the reformed Churches judge necessary and sufficient, and as instituted by Christ and his Apostles for the perpetuall government of his Church, that is, *Pastors, Teachers, Ruling Elders*, (with us not lay but Ecclesiastique persons) and *Deacons.*" *Op. cit.* p. 8, see also John Cotton, *The Way of the Churches of Christ in New England*, pp. 13–38.

have destroyed the possibility of maintaining Puritan unanimity.[132]

The signals for battle had been out early. The proposition was
"That besides those presbyters that rule well, and labour in word
and doctrine, there be other presbyters who especially apply
themselves to ruling, though they labour not in the word and
doctrine",[133] and Lightfoot tells us that when Dr. Stanton,
chairman of the Second Committee, "gave the committee's
mind . . . this helped us forward never a whit".[134] That is understandable, because from the Minutes we learn that Stanton stated
that "it was not the mind of the committee to stampe Jus divinum
upon the ruling presbiter".[135] Very soon after this Alexander
Henderson judged it necessary to enter the debate, which
centred on the proof text, I Tim. 5:17 and then indeed on all the
possible texts that could be brought to support that proposition.

One of the intriguing possibilities, that deserves to be explored
in the light of recent Puritan research although it is somewhat
peripheral to our own major concern, would be to examine how
far Puritan ecclesiology – particularly this division of the Eldership into Preaching and Ruling elders – may be traced to the
system of logic, to the dichotomies and divisions developed by
Peter Ramus.[136] It has been shown that a sermon attributed to

---

[132] It is difficult from the Minutes to say with precision where every speaker stood on
many issues, because some took part in the debates infrequently, and on the few
occasions when they did participate their speeches were either omitted or recorded in a
very incomplete way.

In the debate under discussion, however, we can identify the following men as
speaking in favour of ruling elders: the Scottish Commissioners – Henderson, Ruther-
ford and Gillespie; the Independents – Carter, Bridge, Goodwin, Nye, Simpson,
Burroughes, and Phillips; and of the English Puritans – Herle, Seaman, Calamy,
Walker, Thomas Bayly, Young, Marshall. On the other side of the argument we can
identify Palmer, Smith, Ley, Hoyle, Gataker, Vines, Temple, Hall, Wilkinson (sen.),
Thomas Carter, (Cf. Lightfoot, *Journal*, p. 64,) and also the Erastians – Lightfoot,
Coleman and Selden.

Burgess, Gower, Bathurst and later, Gataker were willing to accept ruling elders as a
'prudential' decision for the church, while Price (and possibly Arrowsmith and Wincop)
appear to have been undecided. It is also difficult to determine where Newcomen stood
on the matter, although as a 'Smectymnuan', we would presume that he was in favour;
Woodcock spoke against setting up the office in a 'prudential' way.

[133] Lightfoot, *Journal*, p. 60.

[134] *Ibid.*

[135] TMs. I. 417 (Ms. f. 212b.)

[136] A considerable amount of research has taken place on the influence of Peter Ramus
(Pierre de la Ramée, 1515–1572), the French Protestant philosopher who attacked the
Aristotelian philosophy of the earlier scholastics. Cf. Walter J. Ong, *Ramus: Method, and
the Decay of Dialogue*, (Cambridge, Mass. 1950,). For the influence of Ramism upon
Puritanism, cf. Perry Miller, *The New England Mind: the 17th Century*, especially
Appendix A, pp. 493ff.; Keith L. Sprunger, *The Learned Doctor William Ames*, and John

Laurence Chaderton, 'the pope of Cambridge Puritanism'[137], had maintained that Romans 12:3–8 established a divine law regarding church government that was perpetual; for St. Paul had declared that he gave this generall law, "in the name of him whose Apostle I am, inuiolably and perpetually to be kept, euen to the comming of Christ."[138] This sermon had been published with a full apparatus of Ramist divisions,[139] and one suspects that in 1643 those who had arrived at the more doctrinaire positions in Puritan ecclesiology, may have reached their distinctions between the different kinds of presbyters – pastor and doctor, teaching elder and ruling elder – in much the same way.

It is an intriguing thought that would be worth careful study, but at this juncture we are more concerned with the attitudes developing in the Assembly, particularly what the debate tells us about the conservative Puritan majority: were these men already committed to a fully Presbyterian ecclesiology in view of the persistent opposition many of them gave to the office of ruling elder? It is questionable. In contrast, the Independents were firmly committed to that office. For example, compare Thomas Goodwin's comments on November 27th, when the debate turned to the consideration of Romans 12:8:[140]

> I desire to confirme that ther is diversity for that of
> proestamenos [i.e. προϊστάμενος = one who rules]
> ther are some parts of ruling, the elder is especially to take care of
> it but he is to doe it with diligence[:] this is the proper
> & peculiar businesse he is allotted too[.]

Herbert Palmer protested that since 'diligence' would apply much more to the pastor "it will not note a perticular office", and Goodwin responded:

> the pastor is not to make it his worke to
> watch over the lives of men[;]
> as the levites ware a gift given to the priests soe
> are they [i.e. ruling elders] to relieve the pastor in this
> service . . .[141]

Dykstra Eusden in the introduction to his edition of Ames's *Medulla Theologica, the Marrow of Theology*, (Boston, Pilgrim Press, 1968) pp. 37–44, etc.

[137] Patrick Collinson, *The Elizabethan Puritan Movement*, 125; cf. also p. 274.

[138] *A fruitfull sermon, upon the 3.4.5.6.7. & 8. verses of the 12 Chapter of the Epistle of S. Paule to the Romanes*, (London, 1586,) p.3; (attributed to Laurence Chaderton.)

[139] I am grateful to Donald K. McKim for drawing attention to Chaderton's sermon. Cf. Donald K. McKim, 'Ramism in William Perkins,' (Unpublished Ph.D. dissertation of the University of Pittsburgh, 1980,) pp. 120, 447.

[140] This verse was from the same passage on which Chaderton had developed his own Reformed ecclesiology in the sermon cited above. Chaderton had classified the Elder with Deacons and 'Attenders on the Poor'; cf. *ibid.* p. 447.

[141] TMs. I. 446, (Ms. I., f. 227.)

He argued that the apostles could not rule with diligence if they were to give their primary attention to exhortation.

Support for the ruling elder was illustrated in speeches by other Independents and the Scottish Commissioners. It was also during this debate that we see the significance of Thomas Bayly's recent conversion to the presbyterian position. On November 30th Henderson had reminded the members that "for reformed churches we should be sparing in speaking too much of that that is received by [other?] reformed churches", and chided them that "since ther is nothing but anarchy in the church of England [I wish] for the present that you would proceed".[142] Then Thomas Bayly said:

I doe not stand up to answer my brother that
first spake but to concurre with him that last spake[.]
when I was young I read Bp. Bilsons booke of government[143]
& I read with great delight & satisfac-
tion for the time & glad to see the discipline by
AB & B soe strongly confirmed & in this opinion I continued to the last year[.]

after my conversation with a gentlewoman some time since
I said I could not see what warrent for this discipline[;]
'she said' strange that you should not see that wch soe many
reformed churches [see clearly.]

As a result of this chance remark, Bayly began a further study and found "the geneva discipline[,] as odiously called[,] most agreeable to the scriptures." He noted that "all the reformed churches are against us in this", and "the[y] will suspect either our heads or our hearts".[144] Samuel Rutherford followed with a warning against any attempt to introduce the elder simply as a 'prudential' measure on the basis of church law:

if it comes to the ears of them that those officers are
made only an ecclesiasticall constitution this
will be a very great preiudice in the hearts of the
reformed churches [for]
then it will follow that in this large ennumeration [of officers]
ther is but one of them a pastor that is of divine
institution. . . ."[145]

---

[142] TMs. I. 453, (Ms. I., f. 230b.) Cf. Lightfoot, *Journal*, pp. 60f.

[143] Presumably Bayly's reference is to Bilson's *The Perpetual Government of Christes Church*, or to *A Compendius Discourse Proving Episcopacy To Be of Divine Institution*, both of which appeared in 1593.

[144] TMs. I. 454–5 (Ms. I. ff. 231, 231b.)

[145] *Ibid.* 455, (Ms. I., f. 231b.) Calvin would probably have had no difficulty in accepting such an office for prudential reasons. In the doctrine of the Church he set down

Bayly's words indicated how he had been impressed by the general agreement of the Reformed churches abroad about the government of the Church, and how this had contributed to his own conversion to the presbyterian position. This belief in a tacit consensus of the Reformed was likely to influence other conservatives as the work continued. Meanwhile, there were still many in the Assembly who had not yet reached Thomas Bayly's new position. When we look at those who were either uncommitted or opposed to the ruling elder, we find every position from that of William Price who declared "I come with a free breast, I am neither for nor against them",[146] to old Henry Wilkinson who remained sceptical even at the very end of the debate. Wilkinson questioned "whether those scriptures doe make to the purpose for wch [they are] alleadged", and he added the tart comment that "when Mr. Calvin did erect the presbiters an[d] discipline in Geneva[,] noe scripture that could be aleadged but he had it, & the helpe of the chiefest divines in christendome as Philip Melanchthon, Bucer, etc." However, perhaps Wilkinson's real fear was a threat to the clergy's status, for he observed, "I have informed myselfe concerning those churches in which the discipline is exercised [-] in some of them 12 lay elders & but one minister & he hath but a single voyce"[!] He wanted to go along with the rest of the brethren, but he was

doubtful till resolved on one or two things[:-]
1. [It was] not lawfull to acte that wch will be a preiudice to the patrimony of the church[.]
2. [They should] consider whether we shall have not necessarily to know how we shall be maintained[.]

At which point, Wilkinson was apparently called to order![147]

The opposition included some of the most respected names among the conservatives whom the Scots were extremely anxious to win over. A common attitude among English Puritans in their

---

in the *Institutes* (IV. iii.) he certainly regarded the ministry as of divine institution, but this was particularly centred in pastors and teachers, offices which, he said, the church could never be without. (Cf. *Institutio Christianae Religionis* (1559) IV. iii. 4.) It is not clear how far he regarded ruling elders as of divine institution. He made a distinction between teaching and ruling elders, and associated the latter in a consistory with pastors for matters of discipline (IV. xi. 6), but it was an office he did not stress in the *Institutes*. He did, however, insist that everything in the church should be done 'decently and in order', which sounds very much like 'prudential reasons'. (Cf. IV. iii. 10 and x. 27–32.)

[146] TMs. I. 419, (Ms. I., f. 213b.)

[147] On December 14th, 1643; *Ibid.* 530, (Ms. I. f. 269b.) Throughout these debates there were those who were worried that this would mean adding another paid officer to each parish, and who were doubtful where the money could be found. Cf. Lightfoot, *Journal*, p. 69. (Dec. 4th.)

opposition to diocesan episcopacy had been to emphasize one essential kind of ministry in the church – pastor, bishop, presbyter all meant essentially the same office, the shepherd of a single congregation, in whom the church's discipline was vested. Thomas Gataker illustrated the position early in this debate.[148] He observed:

> it is well knowne that in the apostels language
> episcopus & presbiter are one & the same . . .
> If therefore ther cannot elsewher be showed an
> Institution of 2 such severall offices it will
> be hard to suppose the apot: doth speake of
> 2 such offices of whose institution we can find
> noe mention[.][149]

Similarly, on November 27th, while they were still occupied with this passage, Herbert Palmer asked "by what argument this may be a distinct officer from a pastor[,] since it is acknowledged by the assembly that the pastor hath a share in ruling";[150] and although by December 5th he was ready to admit the possibility of the ruling elder in apostolic times, he was not willing to accept it as a perpetual office in the church.[151] Henry Hall of Norwich also voiced doubts and the possible encroachment on the pastoral authority:

> If ther be such an officer I desire some grounds of
> scripture laying out the bounds of his calling wher he
> must stop & beyond wch he must not goe[:]
> I doe not know how to give an account of the worke
> that must be cut out for this ruling presbiter . . .
> it is unequall that a man that is but a ruler only should
> have equall [status] to him that is both[.]
> I am inclinable to believe that ther hath been 2 sorts
> of presbiters de facto in the church but then they
> have been both preaching presbiters[.][152]

Reflection on the meaning of Hall's final sentence should have

---

[148] The debate was on I Timothy 5:17: "Let the elders that rule be counted worthy of double honour, especially they who labour in the word and doctrine." The debate had begun on 22nd November and Gataker made this speech on the 23rd.

[149] *Ibid.* I. 424f., (Ms. I., ff. 216–216b.)

[150] *Ibid.* 445, (Ms. I., ff. 226b.)

[151] "if the meaning of this committee be that ther ware such officers in the apostells times it will be granted, but if to be perpetuall it will admitt of debate". TMs. I. 475, (Ms. I., f. 214b.)

[152] On November 27th, *Ibid.* 441, (Ms. I., f., 224b.)

given some pause, because there were still those in the Church of England to whom this would have suggested preaching elders and presiding preaching elders, i.e., bishops.

During the debates on those church officers which the conservatives thought had been brought in as novelties by the Genevan ecclesiology, we detect a growing insistence on clear biblical evidence. Even the lay members of Parliament who attended during the closing sessions of this debate protested at what they felt was over-reliance on Old Testament parallels for 'proving' the necessity of ruling elders in the Church,[153] and men like Dr. Thomas Wincop called for "cleare evident & convincing proofes."[154] Richard Vines, on November 23rd wanted to know "wher is the institution found & the name of the office"[155] in the text that was being discussed, and a few days later declared, "I desire to see my light in the text and begin with that."[156] Dr. Temple held that at least one of Goodwin's arguments was "against the cleare letter of the text".[157] Answering Thomas Young on another occasion, he stated bluntly, "the thing that stickes with me is that I doe not conceive any cleare place to ground this institution upon", and continued, "having search[ed] the scripture I doe not find anything in matter of fact related of them as in [the matter of] excommunication [or] in the councils in acts"; where was there in scripture such a description?[158]

By the time the debate had dragged into December, there were some who were prepared to accept ruling elders on 'prudential' grounds,[159] but on December 7th, 'gracious and learned little Palmer' pointed out that where the scriptures are obscure, our conclusions are only "very sparingly to be imposed on men's consciences";[160] and he gave as one reason why he questioned the

---

[153] Sir Benjamin Rudyard on Dec. 13th thought it "strange that we should seeke for officers of the church in the new Testament out of the ould", while Lord Say, the Independent peer, was obviously troubled by this and said "it ware much better to find out those places that establish a ground for this ruling elder in the new testament wher this constitution was." (14th Dec.) *Ibid.* 527, 536, (Ms. I., ff. 268, 272b.)

[154] *Ibid.* 499, (Ms. I., f. 254.) Cf. also the retort made by William Price on Nov. 23rd after a speech by Rutherford, that they should "adhere to this text in the Interpretation [given] yesterday"; *ibid.* 427, (Ms. I., f. 217b.)

[155] *Ibid.* 428, (Ms. I., 218.)

[156] *Ibid.* 438, (Ms. I., 223.)

[157] *Ibid.* 445, (Ms. I., f. 226b.)

[158] *Ibid.* 464, (Ms. I., f. 236.)

[159] Gataker, Bathurst, Gower, Coleman all expressed their preference for the 'prudential way' which has earlier been suggested by Cornelius Burgess. Cf. *ibid.* pp. 438, 471, 486, 489, 529, (Ms. I., ff. 223, 239b, 247, 249, 269.)

[160] Lightfoot, *Journal*, p. 75.

two forms of eldership that were being put forward, that "if 2 sorts of rulers then 2 sorts of Bishops".[161]

At this point Thomas Goodwin made a very important speech urging that some attempt should be made to reach 'accommodation' to bring the opposing views closer together. His own view was that the officers were of divine Institution, but they should defer a vote on the matter until they had first considered the matter of discipline,[162] Palmer asked the Assembly very pointedly what it would gain by forcing through a vote, for "the thing you seeke for is truth, if it be truth every one will hold the same".[163] Then Alexander Henderson seems to have moved that the proposition should be remanded to the committee to review the extent of their agreement, but not before he had expressed amazement that the Assembly could spend so much time on this single point and "make noe progresse at all". He urged the members "not to stay soe long when Haniball is ad portas", for when they had a properly constituted Church, it was then "that things might be debated at lardge . . ."[164]

There were still several days of debate. The discussion provided the chief item on the Assembly's agenda from November 22nd to December 14th, and even then it was not resolved but "laid by for the present",[165] presumably with the intention of reviving it in connection with some other aspect of church government. The rest of the year 1643 was taken up with the scriptural foundation for other offices in the Church – deacons and widows. Although the debates on these offices[166] did not hold as much latent dynamite as those which had preceded or as those which were to follow, it is interesting to notice that the Independents argued strongly for including the office of 'widows' under the general office of the deacon, that is, as what in a later time would be called 'deaconesses.' The suggestion had been first put forward by John Gibbon, who "would prove out of Phil. i. 1., Rom. Xii. 8, that widows are comprehended under the deacon's title",[167] but he was strongly supported by the

---

[161] TMs. I. 495, (Ms. I., f. 252.) Cf. Lightfoot, *Journal*, p. 75.

[162] *Ibid.* (Ms. f. 252.)

[163] *Ibid.*

[164] *Ibid.* 296, (Ms. I., f. 252b.) Henderson's frustration may be understandable, but his argument contained a basic contradiction, for the reason why so much time was being spent in the debates was precisely to ensure that England would have a properly constituted church.

[165] Lightfoot, *Journal*, p. 83.

[166] December 15th to January 1st, 1643/4.

[167] December 29th, 1643; *ibid.* p. 94. Note that from December 10–February 15th 1643/4 the Minutes are missing.

Independents, Bridge, Simpson and Goodwin.[168] They did not carry their point.[169]

Undoubtedly, some differences had developed during these last months of 1643 between the Independents and the conservative majority in the Assembly, but it is clear that the major theological issues discussed to date did not involve division between Independency and Scottish Presbyterianism, but between those who believed that there was a clear scriptural warrent for Reformed church order, and those who were either willing to accept it, in Baillie's phrase 'in a prudential way', or who were still more than half persuaded that the scriptures justified something different. The Erastians, of course, would be prepared to go along with almost any church order as long as there was no attempt to establish it on *jus divinum*, but the major opponents to the ruling elder suggest that behind the opposition there was English suspicion of a system that was regarded as foreign, a reluctance to concede 'divine right' to any orders regarded as distinctively 'Genevan', and even perhaps a covert desire to leave the way open for a reformed model of Church and Ministry closer to the traditional English forms. The issue for this group in the Assembly was very bluntly stated on December 6th when old Mr. Wilkinson, that exemplar of English Puritan conservatism,[170] asked that "if the place alleaged hold out so clear a ground for a ruling elder, how comes it to pass that it was never seen before Calvin"? and he went on to claim that when Calvin returned to Geneva after his temporary exile, he enlisted the help of four Swiss churches that did not have that church order.[171]

The real issue at this time was between biblical restorationists, Independent or Presbyterian, and the rest of the Assembly; and to discover how this conservative majority eventually closed

---

[168] *Ibid.* pp. 94–8.

[169] January 1st, 1643/4.

[170] Henry Wilkinson, senior, consistently represented the more conservative English view of Church and Ministry. For example, on Nov. 8th, 1643, Thomas Coleman shocked the members by asserting that "Scripture doth not seem to ascribe any particular action to the pastor in the administration of the Lord's Supper", and we read, "Old Mr. *Wilkinson*, senior, did very roundly answer, that he did never hear from the learned such a question, as whether the pastor hath to do more in the sacrament than others." And Wilkinson seems to have had considerable support, for the account continues, "And the rest of the Assembly cried the thing down, as not worthy to be answered." *Ibid.* p. 44; TMs. I. 326–7, (Ms. I., ff. 165, 165b.)

[171] Lightfoot, *Journal*, p. 44. The Minutes are obviously incomplete on this debate, for they do not mention Wilkinson's contribution, although Lightfoot's account of it parallels what Wilkinson said later on Dec. 14th; cf. TMs. I. 530, (Ms. I., f. 269b.)

ranks with the Scots against the Independents, we must perhaps turn away from the theology that was being discussed in the debates to the other things which were exercizing the minds of the men at Westminster and which surfaced during their deliberations.

CHAPTER 6

'IN THE MIDST OF THESE DEBATES'

Lightfoot often introduced a phrase like the title given to this chapter when he wished to tell us about some irritant that entered the Assembly's steady diet of theological eloquence. Several irritants appeared during the period covered by the debate on the Officers of the Church. Indeed, it is remarkable that the members of the Assembly were able to accomplish as much work as they did, for during the three months following the arrival of the Scots Commissioners they had been constantly required to make decisions on practical matters of administration, they had been subject to all sorts of orders and communications from Parliament, and they listened to a sermon by a probationer almost every morning.

The administrative chores included such matters as drawing up rules for the future examination of ministers;[1] but beyond this they had been asked to consider steps to provide for students prevented from continuing studies in Oxford,[2] answer a point of conscience for a minister in Hamburg,[3] draft a letter to be sent to churches in Europe,[4] investigate a schism in the French Church in London,[5] and take a collection for their porter and doorkeepers.[6] Of course, this last item could hardly be called a 'Christmas box' in those Puritan times, but it was very conveniently voted on December 22nd.

But these things were incidental. During the same period

---

[1] October 26th, November 8th, 10th–13th, 1643; cf. Lightfoot, *Journal,* pp. 29, 43, 47–50; TMs. 1. 250, 326, 345–361, (Ms. I., ff. 126, 167, 176b–184b.)

[2] November 20th, 23rd; Lightfoot, *Journal,* pp. 57, 61; TMs. I. 402, 424, (Ms. I., ff. 205, 216.)

[3] Lightfoot, *Journal,* p. 77 (Dec. 11th.)

[4] November 22nd; *ibid.* p. 61, cf. TMs. I. 422, (Ms. I., f. 215.) The letter is in Rushworth, *Historical Collections,* VI, 371–76.

[5] Lightfoot, *Journal,* pp. 89, 93 (Dec. 22nd, 29th.)

[6] *Ibid.* p. 89. Thomas Carter had first proposed this on the 15th, but nothing had been done; *ibid.* p. 84.

other matters intruded that had a more direct bearing on the relationship between the Independents and the other members of the Assembly, for they were issues that touched directly on the Assembly's commitment to an established national Church, to its fear of the sects and its suspicion that Independency was sabotaging any hope of uniformity in religion. The primary concern of the Puritan majority was the disintegration of orthodox religion in London and in the parts of the country under parliamentary control. This was brought to a focus by three issues in which the Independents seemed to be cast in the role of villains – the problem of Antinomianism, the increase of 'gathered churches' outside the parochial system, and irregular 'ordination.'

I

The Problem of Antinomianism

Antinomianism is a term used in Christian theology to describe the view that the gift of grace by faith frees the true believer from any obligation to the moral law.[7] This had been expressly countered by John Calvin in the *Institutes* where he deals with the relationship between Law and Grace, and in which he emphasizes the necessity for the Law.[8] Antinomianism was therefore anathema to orthodox Calvinists, and all the members of the Assembly professed to be orthodox Calvinists.

Antinomianism had begun to surface after the outbreak of war. It seems to have been given some theological credibility in the Reformation period by John Agricola (1494–1566) in 1536, and his doctrines were introduced into England by Tobias Crisp (1600–43).[9] They were carried further in sects like the Libertines, Ranters, Adamists and varieties of the Familists,[10] which showed that the doctrine of free grace could too easily become the excuse for licence. Baxter gave ample testimony to the spread of Antinomian opinions after the battle of Edgehill among the soldiers of the Puritan army.[11] The Independent leaders in the

---

[7] Anti+nomos (law). Antinomianism arises from an overemphasis upon those passages in Paul's writings where he seems to disparage the Law of Moses in favour of faith and the grace received in the gospel. Parts of *Romans* could be interpreted in an Antinomian way (e.g. 2:17–4:25), but not if the epistle is read as a whole (cf. chapter 6.)

[8] *Institutes* II, and particularly chapters vii and viii.

[9] Cf. C. E. Whiting, *Studies in Puritanism from the Restoration to the Revolution, 1660–1688*, London, S.P.C.K., 1931,) pp. 267ff.

[10] *Ibid.* 270, 272ff.; cf. *Rel. Baxterianae* I. 76 (§122).

[11] Rel. Baxt. I. 46, 50f., 53 (§§66, 73, 77). The reference to Baxter given by C. E. Whiting, (*Studies in Puritanism*, p. 268, no. 1.) is incorrect.

Assembly were strict if not rigid Calvinists, but there were other ministers on the radical wing of Independency whose emphasis on free grace pushed them towards Antinomianism – men such as William Dell, John Saltmarsh and Walter Cradock, who became important and influential chaplains among Cromwell's troopers.[12] It is also worth noting that Sir Henry Vane, the leader of the Independent party in the House of Commons had leanings in that direction, and that he had sided with that faction against the more orthodox views of John Winthrop and John Cotton during his brief governorship of the Massachusetts Bay colony.[13] With the death of John Pym on December 8th, Vane was to become the most important statesman at Westminster.

This much is background, but the divines in the Assembly were orthodox Calvinists who feared the sects and detested Antinomianism. They were also firmly convinced that as ministers of the national Church they had a God-given right and responsibility to stamp out all that could be regarded as heresy according to their own standards of orthodoxy. On August 10th, 1643, we find them warning Parliament of its growth in a petition,[14] and although the members of Parliament had enough on their mind with the conduct of the war, on September 12th they ordered

> that it be referred to the Assembly of Divines to compare the Opinions of the *Antinomians* with the Word of God, and with the Articles of the Church of *England*; and to return their Opinions and Judgments upon them speedily. It is further *Ordered*, that the *Antinomian* Books be referred to the Examination and Consideration of the Assembly.[15]

This was followed on the 20th by a speech in the Assembly by

---

[12] *Rel. Baxt.* I. 56 (§81). For these men see also Geoffrey F. Nuttall, *The Holy Spirit in Puritan Faith and Experience*, (Oxford, Basil Blackwell, 1947.)

[13] Young Henry Vane, at the age of twenty-two, had spent two years in New England. He arrived at the same time as the Rev. Hugh Peter in 1635, and they found the young colony of Massachusetts Bay in considerable turmoil. Roger Williams was causing problems for the leaders of the theocracy, and Vane and Peter tried to mediate between the magistrates and some of the dissidents. In 1636, despite his youth, but largely because of his social prestige, Vane unseated the Governor, John Winthrop, and became Governor in his stead, but he failed to be re-elected the following year. This was probably because he sided with Anne Hutchinson in the 'Antinomianan' dispute with the clergy of the colony, and he returned to England in the autumn of that year. It will be seen that religious toleration had been a very live issue in the colony during Vane's time in Massachusetts, and that he had taken a definite position on that matter. Cf. John Winthrop's *Journal 'History of New England'* I. 61f., 69, 180–215, 229; James K. Hosmer, *The Life of the Young Sir Henry Vane*, (Boston, Houghton, Mifflin & Co. 1888,) pp. 32–82, V. A. Row, *Sir Henry Vane the Younger* (London, Athlone Press, 1970.)

[14] Rushworth, *Historical Collections* VI. 376.

[15] *C. J.* III. 237.

Dr. Temple that expressed the antipathy the members felt towards Antinomianism,[16] and two days later a report was read to the Assembly of arguments against the error. That caused John Selden, the jurist and Semitics scholar, to question what constituted heresy in English law.

However, the most important speech for our purpose was that of the Independent, Thomas Goodwin, who declared, "I say I hate them as much as any", but he thought the members ought to consider whether they went beyond their mandate in trying to get these people punished, and he continued:

> persons should first be dealt with soe as to be convinced,
> all wayes [are to be] taken to this end if you can[.]
> magistrates are to deale with persons in matters ecclesiastical
> as a church [deals] in spirituall [matters], if you had power of
> excom[munication] you would first convince then admonish them
> & then I think you should deale with them.[17]

We get a hint in this of the peculiar embarrassment that the Antinomians might become for orthodox Independents. As Calvinists Goodwin and his colleagues abhorred Antinomian opinions, but in strict obedience to the scriptural rule in matters of church discipline, they also believed that the biblical way of dealing with mistaken beliefs was by spiritual persuasion.[18]

The majority was suspicious of the Independents, and this suspicion is seen in charges that were levelled against some of the Independents in the Assembly. On October 9th Herbert Palmer charged Sidrach Simpson with having encouraged the Antinomians and of holding the opinion that we need not confess our sins,[19] and on the following day Simpson produced the copy of a paper that had been put out against him.[20] At the same time Peter Sterry got into trouble with the Assembly for a speech that he made.[21] He was asked to explain himself, and Dr. Temple commented that "much of this discourse intrenches upon those opinions now abroad in the city." The Prolocutor, Dr. William

---

[16] TMs. I. 142, (Ms. I., f. 71b.)

[17] Ibid. 147, (Ms. I., f. 75b.) Cf. Matthew 18:15–22.

[18] For dealing with error, Jeremiah Burroughes said that two things were premised in Congregational ecclesiology: "First, that the onely way the Church hath to keep downe errors or heresiés is spirituall; as for other means they are extrinsecall to the church . . . as for subjection to the Magistrate if he pleases to interpose, to that both they and we must yeeld. Secondly, the vertue of spiritual power works not upon the outward man, but by its prevailing upon conscience . . ." Irenicum, p. 42.

[19] TMs. I. 178, (Ms. I., f. 90.) Lightfoot did not give any account of these incidents.

[20] Ibid. 188, (Ms. I., f. 95.)

[21] October 9th, ibid. 185f., (Ms. I., ff. 93b, et seq.) For more on Peter Sterry see supra p. 84, 125, and Rel. Baxt. I. 75 (§119).

Twisse, seems to have found Sterry's remarks strange, but "only in the close confounding of Justification and Sanctification."[22]

This may have been the opening for which some of the Assembly had been looking and strong action was taken. On the 10th October, Palmer, Burgess, Gataker and Temple, four of the most prominent leaders among the Assembly's conservative majority were appointed a committee to communicate to the House of Commons the Assembly's concern, and to urge that the House should speed up its action against the Antinomians. They were given immediate permission to retire to do this,[23] and we read in the *Journal of the House of Commons* that they were received and their petition and paper read. A committee of the House of Commons was at once appointed:

> This Committee is to consider of the Business concerning the *Antinomians;* and the Paper and Petition presented from the Assembly: And is to take care to hinder those of the *Antinomian* Opinion from preaching: And are to meet this Afternoon, at Three a Clock, in the Star Chamber . . .[24]

The Assembly's representatives reported back the same day, and, as we might expect, the Independent divines wanted the matter to be treated as gently as possible. William Bridge urged the members "to be tender in this", and Thomas Goodwin, although he protested "I am as sensible of the danger as any man", urged the Assembly to be careful of two things – first, that the opinions were put down in a way that was just, and secondly, that the people involved "should be dealt withall to convince them." At that, Gataker then very pointedly asked, "if the opinions be of themselves soe odious[,] is it not high time to require them to be suppressed[?]"[25] There can be little doubt that the majority in the Assembly thought that Independency was harbouring very questionable opinions.

On the following day, October 11th, Cornelius Burgess presented a motion regarding Peter Sterry's alleged Antinomian opinions. The Assembly would "desire him to receive & give satisfaction in this businesse & when [he does] he shall be inabled

---

[22] Ms. I. 187, (Ms. I., f. 94b.)

[23] *Ibid.* 192, (Ms. I., f. 97.)

[24] *C.J.* III. 271. The Commons' committee consisted of Ashurst, Saloway*, Sir Sy. D'Ewes, Knightly, Sir Wm. Strickland, Lord Ruthen, Sir Pet. Wentworth*, Sir Jo. Clotworthy, Erle*, Blakeston*, Lisle*, Tate, Smith*, Barnestone, Sir Chr. Yelverton, Gurdon*, Hill*. Of these seventeen names, the eight marked with an asterisk may be counted to have been political Independents. Cf. George Yule, *The Independents in the English Civil War.* Appendix A, pp. 83–130.

[25] TMs. I. 192, (Ms. I., f. 97.)

& have opportunity to returne backe againe". He was also asked to express himself "more distinctly & clearly in the doctrine of Justification"[26] but he seems to have made amends promptly, for his name appears in the Minutes on the 17th, apparently in good standing.[27]

For some time after this the problem of Antinomianism remained dormant in the Assembly, although the growth of this and all forms of sectarianism was becoming increasingly acute in the City and in the nation at large. When the issue resurfaced in November, the initiatives came from outside the Assembly. On November 3rd the Assembly received an order from Parliament on the subject. Walker, Caryl,[28] Arrowsmith, Gataker, Cheynell, Gouge, Cornelius Burgess, Tuckney and Newcomen were appointed as a new committee to consider it, and at the beginning of the following session (Monday, the 6th) it was agreed that these members should be joined by the members of the former committee.[29] We can only assume that the task of reading the Antinomian literature was proving too formidable for a few men to accomplish quickly.

If the members of the Assembly had any inclination to forget the situation beyond their doors, there were others to remind them. On November 20th, a communication arrived from the ministers of London, which again broached the dangers of Antinomianism together with several other issues in which the conservative majority had been at odds with Independents.

Then was read a letter from the divines of London, in which they urge us for some settlement betimes; as, 1. For ordination of ministers. 2. For distinction of people that come to the sacraments. 3. For catechising. 4. For some cause against Brownism, Anabaptism, Antinomianism. 5. Against scandalous and debauched persons. 6. Against the gathering of churches, for which they desire us to make all possible speed.[30]

---

[26] *Ibid.* 201, (Ms. I., f. 101b.)

[27] *Ibid.* 220, (Ms. I., f. 111.) Sterry was one of the most interesting men associated with the Independents, for he was not only a Calvinist (in the main), but also one of the Cambridge Platonists; cf. F. J. Powicke, *The Cambridge Platonists*, (London, J. M. Dent, 1926,) pp. 174–92, and Vivian de Sola Pinto, *Peter Sterry: Platonist and Puritan*, (Cambridge, Cambridge University Press, 1934.)

[28] Joseph Caryl (1602–73) is the only member appointed to that committee who may have been associated with Independency. He is best known as the author of a voluminous commentary on the Book of Job.

[29] This had apparently been the original intention, but we must assume that in appointing the new committee, Palmer and Temple had been inadvertently omitted. Cf. TMs. I. 307, 316 (Ms. I., ff. 157b, 162,) Lightfoot, *Journal*, pp. 37, 40.

[30] Lightfoot, *Journal*, pp. 56f. Cf. TMs. I. 402, (Ms. I., f. 204b.)

Burgess gave some account of this letter on the 23rd. In their emphasis on regular ordination procedures and in the protest against sectarianism and the gathering of churches the London ministers were simply reiterating the concerns of the conservative majority in the Assembly, but in the question about 'the distinctions of people that come to the sacraments' we detect a distinctly Reformed emphasis. It may be that these London ministers were more ready to adopt presbyterian discipline than were many in the Assembly at that time.

In response to this William Gouge seemed to affirm the traditional position of the Church of England when he said that "none but such as are presented may be kept from the Communion". What he appears to be saying is that only those who have been excluded from Communion by higher authority (in this case Parliament) are to be excluded from the sacrament.[31] Gouge recognized, however, that Parliament might very well pass an order forbidding all celebration of the sacrament *pro tem.*, or give ministers the "power to keepe away unworthy communicators."[32] But the import of his words is that ministers as yet had no power to forbid the sacrament to any but those proscribed by Parliament; and that was a position closer to the traditional Church of England than to strict restorationist Puritanism.

However, the letter from the London ministers reminded those of the Assembly that Antinomianism was still a problem, and perhaps for this reason they began again to be more sensitive to Antinomianism lurking close by.[33] Later in December (the 18th) more members were added to the Antinomianism Committee – Vines, Hall, Lightfoot and Conant.[34] It would almost have been simpler to have made the Committee on Antinomianism a Grand Committee of the whole Assembly.

As we look at the history of the Assembly through these months in relation to the Antinomian problem, the Indepen-

---

[31] The reference is not very clear. It could mean excluding those who had been 'presented' for ecclesiastical discipline, as Puritans had earlier been 'presented' to the bishops for censure; alternatively it might refer to those who had been presented to livings by the bishops.

[32] TMs. I. 424, (Ms. I., f. 216.)

[33] On the 23rd November they raised doubts about a certain Mr. Pretty, who had applied to be appointed to a sequestered living. He was required to undergo another examination. On December 6th, they thought a probationer who preached to them was guilty of Antinomianism. He was cleared by the members deputed to examine him, and submitted a statement condemning the opinions of which he had been accused. Lightfoot, *Journal*, pp. 62, 71–2.

[34] TMs. I. 551, (Ms. I., f. 280.)

dents seem to have suffered from guilt by association, but although the issue remained serious for the London churches, we get the curious impression in the Assembly that it was less pressing in December, 1643, than it had been in October. Perhaps Antinomianism would not have been such a grave issue if the Assembly had been less Calvinist than it was, or if the situation in England had been more settled. The conjunction of those two factors made it the serious problem that it had become. Emphasis on free grace was interpreted not as an attempt to moderate the harshness of extreme Calvinism, but as theological justification for sects that appeared to threaten all religion and morality. Of itself it might not have been of such consequence, but when it is seen in relationship to irregular ordinations, gathered churches springing up everywhere, and the inability of the Church to curb heretical opinions, it was serious enough.

II

Irregular Ordination

There was the embarrassing case of Mr. Anderson. He was a minister who had suffered because of the war, but who had been declined appointment because he could not produce proof of his ordination. John Ley who had been given the responsibility of administering applications for vacant livings, intervened in the debate on November 7th to report on this singular case:

> Mr. *Ley* made a report concerning one Mr. *Anderson*, a plundered divine, who the other week was turned back for want of orders, but now came with a certificate that he had orders; which caused some query how he should come by them: – and in canvassing this business, it was related by Dr. *Stanton* that he was informed that there was some company of ministers in the city that took on them to give orders; which we resolved to inquire after . . .[35]

There had been some protest about John Ley's interruption of the debate,[36] but this was clearly a matter of considerable importance to the members of the Assembly, and the following day witnessed a vociferous condemnation of the 'ordination' episode by the majority. The day had begun with consideration of

---

[35] Lightfoot, *Journal*, p. 42.
[36] TMs. I. 323, (Ms. I., f. 165b.) We suspect it may have been the Independents who lodged this protest, but there is no further information.

some stricter rules for the examination of ministers,[37] but before
the day had finished, there had been further information about
the Anderson affair.

Dr. Stanton was prepared to name names,[38] and reported that
Anderson had been 'ordained' by Dr. Holmes[39] and John Goodwin of Coleman Street.[40] Charles Herle, John White, the
Member of Parliament, and Matthew Newcomen spoke on the
matter, and John White moved

> that it be desired to make the house of
> Commons acquainted with this businesse
> as from the Assembly 'concerning the liberty' & presumption
> that some men take to give orders unto men that
> come for benefices & thereby 'abuse' the Assembly
> toutching their orders when inquiry is made therof[.]

Herbert Palmer followed by denouncing

> a frame of a ministry that doth openly
> preach against this assembly and that the certificates
> to this purpose be delivered unto them[;]
> and that they doe also acquaint the house of commons
> with the liberty that many take in the citty & other
> places in gathering of churches at this time to antici-
> pate the worke of the parliament and assembly[.][41]

John White, the M.P., and Humphrey Salloway were asked to
convey these sentiments to the House of Commons.[42]

Obviously this case of irregular or 'clancular'[43] ordination
cannot be separated from increasing anxiety about a growing
practice of bypassing the parish system and 'gathering' new
congregations, to which we shall refer in the next section of this
chapter, but it must be clear that the Independents found themselves in a particularly delicate situation, for these were both
issues on which their own position was ambivalent. They did not
approve of irregular ordination, and yet in strict Congregational
ecclesiology a pastor could be ordained by the presbytery of a

---

[37] Lightfoot, *Journal*, p. 43.

[38] TMs. I. 332, (Ms. I., f. 170,) cf. Lightfoot, *Journal*, pp. 45–6.

[39] This was probably Dr. Nathaniel Holmes (1599–1678), who published works with
strong millenarian emphases. He had founded an Independent congregation in 1643.
Cf. *The Dictionary of National Biography*, (Oxford, 1906, etc.) *ad loc.* [*D.N.B.*]

[40] John Goodwin (1594?–1665), Vicar of St. Stephen's, Coleman Street, from 1633,
was an Independent in ecclesiology, but his Arminian theology clashed with the prevailing theological views of the Assembly. Cf. *D.N.B. ad loc.*

[41] TMs. I. 332, (Ms. I., f. 170,) Lightfoot, *Journal*, p. 46.

[42] Lightfoot, *Journal*, p. 46.

[43] It is Lightfoot's word. It is obsolete, but meant 'secret' [*clancularius.*]

local congregation with or without the assistance of presbyters from other churches;[44] they wished to affirm their support for a national Church and for the English parish system, but again, within a strict congregational view of the church, the *true* church was essentially a gathered and covenanted company of 'visible saints' whether or not they met within the boundaries of the parish structure. On the 10th and 13th November, Philip Nye would raise that very issue in relation to the regulations that were being proposed by those applying for appointment to vacant livings.[45] The situation was one of acute embarrassment for the Independents, and it was one that could lead to dangerous results unless it could be settled quickly.

The account of what happened on Thursday morning, the 9th November, is extremely fragmentary in the Minutes, and it is obvious that a great deal is missing whether by accident or by design. There is mention of certificates from the Dutch Church, and from Dr. Holmes and John Goodwin, and in the debate that followed it seems that there were some exchanges between Simpson and Thomas Goodwin on the one side, and Palmer and Burgess on the other.[46] Lightfoot's brief comment may be as innocuous a summary as we could expect for what transpired on that occasion:

> The first thing we had in agitation, being set, was that Mr. *Bridges* brought in a paper under the hands of Dr. *Holmes* and Mr. John *Goodwin*, whereby they disclaimed their ordaining of Mr. *Anderson;* which cost some time, more than we had well to spend."[47]

He also informs us that the subject cropped up again, in the next day's debate, but it is clear that there was a good deal of acrimony, of which Lightfoot gives no indication.[48]

Dr. Holmes and John Goodwin had apparently disclaimed any intention of 'ordaining' Anderson and claimed that their certificate had simply been a way of recognizing him in terms of his ability and worthiness to be a minister. As Thomas Goodwin said, "that which they gave certificate of is cleare [and it is clear] that they know nothing of that for wch they are accused". He went on to declare "I thinke ther should be a satisfaction given to

---

[44] Cf. John Cotton, *The Way of the Churches of Christ in New-England*, pp. 6, 39–46.

[45] Cf. *supra* pp. 154ff.

[46] TMs. I. 333–4, (Ms. I., ff. 170b, 171.)

[47] Lightfoot, *Journal*, p. 46.

[48] *Ibid.* p. 47. The Minutes say that a paper from Anderson was received, TMs. I. 344, (Ms. I., f. 176.)

the men for the misreports given concerning them."[49] Later in that same part of the exchange William Bridge challenged the opposition, "let it not seem grievous that you stay in vindication since you stayed in accusation". This led Stephen Marshall to state, against the Independents' insistence that Holmes and Goodwin should be cleared before the House of Commons,

if the names of those had been
carryed up it had been fitt
but the accusation was only layd in the
Assembly & here they are vindicated[.][50]

Stanton claimed he had been informed that whatever had taken place between Holmes, Goodwin and Anderson had been "with prayer & imposition of hands",[51] but it was clear that in view of the disavowals of the men accused, the Assembly had no cause against them, and the matter was not pursued.

The Independents felt that they were being hounded unfairly, and that the incident had been given an importance that it did not warrant – which may have been true enough, but it is understandable in light of the majority's suspicions and the chaotic state of religious affairs in London and the nation. However, the matter did not end there. Tempers were running high; charges and countercharges were being made; and if we can sense something of the frustration of the Independents at their treatment in the Assembly, we can also sense the frustration of the majority because they seemed no nearer solving the ecclesiastical problem in the nation. And meanwhile the sects continued to burgeon and conservative Puritans were as far away as ever from that ordered unity of Church and State that they regarded as their birthright.

Some of these frustrations for the conservatives seem to have come to a head on Monday, November 13th, at the end of the debate on the purity of the Church of England which had been so incautiously launched by Philip Nye.[52] After the Assembly passed the rules to govern the examination of prospective incumbents, Lightfoot records:

This being done, Dr. *Burgess* moved, that we might renew our information afresh to the House of Commons, concerning the clancular ordinations and gathering churches in London: for that Mr. *White* and Mr. *Salloway* have not yet had time and opportunity to do

---

[49] TMs. I. 334, (Ms. I., f. 171.)
[50] *Ibid.* 335, (Ms. I., f. 171b.)
[51] *Ibid.*
[52] Ibid. 361, (Ms. I., f. 184b,) Lightfoot, *Journal*, p. 50.

it: and upon this Mr. *Seaman* moved, that we should fall upon settling the churches in London.

And Mr. *Calamy* related, that, yesterday, there was a ticket sent to him in the church, which infringed the privilege and credit of the Assembly, and that it is not fit to wait or attend upon its determination for settlement.[53]

There was also brought in a note from one Mr. *Arthur Swanwicke,* that relateth that he will justify it, that some have complained that they could not have freedom of speech in the assembly; and that, though they offered disputation six to six, they were denied it; which was also appointed to be informed to the House of Commons.[54]

This incident took place at the end of the debate on the purity of the Church of England to which we have alluded earlier, but it is quoted in this context because it underscores the reaction of the conservative majority to a series of issues that were causing the members to become exasperated with the Independents.

III

The Gathering of Churches

This exasperation came to a focus in the increasing unwillingness of some preachers to wait for the Assembly's proposals and to begin to gather their own separate congregations. It was expressed by Herbert Palmer during the height of the furore about the Anderson affair,[55] but it was addressed again at the end of the debate on November 13, cited above, when a committee of Sedgewick, Palmer, Calamy, Ashe, Burgess, Seaman, Chambers and Herrick[56] were specifically charged

to present the former messadge to the house of
commons in case it be not already done and to present
to the parliament the reports 'gathered & gathering' that goe
concerning the Assembly to the preiudice therof, the
multitudes of churches 'gathered' in the 'city &' countrys
& disorders therupon, & concerning the speedy providing for
the comfortable subsistence of the ministry by
quickening the businesse & other dutyes concerning 'ecclesiasticall'
dues[.][57]

---

[53] The Minutes state that Calamy had said "a paper put into the hands of the clarke in which I was charged for saying . . .", and then the record is blank; but he went on to say that "many places brought to prove that it was not lawfull for a sinod to set up government". TMs. I. 361, (Ms. I., f. 184b.)

[54] Lightfoot, *Journal*, p. 50.

[55] 8th November, 1643; cf. *supra*. pp. 182ff., TMs. I. 332, (Ms. I., f. 170).

[56] *Supra* p. 158. None of these were Independents.

[57] TMs. I. 361, (Ms. I., f. 184b.)

At the end of the debate on November 14th, cited earlier, the matter "concerning the Independents gathering churches in the city and elsewhere" was raised again, and Sir Benjamin Rudyard undertook to bring it before the House of Commons.[58] It also arose, as we have seen, as one of the six points of major concern voiced by the London ministers in their letter to the Assembly on November 20th,[59] which was officially answered by the Assembly to a deputation of the ministers on the 24th.[60] If there were any doubt where the sympathies of a majority in the Assembly lay, Lightfoot tells us that "the prolocutor, in the name of the Assembly, gave them thanks."[61]

The issue had been debated fairly fully on the previous day as arising directly out of Nye's concern about the church's purity in respect of Communion. He had declared then that there was a gathering in relationship to the Church that was proper and wholesome, and suggested that what they were opposed to was "disorderly gathering."[62] This led Henry Painter to address the matter very pointedly:

> the gathering of churches is good as the
> scripture houlds it out, that is gathering of
> churches from pagans & heathens but gathering
> of churches out of churches is disorderly[.]

That does not need much explanation: it is good to gather churches as an extension of evangelism and mission, but it was not legitimate to gather churches out of the parishes to which other ministers are already appointed.

On the other hand, Nye insisted that still "ther may be need of gathering churches",[63] and we should recognize that behind his insistence there was the concern of the Independents about the purity of the Church which had made them reluctant to regard every parish in the Church of England as a true church, and which just as surely caused them to be regarded by the rest of the members to be half-way to separatism.[64]

---

[58] Lightfoot, *Journal*, p. 52.

[59] Cf. *supra* p. 180.

[60] Lightfoot, *Journal*, p. 66.

[61] *Ibid.*

[62] On the 13th November. TMs. I. 424, (Ms. I., f. 216.)

[63] *Ibid.*

[64] This was a major issue between the Congregationalists and the rest of the 17th century Reformed churches, and it is not surprizing that William Apollonius's first question to the Puritans of New England was 'Of the Qualifications of Church Members.' Cf. John Norton, *The Answer*, pp. 1–43. Although Norton obviously de-emphasized the differences, it is clear that the question of visible holiness was very real for the New England churches, as it had been from the first.

When we look at this period in the Assembly, there can be little doubt that horror about the increasing number of sectarian churches in London was a major factor in driving a wedge between the Independents and the conservative majority.[65] It is also clear that the Independents in the Assembly were themselves having to walk a very difficult tightrope between fidelity to their own ecclesiology with its concern for the holiness of the church, and of favouring Separatism. We have the impression that Thomas Goodwin and his friends were doing all they could to minimize their differences with the majority and to prevent scandal, which may explain their extremely prompt action regarding the irregular 'ordination' of Anderson. They were to take similar action with regard to the gathering of churches. Lightfoot informs us that on December 22nd,

> There came in, also, into the Assembly, this day, before it rose, which I had forgot, from one of their committees, certain considerations or arguments against gathering of churches in these times, *consented to by the most of the Independents in the Assembly.* It was urged that they should lay down and resign the churches they had already gathered; but when that could not be obtained, the other was accepted and ordered.[66]

IV

The Scots and the Independents

The Scots had not fully entered into the work of the Assembly until the two important debates on the Doctor (November 14th–21st) and the Ruling Elder (November 22nd–December 21st), and, as we have noted, on both of these issues the ecclesiology of the Independents was a great deal closer to that of the Scots than Presbyterian church order was to the views of many among that conservative majority in the Assembly. Nor was the question of church discipline and the visible holiness of the Church really an issue between the Scots and the Independents, but only as to the best way of achieving it. The Scots limited this quest for holiness to the parochial structures of a national Church, whereas the Independents would have had no

---

[65] On December 1st Seaman reported to the Assembly that "it is reported in the city that we petitioned for the removal of our brethren out of the Assembly." TMs. I. 474, (Ms. I., f. 241.) Although we cannot be absolutely certain that this refers to the Independents, because in the midst of the debate on the ruling elder they were not the ones giving trouble, it seems highly probable.

[66] Lightfoot, *Journal*, p. 92. My italics.

hesitation in seeking it within a gathered community wherever they found parish standards defective.

In some ways the Presbyterians of the City and the Scots had their own standards of Puritan practice that went much further than the majority in the Assembly was prepared to go. For example, on December 22nd, the ministers of the City had a serious discussion about their policy for the coming Christmas season. Edmund Calamy was of the opinion that they should not preach on Christmas day and tried to persuade his colleagues to that purpose. John Lightfoot on the other hand urged that they should not depart from normal English practice – "that letting the day utterly fall without a sermon, would most certainly breed a tumult", and that this year represented only an isolated case because by the following year the matter would probably be decided one way or the other by public authority.

Lightfoot apparently prevailed with Calamy, and it was eventually "voted affirmatively, only some four or five gainsaying, that they would preach, but withal resolving generally to cry down the superstition of the day."[67] Robert Baillie, however, gives us an interesting sidelight on Scottish puritanism in contrast to the English variety. The Scots were wholly opposed to the English tradition of celebrating Christmas and did their best to get the Assembly to schedule a normal working session for December 25th. He talked Alexander Henderson into trying to persuade the members of the Assembly "that for the discountenancing of that superstition, it were good the Assemblie should not adjourne, but sitt on Monday, their Christmas day."[68] This did not succeed, probably because some of the members like Lightfoot, were well aware how unpopular the abolition of the holiday would be with the populace. Baillie continued his account.

> We found sundrie willing to follow our adyvce [sic], but the most resolved to preach that day, till the Parliament should reforme it in an orderlie way; so, to our small contentment, the Assemblie was adjourned from Fryday till Thursday next; yet we prevailed with our friends of the Lower House to carie it so in Parliament, that both Houses did profane that holy day, by sitting on it, to our joy, and some of the Assemblie's shame.

Baillie's joy may seem somewhat strange to us, but at even its lowest level of significance the incident suggests that the Scottish

---

[67] *Ibid.* pp. 91–2.
[68] For Scotland, January 1st, 1644, *Letters and Journals*, II. 120.

Commissioners had a good deal to learn about the conservative temper of the English people.

There were more immediate problems to hand. During these months in the late autumn of 1643 we have the impression that the future antagonists were circling each other, and that the Scots were studiously avoiding anything that would precipitate an open breach with the Independents. Indeed, Robert Baillie informed his countrymen with some pride that it was "my advyce, which Mr. Hendersone presentlie applauded, and gave me thanks for it, to eschew a publick rupture with the Independents, till we were more able for them"; for he went on to admit that "as yet a Presbytrie to this people is conceaved to be a strange monster."[69] But the Scots had their friends, particularly among the London ministers. Whether it was careful or fortuitous timing we shall probably never know, but on the very day when Baillie and Rutherford had been received by the Assembly, (November 20th) the letter from the London ministers had been read; and from the Scots point of view, the contents and timing of that could hardly have been bettered if they had written it themselves. If they and their friends did not want to precipitate an open breach at this point, equally they did not want the points at issue with the Independents to be ignored. Neither did they want the Assembly to drag its feet or forget the direction in which those feet should be set.

The Independents knew themselves to be under pressure, but they too seem to have been anxious not to give offence. If Bridge, Goodwin and their friends spoke often in the debates and 'at large', they appear to have been no more culpable of wasting the Assembly's time than other members. Robert Baillie provides some interesting background behind the paper discouraging the further gathering of churches which had come before the Assembly so unexpectedly on December 22nd with the Independents' support. His first reaction to that measure had been positive:

Also, there is a paper drawn up by Mr. Marshall, in the name of the cheefe men of the Assemblie, and the chief of the Independents, to be communicat on Monday to the Assemblie, and by their advyce to be published, declaring the Assemblies mind to settle, with what speed is possible, all the questions needfull about religion; to reform, according to the word of God all abuses; and to give to everie congregation a person [i.e. 'parson'], as their due: whereupon love-

---

[69] For Scotland, n.d. (but certainly written in December, 1643.) *Letters and Journals*, II. 117.

ing and pithie exhortations are framed to the people, in the name of the men who are of the greatest credit, to wait patientlie for the Assemblies mind, and to give over that unseasonable purpose of their own reformations, and gathering of congregations.[70]

Even with his general approval and the expectation that good would come from this document, Baillie added the cryptic comment that beyond this, "wayes are in hand, which, if God bless, the Independents will either come to us, or have very few to follow them." By the time he wrote his next letter to Scotland on 1st January, he had become decidedly more critical of the pamphlet.[71]

Whatever justification Baillie may have had for his fears does not immediately concern us. The pamphlet's importance was that at the time it was being written and published, (December 22nd,) the Independents were cooperating with their colleagues in the Assembly to the point of permitting a public statement to be published under their signatures discouraging the gathering of separate congregations, and advizing people to wait for the religious settlement that was being prepared by the Assembly. It suggests that at that stage the Independents were almost leaning over backward to prevent a breach between themselves and the majority, and that they were extremely sensitive of being tarred with the sectarian brush.

We can therefore appreciate their anxiety when a mysterious parcel of books was delivered to the Assembly on December 29th, after the Christmas recess. It contained copies of a work written by a Separatist in Amsterdam, in which the author had argued that the Assembly was "bound in conscience to tolerate all sects." This may have represented where the Independents

---

[70] For Scotland, *Letters and Journals*, II. 118. This letter is undated, but it must have been written close to the incident it records. Marshall presented this paper to the Assembly at the end of the session on Friday, December 22nd (Lightfoot, *Journal*, p. 92,) but at the time of his writing Baillie probably still hoped that the Assembly would hold its normal session on the following Monday, December 25th.

[71] For Scotland, 1st January, 1644, *Ibid.* p. 121. The passage reads: "We had a great and sharp debate about the paper I wrote of before. Mr. Marshall, with a smooth speech, made way [f]or it, and got it read once and againe; but sundrie did speak much against sundrie expressions of it, as giving too much countenance to these who gathered congregations, and favour more than needed to the Independents; bot they did avow, that they were much thereby prejudged, and were most willing to suppresse the paper, and by no means would consent to the alteration of any word of it. I truelie wish it had never been moved; for I expect more evill to our cause from it than good; yet since it was moved so much in publick, if it had been rejected, it would have certainlie made a greater heart-burning among the dissenting brethren than yet had appeared: so at last it past with the Assemblie's allowance; but without voyceing. Yow may see it now in print. What fruits it shall produce we know not".

would eventually stand politically, and it would increasingly become their position during the coming year, but it would have been an extremely inopportune, not to say dangerous subject to be argued in the Assembly at that point. We read that when the 'business from Amsterdam' came before the Assembly, "it was very much opposed by the Independent party; and it cost a great deal of agitation and a little hot; and, after all, it was not read."[72]

Baillie's account is even more vivid in recording the reaction of the Independents:

> The Scribe offered to read all [the paper from Amsterdam] in the Assemblie. Here rose a quick enough debaite. Goodwin, Nye, and their partie, by all means pressing the neglect, contempt, and suppressing all such fantastick papers; others were as vehement for taking notice of them, that the Parliament might be acquaint therewith, to see to the remedie of these dangerous sects. The matter was left to be considered as the Committees should think fitt; but manie marvelled at Goodwin and Nye's vehemencie in that matter.[73]

From these events it appears that if the Scots were being careful not to bring matters to an issue until they had the Scottish army behind them, the Independents were being equally careful not to aggravate matters. Perhaps they were waiting for the army of the Eastern Association to prove itself, although we doubt whether anyone was gifted with second sight to that extent in December 1643. At the end of December 1643 there was no open sign of any theological breach between the Independents and the Scottish Presbyterians, although there is evidence to suggest that if the conservative majority had obtained its preferences in church order, the form of the Church of England would have differed significantly from both Independency and Presbyterianism.

At the same time, there were basic points at which these conservative Puritans and the Scots were in total agreement – on the need for religious uniformity in a national Church and determination to suppress the sects. This issue, which was as fundamentally political as it was religious or theological, seems to have convinced the members of the majority in the Assembly that they had less to fear by throwing in their weight with the Scots than from Independency. If England was to have a national Church, and if the traditional unity of Church and State was to be preserved, then it was urgently necessary for the Assembly to

---

[72] Lightfoot, *Journal*, p. 93.
[73] For Scotland, 1st January, 1644, *Letters and Journals*, II. 121.

finish its work, and the question of polity would appear to many to be less important than that there should be an effective system of government established at the earliest possible date.

The breaking point in the Assembly may not have been far away. One curious fact that encourages speculation but does not help accurate history is the complete absence of any notes of the debates in the Minutes from December 20th–15th February, 1643/4. We are therefore forced to rely on sources such as Lightfoot and Baillie, but by the end of December in his letters Baillie was already accusing the opposition of deliberately wasting time: "it's marked by all, that to the uttermost of their power hitherto they have studied procrastination of all things, finding that by tyme they gained". But he went on somewhat ingenuously to remark, "We indeed did not much care for [i.e., mind] delays, till the breath of our armie might blow upon us some more favour and strength."[74] Indeed at this point, the advantages of deliberate procrastination to the Independents are not obvious, whereas the Scots might very well wish to postpone too many official decisions until their army had made its appearance in England.

On the other hand, although it would have demanded superhuman foresight for the Independents in December 1643 to have anticipated the later victories of Cromwell and his troopers, there were also *political* advantages to be gained by not hurrying too much in the Assembly. On December 8th, John Pym, the 'uncrowned leader' of the parliamentary cause, had died.[75]

It was soon clear that political power at Westminster had fallen into the hands of Sir Henry Vane, the younger. In a later letter in which Robert Baillie protested against the "slie and cunning way" in which the Independents made their plea for toleration by publishing *An Apologeticall Narration*, he recognized Vane as "the sweet man, Mr. Pym's successor,"[76] and it appears that Vane managed to keep his private ecclesiastical views hidden from the Scots enough for them to count both him and Oliver St. John as "our greatest friends" even as late as September, 1644.[77] Baillie appears to have been completely hoodwinked by Vane, who had apparently impressed him as one of

[74] *Ibid.* p. 122.

[75] The members of the Assembly and the members of both Houses of Parliament attended his funeral in the Henry VII Chapel in Westminster Abbey on the 15th. Gardiner, *The Great Civil War*, I. 255f.

[76] 18th February, 1644, *Letters and Journals*, II. 133.

[77] To D. Dickson, September 16th, 1644, *ibid.* p. 230.

the main architects of the Solemn League and Covenant.[78] Presumably Sir Henry Vane's ecclesiastical position was no secret to the Independents in the Assembly, and it may be significant that the Independents in the Assembly and the party that carried that name in Parliament rapidly became advocates of religious toleration after Henry Vane's rise to power.[79]

However, whatever illusions Baillie may have had about Vane, he recognized that the continuation of an Independent faction represented a serious threat to the uniformity that the Scots intended for the two kingdoms. "We doubt not to carrie all in the Assemblie and Parliament clearlie according to our mind," he confidently assured his countrymen, "but if we carie not the Independents with us, there will be ground laid for a verie troublesome schisme. Always it's our care to use our utmost endeavour to prevent that dangerous [evil]; and in this our purpose, above anie other, we had need of the help of your prayers."[80] The development of this 'schisme' provided the primary news story in the Assembly during the succeeding months.

---

[78] To William Spang, September 22nd, 1643; *ibid.* pp. 88–90.
[79] Cf. *supra* pp. 49–51, and 121–7; and also the earlier comments in *An Apologeticall Narration*, 1963 ed., pp. 110–112, and notes.
[80] *Letters and Journals*, II. 122.

CHAPTER 7

THE PROBLEM OF ORDINATION: JANUARY 1644

I

The Political and Military Context in 1644

Samuel Rawson Gardiner observed that the Parliamentary leaders had every cause to anticipate the campaigns of 1644 with confidence.[1] But in the parliamentary party 1644 was the year when everything in the nation came to the boil in the over-all struggle for leadership, in military affairs, in Parliament itself, and not least in the religious and theological issues hammered out in the Assembly.

One solid cause for optimism was that by the end of January 1644 the Scots army under the Earl of Leven and his son, David Lesley, had entered England,[2] although this would inevitably increase the influence of the Scots in every phase of the struggle. Early in the previous December Robert Baillie had confessed to his cousin, William Spang, that he and his colleagues were not going to hurry their efforts in the Assembly, "till it please God to advance our armies, which we expect will much assist our arguments."[3] This was true because national suspicions were not far from the surface, and to the English the visible sign of the Scots army would be a powerful supporting argument for the so-far invisible spiritual grace of the Scottish Kirk. With the formation of the Committee of Both Kingdoms at the beginning of February, a new instrument was forged for the supreme direction of the

---

[1] *The Great Civil War*, I. 338.

[2] It was announced to the Assembly on January 29th by Lord Maitland ['Mackland'], Lightfoot's *Journal*, p. 130.

[3] December 7th, 1643, *Letters and Journals* II. 111. Cf. also his letter to Spang, July 5th, 1644, after the initial report of Cromwell's victory at Marston Moor: "Our armie oft signified to us, they conceaved their want of successe flowed most from God's anger at the Parliament and Assemblie, for their neglect of establishing of religion. We oft told them the truth, we had no hope of any progresse here, till God gave them victories; and then, we doubted not, all would run both in Parliament and Assemblie." *Ibid.* p. 201.

war, of which the Scots were constituent members.[4] From this point the Scots were a political force in English affairs.

The Scots were soon chagrined to discover, however, that they were no longer hailed by the English Parliament as the major bastion between itself and defeat. A lot had happened since the Solemn League and Covenant, and if the parliamentary armies under Essex and Waller had not done brilliantly, they had at least staved off defeat by their own efforts. Moreover, there were real grounds for optimism in the stubborn defence of Gloucester, and even more in the talent shown by Cromwell and his troops at Gainsborough – which in terms of its promise may be called 'the turning point of the war'[5] – and at Winceby.

This new-found confidence of the English in their own resources was not pleasing to the Scots Commissioners because inevitably it would have ecclesiastical overtones. Parliament began to realize that in the army recruited from the sectarian congregations of the Eastern counties it had a potent military weapon that was native-grown, and that in the person of the unknown squire, Oliver Cromwell, it possessed a formidable cavalry commander. Furthermore, it took the Scots Commissioners several months to realize just how significant it was that Cromwell's rise coincided with the new regime at Westminster under Sir Henry Vane.

On January 22nd,[6] within a few days of the Scots crossing the border, Cromwell had been appointed Lieutenant-General of the Army of the Eastern Association, and he became a member of the Committee of Both Kingdoms as soon as it was established. Cromwell was known to favour Independency openly and he pushed for a policy of toleration for all who would join in the cause. This meant that across the table of the new agency charged with supreme direction of the war effort, the ecclesiastical lines of the Assembly would be reflected but with a somewhat different balance of power.[7]

The victories in the field during 1644 were to be decisive in Parliament's struggle with the King, but they did not help the

---

[4] The Scots were represented by the Earl of Loudoun, Lord Maitland, Sir Archibald Johnston of Warriston, and Robert Barclay. Cf. Abbott, *Writings and Speeches of O.C.*, II. 275 and note 4.

[5] S. R. Gardiner, *The Great Civil War*, I. 191: 28th July, 11th Oct. 1643.

[6] Jan. 22nd is to be preferred over the date, Jan. 21st, that I previously gave in *The Lord Protector*, p. 69. Cf. Abbott, *Writings and Speeches of O.C.*, I. 272f.

[7] Apart from the Scots, the Committee of Both Kingdoms included on the English side fourteen Commoners and seven peers. It has been noted that the Independents' supporters were a majority among the twenty-one members of the new policy-making agency. *Ibid.* p. 275.

Scottish cause, because most of the honours went to Cromwell and his troopers. It is true that the Scots Major-General Lawrence Crawford had been seconded to the Army of the Eastern Association, where Cromwell's influence had been unchallenged, and that he succeeded in supplanting Cromwell in the esteem of its commander, the Earl of Manchester; but in June, during the attempt to relieve the Fairfaxes in the city of York, Crawford prematurely exploded a mine and assaulted the breach without consulting his colleagues, and this caused the repulse of the parliamentary forces and their temporary withdrawal. Even Robert Baillie wrote bitterly of Crawford's "foolish rashness . . . and his great vanitie" in this episode.[8] For the rest, Cromwell and his men showed their mettle at the battle of Marston Moor (July 2nd), much to the chagrin of Baillie and his colleagues in London who were convinced that the credit for that outstanding victory should have been given to David Lesley and his Scots.[9] It was also the year when Cromwell and the 'saints' he represented expressed their growing frustration at the bigotry of religious uniformity in any form[10] and their disgust with commanders who seemed to be working for military stale-mate rather than for victory.[11]

1644 was therefore a year that revealed deep dissensions in the Parliamentary party, and no disputes were more significant than those that affected the generals in the army – first between the Earl of Essex and Sir William Waller,[12] then, on the heels of that, between Cromwell and the Scottish Major-General Crawford,[13] and finally between Cromwell and his immediate commander, the Earl of Manchester.[14] Much of this was due to the exasperation of men who were determined to carry the war to a clear

---

[8] To Mr. Ramsay, end of June 1644. *Letters and Journals* II. 195. Cf. Gardiner, *Great Civil War*, I. 370, and Abbott, *Writings and Speeches of O.C.*, I. 284.

[9] Cf. Baillie's letter to Spang, July 12th, 1644, *Letters and Journals*, II. 202–4.

[10] Cf. Cromwell's letter to Crawford, March 10, 1643/4, Abbott, *Writings and Speeches of O.C.*, I. 277 f., *L–C*, I. 170f. (XX), *The Lord Protector*, pp. 62–68.

[11] Cf. Chapter III in the Introduction to *An Apologeticall Narration* (1963) and chapter 4 of *The Lord Protector*.

[12] During the early days of the war, Waller had been an extremely popular and successful commander and was known as 'William the Conqueror' (Gardiner, *Great Civil War*, I. 104f;) but after his defeat at Roundaway Down (July 1643) he had been approached by the Independents in Parliament with the offer of raising another army for him, if he would engage to appoint officers whom they could trust. Cf. *The Lord Protector*, p. 77. Essex's foray into the west in the summer of 1644 was obviously dictated in some measure by his jealousy and distrust of Waller. Cf. *The Great Civil War*, I. pp. 338–363, especially pp. 355–358.

[13] Abbott, *Writings and Speeches of O.C.*, I. 277ff. The course of this quarrel may be also traced in Baillie's letters: *Letters and Journals II*. 195f., 200, 229–32.

[14] Abbott, *Writings and Speeches of O.C.*, I. 289–320, *The Lord Protector*, pp. 81–93.

decision in contrast to the hesitant generalship of the aristocratic commanders who simply wanted to bring the King to a negotiated peace. The issue came to a head after the advantages won at the Second Battle of Newbury (October 27th) had been frittered away, and the King had been allowed to relieve Donnington Castle. These disputes led directly, first to the open breach between the Earl of Manchester and his Lieutenant-General, then to the remarkable proposal of the Self-Denying Ordinance and the creation of the New Model Army.[15]

The issue was paralleled among the political leaders: 1644 was the year when the latent tensions between the House of Lords and the House of Commons came to a head, or more particularly between those peers who continued to work for a negotiated peace with Charles, and leadership in the Commons that expected peace to come only through out-right parliamentary victory. It was essentially a dispute about ultimate objectives, and the best method to achieve them. Gardiner made the pertinent comment, that "if the New Model would be in a special sense the army of the House of Commons, the Scottish force would be in a special sense the army of the House of Lords."[16]

But, if the Scottish army was the military wing of the Lords in respect to the struggle between the Houses, it also became the army of the Presbyterian party in both Parliament and the Assembly; and it is clear that the New Model Army would become the military weapon not only of the leadership in the Commons, but also of the Independents and all they represented in the Assembly and in the nation. In 1644 we see these alignments becoming clear – a tacit alliance between most of the conservative Lords, the Scots and the Presbyterians, and a rival alliance that joined many of the Commons, the officers of the New Model Army, and the Independents. This is the political and military context in which the debates on Presbytery took place in the Assembly: they were part of an over-all struggle for power, and it was perhaps for this reason that we notice a decided shift of emphasis during the course of 1644. "The question of Presbyterianism or Independency," observed S. R. Gardiner, "would be thrust into the background, and the question of toleration or no toleration would take its place."[17]

In early January, 1643/4[18] this lay in the future, although there

---

[15] These events are presented in more detail in chapter 4 of *The Lord Protector*.
[16] *The Great Civil War*, II. 120.
[17] *Ibid*. I. 263f.
[18] Cf. *supra* p. 16 note 9 on 17th century dating.

was a mood of change, of uncertainty and even of expectancy, for it was clear that the struggle against the King was moving into a new stage. The Scots army was then well on its way, and its arrival would give the parliamentary forces an advantage that they had not enjoyed to this point, while at Westminster the trusted figure of Pym had been superseded by that of the young Sir Henry Vane, who was barely thirty years old. During the first month of 1644 London was shocked by no less than three dangerous royalist plots to divide Parliament's supporters and subvert its government. So if the Assembly's work throughout 1644 has to be seen against the backdrop of the power struggle within the parliamentary party, the immediate debates of January were conducted within the climate of rumour and plots that kept the capital on tenterhooks. What is perhaps even more important to note is that at the end of December 1643 there was no indication that any unbridgeable gap had developed between the Independents of the Assembly and their Presbyterian colleagues, and little indication that such a break would be final.

II

First Salvoes: Ordination and the Apostles

In returning to the debates we must underline that point. We would remind the reader that December had ended with a reasonable expectation of accommodation and unity in the joint declaration of the Independents and the majority party against any further gathering of churches.[19] Even more significantly, as we look at the debates during the preceding months, we find that the alignment in the Assembly was by no means as clear-cut between the Independents and the 'Presbyterians' as later writers have sometimes suggested. In the debate on the ruling elder, for example, it is clear that the real issue was between an alliance of the Independents, the Scots and a few of the English who can be distinguished as Presbyterians – all strongly in favour of the office – and, on the other side, a considerable number of conser-

---

[19] December also ended with an unexplained gap in the Minutes between Dec. 21st, 1643 and Feb. 14th, 1643/4. The second fascicle of the Minutes ends with several blank pages (ff. 292–5) after the entry for Dec. 20th, and the third fascicle begins with several blank pages (ff. 296–9), but these were not nearly enough for six weeks of debate. It suggests that the notes were either made in a separate fascicle, or were deliberately omitted. It means that for this important period we are entirely dependent on Lightfoot and Baillie.

vative English churchmen[20] who remained unconvinced that the office belonged to the Church, or at least by divine institution: there were members of the Assembly who hankered after a system of government closer to the traditional order of the English Church.[21]

It is important to recognize this, first, because we are forced to ask how, in the days that followed, these traditional English Puritans were persuaded to swing so dramatically and so completely to the Presbyterian side of the argument, and secondly, because it reinforces an impression that there was relative amity in the Assembly at the beginning of January 1643/4. It also suggests that we should keep a keen eye on the discussion during the following weeks to see if we can discern when and how the ultimate break occurred.

In dealing with the debates during this crucial period, we must, however, issue a strong warning to the reader who approaches them with the prejudices of the late twentieth century. We are concerned to show the relationship between religion and politics in the seventeenth century and to indicate their mutual influence, but it would be entirely wrong to accuse these divines of deliberately using their exegesis of scripture, or the theology derived from it, for merely political ends. We would have to say of them, as we said earlier of Cromwell, that "to suggest a fundamental hypocrisy – whether on the grounds advanced by seventeenth century royalists, or on those put forward by twentieth century realists – is to offer a solution too simple to be acceptable";[22] and for the same fundamental reason: the religious issue was too grave for any believer to play fast and loose with eternal destiny. These serious divines came to certain conclusions about the Church, about society, and about the way scripture should be interpreted, and they saw with peculiar clarity the evidence that supported those conclusions; but never in the debates do we find them consciously twisting the biblical material to fit their own convictions. They could be narrow,

---

[20] J. R. DeWitt recognized this alignment in the debate, and is correct when he suggests that David Masson and William Shaw misconstrued the situation from Baillie's account of the debate. But as I have argued earlier, DeWitt does not recognize the significance of that. It indicates that the majority in the Assembly at the time was not as 'presbyterian' as he assumes it to have been. J. R. DeWitt, *Jus Divinum*, pp. 78ff, 81 note 99; cf. David Masson, *The Life of John Milton* (Cambridge, Macmillan, 1859–1894, 7 volumes,) III. 19f, and W. A. Shaw, *A History of the English Church*, I. 161.

[21] E.g., Smith, Temple, Vines, Gataker, Price, Hall, Palmer, and Henry Wilkinson, senior.

[22] *The Lord Protector*, pp. 391f.

unbending and even myopic in their interpretations, but not deliberately dishonest.[23]

High on the agenda was the problem of ordination, and the establishment of an alternative order to that which had been swept away by Parliament. It was a practical problem that could not be indefinitely postponed, but it should have been obvious to all that the Solemn League and Covenant forced the Assembly at least to consider the Presbyterian system as it had been embraced by the Scots.

The touchy subject of ordination was approached somewhat obliquely. A month earlier, on December 5th, the Second Committee had presented a statement on the authority and power of the apostles, but on that occasion the report had been laid aside in order to complete the debate on the regular officers of the Church. In this report the committee put forward three propositions concerning the apostles:[24]

1. The apostles themselves had power to ordain officers in all churches, and to appoint evangelists to ordain, Act. vi. 3, and xiv. 23, Tit. i. 5.

2. They had power to order all the service and worship of God, as might make most for edification. 1 Cor. xi. per totum. especially 23. 28. 34, 1 Tim. ii. 8. 12, 2 Cor. xi. 28, 1 Cor. xiv. 26. 37. 40, 1 Cor. xvi. 1, 2.

3. To determine controversies of faith and cases of conscience in all churches, either 'vivâ voce,' or by writing. Act. xv. per totum, and xvi. 4, and xxi. 25, 1 Cor. vii. per totum, Gal. v. 2, 3.

When these propositions returned to the Assembly on January

---

[23] One occasion when they came close (perhaps by way of omission rather than of commission) was at the end of the debates on the Officers of the Church. On Friday December 29th, the divines, with the strong advocacy of the Independents, considered the New Testament office of 'widow'. Lightfoot says this was accepted as a permanent office in the church by the narrow margin of a single vote, "when it was my unfortunacy to be called into the city before it came to the vote." (Lightfoot, *Journal*, p. 96.) On the following Monday, January 1st, 1643/4, the debate focussed on a text in support of this proposition which, Lightfoot states somewhat redundantly, "was utterly against my mind, and far different from my judgment." (*Ibid.*) Apparently his opposition had some effect, because after "a very long debate, the business was put to the question and voted negatively." (*Ibid.* p. 98).

Only one proof text had been voted down, but although the office of widow had been upheld by an affirmative vote, no attempt was made to revive consideration of the office later. One suspects that this was as much due to conservative prejudices against women holding office in the church as to the paucity of biblical evidence. Some might argue that there is at least as much evidence for 'widows' as for ruling elders; but nobody did, and the Assembly moved on to other things.

[24] *Ibid.* pp. 98f. Cf. p. 70.

2nd[25] the Independents, Sidrach Simpson, William Bridge and young William Carter, together with some other members such as Thomas Coleman, immediately questioned the first of the assertions. It was an extremely sensitive area. Was the power of ordination in the apostles by virtue of their office, or was it simply by virtue of the gospel entrusted to them? Was this power unique to them, or could it be transferred to their nominees and so on through the ages in an unbroken apostolic succession? The whole ecclesiological issue would turn on the way those questions were answered.

The issue here was still not so much the Independents' fear of Presbyterianism as their fear of sacerdotalism, which had been given a new episcopal cast and justified on precisely those grounds.[26] There were, after all, Puritans in England who believed that New Testament episcopacy was the biblical pattern of the Church, and if the form in which this proposition was couched argues the desire of the Assembly to deal honestly with the biblical evidence without Congregational or Scottish presuppositions, it suggests that the arguments for primitive episcopacy may have been presented fairly cogently in the Second Committee.

At the same time, ordination was a subject on which the Congregationalists of the Assembly might appear to be out of step not only with other members of the Assembly but also with a greater part of Puritan sentiment in the country: for an overwhelming majority of Puritans ordination was sacrosanct. The Independents' persistent objections and continual disputing about issues that the rest took as self-evident were bound to bring them into disfavour not only with their colleagues in the Assembly but also with the politicians. The impatience of the politicians at Westminster would be voiced with increasing bluntness and clarity during the month of debates: the nation needed ordained ministers, and Parliament expected the Assembly to expedite that matter without further delay.

It was not that the Independents questioned that ordination properly belongs to the Church, and still less that they were trying to abolish the ordained clergy, but they persisted in raising questions at points where the majority thought questions were unnecessary. They maintained, for example, that within the Church of the New Testament there was no ordination qualita-

---

[25] *Ibid.* pp. 98f.

[26] I.e., in the writings of Bilson, Bancroft and Laud. Cf. the discussion *supra* pp. 20ff., 168 n. 143.

tively different from that which had been given to the Church as a whole, and that the recognition and locus of this ordaining power was in the Holy Spirit's visible choice of gifted individuals through the suffrage of the people rather than in the clerically managed rite of the laying-on of hands. To their colleagues in the Assembly, and probably to the nation at large, this represented an attack on ordination as such, and therefore to many of their contemporaries the Independents appeared to be dangerously wasting time on a matter on which there was already an overwhelming consensus.

So in the debate on January 2nd, Sidrach Simpson immediately asked for definitions of the words 'officer' and 'ordain' in the first proposition, while William Bridge took exception to the proposition "as first including, that the apostles alone had power to ordain; and secondly, that what power other elders have is ubt [sic, 'but'] derived."[27] He "disliked the derivation of ordaining from apostles to evangelists", and William Carter, the younger, asked that the word 'ordain' might be changed; but eventually the matter was voted and passed *nemine contradicente*, which is perhaps in itself an indication that the Independents were not anxious to oppose ordination as such.

However, they continued to make their points as the Assembly moved on to consider the proof texts. Acts vi. 3 and 6 were passed without any trouble, but when they turned to consider Acts xiv. 23, "Mr. *Carter*, jun. spake against it as improper; and Mr. *Gillespie* moved, that this place might be waved, because of the great controversy that is upon it; and he with Mr. *Carter* held that χειροτονία signifieth not *ordination*, but *election*."[28] We note that one of the Scottish Commissioners, George Gillespie, openly agreed with the Independents.

On the following day, January 3rd, the consideration of this text continued, and although Thomas Gataker urged that the members should "not fall upon the point about ordination, and in whose hand it lay, but fall directly upon the thing in hand", Sidrach Simpson insisted that χειροτονείν meant 'to give suffrage', and that "it is an authoritative act of the people; and cannot be shewed that it was an act of the magistrate alone".[29] At this point the debate had simply shifted from consideration of broad theological principles to detailed exegesis of the texts: the issues remained the same.

---

[27] Lightfoot, *Journal*, p. 99.
[28] *Ibid*. p. 100.
[29] *Ibid*. p. 102.

So during the debate on Acts xiv. 23 as a proof text for the first of the Committee's propositions, the Scots joined the Independents in preferring 'election' rather than the 'laying on of hands' as the intent of that verse, but they were opposed by the conservative majority.[30] The issue was not so much the word or the idea of ordination itself – they all believed that there are those in the Church who are to be set apart for ministry – but it was with the act in which the rite of ordination centred and how it was transmitted, and on these matters the English Independents and the Scots Presbyterians appear to have been closer to each other than to the rest of the English divines. Even Stephen Marshall, who usually led the more recognizably presbyterian wing in the Assembly, was solidly of a mind with the majority on this, for we read that after Richard Vines had replied to William Bridge's textual criticisms,

> Mr. *Marshal* moved, that he might leave this criticism on the Greek, and come to consider what it meant by 'ordaining:' or, at least, that we should take in the whole verse, and not lay the stress upon any one particular part of it. This was backed by divers, which held us a very long debate; at last it was voted that this verse should be produced for the proof of the proposition, with this clause added, *'The whole verse:'* and so we adjourned.[31]

The seat of ordination and the power to ordain continued to be a major concern of the divines through the next few days. The question of ordination itself had been relegated to the Third Committee, but in debating the proposition that the "apostles had power to ordain . . . and to appoint evangelists to ordain", and in the rigorous examination of suitable proof texts, the Assembly could not help invading territory that was going to be very hotly disputed again when the Third Committee produced its own proposals on ordination. But a new factor would begin to intrude itself into these theological deliberations, and would become more persistent as the month progressed. Because of the pressing need for ordained ministers in the City and in the nation, political pressure would be exerted, and there are signs that many of the divines were increasingly conscious of that pressure. Lightfoot says that before the debate on Titus i. 5 was resumed on Thursday January 4th, "there were divers motions and reasons made and given to hasten that business [ordination], because of the great necessity of it in the kingdom."[32]

---

[30] We read that William Bridge concluded his speech "with a motion that this place might be waved; and this was backed by Mr. *Henderson." Ibid.*

[31] *Ibid.*

[32] *Ibid.*

Then Thomas Goodwin for the Independents questioned Titus i. 5 as a proof text:

> Mr. *Goodwin* began to speak upon this, and denied the pregnancy of the place; and conceived that ὡς διεταξάμην[33] meaneth not his [Paul's] magisterial appointing, but his prescribing a rule and direction, which Titus received from Paul, and which he was to follow in ordaining, and in other things.
>
> He also found out these three propositions in this one, [i.e. in the proposition before them.]
>
> 1. The evangelists had their power to ordain from the apostles.
> 2. The apostles might appoint them from place to place.
> 3. They had power to give direction for the manner.[34]

One suspects that Goodwin had serious reservations about the proposition and that this was as far as he was prepared to go. His comments show that he did not believe the apostles had power to ordain others by virtue of their apostolic *office*, but by their relationship to the gospel.

The other position was represented by Richard Vines who insisted that "Διαταξάμην is authoritative",[35] and the underlying issue behind the discussion that would be contested inch by inch (or perhaps one should say letter by letter) is whether the apostles had authority to ordain other officers in such a way that they in turn could pass on that right in apostolic succession.[36] John Lightfoot, the Erastian, revealed his preference for the traditional form of the Church. In response to objections voiced

---

[33] "This is why I left you in Crete, that you might amend what was defective, and appoint elders in every town *as I directed you.*" Titus i. 5. (R.S.V.) The words italicized represent Goodwin's quoted Greek.

[34] *Ibid.* p. 103.

[35] During the debate Thomas Bayly made the interesting suggestion that the New Testament evangelists should be regarded as regular officers of the Church. Perhaps this should be seen less as an awakened sense of evangelism in Thomas Bayly, than in terms of the matter under discussion. If the office of 'Evangelist' was a regular office in the Church then (1) the apostles had the power to ordain a continuing office in the Church in such a way that the *office* was self-perpetuating, and (2) it raised the question which office in the Church still carried the authority of the apostolic Evangelist, for it was clearly to be distinguished from (and superior to?) Pastors and Teachers.

[36] The passage under discussion may also be interpreted in several ways according to the content given to the word επίσκοπος (bishop, overseer:)

"This is why I left you in Crete, that you might amend what was defective, and appoint elders in every town as I directed you, men who are blameless, married only once, whose children are believers and not open to the charge of being profligate or insubordinate. For a bishop, as God's steward, must be blameless; he must not be arrogant or quick-tempered or a drunkard or violent or greedy for gain, but hospitable, a lover of goodness, master of himself, upright, holy, and self-controlled; he must hold firm to the sure word as taught, so that he may be able to give instruction in sound doctrine and also to confute those who contradict it." Titus i. 5–9, (R.S.V.)

by Smith[37] and Goodwin he argued that Titus had authority to ordain directly from St. Paul, and "if Titus was not an evangelist, what was he? if of some higher degree, then name it: if of a lower, then a lower than an evangelist might ordain."[38] The implication should be clear: the argument could buttress a view of apostolic succession through regular church officers (presbyters or bishops), according to whatever form public authority decided to establish.

The debate continued in a similar vein throughout Friday, January 5th, and part of Monday, the 8th. On the 5th, "Mr. *Coleman* opposed this text, as improper; for that Paul had no power over Titus, as he went about to prove out of other places", while that doughty champion of tradition, "Mr. *Wilkinson,* senior, proved, that the apostles invested those that they employed, with power for the work, as those that they used for baptizing."[39] To the modern reader it doubtless sounds very abstruse and academic, but it could have extremely important practical consequences. The concern that the Independents and a few others in the Assembly were voicing was lest the texts should be used to justify a plenary power of ordination in the apostles, which then passed to the 'regular' officers of the Church by virtue of their *office*. Such a theory of ministerial succession could very well lead to a hierarchical system not very different from the earlier establishment.

III

Diversionary Tactics?

The Assembly sessions in January 1643/4 present us with a curious problem for which there does not seem to be any satisfactory solution. At some time during the first six weeks of 1643/4 the Independents apparently gave up all hope of comprehension in the new national Church, recognized that their most dangerous enemy was not crypto-prelacy but Scottish Presbyterianism, and appealed to Parliament and the nation at large for religious

---

[37] Dr. Peter Smith was usually on the majority side of the argument in the Assembly, but sided with the Independents on this occasion. He was a minister at Backway, Hertfordshire, and was appointed a member of the Committee for Accommodation in 1645.

[38] Lightfoot, *Journal*, p. 103.

[39] *Ibid*. p. 104.

toleration by suddenly publishing *An Apologeticall Narration*. [40]
This represented a clear break between themselves and the rest
of the members of the Assembly. We know from one of Robert
Baillie's letters that there was an immediate reaction to this
Independent *apologia* from the rest of the Westminster divines,
and especially from the Scots who recognized it was a direct
attempt to undermine the uniformity in religion promised in the
Solemn League and Covenant.[41] The resentment lasted a long
time, for Hetherington, the 19th century Scottish Presbyterian
historian, described the appearance of *An Apologeticall Narration*
as a declaration of ecclesiastical war.[42]

The pamphlet appears to have been registered at the Station-
ers' Company on 29th December, 1643,[43] and George Thomason, the bibliophile, dated his own copy 3rd January.[44] This
would seem to be conclusive – at least conclusive enough for one
scholar to remark that there has been "a vast, entirely unnecessary confusion in the dating of this celebrated tract"[45] and for the
most recent scholars to accept January 3rd or 4th as the date of
publication.[46]

---

[40] It was published under the signatures of the five 'Dissenting Brethren', Thomas
Goodwin, Philip Nye, Sidrach Simpson, William Bridge and Jeremiah Burroughes. The
most recent modern editions are those of William Haller in *Tracts on Liberty of Conscience
in the Puritan Revolution, 1638–1647*, (New York, Columbia University Press, 1933, 3
vols.) II. 305–339, and my own, published under the original title by the United
Church Press (Philadelphia, 1963.) For the Dissenting Brethren see the latter work
pp. 81–112, and Berndt Gustafsson, *The Five Dissenting Brethren*.

[41] To William Spang, February 18th, 1643/4, *Letters and Journals*, II. 129f. "The
Independents, holding of with long weapons, and debaiting all things too prolixlie which
come within twentie myles to their quarters, were taken up sundrie times, somewhat
sharplie both by Divines and Parliament-men; to whom their replyes ever was quick and
high, at will. At last, foreseeing they behooved, ere long to come to the point, they put out
in print, on a sudden, ane Apologeticall Narration of their way, which had long lyen
readie beside them, wherein they petition the Parliament, in a most slie and cunning way,
for a tolleration, and withall lends too bold wypes to all the Reformed churches, as
imperfyte yet in their reformation while their new modell be embraced, which they sett
out in generall so well farded as they are able. This piece abruptlie they presented to the
Assemblie, giving to every member a copy: also they gave books to some of either House.
That same day they invited us, and some principall men of the Assemblie, to a verie great
feast, when we had not read their book, so no word of that matter was betwixt us; but so
soon as we looked on it, we were mightilie displeased therewith, and so was the most of
the Assemblie, and we found a necessitie to answer it, for the vindication of our Church
from their aspersions. What both we and others shall replie, ye will hear ere long in
print."

[42] *History of the Westminster Assembly of Divines*, p. 179.

[43] J. R. DeWitt, *Jus Divinum*, p. 89, note 140.

[44] William Haller, *Tracts on Liberty of Conscience*, II. 305. The copy of *An Apologeticall
Narration* used by Haller is with the Thomason tracts in the British Library.

[45] J. R. DeWitt, *op. cit.* p. 89, note 140.

[46] So DeWitt, *ibid.*, Berndt Gustafsson, who argues for January 4th, (*The Five
Dissenting Brethren*, p. 11,) and Haller, *op. cit.* II. 305; but it should be noted that Haller

Admittedly this is direct evidence that cannot be explained away, but the confusion arises because this evidence is completely at odds with other known facts about the pamphlet and its authors[47] that makes a publication date later in the month more plausible; and there does not appear to be any way in which these two groups of facts can be immediately reconciled. For example, the debates in the Assembly show that during the first week of January, the Independents were still as preoccupied with and concerned about the possible revival of episcopacy as with Scottish uniformity.

Certainly they were concerned about the possibility of Presbyterian uniformity, but hardly to the extent that would justify the kind of absolute break that *An Apologeticall Narration* represented: at this time they had solid reasons for emphasizing concord and friendship with the Scots. We know that they would increasingly become, in the Parliament if not in the Assembly, the party of toleration; but this was not their original position as we know from the history of New England; then why should they declare this change of front as early as January 3rd 1643/4, when prospects for accommodation were still reasonably bright? At this distance that would seem to be an act not so much of treachery as of stupidity, and if there is one quality that no one had ever accused Philip Nye and Henry Vane of exhibiting, it is that. There was simply no apparent reason for issuing the pamphlet and aggravating the breach at that time.

Furthermore, there is no indication in the debates of the Assembly that the booklet appeared. The problem is unfortunately compounded because John Lightfoot's *Journal* is the only original source for those debates during this crucial period.[48] However, Lightfoot is usually reliable and was very clearly opposed to the Independents during those debates. We cannot

---

was vague about the date in a later work, *Liberty and Reformation in the Puritan Revolution*, (New York, Columbia University Press, 1955,) pp. 116f. S. R. Gardiner thought that the appearance of the pamphlet was related to Philip Nye's invitation to Oxford on January 6th, and to Thomas Ogle's attempt to involve the Independents in his plot, but he does not offer any clear evidence for these two events being related at this early date; cf. Gardiner, *The Great Civil War*, I. 264ff. On the other hand they may have been related later; cf. *infra* pp. 228–35.

[47] Although J. R. DeWitt thought the Thomason date conclusive he also recognized the inconsistencies and problems that this early dating causes when we see the publication of the tract in relationship to what was happening in the Assembly. Cf. DeWitt, *Jus Divinum*, pp. 89–91.

[48] As noted, the Ms. Minutes for the period are missing (cf. *supra* p. 199, n. 19,) and Robert Baillie unfortunately seems to have given both himself and his correspondents an extended New Year's break from letter writing from January 1st to February 18th, when we have the first independent acknowledgement of the pamphlet's appearance.

imagine him failing to record anything as significant as the publication and general distribution of *An Apologeticall Narration*, especially if the reaction had been as widespread and decided as Baillie's later correspondence suggests. The problem is that in Lightfoot's record of the debates on January 3rd, or for those of the succeeding days, he never gives us the slightest hint of any radical change or estrangement in the Assembly. There is no mention of any distribution of the pamphlet to the members of the Assembly, no oblique references to publication, no suggestion of any heightened animosity between the Independents and the Scots Presbyterians – in fact, nothing at that point that gives the slightest indication that *An Apologeticall Narration* had yet appeared. On the contrary, we find the Independents and the Scottish Commissioners as often as not on the same side of the debate and evidencing a show of reasonable concord; and that is remarkable, if *An Apologeticall Narration* had been made public on January 3rd as Thomason's notation suggests.

IV

Reconnaissance Probes: the debate continued

We know, of course, that the relative amity did not last long, that at some point before Robert Baillie wrote his letter to William Spang on February 18th *An Apologeticall Narration* appeared, and that something caused the Independents to recognize Scottish Presbyterian uniformity as the major danger to them in the Assembly's work; but as far as we can gather from Lightfoot's account, this still lay in the future on January 8th, 1643/4.

On that date, having voted the first proposition presented by the Second Committee the Assembly moved to the proposition, that "the apostles had power to order all the service and worship of God, as might make most for edification".[49] Although this "cost some debate" and was amended to read that 'the apostles had power to order and settle all the service and worship of God in all churches, etc.,' it was eventually passed with its proof texts "without any debate at all, which", Lightfoot observed, "had not been done since we sat"[50]; and having moved to the third proposition, concerning the apostles' power to determine controversies of faith and cases of conscience, we read that "this proposition was also voted without one word of debate upon it."

---

[49] Lightfoot, *Journal*, p. 105.
[50] I Cor. xi, xiv. 26, 37, 40, xvi. 1, 2; 1 Tim. ii. 8, 12; 2 Cor. xi. 28.

When Charles Herle and George Gillespie objected to Acts xv and xvi. 4 as proof texts, other texts were suggested and either "ordered to pass without any debate at all"[51] or "ordered speedily to pass."[52]

The members then proceeded to the report that had been brought in by the Second Committee on January 2nd concerning the work of pastors and teachers.[53] "Mr. *Nye*", we read, "boggled at this proposition, as doubting it lay too near the business of the apostles; as if it limited their power to descend from the apostles", and again we note the Independents' fear lest apostolic succession should be tied to an ecclesiastical office. Gillespie joined Nye in protesting against the proposition as it stood: he regarded the motion as "too straight, as excluding the ruling elder, and bringing a jurisdiction, possibly into the hands of one man; which may not be tolerated", while Thomas Goodwin criticized the proposition "in regard of it so near following that of apostles, and because of its excluding the people from the power mentioned." Dr. Temple raised questions about the wording, and John Selden, as might be expected, questioned excommunication being vested in ecclesiastical officers of any kind; but the significant point we note about the debate as it has come to us via Lightfoot, is that although the Independents and George Gillespie criticized this proposition from the standpoints of their own ecclesiologies, they were on the same side of the debate and were questioning the same assumption – should ecclesiastical discipline be wholly in the hands of ordained clergy, or are others in the church involved in it?

However, the Independents were not only under attack in the ecclesiological debates in the Assembly. There were those in the nation who were blaming them for the spreading sectarianism, and as we have seen their emphasis upon 'grace' made them particularly vulnerable to a charge of Antinomianism that persisted long after the Westminster Assembly.[54] On January 8th,

---

[51] I Cor. vii, Gal. v. 2 & 3.

[52] Romans iii, iv and v, and I Cor. xv.

[53] " 'Pastors and teachers have power to inquire and judge who are fit to be admitted to the sacraments, or kept from them; as also who are to be excommunicated, or absolved from that censure.' Matt. xxviii. 18, 19, 1 Cor. iv. 1, Matt. xvi. 19, 1 Cor. 5 begin." *Ibid.* p. 106, cf. p. 98.

[54] Later in the century, while Increase Mather was in England to renegotiate the charter of Massachusetts, he helped to engineer the 'Happy Union' between the Presbyterian and Congregational ministers in London in 1691. But the union broke up after only a few years when the Presbyterians accused the Congregationalists of Antinomianism, and the latter responded by accusing the Presbyterians of becoming Unitarians. There were grounds for both charges.

Cornelius Burgess pressed for stronger action against the spread of Antinomianism in the City, which, observed Lightfoot, was pursued "with some heat; for the doctor having said, that those that we looked after to help to quell it, have failed in it", Lightfoot continued, "some of the Independents quarrel it, and thought he spoke of them."[55]

They may not have been too far wrong in that, for another member was even more blunt. "Mr. *Walker* spake plainly, that he heard this week, one member of one of the churches that came out of Holland, maintain Antinomianism most strongly and stoutly."[56] If, as we are suggesting, the break between the Independents and the rest of the Assembly may not yet have taken place, the pressures were building rapidly.

V

Activity on a narrow front: Who can ordain?

The earlier votes cleared the way for addressing the question of ordination directly. On January 9th Dr. Temple brought in a report from the Third Committee raising the issues that should be considered – what ordination is, whether it is a permanent order of the Church, who ought to ordain, who should be ordained and with what qualifications, and how ordination was to be conducted. To this end the following propositions were presented for debate:

> Ordination is the solemn setting apart of a person, to some public office in the church. Numb. viii. 10, 11.14.19.22, Acts vi. 3.5, 6. To the 2d. question, It is necessary to be continued in the church. 1 Tim. v. 21.22, Tit. i. 5. To the 3d, in the New Testament, 1. The apostles did ordain. Acts vi. 6, and xiv. 23, 2 Tim. i. 6. 2. Evangelists did. Tit. i. 5, 1 Tim. v. 22. 3. Preaching presbyters did. 1 Tim. iv. 14.[57]

The procedure, as in the previous debates, was to debate the major proposition first, and then proceed to texts offered in support. The consideration of the texts was therefore a very important part of the process, for if the supporting texts were proved to be inappropriate, the proposition would itself be in jeopardy. Opponents of the propositions therefore had a double line of attack and that meant that the issue was virtually debated

---

[55] Lightfoot, *Journal*, p. 106.
[56] *Ibid.*
[57] *Ibid.* pp. 107f.

twice – once as a simple proposition, and then in relation to the proof texts. The Independents made good use of this, but we can see how opposition would become irritating to those who thought the matter resolved by the first vote. At the same time, some of the growing frustration was at least in part due to the extraneous matters that came to the Assembly's attention.[58]

True to the rule that no issue was to be decided on the day when it had been first presented, the major debate opened on the following day, January 10th; but in order to remind the Assembly of its priorities, immediately after the usual sermon by a probationer, Lord Maitland moved "that the Assembly would declare itself, how far we comply with them [i.e., the Scots] in those points which they put in to us, concerning the Presbyterial government; and that we would draw up what we have done concerning church-officers; that so they [the Scots] might return our minds to them that sent them."[59] If the nature of the Church was now going to be broached via ordination, the Scots wanted the Assembly to remember its obligations under the Solemn League and Covenant.

After Lord Maitland's motion, the members resumed the debate on ordination. To the first of the propositions before them, Dr. Gouge wanted to add 'by imposition of hands,' and Thomas Goodwin, 'by election', which, Lightfoot says, "cost some small debate."[60] Old Mr. Wilkinson suggested that the

---

[58] Consider the 'little extras' that had interrupted the Assembly in this period from the beginning of the year until Jan. 15th: On Jan. 2 Lady Waller had asked the Assembly (through Thomas Case) to pray for her husband, although it was reported the following day that the threat had been averted. On the 4th Lord Wharton had conveyed the order of the Lords that each week a member of the Assembly should pray with them, and on the 5th there was a request from the daughter of the late Dr. Folkes for the Assembly to recommend her father's book to Parliament, and that "they would enjoin every parish in the kingdom to buy one of her." In that matter the members "thought it was not fit for us to meddle withal"! Also on the same day they received a request (order?) from a committee of the House of Commons to consider letters that were to be sent to the European churches explaining the Covenant, and listened to a speech from Dr. Twisse welcoming the General, the Earl of Essex, to the Assembly. On the 8th they gave a lot of time to the problem of Antinomianism, and more time on considering the application of a minister for one of the sequestered livings. On the 15th the Assembly received an order from the Commons to provide a minister for the daily prayers in Parliament, and the members organized a roster for this duty to be performed for each of the Houses. In addition to these interruptions, the members listened to the sermons of at least seven probationers. *Ibid.* pp. 96–111.

[59] *Ibid.* p. 108.

[60] *Ibid.* Again, we must warn the modern reader that Goodwin's insistence on the process of congregational election must not be interpreted in terms of later political democracy, or in terms of the implicitly democratic processes of later Congregationalism. The emphasis of the 17th century Puritans was more in the spirit of Acts xv. 28, where it

choice and ordination of Matthias was the most authentic pattern for them to follow, but that did not seem to meet with any general approval.

The following day there were signs of the impatience that lay members of the Assembly would increasingly exhibit as the month drew on. The debate was on scriptural references in support of the proposition they had voted on the 10th,[61] and since the Independents are usually regarded as responsible for the delays in the Assembly, it is interesting to note that it came in the middle of a debate on the Old Testament proof texts that had been initiated by Lightfoot, Selden, and Gataker. "This held some long debate," observed Lightfoot, "insomuch that Sir *Robert Pie* with a great deal of vehemency, did urge us to hasten, and blamed our long debates". At this point the Independents made the tactical error of prolonging the debate when the politicians had already become irritated at its length. Lightfoot said that "Mr. *Bridges*, who had begun, went on very largely, but at last was stopt", and he was followed by Goodwin, which "again cost some debate."[62]

However, there was no obvious sign yet of any unabridgeable gap between the Independents and the Scots. The concern of Goodwin and his friends still seems to have been more with the possible resurgence of episcopacy than with Presbyterianism.

So on January 11th the divines proceeded to debate the second proposition, that "Ordination is necessarily to be continued in the church", and Philip Nye asked "whether it be necessary, 'necessitate finis'", to which Obadiah Sedgewick retorted "that a minister cannot be a minister without it."[63] This Independent attack continued on Friday 12th during the debate on the scriptural proofs, with Sidrach Simpson arguing against the passages presented, and with Vines and Temple defending them. It is worth noting that the point under discussion was the 'laying on of

---

speaks of a decision that "seemed good to the Holy Ghost, and to us", than upon the majority decisions of secular Liberal democracy: it was the attempt to discover a spiritual consensus.

[61] "Ordination is the solemn setting apart of a person to some public office in the church."

[62] *Ibid*. p. 109.

[63] *Ibid*. p. 109. Nye's concern was whether ordination should be regarded as an ultimate necessity for all ministry, (i.e. something constitutive of the church itself,) and appears to have been directed against the traditional view of ordination held by the conservatives rather than against any specifically Presbyterian view. There is ground for this reading of Nye's comment in Charles Herle's support, and from the fact that Herle "scrupled at the word 'continued,' as inferring non-interruption." *Ibid*. pp. 109f. It suggests a fear lest the Assembly should inadvertently endorse a view of ministry based on historical succession.

hands' in ordination, i.e., the discussion was still concerned with matters more germane to a Reformed/Episcopal or Reformed/Catholic debate than with issues that distinguished Congregational and Presbyterian polities. And this continued.[64]

However, the debates appear to have progressed on a fairly even keel, although they were subject to the kind of time-consuming interruptions that had plagued the Assembly from the first and had little to do with its main responsibility.[65] Then on January 17th we discern a noticeable change. The Assembly began to debate a proposition put forward from the Third Committee: "Because apostles and evangelists are officers extraordinary, and not to continue in the church, and since in Scripture, we find ordination in no other hands,[66] we humbly conceive, that the preaching presbyters are only to ordain." Lightfoot went on to say:

> We took this business in pieces; and first upon apostles and evangelists, whether they be extraordinary officers: and this cost some time to determine whether we should fall upon this point or not: at last it was concluded, that the former part of the report should be laid down for the present, and that we should fall directly upon the latter part, that "preaching presbyters are only to ordain;" or on this proposition, "ordination is only in the hands of those who by office are to attend the preaching of the word, and administration of the sacraments."[67]

A critical shift is indicated in Lightfoot's comment that the Assembly agreed to waive any discussion of ordination in relation

---

[64] On January 15th the Assembly began to discuss the first part of the third proposition offered on Ordination, that "in the Scriptures of the New Testament, 1. The apostles did ordain, Acts vi. 6, and xiv. 23, 2 Tim. i. 6." Dr. Gouge then raised a point that appears to have a very curious echo of the Church's traditional hierarchy. He suggested that because the passage in 2 Timothy was related to the ordination of pastors, that of Acts xiv to elders, and that of Acts vi to deacons, the order in which the proof texts were presented should be reversed. His suggestion was not taken up, but behind it we can discern the pattern of the threefold ministry with its bishops (pastors), priests (presbyters) and deacons. *Ibid.* p. 111. The proposition had been introduced on January 9th by Dr. Temple. *Ibid.* pp. 107f.

[65] A good deal of January 15th was taken up by receiving a deputation from the City of London, which invited the members to join the Common Council of the City and the Houses of Parliament in thanksgiving for their having frustrated several dangerous plots against the government. A service of Thanksgiving was to take place on Thursday, January 18th, to be followed by a City banquet. *Ibid.* p. 112.

[66] I.e., since we find ordination in the New Testament in no other hands than those of apostles, evangelists and preaching elders, and since apostles an evangelists were extraordinary officers limited to the apostolic period, therefore ordination today is to be placed in the hands only of preaching elders.

[67] *Ibid.* p. 114.

to the 'extraordinary officers' in the early church, and to debate the proposal that all such power was in the hands of preaching presbyters. This means that at the committee level a significant understanding had been reached between the Scottish Commissioners and the leaders of the Puritan majority in the Assembly. Those divines whose personal preference we suspect to have been closer to 'primitive episcopacy' than to either of the ecclesiologies represented at Westminster had been convinced that their best hope of national uniformity and curbing the power of the sects lay in that which was implicit within the Solemn League and Covenant – a Presbyterian Church of England on the Scottish model.

Obviously, if such a *rapprochement* had taken place, a clear-cut decision on the form of the Church could not be delayed for long in the Assembly. But if the issue was now clear and the end result almost certain, some Presbyterians began to be concerned about maintaining Puritan unanimity. As Baillie had indicated, they wanted if at all possible to win over the Independents, and his colleagues began to urge that the issue should not be pushed through too quickly:

> When it was ready to go to the question, whether this [the motions restricting the power of ordination to preaching elders] should be debated, there was a motion made by Mr. *Calamy*, and backed by Mr. *Gillespie*, that we might not fall as yet upon it. And so it was moved also by others; and this held us [in] debate, whether we should fall upon this or no, till twelve o'clock: and then upon a motion of Mr. *Seaman's* there was a committee of Independents chosen, that should state the question concerning ordination: and so we adjourned.[68]

The debates had reached a critical point. With a solid majority assured, the Presbyterians could afford to give the Independents the opportunity of stating their case and thus possibly avoid the danger of permanent schism.

Thursday January 18th was taken up with the Thanksgiving celebrations, first at a service at Christ Church[69] with Stephen Marshall as the preacher, and then at the banquet in Merchant Taylors' Hall in Cornhill; but on the following day the Assembly received a series of reports that clearly set the stage for the establishment of presbyterian government in the Church of Eng-

---

[68] *Ibid.* p. 114.

[69] Presumably this was held at Christ Church, Newgate Street. Stephen Marshall preached on I Chron. xii. 39.

land. This session was perhaps so crucial in the history of the Assembly that we give Lightfoot's account somewhat more fully:

> *Friday, Jan.19.*]– This morning the first thing we did, was, that Mr. *Nye* reported from the Independent committee in these two propositions:
>
> 1. Ordination, for the substance of it is the solemnization of an officer's outward call, in which the elders of the church, in the name of Christ, and for the church, do, by a visible sign, design the person, and ratify his separation to his office; with prayer for, and blessing upon, his gifts in the ministration thereof. Acts vi. 3.6, Numb. viii. 3. 10–19, Acts xiii. 1–3.
>
> 2. That the power that gives the formal being to an officer, should be derived by Christ's institution from the power that is in elders as such, on the act of ordination, – as yet we find not any where held forth in the word.
>
> Dr. *Burgess* also reported from the first committee concerning the presbytery.
>
> 1. The Scripture holdeth out a presbytery in a church. 1 Tim. iv. 14, Acts xv. 2.4.6.
>
> 2. A presbytery consisteth of ministers of the word, and such other public officers, as have been already voted to have a share in the government of the church.
>
> Dr. *Stanton* also reported concerning,
>
> 1. There is a power of censuring and absolving from censures to be exhibited in the church by the authority and institution of Jesus Christ. Matt. xiv. 19, John xx. 23, 1 Cor. v. 12, 13, 2 Cor. ii. 6, 7.10.
>
> And for the clearing of his business of church censures, the committee thought fit to inquire into these three things, if the assembly think fit:– 1. What the church is, that is to exercise censures. 2. What kind of censures these are. 3. By whom, and in what manner, they are to be exercised. This cost some opposition from the Independents, which would not as yet have the church meddled withal: but at last it was put to the question, and resolved affirmatively, that the second committee should take these three things in hand.[70]

What is particularly of interest in this passage is that the programme developing out of the work of the committees had assumed a decidedly presbyterian character. We also note that because of Lazarus Seaman's motion on the 17th, the issue can be clearly seen as between a form of government that the majority was now prepared to endorse and the Congregationalism of the Dissenting Brethren.

---

[70] *Ibid.* pp. 114f.

The new mood of the Assembly was indicated in what happened during the rest of that day's debates.[71] The Independents' first proposition was discussed, but eventually laid aside in preference to the original motion that "Ordination is in the hands of preaching elders", with Stephen Marshall claiming that ordination should involve the whole presbytery, and Richard Vines equally insistent that the right of ordaining was restricted to 'preaching elders.'[72] However, Lightfoot observed that just as this debate began, "my Lord of *Manchester* brought in an order from the Lords, which requireth the Assembly to dispatch and make haste concerning the business of ordination." "Then fell we upon our work again," he continued, "and divers were for hastening the business; and a committee was chosen to consider of it; and three out of every committee were chosen for the purpose."[73]

To suggest that the conservative Puritans were now ready to support this emphasis on 'preaching presbyters' does not mean that all the divines were ready to follow the Scots in all things, as Richard Vines's contribution showed here and as other interventions were to show in the future. But a start had been made, and if there were those who still hoped to give this 'Presbyterianism' an English accent, the Scots had every reason to feel confident because fear of ecclesiastical chaos would give them the support they needed. Furthermore the call from the politicians was for expedition, and there would be little sympathy for those who obstructed an effective solution for the problem of ordination. The pressure from the House of Lords was not without its effect, and many members of the Assembly and of both Houses would rapidly reach the point where they would interpret everything that delayed final settlement as factious.

---

[71] *Ibid.* pp. 115f.

[72] Marshall had in mind the Presbyterian position, that both preaching and *ruling* elders should be involved in ordination.

[73] *Ibid.* p. 116. I.e., three members from each of the standing committees.

CHAPTER 8

INTO THE BREACH: JANUARY 1644 CONTINUED

I

Ordination and the London Clergy

The Independents suddenly found themselves backed into a corner, and this feeling must have been more pronounced on Monday January 22nd when Richard Vines reported from the special committee appointed to draw up practical proposals for dealing with the need for ministers. Lightfoot had been absent from the Assembly that day for the first time since its sessions had begun, visiting the parish to which he had been appointed at Great Munden,[1] but he obtained a full report of what happened:

> Mr. Vines reported from the committee, chosen for considering about ordination for the present, in these two propositions:
>
> 1. That, in extraordinary cases, something extraordinary may be done, until a settled order may be had; yet keeping as close as may be to the rule, 2 Chron. xxix. 34.
> 2. It is lawful, and according to the word, that certain ministers of the city be desired to ordain ministers in the vicinity, "jure fraternitatis."
>
> Then did the chairman of the committee, that was chosen to consider of the presbytery, tender a report: but the Independents

---

[1] The Revd. Mr. Coleman, 'preacher at the Tower', had been appointed to the sequestered living at Great Munden, Hertfordshire, but on Jan. 9th, 1643/4 he had been refused appointment by the Assembly because of his participation in an irregular ordination, and Lightfoot had been nominated in his place. Lightfoot, *Journal*, pp. 107, 108, 113. Lightfoot was an active member of the Second Committee, and had a particular interest in what was happening in the Assembly at that time. Although he was usually numbered among the Erastians, he was also a strong supporter of the presbyterian measures, probably as the most likely way of countering the sects. He was consistently in favour of a national church, and against the gathering of churches; e.g., see his action against Separatist books, Dec. 29th, 1643, *ibid.* p. 93.

were most exceedingly opposite to the reporting of it, so that it cost at least an hour's smart debate and more, before the report could be admitted; and not admitted but by putting it to the question. The tenor of the report was, That there may be some congregations under one presbytery, as in the church at Jerusalem.[2]

The Independents might well have wondered what had hit them. Not only was the Second Committee proposing to use the example of the church at Jerusalem – a main argument in Congregational apologetic – as its main biblical support for a presbytery, but the proposals brought forward to deal with the current situation frankly looked like a presbytery under another name. And they were very well aware that once the well-organized group of London ministers began to get under way as an operating 'presbytery', it would be very difficult to unseat it in the capital: a *de facto* system of church government could very easily become *de jure* if it could demonstrate its effectiveness in the eyes of this Parliament. This is the fear that developed during the next week's debates.

However, although there was plenty of spirited debate on Tuesday, the 23rd January, when the first proposition from Vines's committee came before the Assembly, even yet the dispute had not polarized itself wholly along Independent/Presbyterian lines.[3] The Independents appear to have been relatively neutral at first, but became more apprehensive as the proposal unfolded. In the end they were certainly guilty of obstructive tactics, but in the beginning they were not alone in their opposition. Lightfoot, who had spoken in favour of the general proposition, went on to say that after the motion had been called to the question,

> Mr. *Goodwin* interposed and spake at large: and after him Mr. *Rutherford*, who scrupled, whether the proof in 2 Chron. xxix. would come up to the proposition, – but put on the matter to the question: and so did Dr. *Gouge*: and it was ready to it again, when Mr. *Nye* again interposed, again and again: my Lord *Say* also spake, and would have had this clause, "keeping ourselves as close to the rule as may be," – left out. . . .[4]

Then after other speeches from Vines, Marshall and Seaman in favour of the proposition,

---

[2] *Ibid.* p. 116.
[3] Both Thomas Coleman, the Erastian, and Samuel Rutherford, the Scots Commissioner, voiced serious criticisms of the proposition.
[4] Lightfoot, *Journal*, p. 117.

it was called again to the question, and then Mr. *Carter* interposed
again, and so did Mr. *Goodwin* and Mr. *Burroughs*: but at last it was
put to the question, with this variation, "keeping to the ordinary use
of the rule:" which was voted affirmatively; – but then this phrase
being scrupled upon before the negative was given, it was revoked,
and the question put in the terms first laid down, and voted affirmatively.[5]

Such hindrances were precisely what the other members of the
Assembly would remember. Lightfoot with many others
thought these tactics dangerous in view of the situation in the
Church, although he suffered no such compunction when he and
his Erastian colleagues[6] at some length opposed the use of
2 Chronicles xxix. 34 as a scriptural basis for the proposition.[7]
After a proposal to use other Old Testament texts[8] barely
passed, "Mr. *Selden* made a motion, That in our votes, when we
come near an equality, the scribes should take a count of how
many negatives there be, and how many affirmatives: – which
cost very large and very smart discussion, and in conclusion it
was laid aside; and so we adjourned."[9]

Lightfoot went on to say, however, that "in the afternoon,
as we were in committee, there was given to each of us a book
from the Scottish commissioners, touching their own government."[10] This is an extremely intriguing incident, and there
seems no reason to doubt that the pamphlet was *Reformation of
Church-Government in Scotland Cleered from some mistakes and
Prejudices.*[11]

What is much more questionable is Haller's assumption, followed by DeWitt, that this had been written specifically in
response to *An Apologeticall Narration*,[12] for at no point can the
Scots work be shown to be an explicit refutation of the Independent pamphlet. It reads more as a response to positions the

---

[5] *Ibid.* p. 118.

[6] John Selden and Thomas Coleman.

[7] The Erastians were all competent Old Testament scholars, and the motion to use
that verse was carried by only a very small majority.

[8] Numbers ix, and 2 Chron. xxx. 2–5.

[9] Lightfoot, *Journal*, p. 119.

[10] *Ibid.* If we accept the 3rd or 4th January for the publication date of *An Apologeticall
Narration*, it might seem plausible to regard this as the response that Baillie promised
Spang he would "hear ere long in print." *Letters and Journals*, II. 130. Unfortunately that
explanation is not possible, since Baillie did not write his letter to Spang until February
18th, and at that point the Scots' reply to the Independents had yet to be written.

[11] London 1644. This date suggests that the booklet was not published generally until
March 25th, or after. It is usually attributed to Alexander Henderson, although it
appeared as the work of "The Commissioners of the General Assembly of the Church of
Scotland now in London."

[12] Haller, *Liberty and Reformation*, pp. 117f., and p. 367.

Commissioners knew in general, but not as their reply to a published document readily available.[13] It emphasized unanimity among the reformed Churches, and Haller himself commented that a "more dignified or reasonable statement from the Scottish point of view would be hard to conceive."[14] That in itself is strange if we bear in mind the outrage that Baillie and others expressed when the Independent pamphlet appeared.[15] *Reformation of Church-Government in Scotland* may well have been circulated to the members of the Assembly in part to undermine ecclesiological positions that the Independents were rumoured to have had already in a piece of writing which had "long lyen readie beside them,"[16] but of which the Scots had as yet little detailed knowledge: they suspected (often correctly) what that might contain, but did not have it to hand. This is simply another awkward piece that refuses to slip easily into the puzzle that surrounds the appearance of *An Apologeticall Narration*.

There are features of the Scots' pamphlet which suggest that although its author(s) were not forgetting the danger of Independency, their major concern was to prepare the way for the presentation of their own church government by the Assembly, and to ease the way, if that were possible, to a consensus and unanimity.

So on the following day (Thursday January 25th), in the presence of the Lord Admiral, the Earl of Warwick, Stephen Marshall offered a report from the Grand Committee of both Houses and the Assembly, in which he presented a paper from the Scots Commissioners concerning the Scottish form of church government:[17]

> Assemblies are fourfold:
> 1. Elderships of particular congregations, Matt. xviii. 17; 2. Classical presbyteries; 3. Provincial; and, 4. National assemblies; Matt. xviii. 17.

---

[13] Cf. the summary and notes, *infra* Appendix VI.

[14] *Op. cit.* p. 117.

[15] Baillie, *Letters and Journals*, II. 129f. The tone and format of *Reformation of Church-Government in Scotland* is very different from the usual style and tone of literary debate in the seventeenth century. The normal procedure would have been to subject any document by the opposition to the most minute scrutiny, almost paragraph by paragraph. E.g., Thomas Edwards's *Antapologia: or, a Full answer to the Apologeticall Narration of Mr. Nye, Mr. Sympson, Mr. Burroughs, Mr. Bridge, Members of the Assembly of Divines* (1644), which subjected the Independents' 31 page pamphlet to over 300 pages of detailed rebuttal. A similar detailed method of criticism was followed by Robert Baillie in his book, *A Dissvasive from the Errours of our Time*, London, 1646.

[16] In his letter to Spang, *Letters and Journals* II. 130; quoted earlier, *supra* p. 207, n. 41.

[17] Lightfoot, *Journal*, p. 119f.

Elderships particular are warrented; 1. By Christ's institution, Matt. xviii. 17. 2. By the example of apostolic churches; as Acts ii. 41, iv. 4, v. xiv. vi. 2. 7, viii. 1, xi. 22, xxi. 18. 25, &c. instancing in the church of Jerusalem, Antioch, and Ephesus, Corinth, Rome &c. Acts xiii. 1, xv. 13, xix. 17–20, I Cor. xvi. 8, Acts xx. 25. 28. 36, 37, Rev. ii. 12, Rom. xvi. Acts xix. 10, I Cor. iii. 4, iv. 15, xiv. 29. 31, 32.

Then Dr. *Stanton* moved, that public thanks might be given to the commissioners when they came in, for the books they gave us yesterday: but it was declined, because some had not yet received the books.

Mr. *Marshal* also moved, that this paper, brought in by them, might be recommended to the committee that hath to treat concerning the presbytery, to examine and weigh it:– which the Independents something opposed, and so also did Mr. *Selden*: and this cost some large debate: but the matter was left at large.

Dr. *Stanton* also renewed his motion for thanks to the Scots; but before it came to be resolved, the commissioners themselves came in; and so the matter was hushed, and nothing more said of it.[18]

This is an important passage because it defined the area of the future 'Grand Debate concerning Presbytery and Independency', and many of the biblical texts over which the major ecclesiological battles in the Assembly were to be fought. Moreover, the almost over-sedulous gratitude of men like Stanton to the Scots indicated the shape of things to come. The Independents must have known that their real adversary in the Assembly from this point was not any lingering episcopalianism, but the Scots' intention to bring the Church of England into complete uniformity with the Scottish Kirk. This doubtless began to influence their attitude as the Assembly commenced debating the second of the propositions brought in by Richard Vines's committee – that, "'it is lawful, and according to the word, that certain ministers of the city be desired to ordain some ministers in the vicinity,' &c."

The issues began to sharpen. After the wording had been made more precise to specify the city of London and its vicinity, Stephen Marshall and William Bridge defined the issues in the propositions very differently. Marshall reduced them to two questions – was the present situation of the English Church extraordinary? and was it legitimate to do what they now proposed to do in order to meet it? Naturally, he answered those questions affirmatively. Bridge on the other hand discerned four matters worthy of debate in the proposition – first, the assertion

---

[18] *Ibid.*

that in extraordinary circumstances procedures different from the (biblical) norm might be followed; secondly, what those procedures would be; thirdly, whether the current case could be regarded as extraordinary to that extent; and fourthly, whether "this be a proper salve."[19]

Philip Nye's contribution suggests that the pressures of the debate may have been pushing the Independents to lengths they would not have considered previously. He argued that "though jurisdiction of bishops be taken away, yet is not their order; for they are presbyters still, and so may ordain", and he concluded from this that the situation they then faced in the Church was not all that extraordinary.[20]

Although the Independents were the main opponents to the *ad hoc* proposals they were still not altogether alone. Charles Herle, the English Presbyterian, was as much a stickler for the biblical rule as the Independents, and he "proved the case not to be extraordinary". John Selden, the Erastian lawyer and Member of Parliament for Oxford University, also raised the ire of the Scots by arguing that in the English law the right of ordaining was still in the hands of the bishops acting in association with their presbyters, and that the Solemn League and Covenant provided no excuse for ignoring the laws of the land. This produced a considerable furore, and Lightfoot was not altogether pleased with his Erastian colleague:

> This speech of his cost a great deal of debate, and had many answers given it: and among other things Mr. *Henderson*, and the Lord *Mackland* [Maitland] after him, took it to heart, and expressed their resenting of it, that there had been too much boldness with the covenant: but Mr. *Selden* being gone, and the day being far spent, it was referred to be considered on in the morning: and so we adjourned.

Lightfoot then added a significant note to the rest of the day's activities:

---

[19] *Ibid.* pp. 120f.

[20] *Ibid.* p. 121. The Independents were moving to broader positions. A few months later Nye declared in the Assembly that "He thought his ordination by the bishop; with some presbyters contingently met together, to be as good as ordination by a presbytery", and he agreed with those English divines who regarded the Church of Rome as "a true, yet corrupt church." On the same occasion Thomas Goodwin declared that "He would keep communion with all churches in the world, and separate from none." 17th April, 1644, George Gillespie, *Notes*, pp. 52–3.

Of course, there are two ways of interpreting this apparent shift – either it can be seen as a genuine movement to new theological positions, or as an indication that the Independents were now holding the door open for a possible political *rapproachement* with moderate Episcopalians.

Myself, and seven or eight more of the Assembly, went and dined with the Scots' commissioners at the Bridge foot; having invited them thither about two or three days before.[21]

Was that a strategy session between some of the English Puritans and the Scots? Probably, since wheels were obviously beginning to turn very rapidly. We know that such meetings had already taken place from the account Baillie gives us of the way in which their statement on church government had been introduced in the Grand Committee; soon after their arrival at Westminster, after the Scots had become tired of continual delays in the Assembly,

and foreseeing ane appearance of a breach with the Independents, we used all the means we could, while the weather was faire, to put them to the spurrs. After privie conference with the speciall men,[22] we moved, in publick, to have ane ansuer to our paper, anent the officers of the Church, and Assemblies thereof, that we might give account to our Church of our diligence.[23] We were referred, as we had contryved it, to the grand committee, to give in to it what further papers we thought meet, which the Assemblie should take to their consideration. They were very earnest to have us present at their committees, where all their propositions, which the Assemblie debated, were framed. This we shifted, as too burdensome, and unfitting our place; bot we thought it better to give in our papers to the great committee appointed to treat with us: so we are preparing for them the grounds of our Assemblies and Presbytries.[24]

Baillie then gives us a glimpse into the political manoeuvring in which he and his colleagues were involved behind the scenes

---

[21] Lightfoot, *Journal*, p. 121.

[22] Who were these 'speciall men'? Undoubtedly the Scots relied heavily on the 'Smectymnvvs' authors and other London ministers who had consistently advocated Presbyterian ideas. But there were others whose influence they recognized and whose support they courted, such as "gracious and learned little Palmer" (Baillie, *Letters and Journals*, II. 111), and other divines who had been committed to a general Puritan position without any commitment to a particular polity.

The *political* influence of some in the Assembly was noted by Clarendon, who remarked that "the archbishop of Canterbury [Laud] had never so great an influence upon the counsels at court as Dr. Burgess and Mr. Marshall had then upon the houses; neither did all the bishops of Scotland together so much meddle in temporal affairs as Mr. Henderson had done." Of course, we expect Clarendon to be biassed, but it indicates how others regarded the importance of men like Burgess, Marshall and Henderson, and suggests the inter-relationship between religion and politics. Edward, Earl of Clarendon, *The History of Rebellion and Civil Wars in England, together with an Historical view of the affairs of Ireland* (with the notes of Bishop Warburton, Oxford, Oxford University Press, 1849, xvi books, 7 vols.,) iv. 33 (I. 427f.)

[23] January 10th, 1643/4. The motion had been presented by Lord Maitland. Lightfoot, *Journal*, p. 108, supra p. 212.

[24] February 18, 1643/4, *Letters and Journals*, II. 130f.

when he goes on somewhat ingenuously to remark to his friend, "Also we wrote a common letter to the Commission of our Church, desyreing a letter from them to us for putting us to more speed, in such tearms as we might show it to the Assemblie.[25] Likewise we pressed the sub-committee to go on in the Directorie." From this we may gather that even where no pressure already existed, it could be artificially created, and the Scottish Commissioner adds piously, "By this, ye may perceive that though our progress be small, yet our endeavours are [to] the uttermost of our strength. These things must be more advanced by your prayers, than by our paines; else they will stick, and letts will be insuperable."[26] Pains, prayers or both, the Scots were beginning to see some glimmerings of ultimate success.

Bearing in mind what had happened in the Assembly during the previous days, and particularly since Richard Vines's special committee report on the 22nd and the Scots' statement on the 25th, the Independents had good cause to feel themselves beleaguered. Ever since the Solemn League and Covenant the possibility had been present, but perhaps the numerical superiority of English Puritans in the Assembly had obscured the real nature of the threat.

The session of the Assembly that opened on Friday, January 26th therefore might very well represent a watershed in the history of the Assembly, and perhaps the shape of the subsequent debates was foreshadowed when Dr. Stanton finally managed to get the Assembly to pass a motion of thanks to the Scots for their booklet. Later that day thanks were expressed officially by Dr. Burgess – who had certainly not been noticeably 'presbyterian' in the earlier history of the Assembly – and was "briefly and sweetly answered" by the ranking Commissioner, Lord Maitland. It was clear that a whole new set of alignments was coming into being, new understandings about the future of the Church and new alliances made that would make the outcome of the Assembly's work certain.[27]

---

[25] This missive explicitly told Robert Douglas, their correspondent in Edinburgh, how the letter from the Scottish General Assembly should be worded: "ffor helping whereof, wee have thought fitt to communicat our thoughts to yow, that yow may, from your owne motion, procure an earnest Letter from the Commissioners of the Generall Assembly to vs, and that to this purpose following . . ." It was signed by Maitland, Henderson, Rutherford, Baillie and Gillespie. *Ibid.* II. 481–2.

[26] *Ibid.* 131.

[27] Although the Independents were the main group that felt itself under pressure, Erastians, such as Selden and Coleman, who were not willing to concede a *jure divino* view to any polity, were also suspicious of the Scottish strategy. John Lightfoot certainly held a similar position, but he supported presbyterian order as a practical way of meeting the need for a national church and more ministers, and of combating the sects.

Ethyn Williams Kirby had solid grounds for insisting that the 'English Presbyterians' had not been a wholly homogenous group, and that many of them originally had serious criticisms of the Scottish view of the Church. But they had some over-riding anxieties: our own study endorses the opinion that they "were still devoted to the concept of a national church such as that which they had known all their lives", and we suggest that they saw the presbyterian system – and hence, ecclesiastical alliance with the Scots – as the best means of retaining that, of maintaining clerical authority and of combating the spreading religious anarchy.[28] Fear of losing the established role of the parson in the structure of English life should not be underestimated in bringing about this understanding between conservative English Puritans and the Scots, for in Scotland the presbyterian system had endorsed the traditional structures of society. Pressure from the Houses of Parliament, induced by the similar anxiety of many Peers,[29] cemented that alliance.

Philip Nye opened the debate for the Independents against the proposal that the London ministers should be allowed to ordain 'jure fraternitatis' as a kind of vicinage council. There was nothing particularly un-congregational or pro-presbyterian about such a concept. By now, however, the Independents were thoroughly scared that this would be used as a first step towards the establishment of Presbyterianism in the capital, and that once the system was in operation it would be impossible to unseat no matter what biblical evidence the Assembly might discover about the true form of the Church. Indeed this fear was unambiguously confirmed later in the debate on the same day, when in response to Jeremiah Burroughes's argument that the London ministers could not ordain because they did not have the ecclesiastical status, John Ley bluntly declared "that the ministers of London being set upon this work *is a presbytery*", and by Seaman who argued "that materially and *substantially there is a presbytery* in London."[30]

In opposing the motion, Philip Nye pushed himself far

---

[28] Ethyn Williams Kirby, 'The English Presbyterians in the Westminster Assembly', pp. 418–426. The writer summarized the English Presbyterians' position very well in the quotation from Obadiah Sedgewick's Thanksgiving Sermon (preached on April 9th, 1644), when he declared, "I had rather my particular opinion were buried in the dust, and my private interest were laid in the grave, than at this time to pursue either the one or the other, to the hazard of a Kingdome, or of all the Churches of Christ." *Ibid.* pp. 426f, cf. Obadiah Sedgewick, *A Thanksgiving Sermon*, 1644, p.30.

[29] Cf. my Introduction to *An Apologeticall Narration* (1963), pp. 74ff.

[30] Lightfoot, *Journal*, p. 124. My italics.

out on a wing. He doubted whether in a case of extremity ordination itself was necessary,[31] and he pointed out that since the motion proposed that the procedure should be as close to the scriptural rule as possible, this implied that there is a regular 'rule', and that those who had framed the proposition knew what it was. In other words, Nye feared that there was a pre-determined agenda.

Nye's views on ordination would probably not have been accepted by many of his colleagues,[32] and certainly not by the Congregationalists of New England,[33] but it should be remembered that the Independents had been arguing consistently in the Assembly that ordination should be centred in the election of a minister to office in the church, and not in the *rite*. They believed they truly represented the Reformed position in this, but Nye could not have done his cause much good in an Assembly that was still made up largely of those who liked the order (with some modifications) of the national Church. The Scots had apparently been able to convince the leaders of that majority position that the best hope of continuing any semblance of a national Church, and of safeguarding the position of a regularly ordained ministry, lay within the presbyterian system. Nye's more unguarded statements must have confirmed the fears of the majority regarding Independency.

His views were immediately countered by Richard Vines and Stephen Marshall, and then, after the formal exchange of courtesies between Cornelius Burgess, on behalf of the Assembly, and Lord Maitland for the Scottish Commissioners, the way was prepared for Alexander Henderson to signal that a new stage had been reached in the debate by strongly attacking what had been said by those who had opposed the proposition the previous day.

---

[31] On being pressed by Lazarus Seaman, Nye insisted "that ordination is not essential to a minister; but a minister may be a minister to all points without ordination." *Ibid.* p. 122.

[32] Jeremiah Burroughes held a very high view of ministry. He distinguished very sharply between the representative character of officers in a Commonwealth and officers in the Church: "The Officers of the Commonwealth may doe without them . . . But it is not so in the Church; if they be without Officers, they cannot doe that which belongs to Officers to doe, they can have no Sacraments amongst them, neither can they have any Spiritual jurisdiction exercised amongst them; onely brotherly admonition, and withdrawing from such as walk disorderly, for their own preservation." He went on to say that "once a man be chosen as an Officer in the Church, all that power that ever any in that office had since Christ's time, in any Church in all the Christian world, or ever can have to the coming of Christ againe, falls upon him." *Irenicum*, p. 51.

[33] Cf. John Cotton, *The Way of the Churches of Christ in New England*, chapter II, 'Touching Church–Officers, with their election and ordination', especially pp. 39–42; also John Norton, *The Answer*, pp. 114–7.

However his attack on Selden and Nye was perhaps less significant than the baring of bosoms that followed:[34]

> Then Mr. *Henderson* spake his mind wherein and how the commissioners did resent the words that passed yesterday from Mr. *Selden*, that said we had only sworn against the bishops jurisdiction, not ordination; and Mr. *Nye*'s that had said, that bishops might yet ordain, though not as bishops, yet as presbyters.
> Mr. *Ley* first spake, and excused himself for that he had dedicated some of his books to bishops with glorious titles: and disclaimed their ordination.
> Dr. *Burgess* and Mr. *Marshall* also expressed their distaste of their ordination.

Here is an interesting change of direction in view of the preferences Cornelius Burgess had appeared to entertain for moderate episcopacy at the time of the Solemn League and Covenant.

The debate continued with Selden seeking to justify his views of the previous day, with Gillespie attacking Nye's position, and with Herbert Palmer – whose opposition to the office of ruling elder had certainly been distinct enough to raise Baillie's comment at the time[35] – insisting that the Solemn League and Covenant excluded recognition of (episcopal) ordination. Then followed a most intriguing passage in which Nye defended his own words, and Charles Herle raised some questions generally in support of a moderating position, although he specifically dissented from Philip Nye's view of ordination. However, the passage may have an importance beyond the evidence it provides of Herle's conciliatory position:

> Mr. *Nye* answered for himself, and persisted still in his opinion, that ordination is in the power of order [i.e. not of jurisdiction.]
> And then we fill [i.e. fell] upon our work again: and Mr. *Herle* queried, 1. Whether the rule we are to come near, be one.
> 2. Whether this rule will admit any latitude: but yet he disagreed from Mr. *Nye*, and held ordination to be necessary.
> Whilst he was in this discourse there was delivered to every one of us [*][36]

The editor of Lightfoot's *Journal* used the asterisk to indicate that at this point the original Ms. is either illegible or defective. It

---

[34] Lightfoot, *Journal*, p. 123. It should be noted that the Independents and the Erastians had been forced into a position where they seemed to be supporting each other. Nye's speeches here had a decidedly Erastian flavour, although Congregational ecclesiology was certainly not Erastian.

[35] Baillie, *Letters and Journals*, II. 111.

[36] Lightfoot, *Journal*, p. 123.

could hardly occur at a more frustrating time.[37] What was it that was delivered to the members of the Assembly at this time? Could it have been *An Apologeticall Narration*? If December 29th to January 3rd saw its recognition in some form, we cannot help noting that all the internal evidence provided by Lightfoot's account of the debates suggests that January 26th is a much more likely date for its general release and distribution to the members of the Assembly. Furthermore, Charles Herle's speech provides additional significance for this occasion. He was a Presbyterian, but he agreed with the Independents on the absolute necessity of obedience to the scriptural rule in church matters, and his respect for the Independent divines led him to take responsibility for licensing their tract. Furthermore, he raised the radical question – for that time – whether scripture offered justification for any variations in ecclesiology – 'whether the rule . . . be one', and this suggests itself as a much more appropriate occasion for the distribution of the Independents' plea for toleration. By January 26th 1643/4 they had clear reasons for that move which were not apparent on the 3rd or 4th of the month, and we have seen that by the later date they had also been "taken up sundrie times, somewhat sharplie both by Divines and Parliament-men", as Robert Baillie noted.[38] The politicians had begun to present themselves in the Assembly in significant numbers only as the debates of January drew to a climax.

In view of the facts cited earlier,[39] the date of *An Apologeticall Narration* cannot be solved in a way that reconciles all the evidence, and we are frustrated by the silence of the sources at the crucial points. But there is at least enough internal testimony from the work of the Assembly to justify raising the possibility, that whatever the official dates of its being registered, the tract may not have received wider distribution until later in January 1644.[40] Lightfoot's *Journal* clearly indicates the importance

---

[37] It is particularly frustrating because of the complete blank in the Minutes. Cf. *supra* p.199, n. 19.

[38] To Spang, February 18th, 1643/4, *Letters and Journals*, II. 129; cf. *supra* p. 207, n. 41.

[39] Cf. *supra* pp. 206–209.

[40] It was the internal evidence (or the significant lack of evidence) in the contemporary records themselves that led me to prefer 'the end of January or the beginning of February, 1643/4' for the appearance of *An Apologeticall Narration* when I edited the 1963 edition of that tract cf. *op. cit.*, 1963 edn. p. 34. Although we recognize the importance of the Thomason dating (3rd January) I am just as impressed as I was earlier by the way in which all the evidence from the Assembly itself suggests that it was not distributed until later in January, possibly on January 26th. I see no way of reconciling all the evidence.

This still leaves in doubt the date of the dinner party to which Baillie referred, and we know of no other reference to that event. It could have taken place on the 26th, although

its author attached to the debates of the latter half of that month, and hence the seriousness of what happened in the Assembly during that crucial period.

II

'An Apologeticall Narration'

We may never know precisely when *An Apologeticall Narration* was generally released, but we know that it appeared some time during the crucial month of January 1643/4, that it signalled a breach in the Assembly, and that the religious uniformity projected by the Solemn League and Covenant was seriously threatened. This was the reason why it caused an uproar in Puritan circles out of all proportion to its size and content, although the plea for toleration against which Baillie complained so bitterly came only at the end of the booklet and was stated modestly enough.[41] However, it would have far broader implications, and for that reason it becomes a document that has to be considered for any proper understanding of what was happening and what was going to happen in the Assembly and in the nation.[42]

The authors said that they had been forced to put their position in print because of the slanders circulating about them. They claimed they had made an objective attempt while in exile to place all church government and worship under the sole direction of scripture, and affirmed their own basic agreement with other Reformed Churches, notably in the matter of church officers, Pastors, Teachers, Ruling Elders[43] and Deacons. They also practised the censures of Admonition and Excommunication in church discipline, and although they did not apply the latter sentence to churches, they claimed their own practice of

---

the most plausible time for such celebration, coupled with the Independents' plea for toleration, would have been the following day after the announcement of the discovery of Ogle's plot that concerned them so intimately.

[41] The authors asked their readers to think of them as those who had already suffered exile for the common cause, and then concluded:

"And finally, as those that do pursue no other interest or designe but a subsistance (be it the poorest and meanest) in our own land (where we have and may do further service, & which is our birth-right as we are men) with the enjoyment of the ordinances of Christ (which are our portion as we are Christians) with the allowance of a latitude to some lesser differences with peaceablenesse, as not knowing where else with safety, health, and livelyhood, to set our feet on earth." *Op. cit.* p. 31.

[42] The pamphlet is 31 pages and may be found in one of the modern editions; cf. *supra* p. 207, note 40.

[43] "with us not lay but Ecclesiastique persons separated to that service." *An Apologeticall Narration*, p. 8.

withdrawal and non-communion worked as well. They took a position that was between that of the Separatists and that of the authoritative presbyterian government then in vogue, and maintained that their own position differed very little from that of others in the Assembly, "yea far lesse, then they do from what themselves were three yeers past, or then the generallity of this kingdom from it self of late."[44] That was a shrewd blow, for it reminded their readers that while the Apologists had been in exile, most of their opponents in the Assembly had not disapproved of episcopal government sufficiently to leave their livings in the Church of England. They concluded with an appeal that they might be allowed to remain in England "with the allowance of a latitude to some lesser differences with peaceablenesse."[45]

Such was the "slie and cunning way" in which the Independents of the Assembly asked for their differences from the Presbyterian position to be tolerated, and perhaps the very modesty of the request made it all the more objectionable to Robert Baillie. He said that the writing "long had lyen readie beside them",[46] and that may be readily believed because some of the ideas expressed in it had already appeared within the debates.

But perhaps *An Apologeticall Narration* was more significant for the Independents themselves than it was for the reaction it produced among their opponents. They had asked to be granted toleration and having made that request for themselves, they could not deny the same principle to others, especially to those who were risking their lives in the ranks of Cromwell's troopers.

III

The Front established:
a theological theme with political accents

The lines were now clearly drawn. In the Assembly the Independents had their backs to the wall, and from this point on they seem to have organized themselves to block or postpone the establishment of presbyterian uniformity by every means in their power.

This became clear during the last few days in January, but although the policy served their purpose, it did not endear them to the majority, or to the increasing number of Parliamentarians who heard the debates. The exchanges on Friday 26th and Mon-

---

[44] *Ibid.* pp. 30f.
[45] *Ibid.* p. 31.
[46] *Letters and Journals*, II. 130.

day 29th, January, seem to have been a turning-point in the work of the Assembly, and brought the Presbyterian issue into the open where it could no longer be evaded.

It also seems to have been a turning-point in relationships within the Assembly itself. The small body of Independents[47] was increasingly isolated from a majority that had become either reconciled or resigned to Presbyterianism. We have to note the impact of the Independents' opposition and the way they expressed it under the critical eyes of parliamentary leaders who had begun to crowd into the Jerusalem Chamber. The political laymen were more than ready to equate *vox populi* with *vox dei*, and opposition to the will of the majority appeared to be blatant obstruction. The pressure for immediate action had come from the Houses of Parliament, and these gentlemen were not used to seeing their wishes thwarted.

There always seemed to be an Independent on the floor of the chamber or ready to speak. If it was not Thomas Goodwin or Philip Nye, then it was William Bridge or Jeremiah Burroughes, and even Lord Say and Sele came to lend support to his friends. A specially called session was to be scheduled for Saturday 27th at the direct request of the peers, for on the previous day (26th) Lord Howard had appeared and "from the Lords, desired the Assembly should sit tomorrow."[48] The members agreed, and that session would discuss the motion that "Ministers, quâ ministers, have capacity to ordain: which", Lightfoot observed, "being gainsaid by the Independents, Mr. *Salloway*, the Parliamentman, put forward that we might do something today, for that House of Commons have made an order to hasten us". Friday's session eventually concluded with voting *nemine contradicente* 'that preaching presbyters of London may ordain', but when it was proposed that this should be put finally to the question, the Idependents "did mightily deny also", and the issue was left for the special session on the following day.

That is where Saturday's debate began, and Lightfoot says that the "Independents began to cavil at it, and found I know not how many scruples in it." Herle, be it noted, also wanted to be

---

[47] The Independent group in the Assembly was not limited to the five Dissenting Brethren – Thomas Goodwin, Philip Nye, Jeremiah Burroughes, William Bridge and Sidrach Simpson. It included William Greenhill and William Carter, the younger, (who are counted among the 'Septemvirs',) and also John Bond, John Green, John Phillips (the only member of the Assembly to have served in New England,) and possibly Anthony Burgess, Peter Sterry and Joseph Caryl. Cf. my edition of *An Apologeticall Narration* (1963), chapter IV, and particularly pp. 109ff.

[48] Lightfoot, *Journal*, p. 124.

reassured "1. That it is lawful. 2. According to the word. 3. That then the London-ministers are to be desired to do it: and, 4. To do it 'jure fraternitatis.'"[49] Then Dr. Temple suggested that since they had already voted that ministers could ordain, they could proceed directly to discuss whether the civil authority had not the right to direct them to do it, but this did not win much support. We read

> The Independents did still intricate the stating of the question: which held us long discourse, 'pro et contra:' which while we were in doing, the Earls of *Pembroke* and of *Salisbury* came in: but at the first said nothing, but our debates continued still.[50]

However, during the course of the debate Lightfoot reported, "my Lord of Pembroke very urgently desired us to hasten, and come to the question." Then there was a sharp passage between Gillespie and Nye – the former suggesting that since the phrase 'jure fraternitatis' had caused so much discussion, it might as well be omitted and the London ministers simply be allowed to decide among themselves who should be responsible for ordaining. But this, Lightfoot observed, "pinched the Independents, as coming too near a presbytery, which Mr. *Nye* soon expressed"; so George Gillespie insisted that "freedom of debate of the presbytery might still be reserved."

Richard Vines moved that the Independents should bring forward their own proposals for dealing with the immediate need of ministers, "which was well liked of; but," we read, "they were also told, the way must be by ordination or else we answer not the order."[51] The majority of members in the Assembly was in no mood to leave the question of ordination in abeyance, and the parliamentary leaders were bringing all the pressure they could. The Earl of Pembroke again intervened urging the members to haste, "for that the church and kingdom are on fire; and let it not be burnt down before we apply some remedy."

It was at that point that the Independents seem to have openly adopted delaying tactics to prevent any decision:

> Yet did Mr. *Nye* again interpose, and again; and so again did my Lord of *Pembroke*, and called to the question: and then Mr. *Bridges* again interposed; and called for a place of Scripture to prove the proposition. Dr. *Burgess* gave 1 Tim. iv. and Acts iii. 1. Then

---

[49] *Ibid.* p. 125.
[50] *Ibid.*
[51] *Ibid.* p. 126.

Mr. *Burroughs* interposed his part, and repeated the argument he proposed yesterday.[52]

Lightfoot obviously disapproved of the Independents' obstruction, for the argument of national need was a strong one. Yet there was a sense, too, in which the Independents felt they were on legitimate ground, for by insisting on being given scriptural proofs for the proposals they were simply taking their stand on the conditions laid down in the Solemn League and Covenant. It was the perfect stand-off, but it was not likely to impress the noble peers or the majority of the churchmen present, who were quite convinced that the conditions foretold by the apostle in 1 Timothy iv were literally afflicting England at that time.[53]

As the members were facing this *impasse*, Lord Wharton came from the House of Lords with the dramatic revelation of a royalist plot to exploit the dissensions in the parliamentary ranks and to seduce the Independents to the King's cause. Thomas Ogle, a prisoner in the hands of the parliamentary forces, had informed the Earl of Bristol that the King would have a good chance of weakening the opposition "if the moderate Protestant and fiery Independent could be brought to withstand the Presbyterian",[54] and to that end overtures had been made to some of the Independent leaders with the promise of a reformed and moderate episcopacy in the Church of England together with some vague hopes of toleration for themselves. The Independents had not been beguiled. With the full knowledge and support of the parliamentary leaders, Philip Nye and John Goodwin, the Independent vicar of St. Stephen's, Coleman Street, had appeared to be interested, and this had enabled them to discover the ramifications of the plot.[55]

This report took up the rest of the day's business. Lightfoot records –

The relation of my Lord *Wharton* was very long: which being done, Dr. *Burgess* being now prolocutor, returned thanks to him and to the Lords, and made a very long speech. When he had done, Mr. *Nye*, who was used with Mr. *Goodwin* of Coleman-street, the Lord *Wharton*, the Lord-general, and others, to carry on the design in hand, for

---

[52] *Ibid.*

[53] I Timothy iv. 1–5 (cited by Cornelius Burgess) was apposite enough in view of the sects that were making their appearance.

[54] Lightfoot, *Journal*, p. 126.

[55] Cf. Gardiner, *The Great Civil War*, I. 264ff. Ogle had been active in plotting for Charles since October 17th 1643. The plot was also related to a royalist attempt to subvert Colonel Mozley, one of the officers of the parliamentary garrison at Aylesbury.

the more detection, made a speech also to express himself in the undertaking of the business: which when he had done, we adjourned.[56]

One may not be able to say that the revelation of this plot was contrived, since the under-cover manoeuvring had been going on since the beginning of the month with the full knowledge of the leaders in Parliament, but from the Independents' point of view the disclosure could hardly have been made at a more opportune time. If the majority in the Assembly needed any prompting, it not only emphasized their fidelity to the common cause, but it was also a salutary reminder of what might happen if presbyterian uniformity were pushed too far.

On Monday 29th the Assembly returned to the debate that had been interrupted. It was obviously a crucial debate, and the keenness with which the various points were argued comes through in John Lightfoot's summary.

First, we again notice the large number of peers who were present and Lord Pembroke persistently urged the divines to hurry their decision; secondly, we note that Charles Herle, the English Presbyterian, spoke consistently on the Independent side of the argument, not, indeed, in support of Independent ecclesiology, but in support of the Independents' opposition to the measures before the Assembly at that time; and thirdly, we sense that the Independents were reluctant to produce their most telling arguments against Presbyterian polity until that issue was specifically debated in the Assembly.

The importance of this session was indicated when both the Lord Admiral, the Earl of Warwick, and the Lord General, the Earl of Essex, entered the Jerusalem Chamber at the very beginning of the day's work, and very soon afterwards they were joined by the Earl of Pembroke. Lord Say and Sele, the only peer known to espouse the Independents' views, was also present and contributed on their side of the debate. Later in the session Lightfoot specifically noted the entrance of Sir William Waller, the Earl of Salisbury and Lord Howard, and then in a group, the Earls of Manchester and Northumberland, "and some other lords".[57] Apparently the importance of what was happening in the Jerusalem Chamber was fully recognized in the Houses of Parliament.

---

[56] Lightfoot, *Journal*, p. 127.
[57] Lightfoot, *Journal*, p. 129.

Early in the debate Charles Herle defined the issue before them as "Whether the ministers of London not yet formed into a classical or congregational presbytery,[58] may ordain", and Herbert Palmer immediately retorted "that those that deny they may, should prove they may not."[59] Thomas Goodwin pointed out that since this was a matter of conscience, the matter should be set down precisely, and Seaman "urged that Mr. *Goodwin* himself should state it."

Lord Say entered the fray in support of his Independent friends. He thought it was dangerous to set up a system that was not "exactly according to the rule", and he felt that the argument from necessity was not strong enough to justify what was being proposed. The existing needs might be met by simply authorizing young scholars to a kind of licensure that gave authority to preach but not to administer the sacraments.[60]

Richard Vines reminded Lord Say that "the apprehension of this necessity came to us first from the House of Lords", and he maintained that to vary from the normal (i.e. scriptural) rule is not always a sin. Whereupon Say disclaimed any intention of questioning what had been decided in the Lords, but said that he simply wanted to keep to the Word. He also complained that it was not very helpful to take their examples for the Church (as the divines often did) from the Old Testament.[61]

This led the Earl of Pembroke to interpose that "the Lords did not send this order that we should precipitate, but that we should hasten what we can according to the word of God." That brief statement should have given some pause, for it indicated that the leaders in the House of Lords regarded these recommendations as more authoritative and permanent than the Assembly claimed they were at this juncture.

The debate continued along a path that was predetermined by what we know of its participants. Cornelius Burgess criticized Lord Say's suggestion of simply licensing young preachers by reminding him that "one of the greatest complaints of the kingdom is for want of the sacraments", and therefore they needed men who were ordained, while Lazarus Seaman argued against

---

[58] The distinction between Presbyterian and Congregational polity was between church government organized on the basis of 'classical presbytery' (i.e. in a classis) and church government which centered in the 'congregational presbytery' of a local congregation. Cf. John Cotton, *The Way of the Congregational Churches Cleared*, p. 11.

[59] Lightfoot, *Journal*, p. 127.

[60] A few months earlier (19th October, 1643) Thomas Young had made a similar suggestion (*ibid.* p. 24), but it is clear that the stance of the Assembly had changed dramatically from that time. Cf. *supra* p. 143.

[61] *Ibid.* p. 128.

insistence on the biblical rule by pointing to the example of our Lord's disciples plucking corn on the Sabbath.[62] On the other hand Charles Herle supported Say's misgivings because "our coming short of the rule will not excuse us." Several others took part, but the Assembly was no nearer a decision.[63]

The nub of the problem from the Independents' viewpoint was probably expressed most succinctly by William Bridge, when he declared that "either the ministers of London are a presbytery or no; if they be, then are we to treat of the presbytery: if not, then to debate whether ministers out of a presbytery may ordain", and when Seaman again urged "that the Independents might state the question", Philip Nye presented the points of their concern:

1. We conceive it doth really, and 'de facto,' set up the presbytery before discussed, as appeared by divers passages in the debate.

2. Ordination is of jurisdiction; and they that may do it, may excommunicate.

3. If any extraordinary thing is in it, and it must come as near as we can, it evidenceth presbytery to be the rule.

4. We cannot implead this, without the arguments, which we must use against the presbytery.[64]

Jeremiah Whitaker immediately responded, "that for ending of this business it might be entered, That there may be a free debate hereafter of the presbytery," and Edmund Calamy added that the term 'jure fraternitatis' had been inserted precisely to "avoid these jealousies". He tried to get the Assembly to vote that the committee's motion should be debated forthwith.[65]

Then Thomas Goodwin produced a paper in which he proposed that "ordination and other like acts are ordinarily to be done by the ministers and elders of the congregation: but, 1. they must do it in their own congregation. 2. In a 'consessus'." Goodwin probably felt that he was preventing the issue between classical and congregational presbyteries from being decided prematurely, by providing for both forms in any interim arrangements. To the Earl of Pembroke, however, it seemed to be merely obstruction in another form.

---

[62] Cf. Matthew xii.

[63] John Selden seems to have made the practical suggestion that the proposition should be divided up so that the members could know how best to address the issues. He also suggested that they should first discuss "Whether the ministers of London be authorized to ordain?" in which he was supported by Seaman, although John White, the Assessor, who was chairing that session, thought the specific reference to London should be omitted as being "a political thing." Lightfoot, *Journal*, p. 128f.

[64] *Ibid*. p. 129.

[65] I.e. presumably the proposition regarding 'many churches in one presbytery.'

My Lord of *Pembroke* again urged for haste, and yet Mr. *Nye* still and still stopped us.

My Lord of *Pembroke* again urged, and said, "he doubted an 'ignus fatuus' had been among us since Saturday: for that then we were in a good way, and now far out of it:" and yet Mr. *Nye* interposed again.[66]

There was another exchange between George Gillespie, the Scottish Commissioner, and Philip Nye. Gillespie argued that what they were proposing for the London ministers was not a true presbytery, 1. because it would not be done 'ex pacto' by the ministers, but by appointment of Parliament; 2. because they have no powers of church government except this single authority to ordain; 3. because no (ruling) elders were to be associated with the ministers; and finally he thought that a note might be added to their motion "that there shall be free debate left concerning the presbytery.[67] Replying to Gillespie, Nye said that they ought to debate whether the civil magistrate had the authority to require ministers to do this. Gillespie immediately saw the unwisdom of that remark and the chance to make a point in the presence of so many members of the Upper House:

> Mr. *Gillespie* thereupon inferred, That it is apparent by this scruple that the presbyterial government giveth more to the magistrate than some others do.
>
> Here grew some heat: for the Independents would not be stopped from speaking: at last Mr. *Seaman* moved, that we might fall upon the presbytery: and my Lord *Say* followed it; and this cost us a great debate again; and some heat amongst us; at last it was putting to the question, whether we should debate the proposition before us, but it was above an hour before we could determine; and then not neither. But Mr. *Goodwin* was desired that he would state the question . . .[68]

While Goodwin was framing his motion Dr. Burgess asked that Lord Maitland, the Scots Commissioner, be allowed the floor. The Assembly then heard the news that the Scots army had entered England on Thursday January 18th and that by the previous Wednesday (the 24th) it had been near Alnwick, Northumberland. Maitland also

> produced a declaration from the Scots, wherein they justify themselves in their coming in, in their intentions and call, and manner of persuance of it: and after it was read, he related some more passages concerning their armies, and read a piece of a letter from the commit-

---

[66] *Ibid.* pp. 129f.
[67] *Ibid.* p. 130.
[68] *Ibid.*

tee of the general assembly, congratulating the happy progress of our Assembly; and concluded with desire of our prayers for them: and Dr. *Burgess* being now chairman, gave him thanks, and made a speech to him in the name of the Assembly.[69]

Again, as in the revelation of the Ogle plot, although we cannot say that the occasion had been contrived, it certainly did the Scots' cause no harm. We are reminded of Henderson's remark, that the Scots could not have much hope of England's "conformitie to us, before our armie be in England",[70] and of Baillie's hope that the Scottish army's advance would "much assist our arguments."[71] The Scots army had been on its way for some time, and sooner or later it was bound to enter England, but this was another of those happy announcements that could hardly have been given better timing; for it reminded the English of the spirit in which the Solemn League and Covenant had been signed. It had not been all that long ago since Baillie had observed that "all things are expected from God and the Scotts."[72]

Maitland's announcement, however, did not conclude the debate. Goodwin's attempt to rephrase the question did not meet with any success, and the amendments proposed by Cornelius Burgess and Herbert Palmer were no more acceptable. "At last," Lightfoot reported, "it was put to the question, 'Whether our proposition as it lay, should be debated at our next meeting:' – and when the affirmative was given, then was there long and much interposition: but being at last agreed, it was carried affirmatively and so we adjourned till Thursday."[73]

The debate continued on Thursday and Friday the 1st and 2nd of February, but we do not have Lightfoot's eyewitness account of the proceedings in detail because he was visiting his parish at Great Munden. However, with his usual care Lightfoot took the trouble to get some idea of what had happened in his absence:

the work of Thursday, as I understood upon my return, was upon the business where we left, about the London ministers' ordination: which, at last, by the urgency of the Lord *Say*, was laid aside for the present, and they fell upon the proposition brought in by the committee, concerning many churches under one presbytery, which the

---

[69] *Ibid.* pp. 130f.

[70] Robert Baillie to William Spang, November 17th, 1643; Baillie, *Letters and Journals*, II. 104.

[71] To the same, December 7th, 1643, *ibid.* p. 111.

[72] To the same, *ibid.* p. 114f.

[73] Lightfoot, *Journal*, p. 131.

Independents did most vehemently oppose the handling of; but it was voted to be fallen upon, upon Monday.[74]

So the way was at last cleared for debating the basic issue of Presbyterian church government. There were no further excuses for postponement, and although the small group of Independents had kept the Assembly stalled for a month, they could not keep their secret theological weapons hidden any longer. The battle was on.

The critical passage of arms in the great debate between Presbyterian and Independent ecclesiologies occurred from the beginning of February 1643/4 until May 14th of that year. The controversy did not end then, for the issues surfaced throughout the Assembly's active life and the literary battle interested denominational apologists long after the polemic faded from the arena of seventeenth century politics; but the period from 2nd February–14th May was decisive.

The members of the Assembly recognized that because a decision to debate the Presbyterian system had been taken, the debates that immediately followed were likely to decide the issues. George Gillespie must have recognized that the crucial period had begun, for it is hardly an accident that his *Notes* began on February 2nd and continued uninterrupted until May 14th.[75] The 'Minutes' also resumed their uneven account on February 15th after an inexplicable silence for over a month. Add to these the consistent account John Lightfoot gives in his *Journal* and Robert Baillie's lively commentary in his letters, and we have a sudden abundance of source material.

Because of the importance of these debates for our subject, some preliminary warnings may not be amiss.

1.   The Independents in the Assembly suffered from the disadvantage that all these eye-witness accounts were written by those who were among their most determined opponents.[76]

2.   It is impossible to present all the argumentation in a debate of this nature, and it is difficult to present it fairly because so

---

[74] *Ibid.* 586 (Ms. I., f. 305.)

[75] He resumed his account on September 4th, 1644, and it continued in some measure until 2nd February, 1644/5.

[76] Lightfoot had been extremely suspicious of the Independents from the beginning, and strongly supported Presbyterianism in everything but its *jure divino* claims, while the Scottish Commissioners, Gillespie and Baillie, were totally committed to their own Kirk. We might have assumed that the Minutes would be written in a more impartial spirit, but the scribe persistently identifies with the prejudices of the majority and often speaks of 'them' (the Independents) against 'us' (the majority party.)

much depends on the idiosyncracies of seventeenth century scriptural exegesis, as well as upon the unconscious prejudices we have inherited from these seventeenth century battlefields. We must necessarily be selective, but the principle of selection will be to accent the tension between religion and politics in the work and methods of the Assembly.

3.   As we have seen, there is a good deal of internal evidence to show that by the end of January a decisive understanding had been reached between the Scots Commissioners who gave leadership to the relatively small band of English Presbyterians in the Assembly, and the Puritan divines whom we have referred to hitherto as the 'conservative majority.' A recent writer has expressed the situation very well:

> With the Assembly for the most part ill attended, and with those divines who had no very fixed views on matters of ecclesiastical polity anxious above all for order to be restored in the church, it was possible for the minority with strong Presbyterian convictions to dominate the proceedings.[77]

That is accurate enough, except that it needed more than a small minority with strong presbyterian convictions – it needed the special circumstances facing Parliament in 1643, the Scottish alliance and the presence of the Scots Commissioners backed by the Solemn League and Covenant. However it was managed, from this time on this alliance acts and speaks as a united party in the Assembly for the discomfiture of Independency and the early establishment of Presbyterian church government.[78] Scattered through the debates of the succeeding months there were occasional peeps of protest or disquiet from the conservatives, but they were rare and tentative: from the point of view of its voting habits, the majority can now be regarded as 'Presbyterian.'

4.   We become aware that the intensity of this debate had its own effect on the way the two main parties reacted. We have the impression that during the first few weeks of February several of the Independents were at pains to state their case in a way that

---

[77] Michael Watts, *The Dissenters*, p. 93.

[78] So we find Richard Vines and Herbert Palmer, who not much more than two months previously had vigorously opposed the office of ruling elder, now lending their full weight to the Presbyterian position, and Cornelius Burgess, whose loyalty had been under the gravest suspicion at the time of the Covenant, now using his position as occasional chairman of the Assembly to bring an early closure on the arguments presented by the Apologists and hasten the settlement of presbytery.

emphasized their closeness to the Presbyterian position, but that as their views were persistently voted down they began to become more 'Independent' and less 'Congregational' – that just as in the debate with episcopal legalism earlier Puritans had become more literalistic in their appeal to scripture, so the Independents stiffened in reaction to the majority position. This may be seen especially in the reactions of Philip Nye.

Clearly the work of presenting their case in the Assembly was carefully parcelled out among the little group of Independents, with the main advocacy going to Thomas Goodwin, although William Bridge and Jeremiah Burroughes made major contributions, and Philip Nye was always ready to enter the lists as the opportunity arose. J. R. DeWitt observes with good reason that "no general ever approached a campaign in the field with more thorough preparation and more dilligent attention to strategy than did Thomas Goodwin, Philip Nye, and their little company of troops."[79]

5. This was equally if not even more true of the Scots. Writing to William Spang on the events that led to the debates of February, 1643/4, Robert Baillie described how the ordination proposals had been shelved at the urgent request of Lord Say. In this way, Baillie continued, "and upon hope made by him and his followers of the quick despatch of the ordinare way, we fell on the long-wished-for subject of the Presbytrie."[80] With confidence born of an understanding with the English majority, the Scots were prepared for an advance on all fronts to secure the four objectives of religious uniformity promised in the Solemn League and Covenant: they had already presented their expectations in this matter.[81] Therefore from this time forward we witness the interrelatedness of ecclesiology illustrated in the Assembly: the practical problem of ordination had led to the consideration of church order, and the discussion of church order would inevitably lead to debates on church discipline and to a Directory of Worship.

---

[79] TMs. I. 589 (Ms. I., f. 306b.)

[80] February 18th, 1643/4, *Letters and Journals*, II. 139. Baillie erroneously dated this event as 'January' 3rd but David Laing, the editor of the *Letters and Journals*, corrected it to February 3rd.

[81] Lord Maitland had reminded the Assembly of Scottish expectations on January 10th. (Cf. *supra* pp. 212f., Lightfoot's Journal, p. 108.) Moreover, Alexander Henderson had persistently reminded the divines of the distinctive points of church government in the Church of Scotland. The program was very explicitly set out in the paper the Commissioners had sent to the Assembly via the Grand Committee, which Stephen Marshall presented on January 25th. Cf. *ibid.* 119f., *supra* pp. 221f.

IV

'The long-wished-for subject of Presbyterie'

The Scottish program had first been presented to the 'Grand Committee',[82] and this committee may have held a key place in the strategy of the Scottish Commissioners. It had been brought into being because Parliament needed a smaller body to give oversight to its treaty obligations in respect to the Scots. Since these obligations involved religious matters, the Assembly had been asked to appoint a number of its divines to join with representatives of both Houses to receive any communications from the Commissioners.[83]

The Scots managed to turn this into a permanent arrangement, and they appear to have regarded the Grand Committee as the most appropriate agent for introducing their views to the Assembly and most fitting to their dignity as treaty Commissioners. Baillie said that they preferred to go to the "committee appointed to treat with us." They regarded the ordinary committees of the Assembly "as too burdensome, and unfitting our place",[84] however, it is clear from Gillespie's *Notes* that they did not disdain working in the less prestigious committees when their special interests were involved.[85]

It has been noted[86] that at first the Grand Committee failed to be the effective steering committee for the Assembly that we might have expected from the prominence of its members,[87] and this was perhaps due to the strength of the Independents in that committee and "the influence of men like St. John, Vane, and Lord Say and Sele."[88] But the same writer noted that during the

---

[82] Or the 'Great Committee.'

[83] September 11th, 1643; TMs. I. 78 (Ms. I., f. 39b.)

[84] *Letters and Journals* I. 131.

[85] Cf. his notes respecting the sub-committee on the Directory, *Notes*, pp. 101f.

[86] Wayne Spear is one of the few recent writers to pay any detailed attention to the place of the Grand Committee in the history of the Westminster Assembly. Cf. 'Covenanted Uniformity in Religion', pp. 73–82.

[87] The first members of the Assembly appointed to the Grand Committee had been John White, one of the Assessors, together with Philip Nye, Thomas Hill, Edmund Calamy, Lazarus Seaman, Thomas Goodwin, Thomas Temple, Brocket (or Peter) Smith, and Joshua Hoyle; 11th September, 1643, TMs. I. 78 (Ms. I., f. 39b.) Herbert Palmer had been added on September 28th, and on the following day, Charles Herle and Thomas Young. As Spear notes, these twelve were reappointed when the committee gained a more permanent status on October 23rd. (*Op. cit.* p. 75.) Later, after Stephen Marshall's return from Scotland, he was immediately given a place on the Grand Committee. 26th October, 1643; TMs. I. 246, (Ms. I., f. 124.)

[88] 'Covenanted Uniformity in Religion', p. 77. The committee included the following important parliamentarians – Lord Say, Lord Howard of Escrick, Oliver St. John, John Pym, Sir John Clotworthy and Gilbert Gerard. Later, others were added – Lord Wharton, Sir Henry Vane the younger, Francis Rous, Edmund Prideaux and Zouch Tate. Spear noted that of these only Prideaux and Tate were not also members of the Assembly.

debates on church government, "all but three of the twenty or so men who were regular debaters in the Assembly" were members.[89] So although it failed to be as influential as the Scots may have wished, it had the potential for effective action, and during the winter of 1643–4 and the following spring it was consistently augmented from the majority party,[90] from those whom we now denominate 'Presbyterians'.[91]

The Scots were prepared to use any vantage point from which they could bring pressure on the Assembly. Robert Baillie's work behind the scenes is an example of this, and we are fortunate in having ingenuous evidence of his activity from his own hand. Baillie admitted later that he never made any speeches in the plenary sessions of the Assembly – and he tried to get himself recalled on that account[92] – but he proved to be extremely adroit in arranging matters to further the Scots design. He appears to have spent most of his time with the London ministers, developing a strategy to counter the Independents, and promoting presbyterian uniformity. Above all he was constantly writing to influential friends in Scotland and in Europe, urging them to bring the kind of pressures on Westminster that might swing the decision in the Scots direction.

It is with that in mind that his letter to his cousin William Spang on February 18th should be read,[93] but there were other

---

[89] *Ibid.* p. 76. The regular and important debaters who were not appointed to the Grand Committee were the two Independents, Jeremiah Burroughes and William Bridge, and William Gouge.

[90] January 8th John Arrowsmith was added at Stephen Marshall's suggestion, and on 25th April, Cornelius Burgess, Thomas Gataker, Edward Reynolds and Richard Vines. Later in the year, after the question of church government had been decided but when there was still some hope of an accommodation with the Independents, Sidrach Simpson, Jeremiah Burroughes and John Durie were added with the Presbyterians, Anthony Tuckney and Matthew Newcomen.

[91] Even at this time the term 'Presbyterian' should be used for many of the divines with some reserve. On January 26th, at the end of an acrimonious debate and at the insistence of the parliamentarians, the Assembly had voted that "Ministers, quâ ministers, have capacity to ordain". Lightfoot, *Journal*, p. 124. Spear pointed out that "this was a dangerous and inconsistent position for the anti-prelatic Assembly to take, since one of their main objections to episcopal ordination was that it put ecclesiastical control in the hands of one man by virtue of the office which he held." 'Covenanted Uniformity in Religion', p. 298f.
It is less strange when we recognize that although the Assembly opposed diocesan prelacy, the majority of its members could by no means yet be regarded as doctrinaire Presbyterians. On no issues were English divines more loyal to traditional church order than to their ordination and status in the ordained ministry.

[92] See his letter to Robert Blair, 26th March, 1644, *Letters and Journals*, II. 159f.

[93] A careful reading of that missive shows how the Commissioners managed matters once they became convinced that a breach with the Independents was inevitable. They had used every opportunity to put the Assembly "to the spurs", they had negotiated in private with the most influential divines how to get official recognition for their own

ways of exerting pressure. Baillie told William Spang of the letter in which he and his fellow-Commissioners had urged their colleagues in Scotland to write to the English exhorting them to haste.[94] It was an oblique way of getting things done, but it was a favourite method of exerting leverage on the Assembly, and it was effective. Repeatedly Baillie urged correspondents like Spang to use their best efforts in getting letters sent from the continental churches to the Assembly supporting the Scots' proposals.[95] Not only did he urge them to get letters written, but he had no compunction in giving explicit instructions on the matters to be addressed and the way in which the replies could be worded most effectively. After all, he was firmly convinced that the cause in which he was engaged was both that of his nation and of properly Reformed Churches everywhere.[96]

His efforts are not without humour, as when he frankly admitted that the Dutch must not expect a member of the Assembly to write directly to them on these matters, because "it's farr above their power to doe this; and if they assayed it, they would soon be taken up by the Parliament."[97] Baillie was constantly involved in the strategy of the Scots ecclesiastical campaign. He may have left the public debating to Henderson, Rutherford and Gillespie, but he was listened to with respect in matters of policy,[98] and his letters provide ample evidence of his diplomatic activity and expertise throughout this period. His letters at the end of 1643 had been sombre enough,[99] but they became noticeably more

---

paper on ecclesiastical order, and they were naturally referred – "as we contryved it" – to the Grand Committee. In these ways, Baillie admitted, the Scots were preparing "the grounds of our Assemblies and Presbyteries". *Ibid*. pp. 130ff.; quoted *supra* p. 224.

[94] Cf. *supra* p. 225.

[95] See his letter to David Buchanan, who had formerly lived in France, urging him to write to friends in Paris, Geneva and Bern, and to persuade them to write to the Assembly "to beware of that pernicious liberty of all sects, and in particular of these who are enemies to the discipline of all the Reformed. There is a golden occasion in hand, if improved, to gett England conforme in worship and government to the rest of the Reformed." *Ibid*. p. 180. The letter is undated but it belongs to this period; it is extremely explicit about the kind of reply that Baillie wanted the foreign churches to supply.

[96] Practically all the letters he wrote to Spang in Holland reflect this single-mindedness about the Reformed faith, but some particurarly striking examples are to be found in *ibid*. II. 115, 143f, 180f, and in letters to David Buchanan and David Dickson, *ibid*. pp. 179f, 277f.

[97] To Spang, 12th July, 1644, *ibid*. p. 202. Baillie obviously thought his own activities exempt from such prohibitions; and indeed there is some slight justification for his view when we realize that as a Scots Commissioner his presbyterian interests were dictated not only by his churchmanship but also by the diplomatic goals of a national envoy.

[98] *Ibid*. p. 117f.

[99] *Ibid*. p. 122.

cheerful as they progressed into 1644.[100] There might be still cause enough for anxiety in the world of secular politics and military action, but in the Assembly the situation rapidly improved, and late in that year he was able to report to his friends in Scotland, "our Church affaires goes on now apace, blessed be God."[101]

[100] *Ibid.* p. 143.
[101] Publick Letter, 21st November, 1644; *ibid.* p. 242.

Part III

'The Grand Debate'

CHAPTER 9

THE BATTLE FOR PRESBYTERIAN GOVERNMENT: ARTILLERY BARRAGE

I

First Phase: the Case against Presbytery

At the beginning of his own account of the Assembly George Gillespie says that on that day "the Assembly had voted, 1st, That there is a presbytery holden forth in the New Testament; 2d, That it consists of pastors and other church governors. The 3d proposition brought in by the committee was, That the Scripture holds forth that many particular congregations may be under one presbyterial government."[1] On the first and second parts of the proposal there was no argument, but it was with the third of these propositions that the Independents took issue. On February 2nd Philip Nye pointed out that the Scots had handed in a comprehensive paper on church government, and he would have preferred the Assembly to use the method they had followed, beginning with the government of particular congregations. He also criticized the words 'may be' in the proposition, since the Assembly's charge was to discover what 'ought to be.'[2] His remarks drew a bland disclaimer from Gillespie that the Scots had not sought to tie the Assembly to their order, and Richard Vines said that the committee had tried to avoid giving offence by the wording, since "*must be* will make each side condemn [the] other, but *may be* will make each side bear with [the] other."[3]

---

[1] Gillespie, *Notes*, p. 9.
[2] He was supported by Goodwin and Burroughes. Gillespie, *Notes*, p. 9.
[3] *Ibid.*

Lightfoot was absent from the Assembly at his parish[4] but he seems to have kept himself well-informed about what had happened while he was away. He tells us that when the Assembly resolved to debate the proposition concerning presbytery, "they also resolved that the Independents which disliked it, should bring in what they had to say against it."[5] A long time after the debate was over, Robert Baillie gave a somewhat different account when he said that the Independents pressed that they might be heard in the negative before the proposition on presbyterian government was debated positively.[6]

Charles Herle seems to have been the person responsible for getting the Assembly to adopt this method as a concession to the Apologists,[7] but although this may have appeared tactically an advantage for the Independents, it was probably a grave error strategically, because not only were they forced to criticize a system of government that had not yet been debated but also they were pushed into presenting an entirely negative position to the world[8] and into appearing to obstruct the practical results of the Assembly's work.[9]

These were but preliminary skirmishings before the real battle, which began on February 5th, but they must be set within the wider context of national affairs if the significance of the battle itself is to be appreciated. By that date every Englishman eighteen years of age or over had been required to take the Covenant, but there were those even in the parliamentary ranks

---

[4] He was in Munden for the weekend, February 2nd–5th.

[5] Lightfoot, *Journal*, p. 131.

[6] Publick Letter, April 2nd, 1644, *Letters and Journals* II. 145.

[7] Gillespie, *Notes*, p. 9.

[8] It was common policy of ecclesiastical parties in power during the late 16th and early 17th century to force the opposition into the position where it had to attack the accepted order. There was an inevitable tendency for dissenters to over-state their case, to get caught up in details and thus to give the impression of quibbling. The Puritans had suffered from tactical disadvantage in the 1570s at the time of the Admonitions to Parliament, and again at the Hampton Court Conference in 1603/4, and were to suffer the same liability in 1661. Cf. Bard Thompson (ed.), *Liturgies of the Western Church*, (Philadelphia, Fortress Press, 1961,) pp. 376–7.

Whether innocently or not, the Independents were caught in the same trap.

[9] "Here they spent to us many of twentie long sessions. Goodwin took most of the speech upon him; yet they divided their arguments among them, and gave the managing of them by turnes, to Bridges, Burroughs, Nye, Simpson, and Caryll. Truelie, if the cause were good, the men have plentie of learning, witt, eloquence, and above all, boldness and stiffness, to make it out; but when they had wearied themselves, and over-wearied us all, we found the most they had to say against the Presbytrie, was but curious idle niceties". Publick Letter, April 2nd, 1644, Robert Baillie, *Letters and Journals* II, 145. Of the known Independents, Simpson and Caryl do not feature prominently in the records of this period, but we do find John Phillips, William Carter and Lord Say taking part.

who were not enthusiastic about this reminder of Scotland's influence in England.[10]

There had been a show of unity on January 18th at the service of Thanksgiving and the Banquet given by the City, but beneath this appearance of concord cracks were rapidly beginning to appear, particularly among the Generals of the army,[11] and between the two Houses of Parliament.[12] A new instrument for directing the war effort had been created by the formation of the Committee of Both Kingdoms on February 1st,[13] but this was not likely to improve the tempers of the aristocratic leaders who were being manoeuvred out of power. Add to these problems the rumours of plots, and the nervousness of the City lest Charles should use Irish troops to invade Protestant England, and we can understand the political ferment in which the debates on Presbytery took place.

The debate on Monday February 5th was opened by Thomas Goodwin, and the importance of what was happening in the Assembly was indicated by the number of parliamentarians present.[14] If anything, this interest of the politicians increased over the next few weeks which were devoted to the Independents' arguments against the 3rd proposition on presbytery.[15]

---

[10] Cromwell had postponed subscription until that date (5th February). He obviously did not approve of all of its provisions. As Gardiner suggests, he must have had recourse to Vane's saving provision 'according to the Word of God', and his decision to sign must have been dictated to some extent by his recent promotion. He had recently been appointed Lieutenant–General in the Army of the Eastern Association and had been given a seat on the newly created Committee of Both Kingdoms. He had already openly set himself against the inefficient aristocratic control of military affairs when he had denounced Lord Willoughby of Parham on Jan. 22nd. Gardiner, *Great Civil War* I. 304, 310f; Abbott, *Letters and Speeches of O.C.* I., 271ff., 275.

[11] Lord Willoughby of Parham had apparently challenged the Earl of Manchester to a duel. Gardiner, *Great Civil War* I. 304.

[12] The Earl of Essex had taken umbrage because he had not been informed of Charles I's attempt to seduce Sir Henry Vane from his parliamentary allegiance. This had laid the groundwork for friction between the Lords and the Commons, but the incident is important for another reason. Charles had offered liberty of conscience as an inducement for Vane. *Ibid.* p. 274.

[13] Lord Say had managed to get this measure through the House of Lords on February 1st. Gardiner, *The Great Civil War* I. 304–6. The Committee of Both Kingdoms was composed of seven peers, fourteen members of the House of Commons, and the lay members among the Scottish Commissioners. (Cf. Abbott, *Letters and Speeches of O.C.*, I. 275, note 4.)

[14] Lightfoot, *Journal*, p. 131.

[15] On 13th February, John Lightfoot interrupted the normal housekeeping that preceded the day's session to point out that it was then past 10 o'clock 'and here are divers noble gentlemen come in, to hear other discourse than this: and just now came in my Lord–General, the Earls of *Pembroke, Salisbury*, &c.', *ibid.* p. 148.

When he was present, Lightfoot provides us with probably the best account of the

Three main presentations or 'arguments' were put forward by the Independents – that of Goodwin on the 5th and 6th, that of Burroughes on the 8th, and a further argument by Goodwin on the 12th. This was followed by the scriptural proofs against the proposition Goodwin offered on the 14th, further scriptural proofs against the proposition on the 15th, and finally by Bridge's argument based on Matthew 18. This debate lasted until the 21st, by which date the Independents' arguments had been systematically voted down; but by that time the scope had been broadened by John Selden and Thomas Coleman giving notice that any attempt to grant *jure divino* powers to Presbyterianism would be vigorously opposed by the Erastians.

Obviously a detailed account of the arguments would be an unwarrantable burden on the reader. All we shall attempt is to illustrate the ways in which the divines tried to prove their claims, to isolate some of the major issues as they arose, and to recognize problems associated with the major positions represented. It should be noted, however, that before the debate got under way Dr. Stanton's report on behalf of the Second Committee on church censures suggests that the majority party was now poised for an advance on all fronts.[16]

Goodwin's opening speech was cast in rather general terms.[17]

---

debate as a whole, and on the 15th and after, when the Minutes become available, they generally follow Lightfoot's record with some additional details. However, Gillespie's *Notes* often present the major arguments more fully, especially his account of Goodwin's speeches and of his own detailed rebuttal.

[16] The report contained six propositions about church membership and censures:

1) "That there is one general visible church held forth in the New Testament."

2) "The ministry, and all the ordinances of the New Testament, are given by Jesus Christ to the general church visible for perfecting thereof."

3) "Particular visible churches, and members of the general churches, are by the institution of Jesus Christ."

4) "Particular churches, in the primitive times, were made up of visible saints and believers, to wit, such as being of age professed faith in Christ, and obedience to Christ, according to the rule of faith and life taught by Christ and his apostles."

5) In great cities there either were, or might be, more such saints and believers than could meet together in one place to partake of all the ordinances."

6) "So many of these saints as dwelt together in one city were but one church, as touching church censures, whether they were one congregation or not." Gillespie, *Notes*, p. 10.

There were scriptural proof texts added to each of these propositions. Further proofs were added to the last of these propositions, which would obviously be opposed by the Independents.

The report suggests that the Presbyterian position was being orchestrated in each committee. The report is also interesting because it shows that all the Reformed churchmen in the Westminster Assembly – not only the Independents – believed that the church should be composed of 'visible saints and believers.'

[17] Apart from a very brief account at second-hand in Lightfoot (*Journal*, p. 131) the only account of the debate on the 5th is in Gillespie's *Notes*, pp. 9–11.

He contended that a presbyterian government exercized over several congregations "is inconsistent with the scripture and principles acknowledged by reformed churches", because the elders belonging to presbytery should stand in equal relationship to all the churches of the presbytery, and that this "makes a disproportion betwixt the officers of a church" since deacons are obviously limited by biblical warrant to work in a single congregation. Furthermore, he wondered what status pastors bore to other congregations in the same presbytery but in which they held no pastoral office.

He contended that the arguments which Puritans had used against prelates and popes applied here: "The extent of a pastor's power", he declared, "is to one flock, as his whole flock, which he is able to rule and feed constantly", and "pastors' ruling is founded upon their preaching, the jurisdiction [is] founded on the order, so that the one can be no larger than the other". Reformed divines had taken exception to prelacy, because "he that feeds me not should not rule me".[18] The apostles were in a different case to elders because of their universal responsibility. He asked whether under the proposed system all the congregations in the presbytery were to be equally responsible for each minister's call and maintenance, for "if they be elders to all these churches, they must be chosen by all these churches". Moreover, if a minister was called to all these churches he should be ordained in the presence of all.[19]

Charles Herle disagreed, because he said there is a distinction between an officer and a commissioner – a member of presbytery "is not invested with an office over all those churches, but with a commission and power". Stephen Marshall said that Goodwin had assumed that congregations are complete churches, which he implied they are not.[20]

Goodwin continued his presentation the following day, largely – if Lightfoot is to be trusted – along the lines already developed. He was answered by Hoyle, Vines, Marshall and Gillespie, and Lightfoot noted that while Richard Vines was speaking, "the Earls of *Essex*, *Pembroke* and *Salisbury*, and other lords came in", and a little later, "the Earls of *Lincoln*, *Manchester*, and others, and so many of both Houses that we wanted room."[21] Apparently the Commander-in-Chief (Essex), about to plan his attack

---

[18] Goodwin set the same kind of local limitation on the power of a ruling elder.
[19] *Ibid.* pp. 10f.
[20] *Ibid.*
[21] *Journal*, pp. 132, 133.

on Oxford, and the General of the Eastern Association (Manchester), about to purge Cambridge University of its royalists, thought the debate took precedence over their military occasions.

Vines's speech illustrates a distinctive feature of the proponents' case, a tendency to base their understanding of the New Testament church on the ordering of Jewish society in Old Testament times. Vines argued that the head of one tribe in Israel joined with the heads of other tribes in the government of Israel although he had no office in any other tribe, so "the elders in a presbytery have immediate relation to the presbytery, and mediate in, and by the whole, he hath relation only to the particular churches."[22]

The strength of the Presbyterian position in respect to its catholicity comes out in Marshall's statement, "The whole Catholic church is but one body". He also outlined a mature view of the church's development, for he maintained that although there may have been only a small number of apostolic churches at first, as the numbers grew, they were still one church. The scriptures do not say whether individual apostles were deputed to minister to particular wards or whether this ministry was carried on in circuit. This view of the early church's development is particularly interesting because it came to be very much the same as that held by John Wesley a century later.[23] Marshall then proceeded to answer Thomas Goodwin, "and took up an exceeding great deal of time."[24]

The most detailed criticisms of Goodwin's arguments that have survived are those of George Gillespie,[25] probably because Gillespie made a habit of setting down his critical response to any theological argument against the Presbyterian position. He denied Goodwin's major premise by pointing to examples of representative government in civil society – so military commanders unite in a council of war without claiming any authority within other regiments, and he cited political examples in the government of the United Provinces and in the relationship of those elected to Parliament. From this he argued that

---

[22] Gillespie, *Notes*, p. 12.

[23] See Wesley's answer to the question of church polity at the Conference on August 3rd, 1745, in Albert Outler, (ed.) *John Wesley* (New York, Oxford University Press, 1964), pp. 153ff.

[24] Lightfoot, *Journal*, p. 133.

[25] In Lightfoot's account Gillespie's speech is summarized in a very few lines; *ibid.* pp. 133f.

The elders of many congregations may be understood to be joined in one presbytery for the government of all these congregations, either *virtute potestatis ordinis*, [by virtue of the power of order] or *virtute potestatis jurisdictionis* [by virtue of the power of jurisdiction]. We hold not the former but the latter, for *non quatenus presbyteri, sed quatenus presbyteri in presbyterium collecti*, [not in that they are presbyters, but in that they are presbyters gathered in presbytery,] they govern these many congregations.[26]

Seaman said that if a minister could have ecclesial relationship with only one congregation this would prevent any of them from preaching in other congregations. The work they were then doing in the Assembly was an extension of their ministry, so "the work of pastors' feeding is of greater extent than their preaching." Against Goodwin he held that in I Cor. 12:28 the church was not to be identified with a particular congregation, nor with the ideal Church, but it referred to the general visible church, and he continued, "as, by baptism, we are made members of the general church, so, by ordination, we are made ministers of the general church, and need not a new ordination, when we go to another church, no more than a new baptism."[27]

At the end of the debate (on the 7th) Lightfoot concluded with what was to become almost the litany of these sessions: "at last it was called to be put to the question, 'Whether this proposition, or major, of Mr. *Goodwin's* have not been sufficiently debated:' and it was voted affirmatively: and so we adjourned."[28]

On the 8th, Jeremiah Burroughes tried to recast the formal proposition against presbytery in the following terms: "If the presbytery of a classical[29] church stand in relation to that classical church as elders; and there be much incongruity in it, then it ought not to be. But, &c. *ergo*." There was a good deal of logic chopping on this because the divines found the form of Burroughes's proposition to be unclear.[30]

Up to that point the issues had been debated in abstract syllogistic terms without really getting to scriptural interpretation, but eventually the debate focussed on Paul's disciplining the incestuous member at Corinth (I Cor. 5.) Burroughes

---

[26] Gillespie, *Notes*, pp. 11f.

[27] *Ibid*. p. 12.

[28] *Journal*, p. 137.

[29] I.e., a church governed by a classis or presbytery.

[30] *Ibid*. The way in which this was recorded does not help its clarity. Burroughes's argument seems to have been that since there was 'much incongruity' in the order offered in the committee's proposition, it would not stand.

255

insisted that "the only Scripture example holds forth that elders must, in the presence of the church, execute their censures."[31]

At first sight, it is surprising to find the Independents agreeing with their opponents that the word *ecclesia* in the passage referred to the elders rather than to the congregation itself and conceding that the elders performed the act of censure on behalf of the church, but we must remember that they wanted to disassociate themselves from any taint of Separatism, and that Rutherford had already tried to link their views with those of the Separatist, Henry Ainsworth. Their major point at issue with the Presbyterians was that *ecclesia* in this passage could not refer to the elders *alone*, and that an act of jurisdiction must be done at least in the presence of the people. They trod a very narrow line between the pure independency of the Separatists, and the presbyterial understanding of the Church that was now being advanced in the Assembly.[32]

A good deal of the debate therefore focussed on what it would mean for a presbytery to act *coram populo* [in the presence of the people], but by the end of the day Cornelius Burgess, as acting prolocutor,[33] thought they had heard enough and tried, unsuccessfully, to close it down. The following day's debate (9th February) began with his pressing Burroughes to define what he and his friends meant by 'the church' since they denied deputed and representative congregations, and Burgess was clearly not satisfied with the answers given. The day was also noteworthy for William Bridge's unsuccessful attempt to use Calvin and Peter Martyr and to cite others,[34] but "that was cried against. And Mr. *Henderson* said, that if they begin to heap up authors, let us do so too, and we shall outvie them."[35]

At the end of the day the Independents' proposition was routinely voted down, and again there was 'great and hot debate' whether the Independents should be permitted to "go on in objecting against the proposition brought in by the committee";

---

[31] Gillespie, *Notes*, p. 14.

[32] This precarious balance is seen in Goodwin's statement: "the substance of the act of excommunication must be either in the presbytery or the church, as we make the substance of ordination in the presbytery, and the rite only in the people." *Ibid.* p. 14.

[33] The Assessors shared responsibility for chairing the sessions in the absence of the Prolocutor, Dr. Twisse. William Twisse was absent through illness for a great deal of these debates. On 8th February Lightfoot recorded, "I moved 'That since our prolocutor hath been so long absent, we might send to see him as from the Assembly:' and Dr. *Stanton* and myself were appointed for that purpose." Lightfoot, *Journal*, p. 139.

[34] In support of his view that in I Cor. 5 the power of excommunication was exercised by the whole congregation.

[35] Lightfoot, *Journal*, p. 140.

but they were allowed to continue.[36] During this period we notice some tension within the majority party between those who wanted the Independents to be given every opportunity of stating their opposition in the hope that when that failed the Dissenting Brethren would have little excuse for rejecting an accommodation, and those who simply wanted to crush the Independents as quickly as possible in order to get on with the new Establishment. The former was the policy of the Scots Commissioners, while the latter was the position of conservatives like Cornelius Burgess.

On Monday the 12th,[37] after Burroughes tried unsuccessfully to get a reworded version of his proposition accepted for debate, Thomas Goodwin brought in another argument, but Lightfoot says "he went on so obscurely, that the Assembly called for more plainness", and he was asked to present his views in a logical form.[38] Indeed, from the records we agree about the obscurity and this is so contrary to Goodwin's usual clarity that the Independents may have been caught unprepared.[39] He may have intervened somewhat hurriedly to prevent closure on the debate.

The most noteworthy feature of that day's debate was a statement by Philip Nye. He has often been regarded as the most intransigent Independent of all the Dissenting Brethren, but he made frank admission of how near he and his colleagues were to the majority position:

> Mr. *Nye* did confess how nearly they came to us; as that they held classical and synodical meetings very useful and profitable; yet possibly agreeable to the institution of Christ. But the quaere is in this, Whether these meetings have the same power that 'ecclesia prima,' or one single congregation has?[40]

Again the debate concentrated on whether the scriptures required a congregation to be present during a sentence delivered by a superior presbytery that was acting in its affairs. The majority position was indicated in the following exchange that began in response to Goodwin:

> Mr. *Seaman* answered, That none have proper interest in presence; but those that have interest in the jurisdictive power; and if the

---

[36] *Ibid.* p. 143.

[37] *Ibid.* p. 143–7; Gillespie, *Notes*, p. 15.

[38] Lightfoot, *Journal*, p. 144.

[39] I.e., by the failure of Burroughes to get his motion accepted for debate.

[40] *Ibid.* Later in the debate on the rights of the congregation in matters of jurisdiction, "Mr. *Nye* would strive a middle way betwixt no interest and jurisdiction; and prove that those two notions of power and jurisdiction are separable. . . . So our debates here are of authority, but not of jurisdiction." *Ibid.* p. 150 (14th Feb.)

people must be present at the decree, then must they also at the examining of witnesses, which may not be granted or concerned; but when the decree is made, then all the congregations should be acquainted with it, as most fit.

Mr. *Bridges*: But the presbyterian church cannot be present at the publication.

Mr. *Herle*: Every act of censure is not a mere ministerial act, but judiciary, and all that the people have to do in this, is, that after the thing is done, they may offer something to the presbytery, to see whether they [i.e., the presbytery] will suspend or reverse the sentence.

Mr. *Seaman*: The decree and the act of excommunication are acts of power, and the people have nothing to do in it.[41]

That was precisely the point at issue. Lazarus Seaman and many in the Assembly like him, whatever their views on church polity, were determined to maintain the unique status and authority of the ordained ministry. At the end of this day's debate there was an even hotter discussion whether the Independents should be allowed more time, but it was eventually decided to continue as they had started.[42]

On Tuesday, 13th February, Goodwin announced a new syllogistic argument based on I Cor. 5: "If many congregations may be under one presbyterial government, then excommunication; and if excommunication must be before all the people, then cannot the presbyterial government do it, for all the people cannot be present."[43] The rest of the day was spent on his presentation and detailed comments on its exegesis by Thomas Gataker, Richard Vines and George Gillespie. The Scots Commissioner claimed that in 1 Cor. 11 and 14 the 'gathering together' was in acts of worship, here in the 5th chapter it was an act of discipline, "and he proved out of 1 Chron. xiii. 1–4, 2 Chron. i. 2, 3, 1 Chron. xxix. that sometimes all the congregation are put for the elders."[44]

Up to this point there is a feeling of unreality about the debate, because both sides had avoided saying very much about their own positive positions. They seem to have been guarding their theological arguments and scriptural proof texts like military generals afraid of revealing their secret weapons. But obviously, time was running out on that policy for the Independents, and on

---

[41] *Ibid.* p. 145.
[42] *Ibid.* p. 147.
[43] *Ibid.* p. 148.
[44] Again we see the tendency of the Presbyterian apologists to use the institutions of Old Testament society to prove equal institutions in the New Testament church.

the 14th Thomas Goodwin made what was clearly one of his most important speeches in the debates.[45]

He argued, first, that I Cor. 5 gave to the people's presence the force of an apostolic injunction; secondly, "That the presbyterial government makes two sorts of churches: one, merely for discipline, the other for worship."[46] Thirdly, he declared that "discipline doth not constitute a church, nor is it a note of a church."[47] Goodwin here was enunciating an important principle of the Independents' ecclesiology, that the discipline of the Church cannot be separated from the regular life of the Church received in Word and Sacraments. The Church is an obedient and worshipping community, and this is the only proper context in which it can exercise discipline. Later on Richard Baxter was to commend this aspect of Independent churchmanship when he observed that he "found in the search of Scripture and Antiquity, that in the beginning a *Governed Church*, and a *stated worshipping Church*, were all one; and not two several things".[48]

Goodwin also indicated that he and his colleagues came much closer to the Presbyterians than we might have expected, for he was willing to admit that in the matter of ecclesiastical censures the people of a congregation do not vote, "but are to carry things in a tacit and obedient way, unless the conscience be unsatisfied." He suggested that the elders of a congregation exercised the same kind of governance over the congregation as a father had over the marriage of a child: they were to do the judging, "but with the church, and before the church".[49]

The Independents' position between the extremes of democratic Separatism and authoritative presbyterial government left them here in a somewhat ambivalent position with regard to the members of a congregation. William Bridge, commenting on the part played by the members in an act of censure, said that it involved "somewhat more than presence, yea, more than consent, and yet short of jurisdiction",[50] while Goodwin "averred that he conceived the people had a power, yet without authority."[51] Gillespie added a further note by Goodwin:

---

[45] *Ibid.* pp. 151f., Gillespie, *Notes*, pp. 18f.

[46] Lightfoot, *Journal*, p. 151.

[47] *Ibid.* See also Gillespie's account of Goodwin's argument, "A church for discipline cannot have the notes of a church which divines give, from word and sacraments, yea, the people of that church do not communicate neither, but only the elders." *Notes*, p. 18.

[48] *Reliquiae Baxterianae* I. ii. 140 (§5.4.)

[49] Lightfoot, *Journal*, p. 152.

[50] *Ibid.* p. 154.

[51] *Ibid.* p. 155.

Mr. Goodwin said, They differ so far from Brownists, that they hold the people, without the officers, cannot excommunicate; only they hold that, when there is a difference of judgment among the people, the elders should explicitly draw forth the suffrage of the major part.[52]

One feels that the Independents were trying to interpret New Testament ecclesiology in terms of its spirit as well as its letter, but that they were going as far as they could in the direction of the majority.

The debate continued in its predestined way. The Presbyterian, Charles Herle, showed an insightful spirit in his summary of the three objectives of the gospel,[53] while someone seems to have convinced Cornelius Burgess that his policy of trying to secure an early closure was bad public relations, for he had renewed the motion that the debate might be continued the next day, "that we might not seem cruel to our brethren abroad."[54]

New rocks, however, began to appear in the path of the Presbyterian majority. John Selden had already given notice of them when he had denied that I Corinthians 5 had anything to do with excommunication and ecclesiastical censures, but on Thursday the 15th, his Erastian colleague, Thomas Coleman, entered the lists on Selden's side of the argument.[55] He was not an Independent, but he was strongly against the assumption of *jure divino* ecclesiastical discipline.[56] He argued that whatever the Holy Spirit required one congregation to do while requiring another congregation not to do,[57] could be regarded as *jure divino* only for the particular congregation on which it had been enjoined.[58]

In response to this Erastian challenge, Stephen Marshall said that first it must be proved that these were indeed particular congregations, and secondly that even if they had been so originally, "yet this doth not infringe their dilating into pres-

---

[52] *Notes*, p. 20. Goodwin said that "he would prove that there was but one church in Corinth, because if there had been more, the apostle would have mentioned that congregation of which this incestuous person was a member." Lightfoot, *Journal*, p. 155.

[53] He summarized the three ends of the gospel as 1. glory to God, 2. good will to men, and 3. peace on earth. *Ibid*. p. 155.

[54] *Ibid*. p. 156.

[55] *Ibid*. pp. 157–9, Gillespie, *Notes*, pp. 20f., TMs. I. 577–82 (Ms. I., ff. 300b–303.)

[56] The day before he had reported additional proof texts and a further argument in support of the First Committee's propositions on Presbyterian government.

[57] He found this contrast by comparing excommunication in 2 Thess. 3:14 and the church of Thyatira in Revelation 2:18ff. The Minutes pass over his speech.

[58] Lightfoot, *Journal*, p. 157, Gillespie, *Notes*, p. 20.

bytery as they grew."[59] Obviously here Marshall was building on
the understanding of church development he had expounded on
February 6th, but he assumed the onus of proof was on those
who questioned his view of church development rather than on
himself to prove it. He adopted the same attitude to those who
regarded the 'churches' in the New Testament as particular
congregations – it was for them to prove they were.

During the debate Goodwin propounded a further argument,
that the highest obedience is not suitable to a classis.[60] Obedience
and governance relate to each other, and the preaching of pastors
is the only ground for the people's obedience. The crux of his
opposition to the Presbyterian system was in his claim that in that
system "one is bound to obey him that never spake the word to
them".[61] It was centred in the belief that there is an integral unity
between Word, sacraments and discipline. This was the primary
relationship which Independents held between the local eldership and the covenanted congregation – worship and discipline
should not be separated.[62]

An important difference was beginning to emerge in the concept of ministry held by the majority and the Independents.
Pastoral authority for the latter was grounded in the pastor's call
and proclamation, while for the former it was grounded in *office*;
as Richard Vines declared, "The ground of obedience is founded
upon the office."[63] The Minutes present his words a little more
fully:

> the reason of obedience lyes in the office[;] if it be a
> part of the office & principall to preach the word[,]
> yet the ground of it lyes in the office[.][64]

Lightfoot recorded that Goodwin's argument "was judged by
the most to be very weak, and yet it held us a long tug, and very
many pros and contras passed, and the Independents did still
remonstrate: at last it was put to the question, and voted that the
argument was not proved, neither concludeth against the proposition in question." Then at the point when the Assembly was
about to vote to proceed to the Committee's propositions on

---

[59] Lightfoot, *Journal*, p. 157.

[60] Gillespie, *Notes*, p. 20, cf. Lightfoot, *Journal*, pp. 157f.

[61] *Ibid*. p. 158. He used 1 Thess. 5:12f., 1 Tim. 5:17 and Hebrews 13:7 and 17
to establish this important connection between pastoral proclamation and pastoral
authority.

[62] Rutherford immediately seized on this emphasis on the pastoral office and asked if
that were true, what about the obedience due to ruling elders? Lightfoot, *Journal*, p. 158.

[63] *Ibid*. p. 159.

[64] TMs. I. 580, (Ms. I. f. 302.)

presbytery, William Bridge announced that he wished to bring an argument based on Matthew 18, and it was conceded that this should be debated the next day.[65]

Gillespie noted two things of interest on February 15th that were related to what was happening in the Assembly. First Robert Baillie had shown him a letter from the New England minister, the son of Robert Parker, admitting that in New England "they had given too much power to the people; and that, though they hold there is a fundamental power in the people, and the power of electing their ministers, and doing other things in extraordinary cases, when they want officers, yet they found it necessary that the ordinary exercise of jurisdiction should be only in the power of church officers."[66] Baillie's diplomatic net had been cast very wide. Gillespie continued:

> We saw also a petition presented to the House of Peers, in the name of many thousands, desiring the liberty of a congregational way, that they be not forced to leave the kingdom and the parliament's service, to seek the liberty of their consciences elsewhere; desiring also that others of their mind might be recalled from New England and Holland, who might be steadable for the parliament's service.[67]

The Scots were not the only ones who knew how to bring pressure on the English Parliament. If they were willing to exert leverage through their own General Assembly and through foreign churches, the Independents and their friends could touch the political leaders at Westminster where it hurt most, in terms of enlistment for their armies. The appeal to toleration which had been tentative enough in *An Apologeticall Narration*, was rapidly becoming more explicit.[68]

In stating the ground for his opposition on February 16th, William Bridge set down the clearest statement of Congregational ecclesiology to appear in the debates to that point. Indeed, he had to, for time was rapidly running out. He worded his dissent in the following formal proposition: "That government which is not according to the mind of God and his word revealed,

---

[65] Lightfoot, *Journal*, p. 159.

[66] The letter also said that an assembly (synod) was to meet at Cambridge in Massachusetts to regulate these matters. Gillespie, *Notes*, p. 20.

[67] *Ibid*.

[68] In March an obscure and anonymous pamphlet was to appear, *Liberty of Conscience, or the sole means to obtain peace and truth*, and the summer of the same year Roger Williams published *The Bloudy Tenent of Persecution*.

is not to be admitted. But the government, in the proposition, is not according, &c. *ergo.*"[69]

This provided him with the springboard from which he launched what he regarded as the proper New Testament ecclesiology:

> The government according to the mind of God[70] and his word revealed, is this:–
> That every particular congregation consisting of elders and brethren, should have entire and full power of jurisdiction within themselves, Matt. xviii. 15–17.[71]

This gave him the opportunity to expound the Congregational interpretation of this passage – the church mentioned here has power to declare the highest form of church censure and it is in the particular congregation. Against Selden and his friends Bridge insisted that it is a spiritual and not a civil court that is referred to in Matthew 18, and against the Presbyterians he declared that it is a Christian and not a Jewish church. Possibly against Episcopalians, he also insisted that the word 'church' here does not mean a particular bishop.

He argued that a universal or national Church is not intended here because our Lord spoke of 'two or three', and he claimed that although the word *ecclesia* is used forty-eight times in the New Testament, never once is it used simply for a presbytery: the offended brother is not part of a presbytery.[72] During his discourse he stated that Congregational opposition was not to synods. Synods could be used to clarify the faith dogmatically, and to declare against those who were subverters of the faith, "but here and elsewhere a perticular congregation is called a church, & such a church as is to be tould in case of offence, & this by institution. Therefore", he went on, "unlesse ther can be shewed an Institution from Christ to take away this power it may not be done".[73] Since the presbyterian form of government seemed to take it away he was bound to dissent from it. He challenged the opposition to "bring forth the Institution"[74] for their system, and although there were many points at which subsequent speakers presented valid objections to Bridge's

---

[69] Lightfoot, *Journal*, pp. 159f.

[70] The scribe in the Minutes has Bridge speaking more of 'the mind of Christ' than of 'the mind of God'; and this would seem to be closer to the Independents' terminology and the New Testament rule for the Church.

[71] *Ibid.*

[72] *Ibid.* pp. 160f, Gillespie, *Notes*, pp. 21f., TMs. I. 582–6 (Ms. I. ff. 303–305.)

[73] TMs. I. 585 (Ms. I. f. 304b.)

[74] *Ibid.* I. 586 (Ms. I. f. 305.)

ecclesiology, they never effectively met that challenge.[75] It was clearly an important speech.

In responding, Stephen Marshall naturally denied that the Presbyterian system was contrary to the will of Christ. The word *ecclesia* is used in six or seven different senses in the New Testament,[76] and virtually the only thing that had been denied by Bridge was "that we shall not find the word church taken for the governours".[77] Marshall appealed to the Old Testament, in which, he pointed out, the word 'congregation' represents "elders & rulers and not the body of the people,"[78] and he criticized the view that there is no appeal from the particular church.

However, Marshall's speech shows how close he and the Independents were in their understanding of the particular church. His criticism of Independency in its extremer forms was certainly justified by good theology, even if it could not be substantiated by literal New Testament texts, as when he claimed that the powers exercised by a congregation should not rule out its responsibility to act in common with others, or in his criticism of the suggestion that a congregation's Christ-given powers were somehow infringed if it united with other congregations. There must be a way of dealing with an errant congregation as there is for erring individuals.

Perhaps the heart of Marshall's position is in this:

> either Christ hath apoynted a remidy for curing [errors] of perticular churches as [for] men or he hath not[;]
> if he have not [, or] if noe way but a precarious way[,]
> then Christ hath not provided soe effectuall a meanes
> for reclaiming a whole church as for one man. . . .
> all may erre in the end but in the multitude of counselours
> ther is peace[.][79]

We must remember that the basic ecclesiastical problem in England in 1644 was errant congregations, and Marshall stands out as having a very healthy regard for practicality. Clearly, he regarded it as unthinkable that our Lord should have left ecclesiastical matters so much in abeyance, and his Presbyterian convictions were built on that. Through all his speeches there

---

[75] Gillespie offered an extensive answer to Bridge's speech, but never met that specific challenge. He simply stated "It is enough we find the elders called the church." *Notes*, p. 21. The lack of a clear institution for a particular polity was a problem for both sides.

[76] Lightfoot, *Journal*, p. 161.

[77] TMs. I. 587, (Ms. I. f. 305b.)

[78] *Ibid.*, cf. Lightfoot, *Journal*, p. 161.

[79] TMs. I. 589 (Ms. I. f. 306b.)

runs a strong strain of Christian pragmatism that must have been honed sharp in engagements with his son-in-law,[80] but the exchange with Bridge shows that the problems arose because both sides expected to find an infallible pattern for the Church in scripture. Since they placed their primary emphasis at different points in the ecclesiastical system – the Independents, on what they regarded as the rights of the people and the need to guard them from ecclesiastical tyranny, and the Presbyterians on what they regarded as the need to bring congregations into fellowship and conformity with the whole church – they treated the scriptural evidence differently. And where the scriptural evidence seemed to be lacking, it had to be inferred from logic.

So too, if the evidence was not to be found directly in the New Testament, it must be sought in the Old Testament. Richard Vines argued that since the disciples understood only the customs in which they had been raised, "they understood nothing but the Jewish form", and since the word *kahal*, rendered as *ecclesia* in the New Testament, related to officers in the Old Testament, he claimed that the Old Testament understanding must govern the New Testament interpretation of the word 'church'.[81] To him, the words 'Tell the church' (Matt. 18:17) were therefore "properly expressed for officers."[82] William Bridge replied point by point until the adjournment.

For the next three days the Assembly debated Matthew 18. It was a crucial passage that no party could afford to ignore, because if it could be validly applied to ecclesiology, it had the force of a direct dominical institution. After what was probably a weekend of intense preparation, Thomas Goodwin opened for the Independents on Monday, 19th February.[83] He maintained that the passage gave "ultimately the power of excommunication to a particular congregation", and that the phrase 'tell the church' means "to tell the officers before the church".[84]

His speech is particularly important because he attacked the Old Testament premise on which the Presbyterian case

---

[80] Philip Nye.
[81] *Ibid.* p. 591 (Ms. I. f. 307b.)
[82] Lightfoot, *Journal*, p. 162.
[83] The debate is to be found in Gillespie, *Notes*, pp. 22ff. TMs. I. 594ff. (Ms. I. ff. 309–16.) Lightfoot was returning on that day from his duties in Munden. Early in the proceedings on the 19th, it had been ordered that the Rules Committee should, without delay, consider "of a way how this assembly may hasten and speed their advice to the houses of Parliament for the settling of all things that concerne the present discipline of the church". TMs. I. 594 (Ms. I. f. 309.)
[84] Gillespie, *Notes*, p. 22.

depended. Even in the Old Testament, the Hebrew word *kahal* was used only once for elders to every ten times it stood for the people of Israel. Gillespie flatly denied that in his record, asserting that wherever jurisdiction is being exercised, "the word is ever used for the elders."[85]

The battle of exegesis continued. Goodwin also insisted – with some justification – that Christ distinguished his church from the Jewish 'church', and denied any necessity "to expresse the new test[ament] of the gospell by the language of the old testament". He laid down a fundamentally different principle of theological interpretation: "Rather interpret what is meant by churches by what follows than what goes before".[86] So in commenting on Heb. 10:21, 25, Goodwin insisted on the priority of synagogue organization and worship for Christians over the hierarchical structure based on the Jewish Temple:

> our lord & saviour Christ being to gather his church
> out of all nations & those dispersed[,] this synagogue
> frame did better suite it than that nationall way
> before.
> Jewish synagogues in all cittyes wch made way
> for the erecting of like churches in all cittyes when
> the apostells came.[87]

He and his colleagues maintained that a local congregation is to be regarded as "a church and a whole church", because "all instances in the Scripture are but of one perticular church under a presbiteriall government[88] being called a church having elders & speaking". Since the first churches were of necessity such as could meet all in one place, "the institution must needs fall upon those & they must have this power within themselves".[89] All Puritans were agreed on the importance of the local congregation against the claims of diocesan episcopacy, and Goodwin claimed that the Scots paper took much the same position regarding the *ecclesia prima* as he did, but he asked his hearers to reflect on how those earliest churches had lost their original powers. Goodwin was arguing that the same criticism Reformed Churches had levelled against the development of episcopacy and papacy could also be levelled at any modification of the autonomy enjoyed by the primitive churches:

---

[85] *Ibid.* p. 23.
[86] TMs. I. 596 (Ms. I. f. 310.)
[87] *Ibid.* p. 598 (Ms. I. f. 311.)
[88] The Independents also claimed the terms 'presbyterian' or 'presbyterial' to describe their own government by local elders in the local church.
[89] *Ibid.*

those first churches in primitive times wher
ther was but one church with an eldership –
when the churches began to be multiplyed how did
they come to loose their power?
all corporations stand upon their priviledges
soe hath the church reason to doe in this case.[90]

In answer to Marshall's reasonable plea that in the multitude of counsellors there is strength, he declared "let them be as counsellours & we have done", because this was precisely the point of difference between Congregational synods and Presbyterian presbyteries – the former were called for counsel and to exercise spiritual persuasion, whereas the latter claimed effective power to command and to govern.[91] Goodwin held that a local church, equipped with an adequate presbytery of three elders, ought to be allowed to govern its own affairs "till it miscarryes".[92] That position was not strong enough for the majority in the Assembly, for it was the miscarrying that concerned the members most. How could that be met? A hierarchical system could provide for it effectively, and Presbyterianism met the need in its hierarchy of church courts.

Thomas Gataker, who carried the major responsibility for rebuttal on this occasion, claimed there is no ecclesiastical censure in Matthew 18, which in his view simply represents the resolution of a case of conscience, how to deal with an erring brother. The word *ecclesia* here represented neither the Jewish Sanhedrin nor the Christian Church, because at that time there was no church. He questioned Goodwin's speech in more detail,[93] but his response did not satisfy Charles Herle, who said that he would speak on the passage "be[cause] I suppose we shall have use of it upon the affirmative[;] therefore [it is] not soe easy to be waved".[94]

Herle said that they were well aware of what they regarded as a divine institution – "that Christ here or some wher else hath instituted a church government such as is capable of its end", but he admitted that "such a one as sets up the whole forme will hardly be found".[95] If Herle could have convinced the rest of the Assembly of that, the whole basis for the discussion might have

---

[90] *Ibid.* p. 600 (Ms. I. f. 312.)
[91] *Ibid.*
[92] *Ibid.* p. 599 (Ms. I. f. 311b.)
[93] *Ibid.* pp. 600f, (Ms. I. f. 312 et seq.,) Gillespie, *Notes* p. 24. The Minutes are defective, and there are gaps that the scribe clearly intended to fill in later.
[94] TMs. I. p. 605 (Ms. I. f. 314b.)
[95] *Ibid.*

been changed. He disagreed with Goodwin's charge that the presbyterian government was essentially hierarchical, because an arrangement of inferior and superior courts did not place one minister above another minister; if indeed they had placed "a person above a person then this would come up to something neare to prelacy".[96]

Stephen Marshall seems to have forgotten the uproar on February 9th when William Bridge had tried to cite the authority of Calvin and other scholars. He challenged Goodwin's statement that Christ did not allude to Jewish practice by claiming that Goodwin had Calvin, Beza, Junius, Thomas Brightman, Thomas Cartwright, Robert Parker and Thomas Jenner against him, and he drew a different conclusion from Goodwin's argument concerning Jewish synagogue practice. He agreed that power had been originally within the single congregation, "but when they increased[,] it remained but one church that had a presbitery to governe all in common, & we desire noe more".[97]

II

Appeal to Caesar?

The Assembly continued to debate Matthew 18 on February 20th.[98] Edmund Calamy said that Goodwin's view of the church as officers governing "in the presence of the church" was new, and it put too great a burden on people to have to attend all the church's business. He also did not miss the opportunity of pointing to the similarity of what Independents had been saying with the views of the Brownists, and said that if the church in this passage was more than a single congregation, then it supported the proposition.[99] Goodwin responded to some of the criticisms he had received, and there was an exchange between him and Calamy;[100] then Rutherford brushed the opposition aside by remarking that nothing hindered debating "more than when things are proved that are not denied & arguments brought that doe not conclude against the proposition in question".[101]

---

[96] *Ibid.* p. 606 (Ms. I. f. 315.)
[97] TMs. I. 607 (Ms. I. f. 315b.)
[98] *Ibid.* 609ff, (Ms. I. ff. 316–320b); Lightfoot, *Journal* pp. 164–7; Gillespie, *Notes*, pp. 25f.)
[99] TMs. I. 611 (Ms. I. f. 317b.)
[100] Lightfoot, *Journal*, pp. 164f.
[101] TMs. I. 611 (Ms. I. f. 317b.)

A dramatic change to the direction of the whole dispute came through a speech by the lawyer, John Selden.[102] He developed the position that he had taken earlier but with a wealth of erudition that could not be ignored by those who were set on proving *jure divino* Presbyterianism.[103]

He said that if *ecclesia* in this passage meant particular congregations, "then the proposition is sufficiently opposed", but he did not believe there was proof here for excommunication. All churches – Roman Catholic, Episcopal, Presbyterian and Congregational – appropriated this passage for themselves, but for four hundred years none of the church fathers had used this text to prove church discipline. He then used considerable rabbinic and classical scholarship to show that this was essentially a *civil* form of separation and sentence,[104] and that since Jesus was at that time in Capernaum where a civil court sat, the term *ecclesia* simply represented that kind of court.

Herle and Marshall at once countered Selden's arguments, "but so, as I confess," Lightfoot wrote, "gave me no satisfaction."[105] The repercussions of that particular speech and the issues it raised would exercise the *jus divinum* theologians of the Assembly long after the Grand Debate between the Presbyterians and the Independents had been resolved. Gillespie's reaction and the detailed notes he used in his speech against Selden the following day[106] show that the Erastian issue was assuming considerable importance in the minds of the Scots Commissioners.[107]

The final day of objections to the Committee's proposition on presbyterial government (February 21st)[108] began with the rules for better expediting the Assembly's work.[109] It was a day's

---

[102] *Ibid.* pp. 611–14, (Ms. I. ff. 317b–319); Lightfoot, *Journal*, pp. 165f; Gillespie, *Notes*, pp. 25, 26.

[103] A view which had also been expressed earlier by Thomas Gataker, cf. *supra*, p. 267. Gillespie ignored the earlier part of the debate on that day almost completely to concentrate on Selden.

[104] TMs. I. 614 (Ms. I. f. 319.)

[105] *Journal*, p. 166.

[106] *Notes*, p. 26.

[107] Robert Baillie had already noted Selden's position on the matter of church discipline; To Spang, 18th February, 1643/4, *Letters and Journals* II. 129. Philip Nye tried to get the debate back to the main issue, Matt. 18, but the Assembly was in no mood to listen to him. He refused to be silent, even although he was accused of saying "nothing to the question"; but eventually the Assembly adjourned.

[108] TMs. I. 618–29 (Ms. I. ff. 320b–326b;) Lightfoot, *Journal*, pp. 167–70; Gillespie, *Notes*, pp. 26f.

[109] Lightfoot, *Journal*, p. 167.

debate in which all three major positions in the Assembly can be identified. George Gillespie opened his attack on Selden's speech of the day before. It was a well-constructed speech, and it immeasurably enhanced his reputation. He argued that the church in Matthew 18 was a spiritual and not a civil court, because (1) its subject matter was spiritual, (2) the objective was spiritual, 'the gaining of the offender's soul', (3) the persons involved were spiritual, (4) the method was spiritual, (5) the censure was spiritual, (6) our Lord would never have sent his disciples to a secular court, and (7) Jewish custom also recognized spiritual censures.[110]

He then turned to attack the other flank, the Independents, but Gillespie does not provide any summary of this part of his speech, and Lightfoot was called out momentarily, although he reported that Gillespie "spake very home, and sharply, and very largely."[111] The Minutes also are defective, but from them it appears that Gillespie was reluctant to discuss whether a congregation possessed complete power within itself, because that would be debated later. He also was reluctant to use Acts 15 to contradict Goodwin, but he declared "it will be never proved that the whole church of Jerusalem was present at that debate", and added "neither in old testament ware the people present at the Jewish Sanhedrin".[112]

Gillespie held that the passage in Matthew was consistent with presbyterial government in the following ways – first, because it endorsed the light of nature and the normal appeal in human society from a lower to a higher authority; secondly, it was consistent with the Jewish system and its appeal from the synagogue to the Sanhedrin; thirdly, it was consistent with the perfection of Christ's institution and the appeal through his kingly office; and fourthly, it was consistent with apostolic practice as exemplified in Acts 15.[113]

But although the immediate issue was still the Independents' opposition to the committee's 3rd Proposition regarding presbytery, some of the Assembly were now preoccupied with the challenge laid down by Selden, and that is the way the debate turned. Thomas Young joined in the attack on the Erastian position, and that brought in Thomas Coleman on Selden's side of the argument.[114] Coleman began to answer Gillespie point by

---

[110] *Ibid.*
[111] *Ibid.* p. 168.
[112] TMs. I. 619 (Ms. I. f. 321b.)
[113] *Ibid.* p. 620 (Ms. I. f. 322.)
[114] *Ibid.* p. 623 (Ms. I. f. 323b;) Lightfoot, *Journal*, pp. 168f.; Gillespie *Notes*, p. 21.

point until he was called to order by Cornelius Burgess and told that he could not discuss the issue of excommunication till it was actually in debate:[115] the control of the agenda was firmly in the hands of the majority.

At that point in the debate Philip Nye made an extremely controversial speech, which from the point of view of his party must have been regarded as disastrous.[116] Whether it was the emergence of the Erastian issue, the presence of the politicians, or his growing frustration at the way in which the Independents' criticisms had been brushed aside and voted down, he seems to have appealed to pure political expediency. He argued that there is no hierarchical structure in the Church, but if there were there would certainly be a risk in establishing an ecclesiastical power commensurate with that of the state:

> Where two vast bodies are of equal amplitude, if they disagree it is nought; if they agree, it will be worse, one will closely be working against another. And here he read something out of Mr. *Rutherford's* preface upon his assertion of the Scotch government, and would have fetched something out of it: when it was sharply prohibited, and he cried out of, as disorderly and dangerous; and Mr. *Henderson* cried out that he spake like Sanballat, Tobiah, or Symmachus: and Mr. *Sedgwick* wished that he might be excluded out of the Assembly: and here was great heat, and it was put to the question, and voted that he had spoken against order.[117]

If Nye thought he could play upon the politicians' fear of ecclesiastical domination, his speech did not have the desired effect, and William Wheeler, one of the M.P.s present, reminded him that in the Protestation taken by every member of the Assembly they were bound to do and say only those things that would conduce to the peace of the Church. Stephen Marshall, with a much firmer grasp of pragmatic reality, appealed to the members of both Houses present – "which were very many present" – whether presbyterial government was more to be feared "or twenty thousand congregations, none in reference or dependance to another?"[118] Bulstrode Whitelocke, the lawyer, had no doubt when he exclaimed, "what a confusion it will prove to have congregations independent."[119]

---

[115] TMs. I. 623, (Ms. I. f. 323b.)
[116] *Ibid.* pp. 623f (Ms. I. ff. 323b–325;) Lightfoot, *Journal*, pp. 168f., Gillespie, *Notes*, pp. 26f.
[117] Lightfoot, *Journal*, p. 169.
[118] *Ibid.*
[119] *Ibid.* p. 170.

On the other hand, Charles Herle, who did not share Nye's ecclesiastical position, defended Nye's right to express his opinion, and declared that "whatsoever had been said against Mr. *Nye* was against order; because he was adjudged to speak against order".[120] Lord Say also intervened, but he may have been administering a rebuke to Nye when he said that debates became very long and tedious when they were simply about conveniences and inconveniences: "you must", he said, "consider whether the word of God hold out an institution or noe". If there was no clear institution of any particular church order, then civil authority would have to appoint whatever was most conducive to godliness, but let the different opinions be clearly stated. In his view this had been clearly done on one side, but not on the other:

> on the other side ther is a double opinion
> 1. that many congregations are such churches as
>   are compleat & have their officers
> 2. others say that those many congregations doe but
>   make up one church consisting of more pastors
>   & elders not assigned to one congregation as their
>   proper charge but in generall[.][121]

Both sides in the dispute should "bring forth those scriptures upon which they lay this foundation", and if this were done, "it must be imbraced without consideration of Inconveniency".

J. R. DeWitt suggests that Lord Say's speech "was especially calculated to infuriate the presbyterians" because "it was precisely the Independents . . . who had been arguing inconveniencies for two weeks running", and he is particularly scathing with regard to the last part of Say's speech – "one can scarcely believe this was seriously intended" – because the Independent peer seems to suggest that the Independents had been clear in what they believed, whereas their opponents had been vague and were divided in their opinions.[122]

I suggest that this is a misreading of Lord Say's speech. It may have been ingenuous, but it may not have been as completely wide of the mark as DeWitt suggests. In the first place, the matter of 'inconveniences' had not been argued for two weeks: the debate up to that point had been on whether sufficient scriptural evidence could be brought against the presbyterial government to prevent further debate of the 3rd Proposition.

---

[120] *Ibid.*
[121] TMs. I. 629 (Ms. I. f. 326b.)
[122] DeWitt, *Jus Divinum*, p. 114.

The question of 'inconveniences', in the political sense obviously intended by Say, had been raised more or less for the first time – we think, inadvisedly – by Philip Nye on that same day.

Secondly, if the debates of the last few weeks had delayed the Assembly's progress, the majority, for reasons that may not have been entirely free of political motive, had allowed the Independents to continue bringing reasons for their dissent. The faults were not all on one side when it came to wasting time and 'speaking largely'. Thirdly, the Independent position had been fairly clearly set out in the debates, in the speeches of Goodwin on February 14th and 19th, and in the exposition given by William Bridge on the 16th. On the other side, the Presbyterian system had yet to be debated. The Scots system had been presented clearly in their earlier paper, but they were at pains to insist that this should not bind the Assembly. There was considerable vagueness yet about the grounds for claiming a scriptural proof for the presbyterian system, and Gillespie, even as late as that same day, had been most reluctant to reveal the arguments he intended to use later from Acts 15.

There had been considerable coyness on both sides about revealing their proof texts and arguments, but the Independents in the course of attacking the Presbyterian proposition had been forced to divulge some of the major bases of their ecclesiology.

Finally, what Lord Say said about two positions appearing in the majority party becomes more comprehensible when we recognize that the 'Presbyterians' in the Assembly represented an alliance, and a fairly recent alliance, of the Scottish Commissioners and a comparatively small number of English Presbyterians, with Puritan conservatives like Cornelius Burgess, Richard Vines and Herbert Palmer. Palmer, indeed, had expressed the second opinion cited by Lord Say almost at the very beginning of the debate.[123]

The one point at which Say might be accused of being ingenuous was in failing to recognize the extent to which the leaders of that conservative majority in the Assembly were willing to embrace the Scottish system. He was apparently not aware that the opposition had closed its ranks against Independency.

The end of the session was a foregone conclusion. Although Nye and Goodwin intervened "and hindered us a long time", Lightfoot recorded, "at last it was put to the question, and voted that it[124] was not proved. It was also put to the question, That the

---

[123] On 2nd February; Gillespie, *Notes*, p. 9.
[124] I.e., the Independent counter-proposition.

affirmative should be next debated, and voted affirmatively: and so we adjourned."[125]

At the end of this initial barrage, perhaps it is only necessary to point out that the conviction of each side that their own polity could be proved in detail from scripture prevented either from getting to grips with the basic issues for which the other side was contending. On the one hand, the presbyterian system did have an effective means of dealing with stubborn error and persistent sinfulness in the church, and at the corporate level where Independency appeared to be least effective. The Independents never understood the presbyterian principle of equal elders acting corporately in presbytery, the valid contention that whatever else *coram populo* means, it means that every member of the church does not have to be present for all church decisions: church officers can act representatively for the church. Furthermore, in its best light, the presbyterian system maintained, as atomistic Independency cannot maintain, a sense of the church's catholicity and wholeness.

On the other hand Independent church government recognized an important distinction between 'ministerial' (persuasive) authority that is proper to the church, and 'magisterial' (coercive) authority that is found in civil society. The Presbyterians did not understand the Independents' contention that governance in church discipline properly applies only to those who are in a regular pastoral relationship with those they govern, that the exercise of discipline has to be set within the context of worship and life. Nor did the Presbyterians meet the Independent conviction that all decisions should be taken in a way that is open to the people, and that the whole church community should be responsibly involved in actions taken against any one of its members.

These insights could have been justified and perhaps incorporated into the Church in England, if theology could have freed itself from its exclusivity and literalism: but then the theologians would have had to look beyond the letter to the spirit of the Bible that they claimed as final authority.

Meanwhile, although Baillie had admitted that the Independents had presented their case with "plentie of learning, witt, eloquence" and other requisite graces, their arguments made no dent in the audience, and the length of the debates had not done

---

[125] *Journal*, p. 170.

their cause any good. Perhaps by this time both sides were beginning to recognize that the issues would not be finally resolved in any of the halls of Westminster: the final appeal would be to the citizens of London, and even beyond them to Parliament's supporters in the country at large.[126]

---

[126] "Everie one of their arguments, when it had been prest to the full, in one whole session, and sometimes in two or three, was voyced, and found to be light, unanimouslie by all but themselves. By this meanes their credit did much fall in the city, who understood daylie all we did, and fand these men had gotten much more than fair play, a more free libertie than any innovators ever in any Assemblie, to reason their cause to the bottom; but further in the countrie, who know not the maner of our proceedings, their emissaries filled the eares of the people, that the Assemblie did cry down the truth with votes, and was but one Antichristian meeting, which would erect a Presbytrie worse than Bishops'. Publick Letter, 2nd April, 1644, Robert Baillie, *Letters and Journals* II. 145.

CHAPTER 10

THE BATTLE FOR
PRESBYTERIAN GOVERNMENT:
ASSAULT FROM PREPARED POSITIONS

I

Second Phase: the Case for Presbytery

The seventeenth-century was over-stocked with military specialists of one sort and another. What was happening in the Assembly already displayed many of the characteristics of a military campaign, but if we think in those terms the debate that opened on February 22nd, 1643/4 reflects not the flamboyant tactics of Condé, nor even the careful strategy of Turenne, but rather the method of their countryman, Vauban, who systematically reduced every opposing fortification in pursuit of victory as deliberate as it was inevitable. Or perhaps we could mix metaphors with De Witt and observe "from this point on progress was slow but steady, and the planks in the presbyterian platform were laid down one by one."[1] They were not only laid down, but they were nailed in place by a reliable voting majority in the Assembly itself.

The engagement began with the committee's first proof for presbyterian church government in the church of Jerusalem. The church described in Acts (1) was a unified church, (2) it comprised several congregations, and (3) the several congregations were united under presbyterial church government. Obviously, scriptural exegesis was crucial to both the forms of biblical restorationism in the Assembly, for neither the Independents nor the Presbyterians could afford to give ground without undercutting their own ecclesiological foundation. An outline of the ensuing debate may be helpful before we look at the arguments in more detail.

---

[1] *Jus Divinum*, p. 115.

[1] Presbyterian ecclesiology was a rational extension from biblical exegesis, and consisted of a series of carefully articulated acts. So on Thursday 22nd February the Assembly debated and voted that the number of believers mentioned early in Acts "belonged to the church in Jerusalem, as members in that church."[2] This set the stage for all the later debates because it meant that the church in Jerusalem included the 120 believers mentioned in Acts 1:15, the 3,000 and the 5,000 converts of Acts 2:41 and 4:4, the indefinite 'multitudes' mentioned in 5:14, and the additional believers and 'great company of the priests' recorded in Acts vi. 6–7.

[2] This vote therefore prepared the way for the next step, which was to debate that the number of believers "ware more than could ordinarily meete in one place at one time for the performance of all acts of worship [&] government".[3] This second stage began on the 23rd with the Independents naturally trying to minimize the numbers and with the majority arguing that the church would have to be divided into several congregations.[4]

[3] These votes prepared the way for the crucial debate, that began on March 1st, on the proposition "that those several congregations were under one presbytery".[5] From the Ramist type of analysis in Gillespie's *Notes*[6] we can see that this debate moved to the second major branch of the presbyterian argument – from the size of the church in Jerusalem and the number of its congregations, to the presbyterial polity that Gillespie and his colleagues were trying to prove.

[4] On the 4th March the divines returned to a subject that had been touched upon during the afternoon of March 1st when it set out "to prove the multitude of beleivers in the church of Jerusalem after the dispersion",[7] but the major thrust from this point on was presbyterial polity itself. Gillespie's analysis shows that this second major division in his argument for presbyterial government was itself divided into two branches – first, the

---

[2] Lightfoot, *Journal*, p. 174. Based on Acts i. 15, ii. 41, iv. 4, v. 14, vi. 6, 7.

[3] This had been voted as the subject of the next day's debate at the end of the session on the 22nd; TMs. I. 637 (Ms. I. f. 330b.)

[4] The 'proofs' for this were found in the number of preachers and teachers in the church of Jerusalem (the 26th), and by the variety of languages used by the converts (the 29th).

[5] Gillespie, *Notes*, p. 31. The proposition used Acts 8:1, 12:5 and 15:4 as proof texts.

[6] *Ibid.* p. 6.

[7] Based on Acts 9:31, 12:24 and 21:20; TMs. I. 688 (Ms. I. f. 356.)

congregations in Jerusalem were called one church, and secondly, they were under one presbytery.[8]

[5] At the end of the morning session on March 6th the divines argued that this form of government existed at Jerusalem before the dispersion.[9] That debate continued through March 7th, and then the Assembly moved on to affirm that "The severall congregations in Jerusalem being one church & the elders of the church being mentioned 'as meetting together about acts of government' doth prove that those severall congregations ware under one presbitery".[10]

[6] The final debate in this engagement began on March 8th and continued until its climax on the 12th. At one point the similarity between Presbyterian presbyteries and Congregational synods offered some real hope of agreement. It was a debate that had not started too auspiciously when Marshall tried to change the proposition,[11] but the differences appeared narrow enough for a Committee of Accommodation to be appointed to explore those possibilities.[12]

On March 12th the members debated Acts 15 to prove that the presbytery acted authoritatively. The proposition, "to prove elders meeting for acts of government"[13] was vague enough, but on the 13th it was made much more specific by citing Acts 15:4, 6, 22;[14] and so at the end of that debate Herbert Palmer moved that with this vote the proposition on presbyterian government which had occupied them so long, was now proved, and the assembly agreed.[15]

---

[8] The Assembly began to debate this on the 5th, and the proponents based their argument on the fact that "the elders of that church are mentioned, Acts xi. last verse; Acts xv. 4, 6, 22; Acts xxi. 18." Gillespie, *Notes*, p. 33.

[9] TMs. I. 700 (Ms. I. f. 362.)

[10] *Ibid.* 713 (Ms. I. f. 368b.)

[11] There are sometimes significant differences between the accounts we receive through the Minutes, Lightfoot and Gillespie. In this instance the Minutes say that Marshall wanted to debate "That the church of Jerusalem before the dispersion was a true Christian church & had the government of Christ [,] & Christ never apoynted but one forme of government for his Church". This claims a *jus divinum* for the church but leaves open what form of the church it would be. On the other hand Lightfoot and Gillespie indicate that Marshall made the claim specifically for the presbyterian system. Cf. TMs. I. 714. (Ms. I. f. 369) Lightfoot, *Journal*, p. 203, Gillespie, *Notes*, 37.

[12] Despite the Independents' plea that further voting should be suspended until that committee could issue its report, the Assembly decided to press on. Whether or not an accommodation could be reached with the Independents, the majority could see light at the end of the tunnel.

[13] Cf. TMs. I. 731 (Ms. I. f. 377b.)

[14] *Ibid.* 741 (Ms. I. f. 382b.)

[15] Lightfoot, *Journal*, p. 214.

The debate was not a rout, but throughout this time the Independents were pushed into an ever-smaller area by the Presbyterian claims and 'proofs', and this gave them an ever-shrinking area in which to manoeuvre theologically. The initiative was always with the majority, carefully managed by the Scots, and the outcome was never in doubt.

This outline will already give some idea of the deliberate strategy that had been set in train for the debate on the church of Jerusalem, but it does not help us to understand the dispute itself. The twentieth century reader will not assume that theological truth is determined by majority votes, even when voted by such a sincere, dedicated and generally incorruptible body as the Westminster Assembly of Divines. Questions, however, remain: how far was the result due to the quality of the arguments, and how far was it due to political and social concerns unconsciously incorporated into the theological beliefs of English people? There is no way in which a fully objective answer can be given, but it is clear from the record that we slight the divines unjustifiably if we assume that because social and political reasons may have influenced their ecclesiology they took the scriptural evidence with less seriousness or they lessened the rigour of their theological debate.

With the defeat of their case against presbytery on February 21st, the Independents must have seen the handwriting on the wall: what they had failed to get voted out, would now almost inevitably be voted in. The parliamentarians thought that, for they were now noticeably absent from the Assembly – a striking contrast from their interest during the previous few weeks. However, it is clear that the Independents' policy remained unchanged. The case for presbyterian polity had been set out in the Committee's propositions, but it was supported by essentially the same scriptures as those on which the Independents based their own doctrine of the Church. This meant that every inch of the way would be fought hard, and no quarter was given, because none would have been accepted. It also meant that the Independents were regarded by many as wilfully stubborn and treacherously delaying ecclesiastical settlement in England.[16]

---

[16] Were the Independents deliberately stalling? The written authorities give that impression. Almost from the first Robert Baillie was convinced they were, and presbyterian writers ever since have charged the Independents with wasting time and with preventing decisions in the Assembly until such time as Cromwell's power was strong enough to secure religious toleration.

There may have been some small truth in the charge, but there was probably a great

If there were times when an 'accommodation' with the Independents seemed possible, this was not because they had renounced their own ecclesiology – however much Baillie and his colleagues might have hoped for that – but because neither side wanted to admit the possibility that the Bible spoke with less than an absolute and single voice on the form of the Church. They were all Puritans, and as William Bradshaw had written of Puritans much earlier, "They hould and mainetaine that the word of God contained in the writings of the Prophets and Apostles, is of absolute perfection, giuen by Christ the head of the Churche, to bee unto the same, the sole Canon and rule of all matters of Religion, and the worship and service of God whatsoever."[17] It was difficult for the seventeenth century Puritan to believe that perfection could be legitimately interpreted in such varying ways.

II

'Jerusalem the glorious, the Joy of the Elect'[18]

[1] The debate on presbyterian church government began on February 22nd, 1643/4 with the Committee's first proof from the example of the earliest church in Jerusalem. The argument was that the church described in the early chapters of the Book of Acts was (a) one church (i.e., unified,) (b) it was made up of several congregations, and (c) it was under presbyterian government.

---

deal more truth in it after the battle of Marston Moor (July 2nd, 1644) had completely changed the prestige of Cromwell and his troops in respect both to Parliament and the nation. But this had not yet happened and it could not have been foreseen. The Army of the Eastern Association was still in its fledgling stage. In March the Scottish Major–General Crawford was busy replacing Cromwell in the affections of the Earl of Manchester, and purging the officer corps of the Baptists and other radicals Cromwell was employing. Cromwell's letter to Crawford on behalf of the Baptist, Lt. Col. Warner, is a classic and it was a clear indication of the new basis for religious toleration that was arising among Cromwell's troopers. Cf. Abbott, *Writings and Letters of O.C.*, I. pp. 276–9.

There is evidence that the Independents in Parliament had been looking for a military leader and weapon to defend their views. (Cf. Paul, *The Lord Protector*, pp. 76ff.) If there had been a deliberate policy of procrastination in the Assembly they must have had tremendous faith that Providence would work a miracle on their behalf; and that should not be dismissed lightly, for there is good evidence that Cromwell acted on that principle. Cf. *ibid.* pp. 38, 58f, 97, 147–50, etc.

[17] William Bradshaw, *English Puritanisme, Containening the maine opinions of the rigidest sort of those that are called Puritanes in the Realme of England*, Amsterdam(?), 1605, p. 1.

[18] From John Mason Neale's translation of Bernard of Cluny's hymn, 'Jerusalem the Golden.'

On the 22nd the first proposition in this argument[19] simply
tried to establish the numerical size of this church in Jerusalem.
The Independents were clearly on the defensive, although
Dr. Thomas Temple joined them on this issue and opened the
attack on the proposition. He argued that there were "noe presbiters apoynted to teach, but in common[,] not fixed to any
place", that in this church there was "noe exercise of Jurisdiction
but only as Joyned with the apostells".[20] If there was a presbytery
then (in Acts 15) it could apparently act beyond its own boundaries, and to prove the proposition it must be clearly shown that
there was both pastor and ruling elder in that church. He went
on:

> to summe up[:] what will this instance prove[?]
> As much as was then done de facto in the unsetled
> condition of the church that may be done in places
> wher the like necessityes are[.]
> Tim & tit: ware commanded to order churches
> alone in those extraordinary times[,] therfore it
> may be soe now; or this, ther were widdowes
> then upon speciall occasions, soe ther may be now[.][21]

At this point he was called to order by Burgess who claimed he
was debating the negative that had already been rejected.[22] True
or not, Temple's comments were open to objection because they
went considerably beyond a proposition that was simply trying to
establish the numerical size of the church in Jerusalem. His
speech suggests, however, that Temple still believed in a
parochial and pastoral view of the primitive *episcopé*,[23] and unlike
some of his colleagues among the Puritan majority, was unwilling to relinquish this position without a struggle.

Herbert Palmer countered Temple's arguments. He claimed
that the large number of converts would have prevented the
church meeting for worship as a single congregation, and he was
joined by John Lightfoot, who took a leading part in the pres-

---

[19] For the fuller accounts of the debate see TMs. I. 630ff (Ms. I. ff. 327–330b),
Lightfoot, *Journal*, pp. 170–4, Gillespie, *Notes*, pp. 27f.

[20] TMs. I. 631f (Ms. I. ff. 327b.)

[21] TMs. I. 631f (Ms. I. ff. 327b, 328.)

[22] *Ibid*. Cf. Lightfoot, *Journal*, p. 170.

[23] I use the Greek word here because the English words 'episcopacy' and 'episcopate'
carry with them overtones of status and power that were not necessarily included in the
New Testament term. This emphasis on the local, parochial *episcopé* was a position
which, as we can see from Baxter, came very close to the Independents' position at some
points. Cf. *Reliquiae Baxterianae*. I. ii. 140 (§§3–5.)

byterian cause.[24] Lightfoot stated that there were eighty-two preaching pastors in Jerusalem,[25] many languages were spoken, and one part of the church had deacons and the other part did not. For these reasons the church must have consisted of several congregations, and although Christians met from time to time in the temple, he questioned whether they could have met there for regular worship. In his account Lightfoot recorded that, "Dr. *Temple* replied again and again, and I answered him over and over again."[26]

Lightfoot was joined by Palmer, Vines,[27] Seaman, Gouge and Marshall, while Goodwin and Burroughes spoke for the opposition. The debate resolved itself, of course, into a Presbyterian attempt to make the numbers in the early church as large as possible, and an Independent attempt to reduce them to a figure consistent with a single congregation. As DeWitt has said, "it was surely a singularly sterile, fruitless, and unconvincing argumentation which in order to prove its point must depend on a mere counting of heads for the establishment of the unity or plurality of the church in one city."[28] Both sides were equally culpable, because this was the box into which exegetical literalism pushed them.[29]

There seems to have been some uncertainty during this initial presentation of the presbyterian case as to how they could proceed most effectively. Palmer apparently tried to bring the debate to an early issue by offering the syllogism "That government which was lawful in the apostles' times is lawful now; but presbyterial government, &c."[30] He was opposed by Goodwin and Burroughes, who attacked his major premise on the grounds that at that time the church "was not as yet 'ecclesia formata'", that the early church was not yet in its final apostolic form.

---

[24] As in the case of the Independents earlier, responsibility for making the major presentations seems to have been parcelled out among the proponents. So Lightfoot seems to have had responsibility in the debates on the size of the church of Jerusalem, and Stephen Marshall accepted leadership in the debate on Acts 8 (March 1st.) Later, George Gillespie took responsibility for presenting the proofs for presbyterial government.

[25] The Minutes, obviously erroneously, record him as giving the number of preachers as "83". TMs. I. 632 (Ms. I. f. 328.)

[26] Lightfoot, *Journal*, p. 172.

[27] Both Vines and Palmer had been critical of the Presbyterian position earlier.

[28] DeWitt, *Jus Divinum*, p. 115.

[29] The argument from the large number of converts was picked up on the following day by Raynor and others. Cf. Lightfoot, *Journal*, pp. 174ff., TMs. I. 645 (Ms. I. f. 334b,) Gillespie, *Notes*, pp. 28f.

[30] Gillespie, *Notes*, p. 28. The '&c.' was simply a convenient device employed in all the records to abbreviate the argument in their syllogisms. E.g., this one would have gone on to assert that since presbyterial government was lawful in the apostles' time, we could therefore conclude that it is lawful now.

After the exchange between Temple and Lightfoot, Seaman suggested that they should first decide "whether the church of Jerusalem consisted of presbytery" but that had not helped very much, and eventually John Selden applied his legal mind to bring some order into the debate. He laid down four steps that would be needed in order to get the proposition proved.[31] "But here", writes Lightfoot, "was a great deal of debate, before we could settle where to begin; and the Independents opposed with vehemency, and we had some heat: at last we fell upon this, 'that the number of believers in Jerusalem were more than could meet in one place.'"[32]

Even as the debate of the first day was drawing to its close, we read that

> here was a great deal of agitation what the question should be; and at last it was ready for the question, when I desired to stop it a little for that it was not very perfect sense; for it ran thus: 'All the believers mentioned, Acts i. ii. iv, &c. were added to the church at Jerusalem:' now there was no church at all before those in Acts i. and having stopped it thus, Mr. *Burroughs* urged to have something said concerning the five thousand which was done; and it extended to a long debate: at last it was put to the question, and voted affirmatively, that the number of believers mentioned Acts i. 15, ii. 41, iv. 4, v. 14, vi. 6, 7, belonged to the church of Jerusalem, as members in that church.[33]

So the groundwork was laid. Now let the Independents try to prove that such a number of Christians could meet for worship in a single congregation and within the confines of a Jewish city that was still hostile! Despite the somewhat uncertain start, the first round clearly belonged to the Presbyterians.

[2] The theological tourney continued the next day (23rd) with that as the major item of debate,[34] and the Independents were clearly at a disadvantage. Thomas Goodwin admitted that membership in the church at Jerusalem swelled by many thousands, but he insisted that this original church community was unique because it was directly under the supervision of the apostles and

---

[31] Cf. Lightfoot, *Journal*, pp. 170–174. Selden's points were that they must establish:
"1 that ther ware presbiters
2 that those ware as a presbytery
3 that ther were several congregations
4 that those ware governed by that presbitery". TMs. I. 635 (Ms. I. f. 329b.)
[32] Lightfoot, *Journal*, p. 172. Based on Acts i. 15, ii. 41, iv. 4, v. 14, vi. 1.7, xxi. 20.
[33] *Ibid.* pp. 173f.
[34] *Ibid.* pp. 174–8, TMs. I. 638–49 (Ms. I. ff. 331–336b.) Gillespie, *Notes*, pp. 28f.

therefore could not be an exact pattern for normal church government in later times. His position was weakest when he suggested that this large community might have conducted worship in the precincts of the temple,[35] but despite the problems for their case at this point, both Goodwin and later Nye insisted on a very literal understanding of Acts 2:1 where it speaks of the believers being all 'in one place' ἐπὶ τὸ αὐτό: for them this meant that the company gathered was a single congregation.

Lazarus Seaman seized on that, he said that to take the words literally:

> [']they did all meet in one place
> under one consent['] this makes me thinke
> of the argument of transubstantiation be[cause] Christ
> saith [']it is my body['] whatever are the absurd
> ityes[.]

He protested that "this was not a fair way of arguing scripture", which should be interpreted not according to its phrases but "according to the matter".[36] That was just, and Seaman's likening the Independent argument to Roman Catholic exegesis was particularly apt, since the previous day the Independents had accused their opponents of arguing like Episcopalians![37] But the literalism was by no means all on one side; they all did it when it suited their case.

Theophilus Bathurst – surely with a touch of humour? – asked how Christians could possibly celebrate the Lord's Supper in the temple, because "where should they have beds for the purpose"? and he emphasized, what Lightfoot had suggested earlier, that the church was already divided into Hebrew and Greek speaking congregations.[38] George Gillespie was also sceptical about the use of temple premises for the sacraments of the church, because that would mean "the most mixed communion that ever was". The church must have other places for regular worship.[39]

The struggle continued throughout the afternoon. Goodwin maintained his earlier emphasis on the unity of purpose and place in the gatherings of the early church, but he disclaimed any intention of saying that the Christians in Jerusalem had actually

---

[35] Lightfoot, *Journal*, p. 175.
[36] TMs. I. 640 (Ms. I. f. 332.) Nye said later that this was a very different case from the literal interpretation of 'This is my body': there were many places in scripture to indicate that that text should not be understood literally, "but not soe in this" where there was nothing in scripture to throw doubt on it. Cf. TMs. I. 646 (Ms. I. f. 335.)
[37] Lightfoot, *Journal*, p. 172.
[38] Lightfoot, *Journal*, p. 176.
[39] *Ibid.* pp. 176f, Gillespie, *Notes*, pp. 28f.

celebrated sacraments in the temple. He had only maintained that it was possible, and it was for his opponents to prove that it was not. He also disclosed a significant principle by which the Independents interpreted their restorationist view of the Church. His opponents[40] had agreed that the church in Jerusalem "was the first measure of a church", but Goodwin argued that although "in what is ordinary, it[41] is a measure for ever", in some things it was not 'ordinary'. In these things it could not be an absolute pattern, and in particular we read of no act of jurisdiction. For Goodwin, a formally constituted church must hold preaching (i.e., worship) and jurisdiction together, presumably on the basis he had enunciated earlier, that church discipline could properly take place only in the context of full pastoral oversight.

In the same way he hinted at another principle that would be important when the Assembly discussed the Directory of Worship – the unity of Word and Sacrament: he insisted that "wher they preached ther they had the sacrament".[42] It was this principle, perhaps applied too literally to the account in Acts, that led him to suggest that because early Christians had heard preaching in the temple, they must also have found ways to celebrate the sacraments there. As in many cases on both sides of this dispute, the theological principles by which the divines spoke were often better than the arguments by which they tried to establish them.

At the end of the debate it was inevitably voted "that the number of believers in the church of Jerusalem, was more than could ordinarily meet in one place, in one time, in the exercise of worship and government."[43] The Independents thought that this still left them room to manoeuvre, since they insisted that there was nothing 'ordinary' about this pre-dispersion church, but the majority would use that vote in a quite different way.

This was demonstrated on the following Monday (the 26th) when the Assembly addressed the proposition "that the church of Jerusalem was more than one congregation, from the number of teaching-elders."[44]

We have already seen that by adding the number of the apostles to the seventy preachers sent out by our Lord (Luke 10),

---

[40] In this case it had been Rutherford.

[41] I.e., the church at Jerusalem.

[42] TMs. I. 650f (Ms. I. ff. 337, 337b.)

[43] Lightfoot, *Journal*, p. 181.

[44] *Ibid.* The day's debate is to be found on pp. 181–3, Gillespie, *Notes*, pp. 29f. and in TMs. I. 655–61 (Ms. I. ff. 339b–342b.)

Lightfoot had reached the figure of eighty-two preaching elders in Jerusalem.[45] Seaman went further. He maintained that the whole of the one hundred and twenty mentioned in Acts 1:15 were preachers,[46] while Samuel Rutherford pointed out from Acts 6:7 that a large number of Jewish priests had been converted, and since it was part of their function to teach the Law (Malachi 2:7) it would be "unlikely that they should not preach as officers made before".[47] Again we note the tendency to argue for a structural continuity of the New Testament church with the Old Testament Jewish community.

However tenuous some of these arguments were, the motion before them was carried,[48] and before the day was finished they had also added Acts 2:42 and 46 to their proofs that there was more than one congregation in the church of Jerusalem before the dispersion.[49]

On Thursday the 29th the divines began by adding further proof texts,[50] but rapidly moved on to consider a supporting argument for the proposition from the evidence of different languages among the members of the early church. It had originally been suggested by Lightfoot[51] and he was very proud of it. He noted, for example, that when Palmer followed him in the debate on February 22nd, he had taken "my argument about several languages, and of eighty-two pastors there, and followed it close",[52] and again in the middle of the morning session on the 29th, he observed that Charles Herle had apparently urged, that "this argument that I had proposed about the diversity of languages" should be debated and that the Assembly agreed.[53]

However, the argument produced opposition beyond the Independents. Dr. Temple spoke against it, maintaining that they were Jews who happened to speak several languages,[54] and

---

[45] Herbert Palmer was willing to concede that not all the seventy may have remained in Jerusalem, he thought that most of them were there. TMs. I. 657 (Ms. I. f. 340b.)

[46] Gillespie, *Notes*, p. 29. The significance of this for Seaman's view of the ministry presumably was that Pentecost came to this group. The Holy Spirit fell initially on preachers.

[47] TMs. I. 658 (Ms. I. f. 341.)

[48] Gillespie, *Notes*, p. 30.

[49] *Ibid.*, Lightfoot, *Journal*, p. 183.

[50] Acts 12:5, 12, 17; TMs. I. 661 (Ms. I. f. 342b.) and Lightfoot, *Journal*, p. 183.

[51] *Ibid.* p. 171, cf. TMs. 632 (Ms. I. f. 328.)

[52] *Ibid.* p. 172.

[53] *Ibid.* p. 184. The ms. from which Lightfoot's account was taken was defective, but from the Assembly's reaction this is what Herle must have suggested. The accounts of the debate are in pp. 184ff.; cf. Gillespie, *Notes*, pp. 30f., TMs. I. 663–71 (Ms. I. ff. 343b–347b.)

[54] Lightfoot, *Journal*, p. 184.

that there was no evidence that all those who spoke tongues were converts.[55] Francis Woodcock said that Peter must have spoken to the crowd after Pentecost in a single language, while Dr. Gouge thought that all the hearers understood Hebrew to some extent,[56] and even Richard Vines pointed out that when Paul addressed the Jerusalem crowd in Acts 22 all his hearers had recognized what he was saying in Hebrew.[57] But those who had been Presbyterians for longer (e.g. Seaman) had no doubts, and Rutherford insisted that since Pentecost was the fulfilment of Joel (Joel 2:28ff.) there had to be a miracle of this kind.[58] Their cause was helped by the erudition of John Selden, who in a long speech argued "a great deal of probability if not certainty that there was not one language that was understood amongst them".[59]

Again we should notice the curious positions into which Puritans were sometimes forced by biblical literalism. The Presbyterians argued that the existence of many languages among the members of the church of Jerusalem necessitated the formation of many separate congregations. That in itself is a reasonable argument, but because of what they knew would be built on it, it forced the opponents of presbytery to downplay the importance of the language division, and to diminish to some extent the miracle of Pentecost.[60]

The debate was carried into Friday March 1st, but when we look at the debates as a whole it is clear that on that date the Assembly moved from the preparatory ground it had laid for itself in the number of people and the multiplicity of congregations in Jerusalem to attempt the demonstration of presbyterian government in that church.

III

'Jerusalem the Golden . . . What social Joys are there!'[61]

The misapplication of a well-known hymn in the title of this section simply tries to make one point – the Church is a society; and because it is a divine society, each ecclesiology assumed that the way it was organized and administered had been divinely

---

[55] TMs. I. 663 (Ms. I. f. 343b.)
[56] *Ibid.* 666 (Ms. I. f. 345.)
[57] Lightfoot, *Journal*, p. 184.
[58] *Ibid.* p. 185.
[59] TMs. I. 670 (Ms. I. f. 347.)
[60] Cf. the comments of William Bridge; *ibid.* 669 (Ms. I. f. 346b.)
[61] From John Mason Neale's translation of 'Jerusalem the Golden.'

prescribed. Furthermore, it should remind us that because of the traditional ties between church and state, we cannot separate matters of church polity in the seventeenth century from the implications they held for the rest of society. It is no accident that an élitist Parliament with aristocratic leadership felt it had a vested interest in the polity that was being expounded in the Assembly.

[3] By March 1st the probative period had been reached in the struggle for a Presbyterian Church of England, and apparently something of this had begun to leak to the public.[62] The divines debated the proposition that all the congregations in Jerusalem were under presbyterian government because they were called one church.[63] Marshall claimed that none would deny it, but "Mr. *Goodwin* said, it was yet to be proved, that they were one church in respect of government; and he denied any such government to be before the dispersion, Acts viii."[64]

Cornelius Burgess commented tartly that the dispersion did not turn the church into two churches,[65] and then Stephen Marshall came out with a clear statement of *jure divino* Presbyterianism. In response to Goodwin he argued:

1. This church before the scatering being a church
   of Jesus Christ had a government that Christ himselfe
   was the author of it, but Christ never instituted
   any other government but one[,] the presbyteriall
   government[.]
2. Ther is the selfesame reason why they should
   have presbyteriall government before the scattering
   as after the scattering[.]
   the only thing aleadged why not this government
   set up till afterwards [is] be[cause] the apostells
   ware with them[;]
   now that was as much after the scattering as before[.]
3. let but the government of the church before
   the scattering be looked upon & it will apeare
   that the apo: carryed all things before as after
   1 Act: 6 Act.[66]

To the objection that we do not read of elders until the 11th chapter of Acts, he responded that this proved nothing, any more

---

[62] See Marshall's cryptic comment, Lightfoot, *Journal*, p. 186.
[63] It was supported by the texts, Acts 3:1, 12:5, and 15:4.
[64] Lightfoot, *Journal*, p. 187.
[65] *Ibid.* p. 187.
[66] TMs. I. 673 (Ms. I. f. 348b,) cf. Lightfoot, *Journal*, p. 187.

than it would prove that because we do not read of elders in Ephesus until Acts 20, the church in that city had none until then.[67] It was a reasonable argument but it did go beyond the text, and in the battle of what might be legitimately inferred from silence each side read its own ecclesiology into the possibilities.[68]

In response to Marshall, Goodwin simply affirmed that it was not yet a formal church in respect to ecclesiastical discipline because the community was under direct apostolic supervision:

> that wch we desire to be proved in this[:-]
> the paterne must be suted to the presbyteriall govern-
> ment[.]
> those were under the apostells gouernment[;]
> & you must prove that they were fixed churches[;]
> their severall meetings were by accident & soe it
> will make nothing at all against us[.][69]

He admitted that the church before the dispersion was the church 'materially' in that it was composed of saints, and he did not deny that it had a form of government, "but this must be made out that they were under one presbyteriall government".[70] Goodwin also admitted that under persecution a church might indeed be forced to meet in several places, but claimed that the persecution recorded in Acts 8:1 had been general and the apostles had remained "to raise a new seed".[71]

Gillespie in his *Notes* flatly contradicted Goodwin's distinction between the church before and after the dispersion: "the saints materially considered are not a church, but only formally as united or incorporated."[72] The problem here was that the word 'church' was being used in different senses – Goodwin distinguished between the church in the general sense as the company of believers and in the more formal sense as a body with a distinct church order. He regarded the former as closer to the church before the dispersion, whereas Gillespie believed that it existed in the second sense from the beginning.

---

[67] *Ibid.* p. 187.

[68] The 'church covenant' beloved of Congregationalists is a good example on the other side. They argued that the idea of covenant is central to the scriptures and that it is peculiarly appropriate not only in God's relationship to us, but also in the relationship his people bear, through him, to each other. But there is no clear New Testament evidence for any such church covenant. Cf. Champlin Burrage, *Church Covenant Idea: Its Origin and Its Development*, (Philadelphia, American Baptist Publication Society, 1904,) p. ix.

[69] TMs. I. 676 (Ms. I. f. 350.)

[70] *Ibid.*

[71] Gillespie, *Notes*, p. 32.

[72] *Ibid.*

Rutherford argued that if the apostles preached and baptized as elders, "why shall we not say that they did govern as elders?"[73] but this was not allowed by the Independents. The problem was how to distinguish between different aspects of the apostolic office, since it was agreed that the office of apostle was not permanent but had been instituted specifically for that time. Presbyterians tended to think of the apostles essentially as elders who possessed some unique abilities and functions, whereas the Independents thought of the office of apostle as unique and indivisible; so Goodwin held that Acts 8:1 did not prove "one church under a presbytery, but under the apostles."[74]

Before the end of the morning session Acts 8:1 had been added to the proof texts on this part of the proposition,[75] and the debate on this verse was continued into the afternoon session of the same day,[76] although Lightfoot and the Minutes show that the debate was ostensibly on Acts 12:5. In beginning to debate the organization of the church after the dispersion it was necessary to deal with the circumstances of the dispersion. Were all the people scattered as it seems to say in Acts 8:1 or was this to be understood as mainly or even exclusively the preachers and teachers? The Independents stood by the first view, and the majority stood as strongly for the latter. So at the beginning of the debate Dr. Smith declared that those dispersed "were only teachers",[77] while William Bridge declared just as roundly that "the dispersion was of the church and not of preachers" and showed that he was not ready to limit the spiritual gifts for "there were others that had extraordinary gifts besides preachers".[78] On the other side, Richard Vines supported Dr. Smith, and here, we read, "we had a large debate which held us even all afternoon"[79] in which Herbert Palmer, Thomas Case, and others like Thomas Wilson sided with Smith and Vines.

But even Palmer had some trouble with the dogmatic way in which the case was being presented. He stood with the majority, but he still wanted to know

out of any author[,] scripture or other[,]
wher ther is any such an exception as this that that [sic]
all must not be taken for all[.][80]

---

[73] *Ibid.* p. 32.
[74] *Ibid.*
[75] Together with Acts 2:47 and 5:11. TMs. I. 680 (Ms. I. f. 352.)
[76] Gillespie, *Notes,* p. 32f.
[77] Lightfoot, *Journal,* p. 190. Cf. TMs. 680 (Ms. I. f. 352.)
[78] Lightfoot, *Journal,* p. 191; cf. TMs. I. 682 (Ms. I. f. 353.)
[79] Lightfoot, *Journal,* p. 191.
[80] TMs. I. 685 (Ms. I. f. 354b.)

Behind the reading of the text as a dispersion limited to the preachers and teachers of the church[81] we recognize the clerical prejudices of English divines, who still tended to consider spiritual gifts as a clerical monopoly. So Vines believed our Lord had committed the proclamation of the gospel in Judea, Samaria and Galilee to "preachers in office", and the intent of his argument suggested that the persecution was against the appointed preachers.[82] For many it was still inconceivable to think that when, as in Acts 8:4, the writer spoke of those who were scattered going about "preaching the word", he meant ordinary Christians.

This may have been an embarrassment to the more convinced Presbyterians. The Scots were noticeably silent throughout the afternoon, George Walker was clearly perplexed, and even Palmer, as we have seen, entertained doubts. Charles Herle warned his colleagues not to stretch the sense of the passage too far, for more than merely the teachers were scattered,[83] and although Stephen Marshall may have contributed mainly to keep the unity of his party, that also seems to have been his conclusion.[84] When he called for one of the Dissenting Brethren to frame a motion to prove that the 'all' in the text "must signify the church", Jeremiah Burroughes obliged, and observed that if the ministers alone had withdrawn under persecution, "none will Justify such a kind of flying."[85]

There are signs that some of the leading Presbyterians had wanted to go in a different direction. At the end of the morning session John Selden had outlined three basic steps by which they should try to prove the proposition before them,[86] and it seems that Lazarus Seaman had tried to move the debate in that direction. But Smith's interpretation of Acts 8:1 had already been aired, and this led Goodwin to protest that he was now uncertain as to what he should address himself, "for that so many things were a-foot at once before us." This led to more delay until the

---

[81] William Bridge produced a cogent argument against this interpretation of the text. He pointed out that if the main intention of Saul and his helpers had been to attack the leadership of the church, they would have moved first against the apostles. Cf. TMs. I. 682 (Ms. I. f. 353.)

[82] *Journal*, p. 191.

[83] TMs. I. 684f (Ms. I. ff. 354, 354b.)

[84] Gillespie, *Notes*, p. 33.

[85] TMs. I. 683 (Ms. I. f. 353b.)

[86] "Mr. *Selden* moved, That we should go on by these degrees:–
1. To prove that the church at Jerusalem was under presbyters.
2. That these presbyters did make one body.
3. That this body exercised government." Lightfoot, *Journal*, p. 189.

divines decided to try the proposition that there were "divers congregations after the dispersion",[87] but the exchanges about the interpretation of Acts 8:1ff. were not far from the minds of the participants, as their comments show.[88]

When the time came for the vote, the Independents expostulated that "this was not to the business of the report, and that we had been beside our order all afternoon", but finally it was voted that 'those words, Acts viii. 1, &c. do not imply such a [wholesale?] dispersion, but that they might still continue divers congregations.'[89] It was also resolved that on the following Monday they should reconsider Acts 9:31, 12:24, and 21:20 "to prove the multitude of beleivers in the church of Jerusalem after the dispersion."[90]

On Monday 4th March these verses were added to the proofs, but Lightfoot was on his way back from his weekend duties in Munden, and the records for that debate are meagre.[91] The main point of interest seems to have been in the communication from the classis of Walcheren strongly criticizing *An Apologeticall Narration*, and this was the first time the Independents' pamphlet was mentioned in the Minutes. The Assembly voted to forward the communication from Walcheren to Parliament with a translation.

[4] Before the major debate on Tuesday the 5th March got under way, Dr. Stanton, on behalf of the Second Committee, reported a further eight propositions regarding church discipline to add to the six he had communicated to the Assembly on February 5th.[92] Although these provisions left some loop-holes for the

---

[87] *Ibid.* pp. 190f. Goodwin had said that there were three things before them:– 1. The question whether there were many congregations after the dispersion; 2. the arguments regarding the apostles; and 3. the suggestion that there were elders in the church at the time of the apostles. He observed that it would be "good that we singled out some one to speake too that we might not be confused in our debate." TMs. I. 682 (Ms. I. f. 352b.)

[88] See the speeches by Bridge, Vines and Selden; Lightfoot, *Journal*, p. 191.

[89] *Ibid.* p. 192. Lightfoot was less clear than usual. Gillespie makes the vote more explicit:

"It was put to the question, That Acts viii. 1, compared with ver. 2, 3, 4, doth not imply such a scattering as that there might not continue more congregations than one in Jerusalem after the dispersion; and resolved upon the question." *Notes*, p. 33.

[90] TMs. I. 688 (Ms. I. f. 356.)

[91] *Ibid.* 688–91 (Ms. I. ff. 356–357b.) Gillespie, *Notes*, p. 33, Lightfoot, *Journal*, p. 192.

[92] The previous six propositions are given in Gillespie, *Notes*, p. 10; cf. *supra* p. 252, n. 16.

Omitting the proof texts and the arguments, a summary of the additional propositions is as follows:

7. When the number of believers grew too large for them to meet in one place, "it is lawful and expedient that they divide into distinct and fixed congregations."

Independents, they were cast in a decidedly presbyterian framework, and they contained plenty of material for future dispute because they assumed that congregations would be organized along parish lines, that each parish would have a pastor, deacon and ruling elder, that power would be in the hands of the presbytery and not in the parish, and that there would be a fairly liberal interpretation in the sacraments.

The Assembly then resumed its debate. The members voted Acts 12:5 and 15:4 as proofs that after the dispersion the several congregations in Jerusalem were still one church, and they were about to vote that Acts 11:30, 15:4, 6, and 22, and 20:18 were proofs that the elders of the church of Jerusalem are mentioned, when Goodwin interjected to point out that the mention of elders "did not infer one presbytery."[93] This led to an important engagement between himself and Richard Vines,[94] and Goodwin's argument may be gathered from his assertion that "it will not be sufficient to say they ware elders unlesse [they were in] an association of such a government".[95] After a considerable verbal tussle between Goodwin and several members of the majority party,[96] these verses were voted as proofs, and the Assembly then turned to proofs for an authoritative presbytery.

George Gillespie carried the major responsibility for present-

---

8. "We find no other ordinary way of dividing, than by the bounds of their dwellings."
9. Congregations should have "such officers, ordinances, and administrations, as God hath instituted for edification. 1. Officers. One at least to labour in word and doctrine . . . another to care for the poor . . . Another to assent in ruling. 2. Ordinances. Prayer, thanksgiving, and singing psalms . . . the word read . . . Some part expounded and applied . . . Sacraments administered . . . Collections for the poor . . . Censures."
10. The rights of the congregation. Those who publicly profess faith and repentence have a right to the sacraments; and also the right to have no officers imposed on them against whom they can take exception.
11. Congregations need mutual support from each other.
12. "No single congregation may ordinarily take to itself all and sole power in elections, ordinations, and censures; or in forensical determining controversies of faith, cases of conscience and things indifferent."
13. Elders in a city gathered together in the Apostles' time joined together to govern its congregations and for censures.
14. Elders today have similar powers, and because of the need in country places as well as towns, they ought to be joined in presbyteries. Lightfoot, *Journal*, pp. 192ff.

[93] *Ibid.* p. 194.
[94] Vines argued strongly from the collegial relationship of elders in the Old Testament. *Ibid.*
[95] TMs. I. 692 (Ms. I. f. 358.)
[96] Note, however, that Rutherford was willing for Acts 9:30 to be dropped, since it was not certain whether it referred to the elders of Jerusalem or of Judea. He may have been convinced by Lightfoot, who assured him that since Paul was in Jerusalem at that time, it was certainly the former. Lightfoot, *Journal*, pp. 194f.

ing this part of the case. He started from the assumption that the apostles were not only apostles but elders, and that they exercised the powers and functions of eldership in the church before the dispersion. He claimed that they had a common meeting for that purpose (Acts 4:23), and claimed that it is most agreeable to the light of nature that officers should act together in consultation. Further, he argued that if the church had deacons therefore[97] it must also have had elders because people's souls "are more excellent than their bodies."[98]

It was not one of Gillespie's most convincing performances, and Philip Nye declared "that proposed by the R[everend] Commissioner is not enough to prove the proposition, [for] it is not enough to say they mete together & conferred together[;] this they may doe & doe noe act of government".[99] Then Stephen Marshall argued the case in three basic steps. First, he noted that 'presbytery' is used only twice in scripture in relation to the Christian church; but he went on to make this logical jump, that "in other churches, when elders are mentioned, we conclude an eldership; and so must we at Jerusalem." Secondly, he noted that the apostles exercised their powers of government both before and after the dispersion – "not 'ad modum imperii,' but 'ministerii.'" Thirdly, he built on the assumption that those scattered had been church officers – if they appointed an evangelist like Philip, "they sure made presbyters", – and on the fact that the converts had been baptized. Therefore (*ergo*), he reasoned, "they had their elders and officers before their dispersion."[100] It was a case built up on logical inferences. Some of it, such as the ministerial way in which the apostles exercised their apostleship, contained valuable insights, but the inferences were not strong enough to carry the case that was being built upon them: certainly not sufficient to justify the *jure divino* ecclesiology that he claimed.

Herle tried to tighten the argument for a presbytery before the dispersion. The apostles had a double capacity in the church – an extraordinary office (as apostles), and an ordinary office as elders – but since everything described in Acts had been done in an ordinary way, he regarded this as evidence that elders existed in the church from the beginning. Again, it was a reasonable inference, but it did not meet the requirement for explicit scriptural

---

[97] The *ergo* (therefore) in the argument of a seventeenth century logician has all the force of an imperative, and in George Gillespie's case, of a divine imperative.

[98] Lightfoot, *Journal*, p. 195. Cf. TMs. I. 693–4 (Ms. I. ff. 358b, 359.)

[99] TMs. I. 694 (Ms. I. f. 359.)

[100] Lightfoot, *Journal*, p. 196.

proof, or the Independents' demand for proof that the 'elders' had met not only consultatively, but in acts of authoritative government.

Goodwin agreed that the apostles "did act as ordinary elders for the substance of the act: yet", he went on to say, their power was "different from the power of elders, in this, that they had power in all churches."[101] The divines should ask themselves what it would mean to the argument "supposing that the difference & that wherin the essentiall difference lyes[,] is soe great as will never prove a presbitery from thence".[102] What the Presbyterians needed to prove was summarized in Lightfoot's brief summary of Goodwin's speech:

> To make a presbytery, 1. There must be a power over many. 2. An association: now in Jerusalem there needed no association, for they were elders in all churches.[103]

One has the feeling that the Independents won this round on points.[104]

Wednesday 6th March signalled particularly heavy weather. A proposition was before the Assembly that "the several congregations in Jerusalem being called one church, and the elders of that church being mentioned, doth prove that those several congregations were under one presbytery"[105] that might bring all their arguments to their predestined end. It was not likely to impress the Independents, who had already queried its basic assumptions, but the majority party was determined to press its advantage on the basis of the votes already secured.

So Rutherford, responding to arguments put forward by Goodwin the previous day, declared that the apostles baptized

---

[101] *Ibid.*

[102] TMs. I. 695 (Ms. I. f. 359.)

[103] Lightfoot, *Journal*, p. 196. For a longer account of his speech, cf. TMs. I. 695f. (Ms. I. ff. 359b, 360.)

[104] There was one way out of the presbyterian dilemma, but it is one that the proponents were extremely unwilling to take. They might have claimed the continuation of apostolic powers and funcions (i.e., *in toto*) within the corporate presbytery. Their reluctance to make such a claim may have been due to the association of the argument with papal and episcopal claims, or to their recognition that presbyteries did not possess the miraculous power of the apostles, or to the almost unanimous consensus of the Reformers that the offices of apostle, prophet and evangelist ceased with the apostolic age.

[105] Lightfoot, *Journal*, p. 197. For the full debate cf. *ibid.* pp. 197–9, TMs. I. 696–700 (Ms. I. ff. 360–362.) Gillespie mixed the morning and afternoon sessions (Gillespie, *Notes*, pp. 34–6.) He gives us a full summary of his own argument at the end of the day's debate. *Ibid.* pp. 34f.

and governed as pastors, although when they exercised those gifts universally they did so as apostles; that what they did *in collegio* they did as elders, but that their miraculous powers were used as apostles; that what they did *interveniente ecclesia* (by ecclesiastical authority) they did as ordinary elders, but when they acted alone they did so on their authority as apostles.[106]

Gillespie argued that if elders neglected their ruling and disciplinary responsibilities they were neglecting something that belonged essentially to their office. By implication, therefore, if the apostles were elders we must assume that they did not neglect this aspect of their calling, and that therefore there was a presbytery among them. We see here the same distinction that Rutherford had made between the function of 'elder' and 'apostle' within the apostolate.[107]

Herle, Seaman, Palmer, Cornelius Burgess and Marshall all supported the proposition, but none of them produced the kind of evidence the Independents were demanding. Palmer wanted the proposition to be re-phrased,[108] while Marshall justified the distinction between apostolic and presbyterial functions among the apostles by pointing to an analogy in English society: the Lord Keeper of England was a justice throughout the country by virtue of his office, but when he sat with the justices in any county he acted simply as one of them.[109]

Cornelius Burgess simply brushed the opposition aside: "this we may take for granted that ther ware acts of a presbitery done".[110] That may have overawed some, although at one point Thomas Gataker protested that they were talking beside the point and "therefore desired we might return flatly to our proposition."[111]

This intervention by Gataker may have indicated his own unease at the course the debate had taken, for in the afternoon session[112] he sided with the opposition on the ground that the

---

[106] Lightfoot, *Journal*, p. 197; TMs. I. 697 (Ms. I. f. 360b.)

[107] TMs. I. 698 (Ms. I. f. 361.) Cf. Gillespie's account of his own views in the *Notes*, which begins "It seems from Acts vi. that the apostles did act here as a presbytery", and he gives his reasons – 1. because they acted *in collegio*, 2. they acted with the knowledge and consent of the church, 3. what they did is a pattern for us, and 4. the actions confirm it. *Op. cit.* p. 34.

[108] He had wanted it phrased like this: "Church of Jerusalem consisting of divers congregations governed by apostels shall be brought to prove that [a] church consisting of divers congregations may be under one presbiteriall government". TMs. I. 700 (Ms. I. f. 362.)

[109] Lightfoot, *Journal*, p. 198.

[110] TMs. I. 699 (Ms. I. f. 361b.)

[111] Lightfoot, *Journal*, p. 197.

[112] For the afternoon session see *ibid.* 199f, TMs. I. 700–705 (Ms. I. ff. 362–364b.)

ordination of 'deacons' in Acts 6 was an apostolic action and not the ordinary action of presbyters.[113] In view of Gataker's earlier record, this is a further indication that the older English Puritan view may have been submerged, but it was not entirely dead. Men like Gataker voted with the majority for reasons that seemed good enough to them at that time, but they were not yet doctrinaire Presbyterians. Indeed, Gataker had a sharp exchange with Rutherford.[114]

[5] At the beginning of the afternoon session on March 6th there had been considerable uncertainty among the majority as to how they might best pursue their goal.[115] The doubts may be indicated in Palmer's curious suggestion that "it was the institution of Christ, that there should be ruling elders, as well as teachers," and his assumption (*ergo*) that this would prove presbyteries.[116] It was at this point that Gataker had made his own intervention, and the Minutes show that his opposition was not to presbyterian church government as such, but to the validity of Acts 6 as a proof text.[117] The contest continued throughout the afternoon with Rutherford, Seaman, Palmer and Herle supporting the proposition and Nye, Burroughes, Bridge and Goodwin opposing it. Virtually nothing was added to the arguments that had been heard earlier.

One point arose that held significance for future ecclesiology. Philip Nye admitted that sometimes an apostle would act with less authority than he might have assumed as an apostle and he instanced Paul's dealings with Philemon over the slave Onesimus: Paul could have commanded but he preferred to entreat. At that point Nye touched an insight that could have immense importance for church government, for what was more properly characteristic of apostolic authority, to command or to entreat? Nye was coming close to a principle that began to assume great importance in matters of church government for the Independents, the distinction between 'magisterial' authority which is coercive and appropriate to the civil state, and

---

[113] Lightfoot, *Journal*, p. 199, cf. Gillespie, *Notes*, p. 34.

[114] Lightfoot, *Journal*, p. 200.

[115] Lazarus Seaman said he hoped that they might "fix upon some medium by which to prove the proposition, whether by apostles being presbyters, or by their uncertainty of staying in Jerusalem; and consequently they were bound to provide elders, &c." *Ibid.* p. 199.

[116] *Ibid.* Cf. TMs. I. 702 (Ms. I. f. 363.) It was a particularly curious argument in view of Palmer's stubborn opposition to the office of ruling elder the previous November: *supra* pp. 164, 170ff.

[117] TMs. I. 702 (Ms. I. f. 363.)

'ministerial' authority which is persuasive and appropriate to the Church.

Word seems to have gone out for reinforcements, for on March 7th[118] we find names appearing in the records of those who had not been regularly involved in the debates – Herrick, Woodcock and Reynolds in support of the proposition, and Simpson and William Carter for the Independents. That debate produced only variations on themes that had already been well enough rehearsed. William Bridge opened with a long speech,[119] at the end of which he had said that nothing spoken for the proposition had convinced him. What had been argued was contrary to Acts 6 where it says specifically that the Twelve acted, and that this was therefore not a presbytery of elders. He also argued that Paul's words in Galatians (1:16) show that the apostle did not act presbyterially and that the apostles acted according to their commission as apostles.

Seaman responded, and argued that because the apostles were twelve they were a presbytery.[120] When Peter was called to account that had been a presbyter, and Seaman was backed by Marshall who declared that there was nothing to prove that the Twelve had not acted collegially in Acts 6. The onus of proof was on the opposition, but obviously, there was no way in which these two positions could agree. They continued to argue around each other. Jeremiah Burroughes wanted it proved that "what the apostles did, they did it as a presbytery",[121] while Edward Reynolds could not understand why the apostles had joined together in their decision if it were not "to give an example to ensuing churches".[122]

There were at least two attempts to push the vote through, the first prevented by the intervention of Simpson, and the second by Woodcock's attempt to get his own argument for presbytery accepted. There were also small indications of that residual conservatism of the English Puritans. It was to be seen in Palmer's preference for a general ministry common to all the churches. During a speech against Goodwin, he said:

I desire to understand what is meant by presbitery[.]
I am not convinced but if a number of presbiters meete

---

[118] The debate will be found in Lightfoot, *Journal*, pp. 200–203, TMs. I. 705–713 (Ms. I. ff. 364b–368b,) Gillespie, *Notes*, p. 36.

[119] TMs. I. 705–7; cf. Lightfoot, *Journal*, pp. 200f., Gillespie, *Notes*, p. 36.

[120] TMs. I. 707f (Ms. I. ff. 375b, 376.)

[121] Lightfoot, *Journal*, p. 201.

[122] TMs. I. 713 (Ms. I. f. 368b.)

together though not [with] all those formaliyes[,] they may make a presbytery as the 12[.][123]

English Puritans of Palmer's background seem to have placed an emphasis on the clerical *office* that was not altogether shared by the Scots.

We see the same concern in Gouge's strong disapproval of the suggestion that apostles might not be infallible in all matters of government,[124] and even in Dr. Temple's distinction between apostles and elders that caused him on occasion to side with the Independent opposition.[125] But when it came to the division, the majority held firm, and it was voted "that the apostles did the ordinary acts of presbyters, as presbyters, in the church of Jerusalem; and that this shall be brought to prove the presbyterial government at Jerusalem."[126]

[6] There was further uncertainty at the end of the session on March 7th as to how the campaign should proceed,[127] and when the members arrived on March 8th, Stephen Marshall tried to introduce a new proof for presbyterian government in the church before the dispersion.[128] It was rejected by the divines, and eventually the Assembly settled down to the debate that would occupy it until the final vote on the 13th:

> the Assembly now returned to the rest of the Committee's report, that the several congregations in Jerusalem, being one church, and the elders of the church being mentioned, Acts xi. 30; xv. 4, 6, 22; xxi. 18, proveth that the many congregations in Jerusalem were governed by one presbytery, especially these elders being met together for acts of government.[129]

---

[123] *Ibid.* 711 (Ms. I. f. 367b.)

[124] *Ibid.*, Lightfoot, *Journal*, p. 201.

[125] "Dr. *Temple:* Christ doth clearly distinguish the office of apostles and elders, Eph. iv. *ergo*, the apostles could not be formal elders." *Ibid.* p. 202.

[126] *Ibid.* p. 203, (cf. Gillespie, *Notes*, p. 36.)

[127] *Ibid.*

[128] *Ibid.* Cf. Gillespie, *Notes*, p. 37. Why Marshall intervened is uncertain, particularly since he seems to have cast his proposition in the clearest possible *jure divino* terms for presbyterian government in the church before the dispersion. Perhaps at this stage he mistakenly thought that this would be needed to get the recommendations of the Assembly accepted by Parliament. Incontrovertible proof had not been forthcoming, and one suspects that Marshall was concerned about the way the 'proofs' would be received when they left the privileged environment of the Jerusalem Chamber. It is worth noting that when Marshall eventually carried the recommendations on church government to Parliament on July 3rd, 1645, he had revised his position because he was very careful not to claim too much for the scriptural proof presented by the Assembly. Cf. Mitchell and Struthers, *Minutes* III, p. 109, also *infra* p. 478.

[129] Gillespie, *Notes* pp. 36f.

That was a clear case of throwing down the gauntlet to the Independents, for that was precisely what they denied and what they insisted had not yet been proved. They were therefore very much on the defensive.

Their anxiety showed. Lightfoot says that they were reluctant to respond to Gillespie's opening argument, and later on they opposed Selden's motion that the Assembly should address itself to the scriptural evidence in the proposition "for it pinched."[130] But it is difficult to understand the initial hesitation, for there does not appear to have been much that was particularly intimidating in Gillespie's speech. Indeed, it seemed to reflect the same position that the Independents had been attacking all through the debates. Gillespie said that there were two ways of proving the proposition – either by scripture (and he cited Acts 15, 11:21 and 21:8), or by arguing "the necessary consequences." He did not appear to be too anxious to concentrate on the biblical references, in part, no doubt, because he regarded Acts 15 as a synod rather than a presbytery. He therefore thought "the shorter way is to make out this poynt by necessary consequences".[131] However, he built his argument on a principle that the Independents shared "that elders doe not the worke of elders except meet together for acts of government".[132] Perhaps it was this use of one of their own principles that caused the discomfiture noted by Lightfoot.[133]

This 172nd session on March 8th was to take a strange turn.[134] The discussion began to centre on the council in Acts 15, and in the Independents' exposition of Congregational synods a number in the Assembly began to recognize how close these were to the classical presbyteries they had been discussing.

This possibility of accord developed after the Assembly had voted to pursue the following argument:

wher the elders are mentioned those elders must
meete to performe acts of government or they
neglect their office[.]
That church wch by Christs institution hath the power
of government 'the elders of that ch:' must meete to
p[erforme acts of government.][135]

---

[130] *Journal*, p. 204.

[131] TMs. I. 714 (Ms. I. f. 369.)

[132] *Ibid*.

[133] There are no hints of the hesitation in the Minutes or in Gillespie's *Notes*.

[134] For the debate of March 8th see TMs. I. 714–21 (Ms. I. ff. 369–372b,) Lightfoot, *Journal*, pp. 203–6, Gillespie, *Notes*, pp. 36f.

[135] TMs. I. 716 (Ms. I. f. 370.) The items in square brackets are an attempt to give the sense of the passage. Words in the transcript in single quotation marks are underlined in the Ms.

This did not give any hint of what would follow. There was more than a little edge in the first exchange involving Marshall and Gillespie on the one side, and Goodwin and Burroughes on the other, and this apparently caused Selden to make his suggestion about exegeting the texts in the proposition.[136] In response to one of Gillespie's contributions, however, Goodwin said,

> we deny presbiteryes over presbiteryes[137]
> & yet deny them to be independent[.]
> they [i.e. local presbyteries] must have their power till
> they miscarry[.][138]

And a little later he clarified the way in which Independents understood the spiritual power exercised by their synods:

> ther is a power to meete together to
> call the failing presbitery to account & to declare
> their miscarriadge to all churches & withdraw
> from them[;]
> and [this] is as good as the other [sentence.][139]

Lazarus Seaman, who was one of the Independents' most intransigent opponents, dismissed this as lacking ecclesiastical authority and as being no more than any private person might do, but there were others who had begun to think differently as the nature of Independent synods became clearer to them.

Goodwin had said that two things were involved in excommunication (i.e., presbyterial excommunication) – first, to withdraw from the guilty party, and secondly, to deliver that party up to Satan. He and his friends practised the first, but denied the second. Philip Nye expanded this. He said that for them the keys of doctrine were in the hands of a synod because it carries more weight than that of individual persons, and although, properly speaking, a synod did not possess jurisdiction, it did have authority.[140]

---

[136] Lightfoot, *Journal*, p. 204.

[137] It should be remembered that in the Independent view, a 'presbytery' comprised the elders of a local congregation. We need to remind ourselves that those whom we identify as 'Presbyterians' or 'Independents' had originally regarded themselves as members of one movement in the English church. They all acknowledged the term 'presbyterian', and there is a good deal to commend George Yule's suggestion that the more precise term to describe Goodwin and his colleagues in the Assembly is "Presbyterians Independent." George Yule, 'English Presbyterianism and the Westminster Assembly,' *The Reformed Theological Review* (Melbourne, Australia,) XXXIII, No. 2 (May–August) p. 38.

[138] TMs. I. 718 (Ms. I. f. 371.)

[139] I.e., excommunication. *Ibid.*

[140] Lightfoot, *Journal*, p. 205. Cf. TMs. I. 719 (Ms. I. f. 371b.)

These contributions led Richard Vines to list several points on
which the Independents and the Presbyterians seemed to
agree.[141] He conceded that where public opinion supported the
one who was censured, there was not much more that anyone
could do than insist on non-communion, and he continued, "if
only the poynt stickes about this formall part of Jurisdiction . . ." At that point, the Minutes unfortunately break off,
although it is fairly clear what the rest of his sentence would have
implied.[142] He certainly expressed the hope that accommodation
would be possible, and this hope, says Lightfoot, "was backed
by Mr. *Foxcraft*, Mr. *Case*, and others", although Marshall and
Seaman remained unconvinced.[143] Thomas Case's comments
also show his desire to reach agreement. He reminded his colleagues that they were committed not only to truth, but also to
peace. What the Independents held about church censures might
not amount to Jurisdiction in the strict sense, but it did amount
to it "to all those purposes for wch Jurisdictio proprie dicta
serves".[144]

Goodwin declared that the presbyterian system they were
discussing did not exercise any more effective power and authority, and he asked the Assembly to consider the combined influence of a decision in which many people, many churches, and a
divine ordinance were all joined.[145] This led Seaman to observe
somewhat tartly that if they gave more power to presbyteries
than appeared in their book, he wished they would put that in
writing.[146]

---

[141] 1 they consent to presbiteryes [&] sinods
2 they can looke upon a presbitery as an ordinance of Christ
3 they may summon & convent
4 if he doe appeare as he ought to doe [,] a presbitery hath special authority in the
name of Christ
5 if he be refractory they may declare his fault either in that congregation [or
generally]
[6] in matters of doctrine they will ascribe very much [authority to synods.] TMs.
I. 719 (Ms. I. f. 371b.)

[142] *Ibid.* 720 (Ms. I. f. 372.)
[143] Lightfoot, *Journal*, pp. 205f.
[144] TMs. I. 720 (Ms. I. f. 372.)
[145] *Ibid.*
[146] *Ibid.* The position regarding synods that Goodwin and his friends developed in this
debate had been expounded in *An Apologeticall Narration.* pp. 16–22.

The last part of the session was given up to the report of a special committee that had
been entrusted with preparing the Assembly's response to the Dutch churches' comments on the Independent pamphlet. It was a sensitive area. Nye objected to any
implication that the Independents had breached parliamentary order, while Lightfoot
and others wanted Parliament to grant the majority permission to write a complete
rebuttal of the pamphlet on behalf of the Assembly.

No sooner had the afternoon session begun[147] than Alexander Henderson and others urged that they should explore the possibility of an accommodation with the Independents, and a committee was appointed for that purpose.[148] Seaman, Vines and Palmer were nominated for the majority and Goodwin, Bridge and Burroughes for the Independents, but later Marshall and Nye were also added.

Henderson's desire for accommodation should be taken at its face value. There is no reason to think that the Scots had anything but a sincere wish to reach agreement with the Independents, as long as this could be obtained without undermining what they regarded as the proper power and authority of the presbyterian system.[149] The hope was shared by many others in the Assembly although it is clear that some remained sceptical.[150] In view of all that had happened, and was happening, was it possible for these two branches of Reformed churchmanship to reach the unanimity that they assumed should result from their common fidelity to the scriptures?

IV

Proof Positive?

On Monday 11th March Lightfoot says that there was more talk of accommodation, but his account was at second hand because he was still in Munden. The debate was about passages in the 11th, 15th and 20th chapters in Acts as proof that "the several congregations in Jerusalem were under one presbyterial

---

[147] Friday, March 8th. All the accounts of this session are brief or inadequate. Lightfoot (*Journal*, pp. 206f) is much briefer than usual, Gillespie passes the session with barely more than a sentence, (*Notes*, p. 37,) the rest of his account of that time being taken up with the report that Marshall ultimately gave of that committee's work. The Minutes are also very fragmentary: TMs. I. 721f. (Ms. I. ff. 372b–373.)

[148] Gillespie, *Notes*, p. 37.

[149] The Scots had already decided that they had to win accommodation if at all possible, in order to prevent a toleration that they regarded as utterly unacceptable. However, even at this date, Baillie recognized that the Independents' objective was probably such a toleration: "We mind yet againe to assay the Independents in a privie conference, if we can draw them to a reasonable accommodation; for the toleration they aime at we cannot consent." Letter to Spang, 18th February 1643/4, *Letters and Journals* II. 140. When the Assembly agreed on March 8th to set up a committee to explore the possibility of such an accommodation, there was every reason for the Scots to be "glad that what we were doing in private should be thus authorized", especially since those appointed by the Assembly were largely those who had already been involved in the unofficial conversations. Cf. Publick Letter, 2nd April 1644, *ibid*. pp. 145–147.

[150] Marshall, Seaman and possibly Palmer. We also have the impression that Lightfoot was less than enthusiastic.

government",[151] and it was soon apparent that any thought of immediate agreement would have been unduly optimistic.

They were so close in most respects. Rutherford said that he wanted to be resolved in only one doubt. The Independents had agreed that a synod, a meeting of pastors, could do anything that was done in Acts 15, and yet they insisted this was not a juridical action. But, continued the Scots Commissioner, it was

> not meet as Christians to give naked counsell
> but as pastors in an authoritative way[;]
> they that meete as pastors [do they give me mere advice?]
> this is absurd and against their principles[.]
> [They deny] pastors as pastors have any pastorall authority
> over any churches but those over wch they are pastors[. But]
> this [Act 15] is a formall church meeting
> 1 they meete as pastors
> 2 they meete as a court and Judicatory
> 3 to make decrees & canons to bind the churches[.][152]

Underlying all the more obvious differences of polity the basic question was the nature of 'pastorall authority' appropriate in the Christian Church, and we notice that even for the Scots authoritative power within the *office* of ministry was a real issue. The Independents could not fault Rutherford's reading of the apostolic council in Acts 15 except in his understanding of the spirit in which the apostles gave guidance to the infant church. The juridical concept of the church, with the implied threat of coercion behind the use of terms such as 'to bind', was one aspect of presbyterian polity that they were questioning. Certainly they agreed that the decision made in Acts 15 was spiritually binding on the churches, but they questioned whether those churches should be subject to a *spirit* of bondage.

Seaman observed that if the Independents were willing to "grant that ther may be presbyteriall government over more congregations than one, that is all the proposition holds out"; but the problem remained because of what the majority would read into the word 'over.' It was at that point that Philip Nye indicated the breadth of the ecclesiological gap that would open up between them.[153] He agreed with Seaman that "to publish doctrine

---

[151] I.e., in the church after the dispersion; cf. Lightfoot, *Journal*, p. 207. A fuller account of the debate on March 11th is in TMs. I. 723–31 (Ms. I. ff. 373b–378.) Gillespie kept no record.

[152] TMs. I. 725 (Ms. I. f. 374b.) As in most of the Minutes, there are frustrating gaps and almost no punctuation. My insertions in square brackets are an attempt to provide the sense of the speech.

[153] TMs. I. 726 (Ms. I. f. 375.)

as a minister is an act of authority" and that without it "scandalls cannot be stayed", but if there was any jurisdictional power in the church it was with the particular congregation. Although he did not say it here, behind his statement there was the church covenant, with its intimate fellowship in which all the members were engaged in a discipline of mutual ministry.[154] It had been said that to grant the kind of authority that they did in synods was to admit a jurisdiction, but Nye declared: "I deny it[.] I doe not suppose a necessity for pastors to meete in a convention[. There is] noe need to gather in a coetus but for acts of power[.]"[155]

Nye, almost in the tradition of John Wycliffe, was saying that some kinds of power and authority are not appropriate to the Christian Church, and this led Lazarus Seaman to declare that whereas Independents claimed that ministers in this synodical way carry an authority that goes beyond a "morall power & institution[.] I only adde this", he insisted, "they have a politicall power".[156] Stephen Marshall reflected that "we shall hardly draw up a vote to have a generall assent notwithstanding the seeming assent of the brethren".

It was practically back to square one. The issue was not so much in the actual polity, in the instituted form of church government, but in the way by which the two sides believed those forms should be administered. William Price truly understood what was at stake when he said, "that wch hinders us in this debate is the want of acurate distinction betwixt authority & Jurisdiction[.]"[157]

Herle thought they had "lost much time by mistaking one another". The power had to be located somewhere and it could not be anywhere but in the elders of the church, while Burroughes thought that some of the things Herle had said could well have been spared because "he disputed against I thinke none in this assembly". Against Seaman's claim that the minister possesses a political power, Burroughes observed that the word 'political' did not belong to scripture. Whatever the Independents had done, he claimed, "we did not doe it to deceive the assembly".[158] The course that the debate had taken made Richard Vines exclaim, "I feare we are like men upon the welch

---

[154] For the church covenant see Williston Walker, *Creeds and Platforms of Congregationalism*, pp. 18–20, 78, 173 and note 3, and especially the Windsor Creed–Covenant of 1647 (pp. 154ff.) and chapter IV of the Cambridge Platform of 1648 (pp. 207–9).
[155] TMs. I. 726 (Ms. I. f. 375.)
[156] *Ibid.*
[157] *Ibid.*
[158] *Ibid.* 728 (Ms. I. f. 376.)

mountains [who] toutch hands at tope & [are] 2 miles asunder at bottome[.]"[159]

Then the Independents made another of their unfortunate interventions, because it was obviously a political gambit to stall for time. Nye claimed that the Assembly would be going against its own vote if it pushed forward with its decisions about church government until it had received the report of the Committee of Accommodation, and he spoke of "the darke footsteps of church power and authority."[160] Goodwin joined him and said that if the divines persisted with their votes he could not foresee the fate of that committee.[161] On the other hand the majority was not going to be deflected. Marshall observed that he did not think that what they were doing would anticipate the work of the committee, and that "it was not intended [that] the assembly should sit still & not goe on with the argument".[162]

So the debate resumed its earlier mode of wrangling about the texts. Goodwin argued that although several congregations and elders are mentioned in the passages they were considering, "yet unlesse you prove that they did meete in an eldership[,] a tacit principle[163] will only prove this that ther ware many presbiteryes". It was the point that they had made repeatedly – it was not sufficient to use the mere mention of elders and congregations in scripture: to prove presbyterial government of the kind proposed, the supporters of the motion would have to show that the elders met in classical presbyteries and did the governmental things that classical presbyteries were supposed to do.

Gillespie said that this could be very briefly answered. The force of the argument was in the instance of one church[164] acting in relation to government, "be[cause there is] noe other respect for wch [it is] called one church but only for government".[165] When the debate concluded the breach appeared as wide as ever.

A factor entered on the following day (Tuesday March 12th) that diverted the Assembly from its immediate concern with government. The Admiral, the Earl of Warwick, asked the divines to help him meet the urgent need for naval chaplains,[166]

---

[159] *Ibid.* 729 (Ms. I. f. 376b.)
[160] *Ibid.*
[161] *Ibid.* 730 (Ms. I. f. 377.)
[162] *Ibid.* 729 (Ms. I. f. 376b.)
[163] I.e., an inferential principle.
[164] I.e., a church that was one in its unity. He did not mean a single congregation.
[165] *Ibid.* 731 (Ms. I. f. 377b.)
[166] There was also information from De la March regarding the fate of the Assembly's letter to the Reformed churches in France. The French pastors had been afraid to open

and this again reminded them of the urgent need for ministers. It may have been the reason why Dr. Burgess had been so impatient of delays earlier, for he at once moved that after the day's debate the Assembly should return to the matter of ordination.

Once past the interruptions, the Assembly turned its attention again to Acts 15 as proof that the elders had gathered for church government,[167] and both sides retreated behind their prepared positions.

To take the Independents first, Nye held that the passage was not proof of the proposition because it extended beyond the presbytery of Jerusalem, while William Bridge argued that since the meeting in Jerusalem had been convened simply to remove additional burdens from believers, it was not an act of government. Goodwin agreed and he also denied it was proof of the proposition because the decision was not issued for the church at Jerusalem.[168]

On the presbyterian side, Gouge maintained that it was the action of a classical presbytery, but that others had been brought in because "they saw the case so large", while Seaman (responding to Bridge) said that to determine a matter doctrinally was to determine it authoritatively. Rutherford said that it included a juridical censure against those who were trying to enforce the rite of circumcision, and Vines argued that since it was a final and decisive act it must have been an act of government. Herle maintained that the issue was not doctrine, but an offence, while Gillespie reiterated his earlier conviction that "this decree comes not from the apostles as apostles, but as elders among the elders."[169]

Under the pressure of debate both sides had moved a little further apart. Against the Independents one could say that certainly the decree was issued by what most people accept as the

---

the letters because the French government was absolutely opposed to their having any dealings with England at that time. In view of Henrietta Maria's relationship to the royal house of France, we can understand the embarrassment the Assembly's letter must have been to the Huguenot churches.

Both Lightfoot and the Minutes place the request from the Earl of Warwick and the communication from De la March at the beginning of Session 175 (March 12th), while Gillespie (apparently erroneously) places it at the beginning of the session the following day. Cf. Gillespie, *Notes*, p. 39.

[167] For the debates see Lightfoot, *Journal*, pp. 207–210, TMs. I. 732–41 (Ms. I. ff. 378–382b,) Gillespie, *Notes*, pp. 37f. Lightfoot presents us with a clear summary, and it is parallelled by the report in the Minutes. Gillespie presents a very brief report on the debate, but includes at the end a summary of his own arguments.

[168] Lightfoot, *Journal*, pp. 208f.

[169] *Ibid.* p. 208.

first general council of the church,[170] and has been accepted as authoritative and carrying a universal validity.[171] To that extent it was an action of church government. But against the Presbyterians one would have to say that the text hardly proved the proposition as they were claiming. The situation of the apostolic church in Jerusalem was unique, and could hardly provide an exact parallel to regular church government in later times.

There were other points of interest in the debate. We see the difference in the way a biblical passage may be interpreted by two schools of thought holding an almost identical theology but with differing convictions about the Church, in the exchanges between George Gillespie and Thomas Goodwin. In his interpretation of Acts 15, Gillespie insisted that "we must not look upon the apostells only, nor yet as binding other churches[,] but upon the apostells as elders in this action".[172] Goodwin not only denied that, but he insisted from his perspective that not only apostles and elders had been involved but also the people, for "it cannot be authority, unless you give the church authority."[173] He also insisted that such a declaration was intended to be "not coercive but persuasive",[174] but that if there was any power in it, "it is apostolic power."[175]

The engagement between Gillespie and Goodwin was something of a *tour de force* on both sides, but Goodwin's response was particularly pointed. The thing that most convinced him that the decrees in Acts 15 were not an act of government was that, although the false teachers afflicting the church

> ware lyars & had erred fundamentally[,] yet they did not
> at all pronounce any sentence upon them in order
> to excommunicate wch the apost: had power to doe
> if they had been in those churches[.][176]

At the end of the day he asked that the debate should be given more time, and he was backed by the Scots Commissioner, Samuel Rutherford.[177]

There was no change of heart overnight, and when the Assembly came to the last day of this official debate on presbyterian

---

[170] This was denied by Gataker; *ibid.*

[171] Denied by Gillespie, who thought the decree was limited to the churches of Syria and Cilicia; *ibid.*

[172] TMs. I. 737 (Ms. I. f. 380b.)

[173] Lightfoot, *Journal*, p. 209.

[174] TMs. I. 738 (Ms. I. f. 381.)

[175] Lightfoot, *Journal*, p. 209.

[176] TMs. I. 739 (Ms. I. f. 381b.)

[177] Lightfoot, *Journal*, p. 210.

government, Wednesday March 13th, the divines simply produced variations on the themes that had already become familiar.[178] Goodwin asked his opponents to prove that the meeting in Acts 15 had been convened for the purpose of government, and Lightfoot responded by saying that the church at Antioch would never have sent Paul and Barnabas to Jerusalem if they had not known that there was a permanent presbytery sitting there for that purpose. Bridge said that in that case it was not a synod. Those who met in Jerusalem had acted in a governmental sense by discovering the truth, but not to perform a governmental act in the formal sense. This distinction remained completely unclear to several members of the Assembly.[179] Lightfoot replied to Bridge, and he was supported by Seaman, Rutherford and Herle, while Burroughes engaged Seaman. Vines and Marshall entered the dispute, but the featured event in this session as in the last was the confrontation between "that excellent youth" among the Scots Commissioners, George Gillespie,[180] and the theological champion of Independency – whom Baillie had originally regarded as "full of grace and modestie" – Thomas Goodwin.[181]

Gillespie said[182] that the decrees of Acts 15 did not equally bind all the churches of the world and the church of Jerusalem. That meeting was an ordinary synod (in the Presbyterian sense,) and the only churches to be bound by the decrees were those which sent representatives. He made his usual claim that the apostles had not acted here as apostles but as presbyters, for otherwise Paul and Barnabas would not have been sent from Antioch. By going to Jerusalem Paul and Barnabas placed themselves under that presbytery. He added further reasons for thinking that the decrees were issued as an example of normal

---

[178] Lightfoot, *Journal*, p. 210–14, TMs. I. 741–49 (Ms. I. ff. 382b–386b.) Care should be used in reading Gillespie here, because he seems to have mixed parts of the debates on March 12th and 13th. E.g., he reported his own speech, in which he said that the incident in Acts 15 addressed the three evils of heresy, scandal and schism, as taking place on the 13th, whereas Lightfoot and the Minutes agree that it was given on the 12th. Gillespie, *Notes*, p. 40; cf. Lightfoot, *Journal*, pp. 208f., and TMs. I. 738 (Ms. I. f. 381.)

[179] Bridge meant that the final result of the decrees certainly affected the government of the church, but those who participated had not met in a formal way to do that: it *was* the end result, but it had been occasioned by the simple request for advice and help from the church at Antioch.

[180] Baillie, *Letters and Journals* II. 117. Gillespie (b. 1613) was thirty-one years old. Baillie had a tremendous admiration for Gillespie's debating skill and theological ability; cf. *Ibid.* p. 140.

[181] *Ibid.* p. 111.

[182] Gillespie's speech is best followed in Lightfoot, *Journal*, pp. 211f., or TMs. I. 744–6 (Ms. I. ff. 384–385.)

ecclesiastical government, by arguing that during the debate Peter and the other apostles did not speak infallibly by the Holy Spirit, and because they allowed themselves to be moderated by James. Therefore, he concluded:

> Here is the form of an ordinary synod. 1. Here are the commissioners from Antioch. 2. The elders are in it as well as the apostles. 3. Things are carried by debate. 4. After the deliberative voice, they make a decisive voice and promulgate it.[183]

In true seventeenth century polemical style he then refuted Goodwin's arguments point by point. He dismissed the suggestion that 'brethren' in Acts 15 meant the ordinary members of the church: "the word doth not signify the whole church but preachers of the word taken into that counsell",[184] while as for the argument that nothing was imposed but what was over and above what was necessary, he snapped "this is a good answer to be given to papists". He also defended the three-fold power of government he had developed from Acts 15 the day previously.[185]

Lightfoot says that soon after this "Mr. *Goodwin* would have spoken, but for a while could not satisfy the Assembly that he was speaking to the proposition before us: at last he spake to this purpose" – and Lightfoot then goes on to devote over two of the four pages he recorded of this day's debate to a detailed summary of Goodwin's speech. Despite his remark about Goodwin's early hesitation, it appears to have been a closely argued presentation by the Independent theologian.[186] Goodwin responded specifically to Gillespie. He began by pointing out a basic inconsistency in his opponents – if the apostles and others in Acts 15 had been meeting in a synod, then they could not have been meeting as a presbytery of the church of Jerusalem. Both interpretations could not be true.[187] It had been argued that this action rep-

---

[183] Lightfoot, *Journal*, p. 211.

[184] TMs. I. 745 (Ms. I. f. 384b.)

[185] He had argued that those who issued the decress had exercised three functions in ecclesiastical government:

    (1) Dogmatica, which was directed against heresy;

    (2) Diatactica [διατάσσω = to order troops before battle,] which was directed against schism;

    (3) Critica, which was to be used against scandal. Cf. TMs. I. 738 (Ms. I. f. 381.)

[186] Lightfoot, *Journal*, pp. 212–4; the whole debate, pp. 210–4. Cf. also for the whole debate between Gillespie and Goodwin, TMs. I. 744–9 (Ms. I. ff. 384–386b.)

[187] Lord Say's earlier criticism that he did not find a unified position represented in the Presbyterian party, was still true. There were those like Dr. Gouge who thought Acts 15 was simply a classis (presbytery), while Gillespie regarded it as essentially a synod. For Say's speech cf. *supra* p. 272, TMs. I. 619 (Ms. I. f. 326b.)

resented an act of government even although it was concerned with doctrinal clarification, but this was no more an act of government in the sense his opponents meant it than was the pronouncement of a local church that sought to declare 'the mind of Christ:' "it is not an act of Jurisdiction."[188] He questioned whether the elders of Jerusalem were exercising jurisdiction over other churches, because there was no sentence of excommunication and that was more properly a juridical action.[189] At the same time the council in Acts 15 could not have been a synod in the normal sense, because there is no suggestion of elders from other churches accompanying Paul and Barnabas. Furthermore, only two churches were mentioned, and "it would seeme that Jerusalem was the Church that was the Judge".[190] Goodwin was engaging in the same point by point rebuttal beloved by all seventeenth century controversy, and he thought that none of the arguments put forward by the opposition disproved his contention that this must be understood as the apostles acting as apostles.[191]

Little in any of this was new, but one would think that Goodwin's case was at least sufficiently strong to raise reasonable doubts on the other side. It was all to no avail. "As soon as ever he had done", Lightfoot recorded, "it was put to the question, and voted affirmatively, that Acts xv. 4, 6, 22, should be brought to prove that clause in the proposition, 'elders meeting in acts of government.'"[192] The battle for the theological possession of 'the church of Jerusalem' had been won by weight of numbers,[193] and very soon after this we read:

> Mr. *Palmer* moved, that it might be determined, 'That this proposition is proved, which we have had so long in hand;' and this cost some debate; and the Independents opposed it, and again and again spake, and re-spake, and stopt, and it came to a very hot agitation: at last it was put to the question, and voted affirmatively, 'That the instance of the church of Jerusalem shall be brought to prove, that many several congregations may be under one presbyterial government.'[194]

The majority still had to prove the jurisdictional power they claimed for presbyteries, and the Independents were not going to

---

[188] *Ibid.* 746 (Ms. I. f. 385.)
[189] TMs. I. 748 (Ms. I. f. 386.)
[190] *Ibid.*
[191] Lightfoot, *Journal*, pp. 213f.
[192] *Ibid.* p. 214.
[193] I.e., it was essentially decided by a political method.
[194] *Ibid.*

let them forget it. Several weeks later they would maintain very firmly that "the presbytery is not yet determined nor debated"[195] and by that they were very clearly referring to this crucial aspect of presbyterial ecclesiology. At the same time, with the votes of early March behind them, the majority knew its strength, and its supporters were confident that little could stand in their way.

Between the last session of the major debate on presbytery and the renewal of the work on ordination, the Assembly spent March 14th debating the first proposition submitted by the Second Committee on church membership and censures, which affirmed that "There is one general church visible held forth in the New Testament" with the proof texts I Corinthians 12:12 and 13, and 15:9.[196]

It was at once clear that a great deal of suspicion had been carried over from the previous debate. We see it in the opposition that greeted Palmer's report on the Committee of Accommodation[197] and his request that the committee be allowed to continue,[198] but it can also be seen in the Independents' distrust of the proposition on church membership and censures. Their scepticism centred in the fear that the 'church visible' was being identified with a particular ecclesiastical structure, and that power would be concentrated within a hierarchical system leading to a General Council.

Philip Nye at once questioned the terms of the proposition, "for that if we take the church for any political body, he denied it."[199] He asked, "what is meant by visible[?] I understand by visible in their faith & love",[200] while his colleague, Thomas Goodwin, suspected there might be some 'snare' in this proposition, for some people thought of church government as rising

---

[195] *Ibid.* p. 240.

[196] Lightfoot, *Journal*, p. 215. The whole summary of the debates is *ibid.* pp. 214–7, and TMs. I. 749–53 (Ms. I. ff. 386b–388b.) Gillespie carried over the debate of March 14th on Acts 15 to the 14th: *Notes*, pp. 41f.

[197] The points of agreement as reported were:

"1. That there be a presbytery or meeting of many neighbouring congregations' elders to consult upon such things as concern those congregations, in matters ecclesiastical: and such presbyteries are the ordinances of Christ, having his power and authority.

2. Such presbyteries have power in cases that are to come before them; to declare and determine doctrinally what is agreeable to God's word; and this judgment of theirs is to be received with reverence and obligation as Christ's ordinance.

3. They have power to require the elders of those congregations to give an account of any thing scandalous in doctrine or practice." Lightfoot, *Journal*, pp. 214f.

[198] *Ibid.* p. 215.

[199] *Ibid.*

[200] TMs. I. 750 (Ms. I. f. 387.)

'ascendendo' from local congregations to the church universal, whereas others thought of it as moving in the opposite direction. "I thinke it is of great moment", he said, "to hold ther is a universall church politicall".[201]

Rutherford said that apart from the two ways of thinking of the church mentioned by Goodwin, there was a third, that of 'ecclesia presbyterialis', which, he suggested, regarded the church's authority not in terms of ascent or descent, but in terms of power being given "immediately from Christ upon every part".[202] The Independents were not satisfied. Their concern continued in the debate on the proof passages in I Cor. 12, in which both Carter and Goodwin argued that the emphasis on the 'spirit' indicated the Holy Spirit, and that the 'body' in that passage should therefore be understood as the "body invisible". They were afraid of any suggestion that the concept of the Church as the body of Christ should be tied to any physical entity, such as a particular polity: "that it is of the catholique church is certain", declared Goodwin, "but for that term visible I sticke".[203] Although their defeat in the previous debate appeared to be decisive, the Independents had no intention of giving up the struggle. They were giving notice that the majority still had a fight on its hands.

---

[201] *Ibid.* The words are somewhat ambiguous, but from the way the Independents were arguing it seems that Goodwin was warning the Assembly that the concept of a universal visible church order should be accepted only with very great care.

[202] Lightfoot, *Journal*, pp. 215f.

[203] TMs. I. 752 (Ms. I. f. 388.) The proposition was voted *nemine contradicente*, and later the passage in I Cor. 12 was accepted, but, at Vines's suggestion, the rest of the chapter was also added. Lightfoot, *Journal*, p. 217.

CHAPTER 11

"ONCE MORE UNTO THE BREACH . . .:"
CHURCH ORDER AGAIN

From the time of the fresh attempt to deal with ordination (March 15th, 1643/4) until the Assembly took its summer recess on July 22nd that year, everything began to move into higher gear. Not that the Assembly was any less meticulous in dealing with exegetical questions or its members any less verbose, but with the conclusion of the recent debates the Assembly had finally determined on its own ecclesiological track, and whether the journey was long or short, it would move to the appointed end. What separates the earlier from the later discourses is that the presbyterian system, as set down and held by the Scots, was the context in which the discussions on ordination, church order, discipline and worship would take place. This may have been implicitly true ever since the Solemn League and Covenant, but it had never been conceded by the Assembly or Parliament; now it became more openly recognized at Westminster.

All parts of the ecclesiology were interlocked: the new consideration of ordination[1] led directly to the debates on church order and censures,[2] and these in turn to the Directory of Worship.[3]

But if Presbyterian ecclesiology provided the context of work for the Assembly itself in 1644, a very different context was developing in the country. We have already seen the shape of this, and if we sense a quickening pace in the Assembly, that may have been in large measure due to the growing recognition that time was running out. While the divines were solemnly debating in the Jerusalem Chamber, sectarians were flourishing in the city of London, and more ominously, in the army of the Eastern

---

[1] March 15th – April 3rd, 1644.
[2] April 4th – 25th; 26th April – June 4th.
[3] June 4th – July 22nd.

Association under the patronage of Cromwell; radical religion now had a formidable military champion.

The Scots too would discover that 1644, short of establishing their dominance in English affairs, set their fortunes in a different direction. By the end of 1644 their influence would already be waning, and their interests were certainly not helped by the general inactivity of the Scottish army or by Cromwell's growing prestige. At the same time, one has to admire the tireless efforts of Robert Baillie in pursuing the ecclesiastical goals of his nation: for all his silence on the floor of the Assembly, his correspondence reveals how enterprizing he was in that cause.

In ecclesiastical terms the struggle came to its climax perhaps not so much in the battle of Marston Moor itself (July 2nd) as in the battle of pamphlet and rumour that ensued, in which the Independents were clearly the victors on the streets of London and in the nation at large. All this in parliamentarian circles provided a mood for all-out military effort against the King, in which there was not much room for the aristocratic theories of Church and State that, in the final analysis, depended on forces from north of the English border. The Independents might lose every battle in the Assembly, but if they could keep their tempers and maintain their position for long enough, they could still win the war.

I

The Church and its Ministers: Ordination

The optimism that Robert Baillie had felt when the Independents had failed to carry the day in the Assembly against presbyterian polity[4] was amply justified by the later votes in favour of presbytery. The work was by no means finished, but the majority of the members of the Assembly were now ready to move in that direction, and it was reasonable to move back to ordination, for that urgent problem had been laid aside only to address the persistent obstacle of church polity more directly.

The problem of ordination had not grown less urgent. The need for a solution had been presented in the Assembly itself on March 12th in the Earl of Warwick's call for naval chaplains, and it had been seconded a few days later by the Earl of Manchester when, in the course of reporting on his efforts to reform the

---

[4] "Praise to God!" he had written to his cousin, William Spang, "we are all well and cheerful, and hopefull, by your prayers, to see the advancement of a glorious work here." 18th February, 1643/4, *Letters and Journals*, II. 143.

colleges of Cambridge,[5] he had "renewed to the Assemblie his former motion, anent the expediting of Ordination."[6]

Accordingly, on Monday, 18th March, Dr. Temple on behalf of the Third Committee presented the propositions on Ordination:

1. That none ought to take upon him the office of a minister without a lawful call, John iii. 27, Rom. x. 14, 15, Jer. xiv. 4, Heb. v. 4.
2. That none be ordained to that office without a designation to such particular congregation or charge, Acts xiv. 23, Tit. i. 3, Acts xx. 17. 28.

To the full and orderly calling of a minister, are requisite;

1. That he be duly qualified, both for life and ministerial abilities, according to 1 Tim. iii. 2–6, Tit. i. 5–9.
2. That he be examined and approved by them by whom he is to be ordained, 1 Tim. iii. 7. 10, and v. 22.
3. That by them he be recommended to the people of the congregation, where he is to be minister, and have their assent, unless they can show just cause of exception against, Acts vi. 3.
4. That he be ordained by prayer and imposition of hands, by such preaching presbyters, as shall be appointed for the purpose, 1 Tim. v. 22; Acts xiv. 23.[7]

The first of these proposals passed without much trouble,[8] but an unexpected problem developed with the second proposition:

The last four Sessions were spent on an unexpected debate: good Mr. Calamie and some of our best friends, fearing the Separatists objection anent the Ministrie of England, as if they had no calling, for this reason, among others, That they were ordained without the people's election, yea, without any flock; for the fellows of their colledges are ordained *sine titulo*, long before they are presented to any people; when we came therefore to the proposition, That no man should be ordained a minister without a designation to a certaine church, they stiffly maintained their own practise: yet we carryed it this afternoon.[9]

---

[5] Manchester had ejected five Heads of the Cambridge colleges (Cosin of Peterhouse, Beale of St. John's, Sterne of Jesus', Rainbowe of Magdalene, and Laney of Pembroke Hall,) and nominated five members of the Assembly in their places – Palmer, Seaman, Arrowsmith, Young, and Vines. Eventually no less than twelve Heads of Houses and one hundred and eighty-one Fellows were supplanted; Gardiner, *G. C. W.*, I. 302f.

[6] *Letters and Journals*, II. 148; cf. Gillespie,*Notes*, p. 43; TMs. I. 756 (Ms. I. f. 390.)

[7] Lightfoot, *Journal*, pp. 218f.

[8] Lightfoot voted against the use of Hebrews 5:4 as a proof text, "having suspended my vote in all the rest." *Ibid.* p. 219.

[9] Baillie,*Letters and Journals*, II. 148 (Public Letter, April 2nd, 1644.) Although this letter was sent later, Baillie's notes must have been made just after the afternoon session on Wednesday, March 20th, when the scriptural proofs for the second proposition had been voted (cf. Lightfoot,*Journal*, p. 228f.;) but although the vote had gone with the committee on that occasion, the issue was by no means dead. Palmer in particular had not been persuaded. Cf. his contribution on Friday, March 22nd; TMs. I. 782 (Ms. I. f. 403.)

The debate was unexpectedly bitter, and the bitterness reflects the fear of the Puritan majority of anything that threw doubt on the validity of ordination as it had been traditionally administered in England. The Scots, some of the convinced Presbyterians, and the Independents found themselves arguing on the same side of the debate against ordination *sine titulo*,[10] although there were a few exceptions to that general alignment. Edmund Calamy, for example, was one of the Smectymnuans, but he spoke very forcibly against the committee's proposition,[11] while Richard Vines, who usually supported traditional English forms, declared that "a minister that is an ordinary minister is to have a chardge before he be ordained".[12]

Behind the opposition there was a fear of a radical challenge to the orders into which most English clergymen had been ordained. As Herbert Palmer said at the beginning of the debate, "it cannot be unknowne that a great part of the ministers were ordained sine titulo"[13] and Calamy declared that the proposition "will bring in a direct renunciation of our ministry".[14] Probably this was behind Cornelius Burgess's concern lest those under pressure from the Earl of Manchester's Visitation of the University of Cambridge should renounce their ordination.[15]

The proposition implied that election to a charge must precede ordination.[16] Calamy declared that this would introduce "a necessity of alowing men to preach before they be ordained" and thus "layes the foundation in a setled church of preaching without ordination".[17] He said, "I would not have the assembly ty ordination to a setled chardge",[18] and the same concern can be seen in 'old Henry Wilkinson', that doughty champion of traditional English ways, for on the first day of the debate he wanted to know how a person could possibly get a call to a parish before being ordained – since presumably it would be unthinkable to preach publicly before being in orders.[19]

---

[10] I.e., without title, without a specific ecclesiastical charge or incumbency.

[11] Even Lazarus Seaman seems to have leaned to Calamy's position.

[12] TMs. I. 761 (Ms. I. f. 392b.)

[13] *Ibid.* 760 (Ms. I. f. 392.) Monday, March 18th.

[14] *Ibid.* 767 (Ms. I. f. 395b.)

[15] 1st March; "*Dr. Burgess* moved, that his Lordship might be desired to be careful that none . . . renounce their orders and livings". Lightfoot, *Journal*, p. 218.

[16] 18th March; TMs. I. 761 (Ms. I. f. 392b.)

[17] *Ibid.* 767 (Ms. I. f. 395b.)

[18] *Ibid.* 768 (Ms. I. f. 396.)

[19] "Old Mr. *Wilkinson* pleaded, that if none should be ordained, till they be fixed to some place, how will it be possible they should ever get a fixed place, when they have not given any trial of their parts?" Lightfoot, *Journal*, p. 220.

John Ley tilted at the Independents when he reminded the Assembly that the Congregationalist theologian, William Ames, had regarded ordination *sine titulo* as a "ridiculous ordination", and said he "so disgraceth our whole English ministry."[20] Herbert Palmer argued from the example of Apollos, who, in his view, neither had a particular charge nor was an Evangelist,[21] and he tried to get a modifying clause inserted into the proposition.[22] Others, like Thomas Gataker, were uneasy, although Gataker was prepared to accept the proposition "in a prudentiall way," but he was anxious to show that ordination did not cease to be effective when a minister left his charge.[23]

Unequivocal support for the committee's proposition came from the Scots, (particularly George Gillespie,)[24] from some of their consistent supporters such as Stephen Marshall, and from the Independents, although Philip Nye did not quieten the fears of the majority or improve the standing of himself and his colleagues, when he announced that he saw no necessity of ordination.[25] Goodwin insisted that if they were to permit ordination in the more general *sine titulo* sense, then they must find a parallel office in the New Testament. "The evangelists indeed", he said, "had such an office, but no presbyter".[26] The concern for evangelism ought to be incorporated into the regular ministry, for "it belongs to a minister to take care of converting others" and "the question is whether simply to [do] this unlesse he be first ordained to a perticular church".[27]

Rutherford, while maintaining his full support for the proposition, tried somewhat clumsily to pour oil on the troubled waters by disclaiming any intention of questioning the validity of orders *sine titulo*: "it was never our mind to thinke they are null[;] ther may be something unlawfull in an ordination that doth not make it null". On the other hand, he claimed that ordination to specific charge had been the preference of all the most godly ministers, many of whom had suffered in that respect, "because of the

---

[20] *Ibid.*

[21] Gillespie, *Notes*, p. 43.

[22] On March 20th; TMs. I. 772 (Ms. I. f. 398.) He suggested that the Assembly should change the absolute terms in which the proposition had been cast: "that it might be read, 'It is convenient that no man,' instead of 'no man ought' ", but this caused Henderson to ask rather pointedly "Whether this church requireth not reformation in this point?" Lightfoot, *Journal*, p. 227.

[23] TMs. I. 773 (Ms. I. f. 398b.)

[24] *Ibid.* 766f. (Ms. ff. 395–395b;) cf. Lightfoot, *Journal*, p. 223, Gillespie, *Notes*, p. 43.

[25] Lightfoot, *Journal*, p. 222.

[26] *Ibid.* p. 221.

[27] 20th March, TMs. I. 776 (Ms. I. f. 400.)

Iniquity of the times".[28] How far this soothed the fears of the majority we do not know, but the debate did not grow noticeably less intense. The whole debate reinforces the view that there were many in the Assembly who were supporting the Scots on most matters because they were scared of what Independency seemed to offer, but who were still attached to the English tradition. There was a continual concern throughout the Assembly's work about the growth of Antinomianism and Anabaptism in the City,[29] and it was fear of religious anarchy that finally brought the dissidents into line when the second proposition, in a slightly modified form, was voted.[30]

On the day following, March 21st, several things happened that suggest that the peculiar tensions of the past few days should be regarded as no more than a temporary hiatus in the program to establish presbyterian church government as soon as possible. In the first place, there was an attempt to get the Assembly to begin its work at 8.00 a.m. in the morning, "but Mr. *Nye* opposed it exceeding scornfully."[31] Then Stephen Marshall reported further points of agreement in the Committee of Accommodation, but the scepticism and even antipathy of many in the Assembly towards the Independents is indicated by "a very long debate, whether this committee should be continued."[32] Finally it was agreed that it should, but that it should report in two weeks' time. This was followed by Thomas Coleman's report on behalf of the First Committee regarding the duties of a Presbytery.[33]

These actions seem to reflect the resolution of the Scots – to seek a comprehensive church settlement without allowing the Assembly to be deflected from pursuing presbyterian uniformity

---

[28] TMs. I. 771 (Ms. I. f. 397b.)

[29] John Leith pointed out that the refutation of Antinomianism had been one of the primary concerns in the Assembly; *Assembly at Westminster* (Richmond, Va., John Knox Press, 1973,) p. 80.

[30] "It is agreeable to the word of God, and very expedient, that such as are to be ordained ministers, be designed to some particular church, or other ministerial charge". Lightfoot, *Journal*, p. 228. The Assembly voted the proposition in this form on the morning of March 20th, and *then* debated the biblical proofs in the afternoon! *Ibid.* pp. 228f.

[31] *Ibid.* p. 229.

[32] *Ibid.*

[33] *Ibid.* pp. 229f. The acts of a presbytery were four:
"1. Ordination, Tim. iv. 14.
2. Censures and release, Matt. xviii. 17, 18.
3. Resolving of doubtful and difficult cases, Acts xv. 'per totum.'
4. Ordering things concerning the worship of God, 1 Cor. xiv. 33, 40, 2 Chron. xxix. 15, compared with ver. 35."

and its establishment 'with all convenient speed.' The debate also shows that this was made possible by the support of Puritans whose conservatism and 'Englishness' showed through as they adamantly set themselves against the Independents.

The complexity of this alliance was demonstrated in the debate on 21st March. The Assembly had been able to pass very quickly to the third of the propositions on ordination: that the ordinand should be recommended by the ordaining authority "to that congregation, to whom he is to be a minister, and have their consent; uless they can shew just cause of exception against him."[34] This threatened the right of a congregation to elect its own minister, and was bound to arouse reaction from the Independents. Jeremiah Burroughes said that the question ought to be whether a congregation should recommend an ordinand to presbytery rather than the way the proposition stated it,[35] while William Bridge "doubted the proposition comes not up to the privilege of the people". Goodwin thought it placed the whole calling of a minister in question and wanted the Assembly to consider how that call was related to a minister's election to a charge.[36]

The Independents were again on the same side of the debate as the Scots Presbyterians, for both these groups were anxious to see that a right in ministerial selection should be preserved for the congregation. In their view it was simply not sufficient to give the people a right of protesting against an undesirable minister for, George Gillespie asked, what happens if the parishoners have no particular cause to reject the candidate but feel they could profit better by having someone else?[37] Alexander Henderson also wanted the Assembly to "take into consideration the people's interest, in point of election" and thought they should consider what would happen if "the presbytery recommends one, and the people desire another"?[38] Samuel Rutherford was even more forthright. He declared, "The Scriptures constantly give the choice of the pastor to the people. The act of electing is in the people; and the regulating and correcting of their choice is in the presbytery."[39]

The issue was between the proposition that originated with

---

[34] Lightfoot, *Journal*, p. 230.
[35] *Ibid*.
[36] *Ibid*. p. 231.
[37] *Ibid*. p. 232.
[38] *Ibid*. p. 230.
[39] *Ibid*. p. 231.

Palmer, which virtually gave presbyteries the right of appointing ministers to parishes, and an alternative proposal by Gillespie which insisted that ordinands should not be "obtruded against the congregation." Gillespie tried to win support for his proposal against the fears of the majority by claiming that "the prelates are for obtrusion, the separatists for a popular voting: *ergo*, let us go in a medium."[40] Palmer on the other hand had asked that his principle should be established first, and then "when this is done, the power of the people may be handled."[41]

Even Gillespie recorded in his *Notes* that "it grew to a heat in the Assembly."[42] Lightfoot contributed materially to the tension which developed at the end of that debate, as he revealed in his account:

Here we had a great deal to do to state our proposition. At last, it was putting to the question, Whether we should fall upon Mr. *Palmer's* proposition; when the Scots put in for Mr. *Gillespie's*, and the Independents moved to have election taken into consideration. So it was moved by Mr. *Vines*, the matter should be recommitted; but that was not well liked: but divers things over and over again, offered to be debated, which cost us exceeding long time. At last, Mr. *Palmer* offered his again, with this addition, 'The people have this right at least,' to give their consent, &c. This was ready to be ordered as current, but I spake against it, and desired to speak to it before it passed; and so it was delayed from voting: and some other forms of propositions were again tendered, especially this: 'No man that is to be ordained for a particular congregation, is to be set over that people, if they shall allege just cause against him.' This was ready again to go to the question, when I interposed, – that this proposition held out that the dissent of the people did exclude him from being set over them; but it hit not upon the business in hand; viz. Whether that did forbid him to be ordained howsoever: whereupon this was fixed upon in its stead, to be debated next, and so it was voted:

'No man shall be ordained a minister for a particular congregation, if they can shew just cause of exception against him:' and there were two more tendered:–

1. 'He is not to be ordained at all without their consent.'
2. 'The people have the right to nominate:' and these were put to the question, whether they should be next debated, after that that was voted; and it was voted negatively, that they should not be taken next into consideration.[43]

[40] *Ibid*. p. 232.
[41] *Ibid*. p. 231. He had tried to rephrase the proposition, but in such a way that the congregation was expected to give its consent to whomever was appointed as its pastor, "unless they can give just cause to the contrary." *Ibid*. 231f.
[42] Gillespie, *Notes*, p. 45.
[43] Lightfoot, *Journal*, pp. 232f.

The Independents and the Scots had again been on the same side of the debate, because both recognized that congregations should have a right in approving the one to be minister, but neither of them could prevail over the majority's fear of popular control in the Church. It appears that this majority was prepared to invest presbyteries with the same authority, and expected them to act with similar power, as the earlier bishops: for these men, new Presbyter certainly was but 'old Priest writ large.' If the significance of what happened later in English Presbyterianism is to be properly understood, both the existence and the influence of this conservative English Puritanism has to be recognized.[44]

The subject of Ordination was full of potentially sensitive areas. On the following day (22nd), having limited a congregation to the right of refusing a minister against whom it could prove sufficient cause, the Assembly arrived at the fourth of the committee's propositions,[45] and in view of Coleman's report earlier,[46] the divines had arrived at a confluence between their work on ordination and their work on church government. They were agreed that ordination should be in the hands of a presbytery,[47] but the Assembly had not yet declared itself about what kind of presbytery.

---

[44] It is impossible to say at which points in the debate 'English Conservatism' would govern the thinking of these English Puritan divines. For example, Calamy, who had been vigorously 'conservative' in the 'sine titulo' debate, was equally convinced that the "power of the people" should be considered. (*Ibid.* p. 232.) Once we disabuse ourselves of the notion that the members had arrived at Westminster with a fixed ecclesiology, the shifting characteristics of the voting majority can be better understood, and it will be seen that the things which eventually brought them to the Scots' side were fear of the growing sectarianism, determination to maintain an established state church, and a strong desire to maintain the status and authority of the clergy.

We can also appreciate the variety of Puritan opinion in the Assembly. Edmund Stanton, for example, thought that ordination should be conferred with fasting as well as prayer, but Seaman, Lightfoot, and Gataker all opposed that. Seaman's reason for opposing it is significant: "This will make the people say, that those who were not ordained with fasting were not rightly ordained." (Gillespie, *Notes*, p. 45). He opposed any opinion that threw doubts on the existing ordained status of the clergy.

The Scots on the other hand had a clearly formulated scriptural ecclesiology. So Gillespie objected to the committee's proposal that ordination is *'by* imposition of hands' and preferred the more scriptural *'with* imposition of hands.' He also objected to the committee's exclusion of ruling elders in that act. (*Ibid.*) Seaman, who had appeared throughout to be 'a good friend' of the Scots, said in response, that the proposition did not rule them out, but that their rights would be taken up in a further report. Gillespie could not be content with that, but he was not able to get the proposition changed.

[45] Cf. *supra* p. 316.
[46] Cf. *supra* p. 319.
[47] It was agreed easily enough; TMs. I. 780 (Ms. I. f. 402.)

Stephen Marshall raised that pertinent question, and he wanted it to be remanded to the First Committee "to prepare something for the Assembly in what Presbitery they doe fixe the act of ordination."[48] It was agreed that they should debate the motion that "The preaching presbyters orderly associated, either in cities or in neighbouring villages, are those to whom imposition of hands doth apertain, for the congregations within their bounds respectively."[49] It sounds Presbyterian, particularly in the phrase 'orderly associated', but there was enough room in it to include Congregational associations of a similar kind.[50] For whatever reason, the majority was extremely reluctant to declare its final solution, and this may have been due to the moderating influence of the Scots who hoped to achieve unanimity through the Committee of Accommodation.

In the afternoon session of the 22nd March[51] the members debated the supporting texts, Acts 14:23, but whereas Gouge insisted that this verse referred to none but preachers in the act of ordaining, Palmer went much further and insisted that there must have been an Evangelist in that company. He continued

. . . . this is my sense[:]
If it pertains unto evangelists then not to
preaching presbyters except evangelists be
present with them[.][52]

It suggests that Palmer was hankering for ordination by a 'bishop in presbytery,' and later in the same debate he declared that he had not been convinced by any of the arguments set up against him. We are back again at an argument about the office of Evangelist that had appeared earlier in the *'sine titulo'* debate, and Palmer claimed there was "noe reason given why not soe much use [be made] of that office now as well as any other".[53] Evangelists like Timothy and Titus had been given the power to ordain on their own authority, and a man like Timothy "must be president at least".[54]

Samuel Rutherford was quick to recognize the implications:

this argument will prove as well
that noe pastor [at] all by the epistell to timothy have
power to imposition [of hands;]

---

[48] *Ibid.*
[49] Lightfoot, *Journal*, pp. 234f.
[50] E.g., what were later to be vicinage councils, or associations.
[51] The session was omitted by Lightfoot and Gillespie.
[52] TMs. I. 781 (Ms. I. f. 402b.)
[53] TMs. I. 782 (Ms. I. f. 403.)
[54] TMs. I. 783 (Ms. I. f. 403b.)

the epist: to Tim: was written to Tim: either as
evangelist only[,] or as pastor[.]
It is that very argument propounded to make a prelate
Jure divino over a pastor[.][55]

It could have been put more unkindly, although no more
frankly, for it was overt episcopalianism, but perhaps Palmer
was saved from the full weight of Scotch wrath because he was
one of their 'special friends' and wielded a great deal of influence.
They counted on his help.

The time was probably long past when Palmer could have
expected open support in the Assembly for these views, but it is
significant that such views were expressed as late as March 22nd,
1644.[56] There may be significance of a quite different kind in that
all our reverend observers, Lightfoot, Gillespie, and Baillie,
were either absent from the session or found it too embarrassing
to record. In any case, Palmer announced that he had not been
convinced by the opposing arguments; he insisted that he did not
want to change what had been done regarding elders in a presbytery, but he did not think "they[57] have a single power[,] but
[that] he[58] may have a concurrent power [–] to speake plainly[,] a
negative voyce" and that the authority was "shared betweene
them".[59]

By the end of the session, however, it was clear that this body
was not going to be deflected from the presbyterian direction it
had set for itself. Lazarus Seaman called for Acts 20 to be
considered in support of the proposition. It was clear to him that
"a plenary pastorall chardge 'is committed' to the elders of the
church of ephesus", and that "it is one part of the pastorall duty
to provide a succession of ministers".[60] It was position which, if
it placed ministerial authority in the corporate body of presbyters, still emphasized clerical responsibility in authorizing the
ministerial succession.

The Independents were relatively quiet.[61] Thomas Goodwin

---

[55] *Ibid.* 782 (Ms. I. f. 403.)

[56] Why did he state his views at that time? We cannot dismiss the possibility that this
represented a very genuine 'scruple' for Palmer on the biblical evidence. The more
sceptical reader, however, may suspect that Palmer could have been 'flying a kite' for
other interests. The office of Evangelist had been sensitive ever since Savaria, a Dutch
convert to Anglicanism, had used it to justify episcopacy.

[57] I.e., the presbyters.

[58] I.e., the 'Evangelist.'

[59] TMs. I. 786 (Ms. I. f. 405.)

[60] *Ibid.*

[61] Probably in response to Palmer's views, Philip Nye exclaimed "if this be true it will
overthrow the whole state of the polity of the church & all that we have done". *Ibid.*

said one thing he would like clarified was – "whether those congregations ware promiscuous or fixed", but Seaman brushed this aside with the comment that this issue would come before them later, and "what we shall say upon the presbitery finally cannot be said till the whole businesse [is] determined".[62] The leaders of the majority party were still incredibly coy about revealing the proofs for their preferred church order. Rutherford said that he at least wanted to see it proved that at that time there were organized congregations.[63]

The debate on Acts 20:28ff. continued on Monday March 25th.[64] Philip Nye, who had a remarkable facility for expressing himself in ways best calculated to frighten friend and foe alike, said bluntly "we suppose a minister may be a minister that is not ordained". More pertinently he observed that to use these verses in support of ordination was to rely on an assumption not yet granted, "that ordination is an act of Jurisdiction". Goodwin said that John Robinson and his followers "doe not hold the calling to their ministry to ly in the Bips: Imposition [of hands, but] they thinke it lyes in the people choosing & electing".[65] Rutherford immediately claimed that this was simply the Socinian view,[66] but the session ended with Thomas Wilson offering some motions aimed at bringing the work on ordination into systematic form. The Prolocutor and two Assessors were to be a committee for that purpose.

The debates of the next few days act as a bridge between the work on ordination and questions of church order and governance that would next occupy the Assembly's attention. On Thursday, March 28th, the divines debated a proposition drawn from earlier proposals because it impinged on ordination.[67] It had wider implications.

---

[62] *Ibid.*

[63] *Ibid.* 787 (Ms. I. f. 405b.)

[64] Lightfoot was still in Munden and Gillespie made no report of the debate, which may be found in TMs. I. 787–90 (Ms. I. ff. 405b–407.)

[65] *Ibid.* 788f. (Ms. I. ff. 406, 406b.) In view of the way in which the Independents had consistently dissociated themselves from Separatism to this point, it is somewhat surprising to find Goodwin citing Robinson. Perhaps his reason for doing so here was to remind the Assembly that if it wished to avoid criticism from the more rigorous Separatists and wanted the existing ministry to be recognized as authentic, it had better deal seriously with the place of election to the pastoral office.

[66] *Ibid.* 789 (Ms. I. f. 406b.)

[67] The proposition had been submitted by the Second Committee: " 'The ministry, oracles, and ordinances, of the New Testament, were given by Jesus Christ, to the general church visible, for the beginning and perfecting of it in this life, until his second coming;' 1 Cor. xii. 28, Eph. iv. 4, 5, compared with ver. 11–13, 15, 16, which were voted after the debate." Lightfoot, *Journal*, p. 235; cf. *supra* p. 252, n. 16. For the debate see *ibid.* but more fully in Gillespie, *Notes*, pp. 46f., and TMs. I. 790–99 (Ms. I. ff. 407–411b.)

The discussion soon concentrated on what is meant by 'the general church visible,' because although leaders like Marshall and Seaman could not understand why it presented any problem,[68] the Independents were suspicious of identifying that concept absolutely with Paul's metaphor of the Body of Christ in I Cor. 12. Nye said at the beginning, "for the proposition. I shall not at all contradict it if rightly understood", but Goodwin wanted to be satisfied at some points.[69] The discussion inevitably touched a concept of the Church as a company of 'visible saints', which was emphasized by the Independents although, as we have seen, it was held by many others in the Assembly. Indeed, at one point Marshall was led to exclaim, "I doe not know any proposition that we have concurred in that have spoken in it with soe unanimous a consent as in the sence of it".[70]

But the suspicions did not disappear. Goodwin said that if the other members of the Assembly were ready to admit that the power given to the visible church was exercised in 'particulars' (i.e., in particular churches,) then he would have nothing more to say, but he continued, "I only dispute against the exercise[;] it is the exercise only wch we feare";[71] and indeed, having experienced the trauma of exile while others had enjoyed their livings at home, he and his friends had some cause to say that. The proposition was eventually voted on April 2nd with proof texts, but only after the expense of "a great deal of time and heat", for we read that "the Independents mightily opposed it."[72] The Assembly was no closer to unity. Theophilus Bathurst's protest at the end of the session on March 28th was directed against members who habitually arrived late and left early,[73] but it could just as well have been applied to the Assembly's failure to deal with the two major subjects it had been called to address, ordination and church government.

Before Cornelius Burgess on April 3rd presented the twelve propositions on ordination that the Assembly would send up to

---

[68] Marshall thought "the proposition & sence of it is soe plaine that ther need not to be any dispute" while Seaman was surprised that the Independents wanted to make any issue of it. TMs. I. 791–2 (Ms. I. ff. 407b–408.)

[69] *Ibid.* 790f. (Ms. I. ff. 407–407b.)

[70] *Ibid.* 795 (Ms. I. f. 409b.)

[71] *Ibid.* 797 (Ms. I. f. 410b.)

[72] Lightfoot, *Journal*, p. 237. There is some doubt about the additional proof texts mentioned by Lightfoot (Gal. i. 2, 22 and Rev. i. 4, 30.) These must have been taken down in error, since Gal. i. 22 is not particularly apposite, and Rev. i. 30 does not exist!

[73] "It is a great scandall that we are soe bac[k]ward in coming to it & soe forward in going from it". TMs. I. 799 (Ms. I. f. 411b.)

Parliament, the divines argued even more extensively, debated more syllogisms and delved into more exegesis, but the basic positions did not change. On Friday March 29th they had debated proof texts for the proposition moved the day before, concentrating particularly on Ephesians 4. Stephen Marshall claimed that "ther is hardly any place in all the booke of God that doth soe clearly prove our proposition as this text before you",[74] while Bridge thought that the text proved precisely the opposite. Nye wanted to know "under what notion this generall church visible is receptive of those gifts".[75] Nothing had changed, but one of the things that emerged during the debate was the weight of conservative English sentiment, and the closeness of the Scots and the Independents with regard to the rights of particular congregations, as in Rutherford's protest against views expressed by Seaman and Palmer. Seaman had said that because many did not wish "to enter into any Christian society of any kind", the choice should not be left to them because it was Christ's will "that christian people should assemble and associate themselves together". Palmer questioned whether there was an 'institution', but agreed to the pragmatic need for "every one to Joyne himselfe to a perticular visible church".[76]

The debate was ostensibly on 'the visible church general', but behind it was a concern for the rights of a local congregation and evidence for its divine institution. English conservatives like Palmer said that there is no institution for it,[77] others conceded that there is a *virtual* institution for it,[78] while the Independents and the Scots insisted that it is divinely instituted. Nye thought it is instituted through a divine promise, because "it is ordinary in the gospell to institute by promises".[79] At the other end of the

---

[74] *Ibid.* 800 (Ms. I. f. 412.)

[75] *Ibid.* 802 (Ms. I. f. 413.)

[76] Rutherford had expostulated that
"to give noe more to perticular visible
churches but only the word of Alowance
is hard [.]
[As] for the word of Institution, it is not inconvenient to say they are of divine Institution [:]
as the ministry is of divine Institution soe is
the church [.]" *Ibid.* 804 (Ms. I. f. 414.) The strong advocacy of the rights of the local congregation by the Scots Commissioners got them in trouble with their friends at home for leaning too far in the direction of the Independents. Cf. Baillie *Letters and Journals*, II. 182. To Spang, May 14th, 1644.)

[77] TMs. I. 806 (Ms. I. f. 415.)

[78] Whitaker, Vines and Hoyle. *Ibid.*

[79] *Ibid.* 807 (Ms. I. f. 415b.) The exigencies of the debate caused some curious interpretations of the gospel. Herle inverted what most people today would regard as the

spectrum, Palmer thought that separate congregations were simply the result of the Church's historical development.[80]

Monday, April 1st was largely taken up with the rival claims of two men for the Mastership of Merchant Taylors' School,[81] but on Tuesday, the 2nd, the Assembly again addressed the motion that "Particular visible churches, members of the general, are the institution of Jesus Christ,"[82] and this started out to very much the same purpose as before, with Palmer denying any evidence for it, others arguing for it, and with Stephen Marshall insisting that congregations are the result of practical necessity.[83] Cornelius Burgess, seconded by Price, then proposed that they should examine the scriptural evidence, and Whitaker cited the examples of Rome, Ephesus and Corinth as "a virtual institution," while Nye, following his argument of March 29th, said it was a mistake to suppose that only a formal command could constitute a divine institution. Goodwin went as far as to suggest that an institution followed from the Laws of Nature, and that a virtual institution "is as strong as [a] formall; that is, as truly the word of God wch we gather out of the word by consequence",[84] while John Phillips, another Independent, claimed that local churches are divinely instituted because they are prophesied in Isaiah 4:6.[85]

Eventually, after a bitter little tussle about minutiae, it was voted on April 2nd that "particular churches were also holden forth in the New Testament,"[86] and it was ordered "That the report of the matter of Ordination as it is drawn up shall be considered of tomorrow morning & after that to goe on in the report of the 2d committee where we left."[87] So on Wednesday morning, April 3rd, Dr. Burgess presented the twelve propositions that the Assembly was ready to submit to Parliament as the

---

proper relationship of the church to the world: "the visible church generall is by a higher ground than Institution [i.e.] moral necessity from the first purpose that ever God had *in the making of the world for a church*". (29th March) TMs. I. 805 (Ms. I. f. 414b.) My italics.

[80] *Ibid.* 808 (Ms. I. f. 416.)

[81] Lightfoot, *Journal*, p. 235.

[82] *Ibid.* p. 236f.

[83] TMs. I. 810 (Ms. I. f. 417;) Lightfoot, *Journal*, p. 236.

[84] TMs. I. 811 (Ms. I. f. 417b.) In Marshall's emphasis on pragmatism and Goodwin's recourse to the Laws of Nature, we see evidence in both parties that Puritans were having to modify their biblical literalism.

[85] *Ibid.* 813 (Ms. I. f. 418b.)

[86] Gillespie, *Notes*, p. 47.

[87] TMs. I. 814 (Ms. I. f. 419.)

doctrinal basis for ordination in the Church of England;[88] but that is not to say that the propositions had an easy passage, for the tenth proposition had gone from the Assembly without scriptural proof and Burgess had simply added 1 Timothy 4:14 on his own initiative.[89] The Independents protested, and even Palmer wanted more proof. Gouge offered Acts 14:21 and 23, but that was "not fully liked", and eventually the proposition had to proceed without specific scriptural endorsement.[90]

Parliament was not unaware of what had been happening in the Assembly, and at the end of the morning session the Earl of Warwick instructed the divines that since they had completed the doctrinal part of Ordination, they were "to fall upon a Directory for the managing of it: – and also, after that, to fall in hand about a Directory for worship, especially about the administration of the sacrament."[91] Behind this parliamentary directive we discern the politicians' concern to get the practical part of ecclesiastical settlement in operation, and particularly that which touched the life of the religiously conservative population most immediately.

---

[88] "1. No man ought to take upon him the office of a minister of the word without a lawful calling; John iii. 27, Rom. x. 14, 15, Jer. xiv. 14, Heb. v. 4.

2. Ordination is always to be continued in the church, Tit. v. 1 Tim. v. 21, 22. And this they have joined to the former with these words, 'For this purpose,' ordination is to be continued, &c.

3. Ordination is the solemn setting apart of a person to some public church office; Numb. viii. 10, 11. 14. 19. 22, Acts vi. 3, 5. 6.

4. Every minister of the word is to be ordained by imposition of hands, and prayer, with fasting, by those preaching presbyters to whom it doth belong; 1 Tim. v. 22, Acts xiv. 23, xiii. 3.

5. The power of ordering the whole work of ordination is in the whole presbytery; 1 Tim. iv. 14.

6. It is agreeable to the word, and very expedient, that such as are to be ordained ministers, be designed to some particular church, or some other ministerial charge; Acts xiv. 23, Tit. i. 5, Acts xx. 17. 28.

7. He that is to be ordained, must be fully qualified, both for life and ministerial abilities, according to the rules of the apostle; 1 Tim. ii. 3–6, Tit. i. 5–9.

8. He is to be examined and approved of, by them by whom he is to be ordained; 1 Tim. iii. 7. 10, and v. 22.

9. No man is to be ordained a minister for a particular congregation, if they can shew just cause of exception against him; 1 Tim. iii. 2, Tit. i. 7.

10. Preaching presbyters, orderly associated, either in cities or neighbouring villages, are those to whom the imposition of hands doth appertain, for those congregations within their bounds respectively; 1 Tim. iv. 14.

11. In extraordinary cases something extraordinary may be done, until a settled order can be had; yet keeping as near as possibly may be, to the rule, which rule being before laid down, the proposition is proved from 2 Chron. xxix. 34–36, and xxx. 2–5.

13. There is at this time an extraordinary occasion for the way of ordination for the present supply of ministers." Lightfoot, *Journal*, pp. 237–8.

[89] *Ibid.* p. 238.

[90] *Ibid.* p. 239.

[91] *Ibid.*

When the divines met that same afternoon, having instructed members of the Grand Committee to expedite the matters still before that committee, they selected Palmer, Marshall, Tuckney, Seaman, Vines, Gataker and Goodwin to prepare the Directory for Ordination. Then the debate on the tenth proposition was resumed, and after Nye had suggested that the last part should be omitted, Seaman

> desired that we might speak fully and plainly concerning presbytery; and that for that purpose, while the directory is framing and moulding up, we might also go on to perfect the business of presbytery.
> The conclusion was, that the twelve propositions were laid by, till the directory for ordination be ready: and to fall on in the morning upon the presbytery, to shew what presbytery our fifth and tenth propositions mean.[92]

The Assembly could not escape that question, and until a definitive answer was given, ordination and all the practical questions related to it would be delayed.

Later that month the Assembly would have to return to the issue of ordination,[93] and after some extremely important votes,[94] the twelve propositions and the Directory for Ordination were sent to Parliament. On that same day, (the 19th,) Robert Baillie had written to his kinsman in Holland:

> Our Assemblie at last hes perfyted Ordination, both in the doctrinall and directorie parts. I thinke, to-morrow, they shall present it to the Houses. It hes cost us much labour, and above twentie long sessions. I hope it shall doe good, and over all this land shall erect presentlie an association of ministers to ordaine. Our Presbyterie will shortlie follow.[95]

In a subsequent letter he announced that the Assembly had eventually handed in its work on ordination after "above fortie long sessions",[96] but that was not the end of the issue.[97] On August 14th the Earl of Manchester and the Scottish peers, Maitland and Warriston were still urging the Assembly to hurry

---

[92] *Ibid.* p. 240.
[93] On April 18th.
[94] Cf. *Ibid.* pp. 250–3, TMs. II. 31–4 (Ms. II. ff. 17b–19b,) Gillespie, *Notes*, pp. 53f.
[95] To Spang, 19th April, 1644, *Letters and Journals*, II. 168.
[96] To Spang, 26th April, 1644, *ibid.* p. 169.
[97] At the end of June Baillie discovered from his friend, Francis Rous, who was chairman of the Commons committee examining the proposals, that the changes were far more extensive than the Scots had expected. He persuaded Rous that the Commons committee should "confer privately" with him and his friends in the Assembly, and as a result a committee of members of the Assembly was appointed for consultation with the politicians. No Independent was on that committee. Cf. the letter to Spang, 28th June, 1644, *ibid.* 198; Lightfoot, *Journal*, p. 290.

this matter,[98] but the recommendations with its Directory were not sent to the printer until October 3rd.

The stumbling-block throughout was the *jure divino* basis of the system that the Scots and some of their friends wanted to establish. This had yet to be made explicit. There was also the concern of some, among them the Scots Commissioners, that the Assembly's work should manifest a degree of unanimity, and it was to these matters that the Assembly now had to address itself.[99] At the end of the session on April 3rd, the Assembly ordered that

> The votes concerning presbitery already passed shall be returned tomorrow & if 'ther be' enough in them to set forth what 'that presbitery is wch' we intend 'in the propositions' concerning ordination, that that shall be expressed together with the proofe and that this shall satisfy[.][100]

As it turned out, these words were still more than a little optimistic.

II

The Church and its Order: Presbytery

The Assembly had deputed its Prolocutor, the two Assessors and the scribes to bring its previous votes on presbyterian government into some semblance of order,[101] and the divines themselves began to realize that they might have arrived at the parting of the ways. There was a lot of breast-beating and warnings against saying anything nasty to each other, with Stephen Marshall, who had never spared the feelings or opinions of his son-in-law,[102] leading the way. "As I would conscientiously abstaine myself," he said, so he wished "that others would abstaine

---

[98] Lightfoot, *Journal*, p. 303.

[99] There is a series of propositions in the Minutes at the end of the debate on April 3rd that may represent the plan that the Assembly intended to follow, or they could have been alternatives. The Minutes are not entirely clear where these proposals originated:

"To consider the 'seate' of this presbitery soe farre as belongs to ordination.

That ordination may be performed by the presbitery of severall congregations.

Many severall congregations may be under one presbiteriall government for the ordination of their elders.

To goe on with 'debate of the propositions concerning' the Presbitery of more congregations than one in reference to the businesse of Ordination.

To goe on in the debate of the report of the 2d Committee." TMs. I. 816 (Ms. I. f. 420.)

[100] *Ibid.*

[101] *Ibid.* 817 (Ms. I. f. 420b,) Lightfoot, *Journal*, p. 240.

[102] Philip Nye.

from such expressions as doe seeme to chardge any as if they did not speake & doe as in the presence of God",[103] while Burgess piously agreed "we should not reflect upon any other in uncomely speaches".[104]

There was more of the same, but this did not deflect the Independents. They argued that the example of the church of Jerusalem did not apply to the situation in England unless Presbyterians could prove "the consequence from those promiscuous congregations[105] to our fixed congregations".[106] This may explain the significance of Goodwin's words during the debate on the afternoon of March 22nd.[107]

While the officers of the Assembly were occupied with systematizing the earlier work, a proposition was presented to undercut the Independent attack: "that it is all one to the point of ordination, whether the several congregations over which a presbytery governs, be fixed or not,"[108] and we read "at first Dr. *Burgess* fairly cleared the proposition, and desired it might be ordered."[109] But Charles Herle seems to have pleaded with his colleagues that if they had to enter into a debate on fixed (parochial) and unfixed (gathered) congregations, "the best way is to deale with our brethren in an Ingenuous & Just way".[110]

There was little if anything that was new in the arguments of the debate (4th, 5th April) that followed. Burroughes asked the Assembly to produce arguments to prove that it was a matter of indifference whether the congregations of Jerusalem were fixed or unfixed.[111] On the other side, some attacked the idea that a 'presbytery' in a single congregation could ever be large enough to perform valid ordination, since ordination needed more than one preaching elder.[112] The Independents just as stubbornly defended the possibility, and argued for the inclusion of the Teacher and the Ruling Elder in that act.[113] Rutherford was not prepared to go too far – although ordaining belongs to the whole

---

[103] TMs. I. 819 (Ms. I. f. 421b.)
[104] *Ibid.*
[105] Free-floating, ad hoc, and hence 'gathered.'
[106] I.e., from gathered churches to parishes.
[107] Cf. *supra* pp. 324f.
[108] Gillespie, *Notes*, p. 47.
[109] Lightfoot, *Journal*, p. 241.
[110] TMs. I. 821 (Ms. I. f. 422b.)
[111] Lightfoot *Journal*, p. 241.
[112] Cf. the comments of Seaman and Palmer; TMs. I. 824f. (Ms. I. ff. 424, 424b.)
[113] *Ibid.*

presbytery, there are some actions that a preaching presbyter can do – such as the pastoral prayer – that cannot be passed on to other presbyters: "they may as well say ruling elders may administer sacraments in case of defect as well as this".[114]

The debate continued throughout the afternoon of Friday, the 5th, but the only result was that the majority tried to confirm its claims by adding a clause to the fifth of the propositions along the lines proposed earlier by Cornelius Burgess.[115] Further work was postponed until Wednesday, April 10th, because a Fast had been called for Tuesday, the 9th; and thus when the Assembly met again on the 10th it began to debate that addition proposed the previous Friday. Henderson also announced that he had received word that a General Assembly of the Church of Scotland would be held early in May, and wanted to know what progress he could report to that body.[116] He also "desired we would take in hand something for the Directory of worship."[117] This reinforced the Earl of Pembroke's plea that the Assembly should hasten its procedures.[118]

The proposition the divines had been debating passed without any trouble[119] – there was, after all, no argument strong enough to withstand the solid voting majority – but in the afternoon, after Byfield had read the summary of their work on presbyterian government to this point,[120] there was a curious hesitancy in the presbyterian leaders to press home their advantage. From Lightfoot's standpoint this was totally incomprehensible:

> This being done, we fell in debating whether we should send up all these votes or no; and the Independents did mightily oppose it; and it held a very long agitation. Here I spake, and urged that though they were more than the matter of ordination required, yet were they nothing near so much as the parliament's patience, and the kingdom's expectation challenged; and therefore desired to put it to the vote: which the Independents still opposed, threatening to put in their dissenting reasons: this much moved the Assembly, as unwilling of such a business. But I again urged that this was more sorrowful

---

[114] *Ibid.* 826 (Ms. I. f. 425.)

[115] To add: "which, when it is over many congregations, whether they be fixed or not, in regard of officers or members, it is indifferent to the point of ordination." Lightfoot, *Journal*, p. 242.

[116] TMs. I. 832 (Ms. I. f. 428.)

[117] Lightfoot, *Journal*, p. 242.

[118] *Ibid.*

[119] "That it is all one as to the point of ordination, whether the congregation be fixed or not." Gillespie, *Notes*, p. 48, Lightfoot, *Journal*, p. 243.

[120] Gillespie says that the summary of votes was handed in by Burgess, but it appears that Byfield, the scribe, read them. Cf. Gillespie, *Notes*, p. 48 and Lightfoot, *Journal*, p. 243.

than terrible; for that we being so many brought up for study, it was no unexpected thing for us to dissent in judgment. Howbeit, Mr. *Marshall*, Mr. *Herle*, and others, moved for accommodation in this business. I interposed again, 'whether it be fit to delay time to see whether we could give four or five content, which was uncertain, and to neglect to give four hundred thousand or five hundred thousand content, which we should certainly do in transmitting these votes to answer some expectation:' yet it was swayed for a committee to be chosen for accommodation, which was done.''[121]

Lightfoot's position made a great deal of practical sense – the divines had been called, had debated, and had decided – for whatever reasons – that presbyterian polity should be established in the Church of England. What need was there for any further discussion, since the power to act on this advice was in the hands of the civil authority? Why the hesitation?

The Scots wanted to reach an accommodation with the Independents, but there was more behind this than christian charity. Lightfoot did not believe in *jus divinum* for any particular polity, but a *jus divinum* was precisely what the Scots and some others wanted to establish, and on that they and the Independents were agreed. It appears that they were reluctant to send their recommendations to the Houses until they had proofs that would enable their claim to withstand the attack that must surely come

---

[121] *Journal*, p. 244. The propositions were:

1. "1. Prop. The Scripture doth hold out a presbytery in a church; 1 Tim, iv. 14, Acts xv: 2. 4. 6.

2. Prop. A presbytery consisteth of ministers of the word, and such other public officers as are agreeable to, and warrented by, the word of God to be church-governors, to join with the ministers in the government of the church; Rom. xii. 7, 8, 1 Cor. xii. 26.

3. The Scripture holds forth that many congregations may be under one presbyterial government. Proved by instance of the church of Jerusalem.

   1. It consisted of more congregations than one; and one apostle; Acts i. 15, ii. 42. 46, iv. 4, v. 14; this before the dispersion; and after the dispersion, which did not so scatter them, but that they were still several congregations; Acts ix. 31, xii. 24, xxi. 20.

   2. By many apostles and other preachers in that church.

   3. The diversity of language among the believers; Acts ii and vi.

2. Prop. "All these were under one presbyterial government."

   1. All these are but one church, and are so called; Acts viii. 1, ii. 47, v. 11, xii. xv. 4.

   2. The elders of that church are mentioned, Acts xi. 30, xv. 4. 6. 22, xxi. 17, 18.

   3. The apostles did the ordinary act of presbyters, as presbyters in the church of Jerusalem.

   4. The several congregations in Jerusalem being but one church, and the elders of that church being mentioned as meeting together in acts of government, it followeth that those several congregations were under one presbyterial government. They met in acts of government; Acts xi. ult. xv. 6.22, xxi. 17, 18." *Ibid.* pp. 243f. The passage has been indented to clarify the way in which these propositions were related.

once their position was made public. So we read, "It was moved by Mr Marshall and others in the Assembly, That the third proposition, That the Scripture holds forth that many particular congregations may be under one presbyterial government, might not be sent to the Parliament till it go with other arguments to strengthen it."[122] Even George Gillespie, who of all in the Assembly had no doubts about the divine rightness of his cause, argued the unwisdom of allowing their votes to be made public without the strongest possible proofs, not because he had doubts about this ecclesiology, but because he wanted it to be established on a much surer foundation than the decision of the English Parliament:

> I said, there is a danger of holding forth ordination by an associated presbytery, before warrents from Scripture for any such presbytery be holden forth; for many in the kingdom will say, that the Assembly is shuffelling in a matter of highest consequence, without any light from Scripture, and so would engage the Parliament and kingdom *fide implicita*.[123]

Furthermore, this was all the more necessary, since the "Independents said, If that proposition be given in, they must give in their reasons against it, because the proposition infers not only ordination, but other acts of government by a presbytery."[124]

Certainly the Independents were causing obstruction, and they might have no better case; but if they presented their reasons against presbytery, they would not have to make the case for Congregationalism, but they would be free to attack the scriptural weakness of the Assembly's propositions. If they could throw reasonable doubt on the system – and what had happened so far showed that they could – the credibility of the Assembly's recommendations would be undermined, and the criticisms would provide plenty of ammunition for detractors all the way from Laudian Anglicans to the wildest sectaries.[125] This danger seems also to have been behind the reluctance of the presbyterian leaders to send in their votes to Parliament at this stage. Therefore, to the obstructions of the Independents we have to add this

---

[122] Gillespie, *Notes*, p. 48.

[123] *Ibid.*

[124] *Ibid.*

[125] In his speech on April 10th, Gillespie had said that one scriptural proof was as good as a hundred, and that in sending in their votes to Parliament without the full panoply of scriptural proofs, they should "intimate that this necessity of the time did make you [do] soe & you are to add more"; but he warned them that if they sent in their votes without scriptural warrant "many in the kingdome will stumble at it & say here is a proposition & noe warrent from scripture held out for it". TMs. I. 836 (Ms. I. f. 430.)

reluctance of the Presbyterians as a major reason for the continued delay in getting the votes to Parliament.

Robert Baillie admitted as much. In his letter telling Spang of the votes on ordination, he said:

> To prevent a present rupture with the Independents, we were content not to give in our propositions of Presbytries and Congregations, that we might not necessitate them to give in their remonstrance against our conclusions, which they are peremptor to doe when we come on that matter. We judged it also convenient to delay till we had gone through the whole matters of Presbytries and Synods; to send them up rather in their full strength than by pieces; also we suffered ourselves to be persuaded to eshew that rupture at this tyme, when it were so dangerous for their bruckle state.[126]

As a result, the Assembly selected a committee to gather together just so much of the earlier voting as could expedite the matter of ordination. The end of this committee's work, however, on the 11th, was simply to postpone further consideration of the report on ordination until the Assembly had completed its work on a Directory.[127]

On April 11th the Assembly returned to the business of 'fixed' and 'unfixed' congregations. It had proved to its own satisfaction that the distinction was irrelevant to ordination, and now it wished to assert the same with regard to church government.[128] It was back to the church of Jerusalem, and the debate that continued through April 15th was remarkable neither for its theological perception nor for its exegetical acuity. Indeed, on the basis of their strict biblical literalism and scholastic logic, there was no way in which the issue could be resolved one way or the other: strained proof texts and tortuous reasoning were almost inevitable because of the form in which the argument was cast. Like Stephen Marshall in earlier debates, George Gillespie put the onus of proof on the opposition: "it lyes upon them", he said, "to prove that ther was noe such distinction of the congregations in Jerusalem but [that they were] all promiscuous, that ther was not a distinction of the cure",[129] and a little later, in

---

[126] 26th April, 1644, *Letters and Journals*, II. 169.

[127] The anxiety of the Assembly to handle the matter effectively is illustrated in Thomas Hill's suggestion that they should put something in the preface of the Directory to justify what they were doing. He was immediately elected to the committee. TMs. I. 841 (Ms. I. f. 432b,) cf. Lightfoot, *Journal*, pp. 244f.

[128] Lightfoot, *Journal*, p. 245: "Whether they be fixed or not fixed, it is all one to the truth of the proposition:– Many congregations may be under one presbyterial government."

[129] 'Cure' – charge or parish.

response to something Goodwin asked him to prove, he claimed "the assembly may prove the poynt de facto very easy but they[130] are the affirmers in this poynt & the proofe lyes upon them".[131]

The Independents therefore had to respond in those terms. So Jeremiah Burroughes said that the congregations in Jerusalem must have been 'fluid' because the officers of that church were known simply as 'elders of Jerusalem' without any more specific designation.[132] Gillespie brushed this kind of argument aside as hardly worth discussing; "when you speake of fixed & unfixed congregations it seems some great matter & when all is examined it is but putting of hercules shoe upon a childs foot[;] the difference is soe small de facto that it will easily be found de Jure".[133] Goodwin then immediately reminded him that what made the distinction so important was what Gillespie and his friends were trying to build on the lack of any distinction; "that wch makes the distinction is the supposition of a presbyteriall government over many congregations".[134]

Gillespie could use some specious reasoning in making a point. He had argued that the church of Jerusalem was the pattern for all churches, and because the best form of government is by fixed boundaries, *therefore* the church at Jerusalem must have had fixed parishes! The majority seemed wholly unaware of the enormous assumptions in such an argument.[135] As Goodwin exclaimed, "you vote things by parts & then you argue from your owne votes".[136]

In the middle of this debate on the 12th, Hugh Peter came to the Assembly to ask for the divines' support in recruiting men and ministers to serve in the parliamentary forces, but he concluded "with an overture very moderate, that in the work we are about, we should be tender of dissenting consciences."[137] There is no direct evidence that this intrusion had been politically contrived, but in view of the state of the discussion in the

---

[130] I.e., the Independents.

[131] TMs. I. 843 (Ms. I. f. 433b;) Lightfoot, *Journal*, p. 246, Gillespie, *Notes*, p. 49.

[132] *Ibid*. Cf. also Lightfoot, *Journal*, p. 246.

[133] TMs. I. 844 (Ms. I. f. 434.)

[134] *Ibid*.

[135] On the 12th Lightfoot called on the Independents to respond to Gillespie's reasoning that "Those congregations that were to be the pattern of all congregations to come were fixed; otherwise they were not the best governed." Lightfoot, *Journal*, p. 246.

[136] TMs. II. 6 (Ms. II. f. 5.) Gillespie even went so far as to maintain dogmatically that the apostles must have been in fixed churches while they were in Jerusalem: "the apostells soe long as they did stay at Jerusalem ware fixed to the particular cure [;] as we goe out when called soe did they, *otherwise the absurdity of confusion takes place. . . .*" *Ibid*. 13, (Ms. II. f. 8b,) my italics.

[137] Lightfoot, *Journal*, p. 247; cf. Gillespie, *Notes*, p. 50, and TMs. II. 8 (Ms. II. f. 6.)

Assembly and the pluralism in the army,[138] it was a significant reminder of where the nation might be headed. The Assembly was not too sure how to respond to Peter's requests, but in respect to Peter's private remarks about unity Marshall observed "we may declare soe much to him that it is our desire".[139]

The Assembly returned to its debating but not to much purpose. Using the weapons at their command, both parties could deliver a crushing attack against the *jure divino* assumptions of their opponents, but were equally vulnerable at that point themselves, and so they circled around each other without ever getting to grips realistically with the problems of the Church. As Goodwin exclaimed, perhaps almost in despair, "this dispute as it is carried on [-] one gives reasons one way and another another way in a way of reason wch we should not now doe".[140]

The debate ended on Monday April 15th, and the will of the majority was incorporated into two crucial votes – first, "That, whether the congregations be fixed or not fixed, in regard of officers and members, it is all one as to the truth of the proposition", and secondly, the proposition brought forward by Gillespie the day before, that there was no material difference between the congregations in Jerusalem and the contemporary parishes in respect to their 'fixedness.'[141]

The majority had had its way, which is not surprising, but at the end of the debate the question of church membership and discipline had been raised, and this signalled the area in which the next ecclesiastical battle would be fought. Goodwin had asked how proper church discipline and a proper fencing of the tables for the Lord's Supper could be maintained if the congregations were 'fixed' in Jerusalem while the officers were common to the whole Church.[142] There was a point in this debate when Burroughes declared forthrightly "there is a difference[,] for ours are churches[;] theirs are not".[143] We can never be quite

---

[138] "The Independents having so managed their affaires, that of the officers and sojours in Manchester's armie, certainlie also in the Generall's, and, as I hear, in Waller's likewise, more than two parts are for them, and these of the farr more resolute and confident men for the Parliament partie." Baillie, to Spang, April 26th, 1644, *Letters and Journals*, II. 170.

[139] TMs. II. 9–10 (Ms. II. 6b, 7.) The Assembly was not enthusiastic about Peter's recruiting drive. Philip Nye observed that those who had sent Peter had no official position, but although the Assembly's duty was to Parliament, "they doe not forbid us to be civill". *Ibid.* 10 (Ms. II. f. 7.)

[140] *Ibid.* 12 (Ms. II. f. 8.)

[141] Gillespie, *Notes*, p. 51.

[142] TMs. II. 21 (Ms. II. f. 12b.)

[143] *Ibid.* 22 (Ms. II. f. 13.)

sure what the speaker meant from the fragmentary state of the
Minutes, but Burroughes seemed to be pointing to the difference
between the Independent idea of a gathered, covenanted Church
under its own 'presbytery' – for which he and his friends claimed
clear New Testament warrant – and a mixed parish in a national
Church governed ultimately by a presbytery in which the greater
number of elders could not be in immediate pastoral relationship
of word, sacrament and ministerial care to the members of all
particular parishes.

On April 16th the Assembly debated the instance of the
church of Ephesus as proof of a presbyterian government in the
early church, but little new was added. The Independents seem
to have brought a new team into the struggle. Sidrach Simpson,
William Carter and William Bridge represented their cause,
although Simpson's argument based on κατοικητήριον – the
'habitation' (of God) in Ephesians 2:22 – and other exegetical
points was regarded by Lightfoot as "not worth the answering."[144] Lightfoot was, however, immensely impressed by his
own argument regarding the synagogue at Ephesus,[145] "which",
he said, "took so well, that Mr. *Marshal*, Dr. *Gouge*, and
Mr. *Burgess*, and generally the Assembly, desired it might be
taken in."[146] The ready acceptance of this argument suggests the
difficulty those divines were having in finding scriptural proofs
to substantiate their claim.

On April 17th Burgess presented a summary of what the
Assembly had voted concerning ordination and the presbytery
which it was prepared to send to Parliament; but as the Assembly
was preparing to vote on this, Stephen Marshall "moved very
urgently that we should forbear to send up the votes concerning
the presbytery; and", Lightfoot adds, "made a long and strange
discourse about it: which business cost a very large debate".[147]
From the Minutes we discover that Marshall urged that the
doctrinal and Directory aspects of ordination should be submitted at the same time, and that it was "not seasonable to send up
the presbyteriall governmt at this time".[148] The people would
expect it to be brought directly into use, but if it was not, then it
would "ly wholly dead by them", and if that was going to

---

[144] Lightfoot, *Journal*, p. 248.

[145] He argued that since Paul had been invited to the synagogue, and yet called the
Ephesians 'gentiles', there must have been at least two congregations in Ephesus, and
these must have been under a common presbytery.

[146] *Ibid.*

[147] *Ibid.* p. 250.

[148] TMs. II. 29 (Ms. II. f. 16b.)

happen, then "it ware better to ly by us". He said that this was "only the keile of the ship[;] all the rest is yet behind".[149]

We suspect that Marshall's concern and also that of Vines was the same as that which we noted earlier. They were unwilling for any statement concerning presbyterian government to be made public until it could be put into practice as a fully integrated ecclesiastical system, and until the Assembly's positions could be given convincing scriptural proofs. "The conclusion of the business," wrote Lightfoot, "when it held us all the forenoon, was, that all the votes reported, should be drawn up ready, and lie by until the Parliament should call, or the Assembly think fit to send them up".[150]

At this point the Assembly had to complete the work that had been dropped on April 4th. On the 18th April, Dr. Temple reported for the committee preparing the Directory of Ordination. He said that the preface and questions to the ordinand were not yet ready, but he submitted some suggestions,[151] and on the following day he presented the rest of the Directory of Ordination, which was debated in some detail and voted.[152]

The work on Lightfoot's proof of presbytery from the church of Ephesus started on the 16th was picked up on the 25th, and Ephesus was eventually added to the proofs;[153] but at the end of the session it was ordered that:

The committee 'of this assembly' that is apoynted to treat with the committee of lords & commons & commissioners from the church of Scotland [are] to expedite a draught about the whole businesse of discipline, to present to the assembly with all convenient speed[.][154]

Discipline raised the problem of the Church's juridical power, and this remained a basic issue with the Independents.[155] If the

---

[149] *Ibid.*

[150] Lightfoot, *Journal*, p. 250.

[151] *Ibid.* pp. 250f.

[152] *Ibid.* pp. 250–3.

[153] *Ibid.* p. 254. To prove this, Lightfoot says that Acts 20:17, 25:25, 30:36f., Rev. 2:1–6, 17:28 were used. Cf. Gillespie, *Notes*, p. 55. TMs. II. 36–8 (Ms. II. ff. 20–21.)

[154] TMs. II. 38 (Ms. II. f. 21.) Cornelius Burgess, Gataker, Vines and Reynolds were added to this committee.

[155] By the beginning of April considerable progress had been made in the Committee of Accommodation. On April 2nd Robert Baillie had written: "We have mett some three or four times alreadie, and have agreed on five or six propositions, hopeing, by God's grace, to agree in more. They yield that a Presbytrie, even as we take it is ane ordinance of God, which hath power and authoritie from Christ, to call ministers and elders, or any in their bounds, before them, to account for any offence in life or doctrine, to try and examine the cause, to admonish and rebuke, and if they be obstinate, to declare them as Ethnicks and

Assembly was now going to tackle that problem and settle this power in the classical presbytery, the final confrontation between the Presbyterians and the Dissenting Brethren could not be long delayed.

III

The Church and its Order: the particular church

It did not happen that way. Again the Assembly seemed to veer away from a collision path, and instead, the discussion centred in the rights and powers of the local church or congregation. That was a subject in which there was likely to be collision enough, for it was one in which we could expect the Independents to react strongly; but the debates reveal more than that, for they give the impression that the Independents' concerns about the local church and its 'presbytery' were shared, for differing reasons, by important groups within the Presbyterian party. That is the element to watch for in these debates.

Although on Friday, 26th April, the Assembly gave consideration to the 4th proposition on church censures presented by the Second Committee,[156] there was little in the discussion of the first few days that directly affected 'the Grand Debate',[157] but eventually interest began to concentrate on the ecclesiastical

---

publicans, and give them over to the punishment of the Magistrates; also doctrinallie, to declare the mind of God in all questions of religion, with such authoritie as obliedges to receave their just sentences; that they will be members of such fixed Presbytries, keep the meeting, preach as comes their turne, joyne in the discipline after doctrine. Thus farr have we gone on without prejudice to the proceedings of the Assemblie." Publick Letter, *Letters and Journals,* II. 147f.

The Independents had gone a long way to meet the Presbyterians, but some important matters had been left unresolved. That is clear from a later letter in which he gave detailed instructions about the subjects on which he wanted Continental theologians to write. These were concerned with church power and jurisdiction; to Spang, 12th July, 1644, *ibid.* p. 205.

[156] "Particular churches in primitive times were made up of visible saints; to wit, of such as, being of age, professed faith in Christ, and obedience to Christ, according to the rule of faith and life taught by Christ and his apostles, and of their children. Proofs, Acts ii. 38.41, and ult. compared with Acts v. 14; which, being debated all day, was at last voted." Lightfoot, *Journal,* p. 254. The propositions of the Second Committee are summarized, *supra* pp. 252, n. 16, 292, n. 92. The first two of these propositions had offered no problem, and seem to have been incorporated into the propositions on ordination debated on March 28th; cf. *supra* pp. 325ff.

[157] The 3rd proposition seems to have been mislaid in the records, but it would have been accepted without too much difficulty. The 4th was passed without trouble, although Cornelius Burgess wanted more to be said about children. TMs. II. 38 (Ms. II. f. 21;) cf. Lightfoot, *Journal,* p. 254, Gillespie, *Notes,* p. 55. The 5th proposition (April 29th) also seems to have been accepted without much opposition. It was the 6th proposition, which spoke of visible saints in one locality being one church in respect to church government that produced the heat. It appears to have been broached on April 29th but the debate was carried over into Tuesday April 30th.

power possessed by a local congregation and its ministerial 'presbytery', and this was a concern not only for the Independents, but also for the Scots. In the debate on April 30th, for example, it was Rutherford who insisted that "particular congregations have their interest in government",[158] and to maintain that interest "Mr. Henderson desired to put in the word *government* for *censure* in the proposition to be stated concerning congregations, because government implies church censures *non contra*."[159] But it was voted to debate the proposition as it was submitted by the committee.[160]

It was the legitimate power of a properly constituted congregation within the universal Church that emerged as the point at issue, and which, as Lightfoot remarked on May 1st, had been "the *de facto* of the proposition in hand yesterday."[161] What is noteworthy about it is to find the Scots and the Independents speaking once more on the same side.

> Mr. *Henderson* first moved, 'That we might give due to particular churches;' and this moved a large debate, and caused the paper, which the Scots' commissioners had put in long since, concerning their government, to be read. And this point held us a very long time: at last it was concluded to waive this proposition, which had now held us in station these three days.[162]

There seems to have been a growing concern among the Scots Commissioners that in reaction to Independency, the English 'Presbyterians' were going too far in the other direction and were not willing to grant what the Scots believed was the proper place of the local congregation within the whole system of classical Presbyterianism. Gillespie expressed this concern:

> My desire was concerning this debate of the power of congregations, That in regard the French Discipline, chap. v., and the Confession of Bohemia, chap. xiv., and the letter from the Classis of Walcheren, owned and approved by the synod of Zeland in their letter, all these and other Reformed churches give some power of church government and censures to the consistory of each particular congregation, which we have also asserted in our second paper concerning church government given in to the Grand Committee, That therefore the Assembly would either resolve, in the general, that some power of church censures doth belong to the elderships of

---

[158] Lightfoot, *Journal*, p. 255.
[159] Gillespie, *Notes*, p. 55. Gillespie, probably in error, places this on the 29th. Cf. Lightfoot, *Journal*, p. 255, TMs. II. 47 (Ms. II. f. 25b.)
[160] *Ibid.*
[161] Lightfoot, *Journal*, p. 256.
[162] *Ibid.*

congregations, without touching the rocks of the particular bounds of their power; or, otherwise, if there be further debate, that they will lay it aside till further consultation and accommodation in the Grand Committee with which we treat, and which must give us answer to our papers. . . . Now Mr. Seaman's grounds would make but one presbytery in one city, yea, in London itself, in whose hands all censures, less and more, shall be.[163]

The Assembly also debated the 7th and 8th propositions submitted by the Second Committee on that same day (May 1st), and there was no great opposition, although the Independents naturally did not like the assumption in the 8th proposition that the normal form of church organization was by parish boundaries, since that obviously suggested that 'gathered churches' were irregular.[164] But the next major controversy arose from a debate on May 3rd[165] on the 9th proposition in the series the Assembly had been discussing,[166] which asserted that "Single congregations ought to have such officers, ordinances, and administrations, among themselves, as God hath instituted."

This began one of the most significant debates since the debates on church government had first started, because the issue lay in which officers had been divinely instituted for the local congregation. A considerable number among the majority showed its preference for the traditional form of the English parish. They whittled away at the provision made earlier[167] to the

---

[163] Gillespie, *Notes*, p. 56. This second paper on church government that Gillespie mentions may have been the one against which David Calderwood protested to the Commissioners for moving too closely to the Independents. Cf. Baillie, *Letters and Journals*, II. 182.

[164] The Independents thought that mixed parishes must be regarded as an irregular form of the church, if indeed, they could be regarded as a proper form of the church at all. It has been pointed out that the Cambridge Platform, written in response to the Westminster Assembly, did not regard proximity in living conditions as "a proper adjunct of church relation." To bring people into such parish-orientated relationships was therefore something "which the truth of the Gospel doeth not acknowledg." Williston Walker, *Creeds and Platforms of Congregationalism*, p. 197; cf. Perry Miller, *Orthodoxy in Massachusetts*, p. 177.

[165] Items of interest in the intervening days included Lord Warriston (Sir Archibald Johnston, Lord of Warriston) officially seeking a report on progress for him to take to the General Assembly (May 1st), and the debate on May 2nd which was on a fuller form of the 8th proposition that read: "Because they that dwell together, are bound to all kinds of moral duties one to another, by virtue of their dwelling together." (Lightfoot, *Journal*, p. 258 cf. p. 192.) This was passed, but not without some questioning by the Independents for "they felt themselves pinched in the business of gathering their churches." (*Ibid.* p. 259.) It was eventually incorporated (in a modified form) within the proposition debated earlier.

[166] Lightfoot says it was the 7th proposition, but this must be in error; cf. *ibid.* pp. 260, 192–3.

[167] I.e., for each parish to have "one at least to labour in word and doctrine . . . another to care for the poor" and "another to assent in ruling." *Ibid.*

point where virtually the only necessary officer would be the parish minister, a Protestant version of the former parish priest. There was even some debate about whether the ruling elder should be given equal status with the preaching and teaching elders, or simply called an 'assistant', although "the Independents thought that abased him."[168]

It was eventually agreed that it was "requisite that there be at least one to join with the minister in ruling", but there were some who would have gone further in the direction of the traditional form of parish life. Richard Vines said that the work of a ruling elder had not yet been decided, "so that he knoweth not but one may do all", while Lazarus Seaman said that there was no warrant in scripture for a ruling elder to be appointed to every congregation.[169]

The Scots arrived late for this debate, but they were horrified when they realized what was happening, and the Minutes show that they immediately asked to have the floor.[170]

> Then Mr. *Henderson,* being but newly come in, excepted against the oneship of an elder in the congregation; 'for how can there be,' saith he, 'an eldership, where there is but one elder?' This also Mr. *Rutherford* followed him in, and this cost a serious debate: for the Scots' commissioners did conceive that we did not here come near enough to them: we feared that more numbers of elders would bring several inconveniences: Mr. *Rutherford* and Mr. *Gillespie* again and again replied. Mr. *Gillespie* urged these reasons:
> – 1. The custom of the Jews, from Ezra x, elders of the city, and rulers of the synagogue. 2. One man cannot discharge the duty of a ruling-elder. 3. If one be set apart to so great a work, he must needs be maintained.
> This was answered again and again, and the debate raught to a great length, and to a little distaste of the Scots.
> The conclusion of the long business, – for it held us till our rising, – was this, that it came to a temper,[171] and divers things were tendered.[172]

Lightfoot was clearly on the side of the English majority, and he shows us that even a compromise on this matter was not easy to reach.[173] Such a compromise was later worked out by a group of

---

[168] *Ibid.* p. 260.

[169] Gillespie, *Notes,* p. 58.

[170] The account in the Minutes ignores everything that had happened during this session until the intervention of the Scots. TMs. II. 57–61 (Ms. II. ff. 30b–32b.)

[171] I.e., a compromise.

[172] Lightfoot, *Journal,* p. 261.

[173] *Ibid.*

English Presbyterians, with the apparent agreement of the Scots, and (on May 6th) it was voted to modify the earlier proposition.[174]

The thing that stands out in this period from late April through the 5th of May is that although the Independents continued to be suspicious, there was no major Presbyterian/Independent clash. Indeed, the deepest division to appear at that time was that within the 'Presbyterian' party itself, between the Scots, whose ecclesiology in some ways was closer to the Independents, and a large number of the English divines, who were pressing for a simplified form of the traditional English parish. They would have preferred each parish to be under the complete control of its ordained ministers, but with *episcopé* exercised corporately by ministers acting in some kind of presbytery.

On Monday 6th May, having finally cleared away the problem of the local congregation and its eldership,[175] the divines turned to the 11th and 12th propositions brought forward by the Second Committee, and although the first of these passed without any problem,[176] the second was a different matter. It hit directly at the power of a congregation to act autonomously: "no single congregation may ordinarily assume to itself all and sole power in elections, ordinations, and censures, or in judicial determinations of controversies of faith, cases of conscience, and offering things indifferent."[177] That was clearly a 'Presbyterian' state-

---

[174] "Mr. Young offered to the Assembly a form of that proposition so much debated the last session, thus, – For officers in a single congregation there ought to be one at least, both to labour in the word and doctrine, and to rule; it is also requisite that there be others to join in government; and likewise it is requisite that there be others to take special care of the poor; the number of each of which is to be proportioned according to the condition of the congregation.

This he, Mr. Palmer, and Mr. Seaman had agreed on, contriving it so that the first part, *ought to be,* might be held forth an institution, the other part, *requisite,* might be held forth a prudential conveniency for ruling elders in a congregation; for Mr. Seaman holds that there is *jus divinum* for ruling elders, but not *jus divinum* that there should be an elder in each congregation." Gillespie, *Notes,* p. 58.

[175] Unfortunately Lightfoot was in Munden the whole of the week May 6th–10th, but as usual he made sure of getting information about the main theme of the Assembly's work while he was away. He provided an excellent brief summary when he returned from getting his family settled in its new home. Lightfoot, *Journal,* pp. 261f.

The Minutes suddenly become less meagre and fragmentary, and Gillespie begins to provide fuller notes although he was absent for the important debate on the 7th May.

[176] "That when congregations were divided and fixed, they need all mutual help one from another, both in regard of their own intrinsical weakness and mutual dependence, and in regard of enemies without. Proved from Gal. v. 9, all the church of Galatia were leavened by the same false doctrine spreading through them all. Other scriptures added, were Acts xx. 28–30; 1 Pet. v. 8; Heb. xii. 12, 15; Acts xv. at the beginning, was added." Gillespie, *Notes,* p. 58.

[177] *Ibid.* pp. 58f., cf. Lightfoot, *Journal,* p. 193.

ment, but the Scots were beginning to fear that some of their English colleagues were becoming too 'Presbyterian' and not sufficiently Reformed. Even George Gillespie became worried about the rights of a Reformed congregation in electing its own officers. "I desired," he wrote, "to put out the word elections, because the election of officers belongs to those only whose officers they are, but they are not officers or elders in relation to all the congregations under a presbytery", and he noted with regard to one of the Scots' leading English associates:

> Mr. Seaman professed, That in all these particulars the people have no power at all, but are merely passive, that is, they have a measure of liberty, and a privilege of consent, but the power is only in the presbytery.[178]

The debates of the 7th May show that the Assembly was fairly evenly divided on the rights of the congregation in ordination.[179] Thomas Wilson produced six reasons for the ordaining rights of the congregation, and William Rathband (or Rathbone) also spoke generally in favour. When Seaman attacked the Independents, Charles Herle criticized Seaman, but the opposition may have drawn the more conservative leaders like Seaman and the Scots closer together, for Rutherford came out strongly against any suggestion that an individual congregation could perform a valid ordination on its own.

Rutherford stated the Scots position when he said "a single congregation hath some power of government in re propria,[180] but this will be farre from sole power & all power". Although the Church may have been a single congregation in the beginning, this could not be regarded as the ordinary form of the Church from which we are to take our pattern, because a single congregation "is alone[,] a maimed congregation wanting sister and neighbour churches[,] as that of sole men".[181]

---

[178] Gillespie, *Notes*, p. 59. The range of opinions among the English is seen when we compare this with the views of Charles Herle, who observed, "a congregation hath all power, but not sole power." *Ibid.* That session was also concerned about the perennial problem of Antinomianism (in Dr. Holmes's *A Coole Conference*,) and with John Goodwin's plea for liberty of conscience (*M:S to A:S.*)

[179] TMs. II. 64–76 (Ms. II. ff. 34–40.)

[180] I.e., in its own concerns.

[181] TMs. II. 67 (Ms. II. f. 35b.) Both sides were curiously selective in dealing with evidence from the New Testament churches. The Independents claimed to derive their pattern of church government from the most primitive form of the Church, but as we have seen they were unwilling to accept the government of the apostles as normative for the Church in later ages, and they ignored inconvenient evidence that arose from the Church's development. Presbyterians (in this case the Scots) accepted the New Testament evidence as it supported their own system, but ignored the evidence from more primitive or more developed forms.

Rutherford presented the positive side of Presbyterianism when he declared that "the accession of sister churches is noe wayes a losse or diminution of power given to a congregation[,] noe more than when one pastor hath sole power of administering[,] when ther comes 2 to helpe him noe man will say [his power is diminished.]" He thought the fallacy of the Independent position was that "the power of presbyteryes & congregations are conceived to be different specie, whereas I conceive it is only different gradu".[182]

The most bitter antagonism to the Independent position, however, came from the clericalism of many of the English divines. Herbert Palmer objected to the words 'no single *congregation*' in the proposition, because he thought that it should "rather say the *officers* of the single congregation",[183] and a similar desire to preserve clerical privilege is seen in Seaman. In response to the Independents' appeal to the earliest church, (the one hundred and twenty mentioned in Acts 1:15,) Seaman said he did not regard that body as a church but that they were "such as had conversed with Christ more or lesse from the time of John the Baptist upwards",[184] and from the earlier debates on the church of Jerusalem we know that he regarded the hundred and twenty of Acts 1:15 as preachers.[185] Charles Herle retorted that "this opinion is the opinion of few but him that offers it",[186] and Goodwin maintained that "the churches generally called so in the new testament are particular congregations". He wished "the controversy might be reduced to that". Against Seaman's theory regarding the hundred and twenty, he asked, "wher ware ther soe many churches as these to represent them[?] they ware a church & at a church meeting[.]"[187] In effect he was asking, where were the churches to maintain all these preachers at that stage of the Church's life?

Seaman admitted that the last point discussed was "but my own opinion", but Christ had given his power to the Church in general and therefore the argument could not be based on an appeal to the most primitive form, to the fact that these "ware the first in existence".[188] But even Richard Vines was dubious about

---

[182] I.e., Rutherford distinguished between things of different species and two things which represented simply different degrees within the same species. TMs. II. 67 (Ms. II. f. 35b.)

[183] *Ibid.* 66 (Ms. II. f. 35.) My italics.

[184] *Ibid.* 71 (Ms. II. f. 37b.)

[185] *Supra* p. 286.

[186] TMs. II. 72 (Ms. II. f. 38.)

[187] *Ibid.* 73–4 (Ms. II. ff. 38b, 39.)

[188] *Ibid.* 74 (Ms. II. f. 39.)

Seaman's reasoning: "the Argument propounded in the beginning", he said, "was to prove that single congregations have power", and added, "they are not inconsiderable arguments." He continued:

> if you will setle a presbitery[,] then 'how' you will take
> away is [its?] power or halfe it with them will be a businesse
> that will require cleare arguments; yet I should not deny
> but a congregation single with complete officers
> is a church[.][189]

He defined the real issue raised by the proposition as "whether a single congregation be not bound to consociate in government with other congregations in the neighbourhood & vicinity therof", while Palmer, on the other side, wanted to know "what the sufficiency of elders is".[190]

The debate continued the next day (May 8th), and again we notice the wide range of ecclesiological opinion among the English 'Presbyterians,' with Herle, Marshall and Vines arguing, in this instance, generally on the same side as the Independents, while Palmer, Seaman, Reynolds, De la Place and the Scots took up cudgels for the other side. The Independents and their associates had a difficult time producing literal proof for their contention that a single church, with a properly constituted local eldership, had all that was necessary to act as a regular ordaining authority. There was considerable distance between hints and inferences that could be drawn from the New Testament and the kind of literal proof sought by Westminster. Again it must be insisted that they did not suggest a single congregation *ought* to act alone, but that it *might* act alone where necessary. Goodwin stated it in this way, "the congregation hath a power to call others to assist but the power must reside in the congregation": ordination was not "an act of Jurisdiction but of blessing, therfor they may call in others".[191]

On the other side, Palmer declared that no single congregation in apostolic times had assumed power to ordain, and that if the action does not appear in scripture it could not have done so at the time of the apostles. In his view there was "noe manner of intimation in the new testament that it was practised[,] nor is ther any principle for it, that noe single congregation may ordinarily assume [this power.]"[192] Philip Nye said that there might "be an

---

[189] *Ibid.* 75 (Ms. II. f. 39b.)
[190] *Ibid.* 76 (Ms. II. f. 40.)
[191] *Ibid.* 79 Ms. II. f. 41b.)
[192] *Ibid.* 77 (Ms. II. f. 40b.)

Institution of truth wher ther is noe intimation of practise" and spoke of the "precepts wrapt up in promises in the new testament",[193] but that hardly met the demand for specific scriptural examples. The Independents were hampered by the Assembly's appropriation of many of the texts as proof of presbytery which they would have used, but until a rupture became final they could hardly flout the votes of the Assembly, although Goodwin did claim Acts 13 and 1 Timothy 4:14 as instances of congregational ordinations.[194]

Gillespie dismissed both. He denied Acts 13 because he claimed this referred to a classical presbytery and he cited Acts 15:35 as proof of that,[195] while as for Timothy's ordination "with the laying on of hands of the presbytery", he simply said that Goodwin "must prove that that was the presbytery of a single congregation" and that it ordinarily assumed that power.[196] It never occurred to Gillespie that the onus of proof was equally upon him to prove the negative, or to prove that it was a presbytery of the classical kind.

Richard Vines continued to raise questions. With the possibilities of the local congregation in mind, he asked, "if ther ware 7 ministers or 6; why may not they ordaine as well as 7 in a classicall presbytery?"[197] In view of the position taken by Vines generally in the debates, such views could hardly have arisen out of any desire to side with the Independents but must have arisen out of his own conviction about the sufficiency of the 'presbytery' in a properly constituted parish. A similar conviction appears to have been at the root of Marshall's comments, although in regard to the existing situation in England, he admitted that "de facto with us it will be hard to find such a congregation".[198] Henderson at once observed that it would be more fitting to "debate those things that are practicable".[199]

The debate on the claim of a local congregation to have power to ordain was coming to a climax, and at the beginning of the session on Thursday May 9th, there was agitation "to waive the proposition which had so divided the Assembly the two days preceding, and was like to divide the Assembly more and more", but this "was not hearkened to, but the proposition stated thus:

---

[193] *Ibid.*
[194] Gillespie, *Notes,* p. 60.
[195] *Ibid.*
[196] *Ibid.*
[197] TMs. II. 81 (Ms. f. 42b.)
[198] *Ibid.*
[199] *Ibid.*

No congregation which may conveniently associate, ought to assume to itself the power of ordination."[200] It was a reasonable proposition that the rule of Christian fellowship seemed to require, and it was one which in less pressured times Congregationalists would follow to avoid the dangers of atomistic independency; but these were not unpressured times, and the Dissenting Brethren and their associates had been pushed into a corner.

That pressure had a curious effect on the way the men argued. Consider, for example, Rutherford's reasoning when he said that "in the apostels times many congregations associated de facto & therfore they ought to be soe de jure".[201] This declared, in effect, that whatever the apostles did for practical reasons, must be obligatory on the Church now as a divine command. The pressure made Richard Vines more stubborn. No Independent could have expressed the position they were taking more clearly:

> the right to a minister is in the congregation [and]
> the right of ordaining is in a presbytery authoritatively
> combined & soe a company of ministers may be a
> presbytery. suppose a company 'of ministers' in a
> congregation be authoritatively combined I thinke
> they my[may?] ordaine:
> ordination is in a presbytery whatsoever that presbytery
> bee . . .
> the first presbitery is in the congregation and other
> presbyteryes are composed secondarie of those[.][202]

Goodwin, who had objected rather testily to the Assessor, Burgess, being given the floor before him, used the same argument from silence that Gillespie had used against him earlier, for the apostles had left the churches without "giving a word of institution to them for any association".[203] In reply Gillespie declared that there was as much warrant for the two kinds of presbyteries in the presbyterian system as there was for the Independents' "two kinds of sinods".[204] Although there he was probably doing no more than scoring a debating point against his opponents, he put his finger on the real dilemma between the two ecclesiologies: there is no literal, scriptural proof for either.

The proposition was voted on Friday, May 10th, but not

---

[200] Gillespie, *Notes*, p. 60.
[201] TMs. II. 87 (Ms. II. f. 45b.)
[202] *Ibid.* 90 (Ms. II. f. 47.)
[203] *Ibid.* 92, cf, 91 (Ms. II. f. 48, cf. f. 47b.)
[204] *Ibid.* 93 (Ms. II. f. 48b.)

before a hard struggle.[205] Jeremiah Whitaker's remarks may indicate why the proposition succeeded, because of an underlying fear that if it were defeated Antinomians, Anabaptists and others would use it as an excuse to ordain at will.[206] Stephen Marshall denied that consequence, but he said "I grant the inconvenience if all doe it".[207] This fear ran very deeply in most members of the Assembly, and it must never be underestimated as a primary reason why many turned away from Independency towards the other polity. Even more striking was Whitaker's fear of lowering standards in the professional clergy:

> If some congregations may assume the power which this proposition denies them, then all may challenge it as having a like right from Christ; that if all depend on having a sufficient number of pastors, anabaptists having a plurality of ministers in their congregation, and all sectaries will heap to themselves teachers. If every congregation may assume this power, then it shall be, as in Jeroboam's day, priests shall be made of the lowest of the people, and we shall be as, he said, *clerus Angliae, stupor Mundi*.[208]

There may have been a discreet chuckle or two at this erudite play on words,[209] but there was nothing amusing in the practical problem it forecast. It was all too possible. The Assembly had been called into being to discover the scriptural truth about the Church, but its members lived in a society in which the practical results of their actions could not be ignored: no argument was more likely to remind members of where their own best interests lay.

Seaman tried to drive a wedge between the Independents, whom he despised as discredited, and the others who opposed the proposition,[210] and later in the debate both he and Burgess declared that the defeat of the proposition would destroy everything the Assembly had prepared for Parliament. Richard Vines still disagreed. In fact, our interest in this debate is not to rehash the views of men whose theological positions we can now recite by heart, but to notice the concern of those who were for a time ranged in opposition to their normal place within the 'Pres-

---

[205] *Ibid.* 94–100 (Ms. II. ff. 49–52,) Gillespie, *Notes*, pp. 62–4.

[206] TMs. II. 95 (Ms. II. f. 49b.)

[207] *Ibid.* 96–7 (Ms. II. ff. 50, 50b.)

[208] Gillespie, *Notes*, p. 62.

[209] "Clergy of England, the amazement of the world." It is a play on words, because *stupor* can also mean 'stupidity' and 'dumbness.'

[210] "Mr. Seaman said, They who assert that a single congregation may have all and sole power of a presbytery differ in their grounds. Some say so, because a congregation is a church, which, he said, is a deserted argument; others, because a congregation hath a presbytery, a company of preaching presbyters." *Ibid.*

byterian' majority. Charles Herle's stand is perhaps not too surprising, because he always maintained closeness with the Independents, but Vines and Marshall had provided a good deal of the leadership on the other side of the chamber. Marshall denied Whitaker's belief that an ordaining power in congregational presbyteries would overthrow wider associations, and argued that such power simply provided that "some are not bound to associate".[211] Both Marshall and Vines maintained that the earlier votes of the Assembly had left this point "free for a dispute". Both men were realistic about the situation in England, for Vines agreed with Marshall that it would not be "convenient to leave the power of ordination to congregations in England", but he went on to say that "his conscience was straitened with that theological maxim, that no single congregation that may conveniently associate may ordain", and he claimed that "it cannot be said that a classical presbytery hath all and sole power."[212]

The proposition passed; and whatever the rights or wrongs of the case theologically, we may regard it as much a victory for political necessity as it was for scriptural truth. Lightfoot's account admittedly came at second hand, but it was a vivid summary of what happened. Writing of the debate that started on May 6th, he says "this held them tugging with the Independents the rest of that day, Tuesday, Wednesday, Thursday, and Friday: at last, on Friday, it came to the question, and voted 'in terminis,' by twenty-seven, and denied by nineteen. And this business had been managed with the most heat and confusion of any thing that had happened among us."[213]

William Shaw thought that this vote "is to be regarded as one of the severest blows the Independents had yet received", although he recognized that they were not alone.[214] That is the place at which Lightfoot has to be corrected, because he leaves the impression that it was the Independents alone who opposed the proposition. It was not, and perhaps the importance of this vote was not in any defeat of their own ecclesiology, but in the recognition that even with the support of Vines, Marshall, Herle and others, there was no way they could outvote the Pres-

---

[211] *Ibid.* p. 63.
[212] *Ibid.*
[213] Lightfoot, *Journal*, p. 262.
[214] Shaw, *A Hist. of the English Church*, I. 174, cf. p. 240.

byterians politically in the Assembly.[215] To use an Americanism that perhaps expresses the matter with more precision than English usage, "when push came to shove" the Independents had no chance of deflecting the purpose and the program of the Presbyterians.

The vote on the 10th May was not the end of the matter, for on the following Monday (the 13th) Marshall asked for scriptural proofs to be added to the proposition[216] and Vines asserted that there was "noe reason that proves the conveniency of it will prove the proposition as it's now carryed".[217] The events of the past week also seem to have aroused some concern about the way the records were being kept,[218] and the First Committee was charged to study whether there was any scriptural warrant for congregational presbyteries.[219]

The matter blazed again on Wednesday, May 15th, when Dr. Stanton presented the report of the Second Committee. This was couched in such absolute terms that it was clear that those responsible for framing the propositions were determined to slam the door fast against any possibility of ordinations being

---

[215] We do not have precise information about which members took part in the vote, but if we take the known Independents (the five Dissenting Brethren together with William Greenhill, William Carter, Peter Sterry, John Phillips, Joseph Caryl, and possibly Anthony Burgess, John Bond and John Green,) there was a total of 13 possible votes. If we add to this total the 6 divines whom we can identify as speaking on that side of the debate during this week – Marshall, Vines, Herle, Wilson, Rathband and Temple, this provides a total of 19 votes. We cannot say that all these were present on May 10th and voted, and a few who cannot be identified may have voted on that side, but it should have been clear to the Independents and their friends in Parliament that there was no way they could challenge the voting strength of the majority party in the Assembly.

[216] Gillespie, *Notes*, p. 64; cf. TMs. II. 102 (Ms. II. f. 53.)

[217] TMs. II. 103 (Ms. II. f. 53b.)

[218] Cf. the following comments:

"Dr Gouge:– it stands with all assemblys to set downe
propositions, all these reasons produced were voted
by divers of the brethren & they are in the scribes
bookes, & upon record [:] the reasons of the Committee
must be reserved to the close [.]

Mr Gataker:– ther is nothing upon record but the
resolves of the Assembly, not whatsoever is in the
scribes bookes [.]

Mr Marshall:– all our discourses are recorded by
the scribes soe farre as their pens can reach them [,]
but not to be taken as the Judgment of the
assembly [.]" *Ibid.* 102 (Ms. II. f. 53.)

[219] "That the first committee doe consider of the Acts of Presbyteryes already reported by them and not determined by the Assembly, & give an account to this Assembly what presbyteryes 'it is that' they doe intend in that report whether classicall or congregationall, and whether they find any warrant for congregationall Presbyteryes." *Ibid.* 103 (Ms. II. f. 53b.)

conducted legally by single congregations,[220] and this caused some who had supported the original proposition[221] to draw back. For example, Edward Reynolds suggested that the original proposition should be "tempered and qualified", and the Assembly softened its effect, against the strong opposition of Seaman, Lightfoot and others, by introducing it with the words "It is very requisite."

"Now came the Scots' Commissioners in," says Lightfoot, "and they took it not well that the proposition was altered: and this cost again a fresh debate."[222] One guesses that if the proposition had been agreed upon in the committee with their support, they were furious, and their reaction led to a heated debate that carried over to the next day (the 16th). When Gouge remonstrated that "our reasons should not be heightened to such a pitch", Lightfoot replied sharply that he "saw no reason to start at more light, if it may be shewed."[223]

A division had developed in the Assembly in which the Independents had played no more prominent part than several of those who had generally supported the earlier presbyterian proposals.[224] Even old Henry Wilkinson spoke up for the rights of the local presbytery. "I desire to speake to that wch will be matter of fact," he said, "it will be an advantage to have it in a perticular congregation[.] I beseech you that we may[.] wher ther are fit persons to make up in one congregation a sufficient combination amongst themselves[,] may they not doe the acts incident to a presbytery[?]" But he would limit the act of ordina-

---

[220] "1. They do not find in Scripture that any single congregation, which might conveniently associate, did assume to themselves all and sole power for ordination; nor do they find any rule which may warrant such a practice.

2. We read that a presbytery over divers congregations associated, did ordain, as in Jerusalem.

3. We find no reason why a single congregation, which can associate, should divest a classical presbytery of this due to it.

4. This crosseth the first pattern, Acts vi. in two things:

1. In not associating when they may: 2. In ordaining, not being associated." Lightfoot, *Journal*, pp. 265f.

[221] The 12th proposition submitted by the Second Committee.

[222] *Ibid.* p. 266.

[223] *Ibid.* p. 267.

[224] Robert Baillie recognized the extent of this division in the Assembly. On May 9th he had written to Andrew Ramsay of Edinburgh: "The leading men in the Assemblie are much at this time divided about the questions in hand, of the power of congregations and synods. Some of them would give nothing to congregations, denying peremptorilie all example, precept, or reason, for a congregationall eldership; others, and many more, are wilfull to give to congregationall eldership all and intire power of ordination, and excommunication and all. Had not God sent Mr. Henderson, Mr. Rutherford, and Mr. Gillespie, among them, I see not that ever they could [have] agreed to any settled government." *Letters and Journals*, II. 177.

tion to those who were themselves ordained: "I doe not speake of any but such as have taken orders".[225]

The more temperate mood of the Assembly was expressed by Gataker, who pointedly observed that "what arguments [are] used against congregationall may be aledged against classicall presbytery[,] be[cause there was] noe ordination[226] in wch ther was not either an apostell or evangelist".[227] It is clear that some of those who were willing enough to recognize practical reasons for establishing the presbyterian system in England were beginning to have qualms at the dogmatic position the Assembly was taking, and they were not ready to grant to classical presbytery an exclusive divine right.

Lightfoot provides a graphic account of the last stages in the debate of the 16th May:

> Our debate grew long and hot, and there was much 'pro et contra' upon it; and at last we had it very near the question, when Mr. *Carter* interposed, and Mr. *Herle*, Mr. *Nye*, and Mr. *Burroughs*. At last, with extreme tugging, we got it to the question, and was carried so narrowly, that it was thrice put to it before it could be determined; and there arose a great heat; and at last it was carried affirmatively, by four voices, that the first reason should be brought to prove the proposition. – I gave my affirmative.
>
> Then fell we upon the second reason: 'We find that a classical presbytery did ordain,' &c. And this the dissenting party urged to go to the question, thinking this reason not to make a clear conclusion upon the proposition, 'A classical presbytery did ordain;' *ergo*, a single congregation may not. This scoff cost some heat and long debate: and the thing itself spent abundance of time: at last it was put to the question, and voted affirmatively, some five votes difference. There I suspended my vote.[228]

It had been close.

Theological Note on the Debate

There are two theological comments that may be made at the end of the important debate on congregations and the right to ordain.

1. The basic problem arose because both Presbyterians and Independents claimed *jus divinum* for their own polity, and this claim caused them to push the biblical evidence further than it would go.

---

[225] TMs. II. 113 (Ms. II. f. 58b.)
[226] I.e. in the New Testament church.
[227] TMs. II. 116 (Ms. II. f. 60.)
[228] Lightfoot, *Journal*, p. 267.

It may be illustrated by looking at George Gillespie's Memorandum on the necessity of churches being in presbyterial associations with each other. In his Memorandum (*Notes*, pp. 61–2) he offers six considerations:

(1) The institution of our Lord in Matthew 18:17.
(2) The apostolic pattern in which many congregations, not (according to the vote of the Assembly) materially different from those in England, did associate.
(3) The general rules held out in scripture, that two witnesses are better than one, that in the multitude of counsellors there is strength, etc.
(4) The light of nature that applies equally in church and state.
(5) The law of necessity that requires a place of appeal in cases of dispute.
(6) The argument that if people are allowed to choose, "then we should have many who would effect an absoluteness in their own congregation, and despise the fellowship of their brethren, and not join with others in common counsel."

Several of these are excellent arguments, and all of them have validity when not used to impose an 'association' of some predetermined kind; but Gillespie's claim to *jus divinum* is based on the first two of his considerations, which are the two most open to question.

The first is our Lord's command to his disciples regarding their treatment of a recalcitrant brother. If the brother was not willing to listen to a private approach, or to several brethren, then the disciples were told to take the issue to the church. But what does 'church' mean in that passage? It is as plausible that it could represent a company of believers locally associated as that it means a classis. In any case, there is a considerable difference between 'the church' then and the system of church courts envisaged by Gillespie. Every believer is likely to read into that term 'church' his or her own understanding of what the church is.

An even greater objection is possible to the second consideration, because it was ultimately based on a dubious vote in the Assembly. The early churches did associate together and the basis for that association was in the Spirit's call and the common faith that bound Christians together in the love and mutual ministry they exercised towards each other. It was grounded in grace rather than in law, and when that order was reversed, that which should have been a strength and support for congregations, could easily become a new form of bondage.

At the same time we must recognize the practical strength of

Gillespie's position, which must have commended itself to many of the practical-minded English divines. His sixth consideration was particularly telling, since there are indications that that kind of local parochial episcopacy was precisely what several in the Assembly wanted.

2. We should underscore the spiritual issues in the concern for ministry that lay beneath the Independents' insistence on the right of the local church to ordain, and the Presbyterians' insistence on ministers being ordained in presbytery.

When we look at the situation that had arisen in England since the Reformation, we see a struggle between two kinds of ministerial qualities in concepts of what Reformed ministers should be and do. First, there were the spiritual and personal qualities that enabled a person to be a true pastor, to become a good preacher, and to exemplify in life that which was presented in the pulpit and at the Lord's table. Secondly, there was the expertise that came from study, such as a competency in biblical languages that would enable ministers 'rightly to divide the word of truth', and the classical lore that would enable them to study the theology of that time: the emphasis on 'the Word', on preaching and exegesis, and on 'edification' among Puritans is not accidental.

It should be obvious that these two sets of qualities should not be exclusive of each other – indeed, the ideal (as attempted in modern programs to evaluate 'competency for ministry') is to hold them together. It should also be obvious that whereas the first can best be judged by the group of people with whom the minister has entered a close and responsible pastoral relationship, the second can best be judged by a company of peers who have mastered the same disciplines and have had experience in using them.

The victory of the presbyterial over the congregational form of ordination in the Assembly was perhaps the recognition that the 'professional' abilities were given priority in equipping the ministry for a Reformed Church of England: it was a step towards the professionalization of the ministry.

CHAPTER 12

IN AND OUT OF THE ASSEMBLY

I

Church Censures

After all the heat of the past few weeks, the debate on church censures, from the middle of May until Stephen Marshall introduced the work on the Directory for Worship on May 24th, was an anti-climax.[1] In any case, the last two weeks of May were interrupted by a number of administrative but time-consuming matters, such as stricter regulations for those appointed to sequestered livings,[2] the letter to the General Assembly,[3] pressure from the London ministers for the stricter enforcement of the Sabbath, the case of an indigent minister,[4] the reception of newly arrived members,[5] and prayers for Sir Thomas Fairfax during his sickness.[6] There was also an important Fast Day that took up practically the whole of Friday, May 17th, in which exercises Marshall and Seaman were given the responsibility of delivering the prayers,[7] and Arrowsmith and Palmer were deputed to preach. In view of the recent tensions within the Assembly, it is perhaps worth noting that John Arrowsmith inveighed against 'inordinate passion' in their debates,[8] while Herbert Palmer declared that "unity may be a special meanes to find out truth."[9]

---

[1] Lightfoot, *Journal*, pp. 267–77, TMs. II. 107–168 (Ms. II. ff. 55b–86.) The milder climate may be indicated by Gillespie's *Notes*. He took no notes of the debates in the Assembly itself in the period from May 14th to September 4th, 1644. He seems to have taken detailed notes only on those matters in which he felt the Kirk had a crucial interest and in which there was likely to be a theological struggle.

[2] 15th May, Lightfoot, *Journal*, p. 265.

[3] 16th May, TMs. II. 117 (Ms. II. f. 60b.)

[4] Both of these matters arose on the 21st May, Lightfoot, *Journal*, p. 268.

[5] Jasper Hickes and Humphrey Hardwick; *ibid*. p. 273 (22nd May.)

[6] 23rd May, *ibid*. p. 275.

[7] Before his prayer Marshall said he would offer an exhortation of "2 or 3 words", which occupies two pages of the Minutes. TMs. II. 117f. (Ms. II. ff. 60b, 61.)

[8] *Ibid*. 121 (Ms. II. f. 62b.)

[9] *Ibid*. 129 (Ms. II. f. 66b.)

The debate itself was concerned with the censures of Admonition and suspension from the Lord's Supper, and in these matters there was little at issue between the Independents and the rest of the Assembly because the debate stopped short of excommunication. That would certainly have produced a confrontation, because it centred in the problem of where ecclesiastical jurisdiction is to be properly located. As it was, the debate raised no such issue, and although there are intriguing points of interest for the researcher in liturgics,[10] they are largely incidental to the ecclesiological debate. The major issue of the period was in the Lord's Supper – who could properly be admitted to it, and who ought to be excluded from it. John Lightfoot took the Erastian position that exclusion did not properly belong to ministers, and this was a position in which he and the few Erastians in the Assembly were clearly at odds with the rest of this Puritan body. He made a great deal of his own intervention into the debate on the 21st and suggested that it continued to influence the subsequent discussion.[11] The matter is not without interest, but it is of more importance to the later fate of the presbyterian proposals than to the 'Grand Debate concerning Presbytery and Independency.'

II

The Church and its Worship: the Directory

In some ways what was said about the debate on censures was also true for the discussions regarding the Directory of Worship. They ought to be of great interest to the specialist in liturgics, and there are some signs that they may be due to get more attention from that direction than they have in the past,[12] but they do not help us a great deal with the ecclesiological issue – except to underline that when two parties claim *jus divinum* even

---

[10] E.g., many Puritans tried to maintain the unity of Word and Sacrament, but the priority they gave to 'the Word', preaching and 'edification' could lead to some curious results. Lazarus Seaman, for example, in the course of the debate made the offhand remark that "we doe all take it for granted that there is a power of suspending & and thereupon we keepe away children & deafe men". (*Ibid.* 163, Ms. II. f. 83b.) Apparently if one could not understand or hear the Word correctly, the benefits of the Sacrament were to be withheld.

[11] Lightfoot, *Journal*, p. 272. The Minutes dismiss his speech with a brief mention; TMs. II. 149 (Ms. II. f. 76b.)

[12] Cf. 'The Independents and the Westminster Directory', chapter 8 in Bryan D. Spinks, 'The Eucharistic Liturgy in the English Independent, or Congregationalist, Tradition . . . 1550–1974' (Unpublished B. D. Thesis, University of Durham, 1978,) pp. 285–314. [To be published in 1984 as *Freedom or Order* by Pickwick Publications, Allison Park, Pennsylvania.]

irrelevancies assume an importance out of all proportion to their intrinsic significance. They also show how cultural and national prejudices can be caught up into a people's most cherished beliefs and almost invested with divine justification, for Robert Baillie reveals variations in English from Scottish practice that were innocent enough,[13] but which he has no compunction in saying "we must have away."[14]

The records themselves suggest that the participants did not expect matters of worship to cause any insurmountable problems. George Gillespie, who was present and active throughout the period, gave up writing a detailed account of his arguments and has simply left us two pages of notes about the work of the sub-committee on the Directory spanning the months from March to June, 1644,[15] while the Minutes are extremely sparse during most of the debates, and resume more comprehensive summaries only during the later discussions on the Lord's Supper. Lightfoot soldiered on as always, but even he was absent in Munden for a week at a time during two critical periods.

The major source of information is in Baillie's sporadic letters, since he was involved in the committee work, and it was a subject on which he held decided views. He often gives us invaluable intelligence about what went on behind the scenes. The practical matter of providing a substitute for the Book of Common Prayer had been in the forefront of Parliament's concern in calling the Assembly, and it was a matter that needed to be addressed expeditiously. The Scots Commissioners also had particular reasons for pushing for the preparation of the Directory, as Baillie indicated in a letter he wrote to Spang in December 1643.[16]

Within a month of his arrival in England as one of the Scottish Commissioners, Baillie had recognized that their ultimate target in the Assembly would be Independency and the "democratick anarchy and independence of particular congregations".[17] However, he had managed to convince Alexander Henderson and the rest of his colleagues that they should not attack the Independents immediately but wait for a more propitious time. In the

---

[13] Baillie, *Letters and Journals*, II. 122f.

[14] *Ibid.* p. 187. There was no fundamental difference in their understanding of the sacraments and Christian worship, and the variations were largely procedural and culturally inspired.

[15] Gillespie, *Notes*, pp. 101f.

[16] For Scotland, *Letters and Journals*, II. 116ff. The letter was undated, but appears to have been written just before December 22nd, 1643; cf. *supra* p. 191, n. 17.

[17] Cf. the lengthy quotation from his letter dated 7th December, 1643, *infra* pp. 375f. *Letters and Journals*, II. 115.

meantime they should work with them because he realized that the bulk of the English people viewed all reforming churches with suspicion: "As yet a Presbytrie to this people is conceaved to be a strange monster." Therefore the Scots decided "to go on hand in hand" with the Independents in the Assembly, "so far as we did agree, against the common enemie." The Scots used the zeal of the Independents for liturgical reform to attack the Book of Common Prayer, which they were all convinced must be supplanted.[18]

The preliminary work on the Directory was therefore started long before the ecclesiological issue had been resolved. With the approval of some of the most important men in Parliament,[19] a sub-committee of divines had been appointed. Stephen Marshall was to be chairman, and Herle, Palmer, Young and Goodwin were appointed to act with the Scots Commissioners, but although Baillie says that Goodwin had at first "assayed to turn all upside down" by arguing against all directories, after inviting him to dinner, Baillie fell under Goodwin's charm and wrote "we and he seemed to agree prettie well in the most things of the Directorie"[20]

Indeed, there was no reason why they should disagree fundamentally concerning worship since they accepted the same biblical basis. The Independents leaned more in the direction of extempore prayer, but they did not take an exclusive position on that,[21] and they insisted that their "*publique worship* was made up of no other parts then the worship of all other reformed Churches doth consist of."[22] However, Baillie did not appreciate Good-

---

[18] "In the meantime, we would assay to agree upon the Directorie of Worship, wherein we expect no small help from these men to abolish the great Idol of England, the Service-Book, and to erect in all parts of worship a full conformitie to Scotland in all things worthie to be spoken of." *Letters and Journals*, II. 117.

[19] The active politicians had been the Solicitor-General (presumably Oliver St. John), Sir Henry Vane the Younger, Lord Say and Lord Wharton. All of these may be counted as belonging to the political wing of Independency.

[20] "For the help of this evill, we thought it best to speak with him in private; so we invited him to dinner, and spent an afternoon with him verie sweetlie. It were a thousand pities of that man; he is of manie excellent parts: I hope God will not permitt him to goe on to lead a faction for renting of the kirk . . ." To Scotland, January 1st, 1643/4, *ibid.* p. 123.

[21] "Againe, concerning the great ordinance of *Publique Prayer* and the *Lyturgie* of the Church, whereas there is this great controversie upon it about the lawfulnesse of set formes prescribed; we practiced (without condemning others) what all sides doe allow, and themselves doe practice also, that the publique Prayers in our Assemblies should be framed by the meditations and study of our own Ministers, out of their own gifts, (the fruits of Christs Ascension) as well their Sermons use to be. This vve vvere sure all allowed of, though they superadded the other." *An Apologeticall Narration*, p. (12).

[22] *Ibid.* p. (8).

win's freedom in inviting Philip Nye to join him in the deliberations of this committee,[23] and later on he was very critical of the
way in which they celebrated the Lord's Supper. He did not
understand the Independents' practice of conducting communion each week, nor did he understand that where the sacrament is
part of the normal worship in a gathered church of 'visible
saints', the forms might differ from those necessary in a mixed
parish:

> The Independents way of celebration, seems to be very irreverent:
> They have the communion every Sabbath, without any preparation
> before or thanksgiving after; little examination of people; their very
> prayers and doctrine before the sacrament uses not to be directed to
> the use of the sacrament. They have, after the blessing, a short
> discourse, and two short graces over the elements, which are distri-
> bute and participate in silence, without exhortation, reading, or
> singing, and all is ended with a psalme, without prayer.[24]

For all their differences, however, the members of this committee at least had sufficient confidence in the liturgical stance of
their common Calvinistic theology to parcel out among them the
work on the Directory, although we note that the Scots retained
to themselves the crucially important work on the sacraments:

> It was laid on us to draw up a Directorie for both Sacraments; on
> Mr. Marshall for preaching; on Mr. Palmer for catechizing; on
> Mr. Young for reading of scriptures, and singing of psalms; on
> Mr. Goodwin and Mr. Herle for fasting and thanksgiving. *Had not
> the debate upon the main point of differing (the Presbytrie) with-
> drawne all our mind, before this these taskes had been ended.*
> However, we expect, by God's grace, shortlie to end these: What is
> behind in the Directorie, will all be committed the next time to the
> forenamed hands; and if it had past these, we apprehend no great
> difficultie in its passing both the great Committee, and the
> Assemblie, and Parliament.[25]

---

[23] To Spang. 18th February, 1643/4, Baillie, *Letters and Journals*, II. 131. Nye
apparently had some idiosyncratic ideas of his own, of which Baillie made considerable
play: "Mr Nye told us his private judgement, that in preaching he thinks the minister
should be covered, and the people discovered; but in the sacrament, the minister should
be discovered, as a servant, and the guests all covered." *Ibid.* p. 149, cf. p. 195. There is
no evidence that Nye's private opinion was generally accepted among his fellow Independents.

[24] Publick Letter, April 2nd, 1644, *ibid.* pp. 148f. He said much the same in a later
letter regarding Independent practices: "The unhappie Independents would mangle that
sacrament. No catechising nor preparation before; no thanksgiving after; no sacramentall
doctrine, or chapters, in the day of celebration; no coming up to any table; but a carrying
of the element to all in the seats athort the church: yet all this, with God's help, we have
carryed over their bellies to our practice." Publick Letter, n.d. (June 1644), *ibid.* p. 195.

[25] To Spang, February 18th, 1643/4, *ibid.* p. 140. One wonders whether the punctuation here makes the sense clear. The sentence between the asterisks might be

Baillie was a little too sanguine in his hope of a speedy passage. The Scots did not like what had been prepared by Marshall on preaching or by Palmer on catechizing, and they themselves were opposed by the rest on their method of taking communion by coming up to successive tables in the Dutch fashion.[26] A good deal has sometimes been made of the differences in sacramental procedure as if it were only the Independents who withstood the Scots in this matter, but it is clear that although their opposition was stiffer and lasted longer than that of the rest, the Scottish practice was opposed by most if not all the English. Gillespie recorded that "Mr Marshall, Palmer, Herle, and Goodwin too, said it was enough that the elements be blessed on the table, and that some sit at table, but that the elements may be carried about to others in their pews or seats."[27]

Herle, indeed, sided with the Independents throughout in this liturgical debate, and later in the discussions on the floor of the Assembly Baillie complained that "not one of the English did joine with us, only Mr. Assessour Burgess, who then was in the chair, beginning to speak somewhat for us, but a little too vehementlie, was so mett with by the Independents, that a shamefull and long clamour ended their debaite."[28]

The Scots were intransigent on their way of taking communion, which was surely as much a matter of custom as it was of theology. In telling his kinsman, Spang, how the subject of excommunication had been laid aside at the end of May in order to get on with the Directory, Baillie said "the Independents, *and all*, loves so well sundry of their English guyses; which we must have away."[29] As far as Baillie and his Scottish colleagues were concerned, Scottish practices were right and the rest of the Assembly was expected to toe the line.

This is background to the work on the Directory. At the same

---

clearer for us if the comma were placed after the word 'this', rather than where it is; viz. 'Had not the debate upon the main point of differing (the Presbyterie) withdrawne all our mind before this, these taskes had been ended.'

[26] "As for our Directorie, the matter of Prayer which we gave in, is agreed to in the Committee. Mr. Marshall's part, anent Preaching, and Mr. Palmer's, about Catechizeing, though the one be the best preacher, and the other the best catechist, in England, yet we no wayes like it: so their papers are past in our hands to frame them according to our mind. Our paper anent the Sacraments we gave in. We agreed, so farr as we went, except in a table. Here all of them opposeth us, and we them. They will not, and saith the people will never yield to alter their practise. They are content of sitting, albeit not as of a ryte institute; but to come out of their pews to a table, they deny the necessitie of it: we affirme if necessare, and will stand to it." Publick Letter, April 2nd, 1644, *ibid.* p. 148.

[27] Gillespie, *Notes*, p. 101 (March 4th, 1643/4.)

[28] To Spang, June 28th, 1644, Baillie, *Letters and Journals*, II. 199.

[29] To Spang, May 31st, 1644, *ibid.* p. 187. My italics.

time, when the preparatory work was brought to the floor of the
Assembly, there was every indication that the work would move
apace. On May 24th, 1644, Stephen Marshall, as chairman of the
committee responsible for this preliminary work, presented the
general reasons for a Directory and the criteria adopted by his
committee – to find a mean between a completely fixed liturgy
and a form of worship in which everyone would be "left to his
own will". They looked for "a kind of uniformity as great as need
to be looked after in the variety of gifts that God hath given", and
he went on to describe the work:

> This doth not only set downe the heads of things but so lardgly as
> that with the altering of here & there a word, a man may mold it into a
> prayer[.][30]

Many matters were quickly dealt with in the week that followed,[31] so that at the end of May, Robert Baillie had good reason
for optimism. "Already we have past the draught of all the
prayers, reading of Scripture, and singing of psalms, on the
Sabbath day, *nemine contradicente*", he wrote to Spang; and went
on, "We trust, in one or two sessions, to through also our
draught of preaching: if we continue this race, we will amend our
former infamous slowness."[32]

On Monday June 3rd the parts of Preaching were introduced
in the Assembly, and reappeared several times[33] before finally
being completed on the 18th of that month. There are two points
in that debate that should be of interest to students both of
English Puritanism and of liturgics, although they may not have
too much direct bearing on the ecclesiological issue. The first is
the unexpected criticism of Plain Style preaching, which had
been one of the distinctive marks of the Puritan movement in the
first half of the seventeenth century. On June 5th Anthony
Tuckney[34] roundly criticized preaching "by doctrine, reason,
and use, as too strait for the variety of gifts, and occasion doth
claim liberty", and he was apparently upheld by William Gouge

---

[30] TMs. II. 169 (Ms. II. f. 86b.)

[31] Lightfoot was in Munden from the 24th May until June 4th. It should also be
observed that from June 17th–21st the transcriber noted that the Minutes appear in a
different hand, and much of this material remains in untranscribed shorthand. On Friday
June 14th, the scribe, Adoniram Byfield, had been given permission to absent himself;
cf. Lightfoot, *Journal*, p. 285.

[32] 31st May, 1644. *Letters and Journals*, II. 187.

[33] They reappeared, 4th–5th, 7th, 17th–18th June.

[34] Anthony Tuckney (1599–1670) had been assistant to John Cotton at Boston,
Lincolnshire (1627) and had succeeded him when Cotton had emigrated to New England
in 1633.

and Thomas Gataker.[35] This is a further indication that English Puritanism in the Assembly did not altogether follow earlier stereotypes.

The same thing is true about the use of classical languages in the pulpit. The use of classical languages and non-biblical authors in preaching had been frowned upon in Puritan circles ever since William Perkins had uttered his strictures against homiletical ostentation in *The Art of Prophesying*,[36] but the situation was no longer quite the same as it had been at the end of Elizabeth's reign, and although few of the divines wanted erudition to obtrude in preaching, the mood was not as absolute as we might have expected. Samuel Rutherford expressed himself rather graphically on this when he said, "the pot may be used in the bilyng but not brought in with the porridge",[37] and although Nye did not exclude the use of classical languages absolutely, he said that "this is soe poore pedanticall a way as it is not to the honour of ministry nor to the profit of the auditors".[38]

The public reading of scripture raised some debate,[39] with Palmer, Herle and Temple very much in favour of it being restricted to the clergy, and others, including the Scots, wanting more latitude. Gillespie thought that ordinands – 'expectants' – should at least be allowed to try out their gifts in this way.[40] Eventually the differences were resolved in a way which, if it did not satisfy everyone, at least reached a reasonable compromise.

The most serious clash, as we have mentioned, was on the method of receiving the elements in the Lord's Supper. The debate on the supper was introduced on June 6th,[41] on the 10th the Assembly discussed who was to be admitted, and on the 19th it debated who should be excluded.[42] The real confrontation arose on June 20th, when the Scots insisted that those who took the communion should sit around the table, and when the congregation was too large for a single table, that they should come up to successive tables. Nye pleaded "for liberty of posture" in not requiring everyone to go up to the table.[43] This may have

---

[35] Lightfoot, *Journal*, p. 278; TMs. II. 177f (Ms. II. ff. 90, 90b.)

[36] See 'The Art of Prophesying' in *The Works of William Perkins* (London, 1609,) II. 759.

[37] TMs. II. 182 (Ms. II. f. 93.)

[38] *Ibid*. 180 (Ms. II. f. 92.)

[39] Cf. Lightfoot, *Journal*, pp. 282–5, TMs. II. 185–90 (Ms. II. ff. 94b–97.)

[40] TMs. II. 187f. (Ms. II. ff. 95b, 96.)

[41] Lightfoot has a good account of the debate on this date: *Journal*, pp. 279–81.

[42] *Ibid*. pp. 282f., 285f.; cf. TMs. II. 184f., 194f. (Ms. II. ff. 94–94b, 100–101.)

[43] Lightfoot, *Journal*, p. 286.

been the debate to which Baillie referred in one of his Publick Letters, and which caused him to write so disparagingly about the Independents at communion.[44] The debate ended with the addition of a clause about the table that implied what the Scots wanted but was vague enough to permit other modes.[45]

Although this matter of posture seems hardly of sufficient importance to occupy all the time and energy the Assembly devoted to it, it almost tore the Assembly apart and occupied all the time until a compromise was reached on July 10th. But the compromise came about because the issue was seen to have ramifications beyond the Scots' demand. It should be remembered that only a few years previously most of these divines had been ministering in a church where kneeling for the sacrament had been the rule. For some, it was still a question whether to sit, stand or kneel.[46] In that opening debate on June 20th, for example, John Ley said he "consented to any posture", although he thought sitting was probably best in imitation of the example of Christ; but he noted that different practices were followed in different churches.[47] The Scots wanted the matter to be decided forthwith in their favour. Gillespie asked for the issue to be resolved *in terminis* and in favour of sitting at the table, while Rutherford argued strongly that this method was the most convenient.

By this time the English members of the original committee, with the exceptions of Herle and Goodwin, seem to have gone along with the Scots, Marshall said that "The intent of the committee was, that the people should all sit down at the table, company after company", but he balked when Burgess, with Rutherford's backing, suggested that the arrangement of the English parish churches should be changed to conform to this new way of taking communion.[48] The end of that debate, as we have noted, was the addition of a clause that seemed to say one thing, but was probably intended to include everything else.

The following day (Friday, June 21st,) before the debate could be carried to other things, Rutherford interposed, and again strenuously argued for the Scots mode of taking the communion. He also complained that the phrase "Where with conveniency it may be" would "give offence to the church of Scot-

---

[44] Baillie, *Letters and Journals*, II. 195; cf. *supra* p. 363, n. 26.

[45] And about which, where it may with convenience be, the communicants are orderly placed about it". Lightfoot, *Journal*, p. 287.

[46] *Ibid.* p. 286.

[47] *Ibid.*

[48] *Ibid.* pp. 286f.

land."[49] It was therefore suggested after some debate to add a hint in the preface about the possible rearrangement of church furniture. "Yet", said Lightfoot, "when this was drawn up, we could not conclude upon it" and the matter was remanded to the committee.[50]

The debate on the sacrament continued,[51] but behind all the arguments the issue of how the communicants were to receive the communion remained unresolved. During the week from Monday 24th June to Friday 28th[52] the debate was mainly on the consecration of the bread and wine, but on the 28th the divines were again brought back to the problem of the tables. Gillespie again maintained the necessity of sitting at the table for communion, but Nye replied that although the sacrament itself is "an institution & a pure ordinance", a table is simply a consequence.[53] Rutherford declared "We contend for the necessity of a table", and this led Charles Herle to make the comment, "in this debate we may possibly create more Institutions & sacramentalls than ther is cause". He maintained that "all the externall sacramentalls is the eating of bread & [drinking of] wine", and added that "if ther ware no table all[,] that [which] ought to be done may be done without it[.]"[54]

Henderson claimed that in the Church of Scotland they were "all of one mind in this poynt", and that the French churches in London used the same method.[55] Rutherford supported him, but Goodwin said that there were two sorts of signs or symbols in the sacrament – the one sacramental and essential, the other accessory and presumably inessential. William Bridge observed with a certain irony (or sarcasm, according to one's point of view,) "our brethren of Scot[land] have been helpfull to us in reformation, let us helpe them in this poynt by beating of it out".[56] The issue, said Bridge, was whether those who did not actually sit at the table could partake of it, while Goodwin, in making the distinction between essentials and inessentials that

---

[49] *Ibid.* p. 287.

[50] *Ibid.*

[51] On Friday 21st the debate was mostly about the distribution of bread and wine, but the Assembly could not decide whether communicants should break the bread for themselves. *Ibid.* pp. 288f.

[52] Lightfoot was in Munden throughout this week.

[53] TMs. II. 204 (Ms. II. f. 106.) For the whole debate on June 28th, cf. *ibid.* 204–208 (Ms. II. ff. 105–108.)

[54] *Ibid.* 205 (Ms. II. f. 101b.)

[55] He omitted to mention that the French churches in France did it differently.

[56] TMs. II. 206 (Ms. II. f. 107.)

he had made earlier said "Christ doth not put the honour in that sitting at table, but that he serves them".[57]

From the debate on July 1st[58] it is clear that many of the English leaders felt under obligation to their alliance with the Scots and wanted to accommodate them if at all possible. It is also clear that the Scots were fully prepared to use whatever sense of obligation there was to get their way. So Stephen Marshall said "it would be most comely for us to commend the practise of it[,] though we doe not stand upon an Institution". Gataker agreed as long as it could be done conveniently, but he added that he did not think there was "any necessity in the thing".[59] That probably indicates how far the other English leaders wanted to go to meet the Scots demands; they were willing to go along with the method, but they did not believe there was any *jus divinum* attached to it, or that it was in any sense necessary.

That was not far enough for the Scots, who seem to have thought that they had a right to expect the Assembly to endorse their practice. Rutherford, while insisting that he and his colleagues were not claiming a divine institution for their method of taking communion, protested that "the word convenient will hold out to all churches a cleare condemnation of all churches [which do this] & in particular the church of Scotland".[60] Of course, that was nonsense, but the Scots were adept at bringing pressure on the English divines, and if they could not in this instance prey on their fears, they could still exert constraint on the divines' sense of obligation.

The Assembly moved on temporarily to other things on July 2nd,[61] but on the 3rd the issue was revived. Herbert Palmer, on behalf of the committee, proposed that the form of words to be used in the Directory should read, "It is likewise desired, or recommended, that the communicants receive at the table";[62]

---

[57] *Ibid.* 207 (Ms. II. f. 107b.)

[58] *Ibid.* 209–212 (Ms. II. ff. 108b–110.)

[59] *Ibid.* 210 (Ms. II. f. 109.)

[60] *Ibid.* 210f. (Ms. II. ff. 109, 109b.)

[61] The debate on the 2nd was on whether a minister should exhort the communicants (in the Scots fashion) or remain silent during the actual act of taking the bread and wine (as practised by the Independents.) Cf. *Ibid.* 212–216 (Ms. II. ff. 110–112,) Lightfoot, *Journal*, pp. 289ff.

There was an interesting liturgical point in this debate. Herle and the Independents were for receiving the elements in silence, but Henderson spoke up for the 'sursum corda' or something like it. He said that he saw no more wrong with this than for a minister while preaching to call on the congregation to heed his words. TMs. II. 213 (Ms. II. f. 110b.) This is one of the very few references to the traditional words of the liturgy during the debate.

[62] Lightfoot, *Journal*, p. 291.

but when Dr. Gouge spoke out "against many removals", he was immediately lectured by Rutherford, who declared that "the Scots' church indeed holds it a thing most necessary, that all the communicants should come and sit at table; yet, for peace and conformity's sake, they desired that it might be recommended only." This is the first sign that the Scots were beginning to realize that the mood of the Assembly was firmly against their method.

Herle said that anything simply recommended was not *jure divino*, and they were recommending something contrary to the practice in other Reformed churches such as France. In any case, he spoke of "an impossibility of coming up to this in our land", and the contest continued with Herle and Nye 'mightily' opposing the committee's proposal, and with Gouge and Seaman suggesting that the clause should be discarded. When the session ended, the problem was still with them.[63]

A sharp edge appeared in this debate. Earlier, Palmer had tried to smooth over the ruffled feelings of the Scots Commissioners by observing that "we who have been gratified . . . ought to give satisfaction to the church of Scotland",[64] but Nye had stubbornly maintained that "if they simply commanded it, then they held it to be of divine institution";[65] and, of course, if that were so, then the opposition had a right to be given some scriptural proof. The rough edge appeared when Rutherford made the sarcastic comment that if any exception had been taken to the fact that "something [is] granted in favour of us, [there is] noe reason to take exception at this for it is normal in this assembly".[66] Perhaps the most remarkable thing about this somewhat obscure comment is the reaction it produced. The session closed with Humphrey Chambers anxiously trying to mediate, and with Gataker, Hardwick and Wincop at pains to explain why they were opposing the Scots demands.[67] In a more sceptical age we might be tempted to wonder if any members of the Assembly had particular reasons to feel 'gratified' to the Scots Commissioners.

The debate was taken up again on Thursday, July 4th,[68] with the Scots still demanding "it to be done as necessary", and Nye

---

[63] *Ibid.* p. 293.

[64] The sentence in the Minutes is obscure, but at least it says this. TMs. II. 218 (Ms. II. f. 113.)

[65] *Ibid.* 219 (Ms. II. f. 113b.)

[66] *Ibid.* 220 (Ms. II. f. 114.) It is difficult to see how this comment could have been anything but very heavy irony at least.

[67] *Ibid.* 220f. (Ms. II. ff. 114, 114b.)

[68] *Ibid.* 221–6 (Ms. II. ff. 114b–117,) Lightfoot, *Journal*, pp. 292f.

and Herle insisting that the practice was not lawful. Both sides were becoming noticeably more obstinate as a result of the argument in the Assembly, although the leaders of the English Puritan majority tried to take a moderating position while leaning as far as possible in the Scots direction. So Palmer summarized the three positions in the debate:

1. some thinke it necessary to come successive[;]
2. others thinke it is unlawfull to come successive[;]
   these two can never be reconciled or agree in a
   recommendation[.]
3. ther is a third that it is lawfull, lawfull & not
   soe convenient, others lawfull & the best, these
   2 may be reconciled in phrases[.][69]

He then moved – that they should debate whether it was 'lawful' to come successively to the table, and Marshall agreed with him. This may indicate the extent to which Palmer and Marshall wanted to emphasize support for the Scots against the Independents, for if Palmer's motion had stood it would clearly have united the first and third positions outlined above. Others still had reservations. Gouge, for example, thought it would be inappropriate to debate the lawfulness or unlawfulness of the mode, "for certainly it is but a matter of expedience."[70]

Despite their unwillingness to go all the way with the Scots, the English leaders were clearly anxious to mollify them as far as possible. So when Philip Nye said that they had a proposal "that seemes to begin wher institution leaves us", Stephen Marshall sprang to their defence and said "our brethren of Scotland never urged us to take it up of divine Institution but only soe to recommend it as not to cast a blemish upon their practise". Therefore he suggested that they should "inquire not whether [it is] against an Institution but whether against order & decency & edification".[71]

The problem was that in the bitterness of this debate on a relatively non-theological issue, both sides had been pushed to extremes from which it was difficult to extricate themselves. The Scots had so insisted on the necessity of following their method of taking communion that they had virtually put it on the level of a divine institution, even although they knew they could not sustain that position biblically. Their opponents on the other hand had been pushed into the position of representing the method of

---

[69] TMs. II. 222 (Ms. II. f. 115.)
[70] Ibid.
[71] Ibid. 223 (Ms. II. f. 115b.)

communicating by successive tables as unlawful or even as 'sinful', which clearly it was not, and that position was equally untenable. Both sides were now unprofitably busy attacking the more extreme and indefensible features of their opponents' position.

The wind blew from the same inhospitable quarter on Friday, July 5th,[72] when Herle said he was "sorry that the counsell of the pope in [the] councill of Trent is taken[,] to imbitter the partyes as much as may be by making the difference as wide as may be". He thought that "the practise of the church of Scotland was sufficiently secured in the former [wording of the proposition.]"[73] That was probably true, but Herle was on much less certain ground when he argued that the Scots position did not conduce to edification because it separated the church into several congregations by coming to the table in different groups. Edmund Calamy answered that adequately when he said that "the unity of the congregation is the unity of the consecration, the bread is blessed to them all": no more division was caused by coming up to the table in successive groups than by "the handling of the bread & wine from one to another."[74]

On the same date Robert Baillie sent his report to William Spang:

> As for the Assemblie, Mr. Nye, and his good friend, Mr. Herle, hes keept us these three weeks on one point of our Directorie alone, the recommending of the communicants coming up to the table to communicate. Their way of communicating, of some at the table, and some about it, without any succession of companies to more tables, is that whereupon we stick, and are like to stick longer.[75]

Of course, it will be a matter of opinion as to who was responsible for the delay in the Assembly, for if Nye and Herle were obstinate in their opposition, the Scots had been equally adamant in what they demanded, and it had been clear from the start that most of the Assembly did not endorse this particular procedure, although for one reason or another many divines were willing to give the Scots method a trial.[76]

---

[72] *Ibid.* 227–34 (Ms. II. ff. 117b–121.)

[73] *Ibid.* 227 (Ms. II. f. 117b.)

[74] *Ibid.* 228 (Ms. II. f. 118.)

[75] July 5th, *Letters and Journals*, II. 201.

[76] A week or so later Baillie wrote to Spang: "In our Assemblie we goe on as we may. The Independents and others keeped us long three weeks upon one point alone, the communicating at a table. By this we came to debate, the diverse coming up of companies successively to a table; the consecrating of the bread and wine severallie; the giving of the bread to all the congregation, and then the wine to all, and so twice coming up to the table, first for the bread, and then for the wine; the mutual distribution, the table-exhortations,

In the middle of the debate on Monday July 8th Philip Nye finally came to the position he and his friends should probably have taken all along. He agreed that "a thing may be lawfull in some sence or other[,] but not absolutely to be commanded but conditionally", and George Gillespie remarked, "I am glad to have him after 2 dayes debate against it to come to this conclusion".[77]

Having removed the issue of debating a tacit *jus divinum* in regard to the Scots practice, the Assembly began to debate the expediency of this method of communicating, and at once the Independents revealed that behind their opposition there was a similar claim of their own. Goodwin maintained that "according to the institution the bread is to be given to all & then the cup".[78] In practice this would have meant that if successive tables were the method each group would have to come to the table twice, first for the bread and then for the wine. Rutherford at once noted the inconvenience of that, and Marshall remarked ironically that if this were indeed an institution, "then we should be humbled for our neglect[,] for that hath never been observed any[where.]"[79]

So the debate passed from a debate on coming up to the table in successive groups to a debate on whether the whole congregation should partake of the bread before any were offered the wine. This began on Tuesday July 9th,[80] but behind it was the earlier issue, and behind that the confrontation of two ecclesiologies that each claimed *jus divinum*. One suspects that the time had come for the offer of a fair trade, and none was quicker to recognize that than Stephen Marshall. He moved that there should be a new attempt at accommodation, but Lightfoot says that "the conclusion of all which was, that the whole business was recommitted: but a huge business there was upon it before we could conclude upon terms of recommitment: but, at last, the matter was put to the question, and voted to be recommitted, even the whole business about coming up to the table."[81]

---

and a world of such questions, which to the most of them were new and strange things. After we were overtoyled with debate, we were forced to leave all these things, and take us to generall expressions, which, by a benigne exposition, would infer our church-practices, which the most promised to follow, so much the more as we did not necessitate them by the Assemblie's express determinations. We have ended the matter of the Lord's Supper, and these last three dayes have been upon Baptisme." 12th July, 1644, *ibid.* p. 204.

[77] TMs. II. 238 (Ms. II. f. 123.)
[78] *Ibid.*
[79] *Ibid.* 239 (Ms. I. f. 123b.)
[80] *Ibid.* 240–243 (Ms. II. ff. 124–125.)
[81] Lightfoot, *Journal*, p. 294.

Apparently everyone had had more than enough,[82] and on the following day (Wednesday, July 10th), we read:

> Mr. *Palmer* reported from the committee for accommodation, concerning the communicants' coming to the table: which was to this purpose, – that all the business about coming in companies to the table was left out, and the passage was only this, – 'the communicants orderly sitting about the table,' &c. and no more mention of any posture: which the commissioners of Scotland consented to, only desired, that they might impart so much to their General Assembly: and promised to do it with all reverence and respect to this Assembly."[83]

So in the end that was passed, and the only person to vote against it was John Ley, who a month earlier had said that he 'consented to any posture,' but who still felt that the proposal tied communicants "too strictly to sitting."

The debate on baptism lasted from Thursday, 11th July until the Assembly broke for its summer recess on Monday, July 22nd,[84] and although it may not have been all sweetness and light, it did not repeat the frustrating bitterness of the preceding debate on the purely circumstantial aspects of the Lord's Supper. There was a flurry of dissent on the strong stand taken by the committee that baptism should be performed in church, rather than in private houses as was normal in English parishes. However, this time the Scots, their most ardent supporters, and the Independents were on the same side of the debate, leaving the somewhat feeble opposition to be voiced by members of an almost-docile English majority. These men were more concerned with the practical problem of changing the patterns of English custom, for on July 11th Edmund Calamy admitted, "I confesse a great abuse in the citty[:] in 2 or 3 years none [were] baptized in the church [for] the ministers could not get the people to bring them".[85] He recognized that in the parishes they had to deal with the sullen weight of conservative and even 'catholic' prejudice that was only slowly finding its way into the national form of a Protestant Church.

Perhaps this was the reason Calamy argued that, like the rite of circumcision in the Old Testament, "Baptisme properly is noe

---

[82] There was also the problem of members not being paid. Baillie notes some time at the end of June that "many of the Assemblie are departed for want of means." To Robert Ramsay, *Letters and Journals*, II. 196.

[83] Lightfoot, *Journal*, p. 296.

[84] *Ibid*. pp. 296–9, TMs. II. 242–268 (Ms. II. ff. 125–138.)

[85] TMs. II. 244 (Ms. II. f. 126.)

church ordinance",[86] and even Stephen Marshall appears to have been against making baptism in church an absolute rule.[87] With regard to private baptism and its legality, Whitaker said "that which god hath made to be lawfull noe man is to count unlawfull".[88] But the provision was passed, and even Baillie was surprised with the ease with which that happened:

> We have carryed, with much greater ease than we expected, the publickness of baptisme. The abuse was great over all this land. In the greatest parosch in London, scarce one child in a-year was brought to the church for baptisme. Also we have carried the parents presenting of his child, and not their midwives, as was their universall custome.[89]

The opposition was a testimony to the persistence of conservative sentiment in England, and perhaps the relative ease with which the measure for public baptism was passed was due less to the persuasiveness of the arguments on the other side, than to the impatience of the majority for the early settlement of the English Church.

As in the case of the Lord's Supper, every aspect of the administration of the sacrament was debated in the Assembly. The divines considered the time when a child should be brought to church for baptism,[90] the matter of placing the child in the parents' arms and the question of godparents,[91] the rubrics for the minister in the service,[92] and baptismal regeneration.[93] There was also a long debate on the extent to which a child was to be regarded as a member of the church.[94] They discussed the responses to be made by parents,[95] the relationship of inward to outward baptism,[96] the form of benediction,[97] and finally the vexed question of 'dipping.' This was a particularly sensitive subject in view of the numerical growth of Baptists in the City and in other parts of the country, and the anxiety surfaced during the debate. Most of the divines seem to have recognized the legitimacy of this mode and wanted it to be acknowledged in the

---

[86] *Ibid.*
[87] *Ibid.* 248 (Ms. II. f. 128.)
[88] *Ibid.* 249 (Ms. II. f. 128b.)
[89] To Spang, 12th July, 1644; *Letters and Journals*, II. 204f.
[90] 12th July; TMs. II. 251 (Ms. II. f. 129b.)
[91] *Ibid.* 252 (Ms. II. f. 130.)
[92] 15th July; *ibid.*
[93] *Ibid.* 252–5 (Ms. II. ff. 130b–131b.)
[94] 15th–16th July; *ibid.* 255–261 (Ms. II. 131b–134b.)
[95] *Ibid.* 261 (Ms. II. f. 134b.)
[96] 19th July; *ibid.* 261–3 (Ms. II. ff. 134b–135b.)
[97] *Ibid.* 263 (Ms. II. f. 135b.)

Directory,[98] but others, including the Scots, were anxious to exclude anything that might throw doubt on the practice of sprinkling.[99]

So the Assembly reached its summer recess, and the first respite the divines had had from their work since it had started a year before. Lightfoot says that he returned to Westminster from Munden on Monday, July 22nd, "and when I came, I found that the Assembly had met this morning, and adjourned themselves till Wednesday fortnight; having now sitten a twelvemonth, and never adjourned of all the time."[100] They needed the rest.

III

Affairs public and private

Robert Baillie never once spoke on the floor of the Assembly, and yet none of the Scottish Commissioners worked more persistently or more successfully than he to achieve the goals of the Kirk. Throughout this time he was indefatigably carrying on his correspondence with his kinsman, William Spang, and others to win the support and assistance of Reformed churches abroad for what he and his colleagues were doing in the Assembly. Spang as minister of Campvere in the Netherlands was well placed to engage the help of the Dutch churches, but Baillie wanted to enlist the support of all the Reformed churches and scholars of the Continent in the Scots campaign to win the Church of England to the cause of Presbyterian Calvinism. The tone and the import of his later correspondence were set by a letter that he wrote to Spang as early as December, 1643. He not only warned Spang of the communication that the Assembly would be sending to the Dutch churches, but he gave a clear indication of the kind of reply the Scots would find most useful:

I have been thinking yow may doe good service in this particular. There is shortlie to come from the Assemblie here, and us Commissioners from Scotland, letters in Latine to all the Reformed churches, and among the rest, to yow of Zeland and Holland. It is my earnest desyre, if by some of the eminent brether there, yow can obtain, in their answers, which I hope will come, some clauses to be insert, of the churches of Holland and Zeland [their] grave counsell, and earnest desyre, that, according to our profession in our late Covenant, taken now be both the Assemblies of Scotland and England, we

---

[98] E.g., Nye, Burroughes, Tuckney, Gataker, Ley, Seaman.
[99] E.g., Woodcock, Arrowsmith, Palmer; 22nd July, *ibid.* 264–8 (Ms. II. ff. 136–8.)
[100] Lightfoot, *Journal*, p. 299.

would be carefull in our reformation, after the word, to have an eye to that Discipline wherein all the Reformed churches doe agree; and that we be verie diligent to eshew that democratick anarchy and independencie of particular congregations, which they know to be opposite to the word of God, and destructive whollie of that Discipline, wherby they, and the whole Reformed churches do stand. If by your dealing, such clauses could be gotten put into your letters unto us, and in the letters of the churches of France, Switze, Geneva and others, by the means of your good friends Dr. Rivett and Spanheim, or some others, it might doe us much good: for however we stick here on manie things, yet the great and dangerous difference will be from the Independent faction, to whom it would be a great dashe, if not onlie we in Scotland, but they also of Holland, France, and Switze, who are alyke interested, would give a tymeous warning upon the occasion, from this, against the great and common enemies of that Discipline which is common to us all. Think what yow can gett done here.[101]

Baillie kept up his pressure on his Dutch connection. "Faill not when our letters come, as quicklie they will," he wrote to Spang, "to obtaine from your folks, and, if ye can, from these of Switze, France, and Geneva, ane grave and weightie admonition to this Assemblie to be carefull to suppresse all schismaticks, and the mother and foster of all, the independencie of congregations."[102] And the first-fruits from these efforts were seen when a letter arrived in March from the Classis of Walcheren specifically attacking the views expressed in *An Apologeticall Narration*, which Baillie said had been received by the Assembly "with a great deal of respect." He also told Spang that it had come "wonderfull opportunelie" and he thought it would "doe a great deall of good."[103]

But there is evidence in Baillie's letters that some people in Westminster had begun to think the letter from Walcheren was a little bit too true to be good. It was too apposite to the situation in the Assembly, and it had been written almost as if the Dutch churches had been specifically briefed about what had been happening and how to word their reply best to further the Scots' interest! None, of course, had admitted having done anything like that, and therefore Baillie told Spang that the Scots had graciously "let such a calumnie pass, without an apologie." At

---

[101] The letter is dated 7th December, 1643, but Baillie made it clear that this passage had been added after Spang's letter of the 11th December had been received; *Letters and Journals*, II. 115.

[102] To Spang, 1st January, 1643/4, *ibid.* p. 128.

[103] To Spang, 10th March, 1643/4, *ibid.* pp. 143f.

the same time, he thought that many of the divines wished that other churches in Europe would do what the Walcheren Classis had done,

> But I heard them say, in private, that they had no correspondence at all with any forraigne Churches; it might be, that some of them had sometimes letters from the Minister of the Scotts Staple at Camp-veere, but that none of them had sent him either the Apologeticall Naratione, or so much as our Ansuer to it; that they had never motioned any censure of that book by the forraigne Divines. How-ever, in the good providence of God, that letter came. It is expected that the Synod of Zeland will not onlie avow what their brethren hes written, but will give their brotherlie advyce to this Synod, anent all the things in hand; which, I assure you, will be very well taken, and doe much good; especiallie, if with their serious dissuasive from Independencie, and cordiall exhortation to erect Presbytries and Synods, they joyne their counsells for abolishing the relicks of Romish superstition, in their festivall dayes, and Liturgie, etc. and above all, to beware of any tolleration of sects, wherein yow are ane evill and dangerous example. If yow assist us at this time, God may make us helpfull to yow another day.[104]

Baillie was entirely impenitent about his activities, which were obviously intended to give the providence of God a little assistance. However, his words here unconsciously throw light on the religious situation in England at that time, by revealing the major features in that society against which he wanted Spang's friends to raise their protest – first, the idea that all forms of religion should be tolerated, and secondly, the persistence of 'Romish superstition' in the habits, customs, and perhaps affections of the English populace.

Baillie was somewhat chagrined to find that the replies from foreign churches were not always helpful. One passage in the letter from Walcheren had even gone too far in the direction of Independency, and Baillie had asked Spang to see that the sentiment was corrected in the letter he expected from the Synod of Zeeland.[105] On March 12th, De la March, one of the French

---

[104] *Ibid.* p. 144.
[105] "The tenets of Independents yow know: I wrote to yow the great harm of that clause of your Walcheren letter, of the entire power of government in the hands of congregational presbytries, except in cases of alteration and difficultie, &c. Not only the Independents make use of it publicklie against us, but some of our prime men, Mr. Marshall by name, upon it and Voetius, who from Parker hes the same, dissents from us, giving excommunication, and, which is more, ordination, to our sessions in all ordinarie cases. If yow can gett this helped in the Zeland letter, it will be well; for other divines, in the face of the Assemblie, Seaman by name, hes been forced to decline with all reverence your authoritie, saying, that Voetius was bot one man, and the classis of Walcheren but one

ministers in London, had reported the embarrassment which the Assembly's letters had caused the Protestants of France,[106] while the reply received from Hesse-Cassel had been totally unacceptable because it advised the English divines not to get rid of their bishops![107] For all that, the Assembly was anxious to have its efforts known and supported by churches abroad, and on April 2nd it voted to put copies of its letter to foreign churches into the hands of merchants travelling to such places as Sweden and Transylvania.[108]

Baillie himself was indefatigable, although his own efforts were designed not simply to inform the churches about what had been happening in England, but to enlist their support in the program set down by the Scots. Nothing that threatened the full success of the Scots program was to be tolerated,[109] and no fact that could be used to the disparagement of the Independents was ignored,[110] and his communications with Spang end with the refrain, "Be diligent, we beseech yow, with your Synod."[111]

On April 26th he was even more ambitious in his requests to Spang. He said that he and his colleagues were "all very sensible of your prudent diligence" and approved the suggestion to refer some of these questions to Dutch theologians. Indeed, he suggested that "these whom yow have engaged in Zeland" might be encouraged to combine their efforts with the theologians of Leyden to write against the Scots' opponents in the Assembly. They might write what they liked against the bishops and ceremonies, he said,

> but above all, and in earnest, let them exhort to be watchfull against anarchicall schismes, and the heresies of Antinomians and Anabaptists. These three come togidder cordiallie against all the Reformed churches, and increases so much in number and boldness, as easilie they would carry all here to a lamentable confusion, if the fear of our armies did not keep them in order; and, as it is, many fears they shall doe much [evil], if God prevent it not.[112]

---

classis; that the Acts of your General Assemblies, and Harmonie of Confessions, gives the power of excommunication and ordination in ordinarie cases to your Classes, and not to your parochiall Consistories." 12th April, 1644, ibid. p. 165.

[106] Lightfoot, Journal, p. 207. Cf. supra pp. 306, n. 186.

[107] Ibid. p. 245 (April 11th,) Baillie, Letters and Journals, II. 164f.

[108] Lightfoot, Journal, p. 235.

[109] E.g., Baillie strongly disapproved of John Durie's ecumenical efforts. 19th April, 1644, Letters and Journals, II. 166. Cf. supra p. 125, n. 66.

[110] He was at pains to point out that there was "in all New England, no libertie of living for a Presbyterian." Ibid., p. 168.

[111] Ibid.

[112] To Spang, 26th April, 1644; ibid. p. 169.

In that same letter he revealed that it was deliberate policy that caused the Scots and their friends to postpone sending to Parliament the Assembly's recommendations concerning presbyterial government, since they were not anxious for the Independents to publish the reasons for their dissent,[113] and he thought it would be helpful if some French theologians could be persuaded to write privately to Spang and his collaborators on church government. However, they should be very circumspect in writing about the powers of the civil magistrate. "I wish", he advised explicitly, "they might speak home to that yow assure is their practice, of giving ordination only to the classes, and excommunication, at least for regulating of the processe", because that is what the Scots believed: "We count it a *causa communis*, and of so high a consequence as can be, to cutt off a member, not from one congregation only, but the whole church and bodie of Christ."[114]

Lightfoot tells us that on April 29th the Assembly received letters from Zeeland of "the same tenor as those of Walachria [Walcheren]: and the same dislike of the Apologetic narration, and a promise to say something in time to it."[115] In his letter thanking William Spang, Baillie said that "a better turne could not have been done to us",[116] and because of his success with the Dutch churches he enlisted the help of David Buchanan, who had been resident in France. Again he left his correspondent in no doubt about what he wanted:

> I conceive it very expedient, that yow write to some of the ministers of Paris, Geneva, and Berne, the true estate of our affairs, how that a mighty faction is arisen, to press liberty of conscience for all sects, at least a freedom for Morellius's popular government of the Church; that the Scotts, and most of the Synod and Parliament, are for the establishing of the Government by synods and classes. It would encourage them much, if the Divines of Geneva and Switzerland would, in their answers to the synod's letter, as the Divines of Zeland hes done in their letter, and the Divines of Hessia also, exhort the synod at some length, and in earnest, to beware of that pernicious

---

[113] "To prevent a present rupture with the Independents, we were content not to give in our propositions of Presbytries and Congregations, that we might not necessitate them to give in their remonstrance against our conclusions, which they are peremptor to doe when we come on that matter. We judged it also convenient to delay till we had gone through the whole matters of the Presbytries and Synods; to send them up rather in their full strength than by pieces". *Ibid.* pp. 169f.

[114] *Ibid.* p. 170.

[115] *Journal*, p. 254.

[116] 3rd May, 1644; *Letters and Journals*, II. 174.

liberty of all sects, and in particular of these who are enemies to the discipline of all the Reformed.[117]

Surely this letter was a little less than ingenuous, since he had already complained to Spang that the letter from Hesse had been "but a poor short epistle",[118] but doubtless in Baillie's view, the end justified the means. There was, after all, "a golden occasion in hand, if improved, to gett England conforme in worship and government to the rest of the Reformed", although he was careful to say that if the French ministers could not write publicly, Buchanan should get them to write privately to their friends in England or Holland. He had no hesitation in expecting Buchanan to engage in the widest possible activity in promoting the Scots' plan.[119]

But this ecclesiastical diplomacy could backfire. The letter from Zeeland, like the earlier one from Walcheren, contained material that could be used by the Scots' opponents. "The letter of your classes of Zeland," he complained to Spang, "I feare it shall here be drained, as well as that of Walcheren, because the Independents, on the occasion of the clause of the Magistrate, works, by their too many friends, on the Parliament to suppress it."[120] He suggested that Spang should get it printed in the Netherlands and some copies sent over, and he was enthusiastic about Apollonius's plan of publishing certain fundamental queries for the Independents to answer.[121] He also told Spang to

---

[117] N.d., but placed by David Laing at the beginning of May; *ibid.* pp. 179f.

[118] *Ibid.* p. 165.

[119] "You would write for the same purpose to Moulin in Sedan and Spanheim in Leyden. It were good if they writte, that their letters were conceived in the greatest names they could procure; the Theologie of Berne would get a letter from the Switz Church, these of Geneva from their whole Ecclesiastic classes, Moulin from the University of Sedan and Spanheim from the University Leyden. It were not ill, that in all their letters, they congratulate the abolition of Episcopacie and Popish ceremonies, and exhorted to sett up quickly the government of Christ; that so long an annarchie as hes been here, is the mother of Heresies and Schismes, and many more evils." Memorandum to Mr. Buchanan; *ibid.* p. 180.

[120] To Spang, undated, but to be placed in early May; *ibid.*

[121] *Ibid.* William Apollonius, minister of the Dutch church in Middleburg, published a series of questions addressed to the Independents, *Consideratio qvarvndam controversiarum, ad regimen ecclesiae Dei spectantium, quae in Angliae regno hodie agitantur, ex Mandato & Jussu Walachrinae Conscripta*, 1644. [English version published in 1645 as *A Consideration of Certaine Controversies at this time agitated in the Kingdome of England, concerning the Government of the Church of God. Written at the command and appointment of the Walachrian Classis by G. A.*] Baillie speculated that the reply would be written by John Cotton, (*Letters and Journals*, II. 190) but it was actually John Norton's *Responsio*, which appeared in 1648. Cf. Douglas Horton's introduction to John Norton's *The Answer*, and my note in the 1963 edition of *An Apologeticall Narration*, p. 48, note 11.

keep an eye on young Patrick Forbes of Delft, who had written a useful criticism of *An Apologeticall Narration* that Baillie wanted to see in print.[122]

Baillie was absolutely tireless, and in the main he was careful to give his correspondents accurate information. For example, in a postscript he was careful to distinguish between the attitude to liberty of conscience taken by the Independents of the Assembly and the Congregationalists of New England,[123] but he noted that in all other matters they appeared to be of one mind, and that with regard to their polity, "a presbytrie to them is our session, and our presbytrie is their synod."[124] Baillie also tried to keep up with the latest work in theology, constantly asked Spang to send him books, and kept urging him to get distinguished foreign churchmen, like Gisbert Voet, to write in their cause.

He had no moral qualms about any of these activities, although he knew that members of the Assembly were expressly forbidden to reveal any of the Assembly's work or to enter into correspondence about it with those outside Westminster. Even in a letter in which he explained this to Spang, and pointed out that the churches abroad could therefore not expect to get a request for help from any member of the Assembly,[125] he gave his correspondent explicit instructions about the subjects on which he wanted the theologians to write in order to refute the Independents. Against all the rules the Assembly had imposed on its own members he provided a comprehensive summary of the Presbyterians' arguments, so that any foreign writer would know the positions that had to be defended.[126]

Undoubtedly he and his friends would have excused themselves by pointing out that they were not members of the Assembly but Commissioners of a sister church and nation; but in any case, despite Baillie's best endeavours, he did not enjoy the success he had expected, for in September we find him complaining to William Spang that the "unkindliness of all the Reformed churches to us at these times is great. It's England's merit, but it may be the great sin of these who hes no charity, nor so much zeale as prudence."[127]

---

[122] Baillie was able to get it printed; cf. *Letters and Journals*, pp. 181, 193.
[123] 17th May, *ibid.* p. 183.
[124] *Ibid.*
[125] *Ibid.* p. 202. Dr. Daniel Featley had been ejected from the Assembly and had his living sequestered for passing on information of the Assembly's affairs.
[126] *Ibid.* pp. 202–5, but especially pp. 202, 205.
[127] To Spang, 13th September, 1644, *ibid.* p. 227.

IV

The 'Second Battle of Marston Moor'

Writing a letter of condolence to Valentine Walton on the death of his son at the battle of Marston Moor, Cromwell declared, "Truly England and the Church of God hath had a great favour from the Lord, in this great victory given unto us, such as the like never was since this war began. . . . God made them as stubble to our swords, we charged their regiments of foot with our horse, routed all we charged."[128] That is the context in which the presbyterian success in the Assembly and Baillie's diplomatic activities have to be seen: an outstanding victory in which the Independents' sectarian supporters in the army showed that they were indispensable to the Parliamentary cause.

One of Baillie's persistent disappointments in 1644 was the modest performance of the Scots army. They had come in with such high hopes, but a great deal had taken place since the last month of 1643 when Baillie had described the London mood in the words, "All things are expected from God and the Scotts",[129] and there was not much to be credited to the Scots on the field of battle. From the first, Alexander Henderson had recognized what happened in the Assembly was directly related to what happened in the field.[130] Indeed, in spite of all Baillie's grumbling about the delays caused by the Independents, – "they have studied procrastination of all things" – in January he had admitted to his friends in Scotland that "We indeed did not much care for delayes, till the breath of our armie might blow upon us some more favour and strength."[131]

The army had been long enough in coming, and even after its arrival the brisk breeze that Baillie had anticipated was not much in evidence. Baillie had complained in April, "this was our griefe, that little honour would come to our armie, who had so long done so little," although he was quick to remind possible critics that the presence of Scots troops had kept the Earl of Newcastle's forces tied up in the north.[132] But it was not much, and certainly not enough to convince the English that victory for their cause was in the hands of the Scots. The net result of the Scottish excursion into England had been poor. It was true that Major-General Lawrence Crawford managed to oust Oliver

---

[128] W. C. Abbott, *Writings and Speeches of Oliver Cromwell*, I. 287.

[129] *Letters and Journals*, II. 114f.

[130] Cf. the reference *supra* p. 239. To Spang, 17th November, 1643, *ibid*. p. 104.

[131] For Scotland, 1st January, 1643/4, *ibid*. p. 122

[132] To Spang, 19th April, 1644, *ibid*. p. 167.

Cromwell from the affections of the Earl of Manchester, and had begun to purge the Army of the Eastern Association of its sectaries; but in consequence the command of that army had been set at loggerheads, and Crawford's efforts laid the groundwork for dissensions that could have wrecked the entire military enterprise. Then there had been Crawford's foolhardy attempt in early June to gain credit by springing a mine and storming the fortifications of York (unsuccessfully) without consulting his fellow commanders. Even Baillie had to condemn that.[133]

Apparently the Scottish divines had not been slow to express their disquiet to their own officers, but these officers showed how well they understood the principles of Calvinist theology in dealing with their own men of the cloth.

> We hope things in the Assemblie and Parliament may go more after our minde. Our armie oft signified to us, they conceaved their want of successe flowed most from God's anger at the Parliament and Assemblie, for their neglect of establishing of religion. We oft told them the truth, we had no hope of any progresse here, till God gave them victories; and then, we doubted not, all would run both in Parliament and Assemblie.[134]

Whatever Baillie and his colleagues may have said about Providence in the Assembly or from their pulpits, they had a fairly realistic understanding of the material factors that could spell success or failure for their goals.

The situation became all the more problematic for the Scots after the parliamentary victory before York at Marston Moor on July 2nd, 1644. The Royalist cavalry under Prince Rupert was initially so successful that no less than three of the parliamentary generals fled the field in the belief that the battle was already lost,[135] and there was a critical moment when Cromwell's troopers had been halted and Cromwell himself had received a slight wound. At that juncture, it appears, Cromwell's men received help from David Lesley and a small force of Scots cavalry that had been held in reserve, and this had given Cromwell and his men the time to regroup and remount their charge. They had been able not only to destroy the opposing cavalry on their own wing, but then wheeled and cut down the royalist foot in the

---

[133] Letter at the end of June to Robert Ramsay; *ibid.* p. 195.
[134] To Spang, 5th July, 1644; *ibid.* p. 201.
[135] Lord Fairfax, the Earl of Leven, and the Earl of Manchester.

centre, so that by the time Rupert's men had returned from plundering the baggage train, the field was lost for them.[136]

This great victory was followed by what we may call 'the second battle of Marston Moor,' fought not with broadswords by soldiers on a Yorkshire moor but with broadsheets by news vendors on the streets of London. The course of this bitter little struggle for favourable publicity may be traced in Robert Baillie's letters. At first he was sure the defeat of Rupert was a clear case of divine intervention. "But behold, in a moment," he wrote to Spang, "when our credit was beginning sensiblie to decay, God hes come in. Our army foughten Prince Rupert, hes overthrown his forces, taken his cannon and baggage, killed many of his chief officers, and chased the rest within Yorke." At this point Baillie seems already to be claiming the victory for Scottish arms. "We dare not be too much exalted," he said piously, "only we bless God from our heart, that is beginning to shyne on our armie, and make it, after very long expectation, and beating doune of our pride, to be a fountain of joy and hope to these that loves the wellfare of religion." Then Baillie continued with the exchange between the Scots ministers and their army officers in the passage quoted earlier,[137] and it is clear from this that he not only regarded Marston Moor as a great Scottish victory, but there is at least the hint that the victory was due to the determination of the Assembly to set up a Presbyterian Church.

That euphoria did not last long. His mood changed, if not to despair, certainly to very serious concern. To begin with, as the eye-witness accounts of the battle came in, Parliament began to realize how close it had come in that action to losing everything. Baillie's earlier elation was chastened: "God was mercifull to us. We were in sad condition". However, there was another serious reason for concern:

> The Independents sent up one quicklie, to assure, that all the glory of that night was theirs; that they, and their Generall-major[138] Cromwell, had done it all their alone: but Captaine Stuart afterward shew the vanitie and falsehood of their disgracefull relation. God gave us that victorie wonderfullie. There was three Generalls on each

---

[136] For Marston Moor see Sir Charles Firth's article, 'Marston Moor', *Transactions of the Royal Historical Society* (New Series,) 1898, XII; S. R. Gardiner, *G. C. W.*, I. 374–82; Abbott, *Writings and Speeches of O. C.*, I. 283–89; R. S. Paul, *The Lord Protector*, pp. 78–81, and other histories of the civil war.

[137] Cf. *supra* pp. 382f.; To Spang, 5th July, 1644, *Letters and Journals*, II. 201.

[138] Cromwell had the higher rank of Lieutenant-General in the Army of the Eastern Association.

side, Lesley,[139] Fairfax, and Manchester; Rupert, Newcastle, and King.[140] Within halfe an hour and less, all six took them to their heels; this to yow alone. The disadvantage of the ground, and the violence of the flower of Prince Rupert's horse, carried all our right wing doune . . . but the beginning of the victorie was from David Lesley, who before was much suspected of evill designes: he with the Scotts and Cromwell's horse, having the advantage of the ground, did dissipate all before them.[141]

The battle for public credit was no less bitter than the battle for York, and it lasted a long time with the Scots claiming that all the victory was due to David Lesley and even developing the *canard* that Cromwell had not even been present at the height of the action but had been nursing his wound.[142] On the other side, the English, and particularly the Independents, down-played David Lesley's part in the fight and gave the credit to Cromwell. Indeed, one of the Scots charged them with calling Cromwell the Saviour of the three kingdoms.[143]

The truth, as usual, seems to lie between both extreme positions. It was certainly true that David Lesley and his comparatively small force of cavalry arrived at the critical point when Cromwell's initial assault had been halted, and that had given Cromwell and his men time to re-form for the fresh onslaught that would win the day. In that sense 'the beginning of the victorie was from David Leslie'; but it is also clear that once that breathing-space had been gained, major credit for the brilliance of the counter-attack and the disciplined tactics of halting his men at the crucial point to turn them on the Royalist foot-soldiers in the centre, was Cromwell's alone.

What was most true of all, however, was that both parties exploited the news to the full in the capital in order to further their own interests in Church and State; and in that battle the Independents came out the clear victors. It appears that English people of whatever persuasion were more ready to give Cromwell credit for the victory than they were to accept it at the hands of

---

[139] Alexander Lesley, Earl of Leven. Here Baillie mentions only the principal Generals in full command of armies.

[140] James King, Lord Eythin, who had fought in Germany.

[141] To Spang, 12th July; *Letters and Journals*, II. 203f.

[142] E.g., the book by the Scot, David Buchanan, *Truth its Manifest*, published in 1645 persisted in the view that Cromwell was not present at the main action.

[143] Buchanan in *Truth its Manifest*. See Edward Bowles, *Manifest Truths, or an Inversion of Truths Manifest* (1646), and *Vindiciae Veritatis* (1647) attributed to Nathaniel Fiennes, son of William Fiennes, Lord Say. [The relevant passage in this work is quoted in *The Lord Protector*, pp. 401f., but the confusion there regarding its authorship should be corrected.]

the Scots,[144] and the more the latter tried to disparage Cromwell the more they found themselves discredited in the eyes of the public. Simeon Ashe, the Earl of Manchester's chaplain, was a member of the Assembly and no Independent, but to Baillie's disgust his account gave most of the credit of Marston Moor to Cromwell. In writing to Robert Blair,[145] Baillie admitted how crucial this victory had been, and he then went on to protest:

We were both grieved and angry, that your Independents there should have sent up Major Harrison[146] to trumpett over all the city their own praises, to our prejudice, making all believe, that Cromwell alone, with his unspeakablie valorous regiments, had done all that service; that the most of us fled; and who stayed, they fought so and so, as it might be. We were much vexed with these reports, against which yow were not pleased, any of yow, to instruct us with any ansuer, till Lindesay's letters came at last, and Captaine Stuart with his collors. Then we sent abroad our printed relations, and could lift up our face. But within three dayes Mr. Ashe's relation was also printed, who gives us many good words, but gives much more to Cromwell than we are informed is his due. Let good Mr. Ashe know what is the use that generallie here is made of his relations; much I know beside his intention: even in plain terms, the Independents have done so brave service, yea, they [are] so strong and considerable a party, that they must not only be tollerate, but in nothing grieved, and no wayes to be provocked. It seems very necessare, that since none of yow of purpose, and ordinarlie, sends up relations and Mr. Ashe sends to the presse constant intelligence of your actions, which, for the man's known integrity, are every word believed, your proceedings have a great influence in all affaires here both of Church and State; I say, it seems needfull that all Mr Ashe's letters which are sent hither to the presse, should be first seen and pondered by some of yow there. These are my own private motions, which I propone to yow alone, to be made use of as yow think fitt. I blesse God, who graciouslie saved your life in that so dangerous ane hour. Glory to his name. Farewell.

---

[144] This interpretation of the victory prevailed. Cf. Lucy Hutchinson's *Memoirs of the Life of Colonel Hutchinson*, (first published, 1806,) which was written many years later to justify her husband, John Hutchinson, the regicide. She described Marston Moor in these words: ". . . the Scots and my Lord Fairfax were wholly routed, and the battle lost; but that Cromwell, with five thousand men which he commanded, routed Prince Rupert, restored the other routed parliamentarians, and gained the most complete victory that had been obtained in the whole war." *Op. cit.* (London: Ingram, Cooke & Co edn., n. d.) p. 70.

[145] For Mr. Blair, n. d. (but clearly in July, 1644,) *Letters and Journals*, II. 208f. We assume that this was to Robert Blair, but the recipient must have been with the Scottish army at that time, and also in a position of some trust in the Scottish nation and church.

[146] Thomas Harrison (1606–60) was at that time Major in Charles Fleetwood's regiment. He later became a general and a leading Fifth Monarchist. He was executed as a regicide in 1660.

From the point of view of one who had absolutely no doubts about the campaign to win "unanimity in the Scots fashion",[147] and was fully prepared to exercise a little censorship on Simeon Ashe's dispatches to further that end, Baillie had good reason to be concerned, for he had correctly gauged the changing mood in England. The Independents' modest request in their *Apologeticall Narration* that they should themselves be tolerated was now not only backed by a successful army and a charismatic leader, but also by a growing body of public opinion both in the army and in the nation at large that would extend this plea to full liberty of conscience. Baillie had already noted the growth of sectarian opinion in the armed forces.[148] Time now seemed to be on the side of the Independents, and when the debates resumed in the Assembly the divines could expect more dramatic intrusions into their plans from the rough world of politics.

---

[147] Baillie, *ibid*. pp. 186f.
[148] To Spang, April 26th, 1644, *ibid*. p. 170; quoted *supra* p. 338, n. 138.

CHAPTER 13

THE PARTING

If Marston Moor on 2nd July, 1644, was a sign of the King's ultimate defeat, the battle of Naseby on 14th June, 1645, was its seal, and in both battles victory in the face of defeat was won by the generalship of Cromwell and the valour of his troops. At least, that is the way many English people viewed those events, and we must recognize that in a theological climate which saw God's providence in the successes and failures of this life, the meteoric rise of Cromwell could not be brushed aside as irrelevant. According to those principles and one's theological point of view, he had to be either the instrument of God or the agent of the devil. It was in the context of fear or exultation that the debates in the Assembly took place.

During the course of the year between Marston Moor and Naseby the break between the Independents and the Presbyterian majority on church government became final, and the Independents submitted their dissenting Reasons to the Assembly and Parliament. In all other branches of the Assembly's work they continued to participate, and by the end of 1645 the Assembly was well on its way to completing its work on the four parts of ecclesiology set out by the Scots and promised in the Solemn League and Covenant.[1]

---

[1] This four point program had obviously been in the mind of the Scots for a considerable time before the Solemn League and Covenant as the basis of lasting peace with England. Alexander Balfour had written to his brother, Sir James Balfour, during the 1640 treaty negotiations after Charles I's second ill-fated attempt to invade Scotland and impose episcopacy: "Some course is taken that thear may be one Confession of Faith, one Directione for worship, one Catechisme, one forme of Government for God's house in both Kingdomes: and ther is great houps of it; God Almichtie furder it, for our peace sall ne'ar be sure till then." (Baillie, *Letters and Journals*, II. 473.)

The four parts of the ecclesiastical program were again presented by Henderson as Moderator of the General Assembly in 1641. Baillie wrote to Spang, "The Moderator did fall on a notable motion, of drawing up a Confession of Faith, a Catechisme, a Directorie for all the parts of the publick worship, and a Platforme of Government, wherein

Yet throughout whatever was happening we must keep the political and military situation always in mind, for the Presbyterians' success in the Assembly was won within a total context in which initiative was rapidly slipping away from them, because the Covenanted uniformity for which they strove was increasingly disliked by those who were taking charge in the war against the King.

Realization that time was no longer on their side may well have caused the Scots to make a major change in their strategy. It must have been in early July, probably arising from Cromwell's success at Marston Moor and the unwelcome publicity they had received after the battle, that the Scots decided that they need no longer dissemble in their attitude to the Independents, and that they could achieve their objectives directly with the help of the conservative majority in the Assembly. We get a hint of this in a letter that Robert Baillie wrote at the very beginning of December, 1644 regarding their relations with the Independents, when he observed:

> But this four moneth bygone, since we sett our face against them openly, their plotts are so broken, and their strength decayed, that I hope God will make them more plyable to reason than otherwise they were inclyned.[2]

If Baillie's estimate was correct, and no one was more likely to have known of such a change in Scots strategy, the decision must have been taken about the end of July 1644. What the Scots did not recognize, however, was that others could also dissemble, and their own decision may have had a direct bearing on the discomfiture they experienced when the Independent politicians revealed their true objectives in the following September.

I

Political Pressure

The Assembly was never free from outside constraint. Almost from the moment it had resumed its work in August it had been under pressure to hasten its recommendations, and particularly those parts directed to the practical needs of the Church. So on

---

possiblie England and we might agree. All did approve the motion; and thereafter the burden of that labour was laid on the back of the mover, with liberty to vake [i.e. be freed from] preaching whenever he pleased, and to take help of whom he thought meet. He did declyne to undertake it, yet it will lie on him; and readilie in this he may doe some good." August 20th, 1641, *ibid.* I. 365.

[2] Publick Letter, 1st December, 1644; *ibid.* II. 243.

14th August a letter from the Earl of Manchester urged the divines to expedite the work on ordination, and on the same day Warriston and Maitland,[3] in presenting a letter from the General Assembly in Scotland, had emphasized the general desire in Scotland "for hastening of the work in hand."[4] Warriston's words were much more explicit than this, and the pressure was part of Scotland's carefully orchestrated ecclesiastical diplomacy:

> So soon as my Lord Warriston came up, we resolved on the occasion of his instructings, and the letters of our Generall Assemblie, both to ourselves and to this Assemblie, which he brought, to quicken them a little, who had great need of spurrs. My Lord Warriston very particularlie declared in the Assemblie the passionate desires both of our Parliament, Assemblie, armies, and whole people, of the performance of the Covenanted Uniformitie . . .[5]

That whole letter shows how the Scots used their friends to put pressure on the Assembly, and perhaps this needs to be seen in relation to the peace proposals that Warriston had brought back from Scotland; "also", Baillie wrote "we have the grand committee to meet on Monday, to find out wayes of expeditione; and we have gotten it to be the work of the Assemblie itselfe, to doe no other thing till they have found out wayes of accellerating; so by God's help we expect a farr quicker progress than hitherto."[6] On that same day in the Assembly it was moved to despatch practical matters related to the Directory "and to leave the extraordinary till further leisure".[7]

The Scots kept up the pressure. On August 30th Henderson had stressed the urgency of settling church government,[8] but the greatest show of authority came on November 7th when the Earls of Warwick and Pembroke for the House of Lords, and Holles, Strode, Rous and Tate for the House of Commons, came to the Assembly to get immediate action. As a result it was ordered "That what is already voted for the houses as the Advice of the Assembly 'touching church government' shall be transcribed and sent up tomorrow morning to both houses".[9] This

---

[3] Lord Maitland (1616–1682) was soon to become the Earl of Lauderdale. In 1649, however, he changed sides in the war and was captured after the battle of Worcester in 1651. He was imprisoned, but was released at the Restoration in 1660 and created Duke of Lauderdale. Thereafter he worked hard to establish absolute monarchy in Scotland.

[4] Lightfoot, *Journal*, p. 303.

[5] Publick Letter, 18th August, 1644; *Letters and Journals*, II. 220.

[6] *Ibid*. p. 221.

[7] TMs. II. 291 (Ms. II. f. 153b.)

[8] *Ibid*. 315 (Ms. II. f. 165b.)

[9] *Ibid*. 559 (Ms. II. f. 287b.)

simply shows that the Assembly was under constant pressure to get the ecclesiastical aspects of its work completed, as it hastened to fulfil a time-schedule over which it had little control and for ends that were as political as they were religious.[10]

This constant constraint, and the desire of the members to see tangible results for their work, have to be recognized in reading the debates of those months. On November 11th, after the debate about the Sabbath, the work on the Directory for Worship was supposed to be complete, and it was voted that it should be sent up to the Houses, but it is evident from later debates that there were matters that had been left in abeyance, and the Directory would not be passed into law by the House of Commons until 17th April, 1645.

Parliament's interest was in the parts of ecclesiology that touched the life of people in the parishes most closely – those points where a conservative people demanded the presence of the Church and its clergy. Therefore on Monday, December 2nd,

> Mr. *Tate*, of the House of Commons, did, from that House, desire us to hasten the Directory for marriage and burial; for that the House intends to lay by the book of Common Prayer, and cannot do it till these be finished, Whereupon we fell to our work about marriage, where we left; which was in a debate, whether marriage should be on the Sabbath-day or no. It was concluded, that we advise that there be no marriage on the Sabbath-day; and we passed the whole Directory before we parted.
>
> Which when we had done, the Lord Chancellor of Scotland desired that our business of government might be made as ready as possible against that some of their commissioners go down to the general Assembly, which meets in January next. Whereupon it was ordered, that what is already done, should be brought in on Thursday. There was also a committee made for the summing up a catechism.[11]

Again we must emphasize that the Independents were in sympathy with, and participated in the revision of church worship. More often than not, where there was opposition on these matters it came from English conservatives who may still have had some regard for the Book of Common Prayer. Even Baillie recognized those feelings in the Assembly, for he speaks of "one

---

[10] Even if one ignores the political motives behind the demand to stamp out the sects and to get rid of the Book of Common Prayer, there were more immediate political reasons for this demand for haste at the end of 1644: the Scots wanted to have something to take to their own General Assembly that was due to meet on January 22nd, 1644/5, and there was the even stronger desire to have a unified form of church government by the time the negotiators met the King at Uxbridge.

[11] Lightfoot, *Journal*, pp. 337f.

party purposing by the preface to turn the Directorie to a straight Liturgie."[12]

This conservatism is evident in the debates on the Preface to the Directory of Worship,[13] and it withstood some of the wilder ideas such as the Scots' belief that baptism should take place in the pulpit[14] and their determination to have an all-out condemnation of the Book of Common Prayer in the Preface.[15] All English Puritans did not wish to publish such a broadside against the Book of Common Prayer, probably because they were closer to the English parishes, and they knew the respect that many of their countrymen had for the book. Even Charles Herle, who was usually on the Reformed side of any argument, spoke against any outright condemnation of the Prayer Book, for "all the west are exceedingly devoted to this booke."[16]

Conservative English Puritans continued to exist, still present in the Assembly but perhaps even more numerous among parish ministers, who, Baxter had claimed, "had addicted themselves to no Sect or Party at all; though the Vulgar called them by the Name of *Presbyterians*".[17] The Assembly divines were in the process of earning that name at this time, for although we can discern opposition to many of the liturgical preferences of the Scots, there was no doubt that on issues touching the polity of the Church or covenanted uniformity, they closed ranks. On all matters vital to their program in the Assembly the Scots could count on this solid voting majority.

II

August in the Assembly

When the Assembly had adjourned for its brief vacation, Robert Baillie had looked forward to "a happie conclusion of the whole work" in a relatively short time, and although he had hoped that the section on baptism might have been completed

---

[12] Publick Letter, November 21st, 1644; *Letters and Journals*, II. 242.

[13] 28th October – November 7th; TMs. II. 547–560 (Ms. II. ff. 281b–288.) The Minutes are our only first-hand record through most of this period, since Gillespie did not give this subject his attention, and Lightfoot was absent between October 25th and November 7th. However Lightfoot was present on November 7th, and he clearly sided with the English conservatives when he said it was dangerous "to hint anything against a form of prayer" and in his opposition to giving ecclesiastical power to lay people. Lightfoot, *Journal*, p. 323.

[14] October 9th; *ibid*. p. 315, Gillespie, *Notes*, p. 89.

[15] 31st October; TMs. II. 550 (Ms. II. f. 283.)

[16] TMs. II. 552 (Ms. II. f. 284.)

[17] *Reliquiae Baxterianae*, I. 146 (§23).

before the recess,[18] he had every reason to feel optimistic when the divines resumed their work on August 7th, 1644. He could report that the House of Commons had unanimously passed the work on ordination – with some alterations, it was true, but he could confidently say that "the right settling of that business will be a great step to advance our affaires." In the Assembly the mood was for getting the rest of the work done as soon as possible, and so Baillie hoped for "farther progresse quicklie, than for a long time bygone we have made."[19]

The ecclesiastical program seemed to be taking shape, but a number of loose ends had been left hanging before the recess. Baptism, the remaining parts of the Dircctory, ordination, and church government still needed work, and this was largely because church government, with the particularly difficult problem of excommunication at its heart, was central to all the other issues. As long as the Assembly hedged on church government and discipline, either in the hope of accommodation and a show of Reformed unity, or as a means of preventing the Dissenting Brethren from handing in their Reasons to Parliament, not much further progress could be made in the drive to establish presbyterian uniformity in the British Isles. Until that happened there was little hope of decisively suppressing sectarian religion in the way desired by the Scottish Commissioners, by most of the Lords and Commons and probably by all Parliament's conservative supporters in Church and State. Indeed, Robert Baillie shows us that his antipathy to Independency, which became almost an obsession, was because he regarded it as "the mother and true fountaine of all the church distractions here."[20]

Therefore during the first month after the Assembly's recess the problem of sectarianism continually intruded into the agenda, and for the rest the work was concerned with completing the Directory and developing the theological defence of presbyterial ordination. So on August 7th and 8th the Assembly continued its consideration of baptism,[21] on the 9th it moved to Thanksgiving and drew attention to the sects,[22] and these concerns overflowed into the following week. The danger of the sects was given special point by the curious case of Thomas Picot, a preacher of advanced Chiliastic views who had been

[18] To D. Dickson, 23rd July, 1644; *Letters and Journals* II. 213.
[19] For Glasgow, 7th August, 1644, *ibid.* p. 214.
[20] *Ibid.* p. 216.
[21] Lightfoot, *Journal*, pp. 299–301, TMs. II. 267–277 (Ms. II. ff. 138b–142b.)
[22] Lightfoot, *Journal*, p. 302, TMs. II. 277–287 (Ms. II. ff. 142b–147b.)

apprehended by the Admiral[23] in the Isle of Guernsey and sent to London. In view of the widespread popularity of apocalyptic ideas among respectable divines,[24] we can only suspect that the anger against Mr. Picot was less for his Adventist views than for declaring that the reformed church order established on the Isle of Guernsey "was worse than sodomy."[25]

The special interests could not help overlapping in the debates, and there is an enveloping penumbra at the centre, because an as yet undefined church order was presumed by most of the divines.[26] The Scots used Warriston's return as a means "to quicken them a little, who had great need of spurrs," and Warriston "verie particularlie declared in the Assemblie the passionate desires both of our Parliament, Assemblie, armies, and whole people, of the performance of the Covenanted Uniformitie."[27] To that end the Commissioners produced a paper written by Henderson that was introduced in the House of Lords by Lord Say, by Oliver St. John in the Commons, and by Marshall in the Assembly.[28] At this stage, however, the Scots apparently did not realize that beyond a rupture with the Independents in the Assembly the claim of Covenanted uniformity by

---

[23] Lightfoot, *Journal*, pp. 301f. Robert Rich, The Earl of Warwick and Lord High Admiral, was extremely active in the presbyterian interest. See also Stephen Marshall's report against the Anabaptists at this time: TMs. II. 277 (Ms. II. f. 142b.)

[24] Robert Baillie seems to have changed his views. Earlier that summer, just before Marston Moor, he had given vent to expressions of a decidedly Chiliastic flavour: "The times of Anti-christ's fall are approaching. The very outward providence of God seems to be disposing of France, Spaine, Italy, and Germany, for the receiving of the Gospell." However, the unexpected results of that battle in Yorkshire must have been hard for Baillie to accept as wholly the will of divine Providence. Later he expressed his amazement at the popularity of Chiliastic views among some of the most respectable divines in England: "the most of the chiefe divines here, not only Independents, bot others, such as Twiss, Marshall, Palmer, and many more, are express Chiliasts." Cf. his Publick Letter, June 7th, 1644, and his letter to Spang, 5th September, 1645, *Letters and Journals*, II. 192, 313.

[25] Lightfoot, *Journal*, p. 301.

[26] As an example of the overlapping interests, the discussion of 'dipping' as a legitimate mode of baptism almost inevitably became compromised by the practical problem of how far any endorsement would encourage Anabaptists. Lightfoot, Temple and Gataker were opposed to any mention of it in the Directory; cf. Lightfoot, *Journal*, pp. 300f., TMs. II. 275f. (Ms. II. ff. 141, 141b.)

[27] Publick Letter, 18th August, 1644, Baillie, *Letters and Journals*, II. 220; cf. Lightfoot, *Journal*, p. 303.

[28] It is strange to find parliamentary 'Independents' assisting the Scots in this way, but in view of Baillie's astonishment and disappointment later in the year with the policy of St. John and his associates, it seems that the Scots had counted them to be among their 'special friends' in the English Parliament. These men had, after all, been prime movers in agitating for an alliance with the Scots, and if the Solemn League and Covenant had gone beyond what they had hoped for, they had fully supported it. For Baillie's later disillusionment, see *infra* pp. 406ff.

divine right was bringing them into a collision course with the English Parliament.

Robert Baillie was particularly satisfied with the Fast sermons preached by Herbert Palmer and Thomas Hill on August 13th as "two of the most Scottish and free sermons that ever I heard any where." He detested the adulatory way in which most English clergymen addressed the civil authorities, but he noted that this "stile is much changed of late" and "these two good men laid well about them, and charged publicke and parliamentarie sins strictlie on the backs of the guilty; among the rest, their neglect to settle religion according to the Covenant, and to sett up Ordination, which lay so long in their hands. This was a means to make the House of Commons send us doun that long delayed paper of Ordination."[29]

The Scots were far less satisfied with that paper when they had the chance of studying it, and to encourage its rejection by the Assembly they expressly disavowed it themselves and set down their reasons in writing. This had the desired effect, for this "did so encourage the Assemblie, that this day, unanimouslie, they sent a committee to the House, to crave leave to consider their alterations."[30] The discussion in the Assembly on the 16th, when this passage seems to have been penned, had dwelt not so much on the provisions for ordination as on the authority of the Assembly in relation to the Houses of Parliament.[31] In the months that followed the supreme control of Parliament over the ecclesiastical situation in England began to throw a lengthening shadow for the Scots over their successes in the Assembly.

The Assembly had handed in its twelve doctrinal propositions about ordination on April 3rd, and proposals for practical administration on the 19th,[32] but early in the summer Baillie had discovered from his 'good friend', Francis Rous, that the House of Commons had made extensive changes. He had persuaded Rous, who was chairman of the Commons' committee examining the proposals, that his committee should confer with some of the members of the Assembly before taking any further action. Marshall, Burgess, Vines and Tuckney, together with the Assembly scribes, had therefore been deputed to meet with the parliamentary committee, and they discovered that the House of Commons

---

[29] Publick Letter, 18th August, 1644, *Letters and Journals*, II. 220f.
[30] *Ibid.* p. 221.
[31] Cf. TMs. II. 295–8 (Ms. II. ff. 155b–157;) Lightfoot, *Journal*, p. 295.
[32] Cf. *supra* pp. 328–30.

has past by all the whole doctrinall part of ordination, and all our scriptural grounds for it; that they had chosen only the extraordinarie way of ordination, and in that very part had scraped out whatever might displease the Independents, or patrons, or Selden and others, who will have no Discipline at all in any Church *Jure Divino,* but settled only upon the freewill and pleasure of the Parliament. Mr. Henderson, and the rest, reasoned against the dangerousness and disgrace of this their way, so clearlie, that sundry of the gentlemen repented of their alterations; yet the most took all to advysement. We, in private, resolved we would, by all means, stick to our paper; else, this being the first, if we yielded to these most prejudiciall alterations, which the Independents and Civilians underhand had wrought, the Assemblie's reputation was clean overthrowne, and Erastus way would triumph.[33]

Parliament had been in no hurry to return this material on ordination, but when it finally arrived on August 15th the divines discovered that their intervention had achieved practically nothing. The doctrinal part of ordination was still omitted, all reference to a presbytery had been taken from the practical part, and the politicians had even added a preface of their own. Hence the Scots Commissioners' protest and a request that the House should not proceed with any legislation in this matter until it had the chance of studying the reasons for their dissatisfaction.[34] The English divines on the other hand were reminded by Marshall that "we are tyed by an ordinance to debate nothing here but what we receive [as an] order".[35]

The members of Parliament and the divines obviously regarded the ordination proposals very differently. The divines saw them as part of the Church that must be to some extent *jure divino* whatever one might feel about individual polities, whereas the politicians saw them primarily as the practical means of getting ministers into parishes. The divines knew that if they could not justify the orders of those who were to be ordained with solid biblical evidence, they would face a challenge both from the rigorously biblical sects and from the supporters of episcopacy. If the parliamentarians were concerned about any such challenge, it was probably that posed by the conservative opinion

---

[33] To Ramsay, end of June, 1644, Baillie, *Letters and Journals,* II. 198f. How far the Independents in the Assembly shared complicity is uncertain. We may suspect Philip Nye, and certainly the political independents must have been involved; but Congregational ecclesiology claimed *jus divinum* as did that of the Scots, and it was therefore theologically just as much opposed to Erastianism.

[34] The Scots expressed "the great grief that they have by reason of a paper sent from the Honourable House of Commons."

[35] 16th August, 1644. TMs. II. 295 (Ms. II. f. 155b.)

which still pervaded the English parishes; so when Francis Rous commented upon the preface to the new paper on ordination, he remarked that the people "have a certaine opinion of Episcopacie",[36] and it may be significant that a few days later the Assembly voted that "Presbyter and episcopus, in Scripture, are one and the same."[37]

Through the period from August 21st to September 3rd the ordination issue and concern about sectarianism ran parallel,[38] and the divines showed their anxiety about the biblical challenge of the sects. Nothing incensed the members of the majority more than questions about the validity of their own ordination in the national Church.[39] At the same time, in the relative privacy of the Assembly, they recognized the difficulty of finding an explicit institution in the New Testament,[40] and even the Scots based their claims on inferences from the biblical evidence rather than from an explicit dominical command.[41]

The Independents were clearly suspicious that under the cover of attacking sectarianism, the way was being prepared to outlaw their own position. Some of the papers in reaction to the House of Commons' revisions had condemned opinions they had expressed, such as questioning episcopal ordination or refusing to regard ordination as an act limited to ordained church officers. "These", said Philip Nye, "are supposed to be the conceits (?) of those called Anabaptists & Antinomians [,] but in most of our writings we make a distinction of those 2". The two opinions should not be confused, because many Separatists who held high views of the Church "doe directly oppose the others[42] as Ainsworth did & Robinson".[43] In fact, views that were being condemned were uncomfortably similar to those of the Independents themselves, and George Walker pressed the point home. The Assembly was attacking the beliefs of the sects that

---

[36] The Minutes are unclear, but the drift of his remarks seems to have been concern lest the people should think that "ministers may not ordaine". 15th August, 1644, TMs. II. 293 (Ms. II. f. 154b.)

[37] Lightfoot, *Journal*, p. 305. Henderson, however, protested against this "as giving too much to episcopacy." *Ibid.* p. 306.

[38] TMs. II. 303–332 (Ms. II. ff. 159b–169.)

[39] This appears to have been the thrust of Seaman's remarks on September 2nd, in the debate on heresy and schism, and it was certainly the point of what Walker said on August 29th: *ibid.* 332, 312 (Ms. II. ff. 168, 164.)

[40] On 3rd September, *ibid.* 322 (Ms. II. f. 169.)

[41] Rutherford argued that "what the apostells did in ordaining of perpetuall officers we are to hold it the ordinance of Christ as if himselfe had ordained it". *Ibid.* 325 (Ms. II. f. 170b.)

[42] I.e., the Antinomians.

[43] 19th August; *ibid.* 311 (Ms. II. f. 163b.)

were most pertinent, "but those that [hold] we are noe ministers [and] noe church, [and practice] separation from us, are more dangerous than the rest", and he was "sorry that any man should speake one word in defence of those who say [we are] noe ministers, noe churches[;] why should we have anything to doe with such[?]"[44]

This is where the shoe pinched, because this is where the ministers among the majority felt themselves to be most vulnerable in relation to other forms of churchmanship, and even Charles Herle thought the Independents' opposition was out of place because of the threat posed by the sects. This also shows how carefully the Scots were wooing the English Puritans, for by remaining silent they ensured that the Independents would appear as those who questioned the orders of most of their colleagues in the Assembly, and hence as a major threat. On the other hand, the Independents felt that they were being deliberately confused with the Anabaptists and Antinomians, and Goodwin protested because the paper under discussion condemned only those views which the sects happened to hold in common with the Independents. Against the majority he protested, "we doe hold more things with the reformed churches than many of this Assembly doe",[45] and in view of the earlier history of men like Burgess, Palmer and Twisse, he was probably right.

The final clash on church government could not be long delayed. The Scots Commissioners had asked the Grand Committee to expedite matters,[46] and so on August 20th, Herbert Palmer on behalf of that committee presented an agenda for the Assembly to follow:

1. 'That the Assembly appoint a committee to draw up the Directory;' which is already done.

2. 'A committee to join with the commissioners of Scotland, to draw up a confession of faith.

3. 'The committee for the summary hasten their report about church-government.

4. 'The Assembly to return to the government.

5. 'Then to handle excommunication.'[47]

---

[44] *Ibid.* 312 (Ms. II. f. 164.)

[45] *Ibid.* 313 (Ms. II. f. 164b.) Goodwin seems to have become very tired of all the loose talk about Anabaptism and Antinomianism, because on the 9th September he said, "I desire you would first define what is antinomianisme & Anabaptisme", which Burgess immediately interpreted as "an aspersion on the Assembly". *Ibid.* 362 (Ms. II. f. 189.)

[46] Cf. Henderson's comment on September 4th; *ibid.* 327 (Ms. II. f. 171b.)

[47] Lightfoot, *Journal*, p. 305.

This program was immediately set in motion: committees were chosen to put the Directory in a final form and to begin work on the Confession.[48] The committee charged with systematizing the earlier work on church government brought its work to the Assembly on September 4th, although there was considerable debate on how they should proceed, whether to debate the three issues set out by the Grand Committee[49] or to carry on from where the Assembly had left it earlier.

This debate involved rather more than procedure,[50] Marshall had argued that they should begin with the recommendation of the Grand Committee, but this was not to the liking of the Scots who wanted the Assembly first to establish the form of government that it was prepared to recommend,[51] but there was still a considerable body of opinion in the Assembly that wanted to begin with the power of congregations. Marshall, Vines and others argued that whether they started with the subjects set out by the Grand Committee, or with those brought in by the Committee for the summary, they should begin logically with the power of the congregation and progress upward.[52] Herle affirmed that "we all strive to have a government setled & that a presbiteriall [order;] that which is right Indepen[den]cy all of us are opposite to", but they "must dispatch the power of a congregation",[53] and he argued that they should begin with "the presbytery from which one must appeal, before the presbytery to which one must appeal."[54]

---

[48] Nine were initially selected, and it should be noted that Independents were not excluded: Drs. Gouge, Temple, Burgess and Hoyle, together with Gataker, Arrowsmith, Burroughes, Vines and Goodwin. On September 4th, Dr. Temple asked that this Committee should be augmented, and Palmer, Newcomen, Herle, Reynolds, Wilson, Tuckney, Young, Ley, Sedgewick, and Dr. Smith were added. *Ibid.* 305, 308, TMs. II. 300, 327 (Ms. II. ff. 158, 171b.)

[49] "It was the advice of the Grand Committee (at the voicing whereof in the committee we were silent and did not contradict, though we had in the debate advised another method) that the Assembly should fall again upon church government, and therein to handle these three questions in order: 1. Whether there be such an ordinance as excommunication. 2. Whether a single congregation may excommunicate. 3. Whether a classical presbytery may excommunicate." Gillespie,*Notes*, p. 65. The Scots opposition to this method may have been due to their unwillingness to debate the Erastian issue at this juncture.

[50] TMs. II. 327–336 (Ms. II. ff. 171b–176;) Lightfoot, *Journal*, p. 308; Gillespie, *Notes*, p. 65.

[51] Apart from the reason given above, the Scots may also have wanted a clear statement of presbyterian government against the arrival of their Chancellor, the Earl of Loudoun and other Scottish peace commissioners. Warriston had already arrived.

[52] Gillespie, *Notes*, p. 65.

[53] TMs. II. 329 (Ms. II. f. 172b.)

[54] Gillespie, *Notes*, p. 65.

The Scots, however, won the support of men like Palmer, Calamy and Seaman for the Assembly to address itself directly to the several sorts of presbyteries by which the church should be governed. "I doe not expect soe perfect a uniformity in all things", Henderson said, "but if this [church is] all governed by 4 assemblyes", then (we must assume he said) there would be little to fear.[55] The Scots and their supporters said this repeatedly and at considerable length, and Henderson's speech caused William Gouge to protest, "we are all for expedition & we are long disputing about our method. let the question be put".[56] This underlines a feature of the sessions at Westminster that the Minutes make much clearer than the other records. The Scots and their supporters justly blamed the Independents for holding up proceedings, but they could be great time wasters themselves when it suited their purpose.

Not that the Independents were silent in this debate, for both Nye and Goodwin had their say. Goodwin questioned the number of assemblies that were being proposed. He thought national assemblies might occasionally be called, but he was doubtful of their ecclesiastical status, and he could not see the need for provincial assemblies. He did not deny the place of presbyterial assemblies (presumably classes) in cases of congregations miscarrying,[57] but "the question still stickes about the power of congregations".[58]

There were others besides the Independents who were still concerned about this last point. Dr. Temple, in response to those who were trying to push the system of church courts through the Assembly, declared, "I desire to know what the question shall be[:] how will you consider the 4 Assemblyes till you first consider the power of perticular congregations[?]" Charles Herle spoke along the same lines, and when he was called to order for repeating what he had said earlier, he protested, "I am sorry to see how things are carryed here. I have no comfort to sit here."[59] Even Marshall protested at the way the session was

---

[55] TMs. II. 331 (Ms. II. f. 173b.) The notes are incomplete, and we must therefore guess what Henderson continued to say.

[56] September 4th; *ibid*. A similar accusation had been made by Goodwin on August 30th: "you call for expedition & it is only in those thinges [you want passed,] when as you ware 10 or 12 dayes in debate about 'at or about'." TMs. II. 317 (Ms. II. f. 166b.) Goodwin's reference was obviously to the lengthy debate about being 'at or about' the Lord's table.

[57] The word obviously was 'miscarry' or 'miscarrying', rather than the word 'missionary' offered by the transcriber. TMs. II. 332 (Ms. II. f. 174.)

[58] *Ibid.*

[59] *Ibid.*

being chaired, and sprang to Herle's defence: "to take him of[f] for speaking the same thing when you doe not soe to others[,] he may well say he hath noe comfort in it".[60]

The day was managed well enough for the Scots to get their way. It was voted "that this shall be next debated, That it is lawful and agreeable to the word that the church be governed by several sorts of assemblies"; but the heat generated may be indicated by Gillespie's admission that this would not have passed had the supporters of the motion not conceded that "it should be free to the Assembly to debate what they would, and in what manner they please, only to do this first."[61]

Perhaps the Independents saw the handwriting on the wall, for the next day (5th September) Philip Nye pointedly asked when those who dissented from the Assembly's advices regarding the suppression of the sects should present their dissent, and in what way should that dissent be presented.[62] This was an implicit threat, for we can imagine the effect that the open publication of the opposing views would have had on the streets of London, or in the ranks of the Army, where there was growing suspicion of the "Sots [sic.] and with them all Presbyterians but especially the Ministers; whom they call *Priests* and *Priestbyters*, and *Drivines*, and the Dissemby-men, and such like."[63]

The debate on the government of the church by different forms of assembly began on Friday, September 6th, and with a few significant interruptions[64] continued throughout the next few months. It was a campaign planned with logical progression. The vote on the government by different assemblies led directly to the debate on the subordination of assemblies (September 26th), and that in turn to church censures (4th–8th October) and excommunication (14th–25th October). Finally a summary of

---

[60] *Ibid.* 332f. (Ms. II. f. 174, 174b.)

[61] Gillespie, *Notes*, p. 65.

[62] *Ibid.* pp. 65f., TMs. II. 336–8 (Ms. II. ff. 176–177,) Lightfoot, *Journal*, p. 308. Nye seems to have wanted the Assembly to postpone sending in its advice on sectarianism until it had the opportunity of looking at the Independents' objections. Others were not entirely happy with the Assembly's action: "It was put to the question, That the dissenting brethren have been left to their liberty this day of entering their dissent and their reasons. There were no Noes, but the Independents' and Mr. Wilson's; Mr. Marshall, Herle, Calamy, Corbet and young Mr. Wilkinson neither stood up to the ayes nor the noes." Gillespie, *Notes*, p. 66.

[63] *Reliquiae Baxterianae* I. 51 (§73). Baxter's testimony may not date until after Naseby, but there can be little doubt that the mood grew very rapidly after Marston Moor.

[64] E.g., the debate on national humiliation (9th–13th September), the reconsideration of the ordination proposals (16th, 18th September, 3rd October), the concluding work on the Directory (9th October–12th November), and the time-consuming visits of various dignitaries.

the votes on church government was presented on November 8th, and at once the Dissenting Brethren began to register their dissent.

However, the debate was hardly off the ground when the first major interruption occurred, with the news during the weekend of 7th and 8th September of Essex's ignominious defeat at Lostwithiel in Cornwall.[65] On the following Monday this brought all sorts of breast-beating in the Assembly, and everyone had his own favourite reason as to what had caused God to be so provoked against the parliamentary cause.[66] Valentine declared that it was because they had slighted the Covenant, Whitaker blamed the divisions among professed Christians, Seaman pointed to the existence of scandalous ministers, and Henderson to the neglect of reformation. Nye may have been more realistic when he mentioned the miscarriages in the parliamentary armies, and this was also acknowledged by Calamy in making his report to the Assembly on what had happened in the west:

> The King hath an army of sixteen thousand, and now may easily get more; he is got in betwixt the Lord General's horse and Middleton's horse, and is like to cut off either the one or the other very quickly, and then approach to London. There are none to go and meet him but Manchester's army, and they are like to break among themselves, divisions being now grown so great betwixt Cromwell and Crawford, &c., and it may be, come too late. Cromwell and his party have also given a remonstrance of their grievances to Manchester, and begin to show themselves very much. All this falls in when the Parliament makes so great difficulty in passing the ordinance about ordination. Many among them will not acknowledge those particulars voted in the Assembly, That they would put in their ordinance that clause left out, 'That Ordination is an ordinance of Christ,' 'That ministers are set over people in the Lord.' These clauses Sir Harry Vaine and Sir Arthur Haslerig quarrelled mightily at yesternight, in Wareston [Worcester] House; and when these things are opposed, what hopes are there of carrying the whole government and directory?[67]

---

[65] It was a strategic defeat rather than a defeat in battle. On September 1st the Earl of Essex had been in Lostwithiel, where he had been more or less cooped up by the King's army since the beginning of August. He managed to escape with his cavalry by sea, but this left Major-General Skippon and his infantry to make what terms they could. Gardiner, *G. C. W.* II. 10, 13–19.

[66] Gillespie, *Notes*, pp. 67–9; TMs. II. 344–59 (Ms. II. ff. 180–187.)

[67] Gillespie, *Notes*, p. 67. Herle put his finger on one of the practical causes of the trouble when he said that Essex's army "hath been principled to think that this war is only defensive, and that they may not assault, whereas the war is offensive against those who guard and strengthen themselves against the justice of the state." *Ibid.*, p. 68. This was a theme that was to reappear several times throughout the military quarrels of the next few months, and it reflected a fundamental difference of opinion about military policy.

That was a good question, and one that the Scottish Commissioners and their supporters in the Assembly should have pondered. Calamy's account seems to have stimulated some frank words from the Independents:

> Mr Goodwin said, The breach of covenant should not be charged upon men, because men took it in different senses, and each was left to his own sense; and it was often professed that there should be liberty to debate fully from the word of God, and the example of Reformed churches should be no prejudice to that free debate; and that it is a great wrong that it hath been alleged in books, those that admit not the government of Scotland break the Covenant.[68]

Nye bluntly reminded the members of the Assembly that the majority party differed as much within itself "as against his party", for there were within it those who denied any divinely-established form of the Church, others denied the institution of ruling elders or that they should vote in presbytery, while others denied excommunication. With some justification he declared, "that were the government of Scotland laid before us, he and his party would come nearer to it in many things than divers of this Assembly will do in other things."[69] All of this is clearly true from what we have already seen in the debates, but it did not change the fact that within the Assembly Nye and his friends were completely outmanoeuvred and out-voted by a majority that was prepared to go along with the Scots in order to preserve the national organization of the Church of England and the traditional authority of its ordained ministry. The Scots recognized this more clearly than Nye, and that for this reason the Independents' claim to *jus divinum* constituted a much more fearsome threat to the English majority than their own.[70]

The debate that arose out of Essex's débâcle became a review of the moral degeneration of the nation,[71] and a Fast and Day of

---

[68] *Ibid.* p. 67.

[69] *Ibid.* p. 68.

[70] The Independents had strongly supported the alliance with Scotland and the Solemn League and Covenant, and Nye's words suggest that they may well have expected the Scots to be their allies in the Assembly against the less clearly defined views of the English majority. Therefore they may have felt just as deceived by the Scots policy in the Assembly, as the Scots themselves were a little later by the policy of the Independent politicians. The two facts may well be related.

[71] The divines accused everything in sight. Palmer blamed the spread of heresy, schism and liberty of conscience, while he and Temple also castigated the condition of jails, ale-houses and bawdy-houses (Gillespie, *Notes*, p. 68;) Rutherford blamed the Independents for declining an accommodation (TMs. II. 349, Ms. II. 182b;) Gouge spoke of "an indecent carriadge of ministers in regard of long haire and aparell" (*ibid.* 356, Ms. II. f. 186;) and the sins of the Assembly itself were not forgotten: Charles Herle, for example, spoke of "a great deale of time spent in inveighing against long time" (*ibid.*

Humiliation was scheduled for Thursday September 12th. The soul-searching continued on September 10th, and took up both the morning[72] and the afternoon.[73] During this last session there was an interesting change of attitude, when at the instigation of Thomas Goodwin all the Assembly, with the significant exception of the Scottish Commissioners, began to have second thoughts about their criticisms of Parliament. Rutherford was disgusted, and he roundly told the divines that "the lord calls you at this time to dischardge your conscience both to parliament, church & the whole land" and that would be "a testimony to them of the fidelity of the lords messengers & exonerate your consciences in the day of Jesus Christ".[74] The Scots had no doubt that England's troubles were due in the main to Parliament's reluctance to establish Covenanted Uniformity.

III

New Political Intrusions

Essex's defeat at Lostwithiel produced a new injection of politics into the affairs of the Assembly, for it had been caused in part by Manchester's unwillingness to march westward to relieve the senior General. Hearing of that reverse, Manchester contritely promised the Committee of Both Kingdoms that he would fully cooperate in helping to extricate the parliamentary armies from further embarrassment,[75] but he continued to vacillate, and he was later reported to have threatened that he would hang anyone else who advised him to march to the west.[76]

354, Ms. II. f. 185.) Walker told of a woman who had said of the divines, "they sitt with a piece and [are] always sitting [;] but when will they hatch [?] they will hatch in hell". (*Ibid*. 347, Ms. II. f. 181b.)

Parliament came in for rigorous criticism: Gillespie, Tuckney, Case, Herle, Burroughes, Seaman, Calamy, Palmer, Burgess and Chambers all attacked the sins of Parliament. Eventually a committee was appointed to draw up a list of the 'mischefes' in Parliament, Assembly and nation, and report the following day. The general gloom was not lifted for the Scots by the news of a Scottish defeat at Perth at the hands of the Irish. Gillespie, *Notes*, p. 69.

[72] *Ibid*. pp. 69f., Lightfoot, *Journal*, pp. 309f., TMs. II. 350–62 (Ms. II. ff. 187–189.)

[73] Gillespie, *Notes*, p. 70, Lightfoot, *Journal*, p. 310, TMs. II. 362–5 (Ms. II. ff. 189–190b.)

[74] TMs. II. 364 (Ms. II. f. 190.) Baillie was equally disgusted. He wrote that when they were in full hope "of so honest and faithfull a censure, Thomas Goodwin and his brethren, as their custome is to oppose all things that are good, carried it so, that all was dung in the howes, and that matter clean laid by." Publick Letter, 16th September, 1644, *Letters and Journals*, II. 228.

[75] Manchester to the Committee, *The Quarrel between the Earl of Manchester and Oliver Cromwell* (edited by John Bruce and David Masson, Camden Society, 1875) p. 25.

[76] From the depositions of Cromwell and Hammond cited in Gardiner, *G. C. W.* II. 26f.

Cromwell and other officers had been thoroughly exasperated,[77] and the quarrel flared up to the degree that brought most of the contending parties posthaste to London to put their case to the parliamentary leaders. Cromwell laid the blame on the influence Maj-General Crawford was exerting on Manchester and threatened that if this officer were not replaced, he and his senior officers would resign their commissions. This dismayed the Scots:

> At this nick of time, while their service is necessary to oppose the King, they give in a challenge against Crawfurd; they require a committee of warr to remove him. Both the parties wrytes up here to their friends the caise: at last, Manchester, Cromwell, and Crawfurd, come up themselves. Our labour to reconcile them was vaine: Cromwell was peremptor, notwithstanding the Kingdom's evident hazard, and the evident displeasure of our Nation; yet if Crawfurd were not cashiered, his Collonells would lay downe their commissions. All of us, by my Lord Manchester's own testimonie, and the testimonie of the Ministers in the army, finds Crawfurd a very honest and valorous man, in nothing considerable guiltie, only persequuted to make way to their designes on that army, and by it on the Parliament and Kingdome; therefore all here of our friends resolves to see him gett as little wrong as we may. What the end of this may be, God knows.[78]

The account of this military quarrel may be traced elsewhere,[79] but it was clearly related to what was going on in the Assembly. Gardiner has pointed out however, that Cromwell's political tactics seem to have followed very much the same pattern as his military tactics – attack, but always be ready to change direction in order to secure the objective. Within a few hours of returning to the capital, he dropped the demand for Crawford's dismissal – probably in return for a promise that Manchester would prosecute the war more vigorously – but taking advantage of his own presence in the House of Commons and of the debate

---

[77] The exasperation shows in a letter that Cromwell wrote at this time to his brother-in-law, Col. Valentine Walton: "We have some amongst us much slow in action: if we could all intend our own ends less, and our ease too, our business in this Army would go on wheels for expedition. Because some of us are enemies to rapine, and other wickednesses, we are said to be factious, to seek to maintain our opinions in religion by force, which we detest and abhor. I profess I could never satisfy myself of the justness of this War, but from the authority of the Parliament to maintain itself in its rights; and in this Cause I hope to approve myself an honest man and single-hearted." 5th September, 1644, Abbott, *Writings and Speeches of O. C.*, I 292.
[78] To D. Dickson, 16th September, 1644, Baillie, *Letters and Journals*, II. 230.
[79] E.g., Gardiner, *G. C. W.*, II. 25–31, Abbott, *Writings and Speeches of O. C.* I. 290ff., Paul, *Lord Protector*, pp. 81–6.

on the ordination proposals, he persuaded the House to pass an order that

> the Committee of Lords and Commons appointed to treat with the Commissioners of Scotland and the Committee of the Assembly do take into consideration the differences in opinion of the members of the Assembly in the point of church-government, and to endeavour a union, if it be possible; and, in case that cannot be done, to endeavour the finding out some way, how far tender consciences, who cannot in all things submit to the common rule which shall be established, may be borne with according to the Word, and as may stand with the public peace, that so the proceedings of the Assembly may not be so much retarded.[80]

The order had a significance beyond the immediate clash between Cromwell and Crawford, or even beyond the immediate division in the Assembly, for in the debate in the Commons Selden and the Erastians had vigorously opposed the clerical power at which the divines seemed to be aiming, and it has been pointed out that even members of Parliament who detested the sects were entirely opposed to clergymen assuming the kind of 'tyrannical power' previously held by the bishops.[81]

The order from the Commons put the Scots in some disarray. At first Baillie seems to have thought that it might be turned to their advantage,[82] but further reflection eroded that confidence and he was particularly dismayed to realize that "the main procurers of all this" were "our greatest friends", young Sir Henry Vane and Oliver St. John.[83] It had been a totally unexpected setback, and Baillie did not make a speedy recovery. Several times in his later letters he returned to what he felt was the great betrayal that the Scots had suffered by Vane and St. John's open pursuit of religious toleration.[84] On 25th October, for example,

---

[80] Abbott, *Writings and Speeches of O. C.*, I. 294. The motion was introduced by Oliver St. John, but as Abbott remarked, "It was the voice of St. John but the spirit of Cromwell." Cf. *G. C. W.*, II. 30.

[81] See the comments of Sir Simonds D'Ewes quoted by Gardiner, *G. C. W.*, II. 29f.

[82] To Spang, 13th September, 1644, *Letters and Journals*, II., 226.

[83] To D. Dickson, 16th September, *ibid.* 230.

[84] Even later Presbyterian historians found this difficult to forgive. A. F. Mitchell, the editor of the third volume of the Minutes, said that it was "akin to presumption" and "obstruction" for Cromwell and his friends "to demand that the national Church should either be constituted according to the model they advocated, or should get no constitution at all till legal security outside of it were first assured to them. Thus far certainly the Presbyterians had reason on their side when they said: Settle first what the rule is to be; make the national Church as comprehensive as you can, preserving its Protestant character, but do this without more delay, and so give reasonable satisfaction to those who are likely to constitute it, before you proceed to make arrangements for a small minority who are not likely to enter it, and who in fact tell you they are not likely to do so

he wrote a long account to his cousin of the political machinations of the Independents throughout this episode and he referred again to this order of the Commons as "their greatest plott."[85]

The only reasonable explanation for Baillie's sense of betrayal is that the Scots did not recognize any close connection between the Independents they were opposing in the Assembly and the group of politicians headed by Vane and St. John in the House of Commons.[86] To that extent we must assume that Independency, as a political party, was only in the process of being formed, and that it was probably the events of 1644 that began to give this group of politicians their separate identity. But there was no turning back, and for the Scots this meant that they would have to look for new political allies. Bad news from Scotland added to their troubles, for on August 18th James Graham, Marquis of Montrose had set out from Carlisle in disguise and made his way to Scotland to fight in the King's cause. By September 1st he had won the first in a remarkable series of victories that all but brought Scotland to its knees.[87]

Our concern, however, is with the events at Westminster, and Baillie's reaction to the newly declared religious policy of Vane and his associates suggests that it may have been from Cromwell's intervention that the political aspects of Independency and Presbyterianism began to take their shape. Certainly from this time we can see the emergence of two clearly defined political positions. On the one side, most of the peers and the more

---

unless you yield to them in other matters than those of the constitution of presbyteries and the authority of synods." *The Westminster Assembly*, pp. 201f.

This would be fair enough criticism if the setting had been Liberal, Victorian Britain, but it was not. It was seventeenth century England with its rival claims to *jus divinum*, in which the successful ecclesiology was likely to invoke the full power of the State in suppressing all dissent. The Independents had seen their biblical arguments brushed aside for what seemed to them to be inadequate reasons, and it is clear from Baillie's letters that the Scots had no intention of granting toleration to any dissent. Indeed, if liberty of conscience had become the Independents' goal by this stage, they were wise to insist on what security they could before the new Settlement came into effect; for once the Church was established on its new basis, they could not hope for much further consideration.

[85] To Spang, October 25th, 1644, *Letters and Journals*, II. 234–239.

[86] Writing of the Independents on April 2nd, earlier that year, Baillie had confidently stated, "Sir Harie Vane, whatever be his judgment, yet less nor more, does not owne them, and gives them no encouragement." *Ibid.* p. 146.

[87] "We were here for some dayes under a cloud. The dissasters lamentable in Scotland about St. Johnstone and Aberdeene, the prolongation of the siege of Newcastle, the scattering of Essex's army in the west, Sir Henry Vane, our most intime friend, joyning with a new faction to procure liberty for sects; these, and sundrie other mis-accidents, did much afflict us for a fourtnight." Publick Letter, October 1644, *Letters and Journals*, II. 231.

conservative members in the Commons[88] did not want to see any radical change in the constitution of the country, they were jealous for the reputations of their own aristocratic military leaders, and they began to hope for a gentleman's stalemate on the field of battle that would produce a negotiated peace. Those who held these views were naturally drawn to the presbyterian system for the Church, because it guaranteed a national form of religion, the suppression of heresy and schism, support for the traditional social order under the Covenant, and therefore prospects for a negotiated peace. By the middle of August Warriston had returned from Scotland with the proposals that the Scottish Parliament and General Assembly together with the English Parliament were ready to submit to the King.[89]

Such a policy was highly distasteful to the radicals, who distrusted Charles and were convinced that the only prudent course was to pursue the war to all-out victory; and it had become increasingly clear to them that the only men likely to fight such a war were those demanding liberty of conscience, for since that was equally anathema to both the King and the conservatives at Westminster, their only hope was to fight for a victory in which they could impose the conditions. The defeat of Essex and the confrontation between the senior officers of the Eastern Association started a movement that continued throughout the remaining months of 1644, and finally centred in the person of Cromwell. The Scots on the other hand had to make a rapid readjustment, for they found themselves and the covenanted uniformity the Assembly was largely ready to accept[90] at the centre of this political whirlpool. They were now allied to those elements in English society for whom this represented the best chance of preserving a national Church and the traditional orders

---

[88] There are signs that individuals also were reviewing their own personal allegiance during these months. Up to this point, for example, Sir Arthur Haselrig had been prominent in the more radical party, but during the debates that followed the second battle of Newbury and the relief of Donnington Castle seems to have justified the cautious approach of Manchester. From that point on he leaned to the presbyterian side. Cf. Gardiner, *G. C. W.*, II. 54, 57.

[89] "The long-looked-for Propositions of peace, which my Lord Warriston brought down to our Parliament, are now past the Committee of both Kingdoms unanimouslie, with all the additions our Parliament putt to them; also this day they are transmitted to the House of Commons, and from thence it's expected that they will quicklie goe to the Lords, that so they may be sent to the King. If he will accept them, our troubles will shortlie be ended; if he reject them, they will be published, that the world may see which partie refuses, and which hes been misguiding ignorant people with the shew of the desyre of peace." Publick Letter, 18th August, 1644, Baillie *Letters and Journals*, II. 221.

[90] Cf. Baillie's letter, October 1644, *Letters and Journals*, II. 231f.

of society, and they may not have found this an altogether comfortable position.

The curious visit to England of Charles Lewis, the destitute young Elector of the Palatinate, in September 1644 is an event on which it is easier to hazard educated guesses than to provide solid evidence. Baillie mentioned his arrival very casually and dismissed it as no more than the Prince's decision to live in England until he regained his territories;[91] but it was a strange time and place to choose to enlist support for his failing cause, and even more strange to identify himself so openly with Parliament rather than with his uncle, in whose cause both the Elector's younger brothers were enlisted.

The Prince must have been invited. Earlier in the year at York Vane had suggested that Charles should be deposed, and although Gardiner admitted that there is no hard evidence to support this theory, he has made the plausible suggestion that Vane may have initiated the Elector's visit in the hope that Charles Lewis might occupy a similar relationship to Charles I as William of Orange would do a generation or two later to James II.[92] The Prince Elector may have been willing enough, but the situation in September was very different from what it had been at the time of Marston Moor, and the young Prince hinted that on his arrival he had been shunned by those who had earlier encouraged him.[93]

Whatever their earlier complicity in the matter, Vane and St. John indignantly criticized the Prince's visit in Parliament, and a communication was sent to him from Parliament suggesting that his cause would be helped more by his early withdrawal. The point that should interest us, however, is that the Prince "persisted in remaining in spite of the rebuff, and ostentatiously took the Covenant as an outward mark of his sympathy with the Parliamentary party."[94] He was also treated as a distinguished guest of Parliament, given apartments in Whitehall, and in November we find him being given an official welcome when he attended the Assembly for several sessions.[95]

Who had encouraged him to stay? Again we must admit that there is no hard evidence to support this theory, but those who appear to have been in the best position to exploit his presence

---

[91] Publick Letter, 18th August, 1644, *ibid.* pp. 221f.

[92] *G. C. W.*, II. 27f.

[93] *Ibid.* p. 27 note 5.

[94] *Ibid.* p. 28.

[95] October 28th, November 7th, 8th, 11th; TMs. II. 544–547 (Ms. II. ff. 280–281b.) Lightfoot, *Journal*, pp. 322–5.

were the Scots and the Presbyterians, and there are hints that this may now have been the direction in which he was looking. Robert Baillie had been in one of his more sanguine moods, and the Scots had still been associated with Vane and St. John, when he made the comment "We are thinking of a new work over sea, if this Church were settled."[96] It was a cryptic remark, and there is no way of knowing what Baillie had in mind – Ireland? New England? or had there been a suggestion of entering the Continental struggle? The context in which that remark was made in Baillie's letter makes the last suggestion at least a possibility.

To this we may add the Elector's remaining at Westminster despite the express opposition of Vane and his friends, his openly taking the Covenant, and his deliberate attendance at the Assembly. The Palatinate was the home of the renowned Heidelberg Catechism, and until its disastrous entry into the Thirty Years War, it had been one of the foremost Reformed states in Europe. Although it can remain only a suggestion, the Scots and their friends may well have reflected that the Elector's continued presence at Westminster would not only be an embarrassment to the men they thought had betrayed them, but it would be a useful reminder of the ecclesiastical unity of the Reformed churches.

IV

The Breach: Church Government
September to January, 1644/5

Despite the 'very black cloud' that Baillie said had hung over the Scots for a time, the progress in the Assembly had been promising, and almost every one of his letters since the recess had reported advances.[97] If the arrival of the Scottish Chancellor, John Campbell, Earl of Loudon, had coincided with news of the disasters to Essex's army in the west and to the Scots themselves near Perth, it had also coincided with the welcome fact that church government had returned to the Assembly's agenda.[98] "We are again on the Government", he wrote. "We have past

---

[96] 7th June, 1644, *Letters and Journals*, II. 192.

[97] In the letter to Glasgow, 7th August, he reported the unanimous acceptance (with some alterations) of the Assembly's paper on ordination. This had been premature enthusiasm, but struck the note of optimism that continued in his letters. The letter to Spang (10th August) reported the end of the work on Baptism, a letter on the 18th the acceptance of the Directories on Baptism and Thanksgiving, and on August 28th he was optimistic that Parliament "without further adoe" would accept the Assembly's changes in the ordination paper. *Ibid.* pp. 214–227.

[98] 16th September, 1644, *ibid.* pp. 227f.

two or three propositions, that the Church may be governed by three sorts of Assemblies, congregationall, classicall, and synodall. We begin with Synods, and hopes to make quicker dispatch than before, by God's help." And then in a curious juxtaposition of political shrewdness and pious sentiment, he observed, "We have sundry means of haste in agitation with our private friends; one of our speciall helps must be the prayers of the godly there."[99] It is, however, important to recognize that although Church Government was the crucial subject during the next two or three months, it was not the only subject considered, and both ordination and the Directory for Worship were inevitably affected by the polity that the Church adopted.[100]

1. *A Summary of the action*

A few general comments on the course of this crucial series of debates, and a summary of the progression of the ecclesiastical campaign, may not be amiss at this juncture. On August 29th Thomas Coleman had proposed that the Assembly should leave its discussion about suppressing the Antinomians and take up the consideration of church government because "that will setle all", and this had been supported on the following day by Henderson.[101] The subject therefore returned to the floor of the Assembly on Friday 13th September with the debate on synods, and both Goodwin and Marshall wanted synods first to be defined, because whereas in Independent practice "they are occasionall" they were for others "standing", and Goodwin claimed that the distinction "will not ly in this they are greater".[102] But this superior power was precisely what the Scots and their supporters wanted to establish, and as soon as the Assembly had accepted the principle of government by different ecclesiastical assemblies,[103] they moved on to determine the hierarchical structure by introducing 'the subordination of assemblies' as the subject for debate on Monday September 26th.[104]

George Gillespie seems to have been the leading advocate

---

[99] 16th September, 1644, *ibid*. pp. 228.

[100] Ordination was discussed on October 3rd and November 18th, while various aspects of the Directory were considered October 28th–13th November, and occupied a good deal of the rest of November and December.

[101] TMs. II. 311, 315 (Ms. II. ff. 163b, 165b.)

[102] *Ibid*. 366 (Ms. II. f. 191.) Marshall had said, "I think you should explaine your meaning & distinguish it." *Ibid*.

[103] Friday, September 23rd.

[104] *Ibid*. 415–422 (Ms. II. ff. 215b–219.) Gillespie, *Notes*, pp. 78f.

throughout these debates. They continued through October 2nd when the subordination of assemblies was proved to the satisfaction of the majority by inference from Matthew 18. Indeed, the whole line of argument adopted by the Presbyterians during this debate was an example of what De Witt has called "the postulate of necessary consequence", since the system of subordinate assemblies in relation to synods could not be proved conclusively by specific examples in the New Testament church.[105] On October 4th the Assembly proceeded to consideration of the assemblies (or courts) of the Church in relation to discipline and censures, and this led directly to excommunication on the 14th,[106] which with its scriptural proofs occupied the divines until the 24th.

By that time the issue of the Church's government was decided, but on that day an issue arose out of the debate on the church at Ephesus (as a proof of excommunication) that again revealed the differences persisting within the majority party. Marshall wanted the divines to begin by considering this in relation to the authority of the particular congregation, while Newcomen and Seaman thought they should begin with the authority of the classis (or presbytery). It was more than a question of method because it raised the question of where authority in the church is primarily located. The Scots were not anxious to force the issue between these two positions,[107] but the discussion produced a debate on who had the right of suspending church members from the Lord's Supper.[108]

This simply offers a summary of the way in which each plank in the Presbyterian platform was carefully fixed in place before proceeding to the next, but we shall also notice that beneath all the specific questions of polity that appeared to divide Independents and Presbyterians, an even more fundamental cause of division on ecclesiastical power and the way in which spiritual

---

[105] De Witt, *Jus Divinum*, p. 130. The Independents also accepted this principle of 'necessary consequence,' for during the earlier debates on ordination, Thomas Goodwin had used it in supporting Jeremiah Whitaker's contention that there is a 'virtual institution' for the particular church in scripture: "the virtuall institution", he declared, "is as strong as formall; that is, as truly the word of God wch we gather out of the word by consequence." April 2nd, 1644; TMs. I. 811 (Ms. I. f. 417b.) It shows the extent to which all the Puritans who claimed *jus divinum* for their ecclesiology were forced to accept human reason as an authority in the interpretation of biblical evidence.

[106] After a brief return to baptism, 9th–11th October.

[107] Gillespie said, "we maintaine both". TMs. II. 539 (Ms. II. f. 277b.)

[108] 24th–25th October, 1644. There was also a debate on the Preface to the Directory (October 28th–November 8th) in which the Scots Commissioners showed their settled antipathy to the Book of Common Prayer, and the matters arising from that debate continued to occupy most of the Assembly's time until the end of December.

authority was to be exercised in the Church began to emerge during the coming months. We will comment on a good deal more in these debates, but it is important to see that issue emerging for its later confessional significance, and also to notice the careful way in which the program was presented because it shows how the Scots used the guaranteed support of the English divines in winning their objectives in the Assembly.

2. *The Debates on church government*

Although there is much in these sessions worth study it is not necessary for us to deal with them in great detail, for most of the speeches were variations on themes that have already been made familiar through the earlier debates, and both sides repeated arguments that had already been well canvassed. The important aspect of the debates is to see how the strategy of the dispute was handled, and to note the points at which the two ecclesiologies diverged.

From the first there is no doubt about the prominence of the Scots, particularly of George Gillespie, and we get an impression of the great care and planning that the Scots and their leading English supporters had given to the way in which their argument should be presented. As Richard Vines admitted on 26th September during the debate on the subordination of assemblies,

> but this Assembly proceeds upon that wch is consequentiall
> & if we follow the clue of reason for subordination
> of the first to the second then we may follow it from
> the 2 to the third[.][109]

It was a closely integrated, logically worked-out system, and the sequence of subjects had to be carefully monitored. So later, on October 8th, when Calamy, Marshall and Herle wanted to start with the ultimate church censure, excommunication, Gillespie opposed this because he thought that what they were discussing – 'Admonition & authoritative reproofe and suspension' – would "be more unanimously agreed upon".[110]

An example of this concern to control the flow of the debate is seen at the very beginning, on Friday, 13th September, when the debate on synods began. Bridge stated the Independent view that synods were not regular meetings like the meetings of a presbytery, but were occasional and to be called as needed, while

---

[109] TMs. II. 417 (Ms. II. f. 216b.)
[110] *Ibid.* 473 (Ms. II. f. 244b.)

Goodwin, with some perception of the eventual objectives of the Presbyterians, asked "how many degrees of synods we make". Lazarus Seaman immediately brushed that aside, for "we are now on a different notion, betwixt a presbytery and a synod, not betwixt one synod and another."[111] The success of the Presbyterian strategy depended on very careful attention to timing, to when and how subjects were introduced: no subject was to be introduced until the Assembly was ready for it. On this occasion Philip Nye had declared that his opponents would "never find but two sorts of assemblies in Scripture" and that "the Assembly hath not granted any distinction of synods and classes." George Gillespie and the majority thought differently, and at once brought in a proof for their synods based on Acts 15.

The session on Monday, 16th September, was lengthy, and it showed that all sorts of wheels, political as well as theological, were beginning to turn very rapidly. The Scottish Chancellor, the Earl of Loudoun, and the Earl of Manchester both visited the Assembly and received complimentary addresses, which gave them the opportunity to put in their pleas for hastening the work of bringing peace to the Church.[112] Also the Assembly received back its ordination statement from Parliament, and an order from the House of Commons requiring the Grand Committee to consider "how far liberty should be given to tender consciences."[113] All kinds of pressures were beginning to build.

The debate itself was not remarkable because in using Acts 15 the divines were simply returning to the debates on the church at Jerusalem. Goodwin protested that those arguing for synods in the sense intended by the proposition had used the same passage to prove a presbytery, and "it cannot serve both."[114] He questioned whether the meeting in Acts 15 could have been a synod in that sense, and he maintained that it was essentially a meeting of two congregations, in which the church of Antioch had asked the advice of the church at Jerusalem. He spoke at great length, and Gillespie replied in great detail, but at the end of the session it was voted that the arguments for using Acts 15 had not been met, and the debate continued on the following day (the 17th).[115] Bridge brought further arguments from the Independent side,

---

[111] Gillespie, *Notes*, p. 70.

[112] TMs. II. 379, 384, (Ms. II. ff. 197b, 200.)

[113] Lightfoot, *Journal*, p. 311, Gillespie, *Notes*, p. 73.

[114] TMs. II. 376 (Ms. II. f. 196.) For the whole debate see *ibid.* 374–387 (Ms. II. ff. 195–210b;) Gillespie, *Notes*, pp. 71–3; Lightfoot, *Journal*, pp. 310f.

[115] TMs. II. 387–393 (Ms. II. ff. 201b–204b;) Gillespie, *Notes*, pp. 73f.; Lightfoot, *Journal*, pp. 311f.

but it was eventually voted that Acts 15 "proves another kind of assembly for the government of the church besides congregational and classical" and it was resolved that the next consideration should be the pastors, teachers and other church governors who were to make up a synod.[116]

The main thing that arises from the debate is the different way in which the two groups regarded a synod. The Independents thought of a synod as basically a fraternal meeting of several congregations called together for mutual help and advice, but they were not ready to accept a formal authoritative synod in the sense accepted by the majority. As Goodwin said, "ther is a difference betwixt your opinion & ours." The notes in the Minutes are not very clear about the way in which he defined his own view, but he seems to have thought that the church at Antioch simply turned for advice to the church at Jerusalem either as the mother church or as the place where the apostles ministered. Then he continued:

> but your argument tends to a further businesse[,]
> you make a subordination[;]
> that which you call a sinod is to us the second degree[–]
> a presbitery over many congregations, but you stating
> it as a third sort & proving it to be such a formall
> one that is that we argue against[.][117]

Behind these arguments about the number of authoritative assemblies in the Church, there was the deeper problem of 'subordination' lurking in the wings, because this would involve a power over churches that the Independents believed to be foreign to the gospel. They were willing, as Seaman realised, to allow a "'ministeriall' power in determining matters of faith",[118] but they did not find in the New Testament church the kind of power implied in the principle of subordination.

The Independents were not alone in their opposition to the way the Scots and their supporters were exegeting Acts 15. On the 17th Jeremiah Whitaker,[119] and on the 19th Edward Reynolds[120] argued that in the meeting of Acts 15 not only apostles and elders but also ordinary members took part, and this was hotly disputed by the Scots and most of the other English divines. This does not mean that Whitaker and Reynolds were

---

[116] Gillespie, *Notes*, p. 74.
[117] TMs. II. 389 (Ms. II. f. 202b.)
[118] *Ibid.*
[119] *Ibid.* 391 (Ms. II. f. 203b.)
[120] *Ibid.* 397 (Ms. II. f. 206b.)

Independents, but belonged to that form of English Puritanism that preferred a form of parochial episcopacy.[121] However, the Assembly was witnessing an impressive piece of polemical generalship, for the Scots managed to gain their own objectives against the Independents by enlisting the support of men like Whitaker and Reynolds at every vital point: it was a classic case of 'divide and rule.'

The debates progressed from the vote on the 17th September which claimed that there is evidence of synods in scripture, to a vote on the 18th that the constituent members of such synods are pastors and teachers, and thence on the 19th to the consideration of "other fitting persons."[122] This had been proposed by Nye and Reynolds and was supported by several leading members of the Assembly,[123] but it was stubbornly opposed by Gillespie[124] and many of the Scots' supporters, and the dispute carried over into a long debate on the following day (the 20th).[125] It ended in something of a compromise by adding the words "when it shall be deemed expedient", and after the weekend, on Monday 23rd, a qualification was added by limiting such membership of synods to those who had been given a lawful 'call.'[126]

Now the Assembly was ready to take up the question that Goodwin had anticipated at the beginning when he enquired how many degrees of synods they wanted to make. "The next debate", wrote Gillespie, "was of the division of the several kinds of synods. It was ordered that this proposition shall be debated. Synodical assemblies may be of several sorts, as provincial, national, oecumenical."[127] By this means, at the end of that session on the 23rd, the Assembly had reached the crucial point:

> It was put to the question, That subordination of these assemblies, the lesser to the greater, shall be next debated, twenty-one said ay, and eighteen no.[128]

---

[121] Edward Reynolds was the only 'Presbyterian' member of the Assembly to accept a bishopric from Charles II after the Restoration. He became the Bishop of Norwich.

[122] Lightfoot, *Journal*, p. 313. Nye claimed "all idoneous persons" belong to synods, Gillespie, *Notes*, p. 74. For the full debate on the 19th see *ibid*. pp. 74–6, Lightfoot, *Journal*, pp. 312f. TMs. II. 395–404 (Ms. II. ff. 205b–210.)

[123] E.g., Marshall, Vines, and Herle.

[124] Gillespie was at pains to point out in his *Notes* that he was not opposed to such people having "deliberative voices" or even in extraordinary cases ("such as this is") having right to vote, but opposed only that it should be the regular rule for synods; *Notes*, p. 76.

[125] For the debate on the 20th, see *ibid*. pp. 76f., TMs. II. 404–411 (Ms. II. ff. 210–213b.) Lightfoot was in Munden until October 2nd.

[126] Gillespie, *Notes*, p. 77f.

[127] *Ibid*. p. 78.

[128] *Ibid*. In addition, see TMs. II. 411–414 (Ms. II. ff. 213b–215,) for the debate on the 23rd.

This important debate opened on Thursday, September 26th,[129] and lasted until 2nd October, with Thomas Goodwin and George Gillespie as the leading protagonists for the respective sides, but in one of the first exchanges it should have been evident that the basic issue was not 'subordination' itself – indeed, a few days later Philip Nye agreed that there is "a kind of subordination" in the relationship of a local congregation to a synod, "and such a subordination we grant"[130] – but the kind of *power* that the proposals implied.

Nye had begun by suggesting that perhaps they should look for a different word from 'subordination' and asked for clarification. Then after there had been a certain amount of verbal fencing, he observed that they were now "upon 5 sorts of Assemblyes" and that although there might be some evidence in scripture for two he doubted if there was for five, so "if this be acording to gods word then let the word be produced".

At this point Stephen Marshall supported his son-in-law in asking for some clarification about the way the word 'subordination' was intended in the proposition,

> . . . . be[cause] ordinarily we understand
> by a subordination that the superior may doe all
> that the Inferior may doe and something more.
> If the terme ware explained we should find
> the debate not only more cleare but more short[.][131]

In his reply we again see an example of Gillespie's strategy of taking a little and building on that rather than trying to prove everything at once. He suggested that the question of subordination itself should be separated from the question of the power such subordination implied, and that in this way "you may goe on" and "order that this shall be noe preiudice to whatsoever power is due to any of them."[132] It was in this same session that

---

[129] For the debate on the 26th, see Gillespie, *Notes*, pp. 78f., TMs. II. 415–422 (Ms. II. ff. 215b–219.)

[130] On October 2nd; TMs. II. 460 (Ms. II. f. 238.) The Independents' understanding of synods was to be given ecclesiastical expression in Chapter XVI of the New Englanders' Cambridge Platform, but it was a peculiarly sensitive area because there had been those who had questioned the authority of the Cambridge Synod itself. What Philip Nye said here about 'subordination' in respect of local congregations and synods was given some elucidation in the tentative conclusions of the New England delegates in 1646 on 'What is the Power of a Synod', and particularly the following: "The judgement of a Synod is in some respect superiour, in some respect inferiour to the judgment of a particular Church; it is superiour in respect of direction; inferiour in respect of jurisdiction, which it hath none." Williston Walker, *Creeds and Platforms*, p. 192; cf. pp. 191f., 233f.

[131] TMs. II. 416 (Ms. II. f. 216.)

[132] *Ibid.*

Vines made the comment noted earlier about the Assembly proceeding in a 'consequential' way, from one proof to the next; but we can see that the issue of ecclesiastical power was bound to arise as an ultimate question. At the end of this debate Goodwin proposed that the Assembly should next consider the arguments that could be brought against the kind of subordination, and this was agreed.

Most of Friday, September 27th and was taken up with Goodwin's arguments against the subordination of assemblies in the Church.[133] He produced five points against the proposition: (1) such subordination needed express biblical warrant; (2) if in arguing against Episcopalians and Roman Catholics they demanded biblical examples for Archbishops and Popes, then the same thing could be said for the system of courts that was now being proposed. (3) He argued that although the apostle Peter recognized such subordination in civil society as a human institution, a distinction has to be made between this and the church for the Church is a divine society.[134] (4) If Christ laid down express rules for the particular church in Matthew 18, then how much more he would have done so for higher ecclesiastical courts if they had been necessary. (5) To emphasize this latter point, he referred to the explicit rules in the Old Testament for the regulation of the Jewish community.

He then proceeded to consider negative reasons against what was being proposed: (1) there was the silence of scripture; (2) there was no justification for the independent power enjoyed by universal or national synods: it was said that the Congregational way did not hold sufficient remedy for abuse, but the criticism was even more true for this method, since the greater the church, the more likelihood there is of abuse. (3) Such a system was unnecessary. Did these assemblies have the same power or different powers? (4) The higher the court, the more it would draw its constituency from people who are simply representatives of other people, and eventually from those who are representatives of representatives. This argument would justify papacy, and although the principle is accepted in civil society, in the Church we need a specific institution. It was a long speech.

Goodwin was answered first by Marshall who gave "a few thoughts" that occupy over four pages of the Transcript. Against Goodwin's fear of national assemblies he observed:

---

[133] TMs. II. 422–433 (Ms. II. ff. 219–224b.) Gillespie, *Notes*, pp. 79–81.

[134] His argument is not given in full, but this seems to be the sense from the Minutes.

I thinke ther is noe church on earth in any one
nation or 2 nations that ought to looke upon
themselves to be independent soe as not to looke
to all other churches [–] to be ready to give
an account when the providence of god orders it
for their good[.]"[135]

And against Goodwin's contention that the greater a church is
the more likely it is to become corrupt, he said "this is a good
argument against all kinds of association, be[cause] some
Assemblyes may be destructive therfore ther ought to be noe
Association is a non sequitur".[136]

Gillespie said that he had managed to pick up only one positive
argument from Goodwin's discourse, and that was what he had
said about appeals going directly from the lowest to the highest
court in Jewish society. Gillespie thought that this was to be
explained by the small size of the land of Canaan, which permitted witnesses to attend any court with relative ease.[137] In his
Notes he treated Goodwin's speech with more respect, and provided a comment or note on each of his arguments.[138]

On Monday 30th Rutherford declared that enough had been
said already in response to Goodwin, and that there was "noe
need to add anything", but of course he did.[139] He addressed
himself particularly to Goodwin's contention that Matthew 18
set the bounds for a particular congregation while Acts 15 set the
bounds for a synod, and he thought all the arguments used had
concluded "as strongly against the being of sinods as the subordination of them".[140]

Goodwin answered in his own prolix style, and noted with
regard to a national synod, "de facto that it Judges all & is Judged
of none",[141] and in the course of responding to Marshall's criticisms, he declared, "I went upon this ground[,] ther ought to be
an Institution for the subordinations".[142] This point, which
could be regarded as fundamental to the Assembly's commission, had not been answered.

After Goodwin finished his rebuttal the Prolocutor asked that
further speeches should be brief. Marshall noted that some of

---

[135] TMs. II. 429 (Ms. II. f. 222b.) For the whole debate.

[136] *Ibid.* 431 (Ms. II. f. 223b.)

[137] *Ibid.* 433 (Ms. II. f. 224b.)

[138] *Notes*, pp. 79–81.

[139] TMs. II. 334 (Ms. II. f. 225.) The whole debate is to be found *ibid.* 434–443 (Ms. II. ff. 225–229b.) Gillespie, *Notes*, pp. 81–83.

[140] TMs. II. 434 (Ms. II. f. 225.)

[141] *Ibid.* 436 (Ms. II. f. 226.)

[142] *Ibid.*

Goodwin's replies had been directed more to the Scots Commissioners, and he chided the Independent for repeating things he had said earlier: "I thinke he hath spent more time in his reply than he need have done, it is the repetition of his owne former arguments". That was true enough, but Marshall then went on to repeat things that had already been said on the other side.[143] One of the most positive features of this session, however, was a speech by Lazarus Seaman in which he noted the things in which Goodwin and the majority agreed, the points on which Goodwin still had doubts, and the matters in which there were still disagreements.[144] This approach at least held out the possibility of a future accommodation.

The debate continued on Tuesday, October 1st[145] with Nye bringing in fresh arguments against a subordination of assemblies. He held that "if ther be any warrent for any Association Jure divino it is for a parochiall congregation", at which point he was called to order for bringing in new material.[146] It was another lengthy debate, and at the end William Bridge declared that "this subordination is contrary to the 18th of Math: & repugnant to 15 Act & therfore not agreable to the word of god",[147] but the proposition carried:

> It was put to the question, that it is lawful and agreeable to the word of God, that there be a subordination of congregational, classical, provincial, and national assemblies for the government of the church; and so it was voted.[148]

On the final day[149] of this long debate Gillespie attacked the central biblical citadel of the Independent position by using Matthew 18 as a proof for the proposition they had just voted. He began on October 2nd by citing John Cotton's use of Matthew 18 in laying down the principle that "arguments drawne from consequences are as strong as those from expresse scripture[:] quicquid necessario sequitur ex verbi dei esti verbum dei".[150] Christ

---

[143] *Ibid.* 439f. (Ms. II. ff. 227b–228.)

[144] *Ibid.* 442f. (Ms. II. ff. 229–229b.)

[145] *Ibid.* 443–453 (Ms. II. ff. 229b–234b.)

[146] TMs. II. 444 (Ms. II. f. 230.) There is an interesting illustration of the scribe's bias in the report of Nye's speech. The scribe wrote, "another perticular out of 18 of Math. seemed to be made as litel to the purpose" and he added that Nye's answer "was againe mistaken as Mr Marshall shewed by repeating his argument againe." *Ibid.*

[147] *Ibid.* 452 (Ms. II. f. 234.)

[148] Gillespie, *Notes*, p. 84.

[149] October 2nd. Cf. TMs. II. 453–463 (Ms. II. ff. 234b–239b,) Gillespie, *Notes*, pp. 84–86.

[150] TMs. II. 454 (Ms. II. f. 235.) As we have noted, this was a principle fully accepted by the Independents in developing their own ecclesiology. Cf. *supra* p. 412, n. 105.

had laid down the method in Matthew 18, and therefore Gillespie argued "from Christs faithfullnesse in providing for all the necessityes and evills of his Church. Christ's intention was to provide a remedy for offences", and he noted that both Cotton and Robert Parker (another favorite author of the Independents) had used the passage to prove synods in the church.[151] Eventually Matthew 18 was voted as proof of the proposition, and this virtually ended any possibility of the Independents winning concessions in the shape of the future national establishment.[152]

3. Ecclesiastical power and church censures

However, there was one area in which they were expected to put up a fight because of the extreme sensitiveness that had developed in the debates every time the subjects of church discipline and excommunication had been approached. In this the issue for the Independents was perhaps not so much in the subjects themselves as what they implied about ecclesiastical power. This became more evident as the debates continued. The Assembly had moved directly into this delicate area when Dr. Temple, on behalf of the Third Committee, brought in a proposition on the power of church assemblies:

> 1. That they have power to convent and call before them, any person within their bounds respectively; 2. To hear and determine such causes as do come before them; 3. That all these assemblies have some power of censures.[153]

Again we notice that the proposition is phrased not to claim too much at once, but it prepared the way for the debate on the ultimate church censure, the right to excommunicate, and this debate lasted from Friday 4th October[154] until the 25th when the Assembly determined who held the right to suspend persons from the sacraments.

The difference of approach to ecclesiastical power was illustrated in the initial debate on October 4th, when Rutherford was involved in an exchange with the Independents. Because of the way in which the proposition was framed, the debate concen-

---

[151] *Ibid.* 455 (Ms. II. f. 235b.)

[152] Both sides are open to criticism for things they said in the pressure of the debate. On October 1st, for example, Goodwin gave far more power to the civil authorities than his ecclesiology should have allowed, (cf. TMs. II. 446f; Ms. II. ff. 230–230b,) and in the debate on the 2nd October Gillespie could not have been entirely ingenuous when he asserted – in reaction to Nye's charge – that he was not arguing for a *jure divino* position.

[153] Gillespie, *Notes*, pp. 86f.

[154] For the debate see *ibid.*, TMs. II. 464–467 (Ms. II. ff. 240–241b;) Lightfoot, (*Journal*, p. 314,) is in error in making this the responsibility of the First Committee.

trated on the capacity of church officers to perform certain functions, rather than the power they exercised, but the underlying difference can still be discerned. Rutherford insisted that "those that are governours have power to convent & call before them all that are governed", and Nye responded "True if they governed according to a power of Jurisdiction", but he implied they did not.[155] Burroughes expressed the point even more cryptically:

> it is their duty to send for them[;]
> it is not their power[.][156]

One is reminded of John Cotton's statement in the preface he was to write for John Norton's *Responsio*, when he declared that "Church government is not an authority but a ministry."[157]

At the end of the session Goodwin protested against the way the debate was moving: "You cannot argue", he said, "from the subordination to the power, be[cause] you avoyd[ed] that of power in the debate of subordination".[158] He made this point again on the 7th,[159] but beneath all that was being said the real issue was a distinction between juridical power, of the kind exercised within the civil state, and the kind of spiritual power appropriate in the Church. "You have voted assemblyes for government," declared Goodwin, but "you brought noe arguments for a Juridicall government[,] the power was reserved, & therfore for you to argue from it is beyond what should be", while William Carter in pressing that they ought first to debate who had the authority to call assemblies into being, put the issue in this propositional form: "That which is a coercive power those assemblyes have not[;] but this is a coercive power", *ergo*![160]

The debate on Tuesday, 8th October, was hotly contested, for, as we have noted, some members of the Assembly wanted to proceed directly to the ultimate form of church censure, excom-

---

[155] TMs. II. 466 (Ms. II. f. 241.)

[156] *Ibid.* Gillespie, *Notes*, p. 87.

[157] 'Foreword from New England', *The Answer* (1958 edn.) p. 15. Marshall, who was generally on the other side of the argument, was also concerned about the 'ministerial' principle in church government. On October 8th, in reply to some ill-considered words by Nye about the punitive aspect of church censures, he said he was not at all ready to think of them as the infliction of a 'misery': "this I cannot grant, the church doth inflict them under the notion of a medicine". TMs. II. 475 (Ms. II. 245b.)

[158] *Ibid.* 467 (Ms. II. f. 241b.)

[159] For the debate on the 7th the Minutes are the only firsthand authority; since Lightfoot was in Munden and Gillespie offers no report; TMs. II. 468–71 (Ms. II. ff. 242–243b.)

[160] TMs. II. 469f. (Ms. II. ff. 242b–243.)

munication.[161] It is also evident that the Independents were feeling the pressure of being slowly but surely painted into an ever-narrowing corner. Tempers were liable to become frayed,[162] and sometimes in their attempts to get a foothold in the debate, they appear to go beyond their own principles. For example, William Bridge represented church censures as far more punitive than the Independents' own best insights would indicate.[163] Goodwin seems to have been far closer to the mark when he distinguished between censure that is the outcome of ministerial duty and censure that is a judicial act.[164]

At Seaman's suggestion the Dissenting Brethren were asked to put their objections in written form,[165] but it was voted that "it is lawful and agreeable to the word of God that all the said assemblies have some power to dispense church censures."[166]

This left the consideration of excommunication, which was introduced on Monday, 14th October. It was the last issue that directly affected church government, and at once a new element entered into the debates, for Thomas Coleman, an admitted Erastian, and several others denied that any such censure properly belonged to the Church.[167]

At this point the dispute between the Independents and the Presbyterians on church government was somewhat side-tracked, for neither of them agreed with the Erastian position. The debates on excommunication and the proofs for it continued until Friday, 25th October,[168] and throughout this period, although the Independents were present and participated, the major issue seems to have been between those who questioned excommunication in the Church and the rest. Coleman's and Lightfoot's position might be expected because of their Erastian views, but at various times in this series of debates, Whitaker,

---

[161] "The next proposition, That all these assemblies have some power in church censures, was this day ordered to be debated." Gillespie, *Notes*, p. 87.

[162] Nye was very sarcastic in response to something said by Gillespie, but unfortunately the incompleteness of the record in the Minutes prevents us from discovering what that was. Gillespie omitted the incident in his *Notes*. Cf. TMs. II. 472 (Ms. II. f. 244.) Nye also protested later in that debate that "in this Assembly we have affirmed things before we proved them". *Ibid.* 474 (Ms. II. f. 245.)

[163] *Ibid.* 476 (Ms. II. f. 246.)

[164] *Ibid.* 475 (Ms. II. f. 245b.)

[165] *Ibid.*

[166] Gillespie, *Notes*, p. 88.

[167] Gillespie, *Notes*, p. 91.

[168] For these debates see TMs. II. 493–543 (Ms. II. ff. 254b–279b;) Gillespie, *Notes*, pp. 91–96, Lightfoot, *Journal*, pp. 316–322.

Reynolds, Calamy,[169] Temple and Gataker[170] all spoke against the sentence of excommunication or in modification of it; and perhaps their own ecclesiastical position can best be illustrated by Jeremiah Whitaker on October 18th, in his commentary on the words in Matthew 18:17, 'tell it to the church.' With regard to authority to excommunicate, he declared:

> the papists give this to the pope[;]
> Bishops you know what they make of it[;]
> presbyteriall & Independents you know how
> much use they make of it[.][171]

He argued that nothing in this passage should be interpreted as rising to a power of excommunication in the Church. His words suggest that he and others in the Assembly did not regard any particular polity as having divine right.

The work on church government and the work on the Directory came together in the debates on excommunication. It is illustrated in the proposition considered on October 24th, "The presbyteries, which were over more congregations than one, in the apostles' days, in Jerusalem and Ephesus, as they had the power of ordination, so had they of excommunication."[172] This debate on who should have power to suspend offenders from the Lord's Supper continued through the next day (the 25th), and with the vote that this power resides in the ruling officers of particular congregations[173] the work on church censures and excommunication appeared to be complete. A committee was immediately selected to methodize the votes on church government, and the Assembly decided it could now turn its attention to the work remaining on the Directory.

However, on reading the account one feels that the debate on excommunication, for all its promise as a final confrontation, had already lost some of its significance for the larger dispute about church government, because it presaged the Erastian issue. What was then at issue between the Independents and the Presbyterians was not the validity of the act of excommunication, but the proper vehicle of the sentence and the nature of the ecclesiastical power involved. The injection of the Erastian issue into the debate at that juncture may have deflected the debate

---

[169] On October 16th.
[170] On October 17th.
[171] TMs. II. 523 (Ms. II. f. 269b.)
[172] Lightfoot, *Journal*, pp. 320f.
[173] Gillespie, *Notes*, p. 96.

from the course it might have taken. The ultimate principle at issue between the two ecclesiologies was not polity – although there were obvious implications in this area – but it was the nature of ecclesiastical authority, the kind of power to be exercised in the Church. When they could free themselves from preoccupation with polity, the Independents wanted church discipline to be within the context of pastoral care and the offices of regular worship. Goodwin said on October 24th, "the presbitery[174] have not the power of word & sacrament", and he went on, "I am for suspension[,] but for this authoritative power I am against it":[175] it was the prevailing sense of juridical power in the Church that made the Independents uneasy. He declared, "that that I question is the word authoritative,"[176] and Nye, in one of the rare moments when insight triumphed over his tendency simply to react to the opposition, suggested that perhaps the exercise of discipline should be thought of as "rather a suspension of the ordinance from the person than of the person from the ordinance."[177]

4. *Dissent*

The Independents were not threatened by the Assembly's work on the Directory and they were not noticeably active in the period that followed the debates on church discipline. They were obviously considering their options in the light of what had been happening in the Assembly. So on November 7th Philip Nye and William Carter registered dissent[178] from the 3rd proposition on church government.[179] A deeper rupture was, however, signalled when after Jeremiah Burroughes stated his wish to dissent not from the proposition itself but from its 'proofs', the majority stiffly declared that this was "not thought fit."[180] The Assembly

---

[174] I.e., a classis. Goodwin would have defended the right of the presbytery of a particular congregation precisely because it does hold responsibility for word and sacrament in relation to those it disciplines.

[175] TMs. II. 539f. (Ms. II. ff. 277b–278.)

[176] *Ibid.* 541 (Ms. II. 278b.)

[177] *Ibid.*

[178] There is a good account of the break between the Independents and the Presbyterian majority in the Assembly in De Witt's *Jus Divinum*, pp. 125–138. It is the only account that draws on the Minutes in their entirety.

[179] "The Scripture doth hold forth that many particular Congregatons may be under one Presbyteriall Government." The proposition, together with its scriptural proofs, appears at the beginning of *The Grand Debate Concerning Presbitery and Independency*, published in 1647 and again in 1652; cf. *supra* p. 249.

[180] TMs. II. 559 (Ms. II. f. 287b.) The Earl of Pembroke apparently regarded all dissent as simply an attempt to hinder the work of the church; Lightfoot, *Journal*, p. 323.

then tried to set a date by which the reasons for dissent should be received and Philip Nye just as stiffly asserted that it was "in his liberty whether to bring in Reasons for it or noe".[181] The following day he may have been trying to defuse the situation somewhat when he hoped the Independents' action "may not be interpreted that it is out of a desire [to] dissent or disaffection to the cause", but his dissent was followed by that of William Bridge, Thomas Goodwin, Sidrach Simpson and William Greenhill. Jeremiah Burroughes dissented from the proofs, and with these official notices of dissent there was no longer any reason to delay putting the Assembly's recommendations in final form and sending them to Parliament.[182]

Lightfoot reported that on Tuesday, November 12th, the Dissenting Brethren (or Septemvirs) petitioned Parliament for permission to submit their Reasons and had been given until 'Thursday next.'[183] In the middle of the Assembly's debate on Thursday the 14th we read:

> Then did the seven dissenters, the Independents, give in their reasons, of some eight sheets of paper: and it was blotted in divers places, which was soon observed by the Assembly, and it was scrupled, whether these obliterations might not in time be laid to the Assembly's charge: whereupon it was ordered, that an exact account of all the blottings should be taken, and their own hands subscribed to the number of them.[184]

As De Witt remarked, that entry probably illustrates more graphically than anything else "the division and the disharmony which now marked relations within the Assembly itself."[185] The

---

[181] TMs. II. 560 (Ms. II. f. 288.)

[182] So on Wednesday 13th November the Assembly ordered: "That the former votes concerning the church gouernment shall be transcribed to be transmitted to the parliament and brought into the Assembly tomorrow morning[;] and the votes concerning the church of Ephesus". It was also ordered that "The committee to put into method the votes of the Assembly doe meete this afternoone and draw out all the votes concerning the officers and assemblyes, and make report to this assembly upon Monday morning." *Ibid.* 565 (Ms. II. f. 290b.)

[183] Lightfoot, *Journal*, p. 327.

[184] *Ibid.* p. 330.

[185] De Witt, *Jus Divinum*, p. 135. Despite the frustration that the majority felt about the delays caused by the Independents, one cannot help regretting this evidence of mistrust and even petulance; for two days was not an overly generous amount of time to expect them to prepare detailed criticism of the kind required and to have it transcribed into a fair copy. The majority got rather more considerate treatment from the House of Commons, for when Burgess informed the House that the Assembly had been prevented from presenting the answers to the reasons as early as had been hoped, Burgess reported "they refer us to our own time, but desired that we would make what haste we could." 19th November, Lightfoot, *Journal*, p. 333.

bitterness shows through Lightfoot's record. On the following day, November 15th, when Goodwin read the Reasons to the Assembly, we read:

The first reason was this:–

'If many congregations be under one presbyterian government, – then every elder in that presbytery is an elder of every one of those congregations. But he is not, for he preacheth not to them.' This argument they have spent the most of their stock upon: though they have also taken up all the branches of our proofs, and taken on them to give reasons against. The business was so long, that Mr. *Goodwin* read as long as he could, and then Mr. *Nye* took at him.

Which when they had finished and all read over, the dissenters confessed, that, through haste, there had some things slipped them: they desired, therefore, that they might have time to amend them. Mr. *Marshal* moved for a committee to take the business into consideration; and observed that there were some things in the paper, which properly are not against the paper we have sent up: as, about the point of synods; and many things also which were never urged by them before, when we were arguing upon this point: and that those things that they then urged, are newly moulded and newly methodized: so that it will be a work of no small time to answer and conclude upon them."[186]

The Presbyterians were very unhappy about the addition of new arguments, and De Witt agrees that these additions "did not seem fair inasmuch as abundant opportunity had been offered for elaborate discussion."[187] However, he overlooked the fact that the Presbyterians had been guilty of precisely the same fault, for on the previous day Lightfoot had proposed an entirely new argument from the church of Ephesus for the support of presbytery.[188] Furthermore, William Bridge reminded the divines that if they found new arguments in the Reasons, they should remember those times in the debates when he and his colleagues were stopped with this, – "that they should bring in more arguments when they brought in their reasons". The Assembly did not like that, and chose to regard it as an aspersion against itself,[189] but it appointed a committee of twenty to consider the Reasons.[190]

---

[186] Lightfoot, *Journal*, p. 331.

[187] De Witt, *Jus Divinum*, p. 136.

[188] "I moved, that since the example of the church of Ephesus should be brought in for a presbytery, – at the framing of which up, I was absent, – that the Assembly, if they had not already taken notice of it, would observe, for the more confirmation of it, how many ministers were with Paul there of his own company: and I was desired to bring in my notions to the committee." Lightfoot, *Journal*, p. 327.

[189] 15th November, *ibid*. p. 332; TMs. II. 571 (Ms. II. f. 293b.)

[190] Tuckney, Newcomen, Calamy, Vines, Herle, Marshall, Palmer, Young, Whitaker,

Although the major effort throughout the first few weeks of December was to finish matters left outstanding from the Directory, the Platform of Government, the dissenters' Reasons and the Assembly's response were never far from the agenda. So on December 3rd it was reported that the Independents "desired to alter something in their reasons, which were not so exactly done, through their heat",[191] and it was ordered that,

> The dissenting brethren may read over their reasons, and what additions or alterations of words or sentences that were mistaken or omitted in the transcribing shall be set down in a paper and first reported to the Assembly before the alteration be so made.[192]

On December 5th Dr. Temple presented the draft of the votes on church government, and this was discussed in the Assembly on the following day.[193] On the 10th the draft Platform of Government was voted to be sent to Parliament, and Burroughes, Nye, Carter, Simpson and Bridge asked that their dissent regarding the subordination of assemblies should be recorded. Goodwin was absent from that session, but when Simpson tendered dissent in his name, it was refused on the ground that "we would not admit of any proxies."[194] Goodwin was given the following day to register his own dissent,[195] which he did, and the divines considered some alterations in the Reasons. On the 11th Greenhill added his dissent to that of his colleagues,[196] and on the 12th Dr. Burgess conveyed the draft of this Platform of Government to Parliament, and the Assembly heard the Independents' Reasons against the subordination of assemblies read by William Carter. These arguments were referred to the committee appointed to answer the Dissenting Brethren's Reasons.[197] However, it should be emphasized that the rift was only at the point of church government, and while this was going on Dis-

---

Reynolds, Seaman, Lightfoot, Temple, Prophet, Burgess, Sedgewick, Spurstow, Smith, Hoyle, and Arrowsmith, or any seven of them; "the commissioners of the church of Scotland are desired to be assisting to this committee." TMs. II. 570 (Ms. II. f. 293.)

[191] Lightfoot, *Journal*, p. 220ff.

[192] Minutes III. 13. The second volume of the unpublished Minutes ends with session 323 (15th November, 1644,) TMs. II. 571 (Ms. II. f. 293b.) The third Ms. volume, in a clearer hand, was edited by Alexander F. Mitchell and John Struthers; cited as 'Minutes III'.

[193] Cf. Minutes III. 15f. and Lightfoot, *Journal*, p. 339. Goodwin introduced something concerning the Reasons that "cost some debate", but Lightfoot does not enlighten us as to what it was, and the Minutes are silent.

[194] Lightfoot, *Journal*, p. 341.

[195] Cf. Minutes III. 17.

[196] Minutes III. 19.

[197] Lightfoot, *Journal*, p. 342.

senting Brethren were still being appointed to committees related to other aspects of the work.[198]

The Presbyterian Answers to the Reasons were read on December 17th, and this carried over to the following day when Lightfoot read that part of the Answers which he had been asked to draft.[199] Lightfoot's personal *Journal* ends with his report on Session 344 on December 19th, 1644, and from this point, apart from a few sporadic references until January 3rd, 1644/5 in Gillespie's *Notes*, and the occasional references in Baillie's correspondence, the only source we have for the later work of the Assembly is to be found in the third volume of the Minutes. One cannot help feeling that since both Lightfoot and Gillespie virtually ended their personal accounts with 1644, the major ecclesiological struggle had ended.

At the same time, there were other important matters related to it that had yet to be settled. The practical parts and Directory concerning church government and discipline had to be drawn up, and this was ordered on December 20th,[200] and on the 23rd it was indicated that something must be added to the Reasons and Answers on the matter of excommunication.[201]

V

The Breach: Excommunication, January 1644/5

When the Assembly began to consider excommunication in relation to the Directory on December 30th, the Independents again became involved, and the importance of this debate is shown in that it extended throughout January.[202] Having closed ranks with the Scots the English majority tried to produce a Directory in conformity to Scottish practice. So on December 30th, 1644, when Stephen Marshall presented the part of the Directory dealing with excommunication, it had been drawn up by Henderson,[203] and on January 2nd, just before George Gillespie and Robert Baillie left to attend the Scottish General Assembly,[204] the Scots had handed in a paper that was probably intended to reinforce that statement.[205]

---

[198] E.g., on December 14th Nye and Goodwin were appointed to a committee to consider a report of Fasting. Minutes III. 20.

[199] Lightfoot, *Journal*, p. 343; Minutes III. 20.

[200] Minutes III. 22.

[201] *Ibid.* p. 22f.

[202] *Ibid.* pp. 24ff.

[203] To Spang, December 27th, 1644, Baillie, *Letters and Journals* II. 250.

[204] Warriston and Robert Barclay had already left. *Ibid.* p. 251.

[205] Minutes III. 27. Mitchell and Struthers suggested that this was *Reformation of*

However, the Scots and their supporters were conscious of the dangers facing the parliamentary cause because of the Assembly's lack of unity, and how important it might be to the success of the Directory if it could be sent to Parliament with some show of unanimity. Marshall's statement on excommunication had been deliberately worded to be as inclusive as possible, and then it had apparently been submitted to one of the Dissenting Brethren for his approval. Marshall indicated that the draft had been left with that person for 'one night', and the majority assumed it had the approval of the Independents.[206] Later, when it was rejected, the Presbyterians protested that the Independents had had the opportunity then to voice their objections.[207]

When the debate on the part of the Directory dealing with excommunication opened on January 7th, 1644/5, it was clear that the Presbyterians were extremely anxious to have the support of the Independents. Alexander Henderson observed, "I have heard some of our brethren say, if they could get satisfaction in this, they did not see any great difference",[208] while even Cornelius Burgess hoped the material could be discussed without prejudice, because it "was drawn up to prevent heats."[209] Introducing the debate Marshall said three opinions about excommunication were to be found among the members of the Assembly:

(1) some hold it only in the congregational presbytery;
(2) others think that both the congregation and greater assemblies may do it;
(3) others, it may be, think that particular congregations may not do it.

He suggested that although they usually debated a question first and then tried to reach accommodation when divisions appeared, the differences on this issue "did appear abundantly in former debates" and therefore they had tried to present a position that would moderate between different points of view. He hoped that "if at the present we can settle it in such a way as that men of

---

Church-Government in Scotland, Cleered from some mistakes and Prejudices, but we have seen that there are reasons to suggest that this had appeared in the previous January. Cf. supra pp. 220ff.

[206] Minutes III. 31. De Witt blames Goodwin, but there is no clear reason why he should be indicted. Cf. Jus Divinum, p. 143.

[207] The Answer of the Assembly of Divines By the Authority of Parliament Now sitting at Westminster. Unto the Reasons given into this Assembly by the Dissenting Brethren, Of their not bringing in a Model of their Way. (1645), p. 15.

[208] Minutes III. 31.

[209] Ibid. p. 32.

several judgments [could accept it], it would be a great mercy at the present, and it may please God that we may grow up together."[210]

Meanwhile, the Independents were having second thoughts. Goodwin admitted that the "business hath been of long expectation, and needs a great deal of composedness of spirit in the debate about it". He seems to have agreed that the proposal had been "made up so as to satisfy two differing judgments in this Assembly", but he thought the best way to approach accommodation was to debate the issues first, and he observed, "it had been well if you had taken in some of the other [party], that they also might have been consulted with in it."[211] Philip Nye protested that the paper before them was now being treated as if it represented the biblical rule, and he called for new propositions to be formulated without allowing themselves to be limited by the text that was being presented.[212]

The reason for the Independents' opposition appears to have been that they had been excluded from the preliminary consideration of the proposals. The draft had been formulated to the satisfaction of the majority, and then the Independents had briefly been allowed to see what had been agreed on by the others without them. Baillie shows that this policy was deliberately followed by the Scots, who had initially drafted the statement and then discussed it with the leaders of the Puritan majority:

> We have drawn up a directorie for church-censures and excommunication; wherein we keep the practise of our Church, but decline speculative questions. This, we hope, will please all who are not Independents; yea, I think even they needed not differ with us here; but yet it appears they will to separation, and are not so carefull to accommodat, as conscience would command peaceable men to be.[213]

He was even more explicit in his letter to Spang on the following day (the 27th):

> What remains of the Government, concerning the hard questions of excommunication, Mr. Henderson has drawne it up, by way of a practicall directorie, so calmlie, that we trust to gett it all past the

---

[210] *Ibid.* pp. 30, 31.

[211] *Ibid.* p. 30.

[212] *Ibid.* p. 32. Reynolds had suggested that the Independents should indicate how far they could agree with the statement, "and where they stick." It seems possible that Palmer's later intervention, in which he urged that they should speak not of three parties in the Assembly but of two, may have been inspired by the Independents' opposition – a reminder to the Independents that the majority, for all its differences, would vote as one. *Ibid.*

[213] Publick Letter, 26th December; *Letters and Journals* II. 248.

Assemblie the next week, without much debate. The men whom most we feared, professes their satisfaction with that draught. It's certainlie true what yow wrote, of the impossibilitie ever to have gotten England reformed by humane means, as things here stood, without their brethrens help: The learnedest and most considerable part of them were fullie Episcopall; of these who joyned with the Parliament, the greatest and most countenanced part were much Episcopall".[214]

From this it seems probable that the "men whom most we feared" who had been brought into these discussions initially were not the Independents but conservative Puritans who, Baillie recognized, had begun the struggle with decided leanings towards episcopacy.

The upshot of the debate on January 7th was that a committee was appointed with two representatives from each of the three positions set out by Marshall at the beginning,[215] and this committee was to meet with the Scottish Commissioners to explore the chances of agreement. A show of Reformed unity at this time would undoubtedly assist the parliamentary negotiators when they met the King and his advisers at Uxbridge at the end of that month.

The attempt to reach agreement foundered. On Friday, 17th January, the Committee brought in a report on the Directory for excommunication, and the Dissenting Brethren were given the weekend to consider four different forms for giving absolution to the penitent. When they reported their choice on Monday 20th, there still seemed to be a reasonable chance of concord, for although Temple feared it would be "a seed of perpetuall division", Marshall thought very differently, and the session seems to have been relatively amicable.

It is difficult to say from the cryptic comments in the Minutes where the actual break occurred, but it appears to have followed the introduction of a Scots paper on the 23rd listing the sins that warranted excommunication. From the debate it seems that the Independents not only felt that this catalogue of sins was far too wide, but also, more seriously, that it regarded the culpability as centring in the sin itself rather than in the impenitence of the sinner.[216] On the other hand the Scots stated frankly that this was

[214] To Spang, 27th December; *ibid*. p. 250.
[215] Goodwin, Nye, Marshall, Vines, Palmer, Seaman. Later Burroughes, Reynolds and Young were added; Minutes III. pp. 32f.
[216] The issue had arisen previously in this debate, and it pointed to a different way of viewing church discipline and excommunication. At the very beginning of the debate, on December 31st, Philip Nye had declared, "We grant that if any sin come to obstinacy, it

as far as they were willing to go in the matter. Henderson declared, "We cannot accommodate further than we have set down in this paper", and he went on to say with regard to another paper being considered that "If you give way to that paper, I see not how any error can be suppressed."[217]

The record is not very clear, and we no longer have Gillespie's clear analysis or Lightfoot's astringent summaries to help us, and even Baillie was busy in Scotland. There were now two papers before the Assembly – the one apparently penned by Marshall, and material submitted by the Scots on January 21st and 23rd.[218] It seems that the Scots' intervention caused the Independents immediately to react to the way in which the matter of excommunication was now being considered. Bridge at once entered his dissent, and Goodwin protested that the paper before them put the Reformed Churches in a position "which the Scripture doth not put upon any Churches in the world", and he went on to say that "This is to set all truth in the pillory, and the Reformed Churches over them."[219]

From that point on the situation deteriorated, although attempts were still made to bridge the gulf.[220] The major issue was whether excommunication is a sentence to be legally imposed upon specific sins, or whether it is to be reserved for the sinner's obstinate impenitence. Nye insisted on the latter: "sin is not bound in heaven except impenitently persisted in", but Rutherford and others wanted the sentence to be legally invoked – "by sufficient evidence and testimony of the fact" – on some sins automatically. Nye agreed that "atrocious sins may be excommunicated", but he asked, "what will you call atrocious sins, such as are materially so?"[221]

The Assembly ordered its committee to proceed to draw up

---

is liable to excommunication;" but he appears to have been less ready to impose it automatically for specific sins, because "there may be a fundamental error in one age, that is not a fundamental error in another". Minutes III. 25.

[217] *Ibid.* p. 42.

[218] *Ibid.* p. 41.

[219] *Ibid.* p. 43.

[220] E.g., an effort was made on January 30th. Goodwin, Nye, Reynolds, Young, Chambers, Tuckney, Palmer, Herle, and Temple were asked to meet in the afternoon with the Scots Commissioners for what appears to have been a last-ditch attempt to mend the breach.

[221] *Ibid.* p. 45. The difference in their approach to excommunication may have arisen from the difference between a 'gathered' form of the church, in which all the communicants are professed members, and a 'parish' concept in which the communicants may include a mixture of professed, nominal and even indifferent Christians. One can see the need for a more formal listing of sins in the latter, and the emphasis on 'impenitence' as disrupting the fellowship in the former.

the Directory for Excommunication and report after the weekend on Monday, February 3rd, and Rutherford declared "I think this is the saddest session that ever I sat in regard of the reverend brethren's renouncing of the whole accommodation."[222] There were good grounds for his concern, for on the following Monday Goodwin claimed that the whole attempt at accommodation "was professedly ambiguously penned", and he with the rest of his colleagues asked that their dissent on this issue should stand.[223] At much the same time the Assembly was asked to forward to the Houses whatever remained in the matter of church government, because it was needed by the Parliament's negotiators at Uxbridge.[224]

On Thursday, February 6th a committee was appointed to draw up the Directory for Discipline, and on the following day Burgess protested that rumours were circulating in the City to the effect that the Independents had dissented because of the interpretation of accommodation given in the Assembly by himself and others.[225] Naturally the Assembly passed an appropriate motion to exonerate itself and its members, although the Minutes seem to show that the people in the streets of London were not too ill-formed.

By this date there was probably no way of bridging the ecclesiastical differences that had opened up. De Witt says that the final break "entered upon the first lap of its final stage" when Dr. Stanton on February 10th, on behalf of the Second Committee, brought in a proposal regarding appeals to the superior assemblies of the Church, and the Independents countered with a motion that asserted the autonomous rights of the particular congregation. Alternatively we could think of this as the point where the basic cause of the break became clear, for what De Witt and other writers have not seen is that behind questions of the autonomy of the local congregation and subordination there was the fundamental nature of spiritual authority in the Church.[226] Is coercive power necessary or is it foreign to the Church of Jesus Christ?

---

[222] 31st January, 1644/5; *ibid.*

[223] *Ibid.* p. 46. This was somewhat unfair to Stephen Marshall, who had frankly admitted that his paper had been penned in the hope that it might lead to accommodation (cf. *ibid.* pp. 29f.) It was the later Scots paper that caused the rift.

[224] Cf. the intervention of the Earl of Manchester on February 3rd and the Order of the House of Commons the following day. *Ibid.*

[225] *Ibid.* p. 47.

[226] Cf. the proposition "It is lawfull and agreeable to the Word of God, that there be a subordination of Congregationall, Classicall, Provinciall, and Nationall Assemblies for the Government of the Church, that so appeals may be made from the inferiour to the

Even Charles Herle, who had often championed the rights of the Independents, felt that such power was necessary for government:

> An argument against a coercive power is to argue against our Assembly, and the ordinance by which we sit. So government, and what government can there be without coercive power, a power proper to that government? . . . If there be no government, it is not *regnum* but *tumultus* . . .[227]

The issue was particularly acute when the sentence of excommunication was invoked. The Presbyterians argued reasonably enough that the individual should have legal means of appeal against the sentence of a local presbytery,[228] and the Independents with equal reason insisted that church discipline should be exercised only within the context of the church's regular life and worship where the person under that discipline is in the covenant and engaged in mutual ministry with the rest of the fellowship. More particularly they insisted that when a person is to be excommunicated, those who have the duty to perform that sentence must have direct pastoral responsibility for the one under discipline.[229]

The frustration of the Assembly was expressed a few days later during the long debate on appeals. Jeremiah Whitaker had quoted John Cotton's *The Keyes of the Kingdom*, and this had led Samuel Rutherford to exclaim, "When I read through that treatise of the Keys of the Kingdom of Heaven, I thought it an easy labour for an universal pacification, he comes so near to us." Charles Herle's distress revealed itself in his comment, "I conceive it is part of our unhappiness when we are upon disputing we fall accommodating, and when accommodating then disputing."[230] There was little more to be done, since the proof for appeals would clearly follow from the proofs for subordination, as both he and Lazarus Seaman pointed out. Seaman reminded the Assembly that "subordination doth prove the liberty of

---

superior respectively." *Jus Divinum*, p. 146. That is clearly a statement of polity, but behind it there is clearly the question how the subordination of such assemblies is to be arranged for government, and the kind of authority and power by which decisions would be implemented.

[227] 13th February, 1644/5; Minutes III. p. 57.

[228] See Edmund Calamy's arguments, *ibid*.

[229] Hence Goodwin's opposition to including excommunication within the rights of 'superior' assemblies; 13th February, *ibid*. p. 58. Cf. also Nye's comments regarding synods, 3rd March; *ibid*. pp. 66f.

[230] 17th February. *Ibid*. p. 60.

appeals in civil government",[231] and therefore presumably this indicated a similar subordination in the Church. But again, that underscored the issue, for was the government of the Church fundamentally akin to that of the State, or was it to be something radically different?

Furthermore, little compromise was possible because both sides held differing expectations about the work of the Assembly. The Scots and their associates had argued plausibly that it should first determine and establish the new form of the Church of England, and there would then be time enough to consider possible exceptions. Failing the adoption of their own ecclesiology, the Independents on the other hand wanted their right to exist to be granted first, and then they would be ready to explore further points of agreement. William Carter said, "If we can have no security, I hope you will not desire we should withdraw":[232] security was their primary concern as they faced their relationship to the new religious establishment.

By the end of 1644 the divisions between Independents and Presbyterians in the Assembly had become potentially new confessional stances, but we wonder whether this would have become a permanent division if the Assembly had not been subject to constantly intruding influences from outside. Because of the historical context in which the ecclesiastical debates took place, the parties found themselves representing far wider issues within English society and the struggle in which England was locked. The Presbyterians continued to stand for covenanted uniformity and all that would imply socially about the *status quo*, but by this time the Independents were tied to the fortunes of Cromwell's troopers, to liberty of conscience and to all that implied about a different kind of society. Providence had found a strange way of saying that it would not be bound by theology.

---

[231] *Ibid.*

[232] I.e., withdraw their dissent. As far as one can tell, there had been no suggestion that they should withdraw from the Assembly. *Ibid.* p. 47.

CHAPTER 14

COVENANTED UNIFORMITY

I

Uniformity in the Scots Fashion

Robert Baillie left the Assembly soon after the end of December to attend the General Assembly in Scotland, so he had no first-hand knowledge of the further rupture on the matter of excommunication. By the time he left England on this temporary visit to his homeland, the optimism he had had in the spring[1] had been justified. In a letter dated December 26th he reported that the Directory was almost complete, that a good deal of it had already been sent to Parliament, and that the votes on church government had been collated and were ready.

> The Independents have entered their dissent only to three proposi-tions: 'That in Ephesus was a classical Presbytrie; That there is a subordination of Assemblies; That a single congregation hes not all and sole power of ordination.' Their reasons against these three propositions we expect tomorrow. Against the end of the next week we hope our Committees will have answers ready to all they will say; and after all is sent up to the House, by God's help, we expect shortlie ane erection of Presbytries and Synods here; for there appears a good forwardness to expede all things of that kind in both Houses since the taking of Newcastle.[2]

Then the Assembly would proceed to "our great question of Excommunication", the Catechism and the Confession. Baillie agreed that there was enough in these matters to keep the

---

[1] He had written to George Young in April, "daylie we gaine ground". *Letters and Journals*, II. 163.
[2] *Ibid.* pp. 247f.

Assembly busy for a long time "if the wrangling humour which long predomined in many here did continue; but, thanks to God," he declared, "that is much abated, and all inclines toward a conclusion."[3]

It was in this letter, and in the one he wrote to Spang on the following day (the 27th), that Baillie reveals the careful manner in which he and his friends had prepared for the issue of excommunication to be eased through the Assembly. At that time that was still in doubt, but whatever the outcome, he said "we hope to gett the debates of these things we most feared either eschewed or shortened."[4] Baillie's hopes were not entirely fulfilled, but at least the Scots' tactical preparation carried the English majority with them.

The four parts of the covenanted uniformity at which the Scots aimed – 'confessing of faith, form of church government, directory of worship, and catechising' – were an integrated system, and to that extent they were equally important to churchmanship; but special urgency attached to the Directory of Worship and church government not only because of the need in English parishes, but also because church discipline was central to the Scots' understanding of the Church.

For the English the need of the parishes was paramount, and particularly the need for clergymen to be able to fulfil the ecclesiastical (i.e. sacramental) functions expected of them. "The greatest thing this country complains of", declared Herbert Palmer, "is the want of a directory for the sacrament",[5] and behind this we may see the conservative feelings of a population not far removed from its earlier Catholicism. The Puritan suppression of Christmas was detested, and these conservative attitudes of the English public were indicated in the motion "that some of our members should be sent to the Houses, to desire them to give an order, that the next fast-day might be solemnly kept, because the people will be ready to neglect it, being Christmas-day."[6] The demand of such people was for ordained ministers who could be accepted as able to perform valid sacraments and such traditional functions of the clergy as weddings and funerals, i.e., for church order recognizable as a form of 'catholic' Christianity consistent with the English Reformation.

During his time in London Baillie became a shrewd and

---

[3] *Ibid.* p. 248.
[4] *Ibid.* p. 248.
[5] 24th October; TMs. II. 536 (Ms. II. f. 276.)
[6] Lightfoot, *Journal*, p. 344; Minutes III. 21.

accurate observer of English affairs.[7] He may have entered the Assembly with some mistaken notions about the 'presbyterian' convictions of the English Puritan divines, but closer acquaintance for over a year had taught him differently. As we have already seen, in his letters at the end of 1644 he very clearly recognized the episcopal preferences with which many of the English divines had entered the Assembly, and he gives some indication how they were wooed into the Scots' proposals for the Church of England. Baillie's statement that "of these who joyned with the Parliament, the greatest and most countenanced part were much Episcopall",[8] should be put alongside the impressions Baxter gives us about opinion among the Puritan clergy during the early stages of the Civil War.[9] These testimonies explain a great deal in the Minutes that is otherwise inexplicable if that body had been composed of convinced Presbyterians as De Witt and some earlier historians assumed.

In the same letter Baillie mentioned the "unreasonable obstinacy of the Independents" and the "strange confusions" caused by religious anarchy as factors that contributed to the Scots' success in the Assembly. Reading between the lines we can see how these conservative Puritan divines – the English 'Presbyterians' of later history – turned to the Scots to maintain the national character of the Church and to retain the hope of establishing an ecclesiastical discipline enforced by civil authority.[10]

Earlier confessional historians protested that *An Apologeticall Narration* gives the impression that the Presbyterians were intolerant. "This impression", wrote William Beveridge, "was entirely erroneous. No Assembly, guided on questions of

---

[7] For example, he had a very clear and comprehensive understanding of the Independents' ecclesiology, and he strongly advised any who could not write knowledgeably and to the point to remain silent. Cf. his letters to David Buchanan, *ca.* January 1644/5; *Letters and Journals*, II. 152–4.

[8] 27th December. *Ibid.* p. 250; quoted *supra* pp. 431f.

[9] Cf. *supra* pp. 105–18.

[10] On issues that they did not consider vitally important to the covenanted uniformity the Scots were prepared to adjust in order to maintain their unity with the Puritan majority. For example, in the debates on baptism (9th–10th October, 1644,) Rutherford had agreed with Wilson, Marshall and Burroughes that there was no need to catechize parents anew at the baptism of their child; but Calamy represented the position as it was found in the English parishes, and he said that although such questions might not be necessary for believing communicants, they were necessary because "many of the Assembly will baptize the children of those they will not admit [to the Lord's Supper.]" TMs. II. 481 (Ms. II. f. 248b.) Cf. *Ibid.* 480 (Ms. II. f. 248,) Gillespie, *Notes*, p. 90.

Henderson immediately spoke strongly in support of Calamy's position, and followed it with a similar speech the following day. Rutherford was noticeably silent. Cf. Lightfoot, *Journal*, pp. 315f. Gillespie, *Notes*, pp. 90f., TMs. II. 482–489 (Ms. II. ff. 249–252b.)

Church government by such wise and moderate statesmanship as that of Henderson, could have been absolutely intolerant.'"[11] One may agree that Alexander Henderson was the wisest and perhaps most moderate of the Scottish Commissioners, but we should recognize that in putting forward their modest claim to toleration, the writers of *An Apologeticall Narration* were presenting a new and still very unpopular idea. Religious intolerance was not regarded as evil but as commitment, and intolerance was therefore endemic to seventeenth century religion, particularly within churches that expected the support of the civil authorities. Robert Baillie was entirely justified in pointing to the intolerance of the New England Congregationalists,[12] and the New England Puritans never understood the English Independents' claim in this regard.

Indeed it would have been remarkable if, enjoying the power they did, the Presbyterians of that time had been more tolerant, but this was not readily appreciated amid the liberal presuppositions of the nineteenth century when many denominational histories were written. Historians felt they had to dissociate the Presbyterianism of the Assembly from any embarrassing relationship to men like Thomas Edwards.[13]

It would be unfair and inaccurate to suggest that Presbyterians in the seventeenth century held a monopoly on intolerance. The attitude was common to all Churches, especially those that accepted close relationship to the State. Once we recognize that intolerance was regarded as a virtue rather than as a vice, and that liberty of conscience was understood as an excuse for license and immorality rather than as evidence of broadmindedness, we may have less difficulty in recognizing that the attitude of Edwards and Baillie would probably have been endorsed by most people at that time.[14] Baillie had no compunction about using force to secure the establishment of Scottish uniformity, any more than Cromwell had any compunction in using force to prevent it.

---

[11] *A Short History of the Westminster Assembly*, (Edinburgh, T. & T. Clark, 1904,) p. 69.

[12] 19th April, 1644; *Letters and Journals*, II. 168.

[13] W. M. Hetherington, for example, contrasted the 'fiercely hostile spirit' of Thomas Edwards's *Antapologia* with the 'dignified and Christian-like calmness of spirit and manner' in which Charles Herle had written against the Independents, while Beveridge dismissed Edwards as an outrageous fanatic. Cf. W. M. Hetherington, *History of the Westminster Assembly*, pp. 187, 189; William Beveridge, *Short Hist. of the West. Assembly*, p. 86.

[14] It was the almost inevitable result of ecclesiastical *jus divinum* when linked to the power of the State. Belief in a church form as of divine right will produce martyrs who will die for it, but it will also often produce those who think they are justified in persecuting others in order to maintain a church's supremacy.

Furthermore, Baillie believed that once the work of the Assembly was satisfactorily concluded, he and his friends would have no difficulty in getting the Independents and the sects quietened. He was obviously close to Edward's work, for the latter presented him with a copy of *Antapologia* when it was published, and Baillie wrote:

> Mr. Edwards hes written a splendid confutation of all Independents' Apologie. All the ministers of London, at least more than a hundred of them, have agreed to erect a weeklie lecture for him in Christ's Church, the heart of the city, where he may handle these questions, and nothing else, before all that will come to hear.[15]

Thomas Edwards was extremely popular with the London ministers, who were, according to Baillie's testimony, almost to a man Presbyterians. Edwards himself was almost able to build a career out of his opposition to the principle of religious toleration, and the successive parts of his later work, *Gangraena* (1646) reveal the extent to which his views were shared by a very wide public.

Baillie was willing to go to almost any lengths to see the establishment of the covenanted uniformity he and his colleagues sought. Beveridge described him as "the Nye of the Scottish Commissioners" and noted that "he had an undue fondness for little matters of diplomacy – schemes, it has been pointed out, which were peculiarly transparent."[16] However, Baillie's schemes were transparent only because he was such an indefatigable correspondent, and he suffered the curious misfortune of having left his record behind him. At the time his intrigues may have been suspected, but they were unknown except to his intimate friends, and there is a more serious side to these 'little matters of diplomacy', for if they did not always achieve their objectives, they surely contributed to the final breach within the Assembly as well as to its ecclesiastical result.

On the other hand, before we judge Baillie too harshly, we must remember that the Scottish Commissioners, for all the courtesies extended to them, were by their own decision not members of the Assembly. They were present as representatives

---

[15] For Glasgow, August 7th, 1644; *Letters and Journals*, II. 215f. See also the following comments: ". . . bot if once our armie were in such a condition as easilie, if we were dilligent, it might be, all these clouds would evanish, and we would regaine this peoples heart, *and doe with all sectaries, and all things else, what we would.*" *Ibid.* p. 268. My italics.

[16] *Short Hist. of the West. Assembly*, p. 51.

of another Church and another nation, and diplomacy was almost inevitably the condition of their presence in London. To do Baillie justice we must judge him as he viewed himself – he was in London as an official envoy of his Kirk and his nation. His task was to pursue a clearly defined policy that had already been mapped out by Scottish national leadership, and was aimed at preserving the Church of Scotland in its essential character. That could best be secured by bringing the Church of the southern nation into covenanted uniformity with Scottish faith and practice. The location of Baillie's work was the Westminster Assembly, but his goals, whether acknowledged or not, were diplomatic.

So when Baillie secured the help of William Apollonius and the Dutch churches against the Independents, it was a diplomatic victory,[17] and when the Independents were able to persuade Gisbert Voet, the theologian of Utrecht, to write a preface to John Cotton's *Keyes of the Kingdom*, it was a diplomatic reverse.[18] To be fair to Baillie one must see that for all its concern with Reformed theology, his work was essentially an extension of Scottish national policy. Moreover, in light of the earlier relations between England and Scotland in the seventeenth century, its goals are understandable, and to some extent justifiable.[19]

These national goals in relation to the earlier history were very clearly laid out in his speech to the General Assembly on 23rd January 1644/5.[20] He and his fellow Commissioners had for over a year "with all care, attended the Assemblie and Parliament there, for the furthering and advancement of that uniformitie in Divine Worship and Church Government, which both nations have sworn in their solemn League and Covenant."[21] This indicates the priority that the Scots placed on those two branches of the Assembly's work, and the reason why they were so anxious to

---

[17] For more on Apollonius see *supra* p. 380, n. 121; also my notes in *An Apologeticall Narration* (1963 edn.) pp. 47–49, and especially p. 48 note 11. His book *Consideratio*, with a preface by the Dutch Classis of Walcheren, was presented to the Assembly on Wednesday, 4th December, 1644; (cf. Lightfoot, *Journal*, p. 339, Baillie, *Letters and Journals*, II. 246.) On Wednesday, September 10th, 1646, the Assembly held a special session at which Apollonius was received and personally thanked for his work. Cf. the votes on August 29th and September 8th, 1646; Minutes III. 126, 128.

[18] To Spang, November 1st, 1644, *Letters and Journals*, II. 240.

[19] In each subject in which he involved himself, Baillie became a well-informed expert. He made himself very knowledgeable about the earlier history of the relationships between the Church of England and the Church of Scotland; cf. his book, *An Historical Vindication of the Government of the Church of Scotland*, and also his books against the former Archbishop of Canterbury, William Laud.

[20] *Letters and Journals* II. 255–7.

[21] *Ibid.* p. 255.

get them completed. Then he reminded his hearers of the historical background to their enterprise:

When the Bishops of England had put upon the neck of our Church and nation the yoke, first of their Episcopacie, then of their Ceremonies, thirdly, the whole masse of a Service-book, and with it the body of Popery: when both our Church and State did groan under one unsupportable slaverie; to have been freed of these burdens; to have been restored unto the puritie of our first Reformation, and the ancient libertie of our Kingdom; to have had Bishops, Ceremonies, Books and States slaverie reformed, we would latelie have esteemed it a mercie above all our praises: but now beholding the progress of the Lord, how he hes led us be the hand, and marched before us to the homes and holds of our injurious oppressors; how he hes made bare his holy arme, and brought the wheel of his vengeance upon the whole race and order of Prelates in England, and hes pluckt up the root, and all the branches of Episcopacie in all the Kings' dominions; that ane Assemblie and Parliament of England unanimouslie (which is their word) abolished, not only these ceremonies which troubled us, but the whole Service-book as a very idoll (so speak they also,) and a vessell full of much mischiefe; that in the place of Episcopacie a Scotts Presbytrie should be concluded in ane English Assemblie, and ordained in ane English Parliament; as it is allreadie ordained in the House of Commons, that the practise of the Church of Scotland, sett down in a most wholesome, pious, and prudent Directorie, should come in the place of a Liturgie in all the three dominions; such stories latelie told, would have been counted fancies, dreams, meer impossibilities: yet this day we tell them as truths, and deeds done, for the great honour of our God, and, we are persuaded, the joy of many a godlie soull.[22]

We need not begrudge Robert Baillie this moment of patriotic triumph. He had earned it. The national *motif* keeps recurring through his letters in 1645. It is to be seen in a letter written in April after his return to London, in which he emphasized the importance of keeping a strong Scottish army on English soil,[23] a theme that he repeated in his letter to Robert Ramsay on May 4th, for with an adequate army they might in a short time "ruine both the Malignant party and the Sectaries." A rather less than generous note appears later in that letter when he said that they had no need to be bothered by any agitation against themselves,

for if it please God to assist us bot a little, to be at this time serviceable, not so much to defend this people in their present danger, as to fight for Scotland in the midst of their land, at their

---

[22] *Ibid*. pp. 256f.
[23] Publick Letter, 25th April, 1645, *ibid*. pp. 266ff.

charge, and with all the assistance they can make us, we may be assured of satisfaction for any wrong in word or deed that any of our friends pretends to have received, and the full payment of all any can crave, besyde all the contentment we can desyre of them in any matter either in Church or State.[24]

These grim words indicate that by this date the Scots were not popular at Westminster, but the words did not augur well for future relations between the two countries.

Baillie's letters show that to him the Scottish cause and the Presbyterian cause were one, and there is no distinction between patriotism and ecclesiology. He may well have been the source of the information that got James Cranford sent to the Tower for slandering Lord Say and some of the other leading Independents,[25] and as the time of Naseby approached, he wrote a rather ominous series of questions as to what should be their policy if Fairfax was beaten, or "if Cromwell be the victor". He suggested that James Cranford and his associates – probably the ministers and others who supported the Presbyterian cause in and around London – should enlist the help of the Earl of Essex, for by this means "yow put your selfe in that case, that yow may not be enslaved by the Independents, but may be their masters."[26] To that extent Baillie contributed to political Presbyterianism in England. It is also clear from these activities that Baillie was realist enough to know that whatever debates there were about biblical evidence and theological truth in the Assembly, the success or failure of the enterprise would depend on the outcome on the field of battle.

II

"Unanimity in the Scots fashion": the Quest for Accommodation

At the end of May, 1644, Baillie reported that the Scots Commissioners had managed to get their views about church sessions adopted by the Assembly, despite opposition from the

[24] *Ibid.* p. 274.

[25] "In July [19] a Scotch minister named Cranford having been detected in asserting that Say and his friends had carried on unauthorised negotiations with persons at Oxford, was promptly sent to the Tower. It soon, however, appeared that Cranford was a harmless retailer of gossip, and without any long delay he recovered his liberty." Gardiner, *G. C. W.* II. 335. From a letter Baillie wrote earlier to David Dickson (10th June, 1645) it seems that he held the same suspicions about the Independent politicians, and from a letter he wrote to Lauderdale (17th June, 1645) it appears that he could have been the source of Cranford's gossip. *Letters and Journals,* II. 277, 279.

[26] June 17th, 1645, for Cranford; *ibid.* pp. 278f.

Independents and the English conservatives. This, he said, "we have gotten settled with unanimity in the Scots fashion",[27] and we presume that he meant a Reformed consensus that accepted Scots' practice as the mean between two extremes.

There can be little doubt that the Scots genuinely hoped that an accommodation with the Independents would bring "unanimity in the Scots fashion", and there is no reason to think that the attempts to reach agreement, in which Alexander Henderson seems to have taken a leading part, were initiated without a sincere intention of achieving what they set out to do. On the other hand, there is equally no reason to think that Henderson and the Scots Commissioners would allow their own practice to be compromised or even seriously modified: unanimity, if it was to be realized, was to be "in the Scots fashion."

Comparatively soon after his arrival in London, Baillie had spoken of a private conference with Thomas Goodwin, and of how much Goodwin and the Scots seemed to agree on matters of worship,[28] and later he said "We mind yet againe to assay the Independents in a privie conference, if we can draw them to a reasonable accommodation; for that toleration they aime at we cannot consent."[29]

A further attempt to come to terms had been made early in 1644 because the Assembly was getting poor publicity in the City. To prevent the spread of such rumours, the Scots tried to find out "how far we could draw them in a private friendly way of accommodation",[30] and to this end three Independents, Goodwin, Burroughes and Bridge, together with three from the English Puritan majority,[31] met with the Scots Commissioners and the statesmen, Lord Wharton, Sir Henry Vane the younger and Oliver St. John.[32]

Baillie said that there were hopeful signs of possible agreement, but

---

[27] To Spang, 31st May, 1644; *Letters and Journals*, II. 186f.

[28] *Supra* p. 361. Cf. To Spang, 1st January, 1643/4, *Letters and Journals*. II. 123. It is sometimes implied that the Independents were the only ones in favour of extempore prayer. It is true that Baillie held that the Scots were for a moderate position between extempore prayer and a fixed liturgy, but Samuel Rutherford was strongly opposed to read prayers. Cf. his letter to Lady Boyd, Viscountess Kenmure, *Mr. Rutherford's Letters* (3rd edn., 1675), Epist. 49, pp. 221f.

[29] 18th February, 1644, *Letters and Journals*, II. 140.

[30] Publick Letter, 2nd April, 1644, *ibid.* p. 145.

[31] Marshall, Vines and Palmer.

[32] It is interesting to see that the three politicians associated here with the Scots were all later regarded as political 'Independents.' It suggests that in April 1644 it was too early to regard the parties in Parliament as clearly defined.

> Mr. Nye was lyke to spoil all our play. When it came to his turne in the Assemblie to oppugne the Presbytrie, he had, from the 18th of Matthew, drawn in a crooked unformall way, which he could never gett in a sillogisme, the inconsistence of a Presbytrie with a civill State. In this he was cryed doun as impertinent. The day following, when he saw the Assemblie full of the prime nobles and chiefe members of both Houses, he did fall on that argument againe, and very boldlie offered to demonstrate, that our way of drawing a whole kingdome under one Nationall Assemblie, as formidable, yea, pernicious and thrice over pernicious, to civill states and kingdoms. All cryed him doune, and some would have had him expelled the Assemblie as seditious.[33]

This refers to Nye's ill-judged intervention in the Assembly on February 20th and 21st, 1644,[34] and the Scots had immediately conferred on what they should do. At first they were determined to have nothing more to do with Nye until he apologized, but when it had become clear that the other Independents would not negotiate without their colleague, the Commissioners were persuaded by their friends "to shuffle it over the best way might be, and to goe on in our business", and Baillie observed that as a result of this Nye became "the most accommodating man in the company."[35]

It should be remembered that the undisclosed negotiations between the Scots and the Independents had been given more official standing when new possibilities of agreement had arisen out of the debate in the Assembly about synods.[36] This had led to a new Committee of Accommodation being activated on Alexander Henderson's motion of March 8th,[37] and Baillie had remarked that the Scots were glad that what they had been "doing in private should be thus authorized."[38]

This was one of the most determined efforts to achieve agreement and could have become one of the Assembly's crowning achievements. Gillespie's notes of those meetings are particularly instructive.[39] Stephen Marshall brought a list of six propositions that had been accepted in previous consultations,[40] and at the next meeting on March 12th Richard Vines brought in twelve

---

[33] Publick Letter, 2nd April, 1644; *ibid.* pp. 145f.

[34] Cf. *supra* pp. 271ff.

[35] *Letters and Journals*, II. 146.

[36] Cf. *supra* pp. 300–303.

[37] TMs. I. 721–2 (Ms. I. ff. 372b–373.) Goodwin, Bridge and Burroughes had been appointed to meet with Vines, Seaman, Palmer and the Scots Commissioners.

[38] *Letters and Journals* II. 147.

[39] Gillespie, *Notes*, pp. 37, 39f., 40f.

[40] *Ibid.* p. 37.

propositions from the Presbyterian side as a possible basis for agreement.[41] As Gillespie, however, observed, Goodwin and Bridge protested that as a basis for accommodation these proposals left matters "so that all that is left is to see how far they [the Independents] can come up to a presbytery – not how far we can condescend to their principles, but how far they can yield to us."[42] We do not know whether the wording was precisely that of the Independents or Gillespie's own, but it rings true: if agreement was to be reached the Scots Commissioners were determined that it would be by the dissenters accepting the Scots program.

On the following day (the 13th March) the Independents had offered their own seven proposals on church government as a basis for discussion,[43] and the Committee debates developed from these prepared positions. Eventually the first two of the Independents' propositions[44] were revised and expanded and agreed,[45] on March 14th a third article of agreement was added,[46] and on the 19th "other propositions were agreed on."[47] A report was presented to the Assembly on behalf of the committee by

---

[41] *Ibid.* pp. 38f.

[42] *Ibid.* p. 39.

[43] *Ibid.*, p. 40.

[44] "1. Let there be meetings of the elders of several neighbouring church as oft as they have occasion.

2. At these meetings let them pray, expound, resolve difficult cases of conscience, and preach the word." *Ibid.*

[45] They were expanded to this:

"1. That there be a fixed presbytery, or meeting of elders of several neighbouring congregations, to consult and advise upon such things as concern these congregations in matters ecclesiastical, which shall be afterwards expressed, and that such presbyteries are the ordinance of Christ, having authority and power from him.

2. That such presbyteries, in cases that are to come before them, have power doctrinally to declare and determine what is agreeable to the word of God, and this judgment of theirs is to be received with reverence and obligation, as from an ordinance of Christ." *Ibid.*, p. 41.

[46] "Such presbyteries, or meetings of elders, have power to require the elders of any of those neighbouring congregations to give an account of anything scandalous in doctrine or practice." *Ibid.*

[47] "It was added to the first proposition (at these meetings, Let them pray, preach, handle practical cases, or resolve hard questions.)

4. The churches and elderships being offended, Let them examine, admonish, and in case of obstinacy, declare them either disturbers of the peace, subverters of the faith, or otherwise as the nature and degree of the offence shall require.

5. In case that particular church or eldership shall refuse to reform that scandalous doctrine or practice, then that meeting of elders, which is assembled from several congregations, shall acquaint their several congregations respectively, and withdraw from them, denying church communion and fellowship with them.

All these were reported to the Assembly, with this provision added. – These propositions we assent unto, supposing that particular congregations have that power which we conceive respectively to be due unto them." *Ibid.*

Palmer on 14th May.[48] But although it was feared that these discussions might compromise the work of the Assembly itself by anticipating future debates, the divines agreed that the committee should continue and consider "anything that may tend to accommodation".[49] On the 21st May Marshall communicated to the Assembly the matters that had been agreed at the meeting on the 19th.[50]

De Witt observes that Baillie's private account[51] seems to have gone further than the reports actually received by the Assembly, but this would seem to be an almost necessary condition if the Committee of Accommodation was going to explore the possible areas of future friction. He wonders, however, whether this meant that the Independents had compromised their principles, or whether the whole operation was simply "another facet of the many-sided campaign of delay and obstruction in which they had already so long been engaged."[52]

Without doubting the willingness of the Independents to use any means available to postpone decisions if it were politically advantageous to do so, this does seem a rather less than generous way of recognizing that if concessions had been made in the committee of Accommodation, they all seem to have been made on one side. The Independents had gone a long way, although they may not have conceded absolutely the juridical power of presbytery over congregations. If the evidence in the footnotes (45, 51) is compared with the Independents' opening principles (44), it will be seen that the ecclesiastical assemblies had changed their spirit – from that of meetings called for fraternal support

---

[48] The report given by Palmer follows substantially the first three points of agreement as given in notes 45 and 46 above. Cf. Lightfoot, *Journal*, pp. 214f.

[49] *Ibid.* p. 215. On the other hand the vote authorizing the continuation of the committee specified very clearly that it was "The Committee formerly apoynted to consider of Agreement & difference in the poynt of a presbitery over more congregations than one", and it was ordered to report in a week. TMs. I. 749 (Ms. I. f. 386b.)

[50] Lightfoot, *Journal*, p. 229; cf. Gillespie, *Notes*, p. 41.

[51] Cf. Baillie's account: "We have mett some three or four times alreadie, and have agreed on five or six propositions, hopeing, by God's grace, to agree in more. They yield, that a Presbytrie, even as we take it, is ane ordinance of God, which hath power and authoritie from Christ, to call the ministers and elders, or any in their bounds, before them, to account for any offence in life or doctrine, to try and examine the cause, to admonish and rebuke, and if they be obstinate, to declare them as Ethnicks and publicans, and give them over to the punishment of the Magistrates; also doctrinallie, to declare the mind of God in all questions of religion, with such authoritie as obliedges to receave their just sentences; that they will be members of such fixed Presbytries, keep the meeting, preach as it comes to their turne, joyne in the discipline after doctrine. Thus farr we have gone without prejudice to the proceedings of the Assemblie." *Letters and Journals*, II. pp. 147f.

[52] De Witt, *Jus Divinum*, p. 118.

and mutual edification they had been recast in decidedly jurisdictional terms: the spirit is different.

The two parties were, as De Witt recognized, very close, and yet we must agree that these proposals "stop short of that authoritative spiritual power which the presbyterians insisted appertained to the higher courts and assemblies of the church and by virtue of which discipline was possible, but which the Independents denied", and that because of this, "the appearance of closeness and unity is in some measure deceptive."[53] This was the essential difference, and despite the quirks of polity, perhaps it was the only essential difference – one side claimed that there was a governing *power* in the gospel, and the other side thought that such power did not properly belong to the gospel. From that perspective De Witt was entirely right to describe it as the "great continental divide in the history of evangelical church polity",[54] but the division took on these proportions because both sides believed their own position to be *jure divino*, and therefore dared not concede the point to the other.[55]

The dream of Reformed unanimity continued to haunt the Scots and the Assembly throughout 1644. It had been taken up again in April when the attempt to formulate recommendations on ordination led directly into an important debate on the presbytery.[56] The proposition was temporarily dropped, but discussions with the Independents began again, for at the end of the month Baillie wrote to one of his correspondents, "we are hopefull, if God might help us, to have our Presbytries erected, as we expect shortlie to have them, and gett the chieffe of the Independents to joyn with us in our practicall conclusions, as we are much labouring for it".[57] The possibility of Reformed unanimity was worth the effort.

The earlier attempts at accommodation had been conducted within the Assembly itself, but the efforts were put on an entirely

---

[53] De Witt, *Jus Divinum*, p. 119.

[54] *Ibid*.

[55] It is possible to believe in the *jus divinum* of the Church itself without using it to justify the details of a particular polity, but that was something neither side was ready to concede. A more pragmatic approach to church order could have accepted the presbyterian system and administered it with 'ministerial' authority rather than the 'magisterial' authority the Independents rightly feared. There is evidence of this approach in some members of the Assembly, as it was to be found in Baxter; but the members had to make a choice between rival claims to *jus divinum*, and at that point clerical preferences and fears for the nation carried many into the presbyterian camp.

[56] 10th April, 1644; cf. *supra* pp. 333ff.; Lightfoot, *Journal*, pp. 243f.

[57] To David Dickson, 29th April, 1644, *Letters and Journals*, II. 172.

new basis by the vote that Cromwell managed to get past the House of Commons on September 13th, for a parliamentary order of this sort came with the authority of a command. The vote had been joined with a suggestion that must have sounded ominous to the Scots and their supporters, for at the first meeting of the committee on September 20th, Stephen Marshall read the order from the Commons "for endeavouring a union, and, if that be not possible, to consider how far tender consciences may be borne with."[58] Moreover, the scene had shifted from the Assembly and its own committees to the Grand Committee, and at once the politicians were fully in evidence and active. Oliver St. John said that the House had noted the differences about church government that appeared in the Assembly, and thought that the differences should be reconciled or that some other expedient should be found for the peace of the Church.[59]

Gillespie provided us with his own notes for the six or seven meetings of the Grand Committee during the period from September 20th to October 25th,[60] and his record of the first meeting (September 20th) suggests something of the disarray in which the Scots found themselves through the sudden and unexpected 'alteratione' in the position taken by influential politicians like Oliver St. John and Henry Vane. The Scots were relatively quiet,[61] and the open differences that appeared seem to have been between the Independents and English 'Presbyterians' such as Seaman and Palmer. The latter, for example, wanted to restrict discussion to differences already revealed in the Assembly's debates, but Marshall and the Independents argued that this was not the intention of the House of Commons.

The major interest in this debate, is in reinforcing impressions we have from the Assembly itself.[62] It was clear, however, to the

---

[58] Gillespie, *Notes*, p. 103.

[59] *Ibid.*

[60] *Ibid.*, pp. 103–107. The debates were stopped on 25th October by order of the House of Commons. *Ibid.* p. 107.

[61] The Earl of Loudoun urged speed for the peace of the church, while Henderson reacted sharply to mention of 'tender consciences', observing that "tenderness is the best property of conscience, and is to be encouraged rather than tolerated." (*Ibid.* p. 103.) He thought they should first review their agreements, while Warriston pointed out that the work they were presently engaged in was precisely the same as that undertaken by the Assembly's Committee of Accommodation. *Ibid.* Apart from these contributions, the Scots were silent.

[62] First, Palmer showed how far he now identified himself with the Scots when he suggested that the Scots "should give in our Form of the Church of Scotland (it having an existence), and that this Committee shall consider how far they can agree to that." Then Herle pointed out, (as it had already been pointed out in the Assembly,) that there were three interpretations of presbytery to be found among the divines; and again, (as in the

Scots that Oliver St. John, the man whom Baillie described as "our most trustie friend", was backing the Independents' plea for liberty of conscience, and that he would not allow them to be pushed into a corner because of their numerical disadvantage.[63] The upshot of this meeting was that a sub-committee was appointed as St. John had originally suggested, and on 30th September Vines presented nine points of agreement[64] and announced that the Dissenting Brethren had promised to submit their disagreements if any.

These points of agreement were noticeably briefer than the provisions accepted in the Assembly's Committee of Accommodation, but there are two other interesting points. First, there is specific mention of Parliament as reserving the right to select the members of county classes and to call national assemblies;[65] but secondly, we should note the way in which those proposals were

---

Assembly) this had been denied on the grounds that the difference between two of these was purely intellectual. At the same time, Goodwin and Calamy agreed that the order was not intended to explore again all the theoretical points of difference, but only "of practical differences, which may hinder men from living as brethren in peace together." *Ibid.* p. 103.

[63] When Seaman, Burgess and Francis Rous had urged that the Independents should produce a list of their differences from the system of government of the Church of Scotland, St. John said that this put too much on the Independents, but "that now church government is to be looked upon as *in fieri*, in the Assembly." *Ibid.* p. 103.

[64] "In confidence of agreeement in the other three parts of uniformity, we come to points of Government.

1. That a congregation having officers, according to the word, is a church that hath power in all ecclesiastical affairs, which do only concern itself.

2. That these officers are to be so many in each congregation, as that three, or two at least, may agree in every act of government.

3. That these officers have power in those things which are voted by the Assembly to be due to them, as also in suspension and excommunication *non renitente ecclesia* [the church not resisting.]

4. That the elders of the congregation shall take the advice of the classis in all cases of excommunication, before they proceed to it.

5. That the members of a congregation do cohabit within certain precincts of a parish, under the preaching and ruling officers.

6. For associating churches, let there be a select number of able godly ministers in each county, and a certain number of ruling officers joined with them, to determine the causes and differences in each congregation. – The first choice of these to be made by the Parliament, that the election of ministers or governors belongs to them.

7. The ministers and ruling governors of the congregation within that county so associated, shall have power to debate and vote in that classis in such cases as pertain to that congregation, except such . . .

8. A certain number of the foresaid ministers and ruling governors as dwell together in some division, and may conveniently meet together, shall have power to hear and determine the causes within that precinct.

9. That the national assemblies be chosen from time to time, according as shall be appointed by the Parliament, and as the condition of the Church from time to time shall require." *Ibid.* p. 104.

[65] Proposals 6 and 9.

introduced: "In confidence of agreement in the other three parts of uniformity, we come to points of Government." Whatever the differences in the organization and discipline of the church, the unity of the Reformed in other areas of church life and faith was unquestioned.

The rest of the attempt of the Grand Committee to gain harmony does not carry any further than the debates in the Assembly itself, although the presence of the politicians added its own constraints, and there are occasionally intriguing clarifications. The most significant comment, and from the perspective of the ultimate fate of the Assembly's recommendations, probably the most ominous, came from Sir Henry Vane, who said:

> The order speaks of a rule which shall be established; now, if it be meant of the rule established by the Assembly, that cannot be, for the Parliament may alter it. If it be meant the rule established by Parliament, then it will be out of time to talk of differences from the rule, for all must stand to it.[66]

The English Parliament would not regard itself as under any necessity to accept what the Assembly recommended just as it did not feel itself under any obligation to follow exactly Scottish practice; and that point was made very clear a few days later to Gillespie and his fellow Commissioners when we read in his *Notes* that "Sir H. Vaine moved, That this Committee may, according to the nature of treaties, advise among themselves, apart from us."[67] Gillespie then protested that "The parties are not they and we, but the members of the Assembly, who are of different opinions", and of course technically he was right; but one suspects that one of the reasons behind the abrupt change of front on the part of the politicians was that they were beginning to feel that the Scots were having an unwarrantable influence on the deliberations of the Assembly.

Robert Baillie may provide a hint why this quest for Accommodation was abruptly stopped by order of the House of Commons after the session on Friday, October 25th. He tells us that the political Independents[68] wanted to debate the propositions brought forward by the sub-committee, but that the Scots

> refused to consider their propositions except on two express caveats; one, That no report should be made of any conclusion of the commit-

---

[66] October 15; *ibid*. p. 106.

[67] I.e., apart from the Scots Commissioners. October 18th; *ibid*. p. 107.

[68] The peers, Say and Wharton, and the Commoners, Sir Henry Vane and Oliver St. John.

tee, till first it came to the Assemblie, and from them, after examination, should be transmitted to the House of Commons; ane other, That first the common rule of Government should be resolved, before any forbearance of these that differed therefrae should be resolved upon. The first, after many hours sharp debate, we obtained: the second we are to debate tomorrow; and, if we obtaine it not, we have a brave paper readie, penned by Mr. Henderson, to be given in to the Houses and Assemblie, which will paint out the Independents and their adherents so clearlie, that I am hopefull the bottom of their plotts shall be dung out.[69]

For whatever reasons, and perhaps we have to look to the political and military scene to find them,[70] Vane and his colleagues did not want to force an open breach with the Scots at that time.

The dream of reaching a consensus died hard. On Friday, January 3rd, 1644/5, George Gillespie and Robert Baillie took leave of the Assembly to carry a report of its work to their own General Assembly in Scotland. Gillespie gave the speech of farewell on behalf of both. Despite the fragmentary character of the scribe's account, the reader has a glimpse of the real and even passionate desire of the speaker to reach agreement with those Reformed brethren against whom he had been using all his wit, erudition and skill for more than a year. He first acknowledged his own great debt to the Assembly, and noted that although the Assembly had many difficulties, the greatest had been that of getting rid of prelacy and the Book of Common Prayer; and he then went on:

---

[69] To Spang, 25th October, 1644; *Letters and Journals* II. 237. This letter (*ibid.* pp. 235–7) gives a fairly full account of these meetings and the circumstances that led to them. It also seems that the improved military situation since Marston Moor stimulated the Independents to be much more forthcoming about their ecclesiastical situation than hitherto: "We fand the Independents clear for the whole people, every communicant male, to have decisive voyce in all ecclesiastick causes, in admission, deposition, excommunication of ministers, in determining of schismes and heresies. 2. That no Congregation did depend on any superior Synod, so that a congregation falling in all the heresies and crymes of the world, neither the whole nor any member of it can be censured by any synod or presbytrie in the earth, however it may be refused communion by any who finds no satisfaction in its proceedings: but, which is worst of all, they avow they cannot communicate as members with any congregation in England, though reformed to the uttermost pitch of puritie which the Assemblie or Parliament are lyke to require, because even the English, as all the rest of the Reformed, will consist but of professors of the truth in whose life there is no scandall; but they require to a member, besyde a fair profession, and want of scandall, such signs of true grace as persuades the whole congregation of their true regeneration. We are glad to have them declare this much under their hands; for hitherto it hes been their great care to avoid any such declaration; but now they are more bold, apprehending their partie to be much more considerable, and our nation much less considerable, than before." *Ibid.* p. 236.

[70] The letter was written before the second battle of Newbury.

> You have here some dissenting brethren to whom I owe great respect. . . . I wish they prove to be as unwilling to divide from us, as we have been unwilling to divide from them. I wish that instead of toleration, there may be a mutual endeavour for a happy accommodation. . . . There is a certain measure of forbearance, but it is not so seasonable now to be talking of forbearance, but mutual endeavours for accommodation. . . . It is true two are better than one, but it is not true of parties . . . since God hath promised to give His people one heart and one way . . .[71]

It must have been an impressive statement, and it seems to have been a happy inspiration that led De Witt to couple Gillespie's remarks on this occasion with his words to the Dissenting Brethren in his pamphlet *Wholesome Severity Reconciled with Christian Liberty*, which was published within a week of his leaving the Assembly. It is likely that the words he wrote at the end of that tract may have been substantially what he said in the Assembly on January 3rd.

The pamphlet was a strong protest against religious toleration, but at the end he addressed 'A Paraenetick' to the Dissenting Brethren, and it is worth quoting in an extended form because it carries the flavour of Gillespie's style:

> Before I end, I have a word of exhortation for the five Apologists, and such others as shall (I trust) agree with the Churches of both Kingdomes, not only in one Confession of Faith, but in one Directorie of Worship. Methinks I heare them calling to me to say on. *Et tu mi fili?* said *Caesar*. And must you also brethren, give a wound to the body of Christ? Doe not, O doe not involve your selves in the plea of Toleration with the Separatists and Anabaptists. Do not partake in their *Separation*, lest you partake in their suppression. Let us heare no more Paraeneticks for Toleration, or liberty of Conscience: but as many as you will for a *just and mercifull Accommodation*. . . . If you be the Sonnes of peace, you shall be characterized by this *Shibboleth*, you will call for Accommodation, not for Toleration; for one way, not for two. Let there be no strife between us and you, *for we be brethren:* and is not the *Canaanite* and the *Perizzite* yet in the land? O let it not be told in *Gath* nor published in the streets of *Ashkelon*. Let it not be said, that there can be no unity in the Church without Prelacy. Brethren I charge you *by the Roes and Hindes of the field, that ye awake not nor stirre up Jesus Christ till he please;* for his rest is sweet and glorious with his wellbeloved. It shall bee no griefe of heart to you afterward, that have pleased others as well as your selves, and have stretched your principles for an Accommodation in Church government, as well as in Worship, and that for the Churches peace and

---

[71] Minutes III. 28.

edification; and that the eares of our common enemies may tingle, when it shall be said, *The Churches of Christ in England have rest, and are edified, and walking in the feare of the Lord, and in the joy of the Holy Ghost are multiplyed.* Alas, how shall our divisions and contentions hinder the preaching and learning of Christ, and the edifying one another in love! *Is Christ divided?* saith the Apostle. There is but one Christ, yea the head and the body makes one Christ, so that you cannot divide the body without dividing Christ. Is there so much as a seame in all Christ's garment? Is it not woven throughout from top to bottome? Will you have one halfe of Israel to follow *Tibni*, and another halfe to follow *Omri*? O brethren, we shall be one in heaven, let us packe up differences in this place of our pilgrimage, the best way wee can. Nay, we will not despaire of unity in this world. Hath not God promised to give us *one heart and one way*? and that *Ephraim shall not envy Judah, and Judah shall not vexe Ephraim, but they shall flee upon the shoulders of the Philistines toward the East, they shall spoile them of the East together*? Hath not the Mediator (whom the Father heareth alwayes) prayed that all his may be one? Brethren, it is not impossible, pray for it, endeavour it, presse hard toward the marke of Accommodation. How much better it is that you be one with the other Reformed Churches, though somewhat straitned and bound up, then to bee divided though at full liberty and elbow-roome? *Better is a dry morsell and quietnesse therewith, then a house full of sacrifices with strife.* Doth not the Solemne League and Covenant bind you sincerely, really, and constantly to endeavour the nearest (marke *nearest*) uniformity and conjunction in religion; and that you shall not suffer your selves directly or indirectly to be withdrawne from this blessed union and conjunction. I know there is a spirit of jealousie walking up and downe. O beware of groundlesse fears and apprehensions. *Judge not, lest you be judged, judge not according to appearance, but judge righteous-judgment.* Many false rumours and surmises there have beene concerning the Presbyterian principles, practices, designes. *Expertus loquor.* I am perswaded if there were but a right understanding one of anothers intentions, the Accommodation I speak of would not bee difficult. Brethren, if you will not hearken to the wholesome counsell, you shall be the more inexcusable. . . . Consider what I say. The Lord guide your feet in the way of peace. And O that God would put it in your hearts to cry downe *Toleration*, and to dry up *Accommodation*! Amen. Amen.[72]

Certainly to twentieth century mind this sounds like insufferable arrogance, but the modern reader should also realize that it was spoken or written with absolute sincerity. It gives the lie to any suggestion that Protestants had given up belief in the unity of the Church, but it also reveals the dilemma in which many found

---

[72] *Wholesome Severity Reconciled with Christian Liberty* (1644/5), pp. 38–40. Cf. De Witt, *Jus Divinum*, pp. 141–2.

themselves. They truly believed in the oneness of the Church, but they also truly believed that they knew the exact pattern of this unity. Obviously until that assumption was modified it was not possible for a more ecumenical understanding of the Church to develop, or even for any general acceptance of religious toleration.[73]

Both branches of the Reformed churches held that this *jure divino* pattern of churchmanship was expressly prescribed in scripture for all right-minded people to understand and follow, and the assumption was that any who refused to follow it must be perverse. The tragedy was that Presbyterians and Independents differed in their interpretations of the scriptural evidence, and George Gillespie for all his assumption of presbyterian divine-rightness sensed that tragedy. He would make no concessions to the other system, but he respected the Independents in the Assembly, sensed that they were 'brethren' and – let it be said in his favour – longed to have these men in the church with him.

III

Politics and the Military

The final decision whether the Independents would be tolerated or whether this would be waived to gain the wider principle of liberty of conscience would not be left to the divines in the Jerusalem Chamber. It would be decided in Parliament and on the field of battle. Undoubtedly most of the divines regarded the speeches of the politicians and the activities of the soldiers, insofar as they affected the theological discussions at all, as intrusions into their own divinely ordained task, but for any outside observer the work of the Assembly took place within a context that was essentially military and political. By the end of 1644 the Scots were well on the way to achieving all their ecclesiastical objectives in the Assembly, but while this was taking place, two major events in the world outside created conditions that would eventually frustrate the effective establishment of their church government in the Church of England.

---

[73] Recognition that they needed to modify their ecclesiology in this direction is somewhat quaintly expressed by the Congregationalists in their Savoy Declaration of 1658. Article XXX of the Platform of Polity reads:

"Churches gathered and walking according to the minde of Christ, *judging other Churches (though less pure) to be true Churches*, may receive unto occasional communion with them, such Members of those Churches as are credibly testified to be godly, and to live without offence."

(Williston Walker, *Creeds and Platforms*, p. 408; my italics.) The words italicized show the movement from a completely exclusive position.

1. *The Army Quarrel and the Self-Denying Ordinance*

The first arose from the military divisions that had flared up in September in the Army of the Eastern Association. That dispute seems to have ended in a political *quid pro quo* in which Cromwell had dropped his charges against Manchester and Crawford[74] but had seized the opportunity to get the principle of religious toleration raised by the House of Commons.

At the military level, the Committee of Both Kingdoms at Derby House seems to have accepted Manchester's assurances that he would prosecute the war with more efficiency and obey instructions with alacrity. However, in the events that led up to the indecisive second battle of Newbury on October 27th, the three major commanders on the parliamentary side – the Earls of Essex[75] and Manchester, and Sir William Waller had not cooperated with any enthusiasm. Moreover, Manchester followed his usual dilatory methods, and after the action had started, delayed his own attack until the lateness of the day and failing light made it practically useless.[76] The Earl could not have shown more clearly that he did not want the King to be beaten decisively but contained and brought to a negotiated peace.

Indeed, in a later testimony, Manchester was accused of having remarked in a Council of War, "if we beate the King 99 times he would be King still, and his posterity, and we subjects still; but if he beate us but once we should be hang'd, and our posterity be undonne." It was the classic statement of a political conservative who found an all-out victory against Charles just as distasteful as the defeat of Parliament, and Cromwell made the obvious rejoinder that if that were true, then he wondered why they had started to fight in the first place, for to argue as the Earl was arguing was ultimately to justify doing nothing.[77]

Not all Presbyterians in the Assembly would have agreed with the Earl of Manchester – Charles Herle had expressed himself very differently[78] – but their generally conservative attitude to the place of the church in society meant that politically their

---

[74] Baillie took credit for thwarting the dismissal of Crawford: "but we did so manage that businesse, that all their assayes so were in vaine." To Spang, October 25th, 1644; *Letters and Journals*, II. 235.

[75] Essex took no part in the subsequent action. He was ill and remained at Reading. Gardiner, *G. C. W.* II. 44.

[76] For more detailed accounts of the battle and its results, see *ibid.* pp. 42–65, 78–93; Paul, *The Lord Protector*, pp. 86–93. For the partisan accounts given by contemporaries, see, *The Quarrel between the Earl of Manchester and Oliver Cromwell*.

[77] Cf. *The Quarrel between . . . Manchester and . . . Cromwell*, p. 4; *G. C. W.*, II. 59, *The Lord Protector*, p. 88.

[78] Cf. *supra* p. 402, n. 67.

party supported the traditional constitution and was more ready to think in terms of a negotiated peace. The Independents on the other hand, who may have started with ideas that were no less conservative than those of their opponents, now found that because of their opposition to presbyterian uniformity they represented the liberty of conscience for which Cromwell and his troops were fighting, and to some extent they were bound to get caught up in the political egalitarianism that went with that.[79] There is also not much doubt that the political leaders of the 'Independent' party had been actively looking for the military instrument that would advance their aims, and were, as Baillie contended, striving "to advance Cromwell for their head."[80] During the months between Essex's defeat at Lostwithiel and the end of the year these political Independents had been very active in trying to strengthen their position, and in that campaign the work of the ecclesiastical Independents in the Assembly played an important part.

The inept parliamentary generalship in and around Newbury enabled the King to relieve Donnington Castle, so on November 23rd, Charles "entered Oxford in triumph, safe behind the girdle of fortresses which the efficiency of his army and the bad generalship and the bad management of his opponents had enabled him to retain intact".[81] It was evident to those who directed the war effort at Westminster that something would have to be done quickly to remove the ineffectual aristocratic leadership of the Parliament's armies if the King was ever to be brought to a decisive engagement.

Time was extremely important to both the parties at Westminster. On November 8th the Assembly presented its platform of church government to the Houses, and on the same day the peace proposals brought down from Scotland by Warriston were accepted by the English parliamentary leaders. A major offensive for a negotiated peace was being prepared for submission to

---

[79] An Anonymous 'Opponent of Cromwell' later testified:

"I shall declare Coll. Cromwell raysing of his regiment makes choyce of his officers, not such as weare souldiers or men of estate, but such ass were common men, pore and of meane parentage, onely he would give them the title of godly pretious men. . . .

Looke what a company of troopers are thrust into other regiments by the head and shoulders, most of them Independents, whome they call Godly pretiouse men; nay, indeed to say the truth, allmost all our horse be mayd of that faction." *The Quarrel between . . . Manchester and . . . Cromwell*, pp. 72ff. (cf. *The Lord Protector*, p. 84, note 1.)

[80] 10th August, 1644, *Letters and Journals*, II. 218.

[81] Gardiner, *G. C. W.* II. 62.

Charles in which the Scots had clearly taken the initiative.[82] The intense work of the Assembly in the last two months of the year has to be seen in that context.

However, moves were afoot that would send the English Parliament in a very different direction. Cromwell had been disgusted with the part played by Manchester at Newbury, and his quarrel with Manchester was rapidly becoming a national cause célèbre. At the end of November both the principals in this dispute found their way to London to present their cases to the Houses. The difference in national policy that they represented meant that in some measure both men had become symbols for the increasing tension between the Lords and the Commons for control of the war, and of the differences in policy held by the parliamentary 'Presbyterians' and the parliamentary 'Independents.' The cleavage ran through the center of the parliamentary movement, but both sides recognized that their ultimate fortunes depended on adequate military support, and it may be no accident that on the very day when Cromwell took his seat to make his presentation in the Lower House against Manchester, there was a move to get the House of Lords to request the Scots army to march south.[83]

When he made his presentation[84] Cromwell accused Manchester of having "neglected and studiously shifted off opportunities" to press home the army's advantages against the enemy, "as if he thought the King too low, and the Parliament too high", and went on to describe the Earl as "sometimes perswading and deluding the Council to neglect one Opportunity with pretence of another, and that again of a third, and at last by perswading that it was not fit to fight at all."[85]

On his side Manchester delivered an equally damaging attack in the Lords against Cromwell, criticizing in particular his subordinate officer's apparent lack of respect for the social order, his distrust of the Scots and contempt for the Assembly of Divines as

---

[82] *Ibid.* pp. 75ff. Denzil Holles and Bulstrode Whitelocke were in Oxford on November 27th to deliver the conditions to Charles, and on December 3rd the Houses agreed to give a safe conduct to two of the Kings' emissaries to bring his reply to Westminster. *Ibid.* II. 85f.

[83] *Ibid.* p. 82.

[84] Cf. 'Cromwell's Narrative' in *The Quarrel between . . . Manchester and . . . Cromwell*, pp. 78–95, which is also printed in Abbott, *The Writings and Speeches of O. C.*, I. 302–311. Abbott pointed out that the style is somewhat different from Cromwell's usual style in speaking, and was probably worked over by several people; Abbott, *op. cit.* I. 311 note 93. The summary in Rushworth probably provides a more accurate account of what he actually said on this occasion. Rushworth, *Historical Collections*, VI. 732.

[85] Rushworth, *op. cit.* VI. 732.

being persecutors, and his desire to have an army on which he could rely if the Scots attempted to impose a peace which he and his soldiers could not in conscience accept.[86]

The Scots, who were already prepared to believe the worst of Cromwell, were furious. Their antipathy comes through in Baillie's account of what happened:

> Lieutenant-Generall Cromwell has publicklie, in the House of Commons, accused my Lord of Manchester of the neglect of fighting at Newburry. That neglect indeed was great; for, as we now are made sure, the King's armie was in that posture, that they took themselves for lost allutterlie. Yet the fault is most unjustlie charged on Manchester: It was common to all the Generall Officers then present, and to Cromwell himselfe as much as to any other. Allwayes my Lord Manchester hes cleared himselfe abundantlie in the House of Lords, and there hes recriminate Cromwell as one who hes avowed his desire to abolish the nobilitie of England; who hes spoken contumeliouslie of the Scotts intention in coming to England to establish their Church-government, in which Cromwell said he would draw his sword against them; also against the Assemblie of Divines; and hes threatened to make a partie of sectaries, to extort by force, both from King and Parliament, what conditions they thought meet. This fire was long under the emmers; now it's broken out, we trust, in good time. It's like, for the interest of our nation, we must crave reason of that darling of the Sectaries, and in obtaining his removeall from the armie, which himselfe, by his oure [over] rashness, hes procured, to breake the power of that potent faction. This is our present difficill exercise: we had need of your prayers.[87]

We learn what the 'present difficill exercise' was from the English lawyer, Bulstrode Whitelocke. He has recorded how he and another leading English lawyer, John Maynard, were urgently called one night to the Earl of Essex's house in London, where they found that the Earl of Essex had been joined by some of Cromwell's opponents in the House of Commons (Denzil Holles, Sir Philip Stapleton and Sir John Meyrick,) and the Scots headed by their Chancellor, the Earl of Loudoun. At once the Scots took charge of the proceedings, and asked the lawyers if there was any means in English law whereby Cromwell might be proceeded against as an 'incendiary,' for, Loudoun said "It is thought requisite for us, and for the carrying on of the cause of

---

[86] Manchester's defence was apparently made in two parts – first, an attempt to clear himself of the charges levelled against him that may be found in Rushworth, *op. cit.* VI., 733–736; and secondly, his counter-attack on Cromwell, which appears (taken from the Tanner MSS) in the *Camden Miscellany* VIII (1852), edited by S. R. Gardiner.

[87] Publick Letter, 1st December, 1644, *Letters and Journals*, II. 244f.

the tway kingdoms that this obstacle or remora may be removed."[88] However, both the lawyers informed the Scots that this was not possible in English law, and it would be extremely unwise to attempt it in view of Cromwell's popularity. The idea appears to have been dropped.

All these frenzied activities, however, became suddenly obsolete, when on December 9th, the presbyterian member of Parliament, Zouch Tate, who was chairman of the committee investigating the charges and counter-charges, presented his report to the House of Commons. Instead of giving a review of the evidence, he simply confined himself to a general statement to the effect that the main causes of the divisions had been pride and covetousness. Cromwell arose immediately and told the House that the time had come to save the nation by prosecuting the war more speedily, and suggesting that the army should be "put into another method." He also said that they should not pursue particular complaints against any of the commanders, but apply themselves to the remedy. "And", he said, "I hope we have such true English hearts, and zealous affections towards the general weal of our Mother Country, as no Members of either House will scruple to deny themselves, and their own private interests, for the public good; nor account it to be a dishonour done to them, whatever the Parliament shall resolve upon in this weighty matter."

Then Tate arose again, and moved "That during the Time of this War, no Member of either House shall have or execute any office or command, military or civil, granted or conferred by both or either of the Houses."[89] Vane seconded the motion, and the Self-Denying Ordinance was on its way. It was not adopted, particularly by the House of Lords, without difficulty, and it was not until 15th February, 1644/5 that the move became effective as the 'New Model Ordinance', but in light of all the later events it was a masterstroke of statesmanship on the part of those responsible for it, because by this action much of the inefficiency and half-hearted effort that had hampered the parliamentary campaigns hitherto was now confined to the place where it could probably do least harm, the House of Lords.

The Scots seem to have been left completely in the dark. Baillie did not know what to make of it:

---

[88] Bulstrode Whitelocke, *Memorials of English Affairs*, (corrected and enlarged edition, London, 1732,) p. 116.

[89] *C.J.* iii. 718, Whitelocke, *Memorials*, 118; cf. Abbott, *Writings and Speeches of O. C.*, I. 314f; *The Lord Protector*, p. 91.

The House of Commons, in one houre, hes ended all the quarrells which was betwixt Manchester and Cromwell, all the obloquies against the Generall, the grumblings against the proceedings of many members of their House. They have taken all office from all the members of both Houses. This done on a sudden, in one session, with great unanimitie, is still more and more admired by some, as a most wise, necessar, and heroick action; by others, as the most rash hazardous, and unjust action, as ever Parliament did. Much may be said on both hands, but as yet it seems a dream, and the bottom of it is not understood: we pray God it may have a good successe.[90]

Perhaps the most surprising thing about the whole enterprise is how any intimation had not percolated through to Baillie, especially when we consider how close the Scots interests were to those of Zouch Tate and his colleagues in Parliament. Possibly some of the laymen among the Commissioners were consulted and agreed to it, for it seemed that if the Independents would no longer have to worry about Essex and Manchester, the Scots could assume that they had seen the last of Cromwell. If all the parliamentary commanders in both Houses had left the armies for good, that would leave the Earl of Leven as the only really experienced commander to oppose the King, and as W. C. Abbott noted, Leven's troops could be regarded at this stage as "the forces of Presbyterianism and perhaps of the House of Lords."[91] If a few Scots were consulted, they kept their own counsel very well, for Baillie's astonishment appears to have been genuine.

2. *The Uxbridge Proposals*

The other event that was to have an effect on the future of the Assembly's recommendations about the Church was the abortive series of peace negotiations with Charles that began at Uxbridge on January 29, 1644/5. The proposals put forward from the side of Parliament were in three difficult areas – Religion, Ireland, and the Militia – and the meetings were to last for a limit of twenty days, with three days spent on each subject *seriatim* until the time expired.

Our concern is with the first of these, and on no subject was there less likely to be a meeting of minds, because although one may question the depth of Charles I's convictions in several areas, one can have no doubt of his commitment to the episcopal government of the Church of England and the Book of Common

---

[90] Publick Letter, 26th December, 1644, *Letters and Journals*, II. 247.
[91] *Writings and Speeches of O. C.*, I. 328.

Prayer. On the other side there were the presbyterian proposals, forged in Edinburgh, hammered out at Westminster, and presented by Alexander Henderson. Indeed it is not unlikely that the political Independents in London had consented to these proposals because they could be reasonably sure they would be rejected by the King.[92]

All the parliamentary proposals were offensive to Charles, but none more so than those concerning religion. By them not only were all his subjects in the three kingdoms required to take the Covenant, but, as a special demand of the Scots, he was to be required to swear to the Covenant himself.[93] In spite of his expressed determination to maintain the episcopal government of the Church, the propositions from London were taken straight out of the measures recently endorsed in the Assembly,[94] and Alexander Henderson was officially on hand as the theological consultant to the parliamentary commissioners.

The attempted treaty at Uxbridge was doomed to failure, because it was a further example of two theological positions claiming *jus divinum* confronting each other: there was no room for negotiation.[95] However, Robert Baillie shows how far he and his friends were from realizing the small hopes they had of success with these proposals.

We were assured by Richmond and Southampton, that both the King and Queen were so disposed to peace, upon the great

---

[92] As Gardiner has commented, "though no evidence exists on the point, it is most probable that the absence of any resistance on the part of the Independents was mainly due to the conviction that Charles would save them the trouble of a fruitless opposition by peremptorily rejecting the proposal." *G. C. W.*, II. 77.

[93] *Ibid.*

[94] "The commissioners from the two houses of parliament at Westminster, instead of being instructed to treat about a reformation of the hierarchy, were ordered to demand the passing of a bill for abolishing and taking away episcopal government; for confirming the ordinance for the calling and sitting of the assembly of divines; that the Directory for publick worship, and the propositions concerning church-government, hereunto annexed, be confirmed as a part of reformation of Religion and uniformity; that his majesty take the solemn league and covenant, and that an act of parliament be passed, enjoining the taking it by all subjects of the three kingdoms.

The propositions annexed to these demands were these, viz. 'that the ordinary way of dividing Christians into distinct congregations, as most expedient for edification, be by the respective bounds of their dwellings.

'That the ministers, and other church-officers in each particular congregation, shall join in the government of the church in such manner as shall be established by parliament.

'That many congregations shall be under one presbyterial government.

'That the church be governed by congregational, classical, and synodical assemblies, in such manner as shall be established by parliament.

'That synodical assemblies shall consist both of provincial and national assemblies.'" Neal, *Hist. of the Puritans*, III. 215f.

[95] For an account of those negotiations, cf. *ibid.* pp. 215–226.

> extremities wherein their affaires stood, and small hopes from any place to gett them helped, that they would imbrace the substance of all our propositions, with very small and tollerable modifications. This seemed to us not unlyke.[96]

Baillie blamed the divisions in the leadership in London and the victories of Montrose in Scotland for changing the King's mind and convincing him that he need not concede to anything. Whether his envoys, the Duke of Richmond and the Earl of Southampton, had deliberately misled the Scots, we can only surmise, but it would not be beyond the scope of Stuart diplomacy if there were any advantage to be gained by that means.[97] What is certain is that Charles would on no account concede anything respecting the Church and the Scots could not move from their own absolute claims. The tragedy of their position, as Gardiner pointed out, was that "they knew too little and cared too little about the wants of England or the mental characteristics of Charles to ask whether the object of their desire was practicable."[98]

While the negotiations at Uxbridge were moving to predestined futility, there were those at Westminster who would ensure that this diplomatic brief encounter did not deflect Parliament's determination to put its armed forces on a more efficient basis and to pursue the war to decisive victory. The House of Lords had initially rejected the Self-Denying Ordinance but the peers were no longer in any position to wrest direction of the war from the House of Commons, and they played into the hands of the very people they were anxious to oppose, for by rejecting the Ordinance they "had torn down the barrier which the best cavalry officer in England had erected in the way of his own employment."[99] On January 21st, 1644/5, the House of Commons had selected the commanders of the New Model Army, with Sir Thomas Fairfax as General and Philip Skippon as Major-General, and with provision made for men and money. This left the post of Lieutenant-General, with its command of

---

[96] To Spang, 25th April, 1645; *Letters and Journals*, II. 260f.

[97] Gardiner has quoted a letter that passed between the King and the Queen at that time, which shows that Charles had been made to feel unduly confident by the news of the military dissensions in the ranks of his opponents. It also revealed his determination to maintain episcopacy. *G. C. W.*, II. 114f.

[98] *Ibid.* p. 122.

[99] *G. C. W.*, II. 119. When the evidence regarding the Self-Denying Ordinance is examined, it is hard to avoid Gardiner's conclusion that if Cromwell could have foreseen that the measure would have enabled him to retain his commission while leading to the resignation of his rivals, he would have been "more than a sagacious statesman – he would have been an inspired prophet". *Ibid.* p. 91.

the cavalry, significantly vacant, but in the meantime it enabled Cromwell to be active in the parliamentary committees where the work of reorganization was being done.[100]

Possibly it was news of the King's intransigence at Uxbridge that caused the Lords to accept the New Model Ordinance on February 4th, and it was finally passed on the 15th and was effective two days later. The Self-Denying Ordinance was finally passed on April 4th, and by it those members of both Houses who held commissions were required to resign within forty days; but again significantly, nothing was said about the possibility of their re-appointment. The Earls of Essex, Manchester and Denbigh had already handed in their resignations on April 2nd, and Sir William Waller was only too anxious to lay down his commission. He and Cromwell seem to have paid a courtesy call to Fairfax at Windsor before resigning their commands,[101] but before the visit was over the Committee of Both Kingdoms had ordered Cromwell to interpose his forces immediately between the King in Oxford and the royalists in Worcester and Hereford,[102] and just before his forty days' grace had expired, his commission was renewed for a further period.[103]

This enabled Parliament to accede to Fairfax's urgent desire to have Cromwell as his Lieutenant-General as the time of the decisive battle approached.[104] On June 11th Cromwell was greeted enthusiastically when he rode into Fairfax's camp, and on the 14th the battle of Naseby decided the war. It followed a similar pattern to that of Marston Moor, with Prince Rupert's horse cutting through Ireton's cavalry on the parliamentary left wing and plundering the baggage train behind, and with Cromwell successful on the opposite wing and then halting his men to re-form and attack the reserve with the King in its midst. When they had successfully driven the King from the field, Cromwell and his troopers were joined by Fairfax and together they subjugated the royalist infantry in the centre, so that by the time Rupert returned to the battle it was lost.[105]

---

[100] Cf. Abbott, *Writings and Speeches of O. C.*, I. 327–332.

[101] *Ibid.* p. 338.

[102] *Ibid.* p. 339.

[103] *Ibid.* p. 348.

[104] On June 8th Fairfax on behalf of his council of war wrote to Parliament asking for Cromwell to be appointed. Cf. Ibid., p. 355; or *Cromwelliana* (Westminster, 1810,) p. 18.

[105] For accounts of Naseby, cf. *G. C. W.*, II. 234–253; Abbott, *Writings and Speeches of O. C.*, I. 354–360. One of the most damaging results of Naseby from Charles I's point of view was the capture of his personal cabinet which contained a great deal of his correspondence with the Queen. The papers showed that Charles had dissembled at Uxbridge –

This time there was no one to rival Cromwell's reputation, or question what he had contributed to the victory, and in his letter reporting the victory to the Speaker of the House of Commons – possibly, as Abbott suggested, because he no longer felt obliged to avoid antagonizing the Scots – he spoke about liberty of conscience with a new freedom:

> Honest men served you faithfully in this action. Sir, they are trusty; I beseech you in the name of God, not to discourage them. I wish this action may beget thankfulness and humility in all that are concerned in it. He that ventures his life for the liberty of his country, I wish he trust God for the liberty of his conscience, and you for the liberty he fights for.[106]

That was still a provocative subject at Westminster, so that when the House of Commons had the letter printed it appeared without this closing paragraph. However, it was all to no avail, because the House of Lords, "probably in mere thoughtlessness", had allowed a complete copy to go to the printer.[107] From this point on, liberty of conscience was an idea that could not be suppressed.

---

that he would never acknowledge the Parliament at Westminster, that he was negotiating to bring in Irish and other foreign armies into England, and that he was ready to abolish all laws against English Catholics. These revelations discredited those who had hoped for a negotiated peace, and seemed to justify fully those at Westminster who wanted the war prosecuted to final victory. Cf. Gardiner, *G. C. W.* II. 258.

[106] Abbott, *Writings and Speeches of O. C.*, I. 360.
[107] Gardiner, *G. C. W.*, II. 252f.

CHAPTER 15

A BROKEN ENGAGEMENT

I

Romance and Reality

The rupture between the Independents and the Presbyterians in the Assembly should be dated from February and March 1644/5 not because attempts at accommodation ceased, but because it was clear that the issue between the parties would not be settled by theological argument. Despite the work that was to go into the Independents' Reasons and the Assembly's Answers, and although the divines continued to vote their propositions and back them with biblical proofs, what would happen ecclesiastically was more likely to be resolved in the political struggle for power, in diplomacy or (most likely of all) on the field of battle.

For the Independents the issues were relatively simple, although the choice may have appeared hard enough: they might bend a few of their principles to accept accommodation or limited toleration for themselves, but the first would mean assimilation and the second was unlikely in view of the antipathy to toleration in the Assembly. Since either of these alternatives would leave them ecclesiastically and politically isolated, their only other option was to embrace liberty of conscience and align themselves with the political 'Independents' and Cromwell's troopers.

Furthermore, from the time of Marston Moor, but particularly after the formation of the New Model Army, time was on their side, for military success helped to create the myth of the New Model's invincibility. Baxter thought that Cromwell's ambition was served by his embracing liberty of conscience and by crediting his troopers with all the important victories, and he probably made a fair assessment of their worth when he observed, "The truth is, they did much, and they boasted of more than they did."[1] However, in view of the way seventeenth century people equated success with Providence, the military victories were bound to have theological significance.[2] Indeed, as Cromwell's successes continued, even former Royalists began to doubt their earlier allegiance because "they were astonished at the marvellous Providences of God, which had been against that Family all along."[3]

In the Assembly the Independents had been totally thwarted, but after the formation of the New Model Army, they did not need to seek accommodation. As every month made the Army more indispensable to the parliamentary cause, the dissenting brethren were given more time before they needed to enter any plea, until the soldiers established such an impregnable position for them that even Parliament could not withstand their demands.

For the Scots the situation was the opposite: they had won the battle decisively in the Assembly, but they were to lose the 'war' in the English nation. By the time Robert Baillie returned home to Scotland at the end of 1646, he could boast of

> our errand in England being brought near a happie period, so farr as concerned us the Commissioners of the Church; for, by God's blessing, the four points of Uniformitie, which wes all our Church gave us in commission to agent in the Assemblie at Westminster, were alse good as obtained.[4]

They had been frustrated theologically by only one thing, the unwillingness of the English Parliament to accept *jus divinum* as the basis for presbyterian church government, and even on that he had hopes that the London Presbyterians would bring about a change.

However, time had been rapidly running out for the Scots. Not only had the meteoric career of Montrose humbled Scottish military prowess until his eventual defeat at Philiphaugh on

---

[1] *Rel. Baxt.* I. i. 48 (§ 69). Baxter also noted that with one minor exception "all the *Scotch-men* . . . are put out of the whole Army, or deserted it." *Ibid.*

[2] Baxter complained of the army sectaries influencing the countryside so that "the People admiring the conquering Army, were ready to receive whatsoever they commended to them", and that although more intelligent people knew how to evaluate Cromwell's victories, "the Simpler sort" came to believe "that God's Providence brought about all, without his Contrivance or Expectation." In the end, Baxter said, Cromwell believed it himself. *Ibid.* I. pp. 56, 72, 78f. For the influence of the doctrine of Providence in Cromwell's life, cf. Paul, *The Lord Protector, passim.*

[3] *Rel. Baxt.* I. i. 100 (§ 145).

[4] To Spang, 26th January, 1646/7; *Letters and Journals,* III. 1.

September 14th, 1645,[5] but also they had found themselves increasingly isolated and discredited in London. The year of 1644 had ended with Baillie's bewilderment at the news of the Self-Denying Ordinance, but throughout 1645 – not a distinguished year for Scottish arms – he and his colleagues had to listen to the news of Fairfax and Cromwell decisively bringing Charles to his knees. That year had ended with the King feverishly entering into secret negotiations with all parties.

When these diplomatic adventures became known early in 1646, no negotiations were more compromising than those he had engaged in with the Scottish Commissioners.[6] Suspicions were not particularly laid to rest when in May 1646 Charles chose to surrender himself to the Scots near Newark, and the protracted period of bargaining over possession of the King's person and indemnity to the Scottish army did not endear them to the English.

Therefore throughout this period the Scots were also dominated by the politics of the situation as they chased the chimera of a settlement with Charles that would guarantee covenanted uniformity through the abortive negotiations of Uxbridge and the equally abortive propositions of Newcastle.[7]

The situation of the English Presbyterians was a little more complicated, but no less dominated by the shifting scene in politics and on the field of battle. For them it was poised on two contradictory facts that were themselves at least paradoxical – first, the overwhelming success of an 'Independent' army that was the military agent of an English presbyterian Parliament; and secondly, a system of church government claiming *jus divinum* that had been established by Parliament on grounds that were uncompromizingly Erastian. Their situation changed with the changing fortunes of Parliament, for their success or failure was tied to Parliament as the fortunes of the Independents were tied to the army. As the myth of invincibility grew for the New Model Army, so did the conservative fears of those who were scared that it would destroy the fundamental shape of English society.[8]

---

[5] He was defeated by David Lesley.

[6] Cf. Gardiner, *G. C. W.*, III. 3, 45.

[7] 14th July–12th August, 1646; *ibid*. pp. 127–129, 131–137. Alexander Henderson had died on 19th August, soon after returning from his failure to persuade the King to accept the terms. Cf. Baillie, *Letters and Journals*, II. 398f.

[8] Writing of events at the end of 1643, S. R. Gardiner made the shrewd comment that no strong Presbyterian party had yet developed among the laity, and that "it was perhaps

The failure of the Uxbridge negotiations meant that Parliament had to take responsibility for the new ecclesiastical settlement.[9] At first it gave every encouragement to the Assembly by putting the votes into effect and by supporting the establishment of presbyterian church order. For this it had the enthusiastic support of the Scots and the presbyterian supporters in the capital,[10] but it was a very different matter when the Assembly tried to assert *jus divinum* for its proposals. There were those among the Presbyterians of the Assembly itself who, if not wholly Erastian, had shown themselves to be essentially pragmatists on matters of church polity. The one thing that persuaded such men to close ranks with the rest was any threat to clerical privilege; and precisely that arose in the successes of the New Model Army, in hair-raising reports of its sectarian prejudices,[11] and in growing recognition that if it could defeat the King so decisively it could also easily defy Parliament.

It has been observed that throughout 1645 and early 1646 Parliament tended to be "Independent on questions of policy, but Presbyterian on questions of religion,"[12] but as the division between Parliament and the army grew deeper, that distinction became less marked and the objectives for Parliament in political policy and religion came closer together. If the Independent politicians were being pushed into actions which, with their support for religious pluralism, would lead to Pride's Purge in 1648 and the trial and execution of Charles in 1648–9, the Presbyterians were being pushed just as surely into policies that, with the dream of covenanted uniformity, would lead to the Restoration in 1660 and their disappointment in 1662.

II

Breach of Promise?

In spite of the break in relationships that occurred during the debate on excommunication, the Independents continued to be

---

hardly possible to form one till Independency came to be associated with military aggression." (*G. C. W.*, I. 267.) We might set alongside it Clarendon's equally perceptive remark: "they who abhor Presbytery in the Church join with the Independents, and they who tremble at Independency in the State join with the Presbyterians." Hyde to Nicholas, *Clarendon State Papers* (Oxford, 1767–1786) II. 285.

[9] Shaw, *A Hist. of the English Church*, I. 187.

[10] Cf. the extract from Baillie's letter to Ramsay, 4th May, 1645, quoted *infra* p. 476. *Letters and Journals*, II. 271f.

[11] Cf. Baxter's description of the sects in the New Model Army; *Rel. Baxt.* I. i. 50ff., (§§ 73–77.)

[12] Gardiner, *G. C. W.* III. 28.

members of the Assembly and to participate in all matters except in those on which they had registered their dissent.[13] Inevitably the work became preoccupied with the Independents' Reasons and the Assembly's Answers, all of which were published separately and then appeared, together with the papers related to Accommodation in *The Grand Debate Concerning Presbitery and Independency*.[14]

Inevitably we must go to much the same material that has been used exhaustively by previous writers,[15] although the evidence is open to somewhat different interpretations. As the issues became more openly political, we may consider this period of the Assembly in several stages.

1. *Call for a Proposal*

During February and March 1644/5 the Assembly discussed excommunication in relation to synods and classes, but when it reached the particular congregation it resolved that "the dissenting brethren do bring into the Assembly what they think fit for the right, and power, and practice of particular congregations not yet concluded in the Assembly" and named the septemvirs to this task.[16] Within the week, on March 27th, Philip Nye brought in a list of seven principles that the Independents felt would "conduce to the settling of your congregations,"[17] and Seaman's immediate reaction if not positive seems not to have been nega-

---

[13] The Minutes III are fragmentary and often incomplete; apart from them we continue to have Baillie's very partial accounts, and papers the two groups published in their own cause, such as the Independents' *A Copy of a Remonstrance Lately delivered in to the Assembly* (1645) and the Assembly's reply, *The Answer of the Assembly of Divines By Authority of Parliament Now sitting at Westminster Unto the Reasons given in to this Assembly by the Dissenting Brethren, Of their not bringing in a Model of their Way. And since Published in Print, under the Title of A Copy of a Remonstrance* (1645).

[14] Published first in 1648, and reissued in 1652.

[15] The most complete accounts are those of William Shaw, *A History of the English Church . . . 1640–1660*, I, and J. R. De Witt, *Jus Divinum*.

[16] Friday, March 21st, 1644/5. Nye, Goodwin, Bridge, Simpson, Carter, Burroughes and Greenhill were named. Minutes III. 70f.

[17] *Ibid.* p. 72. The list of seven principles was printed in *The Answer . . . unto . . . a Remonstrance*, pp. 17–18:

"1. That there is a platform of Church-Government for the Church, laid down in Scripture.

2. That this is immutable, and binding the conscience to the observation thereof.

3. That the Officers which are to be imployed in those Churches, as Pastors, Teachers, Ruling Elders, and Deacons, are of divine Institution.

4. That the people have an Interest in the choice of those Officers.

5. That these Officers are to be designed each of them to their Functions, by imposition of hands, and by Prayer.

6. That what power these should have, and over whom they should have it, is of divine Institution.

tive, for he said "If they bring in those propositions, with their prefaces (?) annexed, we shall receive them."

The Scots, however, were strongly opposed. Rutherford said that Nye's propositions "concern church government in general", and warned the Assembly "If you create new debates, you will be longer than you have been already," while Stephen Marshall recognized that Nye's paper raised the extremely sensitive problem of *jus divinum* – a subject they had hitherto carefully avoided.[18] He had expected that the Independents would concentrate on the formation of congregational assemblies rather than on the matter of excommunication, and he thought that if they could frame a proposition "tending to the constraining of congregations in their numbers" it would be useful.

At that point Alexander Henderson declared forthrightly against Nye's principles: "This notion crosses, and is contrary to our desires. We thought we had been close to harbour, and now we are sailing out into the deep." At once the English Presbyterians fell into line.[19] Nye said that the Independents' intentions had been mistaken. They had to obey their consciences. All the propositions related to particular congregations, and it was important for the members of congregations to know that they do share in the authority of Jesus Christ.

William Carter also stressed the basic importance of *jus divinum* that the Independents had emphasized from the earliest days of the dispute.[20] The majority had persistently avoided that issue, although the Independents regarded it as fundamental. From the Independents' point of view they had kept within the bounds of the commission they had been given, although from their own later printed account we can see that if any of those seven principles had been taken up by the Assembly, they would certainly have retraced ground already covered in the debates.[21] Clearly, this was the reason for the Scots' displeasure.

---

7. Where there is a sufficient number of Presbyters in any one Congregation, then may the two great Ordinances of Excommunication and Ordination be administered."

[18] Minutes III. 72.

[19] Herle tried to keep some contact with the Independents' proposals by suggesting that they could take up the issue where the Assembly had left it, with the 7th proposition and the last half of it; but Seaman immediately supported the Scots saying that "none of all this was committed to them, or desired of them", while Newcomen echoed Henderson's fear that if any of the propositions were taken up "you hinder the last you have done already." *Ibid.* p. 73.

[20] *Ibid.*

[21] "After this . . . one of us, with consent of the rest, brought in seven Propositions, which contained matter of difference betwixt us, professing, *That if this Reverend Assembly would debate them, or any one of them, we would bring in more, untill we had brought*

The upshot was that the Assembly, possibly stung by outside criticisms, resolved that the "dissenting brethren be desired to bring in a platform of government concerning particular congregations",[22] and on 4th April Newcomen proposed that the Dissenting Brethren should be recognized as an official committee of the Assembly "to bring in the whole frame of their judgement, concerning Church-Government in a Body, with their Grounds and Reasons."[23] The Independents agreed to do this, but asked that they should be allowed to bring in their ecclesiology piece by piece, as the presbyterian system had been presented in the Assembly. The request was refused.[24]

This is another place where we question De Witt's interpretation of the events.[25] His account of this incident makes it appear as if there was something extremely devious in what the Independents had done. He criticizes Nye for having touched on somewhat more than the rights of the particular congregations, implies that he was wrong to bring *jus divinum* into the dispute and that the justice of this criticism is indicated by Henderson's strong reaction to the Independents' 'gesture.'

On the other hand, the terms of the Independents' commission had been clear – they were to bring in what they believed still needed to be explicated by the Assembly in relationship to the particular congregation, but in view of the place occupied by the covenanted congregation in their ecclesiology and the biblical basis they claimed for it, it was perhaps only to be expected that it would be directly related to *jus divinum*. Moreover, they had from the beginning insisted on the priority of *jus divinum* to any debate on church government, but as Stephen Marshall indicated here, and as Baillie was to admit later,[26] this subject had been deliberately evaded in order not to precipitate a quarrel with the Erastians in Parliament. Now the Independents were saying that this was one essential matter that the Assembly had not addressed.

---

in all the Frame, and the Assembly themselves should pick and chuse what they would debate, and what not. But these Propositions were rejected with a refusall to debate any one of them." *A Copy of a Remonstrance*, p. 6.

[22] 27th March, 1645, Minutes III. 73. Later the divines said that this had been done in response to criticisms which had appeared in an 'Epistle to the Reader' in a London edition of John Cotton's *The Way of the Churches of Christ in New England*, which had just appeared.

[23] *The Answer . . . unto . . . a Remonstrance*, pp. 19f.; cf. Minutes III. 76.

[24] *A Copy of a Remonstrance*, p. 6.

[25] *Jus Divinum*, pp. 148–151.

[26] Cf. Baillie, *Letters and Journals*, II. 307; also II. 267, quoted *infra* p. 497.

Why then was Henderson so upset? In some ways what Nye's propositions held out about particular congregations was very similar to what the Scots believed. The major differences lay first in the final article, which could be used to undercut the authority of the classical presbytery; and secondly, in introducing the problem of *jus divinum* at this time.

We concede that the Independents may have intended to use these propositions to delay the recommendations of the Assembly, for by that time they had good reason to do so; but there is another way of interpreting what was happening, for if the Independents had every reason to delay, the Scots had every reason for haste, and there is clear evidence that the leaders in the Assembly were forcing the Independents to produce an extensive statement of ecclesiology that they had no intention of using. Their main concern was to keep the Dissenting Brethren occupied anywhere but in the Jerusalem Chamber, so that the majority could get on with the task of putting its votes on church government into final form. Why else would the members have voted to require a complete platform of church government from the Independents, when they had only just expressed their displeasure at the seven propositions? What guarantee did the Dissenting Brethren have that when their completed ecclesiology was produced it would not be treated with similar disdain?

De Witt picked up William Shaw's suggestion that the Assembly's original request may have been an attempt to get the Independents to focus at least on one of the points at issue,[27] but he might have noted what Shaw went on to say:

> That such a proposal was merely a ruse to get rid of the Independents for a while, or to catch them on the horns of a dilemma, is frankly avowed by Baillie, and was doubtless perfectly well known to the Independents themselves.
>
> Without waiting a moment for this 'platform' from the Dissenting Brethren, the Assembly proceeded in its debate, and from the following session (28th March), discussed the matter of the power of congregational churches on a report by Mr. Reynolds.[28]

Shaw noted that although the result of that debate does not appear in the Minutes, it must have been contrary to the Independents' views, because on 25th April Baillie reported that "the Assemblie hath now, I may say, ended the whole body of the

---

[27] *Jus Divinum*, p. 148; cf. Shaw, *A Hist. of the English Church*, I. 256.

[28] Shaw, *A Hist. of the English Church*, I. 256. Shaw cited Baillie, *Letters and Journals*, II. 266, 271, and *A Copy of a Remonstrance* in support of his contention.

Church Government, and that according to the doctrine and practice of the Church of Scotland, in every thing materiall."[29]

2. *No Answer*

When Baillie returned to London from Scotland[30] he was delighted with the progress the Assembly had made in the absence of the Independents. In the letter cited above he admits that putting them to producing a comprehensive ecclesiology had been a deliberate means of expediting matters in the Assembly:

> The Independents, these six weeks, have not much troubled the Assemblie; for after we had been long time troubled with their opposition to all things, it was found meet to put them to declare their mind positive[ly] what they would be at. This they have shifted to this day, as it was thought, not fully agreeing among themselves; but now being peremptorilie putt to it, they could not gett it declyned. Since, they have been about that task, and we expect daily when they shall present to us their platforme of Church Government.[31]

His next sentence is a clear admission that what the Independents suspected was correct – the Presbyterians had no intention of allowing the Independent statement to be given public debate or to enter into the Assembly's recommendations:

> "The Assemblie purposes not to take it into publick debate, bot to give it to some committee, that they may frame ane answer to it, if so it be found convenient.[32]

The Assembly had the full cooperation of Parliament, and the House of Commons had sought the help of the London ministers in setting up the new ecclesiastical structure for the city. In his letter on May 4th, 1645, Baillie shows how far this had progressed:

---

[29] Publick Letter, *Letters and Journals*, II. 266; cf. Shaw, *op cit*. p. 257.

[30] 9th April, 1645; Minutes III. 77.

[31] 25th April, Baillie, *Letters and Journals*, II. 266f.

[32] *Ibid*. p. 267. Cf. also Baillie's letter to Ramsay, 4th May, 1645: "Church-work here, blessed be God, goes on with less difficultie than it wes wont. The Assemblie having put the Independents to shew what positively is their judgment in things controverted, we have been quyte of their cumber these six or seven weeks. Every day this moneth we have been expecting their positive tenets, but as yet we have heard nothing of them; only in their sermons in the City they are deviating more and more towards old and new errours, especially libertie of conscience: Their wayes are daylie more and more dislyked." *Ibid*. p. 271.

> We have this fourteen dayes been upon our advyce to a sub-committee of the House of Commons, anent the execution of our votes of Government: for it is the work of that sub-committee to draw two ordinances; the one, for the practise of the Directorie, wherein their punishment is as rigorous, if it be not mitigate, for the contemners of any part of that book, as it was before to the contemners of their religion. For preachers, or wryters, or publishers, against it, were they dukes and peers, their third fault is the loss of all their goods, and perpetuall imprisonment. The other ordinance is for the erection of Ecclesiastick courts over the whole Kingdom. For their help herein, they called the ministers of London to advyse them for their city, and they sent to the Assemblie for their advyce anent the rest of the kingdome. The city-ministers have sent them their unanimous advyce (for of one hundred and twenty-one city-ministers, there are not three Independents) for planting, just after our Scotish fashion, an eldership in every congregation; of fourteen Presbyteries within the lines of communication, every one consisting of ministers betwixt twelve and sixteen, and as many ruling elders; and of a provinciall Synod for London and ten miles round about. The Assemblie have presented their advyce this day. We went throw this forenoon – session unanimouslie what concerns provinciall and nationall Assemblies, as yesterday what concerned Presbyteries, and the days before, congregationall Elderships. They have concluded provinciall Synods twice a-year, Presbyteries once a moneth, and nationall Assemblies once a-year, and ofter [oftener], every one of these as it shall be needfull.[33]

Whatever else the majority in the Assembly intended to do with anything received from the Independents, the divines did not intend it to have any influence on the church order they were recommending to Parliament.

Nothing was received from the Independents during the Summer. Indeed, very little of significance happened except the victory of the New Model Army at Naseby, which enhanced Cromwell's reputation. Baillie was particularly disgruntled at the officer Fairfax sent to report the victory, and the use Cromwell made of the success:

> My Lord Fairfax sent up, the last week, ane horrible Antitriastrian; the whole Assemblie went in a body to the Houses to complaine of his blasphemies. It wes the will of Cromwell, in the letter of his victorie, to desyre the House not to discourage these who had ventured their

---

[33] *Ibid.* pp. 271f. By August 20th Parliament was ready to publish *Directions of the Lords and Commons Assembled in Parliament. After Advice had with the Assembly of Divines, for the electing and choosing of Ruling-Elders in all their Congregations, and in the Classical Assemblies for the Cities of London and Westminster, and the severall counties of the Kingdom: For the speedy setling of the Presbyteriall-Government,* (20th August 1645.)

life for them, and to come out expressly with their much-desyred libertie of conscience.[34]

As time went on Baillie began to feel uneasy about the silence of the Independents. In a letter that he sent out on the 1st July he said that

> yet what retardment we may have from this great victorie, obtained most by the Independent partie, and what that modell of government, whereupon Thomas Goodwin and his brethren these three moneths hes been sitting so close, that they very rarely, and he never at all hes yet appeared, we doe not know; only we expect a very great assault, how soone we know not, for a tolleration to we wot not what.[35]

A week later, having commented that Goodwin[36] and Burton, the only two Independents to hold livings in London churches, had been ejected from their charges by Parliament, he said that the Independents had still not produced their statement, and he suspected that the reason for the delay was either their own differences or else "whether to take in or hold out from amongst themselves the rest of the Sectaries."[37]

That was a shrewd understanding of the dilemma in which the Independents found themselves, for they might justify their claim to orthodoxy by accepting accommodation and virtually restricting toleration to themselves, or they could opt to link themselves with the sectarians clamouring for liberty of conscience. In the first case they might establish their othodoxy and become "but a small inconsiderable companie" easily assimilated by the presbyterian majority in the national church, but in the second case they would almost certainly be condemned by all 'honest men' for siding with 'Anabaptists and Libertines.' A twentieth century perspective would commend the latter course, but the Independents must have found it a difficult decision because it would not only cut them off from the Reformed in other national Churches, but also estrange them from many of

---

[34] To Lauderdale, 17th June, 1645; *Letters and Journals*, II. 280.

[35] Publick Letter, *Ibid.* p. 291.

[36] This must have been John Goodwin, Vicar of St. Stephen's, Coleman Street, and not Thomas Goodwin as Baillie said. Thomas Goodwin held no living in a London church.

[37] To George Young, 8th July, 1645; *ibid.* p. 296. Baillie developed the same insight in a letter written on the same day to the Earl of Eglinton: "We hope shortlie to gett the Independents put to it to declare themselves either to be for the rest of the Sectaries, or against them. If they declare against them, they will be but a small inconsiderable companie; if for them, all honest men will cry out upon them for separating from all the Reformed Churches, to joyne with Anabaptists and Libertines." *Ibid.* p. 299.

their friends in New England. In their situation, however, no other decision was politically possible, and the decision was therefore probably as much political as it was religious.[38]

On 3rd July, 1645, the draft of church government was finally debated, voted to be forwarded to Parliament, and on the following day a committee, headed by Stephen Marshall was selected to accompany it.[39] In his presentation of this advice to Parliament Marshall was careful not to claim that everything in these recommendations could be explicitly proved by Scripture, but he urged that the votes were all consistent with scripture. In his statement to the House of Commons he said:

> They had cast their votes into a model and method; and now the House may see all before them. They have left out the proofs both of Scripture and reason, having sent them in with their former votes; but if the House pleased to command the Assembly to give in the proofs, they are ready to do it. Some of these votes are plainly held out by Scripture; others have reasons agreeable to Scripture and have been alleged: And such as have the light of nature are received and practised in all Reformed Churches. This work, though it appears short, yet hath spent much time, by reason of dissenting judgments; that, if possible they might be satisfied. To this short paper of additional votes they have given in the proofs of Scripture; and if those proofs, at first reading, be not convictive, in regard that God hath not laid down the points of Church discipline in such clear texts; they desire they may not be laid aside, but that the House will command them to give in the proofs at large.[40]

That was a politic statement in view of the difficulties that the Assembly would encounter later. At the same time it must be clear that the Assembly had certainly not been delayed from recommending its church order by any failure of the Independents to produce their own: the majority could hardly claim that it had regarded the Independent statement as necessary for its own work on church government. Later Baillie would exclaim that the Independents "have scorned us,"[41] but on balance the scorning seems to have been mutual.

By the middle of July he was beginning to get very worried, for "Cromwell's extraordinar success, makes that partie here

---

[38] Noone detested sectarianism more than Richard Baxter, but he was a pastor under the Stuarts, the Commonwealth, and later the Protectorate. Towards the end of his life he admitted that the hurt suffered by the Church at the hands of sectarian religion was slight compared with what it had received at the hands of the arrogant popes, prelates and councils. *Rel. Baxt.* I. iii. 181f. (§ 15).

[39] Minutes III. 109.

[40] *C. J.* IV. 199. The passage is included as a note by the editors in Minutes III. 109.

[41] *Letters and Journals,* II. 318.

triumph,"[42] and by September 5th he was reporting to Spang that the "Independents and sects are quiet, injoying peaceably all their desyres, and increasing daily their partie: They speak no more of bringing their modell in the Assemblie." Then he complained that the English ingratitude and "unkyndness to us in our deep sufferings for them" by delaying church settlement would cause God's anger; it was also to be deplored because the fortune of all the Reformed churches was bound up in theirs, but he was convinced the English in time "will doe all we desyre."[43]

The Presbyterians did not intend to let the Independents off the hook too easily. On September 22nd the Assembly began to take strong measures: Whitaker moved that the Dissenting Brethren should make their report, and it was noted:

> That this Assembly made the dissenting brethren to be a Committee to bring in the whole frame of their judgments concerning Church government in a body, with their grounds and reasons, April the 4th, and that this was accepted by them, that the advice of the Assembly concerning government was not sent up to both Houses till July 4, that Mr. Goodwin desired to be excused from his attendance here because the Assembly had engaged them upon that work, which work hath been long expected and earnestly desired by the Assembly; therefore it is now ordered that the said Committee shall, by Monday come se'nnight, report to the Assembly what they shall think.[44]

The date went by without any sign of the Independent statement, but on October 6th Philip Nye told the Assembly that at the time its order had been passed, "some of the brethren were out of town," and there had been other matters that they had needed to consult from the scribes' records.[45] Eventually, on October 13th, an event took place that led Baillie to declare "they have scorned us". Sidrach Simpson "made report from the Committee of the Dissenting Brethren concerning reasons why they did not think fit to bring in their model of government."

---

[42] To Lauderdale, 15th July; *ibid.* p. 303. In a Publick Letter, probably written in early August, he said that nothing had been seen of the Independents since April, but that what they were doing was "yet secret." *Ibid.* p. 306.

[43] *Ibid.* p. 315. Baillie's understanding of 'Providence' would be well worth a study. There is an interesting example of it in a Publick Letter he dated 10th August, 1645; *ibid.* pp. 304–6.

[44] Minutes III. 132. The divines also resolved *nem. con.*, "That in the order of the Committee to bring in the whole frame of their judgment . . . is included the business of gathering of churches." *Ibid.* p. 133.

[45] *Ibid.* p. 135.

This was apparently followed by his reading the text of what was later to be published as *A Copy of a Remonstrance*.[46]

It is to be doubted whether the incident was received as dramatically as De Witt suggests,[47] since Baillie's letters show that there had been growing recognition that the Independents did not intend to be bound by the Assembly's limitations. However, the Scots Commissioner's reaction was typical of his fixed suspicion of Independency:

> We were in a long expectation of a modell from the Independents; but yesterday, after seven months waiting, they have scorned us. The Assemblie haveing put them to it, to make a report of their diligence, they gave us in a sheet or two of injurious reasons why they would not give us any declaration of their tenets. We have appointed a committee to answer that lybell. We think they agree not among themselves, and that there is many things among them which they are loathe to professe, which, by God's helpe, ere long, I mind to doe for them in their own words.[48]

Of course, the slighting of the Assembly by the Independents was inexcusable. It was as inexcusable as the original commission to them had been, and it should remind us that not only were the divines influenced by political issues that entered the Jerusalem Chamber from the world outside, but political methods had entered into their dealings with each other.

Why did the Independents fail to present a statement of their ecclesiology? It could not have been that they lacked the capacity to do so as some of the more virulent supporters of presbytery implied,[49] and the Independents had already outlined the major lines in their ecclesiology during the earlier attempts to reach an accommodation.[50] The theological ability of Thomas Goodwin was generally recognized, and there were others who had the ability to do what had been asked of them:[51] Goodwin's later

---

[46] *Ibid.* p. 148. The report was referred to a committee which would report back (14th), and the material was also to be referred to the committee responsible for answering the Independent Reasons: *ibid.* pp. 148f.

[47] *Jus Divinum*, p. 155.

[48] Publick Letter, 14th October, 1645, *Letters and Journals*, II. 318.

[49] Cf. 'To the Reader' in *A Copy of a Remonstrance*.

[50] Cf. Baillie's Letter to Spang, 25th October, 1644, *Letters and Journals*, II. 236; quoted *supra*, p. 453f. n. 69.

[51] Jeremiah Burroughes set out the main lines of Independent ecclesiology a short time later in a book vindicating himself against the attack launched by Thomas Edwards: "If you would know what we would have, it is soon told you. 1. We would have the ruling Power of Ministers not to extend further then their pastorall Charge over their People for the feeding of them by the Word & Sacraments. 2. We would have the Saints separated from the world, not in a negative way only, but in some positive arguments of some work of God upon their hearts that accompanies Salvation, so far as man may be

book on the subject shows that he was well able to accomplish the task.[52] Nor was their hesitation due to any lack of practical models and supporting writers, because the New England experiment was well under way. In the works of earlier Puritans such as Ames, Parker and Jacob, and in the writings of John Cotton, Thomas Hooker, John Davenport and others a flood of apologias for the Congregational way was beginning to appear.

It is possible that the reasons suggested by Baillie had something to do with it. There may have been differences within the group itself – Jeremiah Burroughes may have stood somewhat closer to the Presbyterians than the others – and certainly there was the unwelcome dilemma of cutting themselves off either from other Reformed churches or from their support in the Army. When all is weighed, however, the reasons for delay had to be basically political – as political as the Assembly's decision to hurry its recommendations through in time for the Uxbridge negotiations. There were strong reasons that would make the Dissenting Brethren hesitant of rushing too quickly into print,[53] but there was the overriding political consideration that the longer they waited the more an eventual declaration for liberty of conscience was likely to become militarily and politically viable. That was undoubtedly a political decision, but their own experience in the Assembly had shown them how easily sincere people could differ in their understanding of the biblical evidence. There were theological insights that would also push them to modify their earlier exclusive ecclesiology.[54]

---

able to judge; and that they freely joyn in Spirituall Communion, yet so as the rule of edification be observed amongst others, that there be a cohabitation in those that joyn, and that all that are fit to be members that do cohabit, doe joyn as much as may be. 3. We would have no coactive violence used against such men who carry themselves religiously and peaceably in their differences from others, in such things onely as godly and peaceable men may and doe differ in. Were these three things granted, we might live together as Brethren, in peace and love. Are those the men that are hinderers of Reformation, and the disturbers of the Peace, who would be satisfied with these three things, and if they cannot have the them peceably by the permission of the magistrate, are resolved to sit down quietly to suffer, or to goe to what places in the world liberty may be enjoyed in these, and yet must these be judged the 'disturbers of the peace?" Jeremiah Burroughes, *A Vindication of Mr Burroughes, Against Mr. Edwards his foule Aspersions, in his spreading Gangraena, and his angry Antiapologia, Concluding with a Briefe Declaration What the Independents would have*. pp. 28f. This appeared in 1646, the year of Burroughes's accidental death at the age of 47.

[52] *The Constitution, Right Order, and Government of the Churches of Christ* (1666); reprinted in *The Works of Thomas Goodwin*, D.D., (Edinburgh, James Nichol, 1865,) XI. pp. 208ff.

[53] As the Assembly divines were quick to point out in their *Answer . . . unto . . . a Remonstrance*.

[54] Cf. *supra* p. 456, n. 73.

3. *Remonstrance and Response*

On November 12th, 1645, the Assembly was informed that what Simpson had said in the Assembly had now appeared publicly in print as the work of the Independents, *A Copy of a Remonstrance* "Declaring the Grounds and Reasons of their declining to bring into the Assembly, their Modell of Church-Government."[55] It had been published anonymously and ostensibly without the authors' permission,[56] but the Presbyterians were justifiably suspicious that the material had been 'leaked' to the printer.[57] It is difficult to see how a Ms making five closely printed pages could have been published without either collusion or extremely careless handling. The Assembly immediately called for its committee to produce an answer in two days, and the Houses of Parliament gave it permission to print the reply.[58]

Since there are so few accounts from the Independent side to enlighten us on what happened in the Assembly we should look at *A Copy of a Remonstrance* in more detail. The Dissenting Brethren asserted that from the beginning they had been "willing and ready" to make their views on church government known, and claimed "that constant, free, and open expressing our selves upon all occasions, and in all questions propounded to the debate, with offers to give an open Account at any time, in what ever should be asked us by any Brother." They also protested their readiness to bring in propositions "stated to our sense for the dispute", but that when they had been asked to state their views about ordination and constituted as a committee for that purpose, their work had been brushed aside. They complained that in the way the questions were laid out for debate in the Assembly, "we could not fully argue for our Judgements, we being bound up to the questions as stated by you. The usuall answer to our Complaints heerin being *That the Assembly sate not to argue the opinions of a few men, but that if we had any thing to say to the assertion brought in, we might.*"[59]

They were particularly critical of the Assembly's refusal to deal with the *jus divinum* issue:

> As also our earnest contending to have some questions (*which you all know are the greatest and most fundamentall points*) fairly disputed

---

[55] Minutes III. 162.

[56] The publisher admitted taking the material without the author's permission, but claimed that he had done so to defend their integrity. 'To the Reader', *A Copy of a Remonstrance*.

[57] Cf. De Witt, *Jus Divinum*, p. 157.

[58] Minutes III. 165f. 168f.

[59] *A Copy of a Remonstrance*, pp. 4f.

and debated, is a sufficient testimony of this our willingnesse. As in the entrance into the dispute of *Government*, the first day, we pressed the handling of this, *That there is a platform of Government for the Churches, under the Gospel, laid down in the Scripture,* and desired to have discussed, *what are the sure and certain wayes, whereby we may judge of what Government, is held forth* Jure Divino *therein,* which should have been fundamentall to all the disputes that were to follow: and this was professedly laid aside by you, which therfore in none of the subsequent debates, we could renew, and thus Arguments were cut off, It being that great and necessary *Medium*, by which the particulars should be confirmed, and in a manner, the whole controversie decided; the greatest difference that were likely to grow betwixt us, being this, *That the forms of Government, you pretend to, and we deny, are asserted to be* Jure divino.[60]

They protested that the Assembly had been unwilling to deal with the powers of particular congregations or with their claim that such a congregation can *"have a sufficient Presbytery for all Censures."* This issue had been persistently denied by the Assembly, although it had been argued not only by them, "but by many of those, that are for a subordinate government thereof to Synods."[61] Their willingness to dispute for their own position had been demonstrated in the Committee for Accommodation and the sub-committee that had arisen from it.

They then returned to the specific reason for their taking offence, the way in which Philip Nye's seven propositions had been discarded:

> After this, when upon occasion of something brought in by one Brother, and intertained, we took hold of that example, and one of us, with consent of the rest, brought in seven Propositions, which contained matter of difference betwixt us, professing, *That if this Reverend Assembly would debate them, or any one of them, we would bring in more, untill we had brought in all the Frame, and the Assembly themselves should pick and chuse what they would debate, and what not.* But these Propositions were rejected with a refusall to debate any one of them.[62]

Even after this rebuff, at a time when a good deal had already been sent to Parliament "and there was not much remaining about Church-government", they had still been willing to present their own alternative on being assured that the Assembly intended to submit a complete ecclesiastical system. They had

---

[60] *Ibid.* p. 5.
[61] *Ibid.*
[62] *Ibid.* p. 6.

accepted the assignment to be a committee for that purpose, but when they had suggested that the Assembly should defer further action in one matter until their arguments had been heard, "it was publiquely answered, *that therefore the Assembly should the rather go on to the concluding of it, because we intended to bring it in*".[63] They had not been allowed to submit anything but their complete church order, and the research had taken several months, but the Assembly had still sent its platform of church government to Parliament before they had the time to produce their own. "By all which we perceived," they said, "that that which was the main end and use of presenting such a Modell to this Assembly, would be frustrated."[64]

They charged the majority party with having neglected to answer their Reasons against the subordination of synods, although the material had been in the Assembly's hands for ten months, and even if they were to produce the work assigned and the Assembly its response to it, "we still retain the sense of so much remedilesse prejudice, *by being bound from replying again*, as doth make us justly wary".[65] They therefore concluded,

> Upon these considerations we think that this Assembly hath no cause now to require a *Report* of us, nor will that our *Report* be of any use, seeing that *Reports* are for *Debates* and *Debates* are for *Results* to be sent up to the Honorable Houses, *who have already voted another form of Government then what we shall present*. However it may be of more use some other way, which by this course may be prevented, And therefore we are resolved to wait for some further opportunitie, to improve what we have prepared.[66]

The Answer of the Assembly of Divines By Authority of Parliament Now sitting at Westminster Unto the Reasons given in to this Assembly by the Dissenting Brethren, Of their not bringing in a Model of their Way, And since Published in Print, under the Title of A Copy of a Remonstrance,[67] was a point-by-point rebuttal of over twenty closely-printed pages. It is perhaps unnecessary to deal

---

[63] *Ibid.* p. 7.

[64] *Ibid.*

[65] *Ibid.* p. 8.

[66] *Ibid.*

[67] This must be carefully distinguished from the other Answers of the Assembly that were later incorporated into *The Grand Debate*:

(a) *The Answer of the Assembly of Divines, unto the Reasons of the seven Dissenting Brethren, against the Proposition of divers Congregations being under one Presbyteriall Government* (1645),

(b) *The Answer of the Assembly of Divines to the Reasons of the Dissenting Brethren Against the Proposition concerning Ordination* (1648).

with it in the same kind of detail, except to show the thrust of the divines' counter-attack and to illustrate how far the two parties were from being able to meet each other.

The Westminster divines expressly denied that the Dissenting Brethren had been willing to submit a statement on their ecclesiology, and instanced Apollonius and other writers who had asked them for such an account, but "he could not yet obtain it from them, as he himself hath complained, and as themselves well know."[68] They went on:

> 'Yet as a proof of their pretended Willingness, they tell us of that constant, free and open expressing of themselves, upon all occasions, and in all questions propounded to the debate.
>
> These are but words; we could as easily, and might more truely say, they have been inconstant, obscure, reserved in expressing themselves, as they can say they have been constant, free and open. And whereas they say, *They have done thus in all questions and upon all occasions*, we desire them to ask their own hearts, Whether they did soe clearly, and openly expresse themselves.

The divines pointedly asked the Independents whether they had ever clearly and unanimously expressed themselves in the question of "*Gathering Churches*, or in the question of the *Power of the People*, or in that of the qualification of *Church Members*, or Whether they did ever clearly and directly endeavour to prove that way of Church-Government, which they practise, to be the onely way *Jure divino*?"[69]

These were shrewd blows, because these aspects of Independent polity had obvious political overtones that could stimulate damaging publicity in the inflamed state of the nation: the idea of the 'gathered church' was not altogether amenable to the traditional parish system, the 'power of the people' in church government had dangerous analogies for civil government, the rigorous standard of communicant church membership was at variance with the parochial inclusiveness of a national church, and the claim to *jus divinum* would be the quickest way to frighten many of the politicians as the Assembly itself had realized.

(c) *The Answer of the Assembly of Divines to the Reasons of the Dissenting Brethren, against the Proposition concerning the Subordination of Congregationall, Classicall, Provinciall, and Nationall Assemblies, for the Government of the Church. (1648)*.

[68] *Op. cit.* p. 4.

[69] *Ibid.* Some of these matters had been specifically addressed in the earlier meetings of the Committee of Accommodation, but these negotiations had not been made public. Cf. *supra* pp. 444–56, and especially p. 453, n. 69.

The divines followed this with their own detailed account of the circumstances that led to the Dissenting Brethren being required to present their own form of government, but they returned to those aspects of Independency that seemed most threatening to a national settlement in religion:

1. Whether their gathering of Churches here in *England* was just, necessary, seasonable.

2. How far every particular man and woman may go according to their own judgment, in separating from those Congregations wherein they have orderly Communicated.

3. What power single men and women have of Congregating themselves together to become a Church as their own discretion leads them, without the guidance of the Ministers, and Authority of the Magistrate.

4. Whether people so congregated of their own accord, have all power within themselves for admitting or refusing Members, chusing or ordaining Officers.

5. Whether people are to rule over their Officers.

6. Whether every Congregation ought to have a distinct Presbytery, or whether many may not lawfully have one common Presbytery ruling immediately over them.

These and the like questions we know to be some of the greatest and most fundamental points (as to their way) but we do not remember, that ever they did exactly contend to have these questions fairly disputed and debated: Neither do themselves we think remember it.[70]

In reply to the charge that the Assembly had evaded consideration of *jus divinum*, they claimed that it had been asserted by Presbyterians "long before this way of our Brethren was thought upon", and reminded them that it had also been urged at the beginning by the Scots Commissioners, but that the Assembly in its wisdom had preferred to start with the scriptural evidence before deciding whether or not it amounted to a divine warrant.[71] The *Answer* dealt in detail with the Independents' relationship to the Committee of Accommodation, and then turned to the incident of Philip Nye's seven propositions. The divines charged that the propositions "were not to the purpose of what was then before the Assembly, nor what was desired, and expected from us," namely, what should be further reformed in congregations. They criticized the proposals because they were not in a proper

---

[70] *Ibid.* p. 10.
[71] *Ibid.* pp. 10f.

form for debate, because they had not been presented with proof texts, and because Nye had not left them any record in writing.[72]

The divines concluded that far from absolving the Dissenting Brethren from the need to produce their church order "the Assembly hath still great and just cause" to expect it of them, since it had been claimed publicly that they were ready to do it, the Assembly had ordered it, and it had been used as an excuse for absenting themselves from the Assembly. In any case, it had been rumoured that it was already finished.

They charged the Dissenting Brethren of having "some other cause then what they pretend to, and that something lies behinde the curtain, which doth not yet appear."[73] Perhaps the Independents were not too certain where they stood, or possibly they could not agree among themselves, or maybe those "who at present are a strength to them" might disapprove, or possibly they were waiting for a more propitious time.

Obviously there was right and wrong on both sides, but there is little to be gained by trying to apportion praise or blame, except by those who would try to make denominational capital out of it. What stands clear, however, is that there were political motivations on both sides – there were political reasons both inside and outside the Assembly that might cause the majority to press the Independents for a public statement of their church order at this time, and political motivations that were just as strong for the Independents to draw back from it. We are out of the realm of theology, and we are deep in the mire of politics.

III

The Final Choice: 'A Toleration, A Toleration'

As a result of this open acknowledgement of a serious breach in the Assembly, the Houses of Parliament decided to intervene, and after a year of inactivity the Committee for Accommodation was revived in November 1645, but we must agree with De Witt that this committee "had the now almost hopeless task of bringing together two parties apparently irreconcilably sundered."[74]

---

[72] *Ibid.* p. 18. To put the best construction on this, we must say that there was a complete misunderstanding on the part of both parties regarding this assignment. The Independents claimed they were free to state what they felt needed to be discussed about the rights and power of congregations; the Presbyterians expected the Independents to say what they wanted for congregations *within* the church order that had been voted – i.e., what they would need for an accommodation.

[73] *Ibid.* p. 24.

[74] De Witt, *Jus Divinum*, p. 161.

However, the task of the committee was not restricted to the single point of discovering how the Independents might be included in the new church establishment. It was instructed to

> take into consideration the differences in opinions of the members of the Assembly in point of Church-government, and to indeavour an *union* if it be possible: And in case that cannot be done, to indeavour the *finding out some way how farre tender consciences*, who cannot in all things submit to the Common Rule, which shall be established, may be borne with according to the Word, and as may stand with the publike peace; That so the proceedings of the Assembly may not be so much retarded.[75]

The major concern of the members of Parliament was a quick settlement.

The first meeting of the committee took place on November 14th, 1645, and at the following meeting three days later, the divines who had been members of the previous sub-committee for accommodation were asked to prepare an agenda for future debate.[76] However, when the committee met on the 24th, the chairman of the sub-committee reported that they had nothing to present, "because the Dissenting Brethren, did wave the first part of the Order of the Houses touching accommodation." The Independents proceeded to say the same in a position paper.[77] They had clearly reached the decision not to consider accommodation in the national settlement, but to press for toleration. What was not yet revealed was the extent of the toleration for which they would be working, although Baillie, writing on the 25th, said, that the "Independents in their last meeting of our grand committee of accommodation have expressed their desyres for tolleration, not only to themselves, but to other Sects." At the same time he thought "Parliament has no great inclination to satisfie either."[78]

The extent of the Independents' concern for toleration was not stated as baldly as that, although it may have been implicitly their goal for some time. At the meeting on the 24th November, the

---

[75] From the Order of the Two Houses of Parliament, Thursday, 6th November, 1645, printed in *The Papers and Answers of the Dissenting Brethren And The Committee of the Assembly of Divines. Given in to the Honorable Committee of the Lords and Commons, and Assembly of Divines with the Scotch Commissioners, for Accommodation, At the Reviving of that Committee, 1645.* (1648) p. 12. This group of papers was printed in *The Grand Debate.*

[76] *Ibid.* p. 14.

[77] *Ibid.*

[78] Publick Letter, *Letters and Journals,* II. 326. In the same letter Baillie announced that his book, *A Dissvasive from the Errours of the Time,* had appeared in print.

five original apologists were asked to present the matters "they desire to be born with in point of Church-government, in all those things wherein they cannot submit unto the common Rule that is established", and they were given until Thursday, December 4th to prepare this statement.[79]

In their statement on December 4th they reaffirmed their support for what the Assembly had done in the Directory and said they were "confident that we shall agree in the confession of faith", but they asked for indulgence respecting the validity of congregational ordination, and asked that their congregations should be free from presbyterian discipline. They also asked that they should have liberty to gather churches from any who could not conscientiously join in the parish structure, and that such congregations should be free to set up competent elderships.[80]

Further meetings were held[81] that considered the response of the Presbyterians in the sub-committee to the Independents' requests, the Dissenting Brethren's replies to the Presbyterians, and the presbyterian answers to those replies. After the last meeting on March 9th, 1645/6, the Committee adjourned with the intention of meeting again, "but being diverted by other occasions," did not meet any more and "there was no further proceeding in that business."[82]

Other influences entered to strengthen the Assembly's stand against toleration. A letter that the London ministers presented to the Assembly on 1st January, 1645/6, was published protesting against the toleration for which the Independents had asked.[83]

In that letter the London ministers said that such a toleration would be "extreamly unseasonable and praepoperous", first, because the proposed reformation of religion had not yet been perfected and settled "according to our Covenant", secondly, because it was "not yet known what the government of the *Independents* is", and thirdly,

> Wee can hardly bee perswaded, that the *Independents* themselves (after all the stirres they have made amongst us) are as yet fully resolved about their owne way wherewith they would be concluded,

[79] *The Papers and Answers*, p. 15.
[80] *Ibid.* pp. 15–17.
[81] 15th, 23rd December, 1645; 2nd, February and 9th March, 1645/6.
[82] *Ibid.* p. 123.
[83] *A Letter of the Ministers of the City of London, Presented the first of Jan. 1645. to the Reverend Assembly of Divines Sitting at Westminster by Authority of Parliament, against Toleration.* 1645 (i.e., 1645/6). The letter was signed as from Sion College, and dated December 18th, 1645. Cf. Minutes III. 174.

seeing they publish not their modell (though they are nimble enough in publishing other things) and they professe Reserves, and New lights, for which they will (no doubt) expect the like toleration, and so *in infinitum*. It were more seasonable to move for toleration when once they are positively determined how farre they meane to goe, and where they meane to stay.[84]

This was a good point, and the ministers went on to make another telling blow when they declared that "to grant to them and not to other Sectaries who are free born as well as they, and have done as good service as they to the publike (as they use to plead) will be counted injustice and great partiality; but to grant it unto all will scarce be cleared from great impiety."[85] The ministers probably did not realize that the Independents were moving to a position where the last option did not seem such a great impiety.

The London ministers said that Independency was schism, and they listed no less than eleven dire results that they saw arising from toleration. It was contrary to the Solemn League and Covenant, and in conclusion they declared:

> These are some of the many considerations which make deep impression upon our Spirits against that great *Diana* of *Independents*, and all the Sectaries so much cryed up by them in these distracted times, *viz. A Toleration, A Toleration*. And however, none should have more rejoyced than our selves in the establishment of a brotherly, peaceable and Christian Accommodation; yet this being utterly rejected by them, wee cannot dissemble how upon the forementioned grounds, wee detest, and abhorre the much endeavoured Toleration.[86]

There is no way of proving that Robert Baillie had any hand in compiling this letter, but it echoed his sentiments throughout and we know that he was actively stimulating elements in the City against toleration.[87] By this time, the ministers of London working out of Sion College were to a man supporters of the covenanted uniformity towards which the Scots Commissioners had been working.

The message of this new failure to reach accommodation was that this had finally been laid to rest. The Independents now

---

[84] *Op. cit.* pp. 2f.

[85] Perhaps the Independents would have had little difficulty in presenting their church government if it had been identical with that of New England; but it could not follow that precise pattern without denying the very principle of liberty of conscience that was now the political necessity for their survival.

[86] *Ibid.* p. 6.

[87] Cf. Baillie's letter to Ramsay, January 15th, 1645/6, *Letters and Journals*, II. 337.

demanded toleration, and it is difficult to see how toleration could be limited to themselves alone: in that, the London ministers correctly assessed the situation. It is also difficult to see how either side could have taken any stand other than they did, for if the Independents could not enter into the presbyterian system without relinquishing some of their scriptural insights, the Presbyterians could not grant them the right of opting out of the established church without undermining their own. Toleration would create a permanent schism in the national church, as the Presbyterians had declared in an earlier statement to the Committee for Accommodation:

> This would give countenance to a perpetuall Schisme and division in the Church, still drawing away some from the Churches under the Rule, which also would breed many irritations between the parties going away and those whom they leave; And againe, between the Church that should be forsaken, and that to which they should go.[88]

It would produce a serious practical problem, and we must remember that although there were many examples elsewhere of the presbyterian system in a national establishment and the example of Congregationalism in New England, there was no model anywhere in the world of the kind of new ecclesial relationship that the Independents were demanding. The theology of that time simply could not envisage such a concept of 'churches' within the Church. We agree with De Witt's judgment that the "project of a Reformed, biblical church government in England was thus formally wrecked upon the rocks of a mutually exclusive *jus divinum*."[89]

But we question whether in view of the theologians' own limitations that was altogether a matter for regret, and the failure to reach agreement perhaps indicates the limitations of such exclusive ecclesiologies. The world outside the Jerusalem Chamber had a strange way of revealing that it was a part of Providence, and even of intruding itself into the Church's understanding of 'the mind of Christ.' When toleration became a reality in England, it would be imposed on the theologians from without.

---

[88] *Papers and Answers*, pp. 20f.
[89] De Witt, *Jus Divinum*, p. 166.

CHAPTER 16

'MARIAGE DE CONVENANCE'

I

An Uneven Match

As far as the confrontation between the Presbyterian and Independent ecclesiologies is concerned, the abortive attempt to reach agreement in 1645–6 is virtually the end of our immediate story; but obviously, although some of the actors change and the stage is broader, the dispute of the presbyterian majority and the English Parliament over *jus divinum* raises the curtain on a broader ecclesiological drama.

The issue was implicit within the very circumstances of the Assembly's call, although there is only occasionally any indications in the debates of the problem that it could become.[1] On the other hand the leaders were certainly conscious of it when they deliberately refused to tackle *jus divinum* head on.[2] A plausible case could be made out for the Assembly's method of arguing inductively from the instances in scripture to the formulation of a 'rule'; we have to agree with William Shaw's judgment that "the Assembly had not yet formulated a claim to the *jus divinum* – not from any want of desire, but from what can only be described as policy."[3]

---

[1] There were a few significant hints of the *jus divinum* issue in the earlier speeches of Erastians like Lightfoot: e.g., in the debate on the power of the Keys (at the end of October, 1643,) Lightfoot had argued that the disciplinary power of the church was only in teaching. He was alone in his argument, but his major thrust at that time seems to have been not against *jure divino* Presbyterianism, but against the Independents. There does not seem to be sufficient in that or similar incidents to suggest that the Erastian issue had yet surfaced properly, although obviously the threat of it was present. Cf. Beveridge, *Short Hist. of the West. Assembly*, p. 58; Lightfoot, *Journal*, pp. 30–33, TMs. I. 255ff (Ms. I. ff. 218 et seq.).

[2] 17th October, 1643; cf. Lightfoot, *Journal*, pp. 19–21; TMs. I. 213–224 (Ms. I. ff. 107b–113.) Cf. the care with which Marshall eventually introduced the Assembly's propositions on church government, 4th July, 1645; Minutes III. 109 n. Cf. 72; *supra* p. 478.

[3] *A Hist. of the English Church*, I. 301.

Political considerations swayed the Scots in accepting this line taken by the leaders of the English majority, for all the Scots were convinced about the *jure divino* basis of their Kirk. Their strategy was first to get the presbyterian system established in England, and leave the question of its *jus divinum* until circumstances were more favourable. That had been the advice the Scottish Commissioners gave their English associates when the issue blew up in the early autumn of 1645. Parliament had refused to grant the divines the discretionary powers they demanded in excluding wrong-doers from the Sacrament, and Baillie observed:

> The generall they would not grant, as including ane arbitrarie and illimitat power. Our advyce wes, that they would goe on to sett up their Presbyteries and Synods with so much power as they could gett; and after they were once settled, then they might strive to obtain their full due power.[4]

That was a political decision. It would be easier to deal with the English Parliament when they could present the case for *jus divinum* from a position of greater strength – for example, after a Scottish victory or a reverse suffered by the New Model Army. Meanwhile, the important thing was to get the presbyterian system established throughout English parishes and backed by English law.

However, because of the conditions of its call, there was an inconsistency in the Assembly's approach to *jus divinum*.[5] It was explicitly claimed by both the Independents and the Scots for their respective views of the Church, and it was implicit in opinions held by many of the others, but in view of the Assembly's dependence on and responsibility to Parliament, the divines either evaded the subject or treated it with great circumspection. Although it remained unacknowledged, it had always been present during the 'Grand Debate' with the Independents.

The Assembly had a glimpse of the ultimate struggle with Parliament in the clash in February 1643/4 between the learned Semitist and Member of Parliament for Oxford, John Selden, and George Gillespie.[6] It foreshadowed the future struggle,

---

[4] Publick Letter, August 1645, *Letters and Journals*, II. 307.

[5] The most comprehensive treatment of this is J. R. De Witt's *Jus Divinum*, since he was the first to use all the available sources. For this period see especially pp. 169–246.

However, although we cannot go beyond the sources used by De Witt, we feel that his own theological position sometimes colours his interpretation of the evidence he presents.

[6] 20th and 21st February, 1643/4; cf. *supra* pp. 269ff., Lightfoot, *Journal*, pp. 165–8, TMs. I. 611f., 618–21 (Ms. I. ff. 317b–318, 321–2.)

because the Scots had to take note of Selden's views,[7] since he could also defend his position in the House of Commons where the final decisions about the Church would be made. The Assembly and its Scottish advisers might have taken notice that when, in March the same year, Parliament had published the Assembly's letter to foreign churches, it had very pointedly omitted to print the reply which Baillie had worked so hard to get from the classis of Walcheren precisely because it contained an assertion of ecclesiastical divine right.[8] It should also be remarked that during the Commons debate on this, it was John Selden who spoke

> earnestlie against it, shewing that in that letter they challenged an ecclesiastical or Church government to be *jure divino*, with which the civil magistrate had nothing to do, and this he saied was contrarie to the ancient law of England and the use heere received, and therefore advised that we should forbeare to print that letter, which after some debate was thought to be the best way.[9]

Baillie lamented the bias of the English Parliament. Writing to his kinsman, Spang, on its treatment of the Assembly's ordination proposals in the summer of 1644, he said that the politicians "had scraped out whatever might displease the Independents, or patrons, or Selden and others, who will have no Discipline at all in any Church *Jure Divino*, but settled only upon the free-will and pleasure of the Parliament."[10] He and his colleagues may have underestimated the fixed determination of the Commons on this matter.

The clash occurred in respect to four discrete but often closely related issues. First, in the spring of 1645 it arose out of the divines' claim that church officers should have discretionary rights of excluding from the sacrament those they judged to be guilty of 'scandalous sins.' Secondly, out of this dispute, Parliament asserted its own ecclesiastical control as the final court of appeal for such cases; and thirdly, this in turn led to the divines being charged with a breach of parliamentary privilege and to Parliament's nine Questions regarding the claims to ecclesiastical divine right. Fourthly, there was the claim to *jus divinum* based on the Lordship of Christ which the Assembly incorporated into the Confession of Faith.

---

[7] To Spang, 18th February, 1644/5; *Letters and Journals*, II. 129.

[8] *Jus Divinum*, p. 179.

[9] From D'Ewes's *Diary*, as quoted by Shaw, *Hist. of the English Church*, I. 301.

[10] 28th June, 1644; *Letters and Journals*, II. 198.

However, before we consider this progression of events, we should note that there are two curious incidents related to the claim to *jus divinum* recorded by the lawyer and Member of Parliament, Bulstrode Whitelocke, which he placed within the year 1644, although it is difficult to see precisely when they took place. The first is a speech that he claims to have delivered in the Assembly, in which he advised the Assembly not to tie its recommendations on church government to *jus divinum* but to recommend "that the Government of the Church by Presbyteries is most agreeable to the word of God, and most fit to be settled in this Kingdom, or in what other expressions, you may much better know than I, it is fit to Cloath your Questions".[11] Hetherington suggested that this incident took place at the time when the Assembly was ready to present its Directory of Ordination in August 1644.[12]

The second incident is even more difficult to date precisely. Whitelocke claimed that it was an attempt by the Assembly to get its recommendations respecting church government through the Commons with the *jure divino* claims intact.

> The Assembly of Divines as soon as the House of Commons were sate, and before they were full, came to the House, and presented them with the Assemblie's Advice and Opinion, *for the Presbyterian Government to be settled,* and an expression was in their Advice, *That the Presbyterian Government was* jure divino.
>
> *Glyn* and *Whitelocke* were then in the House, and few others, but those who concurred in judgment with the Assembly, and had notice to be there early, thinking to pass this business before the House should be full.
>
> *Glyn* stood up and spake an hour to the point of *jus divinum*, and the *Presbyterian Government,* in which time the House filled apace, and then *Whitelocke* spake to the same Points, inlarging his discourse to a much longer time than ordinary; and purposely that the House might be full, as it was before he had made an end.
>
> And then upon the question it was carried, to lay aside the point of *jus divinum*; and herein *Glyn* and *Whitelocke* had thanks from divers, for preventing the surprisal of the House upon this great question.[13]

It is an intriguing incident, but unfortunately Whitelocke was not specific about dates. Hetherington thought that must have taken place on November 15th, 1644, when the papers concerning church government were first laid before the House of Com-

---

[11] Bulstrode Whitelocke, *Memorials of English Affairs,* p. 95.
[12] Hetherington, *Hist. of the West. Assembly,* p. 241. The Assembly presented the material on the Directory to Parliament on August 15th, 1644.
[13] Whitelocke, *Memorials,* p. 106.

mons,[14] and in view of Whitelocke placing it in 1644, this date must probably be accepted. At the same time, it seems early for the *jus divinum* issue to have surfaced as specifically as that. Whatever hints we get in 1644 of an impending battle over this issue, it was in the following year that the real struggle between the divine right of presbytery and the claims of Parliament commenced in earnest.

II

The Right to Exclude from the Lord's Supper

During the first two months of 1645 the Assembly was fully occupied with the Reasons of the Dissenting Brethren and with getting its church order approved in time to be of use at Uxbridge, but as Shaw pointed out, the claim to *jus divinum* and the counter-claim to civil control of the national church were bound to arise with the question of ecclesiastical discipline and jurisdiction.[15]

Even before the Directory had been presented, the Assembly had urged the Houses to prepare an ordinance to settle the ministry and take steps to prevent 'ignorant and scandalous persons' from taking the Lord's Supper,[16] and in line with their policy of lending full support to presbyterian proposals in the Assembly, the London ministers had followed this with a petition to the same effect a few days later.[17] However, this pressure caused the House of Commons to request the Assembly to be more specific on what sins or disabilities should disqualify a person from the sacrament.[18]

> Hereupon, [observed Shaw] on the 17th of April, Whittaker reported from the Grand Committee of the House its votes concerning the point of the ignorant and scandalous, and they were immediately adopted by formal resolution of the House. In brief, this series of votes excluded from the Sacrament (1) adulterers, etc., drunkards, swearers, blasphemers; (2) such as have not a competent measure of understanding concerning the state of man by creation, etc., the redemption of Jesus Christ, etc., the way and means to

---

[14] *Hist. of the West. Assembly*, pp. 243f.

[15] *Hist. of the English Church*, I. 302.

[16] March 6th, 1644/5, *C. J.*, IV. 71; cf. De Witt, *Jus Divinum*, p. 180, A. F. Mitchell, *The West. Assembly*, pp. 289f.

[17] March 10th, 1644/5, *L. J.*, VII. 268.

[18] 28th March, 1645: "Sir Robert Harley and Mr. Tate brought an order from the House of Commons, to set down what we mean by a competent measure of knowledge, and understanding concerning God the Father, etc." Minutes III. 74.

apply Christ, etc., the nature and necessity of faith etc., repentence, etc., the nature and use of the Sacraments, etc., the condition of man after this life, etc., In each case the particulars of the 'competent knowledge' were set out in explicit words in the resolution.[19]

The House then appointed a committee to draft an ordinance along these lines and passed explicit resolutions at the beginning of May,[20] but the key to the later dispute between the Assembly and the Commons came with two Commons' resolutions regarding the right to appeal from the decisions of a local eldership through the higher church courts to Parliament.[21]

Baillie's reaction reveals the ultimate objective of the divines that would lead to the later dispute:

> The Parliament have passed many of our votes of Government, purposing quicklie to erect the Ecclesiastick courts, of Sessions, Presbyteries, and Synods, and thereafter to pass so much of our government as they think necessare. We will have much to doe with them to make sundrie of our votes pass; for most of their lawyers are strong Erastians, and would have all the Church Government depend absolutelie on the Parliament: for this end they have past a vote in the House of Commons, for appeals from Sessions to Presbyteries, from these to Synods, from these to Nationall Assemblies, and from these to Parliament. We mind to be silent for some tyme in this, least we marr the erection of the Ecclesiastick courts; bot when we find it seasonable, we mind to make much adoe before it goe so. We are hopefull to make them declare, they meane no other thing, by their appealls from the Nationall Assemblie to a Parliament, than a complaint of an injurious proceeding; which we did never deny.[22]

Again we note the Scots' decision to remain quiet on the *jus divinum* for a time in order to get the church government established, but equally their determination not to leave that matter in the control of the English Parliament.

The Assembly did nothing more until June 4th, when "it was moved to add something concerning scandalous sins" and Palmer and Hill were added to a committee of the Assembly that

---

[19] *Hist. of the English Church*, I. 260f.

[20] Cf. Shaw, *ibid.* p. 262.

[21] "1. Satisfaction shall be given to the eldership of every congregation by sufficient manifestation of the offender's repentance or the party's innocency appearing, before the suspended, as above, shall be readmitted to the Sacrament.

2. If any person suspended from the Sacrament of the Lord's Supper shall find himself grieved with the proceeding before the eldership of any congregation, he shall have liberty to appeal to the Classical Assembly, from thence to the Provincial, from thence to the National, and from thence to the Parliament." *C. J.* IV. 140; as cited also by Shaw, *Hist. of the English Church*, I. 263.

[22] 25th April, 1645, Publick Letter; *Letters and Journals*, II. 267.

was advising the responsible sub-committee of the House of Commons. On the following day that sub-committee asked the Assembly to add any further sins that warranted exclusion from the sacrament,[23] and the divines appear to have gone to work with a will, for on June 12th they appointed a committee of their own to review the catalogue of such sins "and to draw up something to be added by way of desire that there may be some general proposition to leave it to presbytery to proceed in other cases or scandals of the like nature as in those, and some reasons for such a clause."[24]

That led directly on the following day (13th June) to the claim of *jus divinum*, for there was a debate "about adding another reason to show and hold out the *jus divinum*. We claim our power from Jesus Christ."[25] The parliamentary sub-committee, however, seems to have declined this paper as extending beyond its powers, and the claim to a discretionary authority in church officers and courts was dropped at the last minute before the material reached the House of Commons.[26] The Assembly still walked warily, for as Baillie observed, "the Erastian partie in the Parliament is stronger than the Independent, and is lyke to work us much woe"; and he added, "Selden is their head."[27]

III

Parliament and Ecclesiastical Appeals

The matter was revived at the end of July when the House of Commons pressed the Assembly further regarding exclusion from the sacrament, and on the same day (25th) the Assembly appointed a committee to prepare a petition "and a narrative to be presented to both Houses for the hasting of business of the sacraments." This was debated during the following sessions,[28] and the only note of dissent came from Thomas Coleman. Perhaps it was the new aggressiveness of the Assembly in this matter that stimulated Thomas Coleman to preach a sermon strongly against *jus divinum* to the House of Commons on July 30th, and this got him into serious trouble with the Assembly and particularly with the Scots.[29]

---

[23] Minutes III. 100.
[24] *Ibid*. p. 103.
[25] *Ibid*.
[26] 16th June; cf. Shaw, *Hist. of the English Church*, I. 265f.
[27] To Spang, n.d. but placed in June 1645; *Letters and Journals*, II. 277.
[28] Minutes III. 116f. It was debated on 28th and 31st July.
[29] Cf. *infra* pp. 513–15.

The Assembly's paper apparently included a plea for a discretionary power in the clergy to allow or refuse the sacrament on the basis of their divine right to act in such cases. It was presented on August 1st, but this does not seem to have moved the parliamentarians, for on August 6th we find Richard Vines urging the Assembly to "consider of something to move the Houses for the preserving of the sacraments pure, be[cause] the ordinance is drawing up only for seven sins."[30] The divines were alarmed, and on the following day a new or re-worded statement of their position was debated, and voted to be sent to the Houses.[31] It was presented to the Commons on the 8th[32] and to the Lords on the 12th.[33]

This was the most strongly worded document on the divine right of the Church that the Assembly had hitherto addressed to Parliament, and it has received its due number of encomiums from denominational historians – "so faithful, yet respectful, so cogent in argument, yet calm in tone, so importunate, yet truly dignified"[34] – but it ended with the clear threat that if they were forced to receive at the sacrament those they deemed unworthy,

> we do evidently foresee that not only we, but many of our godly brethren, must be put upon this hard choice, either to forsake our stations in the ministry, which would be to us one of the greatest afflictions, or else to partake in other men's sins, and thereby incur the danger of their plagues; *and if we must choose one, we are resolved, and we trust our God will help us, to choose affliction rather than iniquity.*[35]

One of Baillie's letters of that period shows that the Scots advised their English colleagues to walk carefully until at least they were sure of the official establishment of the presbyterian system;

> Bot the Synod wes in ane other mind; and after diverse fair papers, at last they framed a most zealous, clear, and peremptor one, wherein they held out plainly the Church's divyne right to keep off from the Sacrament all who are scandalous; and if they cannot obtaine the free exercise of that power which Christ hath given them, they will lay downe their charges, and rather choyse all afflictions than to sinne by

---

[30] Minutes III. 118.

[31] *Ibid.* 119.

[32] *Ibid.* 120, *C. J.* IV. 234.

[33] *L. J.*, VII. 534–5.

[34] Mitchell, *The West. Assembly*, p. 300.

[35] Much of this appears in a lengthy extract in Mitchell, *ibid.* pp. 297–300, from which this quotation is taken (p. 300). The original is to be found in *L. J.*, VII. 534f. In spite of Parliament's continued opposition the divines did not relinquish their livings.

prophaning the Holy table. The House is highly inflamed with this petition, and seems resolute to refuse it. The Assemblie is also peremptor to have it granted; for upon this point, they say, depends their standing, all the godly being resolved to separate from them, if there be not a power, and care, to keep the prophane from the Sacraments. If the Lord assist us not in this difficultie, it may be the cause of great confusion among us.[36]

However, Baillie also reported that during that week deacons and elders would be chosen for parishes all over London, and that in a few weeks presbyteries and a provincial synod would be established.

On August 11th the Assembly strengthened its committee further, and passed a series of Orders that illustrate its own stiffened resolve:

Ordered – The Committee are to move the sub-Committee that the Commissioners of the Church of Scotland may be by them desired to be assistant to this Committee of the Assembly in this business.

Ordered – Mr. Ny, Mr. Goodwin, Mr. Philips, Mr. Sterry, be added to this Committee.

Ordered – This Committee is to advise and debate with the sub-Committee of the House of Commons concerning a course to be settled touching suspension from the sacrament of the Lord's Supper.

Ordered – This Committee is not to present any list of scandalous sins till they have further order from the Assembly, nor in the debate and advice to reced[e] from the sense of the Assembly declared in their votes, and in those petitions presented formerly by the Assembly to the Honble Houses, till the Assembly be acquainted therewith.

Ordered – Nor to conclude anything *de novo* till the Assembly be acquainted with it.

Ordered – The Committee are to apply themselves especially to those two particulars in their advice and debate:

(1.) The *jus divinum* of a power in Church officers to keep scandalous persons from the sacrament of the Lord's Supper; (2.) The impossibility, by any enumeration of sins, to make a catalogue so sufficient as to preserve the sacraments pure.

Ordered – Mr. Reynolds. This Committee is to prepare a character of scandalous sins, and to report it to the Assembly with all convenient speed.[37]

Not the least interesting feature of this series of Orders is to note the Assembly's specific addition of Nye, Goodwin, Phillips

---

[36] Publick Letter, n.d. but placed in August 1645, *Letters and Journals*, II. 307.
[37] Minutes III. 120f.

and Sterry – all Independents[38] – to the committee: on this point Independents and Presbyterians were not divided.

However, despite its own specific Orders, the Assembly was sucked into the confusing vortex of producing ever-longer lists of 'scandalous sins,' and although it seemed that the politicians on the Grand Committee had bowed briefly to the pressure and granted the clergy a modest discretionary power by including the saving phrase "and other notorious scandalous sins", by the end of the first week in September they had pulled back.[39] Baillie thought matters were still very much in the balance. The divines were weakened by the delay in answering their petition, and the major stumbling-block to the program of ecclesiastical settlement was the legal fraternity in the House of Commons,[40] although he was still optimistic that "in tyme they will doe all we desyre."[41]

The attitude of the Members of Parliament stiffened, possibly in reaction to the pressure put upon Parliament by the Assembly's supporters in the City. On September 26th the Grand Committee presented its votes concerning suspension from the sacrament which simply added a list of additional sins,[42] while the House of Commons produced a clause to prevent abuses and deal with appeals.[43] This provided that there would be a standing committee of the Houses to consider any further reasons for suspension not included within the ordinance, and this would be the body to which any local eldership could refer cases that were not otherwise covered.

That was precisely the kind of subordination of the church to Parliament that the divines wanted to avoid. Baillie was dismayed:

> our greatest trouble for the time is from the Erastians in the House of Commons. They are at last content to erect Presbyteries and Synods in all the land, and have given out their orders for that end; yet they give to the ecclesiastick courts so little power, that the Assemblie finding their petitions not granted, are in great doubt whether to sett up any thing, till, by some powerfull petition of many thousand hands, they obtaine some more of their just desyres.[44]

---

[38] Cf. the comments in *An Apologeticall Narration* (1963 edn.), especially pp. 109ff.

[39] Cf. Shaw, *History of the English Church*, I. 272–4, De Witt, *Jus Divinum*, p. 186.

[40] He named William Prynne. It might be noted that many of these men strongly supported the Presbyterians on pragmatic grounds, but opposed *jus divinum*.

[41] To Spang, 5th September; *Letters and Journals*, II. 315.

[42] Cf. Shaw, *Hist. of the English Church*, I. 275.

[43] *Ibid.* p. 276.

[44] Publick Letter, 14th October 1645; *Letters and Journals*, II. 318.

In another letter written at much the same time to George Young, Baillie said that the "Assemblie is much discouraged; they find their advyce altogether slighted; a kind of [nominal] Presbyterie sett up."[45]

The Ordinance appeared on October 20th, 1645, and it included a whole catalogue of sinners who were to be automatically excluded from the sacrament. By denying discretionary powers to the clergy the politicians had put the divines in the impossible position of having to name every form of wrongdoing or disability that could possibly disqualify a member of the church from the Lord's Supper. Granted that the divines at that time intended to use such discretionary powers in a more repressive way than Parliament thought fit, we must admit that pastoral responsibility could not be reduced to the clear-cut administration of legal provisions:[46] by forcing the Assembly to list anything that might exclude a sinner from the sacrament, the Commons' lawyers had made the whole operation, as De Witt justly observes, a *reductio ad absurdum*.[47]

At the instigation of Stephen Marshall the Assembly decided to make a further approach to Parliament, but the Commons continued to deal with the issue as if it were simply a matter of formulating a more complete list of sins, rather than as the question of a minister's power to act pastorally. Perhaps if the divines had not been so concerned with exclusion in the name of purity, they would have gained the discretionary power they were demanding: by adding to the list of sins to the extent they did, they more or less proved to the politicians that they were right to deny ministers any wider powers.

The Scots had other ways of working to the desired end. They could make their will known directly to the Houses, and they did so in a strongly worded paper protesting the need to safeguard the purity of the Lord's Supper, which was handed in on October 1st. But the same paper showed their complicity in less orthodox methods. Sir Robert Honeywood wrote a letter in early October to Sir Henry Vane, senior, in which he had said:

> The chief thing of moment which has lately been agitated was the debate yesterday in the House of Commons upon a paper some days since delivered in by the Scots, containing a reproach to the Parlia-

---

[45] October, 1645, *Letters and Journals*, II. 320.
[46] However, it should be remembered that the Scots had argued along that line against the Independents during the debates on excommunication. Cf. *supra* pp. 432f.
[47] *Jus Divinum*, p. 188.

ment for the ill payment of their army, their not settling the Presbyterian government as they intimated the House had consented to; in which business they used some sharp language, *and the very words of a petition projected to have been delivered from the City to the House for the settling of the said Government, which petition the House, upon precognizance had voted to be false and scandalous* . . .

From the same letter we learn that under the guidance of young Sir Henry Vane, the House had decided to set up the presbyterian order, "but not with that latitude of power which the Assembly of Divines desired, which the sense of the House could not admit, nor ought the Kingdom of Scotland to press."[48]

It was clear to all that the Scots were working in collusion with the London ministers to bring pressure on the English Parliament. Baillie says that after many exchanges, "we gave them in ane enumeration of many particulars, but withall craves a generall clause to be added", and from the same letter we learn that the London clergy were going slow on setting up the new ecclesiastical system, "for the ministers refuises to accept of Presbyteries without this power."[49] The Scots and the English Presbyterians also extended their influence to other elements likely to sway the politicians at Westminster, for at much the same time as the Assembly was producing a supplementary list of scandalous sins and listening to Sidrach Simpson's statement why the Dissenting Brethren did not intend to present their model of church government,[50] the Common Council of the City of London was induced to add its own petition to those of the Assembly, the London ministers and the Scots.[51]

Early in January 1645/6 Baillie told a friend in Scotland that the settlement of presbyterian church order had been frustrated by the machinations of the Independents, the Erastian lawyers in Parliament and the "worldlie profane men, who are extremelie affrighted to come under the yoke of ecclesiastick discipline".[52] Certainly there were those among the politicians who would have regarded the rigours of this church discipline with no great enthusiasm, but there was rather more to the issue than Baillie allowed. The Puritans themselves had engaged in a longstanding protest against the arbitrariness and pettiness of church discipline under the bishops, and against ecclesiastical sentences being handed down from superior courts without any reference

---

[48] *S. P. Domestic,* Charles I, DXI, No. 9, October 7th, 1645; my italics.
[49] Publick Letter, 25th November, 1645; *Letters and Journals* II. 325.
[50] 12th November, 1645; Minutes III. 162.
[51] 19th November.
[52] To Robert Ramsay, 15th January, 1645/6; *Letters and Journals,* II. 336.

to the pastor of the parish in which the accused person normally worshipped. The Millenary Petition submitted to James I (VI), on his arrival in England in 1603, had urged "that men be not excommunicated for trifles, and twelve-penny matters: that none be excommunicated without consent of his pastor".[53] The Members of Parliament had some grounds for thinking that in this stand against the Assembly they were defending the principles of the earlier English Puritans.

Baillie could not be expected to understand that. As far as he was concerned the opposition was due to an unholy alliance between the three kinds of people whom he detested most, the Erastians, the Independents, and the 'worldlie profane men'. He said that these three groups comprised two parts of Parliament, and "there is no hopes that ever they will settle the Government according to our mind, if they were left to themselves." The specific assignment that Baillie and his colleagues had been given, does not suggest that the Commissioners had any intention of leaving the English Parliament to its own devices in this matter.

> The Assemblie hes plyed them with petition upon petition, the City also, both ministers and magistrates; bot all in vaine. They know that schismes and heresies doe daily encrease in all the corners of the land for want of discipline; yet the most of them care for none of these things. Had our army been bot one 15,000 men in England, our advyce would have been followed quicklie in all things; bot our lamentable posture at home, and our weakness here, makes our desyres contemptible. . . . In this case our last refuge is to God, and under him to the City. We have gotten it, thanks to God, to this point, that the mayor, aldermen, common counsell, and most of the considerable men, are grieved for the increase of sects and heresies, and want of Government. They have, yesterday, had a publick fast for it, and renewed solemnly their Covenant by oath and subscription; and this day have given in a strong petition for settling of Church-government, and suppressing of all sects, without any toleration. No doubt, if they be constant, they will obtain all their desires, for all know the Parliament here cannot subsist without London: so whatsomever they desyre in earnest, and constantlie, it must be granted.[54]

In the same letter Baillie reveals the extent to which he was implicated in these attempts to bring pressure on the English Parliament, and in particular with the London Ministers, for although "They are but very few of the city-ministers about the

---

[53] J. P. Kenyon, (ed.) *The Stuart Constitution*, p. 133.
[54] To Ramsay, *op. cit.* p. 336f.

first and secret wheeles of the businesse", he said, "I make it part of my task to give them weekly my best advyce and incouragements; and, blessed be God, with such successe hitherto that it is worth my stay here."[55]

Baillie was extremely active in stimulating this agitation. A few days later in the same month, at the time when the Independents were pressing for toleration in the Committee for Accommodation,[56] he had informed Spang that "some good friend hes so informed the citie-ministers", that the ministers "in their meeting at Sion Colledge, have resolved unanimouslie to petition the Assemblie against all such tollerations."[57] This petition had taken a leaf from the Independents' book by appearing in print almost before it had been presented, and about the same time Baillie wrote to one of his ministerial friends in the city, Francis Roberts, giving clear evidence of his complicity.[58]

Further evidence of Baillie's involvement in the agitation of the London ministers and in the manoeuvres of sympathetic members of the House of Commons like Francis Rous and Zouch Tate is to be found in his correspondence of this period.[59] In another letter he suggested to Roberts that he should persuade the Earl of Manchester's former chaplain, Simeon Ashe, to intercede with the earl to get the offending portions of the bill killed in the Lords. "If God help yow to keep on the City's zeale," he said, "more is like to be done in a week than hitherto in a year. Be diligent in this happie nick of time.[60]

Baillie could be devious, but the House of Commons for all its

---

[55] *Ibid.*

[56] The movement of the Independents towards the more inclusive principle of liberty of conscience is seen in Baillie's comment to Spang that at the last meeting of that committee, Thomas Goodwin "declared publicklie, that he cannot refuse to be members, nor censure when members, any for Anabaptisme, Lutheranisme, or any errors which are not fundamentall, and maintained against knowledge." To Spang, n.d. but placed between 20th–22nd January, 1645/6; *Letters and Journals*, II. 343.

[57] *Ibid.* p. 344. The same letter said that the political Independents, Lords Say and Wharton, had recently tried to get the House of Lords "to adjourne, that is reallie to dissolve, the Assemblie." *Ibid.* This was the petition of the London ministers mentioned previously; *supra* pp. 489f.

[58] Roberts was minister of St. Augustine's, London. "I wish, by all means, that unhappie court of commissioners in every shyre may be exploded. If it must be so, let the new cases of scandals come to the Parliament by the letters of the eldership, or any other way, but not by a standing court of Commissioners. Yow had need be at your witts and quicklie . . . I pray yow advyse what is to be done: no man knows that I have given yow any information, and yow must keep your informer from all. I purpose to see yow this night after our meeting at Dr. Burgess's house. Yow, and some two or three whom yow trust most, had need to advyse weell and quicklie, for now matters are very near some issue." 22nd, January, 1655/6: *Letters and Journals*, II. 346.

[59] *Ibid.* pp. 358–9.

[60] To Roberts, n.d. but placed in March, 1645/6; *ibid.* p. 359.

readiness to establish presbyterian church government, was determined that this should be on its own terms. On March 5th a new ordinance was voted for remedying defects in the earlier legislation on church government and discipline,[61] but it contained the provision that "In every Province persons shall be chosen by the Houses of Parliament, that shall be Commissioners to judge of scandalous offences (not enumerated in any Ordinance of Parliament) to them presented", and gave those commissioners the final determination of any further offences incurring a suspension from the Lord's Supper.[62] The civil authority was determined to maintain its own control over the national church.

IV

Breach of Privilege and the Nine Queries

The Divines reacted by asserting the *jus divinum* of the Church. On March 19th, 1645/6, the Assembly resolved that "There shall be a Committee to prepare something for the Assembly to assert the *jus divinum* of Church censures, and in whose hands *jure divino* these censures are."[63] Vines, Palmer, Temple, Tuckney, Newcomen, Seaman and Reynolds were selected, and were to confer with the Scots Commissioners, while on the following day Marshall, Vines, Seaman and Newcomen were charged with considering "what in point of conscience may press this Assembly to make their humble address to the Parliament, by way of petition; and they are to prepare a petition to that purpose, and to make report to this Assembly."[64] The petition was presented on Monday, 23rd March, 1645/6, by the Assembly in a body. In that petition, having paid compliments to Parliament for its reformation in religion, the divines continued:

> Yet are we, to our grief, constrained at this time, in all humility and faithfulness, to represent to the Honourable Houses, that there is still a great defect in the enumeration of scandalous sins . . . and that the provision of Commissioners to judge of scandals not enumerated, appears to our consciences to be so contrary to that Way of Govern-

---

[61] *An Ordinance of the Lords and Commons Assembled in Parliament for Keeping of Scandalous persons from the Sacrament of the Lord's Supper, the enabling of Congregations for the choice of Elders, and Supplying of Defects in former Ordinances, and Directions of Parliament Concerning Church-Government.* (1646).

[62] Article XIV of the Ordinance in full may be found in De Witt *Jus Divinum*, p. 192.

[63] Minutes III. 207.

[64] *Ibid.* p. 208.

ment which Christ hath appointed in His Church . . . that we dare not practise according to that provision.[65]

Noone knew what would happen next, because some of the London citizens were beginning to have second thoughts about their opposition to Parliament in this matter:

> The Assemblie hes given in a very honest petition; bot it's like shall have no good answer. The city-ministers are to give in one much higher, not so much upon hope of success, as resolution to deliver their conscience. The citizens say, they will give in ane other for the same end, but we doe not believe them: their fainting hes given our cause one of the greatest wounds yet it has gotten. The nixt week will, it's thought, declare much.[66]

It did. The House of Commons voted that the Assembly had been guilty of a breach of parliamentary privilege,[67] and appointed a committee to address pointed questions to the Assembly on the matter of church discipline.[68] By 16th April those questions had been formulated, and on the 30th a delegation of the Commons formally presented them to the Assembly. The delegation also conveyed the House of Commons' censure to the Assembly, and the reasons for it. Furthermore, Parliament for all its readiness to establish the presbyterian order in the Church was getting thoroughly tired of Scots interference in its affairs. While it had been preparing its queries to the Assembly on *jus divinum*, the Scots had allowed one of their Remonstrances to appear in print, and the Houses had it burnt publicly by the common hangman.[69]

Baillie was disgusted with the way things were going, and particularly at the way the City authorities had folded under the threat of parliamentary disapproval.[70] However, when the parliamentary delegation, Sir John Evelyn, Nathaniel Fiennes,

---

[65] The petition appears in Minutes III. 209–11, note 1, and has been extracted from *L. J.*, VIII. 232.

[66] Baillie to Spang, 23rd April, 1646; *Letters and Journals*, II. 365.

[67] 11th April, 1646.

[68] This had been appointed on 27th March. It was later identified as the sub-committee of the Grand Committee on Religion. Cf. Shaw, *Hist. of the English Church*, I. 305.

[69] 21st April, 1646. *Some Papers of the Commissioners of Scotland Given in lately to the Houses of Parliament, Concerning the Propositions of Peace* (11th April, 1646). Cf. C. V. Wedgwood, *The King's War* p. 547; Hetherington, *Hist. of the West. Assembly*, p. 263, De Witt, *Jus Divinum*, p. 225.

[70] "While we were in great hopes that the City would for all stand to their petition, that we should learn to trust in no flesh, they shamefullie succumbed: by a few fair words from the Houses, they were made all alse mute as fisch." For Scotland, 24th April, 1646; *Letters and Journals*, II. 366.

Samuel Browne and Sir Benjamin Rudyard, delivered the Commons' message to the Assembly, there was no doubt who was in control: whoever backed down it would not be Parliament.[71]

Sir John Evelyn introduced the Commons' statement and said that the House had found in the Assembly's petition things "that did strike at the foundation and roots of the privileges of Parliament", and he pointedly reminded the divines that if they allowed division to develop between the Houses and the Assembly at this juncture, "you will give occasion to all the world to say that, as you were willing to serve the Parliament a while, so you were willing to have them serve you for ever after." He also said, "Do not think the Parliament is unwilling to submit their yoke[72] to Jesus Christ; his yoke is easy. If it be a galling vexing yoke, it is not his, and we [will not bear it]."[73]

Evelyn was followed in a long speech by Nathaniel Fiennes, the son of Lord Say,[74] who asserted that by petitioning Parliament in terms that represented one of Parliament's laws as "contrary to the will of God and the national Covenant", the divines had assumed far more authority than their commission to give advice. "Did the Houses of Parliament give any colour of power to this Assembly to give any interpretation of the national covenant, especially in relation to making of laws? Did it give authority to this Assembly to give their judgment after a law settled?" He pointed out that in Parliament no "particular member may speak against a vote without leave, and shall [you claim] not only to debate, but to arraign and condemn it, nay to pass the highest doom upon it, that it [is] contrary to the will of

---

[71] For the account of this session see Minutes III. 448–456.

[72] The editors suggest this word may have been 'neck'; *ibid.* p. 449, note 1.

[73] *Ibid.* pp. 448f. Cf. also the Commons' *Narrative* of the case, as extracted from the *Commons Journals; ibid.* pp. 456–8, note 1.

[74] This may have represented sweet revenge. In the summer of 1643 Bristol had been assaulted by Prince Rupert, and three days after (26th July) Nathaniel Fiennes, the commander, surrendered the city. He was bitterly attacked in London by the presbyterian apologists, Clement Walker and William Prynne, who cooperated to publish *Articles of Impeachment and Accusation, Exhibited in Parliament, Against Colonel Nathaniel Fiennes, Touching his dishonourable surrender of the City and Castle of Bristoll.* The case was reviewed by the House of Commons (13th November) and as a result Fiennes was court-martialled and condemned to death, but he had been pardoned by the Earl of Essex. However, it finished his military career. Later, when Fairfax and Cromwell occupied Bristol, and "upon a view of the place, comparing the present strength of it with what it was when he [Fiennes] delivered it, and other circumstances, freely expressed themselves as men abundantly satisfied concerning the hard misfortune that befell that noble gentleman." (Joshua Sprigge's, *Anglia Rediviva*, 1647, p. 129.) Clement Walker, of course, dismissed Sprigge's account as merely a front for the Independent Fiennes family. Cf. Clement Walker, *The History of Independency*, Part I, p. 32; Gardiner, G. C. W., I. 179f.

God and the national Covenant?" They had not only exceeded the power granted to them by Parliament, but what they had done "amounted to the breach of privilege of Parliament"; and after a good deal more of the same he concluded, "Those things are not the way of Englishmen, Christians, and Ministers of Christ. . . . We come to speak plainly to you, and plain English; it is not in the thoughts of the House to disgrace or discourage you in your ministry."[75]

The castigation became worse, for Samuel Browne, a lawyer, did not hesitate to remind the divines of the legal jeopardy in which they placed themselves by the breach of privilege.[76] He mentioned the Act of *praemunire* that previous rulers had invoked against ecclesiastics who questioned their authority, and said it was "the doctrine of the Pope to take from princes the power that God committed to them". He raised this pertinent question about the Assembly's debates:

> It is much pressed for the point of the Covenant. We all agree that the Word of God is the rule, and must be the rule; but say there be no positive rule in the Word, are we by the Covenant bound to follow the practice of Reformed churches in case it be against the fundamental law of the kingdom? You must interpret the Covenant so as that all parts may stand. We are bound to maintain the liberties of Parliament and kingdom. If I do any act against this I am a breaker of the Covenant.[77]

After Browne's speech Evelyn read the nine queries that the Parliamentary committee had prepared, and said that they would be left for the Assembly to study and answer.[78] The session

---

[75] Minutes III. pp. 449–52.

[76] *Ibid.*, pp. 452–55.

[77] *Ibid.* pp. 454f.

[78] The queries were published as, *Questions Propounded to the Assembly of Divines by the House of Commons, April ult. 1646. Touching the Point of Jus Divinum in the matter of Church-Government.* In the following pages the nine queries are cited as 'Questions', since this is the form in which they were printed. The text is as follows:
"Whereas it is Resolved by Both Houses, That all persons guilty of Notorious and Scandalous Offences shall be suspended from the Sacrament of the Lord's Supper, The House of Commons desires to be satisfied by the Assembly of Divines in these questions following:

I   Whether the Parochial and Congregational Elderships appointed by Ordinance of Parliament, or any other Congregational or Presbyterial Elderships are *Jure divino*, and by the Will and Appointment of Jesus Christ? And whether any particular Church-Government be *Jure divino*? And what that Government is?

II   Whether the Members of the said Elderships, as Members thereof, or which of them are *Jure divino*, and by the Will and Appointment of Jesus Christ?

III   Whether the superior Assemblies or Elderships, (*viz.* the Classical, Provincial and National;) whether all or any of them, and which of them are *Jure divino*, and by the Will and Appointment of Jesus Christ?

wound up with Sir Benjamin Rudyard laying down the Assembly's immediate task in the most explicit terms:

> The matter you are now about, the *jus divinum*, is of a formidable and tremendous nature. It will be expected you should answer by clear, practical(?), and express Scriptures; not by far-fetched arguments which are commonly told before you come to the matter. . . . I have heard much spoken of 'the pattern in the mount' so express. . . . I could never find in the New Testament [such a pattern]. The first rule is, 'Let all things be done decently and in order,' to edification. Decency and order are variable, and therefore cannot be *jure divino*; discipline is but the hedge. I desire you would make your answer in plain terms.[79]

IV   Whether Appeals from Congregational Elderships to the Classical, Provincial and National Assemblies, or to any of them, and to which of them are *Jure divino*, and by the Will and Appointment of Iesus Christ? And are their powers upon such Appeals *Jure divino*, and by the Will and Appointment of Iesus Christ?

V   Whether Oecumenical Assemblies are *Jure divino*? And whether there be Appeals from any of the former Assemblies to the Said Oecumenical *Jure divino*, and by the Will and Appointment of Iesus Christ?

VI   Whether by the Word of God, the Power of Judging, and Declaring what are such Notorious and Scandalous Offences, for which persons guilty are to be kept from the Sacrament of the Lord's Supper, and of conventing before them, trying and actual suspending from the Sacrament of the Lord's Supper such Offenders, is either in the Congregational Elderships, or Presbytery, or in any other Eldership, Congregation or persons; and whether such Powers are in them only, or any of them, and in which of them *Jure divino*, and by the Will and Appointment of Iesus Christ?

VII   Whether there be any certain and particular Rules expressed in the Word of God, to direct the Elderships or Presbyteries, Congregations or Persons or any of them, in the Exercise and Execution of the Powers aforesaid, and what are those Rules?

VIII   Is there anything contained in the Word of God, that the Supreme Magistracy in a Christian State may not judge and determine what are the aforesaid Notorious and Scandalous Offences, and the manner of suspension for the same; and in what Particulars concerning the premises is the said Supreme Magistracy, by the Word of God excluded?

IX   Whether the provision of Commissioners to judge of Scandals not enumerated (as they are authorized by the Ordinance of Parliament) be contrary to the Way of Government which Christ hath appointed in his Church; and wherein are they so contrary?

X   In answer to these particulars, the House of Commons desires of the Assembly of Divines, their proofs from Scripture, and to set down the several Texts of Scripture in the expresse words of the same: And it is Ordered, That every particular Minister of the Assembly of Divines that is or shall be present at the Debate of any of these Questions, do upon every Resolution which shall be presented to this House concerning the same, subscribe his respective Name, either with the Affirmative or Negative as he gives his vote; And those that do Dissent from the major Part shall set down their positive Opinions, with the expresse Texts of Scripture upon which their Opinions are grounded. Finis.

The Nine Queries will also be found printed in De Witt, *Jus Divinum*, pp. 206f., Shaw, *Hist. of the English Church*, I. 306–8.

[79] Minutes III. 455f.

This recalls the explicit demand of the tenth article after the Commons' questions: if there was a *jus divinum* for a particular polity, they were required to set down "their proofs from Scripture, and to set down the several Texts of Scripture in the expresse words of the same".

We also note that the questions were directed as much against any Congregational claim to *jus divinum* as to the Presbyterian assertion,[80] and this may have been one of the reasons why the Assembly never made any formal response to the questions because on this matter Presbyterians and Independents agreed on the principle but not on the order.

There is obviously a great deal of difference between the Church's proper claim to *jus divinum* over its own members – an authority accepted in faith by the individual believer in the confidence that it will be exercised ministerially – and a similar *jus divinum* asserted by the Church over the whole of society and using the power of the state to enforce ecclesiastical discipline on every citizen; and the distinction is particularly acute when that claim over society is made in the exclusive interest of a particular polity.[81]

Both Presbyterians and Independents could agree in asserting the *jus divinum* of the Church against the Erastian politicians, but their disagreements probably prevented the divines from producing answers to the Questions, since neither side would concede the exclusive claims of the other. The earlier debates had shown that it was easier to attack the *jus divinum* claimed by another polity than it was to bring conclusive proof for one's own, and any disunity in the Assembly's reply to the Questions would have played directly into the hands of the politicians.

The Assembly's first reaction to the Commons' Questions was to do what came naturally to it, it declared a solemn fast for

---

[80] Questions I, II, VI and VII were addressed equally to the Independents, while the questions relating to the civil magistrate (VIII and IX) were applicable to all ecclesiologies that opposed the Erastian position of Parliament.

[81] This must be remembered in assessing Warriston's speech in the Assembly on May 1st, 1646. He was entirely right to assert the crown rights of Jesus Christ over his Church, and to remind the divines that their primary allegiance was to their Lord and his revealed truth. De Witt is right in insisting that the speech should not be dismissed as madness or fanaticism (*Jus Divinum*, pp. 210–14.) However, this does not mean that we have no right to be critical. The problem with the speech is not in what Warriston said, but in what he implied; for beyond the crown rights of Jesus Christ over his Church, he was asserting the divine right of the Church over the whole of English society; and not only the Church in general, but his own Scottish understanding of the church. At that point, the claim of the Church to *jus divinum* became improper, and could easily end in a contradiction of the gospel. For Warriston's speech cf. Minutes III. 458–60, and the fuller version in Mitchell, *The West. Assembly*, pp. 314–19.

Wednesday 6th May. It then began to tackle its formidable assignment. A good deal of work was done on the Questions intermittently through the period 15th May–July 6th, 1646,[82] and at the end of that time the divines adopted *nem. con.* the proposition "That Jesus Christ as King and Head of His Church hath Himself appointed a Church government."[83] Both the major parties could agree on that.

In the second week of July, 1646, Baillie reported that the Assembly's answers to the queries had been its major concern during the previous few weeks,[84] but he went on to say how he had contrived to remove the pressure by getting some of his friends in the House of Commons to urge that the Assembly should first complete the work on the Confession and the Catechism.[85] As a result no official response was made to the Questions, although the work was briefly revived in May 1648.

The reasons one accepts for the failure to respond to the Commons' Questions will depend largely on one's own scepticism about the divines' ability to produce cogent answers. John Selden was entirely sceptical.[86] Alternatively it might be explained by the importance of unanimity in this matter for the Assembly, for there can be little doubt that either side of the ecclesiological dispute could produce answers that were cogent enough for its own supporters: both the Presbyterians and the

---

[82] Cf. Shaw, *Hist. of the English Church*, I. 311.

[83] Minutes III. 251.

[84] "It wes thought it would be impossible to us to answer, and that in our answers there should be no unanimitie; yet, by God's grace we shall deceave them who were waiting for our halting. The committee hes prepared very solide and satisfactorie answers allready, almost to all the questions, wherein there is like to be ane unanimitie absolute in all things materiall, even with the Independents." For Glasgow, 14th July, 1646; *Letters and Journals*, II. 378.

[85] *Ibid.* p. 379. In a letter to Henderson some time later he said: "In the Assemblie we were like to have stucken many moneths on the questions; and the Independents were in a way to gett all their differences debated over againe. I dealt so with Mr. Rous and Mr. Tate, that they brought us ane order from the House to lay aside the questions till the Confession and Catechise were ended." He confidently added that many had taken the Questions as "a trick of the Independents and Erastians for our hurt; but I knew it wes nothing less." 13th August, 1646; *ibid.* p. 388.

[86] "When the Quaeres were sent to the Assembly concerning the Jus Divinum of presbytery, their askeing time to answr. them was a satyre upon themselves, for (if) it were to be seene in the Text, they might quickly turne to the place & shew us it; their delaying to answr makes us think there's noe such matter there. They doe just as you have seene a fellow att a Taverne reckoning; when hee should come to pay his share hee putts his hand into his breeches, & keepes a grabling & fumbling & shakeing, & att last tells you, he has left his money att home: When all the Company knew att first, hee had no money there, for every man can quickly find his own money." From John Selden's *Table Talk* (edited by Pollock, London, 1927,) pp. 113f.

Independents could produce convincing apologia for those who accepted their presuppositions.

Shaw thought the answers of the majority may have been represented by an anonymous tract that appeared in the summer of 1646, and observed that "the answer is comprehensive" although more attention was given to the first of the queries.[87] It is more probable, however, that *Jus Divinum Regiminis Ecclesiastici*, written by the London ministers and published from Sion College in December 1646, represents a much closer identification with the views of the presbyterian majority in the Assembly.[88] Both these works, however, show that far from being unable to make any reply as Selden believed, the Presbyterians were well able to make a significant response when freed from the embarrassment of having to deal with rival claims to *jus divinum*, and when removed from their subordination to Parliament.

If we consider the Assembly's unwillingness to produce answers to the Questions in relation to Baillie's activities, we may more readily recognize that – in a way very similar to the Independents' refusal to produce a model of church government for the Assembly – the theological disputes were themselves essentially set in a political situation and the divines could not avoid acting politically. The unwillingness of either side to respond to a direct challenge was due not to any lack of confidence that the divines had in their respective theological positions, but to a political situation in which a united Reformed movement that had been generally in agreement about the divine right of church order in the scriptures had now separated into rival ecclesiologies based on polity. It was practical recognition that unamity was no longer possible.

V

The Crown Rights of Jesus Christ

The issue of *jus divinum* was bound to arise at other points in the Assembly's work, and particularly in the Confession where

---

[87] Shaw, *Hist. of the English Church*, I. 315. The pamphlet was *An Answer to those Questions Propounded by the Parliament to the Assembly of Divines, Touching Jus Divinum In Matter of Church-Government. Wherein is clearly proved from Scripture, That the Presbyterial Government is Jure Divino, of Divine Institution, and according to the will and appointment of Jesus Christ* (London, 17th June, 1646.)

De Witt rejects Shaw's suggestion because Thomason, the bibliophile had noted that it was by a certain Thomas Bakewell, a 'woodmonger in Fleet Street'. Although that does not conclusively disprove Shaw's contention, since Thomason was not infallible, we must agree that the *Jus Divinum Regiminis Ecclesiastici* of Sion College is more likely to have corresponded to the Assembly's views. Cf. De Witt, *Jus Divinum*, p. 230, note 64.

[88] *Ibid.* pp. 230–234.

the crown rights of our Lord over his Church were asserted. The only acknowledged Erastians among the divines were Thomas Coleman and John Lightfoot, and both were strong supporters of the presbyterian position.[89] Coleman, however, had already given offence by his outspoken opposition to *jure divino* claims,[90] and on 30th July 1645, possibly reacting to a fresh assertion of *jus divinum* in the Assembly, he had vigorously attacked this position in a sermon preached before the House of Commons. As a result he found himself in trouble, and on August 1st had to give an apology for offending the Scots Commissioners. A few weeks later when George Gillespie had the chance of preaching before the House of Lords on a Day of Humiliation, he used the publication of his sermon as an excuse for appending 'A Brotherly Examination of some passages of Mr. Coleman's late Sermon . . . by which he hath to the great offence of very many, endeavoured to strike at the very root of all Spiritual and Ecclesiasticall Government, contrary to the Word of God, the solemn League and Covenant, other Reformed Churches, and the Votes of the Honorable Houses of Parliament, after advice had with the Reverend and Learned Assembly of Divines.'[91] The Scots were annoyed.

In his sermon Coleman had said that the only thing that hindered union in the Assembly was that "Two parties came biased, The Reverend Commissioners from Scotland, were for the Jus Divinum of the Presbyteriall; The Independents for the Congregationall Government. How should either move?"[92] It was a good question and it led to an interesting literary debate,[93] but it is important here because it indicates that *jus divinum* was bound to arise again in the Confession's affirmation of the Church.

The passage in the Confession dealing with the institution of the Church was due for debate in March 1646 when the quarrel of the divines with the House of Commons was beginning to come to a boil. On March 6th the debate was on the proposition "That J[esus] C[hrist] as K[ing] and H[ead] of His Church hath appointed an ecclesiastical government in His Church in the

---

[89] I.e. They supported the presbyterian system ecclesiastically as distinct from ecclesiologically.

[90] Cf. *supra* p. 498.

[91] *A Sermon preached before the Right Honourable the House of Lords. In the Abbey Church at Westminster, upon the 27th, of August. 1645 . . . Whereunto is added a Brotherly Examination . . .* (1645), p. 31.

[92] As quoted by Gillespie; *ibid*. p. 33.

[93] Cf. De Witt's note, *Jus Divinum*, p. 197, note 106.

hand of Church Officers distinct from the civil government."[94] It was an excellent platform from which to launch the *jure divino* claims that the Assembly was trying to assert against the House of Commons.

The proposition was opposed by Coleman and Lightfoot, but the major responsibility for withstanding the claims of the Assembly seems to have been taken by the former, and – perhaps because of the offence he had given earlier to the Scots – he was vigorously attacked by Gillespie and Rutherford.[95] By March 17th the Erastian arguments were regarded as sufficiently answered,[96] but on the following day Coleman fell ill of a sickness that was to prove fatal. He was not to know that, and he asked permission to speak again when he had recovered,[97] but by March 30th he had died and the Assembly was invited to his funeral. The attitude of Baillie to any who opposed the Scots' program is shown in his comment, "God hes stricken Coleman with death; he fell ill in ane ague, and after four or five dayes expired. It's not good to stand in Christ's way."[98]

VI

"This ended, we have no more adoe"

When Baillie returned to Scotland at the end of 1646,[99] he gave an account of his kinsman, William Spang, of how he and his fellow Commissioners had fulfilled their trust in England; and he had solid grounds for satisfaction:

> I have made my report in the Commission of the Church to all their contentment; our errand in England being brought near a happie period, so farr as concerned us the Commissioners of the Church; for, by God's blessing, the four points of Uniformitie, which wes all our Church gave us in commission to agent in the Assemblie at Westminster, were alse good as obtained. The Directorie I brought down before. The modell of Government we have gotten it through the Assemblie according to our mind: it yet sticks in the hands of the Houses. They have past four ordinances at least about it, all prettie right, so farr as concerns the constitution and erection of Generall

---

[94] Minutes III. 193. On November 26th, 1646, this became Article XXX.

[95] For the debate on March 16th cf. *ibid.* 424–29, and for Gillespie on Christ's Kingly Office, *ibid.* pp. 430f.

[96] *Ibid.*, p. 206; cf. Baillie, *Letters and Journals*, II. 360f.

[97] Minutes III. 208.

[98] To Spang, 3rd April, 1646; *Letters and Journals*, III. 364. De Witt dismisses this piece of callous humbug with the comment that "Baillie did not mince words!" *Jus Divinum*, p. 200, note 118.

[99] He took final leave of the Assembly on December 25th, 1646; Minutes III. 315.

Assemblies, Provinciall Synods, Presbyteries, and Sessions, and the power of ordination. In the province of London and Lancashyre the bodies are sett up. That the like diligence is not used long agoe in all other places, it's the sottish negligence of the ministers and gentrie in the shyres more than the Parliament. That the power of jurisdiction in all things we require, excepting appealls from the General Assemblie to the Parliament, is not put in ordinances long agoe, it's by the [cunning] of the Independents and Erastians in the House of Commons; which obstacle we trust will now be removed by the zeale of the city of London. . . .

The third point [of Uniformity], the Confession of Faith I brought it with me now in print, as it wes offered to the Houses by the Assemblie, without considerable dissent of any. It's much cryed up by all, even many of our great opposites, as the best Confession yet extant; it's expected the Houses shall pass it, as they did the Directorie, without much debate. . . . The fourth part of our desyred and covenanted Uniformitie is the Catechisme. A committee hes drawne and reported the whole: the Assemblie ere I came away had voted more than the halfe; a short time will end the rest; for they studie brevitie, and have voted to have no other head of divinitie into it than is sett doune in the Confession. This ended, we have no more adoe in the Assemblie, neither know we any more work the Assemblie hes in hand, but ane answer to the nine Queries of the House of Commons about the *jus divinum* of diverse parts of the government. The Ministers of London's late *Jus Divinum* of Presbytery does this abundantly. . . .[100]

That represents a remarkable achievement for the Scots Commissioners in an English ecclesiastical Assembly. They had almost complete success on all the major points for their programme of covenanted uniformity.

The one exception was the failure to get their system of church government legally recognized as of divine right. The claim was incorporated into Article XXX of the Confession, but it was never accepted by Parliament, and this was one of the two articles to be omitted when the Westminster Confession was re-affirmed by the Rump Parliament just before the Restoration. There was no way that any ecclesiology could have carried a claim to *jus divinum* past that English Parliament.

Note on the later history of the Assembly

It is not the intention of the present work to record the history of the Assembly's programme in detail. That can be better traced

---

[100] 26th January, 1646/7, *Letters and Journals*, III. 1f. Baillie's reference in the last sentence was clearly to *Jus Divinum Regiminis Ecclesiastici*.

elsewhere.[101] However, some brief account of the later history is necessary if the reader is to understand the comprehensiveness of the ecclesiastical system that attempted to set up covenanted uniformity throughout the British Isles. In line with our own primary interest we would emphasize the priority that the Assembly gave to those aspects of its work dealing with the practical organization, government and worship of the Church. The ecclesiological issue was the reason for the Assembly's call, and it was the area of the Assembly's first concern.

(1) The first segment of its work to be offered to Parliament had been the Directory for Ordination which had been sent to the Houses on 20th April, 1644, and 'Propositions concerning Church Government' were added in the winter of that same year.[102] These were essentially practical steps to get a reformed Church of England into operation, but they had already produced some of the most heated debates. More complete recommendations followed later by the same route, for the Scots persuaded the rest of the Assembly to postpone dealing with the doctrinal aspects of church order so that a 'Practical Directory for Church Government' could be sent up to Parliament on July 7th, 1647, and this eventually went into law in a modified form as a parliamentary ordinance on 29th August, 1648: 'The form of Church Government to be used in the Church of England and Ireland.'

The *jus divinum* dispute, which dogged the Assembly and the House of Commons throughout, but became its major preoccupation during 1645 and a large part of 1646, delayed effective implementation of the Assembly's votes and Parliament's readiness to establish presbyterian order. Eventually on June 22nd, 1646, the London ministers declared that although they did not altogether approve of Parliament's provisions for church government, they were ready to comply with the ordinance of March 5th, and this enabled the presbyterian system to move into operation. It should be emphasized, however, that although the Presbyterians won a resounding victory on church government in the Assembly, they failed entirely to make that system effective in England because the House of Commons was determined

---

[101] Cf. Shaw's *Hist. of the English Church* Volume I; also the recognized histories of the Assembly by A. F. Mitchell, W. M. Hetherington, William Beveridge. There is a particularly succinct account in B. B. Warfield's *The Westminster Assembly and its Work*, chapter 1 (pp. 3–72.)

[102] November 8th, December 11th, 1644.

to withstand future clerical domination in any form. The Scots failed to recognize how deeply rooted that determination was among the influential classes of English society.

(2) The Directory for Worship had an easier passage because there were no fundamental differences about it in the Assembly, and if the Scots had to bend a little in the administration of the Lord's Supper, that is all they did. The Directory was presented to the Houses at the end of 1644 and became law for England and Wales in a parliamentary ordinance of January 3rd, 1644/5. Since the work on the Directory had been begun on the previous August 20th, the expedition with which the Directory was passed says a good deal about the demand for a form of worship to replace the Book of Common Prayer, and also about the preparatory work done by the Scots to iron out major problems before the issues arrived on the floor of the Assembly.

(3) The Confession of Faith had a slightly more difficult passage, not because of basic doctrinal differences within the Assembly, but because of the claim to *jus divinum* which impinged upon the relation of Church and State. The Confession had begun in committee in August 1644, and by April 25th, 1645, the first drafts were being presented to the Assembly. The first draft was completed by the middle of 1646 and the whole Confession was sent to Parliament on December 4th that year. Parliament then called for the proof texts which were presented in April, 1647,[103] and eventually the Confession in a somewhat truncated form was officially approved on June 20th, 1648.[104] It was reaffirmed by the Rump Parliament when it met again[105] during the confusing days that followed Cromwell's death and preceded the Restoration of the monarchy.

(4) The Catechisms had a similar story. The work had begun relatively early, but because little opposition was expected, it was postponed until practically all the more controversial work of the Assembly had been completed. There is evidence of material related to the Catechism being debated in August, 1645, but little more was done about it until September 11th, 1646, and we know from Robert Baillie that the first attempt to produce a catechism had been abortive.[106] However, practically the whole

---

[103] 29th April, 1647.

[104] Parliament omitted chapters XXX and XXXI on 'church Censures' and 'Synods and Councils'; and passages from XX 'Of Christian Liberty and Liberty of Conscience,' XXII 'Of the Civil Magistrate,' and 'Of Marriage and Divorce).

[105] March 1659/60.

[106] For Glasgow, 14th July, 1646; *Letters and Journals*, II. 379.

of the work on the catechism was finished by January 4th, 1646/7, but at that point the Assembly had the inspired idea of separating the work into two catechisms. In the Minutes for January 14th, 1646/7 we read:

> Upon a motion made by Mr. Vines it was *Ordered* – 'That the Committee for the Catechism do prepare a draught of two Catechisms, one more large and another more brief, in which they are to have an eye to the Confession of Faith, and to the matter of the Catechism already begun.'[107]

The Larger Catechism was sent to Parliament on 15th October, 1647, and work on the Shorter Catechism was not effectively begun until after that date. It was completed and sent to Parliament on November 25–26th the same year, and the proof texts for both sent up on 14th April, 1648. The Shorter Catechism was approved by Parliament 22nd–25th September, 1648, and the Larger Catechism was approved by the House of Commons but was never finally accepted by the House of Lords.

(5) The Psalter was not one of Baillie's four points of covenanted uniformity, but it became a part of the Assembly's work, and it was obviously related to its work on worship and the Directory. It had first been considered in November 1643, and against rivals, the translation of Baillie's friend, Francis Rous, was finally recommended to Parliament in the Autumn of 1645. In a somewhat revised form this was accepted by the Commons and printed in February 1646/7, but the House of Lords demurred.

* * * * *

The presbyterian system began to go into operation some time before it became law in August 1648. Classes (presbyteries) had begun to meet in London in November 1646, and the first London Provincial Assembly met in the Convocation House at St. Paul's on May 3rd, 1647, but at the second session (May 20th) the assembly turned itself into a Grand Committee so that it could meet a few days later in Sion College. The London ministers were then given leave by Parliament for all subsequent meetings to be held in Sion College, and it began to meet there on June 28th, 1647. It continued to do so until August 15th, 1660, when it was disbanded as a result of the Restoration.[108]

---

[107] Minutes III. 321.
[108] Cf. 'The Records of the provinciall Assembly of London[.] Begunne by ordinance of Parliament' (1647). These are held in manuscript in Sion College Library, London, and carry the name of Thomas Granger.

The presbyterian establishment was fully operational only in London and Lancashire, but William Shaw argued persuasively that it was "adopted voluntarily much more widely than has been hitherto supposed,"[109] and he suggested that if it had not been for the events of 1648–9, there is every probability that it "would have been much more widely enforced, and that it might have become what it from the first designed and desired to become – a national church system, as complete and as uniform as the Episcopal system which had preceded it, and had been swept away to make room for it."[110]

As it was, it did not last for reasons that seem to have had little to do with the truth or falsehood of the theology debated in the Assembly, and perhaps had as little to do with differences between the English and Scottish national temperaments which Shaw regarded as responsible for the failure. We have certainly offered evidence that English people, even within the ranks of Puritanism, retained considerable affinity for traditional practices rooted in medieval society, but when all due allowance is made for this conservatism, the fundamental reasons for the failure of the presbyterian system in England appear to be grounded in the politics of the period and the struggle for power.[111] Indeed, this study suggests what may be an unpalatable lesson, that ecclesiastical systems are set in history, and their 'success' or 'failure' within that society has as much to do with political reality as with theological truth.

The effective work of the Assembly ended with the work on the Catechisms in the first few months of 1648, and on the day when Samuel Rutherford, the last of the Scots Commissioners to remain in London, took his leave (November 9th, 1647), we find the Assembly appointing a committee "to consider of what is fit to be done when the Catechism is finished."[112] For a time the divines occupied themselves in a desultory way with revising the Answers they had given to the Independents' Reasons, and some attempt may even have been made to reconsider the Questions sent to them by Parliament,[113] but with the conclusion of its

---

[109] Shaw, *History of the English Church*, II. 28; cf. M. R. Watts, *The Dissenters*, pp. 115f.

[110] Shaw, *op. cit.* II. 33.

[111] Cf. George Yule, 'English Presbyterianism and the Westminster Assembly', *The Reformed Theological Review*, (1974) pp. 33–44.

[112] Minutes III. 487–8.

[113] On April 18th, 1648, we read that the Assembly put itself into Grand Committee to discuss the Queries. *Ibid.* p. 513.

major theological assignments the *raison d' être* of the Assembly
had practically disappeared. Near the end of the numbered
sessions there is a rather pathetic little note that after Mr. Carter
had prayed, the "Assembly met and adjourned to the scribe's
chamber in a Committee."[114] Obviously the time was long past
since those days when noble peers and important Members of
Parliament had crowded into the Jerusalem Chamber to listen to
the debates. By the time of its final recorded plenary session,[115]
the Assembly had been in existence for over five and a half years,
and it had become largely an office for examining prospective
ministers. With the establishment of Cromwell's Protectorate in
1653 even this minor responsibility came to an end.

---

[114] 8th February, 1648/9, *ibid.* p. 538. When no quorum (40 members) was present,
the Assembly had decided to resolve itself into a Grand Committee to discuss whatever
was in progress, and then to report in plenary once the quorum was obtained. Cf. C. A.
Briggs, 'The Documentary History of the Westminster Assembly', *The Presbyterian
Review*, I (January 1880), p. 138.
[115] 1163, 22nd February, 1648/9.

CHAPTER 17

END OF THE AFFAIR

How is the modern reader to assess the Westminster Assembly? Richard Baxter did not regard himself as a Presbyterian, nor was he a member of the Assembly, and yet he spoke of the Assembly and its divines in terms of the highest respect.[1] Clarendon entertained a very different opinion;[2] and that should remind us that we have to treat seventeenth century plaudits and imprecations with equal care. The Assembly took place in the midst of a bitter civil war, which meant that it was almost impossible for the partisans to speak of their own convictions or those of their opponents in anything but extravagant terms. We may do Baxter an injustice to set his opinion alongside that of Clarendon, and much more than injustice to measure his assessment by the diatribes of Sir John Berkenhead's pamphlet, *The Assembly-man*,[3] but we must recognize that behind such

---

[1] "The Divines there Congregate were Men of Eminent Learning and Godliness, and Ministerial Abilities and Fidelity: And being not worthy to be one of them my self, I may the more freely speak that Truth which I know even in the Face of Malice and Envy, that, as far as I am able to judge by the Information of all History of that kind, and by any other Evidences left us, the Christian World, since the days of the Apostles, had never a Synod of more Excellent Divines (taking one thing with another) than this Synod and the Synod of Dort were." *Rel. Baxt.* I. i. 73 (§117).

[2] Clarendon said, "there were not above twenty who were not declared and avowed enemies to the doctrine or discipline of the church of England; many of them infamous in their lives and conversations; and most of them of very mean parts in learning, if not of scandalous ignorance; and of no other reputation, than of malice to the church of England; so that that convention hath not since produced any thing that might not then reasonably have been expected from it." *The History of the Rebellion and Civil Wars* V. 135 (II. 88).

[3] Sir John Berkenhead wrote it in 1647, although he did not acknowledge authorship until after the Restoration. It was circulated in manuscript and first published 1662/3. It did not sink quite as low as Berkenhead's obscene verses, *A Four Legg'd Elder*, but it does not rise above caricature and bitter satire. Cf. Peter W. Thomas, *Sir John Berkenhead, 1617–1679* (Oxford, Clarendon Press, 1969,) pp. 145ff.; Charles Clay Doyle, 'The Poetry of John Birkenhead', (Ph.D. dissertation, University of Texas, 1969,) pp. 65–70.

extravagant opinions there was more than social and political prejudice; beneath the bitterness there were theologies grounded in rival claims to *jus divinum*.

This issue must be recognized in our assessment of the Westminster Assembly and of the 'Grand Debate' between the Presbyterians and the Independents. It was simply an example of the basic theological issue that was convulsing England, and which claimed not only to determine the shape of the church but also inevitably to influence the future shape of English society. When we see the debates in their seventeenth century context, we see that the issues that brought the Assembly into being focussed in the problem of ultimate spiritual authority that had engaged Europeans since the Reformation, and were then to be given ecclesiological expression in rival claims to *jus divinum*. In the religious context of that time the Bible, the Church (Tradition), personal religious experience and human reason could all make plausible claims to represent that authority, but they were seen by the participants as exclusive contestants rather than as contributory testimonies to the same essential truth.

One of the primary lessons we can learn from the Assembly is the incompleteness of such exclusive claims. Certainly all the English Puritans who took part recognized the unique authority of the Bible, but during the course of the debates we see rival ecclesiologies emerging that made virtually identical claims based upon the biblical evidence, and, in the face of equally honest but conflicting interpretations of that evidence, other more 'humane' testimonies began to be pressed into service.

They would have agreed that reason is subservient to faith, but in that century it could no longer be wholly subjected to ecclesiastical dogma. Indeed, during the following century there would be many who would discard all the claims of revealed truth and turn to reason as the ultimate authority. J. N. Figgis was surely right when he suggested that the struggles over *jus divinum* were a stage on the road to asserting "the Divine Right of majority rule."[4] The seventeenth century was on the way to the Age of Reason and the secularized society that it helped to produce, but in the first half of the seventeenth century that of necessity led *through* theology, and in particular through the problems caused by the proliferation of claims to divine right.

We cannot ignore the persistent element of human perversity. After a lifetime of theological disputes Richard Baxter reflected that when he had been younger he had not appreciated how many

---

[4] *The Divine Right of Kings*, pp. 283f.

of our controversies are grounded in 'mutual Mistakes'. He also said he had not realized "how impatient Divines were of being contradicted, nor how it would stir up all their Powers to defend what they have once said, and to rise up against the Truth which is thus thrust upon them, as the mortal Enemy of their Honour." It is difficult, he noted, to move people from their prejudices, "be the Evidence never so plain."[5] Persistent obstinacy exists, and perhaps Philip Nye was right to regard it as the only fundamentally damning kind of sin.

Such human perversity, however, rarely starts as the intention of being perverse: it starts from convictions that the individual has accepted as truth on what appear to be sufficient grounds. We are back again at the rival claims to ecclesiastical divine right, and the significance of those elements of human obstinacy that we may detect from time to time in these debates is that it hardened the views expressed into denominational attitudes that lasted for well over three hundred years.[6]

I

Presbyterians and Independents

For most of those who have inherited this ecclesiastical lineage at the end of the twentieth century, the problem of an ultimate theological authority is not to be resolved in the absolute and exclusive way followed by many Puritans in the seventeenth century: the ecclesiological questions are not to be answered simply be extrapolating forms of government from the scriptures and backing them with a sufficient number of proof texts. This means that from the point of view of many making a theological appraisal of the polity issue in the Westminster Assembly today, the results may be interesting but the arguments are often wholly unconvincing. At the same time the disputing genes still persist and enjoy a vigorous life in some places, and for this reason we cannot leave the Westminster divines and their Dissenting Brethren without attempting some evaluation of their ecclesiological concern and the insights about the Church that they were trying to safeguard.

It should be clear that such an evaluation must inevitably differ from both sides in the dispute as it differs from their

---

[5] *Reliquiae Baxterianae* I. i. 125 (§213).

[6] The Congregatonal Union of England and Wales and the Presbyterian Church of England have united to become the United Reformed Church. This union was consumated on October 5th, 1972.

resolution of the authority issue. What follows is inevitably a personal evaluation by one who is indebted to both sides of this Reformed dispute; we find ourselves in the curiously ambivalent position of wanting to affirm or deny things said on both sides but not for the reasons given at the time.

For example, on the positive side of the Independent position their concern for religious toleration would be generally affirmed. Many people today would also approve their concern that church members should exercise some responsibility at the local level in church government, their desire to place church discipline in the context of the worshipping community, their emphasis on a close covenant relationship between members of the Christian Church, and their insistence that ecclesiastical government and administration should be consistent with the spirit of Jesus Christ. This does not mean, however, that in agreeing with the Independents on any of these points, the modern Christian would necessarily accept the exegesis they used to support these opinions in the Assembly.

That kind of literalism produced other aspects of their ecclesiology that would be open to fundamental theological question today. Perhaps the most striking illustration of that was their emphasis on the church's purity to the point where membership was restricted to those who conformed to spiritual standards regarded as morally acceptable by the leadership of that time. In the same way, while we may recognize the biblical reasons why the Dissenting Brethren regarded the local covenanted congregation as the basic form of the Christian Church (*ecclesia prima*), we can also recognize how, if it is allowed to degenerate into atomistic independency, it can become a denial of christian fellowship with other congregations. The Independents' emphases on the purity of the Church, on proof of 'election', and on the covenant fellowship of 'visible saints' could easily assume a spiritual arrogance that would be a visible denial of the very saintliness it strove to protect. Certainly the concern for 'ministerial' (as distinct from 'magisterial') authority in the Church for which the Independents argued so eloquently implied the need for a regular, integral, caring relationship between congregations, an organic expression of mutual ministry and responsibility.

Obviously some of the things that the modern believer would criticize in the Independents were criticized for sufficient reason by the Presbyterians, and *vice versa*, but these two groups were so close to each other theologically that their shared characteristics were simply given a slightly different form. For example, the

Presbyterians were no less concerned than the Independents for a church of 'visible saints' under discipline, but they were committed to applying this to a church made up of geographical parishes. We have seen that this produced a legalism that got them in serious trouble with Parliament in 1646, but at least the Presbyterians were trying to relate the Church to the whole of English society and to place the local parish community on as broad a base as their theology would allow. The experience of Baxter shows that their system would enable their clergymen to minister to the parishes in a way that was far less possible for rigorous Independents.[7]

The strongest features of Presbyterianism presented by George Gillespie and his friends were in the corporate sense of mutual ministry among the church officers in a presbytery (classis), and in their insistence that the Church's catholicity needs to be given structural forms: it is one thing to affirm the 'Holy Catholic and Apostolic Church' of the creed, but it is as important for faith that this holiness, catholicity and apostolicity should be made visible in tangible ecclesiastical relationships. In presenting their carefully integrated system of church government the Presbyterians seem to have held a more universal sense of the Church than their opponents, although again we would have to insist that in endorsing their position on this and other matters we are not often tempted to endorse their exegesis or the theological rationalizations they accepted as 'proofs.'

As we have said, the Presbyterians and the Independents were so close theologically that common tendencies surface in only slightly different forms. If in their pursuit of ecclesiastical purity the Independents could manifest spiritual arrogance by cutting themselves off from other Christians, Presbyterians could be guilty of similar arrogance in the standards they were prepared to impose upon society in the name of church discipline; if the Independents were threatened by the danger of Antinomian spiritualizing, the Presbyterians could easily become guilty of legalism; if Independent polity held the possibility of lay control, the Presbyterians could become bound by the domination of the clergy.

The debates seem to show that polity was simply the issue around which the differences in approach to Reformed theology naturally gathered. Perhaps both polities could have been made to work in a more inclusive way if those taking part in the debates

---

[7] This was dramatically illustrated in the contrast between Richard Baxter's and Philip Nye's pastorates in the parish of Acton. Cf. *supra* p. 154, n. 81.

had really heard the basic concerns of their opponents. At the deepest level the issue was less a matter of polity – although that is how it obtained visibility – than of the relationship between law and grace. Both sides wanted to maintain the balance between these essential elements of biblical faith and practice, but in reaction to each other they tended to go further than they would otherwise have gone. The polity issue was bound to become predominant in later history, because with the necessity of developing denominational apologetic both sides were pushed further into biblicism: the argument became centred in trying to find proof texts and biblical arguments to justify the institutions and agencies of their church government.

John Leith has pointed to this biblicism in relation to the doctrinal works of Westminster, which, he says, "became increasingly isolated from life and from the world." Writing of the Confessions and the Catechisms he pointed out that one of the primary concerns of the majority group in the Assembly was to refute Antinomianism, but then he goes on to observe that "the dropping of the rule of charity as an interpretative principle had devastating consequences in the future as doctrine would tend to become divorced from practice."[8] If that became true for Westminster's doctrinal statements, it was probably even more true for its ecclesiologies, for denominations tend to remain literalist in respect to their distinctive forms of church order long after they have ceased to be literalist in anything else.

So the modern reader may have difficulty in taking sides, because for many who by reason of an accident of birth or residence find themselves relegated to one or the other side of this seventeenth century dispute, the attempt to restore the New Testament church in precise detail, and the understanding of the bible on which those claims were made, no longer appear valid. We may recognize that the Church has a proper *jus divinum* in relation to those who belong to it, but we no longer believe that the Church has the right to impose its standards on the whole of society, and we may be even less convinced that this is to be limited to the Church of a particular polity. Many who are proud to acknowledge the legacy they received from the Dissenting Brethren would have difficulty today in justifying the Cyprionic terms used by Henry Jacob,[9] and I doubt whether many who are

---

[8] *Assembly at Westminster*, p. 80.

[9] Cf. his fourth assertion about church government, "The ordinury forme of Church-governement set forth vnto vs in the New Testament, ought necessarily to be kept still by vs; it is not changeable by men, and therefore it only is lawfull." *Reasons*

loyal to their inheritance from Westminster divines would endorse the equally Cyprionic terms of the London ministers when they declared that the presbyterian church order was the form that all church members "ought to observe and submit unto, till the end of the world".[10] The real problem for the twentieth century believer is with the absoluteness with which these rival ecclesiologies claimed to know the exact will of Christ for his church, and sought to fix that form exclusively for all time.

II

The Problem of 'Jus Divinum'

The clashes between Presbyterians and Independents, Parliament and the Assembly, on *jus divinum* emphasize that our contemporaries do not see the issue in the terms demanded by these seventeenth century divines. The contest between Parliament and the Assembly should not be dismissed as the ministers' desire to maintain personal control of the Church. That motive was certainly not absent, but the protest was also based on the Assembly's valid claim that the Church derives its authority directly from Jesus Christ and that this *jure divino* authority has to be preserved.

Obviously, on the basis of ecclesiology the divines were right, both in their claim of *jus divinum* for the Church itself, and in maintaining pastoral authority over church members. However, the claims were vitiated in several ways. When the divines allowed themselves to be pushed into compiling ever longer lists of sinners to be excluded from the Lord's Supper, Parliament began to realize that the clerics intended to use their authority over the population not so much in terms of grace that understood human frailty, but in terms of strict law: Parliament was facing a new manifestation of the canon law that had been so feared and detested in the past.[11] Furthermore, although the divines had been on firm enough ground when they asserted the divine right of the Church over its own members, they were on far less firm ground when the claims were made for a specific

---

taken out of Gods Word and the best humane testimonies proving a necessitie of reforming Ovr Chvrches In England, 1604, p. A2 verso, pp. 70–78.

[10] *Jus Divinum Regiminis Ecclesiastici,* p. 47.

[11] A hierarchial system was bound to strengthen a system of canon law, since it removed cases from the parish where the participants were known and could be dealt with pastorally, and put juridical power in the hands of superior courts where the cases had to be conducted in legal terms.

polity in view of the questions regarding the biblical evidence. The evidence was obviously not all that clear and unambiguous. It was not possible to lift church order directly out of the 1st century A.D. and transpose it unchanged into the 17th century, because the presence of apostles in the earlier time made that situation unique. Thomas Gataker recognized this when he had declared that "what arguments used against congregationall [presbytery] may be alleadged against classical presbytery be[cause] noe ordination [in apostolic times] in wch ther was not either an apostell or an evangelist",[12] and even Lazarus Seaman had realized the danger of the verbal gymnastics into which they were being forced when he observed "it is the weakest argument in matters of divinity to build our opinions upon dictionaries and grammars."[13]

Each view of the Church had its own vulnerability, for if Independent polity relied too much on extrapolating specific examples from the New Testament, the Presbyterians relied on rational arguments based on the defective knowledge and exegesis of their own time. To suggest that the knowledge and insights of that century were somehow made perfect for all time by the votes of the Assembly was to invest the decisions of the Assembly with an absoluteness to rival that of scripture itself.

Then again, the Assembly expected the full support of the civil magistrate – Parliament – in establishing its system of church government over the whole of English society; but Parliament held responsibility for all English subjects, saints and sinners, and the standards that might by willingly accepted by 'saints' represented an injustice when enforced upon 'sinners'. As Sir Benjamin Rudyard reminded the Assembly, "a Parliament is to make laws for all sorts of men," and he may have gone on to say that the discretionary powers demanded by the divines had been refused because Parliament feared they would impose too strict a discipline on English society.[14] The rules that might be pastorally appropriate and voluntarily undertaken in a church as a covenanted community of faith, would not necessarily be appropriate in a church where membership was a civic duty and in which the discipline was enforced by civil power. The divines did not see, and were perhaps unwilling to see, that church

---

[12] On May 15th, 1644; TMs. II. 116 (Ms. I. f. 60.)

[13] 10th February, 1644/5; Minutes III. 51.

[14] *Ibid.* p. 456. He said "It hath been often objected this power is so strongly opposed be[cause] it makes a strict discipline. . . ." At that point the Minutes are incomplete, and we can only guess at what he then said; but the tenor of his comments was on Parliament's responsibility to the whole country.

establishment by the state removed the churches of their century effectively from any close identity with church government in New Testament times.

There are indications that during the next decade the London clergy moved away from their strong advocacy of *jure divino* Presbyterianism to a more inclusive position. We have already noted that in 1646 the divines of Sion College produced an impressive defence of *jure divino* Presbyterianism in *Jus Divinum Regiminis Ecclesiastici*, that represented, if not the Assembly's official response to the nine queries of the House of Commons, a fairly clear indication of the line that response would have taken and of the arguments that would have been used. Several historians have regarded it either as substantially what the Assembly had perpared for its answers, or as an expanded version of them,[15] and we agree that if the leading divines in the Assembly had no direct hand in it, they almost certainly knew of it and approved of its contents. The title-page of the book makes the presbyterian claim to *jus divinum* explicitly, comprehensively and exclusively.[16]

However, the Records of the Provincial Assembly of London, now preserved in the library of Sion College, London,[17] include data about later books written by the London clergy on this subject and published under the aegis of the college. This evidence suggests that during the years that followed the effective work of the Assembly the London ministers themselves moved away from the *jus divinum* of presbyterian polity to a more inclusive stance.

The first book is the manuscript of a work produced at the end

---

[15] Hetherington, *Hist. of the West. Assembly*, p. 371, cf. pp. 271f.; Mitchell, *The West. Assembly*, p. 320; Beveridge, *Short Hist. of the West. Assembly*, p. 98. De Witt says it cannot be absolutely proved to represent the Assembly's answers to the nine Questions, but regards it as likely: *Jus Divinum*, pp. 231f. See also his note that ties the book directly to the nine Questions; *ibid*. pp. 232f., note 72.

[16] The title-page reads: "*Jus Divinum Regiminis Ecclesiastici: or, The Divine Right of Church-Government, Asserted and evidenced by the holy Scriptures:* According to the Light whereof (besides many particulars mentioned after the Preface)

1. The Nature of a Divine Right is delineated.
2. The Church-government which is of Divine Right is described.
3. This Description in the severall branches of it is explicated and confirmed.
4. The Divine Right of Ecclesiastical Censures, Officers, and Ruling Assemblies is manifested.

In all which it is apparent, That the Presbyteriall Government, by Preaching and Ruling Presbyters, in Congregationall, Classicall and Synodall Assemblies, may lay the truest claime to a Divine Right, according to the Scriptures."

[17] 'The Records of the Provinciall Assembly of London, Begunne by ordinance of Parliament May the 3d in the convocation house in Paules, London, 1647'.

of 1649,[18] that bears the title, *A Vindication of the Presbyteriall Gouernment and Ministry, together with an exhortation, to all the Ministers, Elders & people, within the bounds of the province of London, whether ioyning with it, or seperating from us, published by the ministers and Elders, met together in a provinciall assembly. November 2d 1649.* Although the rest of the manuscript title-page suggests a straight-forward assertion of divine right Presbyterianism and still maintains that separation "is iustly charged with schisme",[19] it had lost much of the arrogance of the earlier work, for in addressing not only the churches of the provincial assembly but also those "seperating from us", it at least tacitly accepted the principle of toleration.

One of the most significant matters listed for debate in that Ms was the proposition that "ministers formerly ordained by Bishops, need no new ordination", for that indicates the same lingering defensiveness about their earlier ordination in the Church of England that we noted among the 'presbyterian' majority in the Assembly. It suggests that there were still ministers in presbyterian London in 1649 who were anxious to justify their episcopal ordination, and who were sufficiently aware of criticism to produce a defence of episcopal ordination as part of their apologia for Presbyterianism!

In a later manuscript to appear in the Records of the Provincial Assembly, the mood of the London ministers shifted even further in the direction of a more inclusive view of *jus divinum*, and it re-emphasized their concern to justify both presbyterial and episcopal forms of ordination. Its inclusiveness is shown in that it altered the claim to divine right from explicit Presbyterianism to the whole gospel ministry: "Jus Divinum Minis-

---

[18] It bears the notation, "printed 1650 for Charles Meredith in Pauls Church yard in 4⁰".

[19] The subjects dealt with in the book were listed on the title-page:
1. That there is a church-Government by Divine Right.
2. That the presbyteriall Government is by Divine Right.
3. That the Magistrate is not the foundation of church Government.
4. The Inconveniences of the congregationall way.
5. That the Ruling Elder is by Divine Right.
6. That it is the will of Jesus Christ, that all souls of persons should give an account of their faith, to the minister, and elders before admission to the Lords Supper; together with answers, to the usuall obiections made against it.
7. Directions to the elders, for the right managing of their office.
8. Directions to such as are admitted to the Lords Supper, for the right sanctifying of Gods name in that ordinance and for their carriage one towards a nother.
9. Rules to preserve people, from the errors of these tymes.
10. That seperation from our churches, is iustly charged with schisme.
11. That ministers formerly ordained by Bishops, need no new ordination.
12. The necessity and usefulness of catechizing."

terij Evangelici Or the Divine Right of the Gospel Ministry".[20]
The title-page indicates that the work is divided into two parts –
the first is a justification of:

> The Gospel Ministry in generall[;]
> The necessity of Ordination thereunto by Imposition of hands –
> The unlawfulnes of private mens assuming to themselves,
>   either the office or the Worke of the Ministry without
>   a lawfull Call & Ordination[.]

Even more significantly, the ministers appear equally concerned
to justify not only presbyterial ordination but also episcopal
orders, for the second part is summarized as:

> A Justification of the present Ministers of England, both such
>   as were ordained during the prevalency of Episcopacy from
>   the foul aspersion of Antichristianisme, And those who
>   have been ordained since its abolition from the unjust
>   imputation of Novelty. Proving that a Bishop & Presbyter
>   are all one in Scripture; & that Ordination by Presbyters
>   is most agreeable to the Scripture-Paterne.
> Together with an Appendix, wherein the Judgement & Practise
>   of Antiquity about the whole matter of Episcopacy & espe-
>   cially about the ordination of Ministers is briefly discussed.[21]

This represents a distinct movement away from the earlier *jure
divino* presbyterian position. To claim that "Ordination by Presbyters is most agreeable to the Scripture-Paterne" is far less than
the absolute claims made for it in earlier works – it represents a position closer to that of the 'presbyter-bishop' – that had
been held by many English divines earlier.[22] Perhaps the removal
of the Scots Commissioners and recent relations of England and
Scotland had left the London ministers somewhat less

---

[20] Published by the Provincial Assembly of London and printed for "G. Latham, Jr. Rothwel, S. Gellibrand, T. Underhill, & J. Cranford. 1654."

[21] The theme of this book seems to run parallel to that of another that appeared anonymously about this time, but which was actually written by Clement Writer: *The Jus Divinum of Presbyterie. Or, A Treatise Evidently proving by Scripture, All true Ministers or Embassadors of the Gospel, to be endued with Divine Power from on High, do personate Christ, and are to be heard and esteemed accordingly* (1646). In a second edition of Writer's book, published in 1655, the author also offered reasons 'Justifying the present Government in not giving Power to any to judge Errors and Heresies, &c.' This suggests that the theological concern beind the Erastianism of the lawyers in Parliament had persisted, and that it had been caught up into a new mood favourable to toleration.

[22] John Reynolds, one of the Puritans at the Hampton Court Conference, had contributed to a book on the origins of episcopacy: *The Origen of Bishops and Metropolitans briefly laide downe*, by Martin Bucer, John Reynolds and James Ussher (Oxford, 1641). Edward Reynolds, one of the 'Presbyterians' in the Assembly, became Bishop of Norwich after the Restoration.

enamoured of the presbyterian claim to divine right. The major concern in this work appears to have been as much to defend the legitimacy of their own ordination and ministry as to justify the presbyterian system. It suggests that behind the earlier assertions of *jure divino* Presbyterianism, a considerable number of ministers even in London had been at least as anxious to maintain the national character of the Church and their own ministry as to maintain the claims of that particular polity.

III

The Clerical Majority

This reinforces the view presented in this study that the Scots had been able to gain the support of the majority of Puritans by playing on these anxieties, for the earlier debates in the Assembly show that whenever this claim to *jus divinum* had been approached, a number of the divines had been lukewarm at most. Some may have gone too far in emphasizing the distinction between English and Scottish Presbyterianism,[23] for there were those in the Assembly who fully supported the Scottish pattern, but the English majority in the Assembly had certainly represented more than one point of view in matters of church government during the first year of the Assembly's activities. William Beveridge said that there were two kinds of English Presbyterians, those who accepted the *jure divino* justification of presbytery, and those whom he calls the "presbyterians of expediency":

> The *shibboleth* of the one party was the *jus divinum*; the *shibboleth* of the other the *jus humanum* of Presbyterianism. On the one side were prominent the Smectymnuans (Stephen Marshall, Edmund Calamy, Thomas Young, Matthew Newcomen, and William Spurstow), who were afterwards to be greatly aided by the Scottish Commissioners; and on the other, were such men as Twisse, Gataker, and Palmer.[24]

It was a shrewd observation, although the lines were not always so clearly drawn – we suspect that the preferences of men like Twisse and Palmer may have lain originally in a somewhat

---

[23] E.g., Alexander Gordon, 'English Presbyterianism', *Christian Life*, 15th December, 1888; *Freedom after Ejection: A Review (1690–1692) of Presbyterian and Congregational Nonconformity in England and Wales* (Manchester, the Universty Press, 1917,) and also Jeremy Goring in *The English Presbyterians* (edited by C. Gordon Bolam et al., Boston, Beacon Press, 1968). Cf. M. R. Watts, *The Dissenters*, p. 90.

[24] *Short Hist. of the West. Assembly*, pp. 21f.

different direction and on occasion there was no greater pragmatist than Marshall.[25]

Nevertheless, leaders among the Puritan majority did eventually support Presbyterianism for essentially practical reasons, and Marshall – for all his political reluctance to press it too soon – was a supporter of the *jure divino* position. The comment was acute because it recognized that on matters of church government there were differences of approach to ecclesiology among the English Puritans, and the case has been made for suggesting that those who came to accept Presbyterianism – even *jure divino* Presbyterianism – for pragmatic reasons,[26] had entered the Assembly without clearly formulated views on church government. They accepted the position *force majeure*, because it was the condition of the Scottish alliance, because it was the only ecclesiastical position that stood a chance of withstanding the *jure divino* claims of Independency and thus of controlling the growth of sectarianism. Finally they accepted it because it could sustain a national establishment and the continuation of their own clerical authority.

William Shaw recognized that and spoke disparagingly of "the clerical spirit", but he also noted that there was considerable support for it even among lay members in the Commons,[27] and because of this we may suggest that this is too narrow a mould in which to cast it. In the Assembly it was certainly clerical and concerned with maintaining the privileges of the clergy; at the lowest level we might speak of the 'Vicar of Bray' syndrome that has continually plagued national churches, particularly in England. But that is not all that must be said, for this conservatism was concerned with maintaining the control over national belief and morals that had been exercised at the parish level for as long as Englishmen could remember: and this was now threatened by the spread of heterodox beliefs and sectarian religion. It might be more accurate to regard the divines' reaction as manifestation of a conservative mood that was still not much more than a century away from medievalism and less than a century from Catholicism.

J. R. De Witt seems to think that all the Puritans in the

---

[25] E.g., in the practical reasons for opposing the Scots method of taking Communion, and in the reasons for *not* presenting Parliament with a *jure divino* argument for church government.

[26] That appears to be a contradiction, but in view of the Scots demands and the intransigence of the House of Commons, the support of *jure divino* Presbyterianism appears to have been the only option left to them.

[27] *Hist. of the English Church*, I. 265.

Assembly, with the exception of the few Independents, were Presbyterians from the beginning and that the notion of 'primitive episcopacy' held by some of them "is in reality much more a variation upon the presbyterian theme than upon the prelatical one".[28] We may concede that it is closer to the presbyterian view than it is to prelacy, but not that it is closer to Presbyterianism than to episcopacy. Indeed, in terms of church government this position was in many ways closer to Independency than to either of the other polities,[29] and perhaps the major success of the Scots at Westminster had been in convincing these English Puritans that the traditional authority of the clergy would be safer with them than with Independency. We have seen that despite its unpopular features, many of these same men had been extremely anxious to justify the ecclesiastical integrity of their own episcopal ordination. The Minutes reveal that leanings towards 'primitive episcopacy' can be traced in some of the divines throughout the first year of the Assembly's life, and that they continued to surface sporadically during the rest of the ecclesiological debates.

If this evidence is taken cumulatively, then it suggests that most of the Puritan divines could not have been convinced Presbyterians when they entered the Assembly and had certainly not been ready to endorse the presbyterian system as of divine right. However, the same evidence also shows that by the time the vote on *jus divinum* had been taken on July 6th, 1646,[30] the majority had been persuaded to accept that position, not only for the crown rights of Jesus Christ over his Church, but also specifically for presbyterian church government.

To approach the same issue from another direction, we might ask how 'uncongenial' was the earlier 'prelatical establishment' to these English churchmen? We may concede that it was uncongenial in that it was prelatical, but it was not necessarily uncongenial because it was episcopal, and it was certainly not uncongenial in that it was established nationally by the state. From the point of view of the Puritan majority in the Assembly this last was crucial to the form of the church they wished to see

---

[28] *Jus Divinum*, p. 171. Even De Witt recognized that the English divines "did not identify a biblical form of church government with the church itself, as they had shown previously by their presence in what was for them a most uncongenial prelatical establishment." *Ibid.* p. 246. If one gives full weight to this, it is difficult to see how he could still give the impression that they entered the Assembly as Presbyterians.

[29] I.e., in placing effective spiritual control in the hands of the local 'bishops', acting either independently or in relation to a local presbytery.

[30] Minutes III. 251.

settled. Very early in their London enterprise the Scots had realized that their best hope of success would be to gain the support of men like Herbert Palmer and Cornelius Burgess. These
men had not been conspicuous for presbyterian convictions
hitherto, but the Scots recognized the importance of a national
establishment not only for the covenanted uniformity they
sought, but also in winning the support of the English Puritan
leaders. This united front had been proof against all opposition
save that coming from Parliament itself. However if English
Presbyterianism in the seventeenth century had this mixed
character, it may shed a good deal of light on the history of that
movement during the following century.

There was also an unresolved paradox in the intention of
establishing a Reformed church of the kind they desired. It
contained the problem of superimposing upon a society that still
held substantially medieval views of the relation between church
and state a church order drawn wholly from the New Testament.
The former looked for priestly control over the whole of society,
while the latter pointed to a stricter view of the church and its
sacraments. The realists in Parliament recognized the problem of
trying to establish Puritan standards in a society where membership of the national church had been regarded as the right of
every citizen, and for a national church in which citizens had
traditionally expected their participation in the sacraments to be
regarded in much the same way. Moreover, because church
discipline was oriented juridically the system demanded the
possibility of appeals, and this raised the problem of the ultimate
court of appeal on which Parliament would not give way. The
divines' attempt to retain that right appeared to the members of
Parliament to be simply a new manifestation of the old clerical
arrogance that they had expected to be excised from a Reformed
Church of England. In that impasse the divines' claim to *jus
divinum* was bound to suffer.

Perhaps the acuteness of the dilemma owes something to the
difference of ecclesiastical history and the religious climate in
England and Scotland, as Sir Benjamin Rudyard suggested.
S. R. Gardiner has said much the same.[31] Perhaps the most satisfactory way of stating this difference is to suggest that in their

---

[31] *G. C. W.* II. 66. However we question whether this difference should be traced to
Scottish respect for the clergy in contrast to England favouring 'the predominance of the
laity.' It is true that there had been a tradition of healthy anticlericalism in England that
dated at least from the time of the Lollards, but we could as plausibly argue the opposite.
If England remembered something from Lollardy, there is still more evidence of its
residual Catholicism, which Gardiner had recognized earlier in his study. *Ibid.* I. 261–4.

different histories the English and Scottish peoples had found different ways in which to express their national character and religious aspirations. There was an attachment in the southern kingdom to medieval ideas and customs, particularly in relation to the sacraments, that had not survived as vigorously in Scotland.[32]

William Shaw made the plausible suggestion that the conflict between Parliament and the Assembly had arisen from the ancient antagonism between the canon law and the common law, and there could well be some truth in that.[33] Undoubtedly the lawyers in Parliament would recognize in Presbyterianism a more congenial logic for their purposes than in episcopacy, for a hierarchical system of church courts ultimately responsible to the High Court of Parliament was bound to be more attractive to lawyers than a hierarchy of prelates finally responsible to an absolute monarch. They were anxious enough for the Church to reform its structure and practices, but they did not want it to become something radically different from what it had been traditionally within the English constitution, or fail to meet the expectations of the English people of what the Church should be like. They certainly did not want to establish an ecclesiastical system more autonomous and autocratic than that which it had replaced.

We therefore suggest that the *jus divinum* dispute manifested itself as it did because the Presbyterian majority in the Assembly, urged on by the Scots, were trying to superimpose a restorationist view of the autonomous church and its sacraments upon an essentially traditionalist view of the ministry and of an established national church. This brought them into conflict even with many of their lay supporters in Parliament. Both parties in this dispute represented a mixture of reforming zeal and conservative prejudice in respect to the Church of England, but their willingness to be radical and their determination to remain conservative did not quite coincide.

IV

The Paradox of the Secular

Europe was on its way to becoming a more openly secular society, and although the Civil War in England may have hidden the shape of that new world and postponed its disclosure, the

---

[32] Cf. *supra* p. 43, n. 85.
[33] Shaw, *Hist. of the English Church*, I. 237.

signs of it were there as surely as they were in the realism of French political objectives and Dutch trading policies. They are present in the history of the Westminster Assembly, although the evidence is not seen on the surface and would not have been acknowledged by the divines themselves. John Leith has commented on their complete lack of concern about the cultural, philosophical and scientific issues that were beginning to excite people in the world at large, and he says that the "only conclusion that seems possible is that the Westminster Assembly stands at the climax of an epoch, and that those members, who must have been aware of the changes that were underway, did not significantly relate these changes to the theological task"[34]

That is a perceptive comment. It recognizes and underscores the extent to which these men were still bound by presuppositions that were largely medieval, and we see that not only in the assumption of most of them that the church should be established by the state, but also in what they assumed about the proper relationship of theology to the rest of human knowledge: it was still the Queen of the sciences, and they insisted that it should exercise its regal rights.

Nevertheless, the new world was pressing hard to make itself known, and the signs of that too are to be seen in this history. They are to be seen in the place that reason occupied in these debates, and the way in which it became an almost independent authority in extrapolating the meaning of the texts of scripture; and they are to be seen not only in the way political considerations constantly intruded and influenced the divines' objectives, but also in the political way they pursued those objectives.[35] This is true for all sides in the disputes, and we are unable to identify all the honesty as Presbyterian and the dissembling as Independent, or *vice versa*. Nor can we say that all the theological truth and insight was on the side of the Assembly in the dispute with Parliament.

This intrusion of the political into theology was itself ambiguous. Clearly it did prevent the establishment of a united Reformed Church of England, just as it also hindered the establishment of an effective Presbyterian Church of England;[36] and the churchman is tempted to deplore this, because political

---

[34] *Assembly at Westminster*, p. 43.

[35] This political realism might produce reaction after the failure of Puritan hopes and the persecutions that followed the Restoration. Many of those who held the faith of the earlier Puritans would veer towards the 'otherworldliness' that we find in the writings of the imprisoned, ex-parliamentary soldier, John Bunyan.

[36] Cf. B. B. Warfield, *The Westminster Assembly and its Work*, pp. 70ff.

considerations frustrated the serious attempt to reform the Church according to the biblical pattern and undermined the work of the best theological minds of that time.

At once, however, we are faced with a further paradox, for if these theologians had had their way, and if they had been totally united in their views on church government, the new establishment could have become one of the most repressive in the history of the Reformed churches. The story of Cromwell's Major-Generals shows the direction in which many were prepared to go. We have to recognize that although the divines of the Assembly represented the best minds available, by later standards their knowledge was limited and their understanding of the biblical material was defective; yet they often propounded their answers as if they had infallible knowledge of the mind of Christ not only for their own day, but for all time.

Church historians should recognize that there is a testimony to the truth that the secular world makes to dogmatic religion through events, and it is to be seen in the reaction of the House of Commons to the Assembly's demand for *jus divinum*. From a later perspective we can see how a plea that was entirely right for the Church in the circumstances of the New Testament, would have been an unwarranted imposition if it had been enforced by the State upon seventeenth century English society. Parliament was right to prevent the ecclesiastics from imposing their own ecclesiastical control over English society, and right even to expect a less prohibitive attitude to the Lord's Supper. One of the rather sad features of the restrictions the Reformed theologians would have placed on those who presented themselves for the sacrament was their emphasis on the communicant having a 'competent knowledge' of the doctrines of the faith.[37] It was obviously a reaction from the dangers of medieval superstition, but it is difficult not to think that if any persons needed the assurance of God's grace to be mediated to them in simple action when they were prevented from understanding it in words, it would be the simple-minded and mentally defective.[38] At this

---

[37] Cf. March 28th, 1645. Cited previously, *supra* p. 496, n. 18; Minutes III. 74.

[38] There is a certain parallel in children coming to the sacrament, but the cases, although similar, are significantly different. Eventually children may be expected to reach their own decision about the faith, and the sacrament to them represents the challenge to Christian discipleship; the Church has not only the right but the duty to be sure that this is not taken lightly. In the case of the weak-minded or imbeciles the situation is very different, for the Church is then dealing with those who will never have 'competent knowledge.' To them, therefore, the sacrament cannot represent all the challenge of discipleship, but mainly the assurance of God's compassion and love in Jesus Christ.

point there was a gnostic tendency in Reformed faith and practice that too readily tended to equate salvation with 'competent knowledge'. Sir John Evelyn's protest to the Assembly that "his yoke is easy; if it be a galling, vexing yoke, it is not his", might easily become an excuse for laxity in the church, but it was also a reminder to the divines that the Christian faith is for ordinary sinners and is not reserved for spiritual giants. That was an insight into the nature of Christian faith that came from the secular.

Something similar might be said with regard to the principle of liberty of conscience. Apart from the insights of a few religious radicals like Roger Williams, it was political pressure that forced the issue into the open. This may be seen with respect to the Independents, who it has been said, claimed the same *jure divino* for the Church as did the Presbyterians, but "without any Civil Sanctions or Penalties annexed."[39]

That must be received with some reserve, at least as far as their original position was concerned, for in view of what happened in New England we have no reason to suppose that if they had gained control of the Assembly and had won the support of Parliament their views on liberty of conscience would have been any more enlightened than those of the majority. In the providence of God, however, they were not given that choice, and for political reasons they were forced to broaden their concept of the church and their ethical horizon to include a wider concept of toleration.

A political rationale for liberty of conscience was beginning to gain some credence in the country. Early in 1645 an anonymous writer set out the political reasons for tolerating the Protestant sects, and this found its way into the papers of John Thurloe, who was to become the Secretary of State during the Protectorate.[40] The writer suggested that although papists and prelatists could not be tolerated because their principles made them a threat to everyone else, other sects posed no such threat, and it concluded:

I offer only the view of the flourishing and security of Holland; and the most urgent necessity, that a preaching ministry all over the

---

[39] Neal, *Hist. of the Puritans*, III. 284.

[40] Since the memorandum appears in Thurloe's papers, it may have been sent originally to Cromwell. It was undated, but was placed between letters dated 10th and 13th January, 1644/5: *A Collection of the State Papers of John Thurloe, Esq., Secretary First, to the Council of State, and afterwards to the Two Protectors Oliver and Richard Cromwell*, (edited by Thomas Birch, London, 1742, 7 vols.) I. 54f.

kingdom be encouraged, rather than the many punctitios of the desired uniformity prosecuted; and that if we drive from among us the dissenters (supposed erroneous, which cannot be absolutely concluded by us of them all, by any rule, we yet have, and they want, whereby to try our own certainty) we may indeed ease ourselves from the trouble of them, but we put it upon our neighbours where they shall go, and possibly occasion the dishonour of God more by sending them where they may do more harm, and repelling them from better instruction, which here might be afforded them.[41]

That was essentially a political approach to the problem, but it could also be argued that it was true to the spirit of the New Testament. Similarly when Nathaniel Fiennes protested that the recent activities of the Assembly in respect to its petition "are not the way of Englishmen, Christians, and ministers of Christ" he may in the first instance have been tilting at the Scots, but he was also voicing the layman's criticism of the clergy when concern for orthodoxy caused them to countenance behaviour that contradicted Christian ethics.

The same concern enabled Cromwell when he came to power to cut through the opposing claims of the different theologies to arrive at more equitable principles of political action.[42] The reasons that impelled him to enunciate the principle that "the State is choosing men to serve them, takes no notice of their opinions; if they will be willing to serve them, that satisfies", were essentially military and political,[43] and later, during his Protectorate, he declared that the duty of a Christian magistrate was to oppose all forms of ecclesiastical persecution and to preserve the right of anyone to worship according to conscience.[44]

This is a difficult area for historians to write about without exhibiting their prejudices. Church historians have written about their orthodoxies and pointed to the real contribution that the churches have made to the betterment of human society, while secular historians with equal justification can point to the

---

[41] *Ibid.* p. 55.

[42] In 1656 Cromwell argued against the theologians for the readmission of the Jews into England, and he used virtually the same argument as the anonymous writer in the *Thurloe State Papers* at the end of the quotation cited above. Cf. Abbott, *Writings and Speeches of O. C.*, IV. 51–4; Paul, 'Oliver Cromwell and the Jews', *The Jewish Chronicle* (Special Supplement) 1956.

[43] Letter to Lawrence Crawford, 10th March, 1644; Abbott, *Writings and Speeches of O. C.*, I. 278.

[44] Cromwell told the Fifth Monarchists, John Rogers and Christopher Feake, "Why I tell you, there be Anabaptists and they would cut the throats of them that are not under their forms; so would you Fifth-Monarchy-men. It is fit to keep all these forms out of power." *Ibid.* III. 607–616; for Cromwell and toleration see Paul, *The Lord Protector*, pp. 324–333.

places in history where the same churches were repressive and persecuting. Perhaps the time is overdue for a reappraisal of human history more holistically. There is a sense in which western society and the standards that it admires, even when it fails to follow them, have roots in an essentially Christian history, but it is surely time to admit from the perspective of our present understanding of Christian history that there were issues on which the churches were totally wrong, and in which testimony to a more 'christian' understanding of human relationships was made to the churches by the 'secular' world. True, in the West it has been a secular world largely formed and continuously informed by Christian values, but it was still secular in its political and social objectives. This interplay between the churches and society is seen in the history of the Westminster Assembly.

A further problem to which we have been pointing may be illustrated in the words of Richard Baxter. On the one hand, he acknowledged the highest admiration for the Assembly and its work,[45] but he recognized the problems associated with synods such as Westminster and Dort in trying to establish standards of orthodoxy for all time. Some years later he was asked by a bookseller to write an introduction to the papers of the Assembly, with a view to commending their use to families, and he asked that his introduction should be examined by other divines to obtain their opinion. He said that they could either publish it or not as they wished, but he asked that the introduction should either be printed in its entirety or not at all. He then tells us:

> The bookseller gets Dr. *Manton* to put an Epistle before the Book, who inserted mine in a different Character in his own, (as mine, but not naming me): But he leaveth out a part, which it seems, was not pleasing to all. When I had commended the Catechisms for the use of Families, I added, That *I hoped the Assembly intended not all in that long Confession and those Catechisms, to be imposed as a Test of Christian Communion; nor to disown all that scrupled at any word in it; if they had I could not have commended it for any such use, though it be useful for the instruction of Families*, &c. All this is left out, which I thought meet to open, lest I be there misunderstood.[46]

Of course, from the point of view of what many in the seventeenth century regarded as 'orthodox' Calvinism, Richard Baxter held some opinions that were suspect, although he was regarded as the leading English 'Presbyterian' during the last half of the seventeenth century; but he was pointing to the

---

[45] *Supra* p. 522, n. 1; *Rel. Baxt.* I. i. 73 (§117.)
[46] *Ibid.* p. 122 (§210.)

problem in church history that always occurs when doctrinal statements, which may justly be regarded as the best possible formulations for a particular period, are then regarded as sacrosanct for all time.[47] This is to invest the interpretive and *serving* work of the theologian with a divine authority it should never claim, and it is secular society which has often been the vehicle of judgment against such pretensions. When society addresses the Church in that way it seems to be echoing if not the precise words then certainly the sentiments of Cromwell's protest to the Scottish General Assembly in 1650, "Is it therefore infallibly agreeable to the Word of God, all that you say? I beseech you, in the bowels of Christ, think it possible you may be mistaken."[48]

This is not to say that the Church should give up its claim to be heard in society. The secular world always needs to listen to the Church's prophetic voice, and we suspect that it is itself most responsible when it has both listened and learned from the best spiritual insights available to it. Cromwell himself was a good illustration, for although he is remembered in history as a general and a statesman, his whole life had been nurtured in a culture nourished by christian values, and his ethical judgments were wholly determined by biblical faith and Puritan convictions. Our argument, far from suggesting that the Church is irrelevant to the world in which it is set, would emphasize that there is an inescapable relationship between the Church and its world, but it also reminds us that in this necessary interrelationship and dialogue we must not assume that all the truth is invariably on one side. God does speak to the world through the Church, but we dare not assume that every time the Church speaks it is God's voice that is being heard; and neither can we assume that when the world protests to the Church in the name of justice or truth that the voice of God is not to be heard. The story of the Westminster Assembly is a reminder to later generations that God is not bound by our definitions of the divine nature or our partial understandings of divine truth. It is a testimony to the patience, loyalty, faith and spiritual perception of devoutly

---

[47] He had the same problem with the orthodoxy of the Congregationalists. In 1653 the 'Instrument of Government' became the new constitution of English government, and some divines, headed by John Owen, were called together to define the 'Fundamentals of Religion' in that document. Baxter differed from the rest. In his account he says, "My own Judgment was this, that we must distinguish between the *Sense* (or *matter*) and the *Words*; and that it is only the *Sense* that is primarily and properly our Fundamentals: and the *Words* no further than as they are needful to express that *Sence* to others, or represent it to our own Conception . . ." *Ibid.* pp. 197f. (§51.)

[48] To the General Assembly of the Scottish Kirk, 3rd August, 1650; W. C. Abbott, *Writings and Speeches of O. C.* II. 303.

serious scholars at that time in history, and because of that its work "is entitled to be taken with utmost seriousness but not with idolatry"[49] – and most of all by those who in some sense count themselves to be its spiritual heirs.

However, the ambivalence between church and society, between spiritual and ethical perception and political action, persists, and the necessary juxtaposition needs to be more frankly recognized on both sides. John Leith is surely right to remind us that the theological reconstructions of the Assembly ignored the elements of radical change that were even then erupting into the world, and that the event can therefore be regarded rather as the climax of an epoch that was already passing than as the harbinger of the new age.[50] From that perspective the work of the Assembly was limited. However, when this work is placed within the context of its time, William Shaw could point out with equal justification that "there is hardly a parallel in history to such a constitutional revolution as this."[51]

These evaluations by responsible historians illustrate the paradox with which we are left at the end of this study. It points to the continuum of history in which it is not possible in any society to separate neatly the sacred from the secular, or to unravel completely their mutual influence and relationships. We see that we cannot exclude elements of the sacred (or at least the ethical) that appear in the secular arena, and it is not possible to exclude all aspects of the secular from the sphere of the professedly sacred. It also reminds us that it is often not possible in history to distinguish precisely between the influences in church and society that make for reformation and change, and those which at first sight seem to be uncompromisingly in support of conservatism and *status quo*. The history of the Westminster Assembly suggests that radical change may not always be in the hands of those who seek novelty for its own sake, but that it may spring from those who, on the basis of their own traditional and even conventional convictions, bring a new intensity to that faith as they try to respond to the challenge of their own time.

It is generally known that in answer to Question 1 on the primary end of mankind, the Catechisms declare that the chief end of man is to glorify God and enjoy him for ever. It may be less generally recognized that in ending with the final ascription in the Lord's Prayer the Catechisms bring us full circle to where

---

[49] John Leith, *Assembly at Westminster*, p. 109.
[50] *Ibid.* p. 80.
[51] *A History of the English Church . . . 1640–1660*, p. viii.

they began,[52] because the words of that closing part of the prayer "teacheth us to take our encouragement in prayer from God only, and in our prayers to praise him, ascribing kingdom, power and glory to him. And, in testimony of our desire, and assurance to be heard, we say, *Amen.*"

That when you reflect upon it, is where godly revolution in church and society often begins.

---

[52] Question 107 of the Shorter Catechism; cf. Question 196 of the Larger Catechism.

APPENDIX I.

A.

Note. The members of the Assembly presented in these lists are based on A.F. Mitchell's lists in *The Westminster Assembly*, pp. xii-xx. The divines, however, have been placed first and arranged alphabetically. The reader should also note:

1. Alternative spellings of the names are possible (e.g., Rathbone, Wrathbone, Rathband, etc.) but are not normally given.
2. That the number in parentheses at the end of each entry represents the order in which the divine was nominated to the Assembly.
3. The names of those who did not attend the Assembly appear in square brackets. Those marked * were added later.
4. In addition to the normal use of italics, we have also used this to indicate the elected officers of the Assembly.

For A. F. Mitchell's reasons for not including the names of Dr. Manton, Love, Moore and Newscore, see his note, *op. cit.* pp. xx.

Divines of the Westminster Assembly

John Arrowsmith, B.D., of King's Lynne, Norfolk; later successively Master of St. John's and Trinity, Cambridge, and Professor of Divinity. (58)

Simeon Ashe, of St. Bride's, afterwards of St. Michael's, Basingshaw; appointed in place of Josiah Shute, who died before the Assembly met. (91)

Theophilus Bathurst, of Overton Waterville, Wilts. (29)

Thomas Bayly, B.D., of Manningford-Bruce, Wilts. (80)

[John Bond, D.C.L.], Master of the Savoy; *v.* Archbishop Ussher, (restored 1647.) (129)*

[Samuel Boulton], of St. Saviour's, Southwark; afterwards D.D., and Master of Christ's College, Cambridge, *v.* Burroughes, deceased 1646. (139)*

Oliver Bowles, B.D., of Sutton, Bedford (2)

William Bridge, M.A., of Yarmouth. (10)

[Ralph Brownerigg, D.D.], Bishop of Exeter; sent excuse
for non-attendance. (19)

[Richard Buckley, or Bulkley, B.D.] (89)

Anthony Burgess, M.A.; of Sutton Coldfield, Warwick-
shire, and St. Lawrence Jewry, London. (85)

Cornelius Burgess, D.D., of Watford, Herts, *Assessor;* later
of St. Andrew's, Wells. (32)

Jeremiah Burroughes, M.A., Lecturer at Stepney. (44)

Richard Byfield, of Long Ditton, Surrey; *v.* Dr. Featley,
deceased 1647. (135)*

Edmund Calamy, B.D., of St. Mary's, Aldermanbury,
London. (45)

[Richard Capell, M.A.], Pitchcombe, Gloucester. (28)

[John Carter, M.A.], of York; later of Camberwell or St.
Peter's, Norwich. (25)

Thomas Carter, M.A., of Dynton, Bucks; then of St.
Olave's, Hart Street. (105)

William Carter, of London. (56)

Joseph Caryl, M.A., Preacher at Lincoln's Inn; then of St.
Magnus, London. (47)

Thomas Case, M.A., of St. Mary Magdalene, Milk Street,
London. (14)

Daniel Cawdrey, M.A., St. Martin's in Fields; *v.* Dr.
Harris, of Winchester, (who was excused
attendance.) (125)*

Humphrey Chambers, B.D., of Claverton, Somerset;
afterwards of Pewsey, Wilts. (75)

Francis Cheynell, or Channell, of Oxford; later Master of
St. Johns, D.D., and Lady Margaret Professor of Divinity. (98)

[Thomas Clendon], of All Hallows, Barking; *v.* Nicholson,
(did not attend.) (124)*

Peter Clerk, M.A., of Carnaby; afterwards of Kirkby, York. (26)

[Richard Cleyton, M.A.], of Shawell, Leicester; aft. Easton Magna, Essex. (41)

[Francis Coke, or Cooke], of Yoxhall, Staffordshire. (67)

Thomas Coleman, M.A., of Blyton, Lincoln; aft. of St. Peter's, Cornhill. (38)

John Conant, B.D., of Lymington, Somerset; aft. of St. Stephen's, Walbrook. (76)

Edward Corbet, of Norfolk; v. H. Hall, of Norwich. (132)*

Edward Corbet, M.A., of Merton College, Oxford, and Rector of Chartham, Kent, succeeded Dr. Hammond as University Orator and Canon of Christ's Church, Oxon. (69)

Robert Crosse, B.D., of Lincoln College, Oxford. (60)

John De la March, of French Church, London. (102)

Samuel De la Place, of French Church, London. (101)

Philip Delmé, or Delmy, of French Church, Canterbury; v. Rathbone, deceased (?). (133)*

[Calibute Downing, LL.D.], of Hackney, Middlesex. (43)

[William Dunning, M.A.], of Cold Aston, Glouc., or Godalston, Notts. (121)

John Dury, (or Durie,) v. Dr. Downing, deceased 1644. (136)*

[Edward Ellis, B.D.], of Guilsfield, Montgomery. (99)

[John Erle, D.D.], of Bishopton, Wilts; afterwards Bishop of Worcester, then of Salisbury. (113)

Daniel Featley, D.D., of Lambeth; also of All Hallows, Bread St., and Acton, Middlesex. (66)

Thomas Ford, M.A., of St. Faith's, London, v. Bowles, deceased. (134)*

John Foxcroft, M.A., of Gotham, Notts. (54)

Hannibal Gammon, M.A., of Mawgan, Cornwall. (7)

Thomas Gataker, B.D., of Rotherhithe, Surrey. (93)

John Gibbon, (Guibon,) M.A., of Waltham. (114)

George Gibbs, of Ayleston, Leicester. (42)

Samuel Gibson, of Burleigh, Rutland. (63)

William Good, B.D., of Denton, Norfolk. (128)*

Thomas Goodwin, B.D., of London; later President of Magdalen College, Oxford. (12)

William Gouge, D.D., of Blackfriars, London; *Assessor* after Palmer. (18)

Stanley Gower, of Brampton Bryan, Hereford; and St. Martin's, Ludgate. (34)

John Green, of Pencombe, Hereford. (33)

William Greenhill, M.A.; Lecturer at Stepney. (87)

[John Hackett, D.D.], of St. Andrew's, Holborne; later Bishop of Lichfield. (100)

Henry Hall, B.D., of Norwich. (77)

[Henry Hammond, D.D.], of Penshurst, Kent; and Canon of Christ's Church. (110)

Humphrey Hardwick, of Hadham Magna, Herts. (130)*

John Harris, D.D., Warden of Winchester College. (49)

Robert Harris, B.D., of Hanwell, Oxford; then of Trinity College, Oxford. (59)

Charles Herle, M.A., of Winwick, Lancashire; *Prolocutor* after Dr. Twisse. (39)

Richard Herrick, (Heyrick,) M.A., Warden of Christ's College, Manchester. He conformed at the Restoration. (40)

Jasper or Gaspar Hickes, M.A., of Lanrake, Cornwall. (8)

[Samuel Hildersham, B.D.], of West Felton, Shropshire. (70)

Thomas Hill, B.D., of Titchmarsh, Northampton; later D.D. and Master of Trinity College, Cambridge. (52)

Thomas Hodges, B.D., of Kensington; then later Dean of Hereford. (107)

[Richard Holdsworth, or Oldsworth, D.D.], Master of Emmanuel College, Cambridge. (120)

Joshua Hoyle, D.D., of Dublin, then of Stepney, and later Regius Professor of Divinity at Oxford. (9)

[Henry Hutton, M.A.], of Caldbeck, Cumberland; and Prebendary of Carlisle. (78)

John Jackson, M.A., of Marske, Yorkshire; Preacher at Gray's Inn. (55)

Robert Johnston, of York, *v*. Carter, deceased. (138)*

William Lance, of Harrow, Middlesex. (106)

John Langley, M.A., of West Tuderley, or Tytherley, Hampshire. (71)

John Ley, M.A., of Budworth, Cheshire. (13)

John Lightfoot, M.A., of Ashley, Staffordshire; later D.D. and Master of Catharine Hall, Cambridge. (68)

[Richard Love, D.D.], of Ekington, and Corpus Christi College, Cambridge. (17)

[William Lyford, B.D.], of Sherborne, Dorset. (104)

Stephen Marshall, B.D., of Finchingfield, Essex. (23)

John Maynard, M.A., of Mayfield, Surrey, *v*. H. Nye, deceased. (123)*

William Mew, B.D., of Easington, Gloucester. (27)

Thomas Micklethwaite, M.A., of Cherry Burton, Yorkshire. (116)

[William Moreton], of Newcastle. (88)

[George Morley, D.D.], of Mildenhall, Wilts; later Bishop of Winchester. (50)

Matthew Newcomen, M.A., of Dedham, Essex. (103)

[William Nicholson, M.A.], Archdeacon of Brecknock. (92)

[Henry Nye], of Clapham. (82)

Philip Nye, M.A., of Kimbolton, Hunts. (30)

Henry Painter, B.D., of Exeter. (115)

Herbert Palmer, B.D., of Ashwell, Herts; *Assessor* after White, and Master of Queen's College, Cambridge. (1)

[Christopher Pashley, D.D.], of Hawarden, Flintshire. (95)

Edward Peale, of Compton, Dorset. (22)

Andreas Perne, M.A., of Wilby, Northampton. (108)

John Phillips, of Wrentham, Suffolk, brother-in-law of Dr. Ames. (74)

Benjamin Pickering, of East Hoateley, or of Buckstead, Sussex. (81)

William Price, B.D., St. Paul's, Covent Garden, and of Waltham Abbey. (118)

Nicholas Prophet, or Proffet, of Marlborough, Wilts; aft. of Edmonton. (111)

[John Pyne], of Bereferrers, Devon. (15)

William Rathbone, (Wrathbone or Rathband,) of Highgate, v. Morley, who did not attend. (126)*

William Raynor, B.D., of Egham, Surrey; then of St. John Baptist, London. (6)

Edward Reynolds, M.A., of Braunston, Northampton; later D.D., Dean of Christ Church, Oxf., and Bishop of Norwich after the Restoration. (51)

Arthur Sallaway, or Salway, M.A., of Seavern Stoke, Worcester. (83)

[Robert Sanderson, D.D.], of Boothby Pannell or Pagnell, Lincoln; afterwards Bishop of Lincoln. (53)

Henry Scudder, of Collingborne, Wilts. (79)

Lazarus Seaman, B.D., of All Hallows, Bread Street, London; then Master of Peter House, Cambridge. (48)

Obadiah Sedgewick, B.D., of Coggeshall, or of Farnham, Essex. (24)

Sidrach Simpson, of London; afterwards he succeeded Vines as Master of Pembroke Hall, Cambridge. (84)

Brocket (or Peter) Smith, D.D., of Barkway, Herts. (31)

William Spurstow, D.D., of Hampden, Bucks; later Master of Catharine Hall, Cambridge, and later of Hackney. (97)

Edmund Stanton, D.D., of Kingston-upon-Thames; later, President of Corpus Christi College, Oxford. (65)

Peter Sterry, B.D., of London; later Cromwell's chaplain at Whitehall. (112)

John Strickland, of New Sarum; *v.* Dr. Ward, deceased, 14 Sept. 1643. (127)*

William Strong, preacher in Westminster Abbey, *v.* Peale, deceased. (137)*

Matthias Styles, D.D., of St. George's, Eastcheap, London. (62)

Francis Taylor, B.D., of Yalding, Kent. (35)

Thomas Temple, D.D., of Battersea, Surrey. (90)

Thomas Thoroughgood, of Massingham, Norfolk. (57)

Christopher Tisdale, or Tesdale, M.A., of Uphurstborne, or Hurstborne-Tarrant, Hampshire. (72)

Henry Tozer, B.D., Fellow of Exeter College, Oxford. (96)

Antony Tuckney, B.D., of Boston, and St. Michael Quern; afterwards Master successively of Emmanuel and St. John's Colleges, Cambridge; Professor of Divinity following Arrowsmith. (37)

William Twisse, D.D., of Newbury, Berks; *Prolocutor.* (5)

[James Ussher], Archbishop of Armagh. (61)

Thomas Valentine, B.D., of Chalfont St. Giles, Bucks; later of London. (4)

Richard Vines, M.A., of Calcot; Master of Pembroke Hall, Cambridge, and later a minister in London. (86)

George Walker, B.D., of St. John's Evangelist, Watling Street, London. (46)

John Ward, of Ipswich and of Brampton, *v.* Painter, deceased. (131)*

[Samuel Ward, D.D.], Master of Sidney Sussex College, Cambridge, and Lady Margaret Professor of Divinity. (20)

James Weldy, or Welby, of Selattyn, Shropshire. (94)

Thomas Westfield, D.D., of St. Bartholomew the Great; Bishop of Bristol; (attended only the first meeting.) (109)

[Francis Whidden, M.A.], of Moreton-Hampstead, Devon. (16)

Jeremiah Whitaker, M.A. of Stretton, Rutland; afterwards of Bermondsey. (64)

John White, M.A., of Dorchester; *Assessor.* (21)

Henry Wilkinson, sen., B.D., of Waddesdon, Bucks, and St. Dunstan's in East. (3)

[Henry Wilkinson, jun., B.D.], Epping, Essex; later D.D., and Principal of Magdalen Hall, Oxford. (119)

Thomas Wilson, M.A., of Otham, Kent. (36)

John Wincop, D.D., of St. Martin's in the Fields, and Clothall, Herts. (117)

[Thomas Wincop, D.D.], of Ellesworth, Cambridge. (11)

Francis Woodcock, B.A., of St. Lawrence Jewry, *v.* Moreton, of Newcastle, deceased. (122)*

Thomas Young, M.A., St. And., of Stowmarket, Suffolk; afterwards D.D., and Master of Jesus College, Cambridge. (73)

Peers

Algernon, Earl of Northumberland
[William, Earl of Bedford.]
Philip, Earl of Pembroke and Montgomery.
William, Earl of Salisbury.
[Henry, Earl of Holland.]
Edward, Earl of Manchester.
William, Lord Viscount Say and Seale.
[Edward, Lord Viscount Conway.]
Philip, Lord Wharton.
Edward, Lord Howard of Escrick.
[*Basil, Earl of Denbigh; *Oliver, Earl of Bolingbroke; *William, Lord Grey of Warke; *v.* Bedford, Holland and Conway.]
*Robert, Earl of Essex, Lord General.
*Robert, Earl of Warwick, Lord High Admiral.

Members of House of Commons

John Selden, Esq.
Francis Rous, Esq.
Edmund Prideaux, Esq.
Sir Henry Vane, Knt., senior.

John Glynn, Esq., Recorder of London.
John White, Esq.
Bulstrode Whitlocke, Esq.
Humphrey Salloway, Esq.
[Mr. Serjeant Wild.]
Oliver St. John, Esq., His Majesty's Solicitor.
Sir Benjamin Rudyard, Knt.
John Pym, Esq.
Sir John Clotworthy, Knt.
John Maynard, Esq.
Sir Henry Vane, Knt., junior.
[William Pierpoint, Esq.]
William Wheeler, Esq.
Sir Thomas Barrington, Knt.
[Walter Young, Esq.]
Sir John Evelyn, Knt.
* Sir Robert Harley, v. Pym, deceased.
* Sir William Massam, or Masson, v. Barrington, deceased.
* William Strode [Stroud], v. White, deceased.
* Sir Arthur Haselrig.
* Robert Reynolds, Esq.
* Zouch Tate, Esq.
* Sir Gilbert Gerard (?).
* Sir Robert Pye (?).
* Sir John Cooke.
* Nathianiel Fiennes (?)

Scribes or Clerks of the Assembly

Henry Roborough, of St. Leonard's, Eastcheap, London.
Adoniram Byfield, M.A., afterwards of Fulham.
Amanuensis or Assistant:–
John Wallis, M.A., Fellow of Queen's Coll., Cam.; afterwards
    D.D., Savilian Professor of Geometry, Oxford.

Scottish Commissioners

Ministers
Alexander Henderson, of Edinburgh.
Robert Douglas, of Edinburgh (never sat).
Samuel Rutherford, of St. Andrews.
Robert Baillie, of Glasgow.
George Gillespie, of Edinburgh.
* Robert Blair, of St. Andrews.

Elders

John, Earl of Cassilis (never sat).
John, Lord Maitland, after Earl of Lauderdale.
Sir Archibald Johnston, of Warriston.
Robert Meldrum, in absence of Johnston.
*John, Earl of Loudon.
*Sir Charles Erskine.
*John, Lord Balmerino, *v.* Loudon.
*Archibald, Marquis of Argyll.
*George Winrham, of Libberton, *v.* Argyll.

B.

The Three Standing Committees
(as originally constituted)

Note. The information in these lists (Appendix I. B.) is based upon that given in W. M. Hetherington's *History of the Westminster Assembly*, pp. 429f, and A. F. Mitchell's *The Westminster Assembly*, p. 145.

First Committee

Mr. Herbert Palmer	Mr. Theophilus Bathurst
Mr. Oliver Bowles	Mr. Philip Nye
Mr. Henry Wilkinson, (Sen.)	Dr. Peter (or Brocket) Smith
Mr. Thomas Valentine	**Dr. Cornelius Burgess
Mr. William Raynor	Mr. John Green
Dr. Joshua Hoyle	Mr. Stanley Gower
Mr. William Bridge	Mr. Francis Taylor
Mr. Thomas Goodwin	Mr. Thomas Wilson
Mr. John Ley	Mr. Antony Tuckney
Mr. Thomas Case	Mr. Thomas Coleman
Dr. William Gouge	Mr. Charles Herle
Mr. John White	Mr. Richard Herrick
Mr. Stephen Marshall	Mr. William Mew
Mr. Obadiah Sedgewick	Mr. William Rathbone
Mr. Peter Clerk	Mr. Jasper Hickes

Second Committee

Mr. Richard Cleyton	Mr. Edward Reynolds
Mr. George Gibbs	Mr. Thomas Hill
Mr. Jeremiah Burroughes	Mr. John Jackson
Mr. Edmund Calamy	Mr. William Carter
Mr. George Walker	Mr. Thomas Thoroughgood
Mr. Joseph Caryl	Mr. John Arrowsmith
Mr. Lazarus Seaman	Mr. Samuel Gibson

Second Committee – *(Continued)*

Mr. Jeremiah Whitaker
** Dr. Edmund Stanton
Mr. John Lightfoot
Mr. Edward Corbet
Mr. John Langley
Mr. Christopher Tisdale
Mr. Thomas Young
Mr. John Phillips
Mr. John Conant

Mr. Humphrey Chambers
Mr. Henry Hall
Mr. Henry Scudder
Mr. Thomas Bayly
Mr. Benjamin Pickering
Mr. Daniel Cawdrey
Mr. John Strickland
Mr. John Bond
Mr. Robert Harris

Third Committee

Mr. Arthur Sallaway
Mr. Sidrach Simpson
Mr. Anthony Burgess
Mr. Simeon Ashe
Mr. Richard Vines
Mr. William Greenhill
** ?Dr. Thomas Temple
Mr. Thomas Gataker
Mr. William Spurstow
Mr. Francis Cheynell
Mr. John De la March
Mr. Matthew Newcomen
Mr. Thomas Carter
Mr. Thomas Hodges

Mr. Andreas Perne
Mr. Nicholas Prophet
Mr. Peter Sterry
** Mr. John Gibbon
Mr. Thomas Micklethwaite
Dr. Wincop (¶)
Mr. William Price
Mr. Henry Wilkinson (Jun.)
Mr. Francis Woodcock
Mr. Samuel De la Place
Mr. John Maynard
Mr. Henry Painter
Mr. William Good
Mr. Humphrey Hardwick

** Chairman or Convenor. For the chairmanship of the Third Committee, however, cf. *supra* p. 80, n. 27.

(¶) Could have been either Dr. John Wincop or Dr. Thomas Wincop.

APPENDIX II.

Robert Baillie's Description of the Assembly

Note. From Baillie's Letter to Spang, 7 December, 1643, *Letters and Journals,* II, pp. 107–109.

. . . The like of that Assemblie I did never see, and, as we hear say, the like was never in England, nor any where is shortlie lyke to be. They did sit in Henry the 7th's Chappell, in the place of the Convocation; but since the weather grew cold, they did go to Jerusalem chamber, a fair roome in the Abbey of Westminster, about the bounds of the Colledge fore-hall, but wyder.[1] At the one end nearest the doore, and both sydes are stages of seats as in the new Assemblie-House at Edinburgh, but not so high; for there will be roome but for five or six score. At the upmost end there is a chair set on ane frame, a foot from the earth, for the Mr. Proloqutor Dr. Twisse. Before it on the ground stands two chairs for the two Mr. Assessors, Dr. Burgess and Mr. Whyte. Before these two chairs, through the length of the roome, stands a table, at which sitts the two scribes, Mr. Byfield and Mr. Roborough. The house is all well hung, and hes a good fyre, which is some dainties at London. Foranent the table, upon the Proloqutor's right hand, there are three or four rankes of formes. On the lowest we five doe sit. Upon the other, at our backs, the members of Parliament deputed to the Assemblie. On the formes foranent us, on the Proloqutor's left hand, going from the upper end of the house to the chimney, and at the other end of the house, and backsyde of the table, till it come about to our seats, are four or five stages of fourmes, whereupon their divines sitts as they please; albeit commonlie they keep the same place. From the chimney to the door there is no seats, but a voyd for passage. The Lords of Parliament uses to sit on chaires, in that voyd, about the fire. We meet every day of the week, but Saturday. We sitt commonlie from nine to one or two afternoon. The Proloqutor at

---

[1] A. F. Mitchell pointed out that although it has sometimes been assumed that Baillie had been comparing the Jerusalem Chamber with the Hall of Glasgow College, the dimensions of that hall were completely different. He suggested that "Baillie spoke of a fore-hall or high hall which was demolished even in his own life-time, and was of different proportions." *History of the Westminster Assembly,* p. 170, note 2.

the beginning and end hes a short prayer. The man, as the world knows, is very learned in the questions he hes studied, and very good, beloved of all, and highly esteemed; but merelie bookish and not much, as it seems, acquaint with conceived prayer, [and] among the unfittest of all the company for any action; so after the prayer he sitts mute. It was the canny convoyance of these who guides most matters for their own interest to plant such a man of purpose in the chaire. The one assessour, our good friend Mr. Whyte, hes keeped in of the gout since our coming; the other, Dr. Burgess, a very active and sharpe man, supplies, so farr as is decent, the Proloqutor's place. Ordinarlie there will be present above three-score of their divines. These are divided in three Committees; in one whereof every man is a member. No man is excluded who pleases to come to any of the three. Every Committee, as the Parliament gives order in wryte to take any purpose to consideration, takes a portion, and in their afternoon meeting prepares matters for the Assemblie, setts doune their minde in distinct propositions, backs their propositions with texts of Scripture. After the prayer, Mr. Byfield the scribe, reads the proposition and Scriptures, whereupon the Assemblie debates in a most grave and orderlie way. No man is called up to speak; bot who stands up of his own accord, he speaks so long as he will without interruption. If two or three stand up at once, then the divines confusedlie calls on his name whom they desyre to hear first: On whom the loudest and maniest voices calls, he speaks. No man speaks to any bot to the Proloqutor. They harangue long and very learnedlie. They studie the questions well before hand, and prepares their speeches; but withall the men are exceeding prompt, and well spoken. I doe marvell at the very accurate and extemporall replyes that many of them usuallie doe make. When, upon every proposition by itself, and on everie text of Scripture that is brought to confirme it, every man who will hes said his whole minde, and the replyes, and duplies, and triplies, are heard; then the most part calls, To the question. Byfield the scribe rises from the table, and comes to the Proloqutor's chair, who, from the scribe's book, reads the proposition, and says, as many as are in opinion that the question is well stated in the proposition, let them say I: when I is heard, he says, as many as think otherwise, say No. If the difference of I's and No's be cleare, as usuallie it is, then the question is ordered by the scribes, and they go on to debate the first Scripture alleadged for proof of the proposition. If the sound of I and No be near equall, then sayes the Proloqutor, as many as say I, stand up; while they stand, the scribe and others number them in their minde; when they sitt down, the No's are bidden stand, and they likewise are numbered. This way is clear enough, and saves a great deal of time, which we spend in reading our catalogue. When a question is once ordered, there is no more debate of that matter; but if a man will vaige,[2] he is quicklie taken up by Mr. Assessor, or many others, confusedlie crying, Speak to order, to order. No man contradicts another expresslie by name, bot most discreetlie speaks to the Proloqutor, and at most holds on the generall, The Reverend brother, who latelie or last spoke, on this hand, on that syde, above, or below. I thought meet once for all to give yow a taste of the outward form of their Assemblie. They follow the way of their Parliament. Much of their way is good, and worthie of our imitation: only their longsomenesse is wofull at this time, when their Church and Kingdome lyes under a most lamentable anarchy and confusion. They see the hurt of their length, but cannot get it helped; for being to establish a new Plattforme of worship and discipline to their Nation for all time to come, they think they cannot be answerable, if solidlie, and at leisure, they doe not examine every point thereof.

---

[2] I.e., wander from the subject.

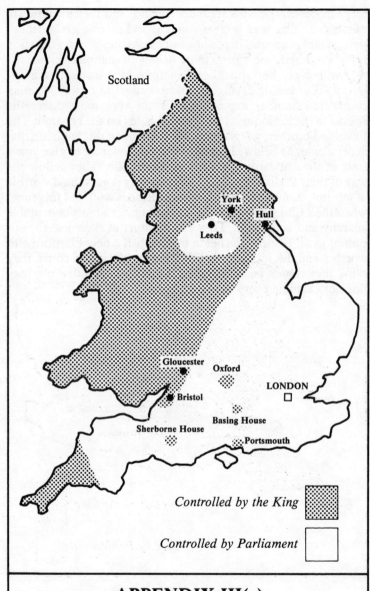

Scotland

York
Hull
Leeds

Gloucester
Oxford
LONDON
Bristol
Basing House
Sherborne House
Portsmouth

Controlled by the King

Controlled by Parliament

APPENDIX III(a)

ENGLAND AT THE OUTBREAK
OF THE CIVIL WAR

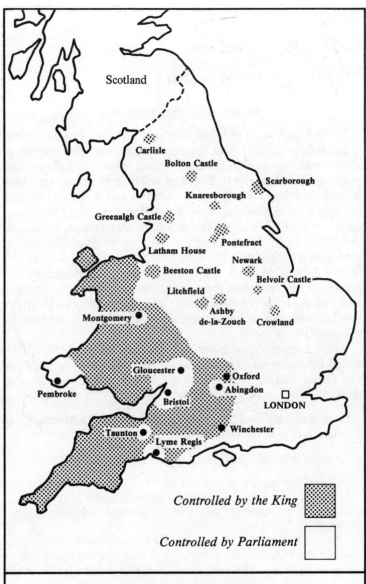

Scotland

Carlisle

Bolton Castle

Scarborough

Knaresborough

Greenalgh Castle

Pontefract

Latham House

Newark

Beeston Castle

Belvoir Castle

Litchfield

Montgomery

Ashby
de-la-Zouch   Crowland

Gloucester   Oxford
                    Abingdon

Pembroke   LONDON

Bristol

Taunton   Winchester
       Lyme Regis

Controlled by the King

Controlled by Parliament

APPENDIX III(b)
ENGLAND AT THE END OF
NOVEMBER 1644

APPENDIX IV.

Interpreting the 'Minutes'

In the scanty and obviously hurried notes that we know as the 'Minutes', punctuation is almost non-existent, and the use of abbreviations and capitalization is erratic at best. For all practical purposes the transcript by E. Maunde Thompson is the only help we have in trying to decipher the debates, and he did not attempt to supply punctuation or to make radical changes at that juncture, but kept faithfully to the text in the manuscript. Because of the difficulties of interpreting the text accurately, and because of the varying meanings that can be read into the notes we have, we have followed Maunde Thompson's method throughout the present work: we retain the original spelling and capitalization, and we have supplied punctuation and other additions in square brackets only when they appear to be essential to make sense of the text.[1]

There is an interesting passage recorded for May 13th, 1644, which throws some light on the way the Minutes were written. Dr. Gouge had said that the propositions were "in the Scribes bookes", but Gataker replied:

> "ther is nothing upon record but the resolves of the Assembly, not whatsoever is in the scribes bookes[.]"

Stephen Marshall also pointed out that

> "all our discourses are recorded by
> the scribes soe farre as their pens can reach them[,]
> but [these accounts are] not to be taken as the Judgment of the
> assembly[.]"[2]

The form in which the notes appear may help us in the task of interpretation, for although there was not much system to the

---

[1] Robert Norris, in 'The Thirty-Nine Articles at the Westminster Assembly', introduced his own punctuation and capitalization. In view of the problems involved, we have not done this in the present work, but we have felt that as far as possible readers should be able to judge the interpretation given by the text itself.

[2] TMs. II. 102 (Ms. II. f. 53.)

scribe's original method, he does seem to have adopted some unconscious conventions in style.

1. Paragraphs usually indicate a new step in the argument, and often this was indicated by a penstroke.

2. Where there are obvious gaps, or where an argument is left incomplete and space left at the end, the scribe may have intended to add fuller notes after the debate, either after consultation with his colleague or from the notes of the speaker.

3. Whenever a new line in the notes does not follow the sense of the one that preceded it, it usually begins a new sentence, and this is often a sentence that is more or less in apposition to the thought it follows – as if the previous idea had been concluded with a colon, and the new idea introduced by 'e.g.', 'i.e.' or some similar connecting phrase.

4. When the words 'for yt' (for that) introduce a new stage in the argument, it usually means that the speaker is about to comment (often in rebuttal) on something that has just been propounded by an earlier speaker. The words are therefore the equivalent of a phrase such as 'As for that question of. . . .'

Two examples may help to illustrate some of these points.

(1) In the debate on February 26th, 1643/4, we would read Lazarus Seaman's response to the Independents' earlier argument in this way:

"[As] for that [matter] of love feasts[, it is] true the apostell did reiect them de futuro, but it proves that for the time past their love feasts ware in their publique meetings[:]
when they had their common nourishment[,] ther they
had their sacrament[.][3]

(2) The second example illustrates how the scantiness of the Minutes can affect (or be affected by) one's interpretation of the issues. On October 19th, 1643, Cornelius Burgess had reported how the Assembly's Committee on Antinomianism had been received by the House of Commons, and he then moved on to address the matter of ordination which was under consideration. His speech may be interpreted like this:

"[Now as to] the thing in question, [which must be] a pro-

[3] TMs. I. 661 (Ms. I. f. 342b.)

vision against blind guid[e]s, [being] admitt[ed] into
the ministry[,]
[and] to provide for [the regular] institution [of the ministry:–]

[Regarding] Institution and Ordination[:]
I durst not presume to offer anything positively in this businesse[,]
[but] ther hath been [times] when bishops are standing [in]
a presbytery to ordaine presbiters[,] as some [scholars] counsell[.]
[But] what if here in London ther might be something in the
nature of a presbytery[?]

[–So] some members of this Assembly, [might join with]
some other grave and godly ministers[:]
[I.e.] for ordaining of ministers and giving of [regular]
Institution [. But if this is not desired,] either discharge
me or give me your further instructions[.][4]

That reading makes connected sense of Burgess's speech, but
we cannot be certain that it is true to what he actually said,
because a great deal will depend on how far the reader feels
Burgess was already prepared to go to establish the presbyterian
system. A great deal, for example, could depend on whether we
hear him speaking of ordaining bishops as 'standing *in* (or *with*) a
presbytery' or of ordaining bishops 'standing *as* a presbytery',
and there is little apart from one's own decisions about Burgess's
churchmanship at that time to indicate which would be the
proper reading.

This simply illustrates the problem of interpretation that persists in the Minutes, and the need for a great deal more work to be
done in that area.

---

[4] TMs. I. 231f. (Ms. I. ff. 116b–117.)

APPENDIX V.

'Independent' and 'Presbyterian' as Political Terms

It has been pointed out that 'Independent' and 'Presbyterian', can be applied to the two major parties in Parliament only with very great care, since we cannot assume that the supporters of either were automatically consistent adherents to the ecclesiologies that bear those names in the Westminster Assembly.[1] The complexity of this issue is another of those places in history where denominational partisanship would have benefited from the cool correctives of the secular historians, for since J. H. Hexter began in 1938 to undermine the too-facile identification of political Independency with its ecclesiastical counterpart in the Assembly,[2] the matter has received a great deal of attention. Hexter pointed out that of the two hundred Members of Parliament who seem to have the best claim to be regarded as political 'Independents' by reason of their political activities, no less than thirty-nine had also been Presbyterian elders, and he went on to show that a significant number of those who supported the 'Presbyterian' party in Parliament were apparently neither Presbyterian nor Independent in the ecclesiastical sense. "We thus emerge from our investigation", he observed, "with 'Independents' who were not Independents adhering in a larger proportion than 'Presbyterians' who were not Presbyterian to a 'Presbyterian Church' that was not really Presbyterian." He admitted that this conclusion appeared to be simply destructive, and that it still leaves us with the anomaly of how the ecclesiastical and the political parties were actually related.[3] The issue was well canvassed in a series of important monographs and articles that began with George Yule's book, *The Independents in the English Civil War*,[4] and came to a head in

---

[1] E.g., John F. Wilson, *Pulpit in Parliament*, pp. 106f, note 25.

[2] 'The Problem of the Presbyterian Independents', *The American Historical Review*, XLIV (October 1938), pp. 29–49.

[3] *Ibid.* p. 42.

[4] Cambridge University Press, 1958. See also, David Underdown, 'The Independents Reconsidered', *Journal of British Studies*, III. No. 2 (May 1964) pp. 57–84; Valerie Pearl, 'The "Royal Independents" in the English Civil War', *Transactions of the Royal Historical Society* (5th Series) 18, 1968, pp. 69–96; George Yule, 'Independents and Revolutionaries', *Journal of B. S.* VII, No. 2 (May 1968), pp. 11–32; David Underdown, 'The Independents Again', *Journal of B. S.* VIII, No. 1 (November 1968), pp. 83–93.

Stephen Foster's criticism of the Hexter thesis[5] and the response it stimulated.[6] The result of this debate led, in the view of one recent church historian, "to seemingly endless confusion among the historians and should be abandoned."[7]

It is difficult to see how any continuing historical anomaly can ever be abandoned by historians, and perhaps there is confusion only for those who expect or desire the neat, precise identification of churchmanship with political parties as it was assumed by most of the earlier writers. The debate also tends to support the contention that runs through our present study, that the greater number of parliamentary supporters entered the struggle with Charles without any clear ideas on ecclesiastical polity, except for certain features in the existing Establishment that they were determined to avoid. As Hexter observed, "The minimum of reform acceptable to all Puritans involved the abolition of ritualism and drastic revision of the prayer book, the reaffirmation of pure Calvinist doctrine, an increased emphasis on the preaching of the Word, radical alterations in the existing church government, and the embodiment of these reforms in a unified national church. Probably the aspirations of the bulk of Puritan commoners were no more specific than this."[8] We have to agree that in view of the exigencies of the political situation, 'the average Puritan Commoner' did not have the luxury of choosing between ideal Presbyterianism and ideal Independency and had "to pick his way among an infinite variety of grays – shifting, unstable, uncertain."[9] Their support for what became political Independency or Presbyterianism was inevitably more likely to be influenced by the political policies of the two parties than by their own serious consideration of the ecclesiological issues.

However, they *were* related. There seems to be a general agreement that we cannot entirely jettison Puritanism as one of the major causes of the seventeenth century struggle;[10] and if it remains as a factor, then because of the rival view of theological authority, we cannot dismiss the ecclesiological issues as irrelevant, although the points at which they intersect with politics are

---

[5] 'The Presbyterian Independents Exorcised. A Ghost Story for Historians', *Past and Present*, Vol. 44 (August 1969), pp. 52–75.

[6] Cf. the symposium in which Blair Worden, Valerie Pearl, David Underdown, George Yule and J. H. Hexter contributed, together with a reply from Stephen Foster, *Past and Present*, Vol. 47 (May 1970), pp. 116–146.

[7] Michael Watts, *The Dissenters*, p. 108.

[8] 'The Problem of the Presbyterian Independents', p. 43.

[9] *Ibid.* p. 46.

[10] Cf. the articles by J. H. Hexter and Lawrence Stone in the *Journal of B. S.* VIII, No. 1 (November 1968).

nowhere nearly as precise as earlier historians thought them to be. We must accept Yule's modification of his earlier conclusions when he declares that in view of the debate about the political 'Independents', "a religious split *simpliciter* just will not do",[11] but the problem of the interrelationship persists, so that, as Hexter remarked, "a member might start to examine his belief on the proper organization of the church and end by examining his belief on the proper organization of the state. Or he might start with the state and end with the church."[12] The problem remains of trying to understand the interrelationship between social and political imperatives that face the Puritans, and their insistence on biblical precedent "which forced them," as Yule noted, "often against their inclination, to take up a positive attitude to the schemes of church government brought forward by the divines." It is certainly true that "having overthrown prelacy, the parliamentarians could not dodge the issue of church government."[13]

It is rather like Max Weber's thesis about the relationship of Protestantism and Capitalism – it is difficult to make specific, and yet we sense there is something there. To determine exactly the churchmanship of the politicians, or to tie any one of them to ecclesiastical Independency, may be almost impossible, since apart from Sir Henry Vane's experience in Massachusetts, none of them had much chance of joining an Independent church before the outbreak of war, although I am not sure the later possibilities have been adequately recognized.[14] However, despite the lack of conclusive evidence, we sense that there was a real connection between the political and the ecclesiastical wings of the parties, perhaps for the most obvious and mundane reason that it is difficult to see how the sobriquets 'Independent' and 'Presbyterian' could have stuck to certain people if there had been no connection at all. Just as Cromwell became known as 'the Great Independent', so the party that was eventually led by Sir Henry Vane and Oliver St. John became known as 'Independent' and worked in close relationship with the Dissenting Brethren of the Westminster Assembly. The names were forged in the heat of ecclesiastical battle, but they were thrown at certain politicians, and they stuck.

---

[11] 'Presbyterians and Independents: Some Comments', *Past and Present* 47 (May 1970) p. 132.

[12] Hexter, *op. cit.* p. 47.

[13] 'Presbyterians and Independents: Some Comments', p. 133.

[14] E.g. I have indicated earlier that the question of Cromwell's church allegiance may have been brushed aside too cavalierly. Cf. *supra* pp. 49f., n. 97.

It appears that the political parties began to take their form in the events of 1644. J. H. Hexter pointed out that during that year the 'godly party', which seems to have had the confidence of the Scots and included all the more rigorous Puritans of whatever stripe, set out "to harrass the moderates and discredit the earl" (Essex), and that they "attained their latter objective" when Essex's army surrendered at Lostwithiel. "Immediately thereafter," he went on to observe, "toward the end of 1644, the 'godly party' was torn asunder."[15] This conclusion seems to be strikingly endorsed by our own studies of what was happening in the Assembly.

Such a reading of the year in which most of 'the Grand Debate' took place would explain a great deal that is obscure in that crucial period – the early cooperation between the Scots Commissioners and the Independents, the concern to prevent too precipitate a break between them, the use the Scots made of the Puritan majority, their dismay at the duplicity of Vane and St. John, and the repeated attempts to reach an accommodation. This all happened in 1644, and we suggest that in considering the reasons for the development of the two political parties, the events that produced *An Apologeticall Narration* and the subsequent debates on church polity should not be ignored. It may still be difficult to document exactly the relationship between religion and politics in those pre-Enlightenment days, but that relationship is still vital to our understanding of that century and the people involved in it.

---

[15] 'The Problem of the Presbyterian Independents', pp. 42–43.

APPENDIX VI.

Two Scots Pamphlets of 1643/4

Two pieces of writing from the pen of the Scots Commissioners have sometimes been associated with the appearance of *An Apologeticall Narration* in early 1643/4.

A. Recently Robert Norris wrote that "on Christmas day Alexander Henderson, in a sermon to Parliament, felt himself strong enough to assert that there could be no place for an accommodation with the Independents within the National Establishment", and he added that "This action by the Presbyterians led to the publication by the Independents of the 'Apologeticall Narration' on December 30th." ['The Thirty-Nine Articles and the Westminster Assembly', p. xxix.]

I find no evidence that Henderson preached on Christmas Day – the Scots had managed to persuade the politicians to work on that day – but he did preach to the House of Commons at the regular Fast on December 27th, and we presume this is the sermon to which Norris refers. It was later published, and we believe a summary will show that it was not likely to have triggered the publication of *An Apologeticall Narration*.

B. As mentioned earlier (*supra* pp. 220f), William Haller thought the Scots Commissioners' pamphlet, *Reformation of Church-Government in Scotland, Cleered from some mistakes and Prejudices*, was a modest reply to the Independents' *An Apologeticall Narration*.

Again, a summary is provided, and we believe it will show that it is not possible to state that categorically. The evidence could equally go the other way – the Scots pamphlet could have stimulated the Independent apologia.

A.

Summary of 'A Sermon preached to the Honourable House of Commons, At their late solemne fast, Wednesday, December 27th, 1643.
By Alexander Henderson, Minister at Edenbrugh (1644)

The sermon was based on the text: 'Whatsoever is commanded by the God of heaven, let it be diligently done, for the house of the God of heaven; for why should there be wrath against the Realme of the King and his Sonnes', Ezra 7:23. It followed fairly closely a pattern of Plain Style preaching, beginning with a careful 'opening' of the text, a division of the text into its parts, and then the extrapolation of the Uses.[1]

Henderson began with examples of how God works differently in people – so he dealt very differently with Nebuchadnezar, Balaam, Caiaphas, Paul, Laban, Judas and Herod.

In dividing the text he declared that it was concerned first with God's wrath as it might be declared against the King, the Kingdom and the King's sons; secondly, the requirement that "whatsoever is commanded by the God of heaven, let it be diligently done, for the house of the God of heaven", and thirdly that this divine threat is conditional: *why* should there be judgment if what God commanded was diligently accomplished? (p. 4).

Developing this theme, he said "Amongst all the great things which the honourable Houses of Parliament have done, there is none more acceptable to God, or more promiseth peace and happinesse to this Land, then that a Church-assembly is called, for searching into the will of the God of Heaven, *that whatsoever is commanded by him may be diligently done*"; and in illustration of their diligence he instanced, "First, Your frequent and continued fasting and humiliation. Secondly, Your entring into a solemne Covenant with God for obtaining mercy. Thirdly, Your begun Reformation, and the course You have taken for perfecting the same." The main thrust of his sermon was summarized in the comment, "If these three be performed in truth, You may expect a blessing: True humiliation, Covenanting with God, and Reformation, are the Harbingers of peace and happinesse: But when they are not in truth, the hypocrisie threatneth more then the performance promiseth." (p. 5).

The breadth of God's dealings was that it involved not only the king but the whole kingdom, and the length was indicated in that it extended to the king's posterity. (p. 6). He applied the threat

---

[1] The 'doctrines' were missing.

of judgment first to the wicked, and then to the godly, whom it should "stirre up in themselves their zeal and just indignation against false worship, and the contempt of the true worship of his name." (p. 9). He charged his congregation to note that the wrath of God extends to both king and kingdom: "It is a miserable debate betwixt a King and a people, when in the time of a publike judgement, both of them stand to their owne innocency, and the one accuseth the other of guiltinesse: But it is a sweet contest and promiseth much mercy and comfort: when the Prince saith; I have sinned and done wickedly, but what hath the people done? and when the people say, we have sinned and done wickedly, and thereby drawne wrath upon our selves." (pp. 11–12).

He charged his hearers that England had not pursued reformation in the church with the earnestness it should have had: "yee have been for the greater part more pleased with things which were not reformed, then the things which were reformed in the worship of God; and this sinne hath beene the cause of many other sinnes, for where God is not served aright, all other duties are but neglected or performed without sincerity." (p 12)[2]

God's judgment also embraced not only the kingdom but the king's posterity: "The greater the persons be, the more grievous in the justice of God is the punishment; because the sinnes of great ones are not onely sinnes, but examples of sinning, and proclamations of liberty to inferiours". (p.13).

So he came to the uses he would draw from the text. His hearers should remember the former sins of their country (p. 15), for "there is nothing more necessary, nothing we should desire more earnestly to know, then by what means this great wrath of the great God may be prevented where it is imminent & feared, or averted wher it is incumbent and felt". (p. 16). Three measures were to be taken to avoid that judgment – first, "publick fasting and solemne humiliation joyned with Confession of sin"; secondly, "a solemne Covenant"; and thirdly (which was the burden of his discourse) "the doing of the work of God; the building of the Temple, the reformation of Religion, the ordring of the worship & service of God". "Their fasting and praying was not sufficient, they behoved to enter into Covenant. Their praying and Covenanting was not enough, nor were they to rest there. They behoved to build and reforme." (p. 17).

Still more needed to be done. With respect to public penitence

---

[2] It should be noted that his criticisms were directed against the incompleteness of reformation in the Church of England to that point.

for national sins, he was afraid "that a great part of the people of the Land are not yet brought to this Confession, but are still fond of a formall Service, and a proud Prelacie; and therefore as ye are your selves in humilitie to acknowledge this sin as high provocation, so would all good meanes be used for bringing the people to the sight and sense of it."[3] The Lord also required "a more direct, open and plain confession" of the Covenant (p. 18). Henderson then stressed the third step, which was his primary concern, and without which, he insisted "the former two are not sufficient: And this is, *Whatsoever is commanded by the God of heaven, be diligently done for the house of the God of heaven*: A dutie which in it self is necessary, and which to us who live under the Gospel, is no other thing, but the reformation and setling of Religion." (p. 19). This was the theme of the last part of his sermon, and the major point that he wanted to impress on his congregation.

Civil magistrates had special responsibility in the matter of religion (p. 20) – they were to defend it from attack, support its authority, and they "also may and ought to call Assemblies of the Church, when the case of Religion doth require, praeside as Civill Presidents, and examine Church-Constitutions, not onely as they are Christians for satisfying their own souls, but as Magistrates for the good of the people." But in the exercise of these powers "they are to do nothing but according to the Commandment of God", (p. 21) for the extent of reformation was to be "*Whatsoever God hath commanded.*" Therefore it must be a "through[4] and perfect reformation", (p. 22) because God is not honoured by half-measures. (p. 23).

To the English parliamentarians he declared that "No Nation under the Sun hath more need to take heed of this then England" (p. 24), because the English Reformation had not been a thorough reformation. They had another chance to accomplish this necessary reform, and the work should be done diligently, zealously, prudently, speedily and constantly (p. 26). Two reasons should provoke them to this duty – first, the greatness and majesty of the God they served (pp. 26–29), and secondly, recognition that "the Church of Christ is the House of the Living God": God is present in the Church and therefore his rule should be established. (p. 29). Such considerations could cure two evils

---

[3] Here Henderson frankly recognized the conservative tendencies of the English people that preferred the Prayer Book and the episcopal order of the former Establishment.

[4] I.e., thorough.

afflicting the country – the denial that the Law of God was Christian, and will-worship.

Henderson was candid in his criticisms. No kingdom anywhere, he said, had a greater need to take warning than England, and his reasons offer an interesting insight into the changes that the Scots hoped would take place in England. First, the English church had been plagued with superstitions and superfluous ceremonies, and secondly, the Sabbath had been profaned. His third reason is of particular interest in view of the holiday season in which this sermon was preached: he said, "God hath called this Land to mourning and fasting, as we professe this day, and I pray God that the unseasonable keeping of this festivitie. . . . be not more prevalent for evil, then the humiliation of this day for good; and yet", he admitted, "the keeping of this day of humiliation in such a time of festivitie, is a presage that by the blessing of God upon the proceedings of the Honourable Houses of Parliament and Assembly, this superstition shall shortly expire, and that it is now at the last gaspe." (p. 31)[5]

The interrogative form of the warning in the text showed that God's judgment was conditional: his wrath would not necessarily fall, and he suggested "it is a speciall wisdom in these that have place and power, to prevent or turn away the wrath of God from the present and future generation by establishing true Religion, and ordering the house of God aright. I confesse it is a higher point of wisdom to have a care of Religion . . . and thereby to prevent everlasting wrath", (p. 32) and he cited several biblical examples.

Religion provided "the touchstone" of who were the real "Malignants and Enemies to the peace and prosperity of the Kingdome", (p. 34) and he declared, "I must therefore take the boldnesse according to the charge and trust committed unto me at this time, in the name of God to exhort, & in the bowels of Jesus Christ to intreat, that the house of God be diligently looked unto, and that first of all, Religion be reformed and setled." Therefore "all men ought to bend themselves to the setling thereof by all good and lawful means, Nor must yee in this work linger or delay upon any consent or concurrence whatsoever: It is true, where matters are darke or doubtfull, yee should seek for light and resolution, and yee have to that end a learned and godly

---

[5] It will be remembered that Baillie had been unsuccessful in his attempt to persuade the Assembly to supress Christmas at that time, but that the Scots had managed to get Parliament "to profane that holy day". For Scotland, January 1st, 1643/4, *Letters and Journals* II. 120; cf. *supra* pp. 189f.

Assembly, but where matters are clear & manifest, if yee lye still waiting for the consent of others, yee are like to lose both the oppertunity and the thing it selfe, as many have done, and repented themselves too late." (pp. 35–36). In some things we must be "subject to God alone, and in things of this kind, we are not to wait for counsell or consent from others."[6] In the time of Ezra and Nehemiah the people of God wrought for the re-building of Jerusalem with one hand while holding weapons to defend it in the other. "In this posture I leave you," he con-cluded, until God's house was complete, "& your swords be turned into plough-shares, and your speares into pruning-hooks; that is, till truth and peace be established in your borders. The Zeale of the Lord of Hosts will perform it: To him be praise for ever, Amen." (p. 36).

* * * *

Such was Henderson's sermon in the Christmas season of 1643. There was nothing in it with which any Independent could not have agreed wholeheartedly, and therefore we cannot think that it was the immediate cause of *An Apologeticall Narration*.

The sermon was a straightforward plea for Parliament to push forward the reform of the Church of England, as Henderson made clear in his preface 'To the Reader' when the sermon was published in 1644.[7] By that time he had also included in this preface a protest against "the present Epidemicall disease of this Land, which threatneth changes & Armies of sorrowes; so it pleaseth the Lord to give more then a taste of the bitter fruits of bad Church-government and a sad representation of the face of the Kingdom, if every man should be left to preach, professe and print what he will."

But that was later, and at the time when the sermon was delivered, Henderson's primary concern was to get church gov-ernment settled as speedily as possible, and his main criticisms were not levelled at the Independents but at the conservative preferences of the English population that still liked the old rituals, enjoyed playing games on Sundays, and persisted in celebrating Christmas as a feast!

---

[6] This oblique reference could possibly mean the concurrence of the Independents; but if it is read carefully, particularly the passage that reminds them that they were 'subject' to God alone, it is more likely to have been directed against the politicians' attempt to win the agreement of the King.

[7] "The desire & endevor of the Preacher was, according to the scope and nature of the Text, to shew, that after so often renued and long continued humiliation; and after solemne entring into Covenant with the most high God, The true reformation of Religion, is the readiest meane to turne away the still pressing wrath of God from the Kingdome . . ."

B.

Summary of 'Reformation of Church-Government in Scotland, Cleered from some mistakes and Prejudices,' 1644

The authors had been sent into England for public employment, and they were waiting patiently for the Reformation of religion "so much desired by all the godly in the three Kingdomes". They had found it necessary to respond to the prejudices of those who were afraid of something about which they had no direct knowledge (p. 1), and to the aspersions of those advancing their own views to the disparagement of the Reformed churches. Therefore they bore testimony to "the order and government of the reformed Churches, and particularly of the Church of *Scotland*"., and also to honour those whose work had been honoured by God in the salvation of so many souls and in the suppresssion of "a world of corruptions, heresies and Scismes, by his wonderful blessing upon their order and Government." They wished to give offence to none, "to unite and not to divide, to compose rather than to create differences; which we conceive to be one principall end, of the calling of the Assembly of Divines, and which all members of the Assembly, against all particular interests, are after a speciall manner ingaged, to aime at and endeavour." (p. 2).

"The order and Government of the reformed Churches in the beauty and strength thereof" was not hidden, but was clear to all nations, and it had obviously been blessed by God "with the preservation of the truth and unity of Religion against Heresies and errours in Doctrine, Idolatry and corruptions in worship, and all sorts of sects and schismes, wherewith it hath been continually assaulted". (p. 3). The instruments of this reformation in Scotland had been extraordinary men, some of whom had been martyred,[8] and as the result of their labours "there was to be seen a representation of the Primitive and Apostolicke times and a new resurrection from the dead." The Scots Reformers had been followed by others of similar spirit, "mighty in converting of soules, walking in the same way, and who communicated their Counsels & and kept correspondence with Divines of other nations, and with the greatest and purest lights in the Church of

---

[8] It was a reminder that Scotland too had suffered in its struggle against the threat of prelacy. Cf. *Ap. Narration*, p. 5.

England, in the point of Reformation and setling of Church-government." (p. 4)[9]

They claimed that none could have been further from "partiality and prejudice in the matters of God, then their wayes witnesse them to have been", and the writers claimed precisely the same biblical authority for their system as the Dissenting Brethren made for their own. "They had no other rule and patterne of Reformation, but the word of God, and the practice of the Apostolicke Churches in the Word."[10] All the books of God are perfect, the book of life, the book of nature, the book of providence, and especially the book of scripture, "which was dyted by the Holy Ghost to be a perfect directory to all the Churches unto the second comming of Jesus Christ". However, it presupposed the exercise of common prudence, first in the need to temper action with the immediate possibilities of the situation, and secondly to recognize that "when the change is not to the better, it is both without and against reason to make a change". (pp. 5–6)[11]

However, what the Scots reformers "had once received, not upon probable grounds in way of conjecture, but upon the warrent of the word, and by the teaching of the spirit with certainty of faith, that they resolved to hold fast and did hate every false way contrary unto it." They did not, like Arminians and Socinians, maintain a sceptical attitude, which is "an open door to all heresies and schismes to enter by," although because nobody can attain to full assurance of faith in religious matters, the believer "should always have his mind open & ready to receive more light from the word and Spirit of God". (p. 6)[12] They declared "we are most willing to heare and learne from the word of God, what needeth to bee reformed in the Church of Scotland: Yet God forbid, that we should never come to any certainty of perswasion, or that we should ever be learning, and never come to the knowledge of the truth; we ought to be resolute and unmoveable in so far as we have attained". (p. 7).

---

[9] The Scots continually emphasized their unity with all other Reformed churches in Europe, and extended this claim to their church government.

[10] One of the places where the writers might be interpreted as answering the claims of the Independents (cf. *Ap. Narration*, pp. 9f.;) or *vice versa*.

[11] These comments seem to be directed more towards assuaging the fears of the English conservatives than to answering the Independents.

[12] The writers almost quote John Robinson here. Cf. Winslow's account of Robinson's sermon at the departure of the Pilgrims: "he charged us before God and his blessed Angels . . . if God should reveal any thing to us by any other instrument of his, to be as ready to receive it, as ever we were to any truth by his Ministry: For he was very confident the Lord had *more truth and light yet to breake forth out of his holy Word*." My italics. *Hypocrisie Unmasked*, p. 97.

The Scots reformers honoured Luther and Calvin, but the writers protested that "for this to call us *Calvinians* & the reformed Churches, *Calvinian reformed churches*, is to disgrace the true Churches of Christ", and to do what the papists did when they assumed the name Catholic for themselves and condemned as Antichristian all who are called by particular names of men. Brownists and Anabaptists might properly be known by their distinguishing names, but those who recognize the danger in such names "ought not to appropriate unto their own opinion, that which is common to al the reformed Churches, nor to joyne with Papists in giving names of Sects unto the reformed Churches". (p. 9)[13] If differences should be noted, then "charity commands the mildest names, such as hint most clearly at the difference and are farrest from reproach".

Nothing could be further from the mind of the Scots than to make their ecclesiastical provisions conform to any form of civil government,[14] for their spiritual forefathers had looked "with singleness of mind to the rule of Scripture", and the writers instanced the grave problems their reformers faced from civil authorities because of their faithfulness to the biblical norm. The Scottish reformers had been educated in other churches where they had experienced reformation in the church (p. 10) and received help from other reformers. The writers were grateful for their own education in the Scottish Church, and were thus "acquainted with the practice of Church-government there, which giveth us much light and confidence against such scruples and doubtings as are powerfull enough to suspend the assent of others, who . . . are strangers unto it."

Their reformers had "intended & designed from the beginning, the government of the Church by Assemblies and Pres-

---

[13] The Apologists had declared "we do professedly judge the *Calvinian* Reformed Churches of the first reformation from out of Popery, to stand in need of a further reformation themselves; And it may without prejudice to them, or the imputation of Schisme in us from them, be thought, that they comming new out of Popery (as well as *England*) and the founders of that reformation not having *Apostolique infallibility*, might not be fully perfect the first day." *Op. cit.* p. 22. But who responded to whom? Is this a direct reaction to this single reference in *An Apologeticall Narration*, or is it reaction to a slur that they had heard often enough, and particularly, perhaps, from some radical preachers?

[14] Here the writers hit on another Independent claim in *An Apologeticall Narration*: "We had no new Common-wealths to rear, to frame Church-government unto, whereof any one piece might stand in the others light, to cause the least variation by us from the Primitive pattern; We had no State-ends or Politicall interests to comply with; No Kingdoms in our eye to subdue unto our mould. . . . We had nothing else to doe but simply and singly to consider how to worship God acceptably, and so most according to his word." *Op. cit.* pp. 3–4.

byteries, although they could not attain that perfection at first in the infancy of reformation, but gave place to necessity," and they claimed that in this they had simply followed the route taken by the apostolic churches, for "if not at first" yet eventually they were governed by a plurality of pastors and teachers in a presbytery. (pp. 11–12)[15] They also established Pastors, Teachers, ruling Elders and Deacons as the officers of the Church, and they did not allow lay people to preach.

The honour that reformed churches gave to civil magistrates was known to all. They held that there should be no fundamental opposition of church to state, but they judged both "by the word, & therefore deny not unto the Magistrate what God giveth them; and more then this, dare we not professe for any respect to our selves, or to the forme of Ecclesiasticall governement professed by us". The Scottish reformers had been fortunate in that while most of the energies of the English reformers had been "for the greater part taken up with Doctrine", (pp. 13–14) in the Church of Scotland doctrine had been readily established and they had been able to concentrate on the church and its discipline. So their way "lay in the middle betwixt Episcopacy upon the one hand, & popular confusion on the other."[16] The Church of England was a true church, but it was blemished. (p. 14) The writers were "neither so ignorant nor so arrogant, as to ascribe to the Church of *Scotland* such absolute purity and perfection, as hath not need or canot admit of further Reformation", but there was a considerable difference between the two churches. They cited the English Puritans, Thomas Brightman and Thomas Cartwright, in their favour. (p. 15).

The Church of Scotland forbade those who were ignorant or unworthy to partake of the Lord's Supper, and those who had removed themselves to New England might quite happily have settled in Scotland. The need of the church earlier had been to protest against prelacy, but now the danger was from the oppo-

---

[15] This passage might possibly be interpreted as a response to what the Apologists said about the church at Jerusalem (*Ap. Narr.* pp. 13f.) but might just as easily be interpreted in the opposite way – i.e., that what was said by the Apologists about the church at Jerusalem had been a response to what the Scottish Commissioners were saying here. Perhaps each group of writers was simply responding to what was common knowledge about the views of their opponents.

[16] This is another ambiguous place where the writers of either pamphlet could be reacting to the other, because in repudiating the name and polity of Brownism, the Apologists had declared, "And wee did then, and doe here publiquely professe, we beleeve the truth to lye and consist in a *middle way* betwixt that which is falsely charged on us, *Brownisme*; and that which is the contention of these times, the *authoritative Presbyteriall Government* in all the subordinations and proceedings of it." *Op. cit.* p. 24.

site view of the church, "Brounisticall and popular Anarchie". (p. 17). Two National Synods in France had illustrated the issue, and had determined "that where a whole Nation is converted to the Christian faith, every particular Church is not to be left to it selfe". (p. 18).

They recalled the persecutions suffered by their countrymen for the sake of church government (p. 19) and proper discipline. In common with other properly reformed churches, the Church of Scotland exercised the power of the Keys "with such sharpnesse, and severitie, and yet with such caution, and moderation; as it hath been very powerfull and effectuall to preserve the Name of God from being blasphemed, the Church and people of God from contagion, and the Delinquents brought under censure, from destruction". (p. 20)[17] To limit censure to those who contravened general standards of morality and "the common and universall practices of Christianitie" was an Arminian and Socinian error and "openeth a wide dore".

Two main objections to their polity were heard. It was first argued that there is no need for the authoritative power of presbyteries and synods, but that withdrawal of Communion would be sufficient. (p. 21).[18] The writers responded that excommunication against a whole congregation had never been exercised in Scotland, and indeed it was never heard of except among the Separatist churches. They argued that a presbytery was necessary to mediate between different congregations, and that the practice of withdrawal and non-communion was no more than any private individual might do. (p. 22). They urged that their own system provided a remedy when civil magistrates neglected their duty to the church, and that there could not be as much effective authority in simply withdrawing from the errant (p. 23).

The second major objection to authoritative presbyterianism was that in it, "one Church hath power over another, which is contrarie to that libertie and equalitie Christ hath endewed his Churches with, and is no other but a new Prelaticall dominion over the Churches of Christ." To this the writers replied that (1) they were far from wanting to destroy the proper equality of particular congregations, but that the power they maintained "is aggregative of the Officers of many congregations over the par-

---

[17] Here the writers were toeing a very narrow line – they wanted to show their church to be sufficiently rigorous not to need further reformation in the name of purity, but not so severe that they alienated the English moderates.

[18] Cf. *An Apologeticall Narration*, pp. 16–22. Again we have to ask, was this passage a direct response to the Apologists, or was it simply in response to their known views?

ticular members of their Corporation. . . . All the Reformed Churches acknowledge the Independencie of one particular Church upon another." (p. 24) (2) They declared that it is "as miserable a mistake to compare Presbyteries and Prelates together", because the prelatical courts were totally unrelated to the churches they ruled. The power of presbyteries "is intrinsecall and naturall, they being constitute of the Pastors and Elders of the particular congregations over which they are set". It was a collegial system, since "they neither ordaine nor depose Ministers, they discern no censure nor sentence of Excommunication of any Member without the knowledge and consent of the congregation which is particularly concerned therein". The Ministry and local Eldership "are advised, assisted, and strengthened rather then commanded, enjoyned, or forced". (p. 25).

What they had presented was offered "not for confutation; but meerely for justifying our owne, and other Reformed Churches against such misrepresentings & mistakings", and they threw a broad hint in the direction of the grandees in Parliament: "Were Magistrates and civill powers acquainted with the power thereof, they would finde their authoritie increased, their work more easie, and their places more comfortable thereby." They ended with a comment that could have bearing on the Apologists' appeal for toleration at the end of their own pamphlet, when they said that "such as are most adverse to this order and government (if they allow no materiall difference in doctrine, worship, or practise) might enjoy their peace, and all the comforts of their Ministry, and profession under it, without controlment, from that authoritative power which they so much apprehend." (p. 26).

* * * * *

Where does this pamphlet fit into the course of events in early 1643? Was it the moderate reply from the Scots Commissioners to *An Apologeticall Narration* as Haller suggested,[19] or was it an apologia of their own that stimulated the Independents to publish the work that Baillie knew had "long lyen readie beside them"? Was it the reply that Baillie promised William Spang "ye will hear ere long in print", or something issued earlier?[20]

A good case could be made either way. There are references in this booklet to matters discussed in *An Apologeticall Narration* – even phrases and expressions that appear similar – but none of

---

[19] Cf. *supra* pp. 220f.
[20] *Letters and Journals*. II. 130.

them is so precise that it could not have been taken out of what was already known of the Independents' position from writings and recent sermons, from Baillie's intelligence network, and from what was already known of the pamphlet that everyone recognized had been ready for print for some time.

What makes it difficult to see this work as a direct reply to *An Apologeticall Narration* is precisely its moderation. In view of the reaction that little work stirred up among people like Robert Baillie, Thomas Edwards and the London ministers, this would have been a masterpiece of Christian restraint if the Apologists' work had already appeared; and in addition, in light of the normal method of rebuttal taken by seventeenth century authors – of which Thomas Edwards' *Antapologia* became an excellent example – we wonder why the undertaking was on such a modest scale and why the references were not far more specific. There is probably no answer to these questions, and perhaps the most appropriate verdict on either of the two positions taken above is the one known to Scottish law, 'Not proven.' The appearance of *An Apologeticall Narration* is still surrounded with a great deal of mystery.

On balance, however, I feel that the problems raised by regarding *Reformation of Church-Government in Scotland Cleered* as a reaction to *An Apologeticall Narration* are particularly difficult to resolve. The tone of the Scottish pamphlet is in complete contrast to the known sentiments of the Scottish Commissioners, and seems to have been designed more to defuse criticisms and mollify apprehensions from whatever quarter – including that of the Independents – than to present a specific rebuttal of the Independent apologia. At some points the pamphlet certainly hits upon views and expressions used in *An Apologeticall Narration*, but that may not be so remarkable when we reflect that these ideas were being widely canvassed in sermons and lectures, and that some of them had already appeared in the Assembly's debates.

But perhaps the most telling reason against accepting the Scots pamphlet as a direct reaction to the Independent publication is that its promise of limited toleration at the end is completely at variance with the fixed determination of the Scots against toleration after *An Apologeticall Narration* appeared. *Reformation of Church-Government in Scotland Cleered* therefore gives the impression that the writers were still more concerned with quietening the fears of their critics, and winning support for their own ecclesiology, than with issuing a vigorous rebuttal of the Independent pamphlet.

Subject Index

Accommodation (Cf. also Assembly: Committees of Accommodation) 50, 124, 257, 280, 302, 303 & n, 306, 334, 340f.n, 372f, 393, 403n, 420, 430f, 434 & n, 435, 444ff, 449f, 451, 452, 453f, 467, 471, 477, 480, 487n, 488, 490, 568, 569.
proposals for: 446-56.
The Papers and Answers . . . for Accommodation (cf. *The Grand Debate*) 488n.

Adamists 176.

Admonitions Controversy 27, 141.

Anabaptists/Anabaptism (cf. also Baptists) 8n, 54, 87, 123n, 149, 150, 151, 155, 180, 319, 351, 378, 394nn, 397, 398 & n, 454, 477 & n, 505n, 577.

An Apologeticall Narration 124 & n, 125, 153, 165n, 193, 206-9 & nn, 220f & nn, 228-31 & nn, 262, 292, 302n, 376, 377, 379, 381, 387, 439-41, 568, 569, 574, 575-81 & nn.

Anglicanism (cf. also Episcopacy) 5, 7, 19.

'Answers' of the Assembly (cf. *The Grand Debate Concerning Presbitery and Independency*) 430 & n, 467, 471 & n, 475f, 484-87 & n, 520.

Antinomians/Antinominanism 47, 50, 82-4, 123n, 126f & n, 135, 143, 176-82, 210f & n, 319 & n, 346n, 351, 378, 397f & n, 411, 526, 527.

Apocalyptic (cf. Eschatology)

Apologists 113, 124, 127n, 454, 489, 578n, 579n, 580f.

'Apostles' 102n, 106f, 140, 146-54, 199-206, 209f, 211, 214n, 280ff, 288, 289f, 290, 291n, 292n, 293n, 294ff & nn, 296-99, 304, 307f, 310, 348, 350, 355, 415, 522n, 529.

Apostolic Succession 20, 205f, 210, 213f & n, 295n, 324.

Armada 42.

Arminians/Arminianism 48n, 82f, 215n, 576, 579.

Army of the Eastern Association 196ff, 251n, 279fn, 382-87, 404ff, 408, 457.

Assembly of Divines ix, 1-9, 23, 30, 31, 38, 44f, 49, 50, 62, 63, 64, 72-100, 111, 114, 115, 127, 130, 131, 135-581 *passim*.
its Call: 4, 30, 52-72, 78f.
control by Parliament: 62, 69f, 76, 100, 108, 131f, 395f, 492-511, 513.
biblical base (cf. Sol. League and Covenant): 75, 109, 509.
Calvinism: 79f, 82, 105, 140, 176, 182.
rules: 70f, 75f, 269, 521n.
procedures (cf. Committee Structures): 78ff. 138f.
urgency and procrastination: 74, 190, 193, 211-13, 217, 219f, 231, 232ff, 250 & n, 272f, 275n, 279f & n, 306f, 326, 335f, 400 & n, 426n, 512n.
interruptions (cf. also Fasts, and 'piety and worship' below): 100, 175-94, 212 & n, 214 & n, 234f, 238f, 306f, 328, 343n, 358, 371fn, 401 & n, 402-4 & nn, 406fn, 409, 414, 442n, 475-87.
recess: 191, 375.
piety and worship (cf Fasts/Thanksgivings): 77 & n, 99 & n, 135n.
participants: 546-56 (Appendix I.)
description of: 557-59 (Appendix II.)
significance and assessment of: 1-5, 522-45.
'Answers' to Independents' 'Reasons': 426n, 427f, 437, 467, 471 & n, 484f & n, 520.

'Elders'/Eldership 102, 140, 158,
163-74, 221f, 230, 254ff, 258, 260,
264n, 272, 278n, 288f, 293-96,
297n, 300, 305-308, 324, 332f, 337,
339, 342ff, 348, 415, 447n, 448n,
476, 500, 580.
Preaching & Teaching Elders
(cf. Pastors, Doctors) 103,
168-9n, 211, 214n, 215,
217 & n, 282, 285f & n, 291,
297, 310, 323, 332, 344.
Elizabethan Settlement 19 & n,
20f & nn, 26f, 34ff, 51, 57n.
England/English People & Society 3f,
17, 19, 23-32, 109f, 129, 131, 279,
352, 361, 380, 385f, 442ff, 461,
468, 478f, 493f, 511n, 517, 523,
526, 529, 532f, 534-37, 539, 571.
English conservatism: 14f, 34f,
41ff, 43n, 45f, 77n, 93, 329, 374,
377, 380, 391, 393, 396f, 438,
511n, 520, 536, 539, 571,
572 & n.
relationship to Scotland: 32-40,
40-43, 96, 173, 189, 442ff, 520,
532f, 536f & n.
English Ecclesiastical Tradition
(cf. Puritan Majority) 30, 93.
attitudes to ecclesiology: 110, 114,
117f, 535n, 566.
desire for a national establishment:
cf. Church.
defence of clerical privilege: 261,
265, 298f, 304, 347, 470, 534,
535.
ministers and ordination: 244n.
sine titulo ordination: 316-19, 322n,
323f & n.
significance of English
ecclesiastical traditions: 323f,
344f & n, 373f.
Cf. also Christmas.
sensitivity re episcopal ordination:
397f, 531 & n, 531-33, 535.
residual episcopacy: 30, 90-94,
102, 105-10.
preference for moderate
episcopacy: 90f, 105, 110, 119,
124.
Episcopacy/Episcopalians 8f, 17f, 28,
30, 48n, 56, 78, 79, 85, 86, 101,
102, 105 & n, 106f, 114, 117, 124,

223n, 284, 396, 443, 462ff & nn,
537, 540.
Episcopal Ecclesiology 20-23, 42f,
43f, 46, 67n, 102, 105, 322-25,
397f.
as prelacy: 3, 7f, 28, 36ff, 67-74,
90-94, 100, 113, 115, 121n, 131,
226f, 275n, 380n, 396f, 443, 462,
463 & n, 464 & n, 535ff, 540,
567, 572, 578ff.
diocesan episcopacy: 53, 90, 106,
107, 131, 169, 320f, 378, 535ff.
puritan episcopacy: 29n, 64, 70n,
90-94, 104, 105-110, 111f, 114,
118, 141, 323f, 397.
primitive (N.T.) episcopé: 30,
90n, 91, 106 & n-110, 114f,
136-37n, 202, 215, 266f, 281 &
n, 535.
corporate episcopé: 59, 90f, 345,
564.
parochial episcopé: 107, 110, 215,
345, 356-7, 415f, 535 & n.
Episcopate (cf. Bishops.)
Erastians/Erastianism 9, 19n, 30, 57,
70, 75, 102, 119, 127-132, 138f,
173, 218n, 220n, 223, 269, 271,
359, 396 & n, 399n, 403, 406, 421n,
423f, 469, 470, 473, 492-515, 516,
532n.
scepticism re scriptural rule: 137,
396, 399n, 473, 510f.
Eschatology 24 & n, 29 & n, 183n,
393f & n.
'Et Caetera Oath' 52f, 106.
'Evangelist' 102n, 106f, 140, 204,
205f & n, 211, 214n, 294, 295 & n,
318, 323f & n, 355.
Excommunication (cf. 'the Keys',
Discipline, etc.) 103, 129, 139,
171, 210, 230, 237, 256n, 258, 260
& n, 265, 269, 271, 301, 308, 311,
359, 363, 377-78n, 379, 393, 399 &
n, 401, 403, 412, 413, 421-25,
429-36, 437f, 451n, 453n, 470, 471
& n, 579.
Delivery to Satan: 301.
Directory for Excommunication:
433f.
'Extraordinary offices'
(apostles, prophets, evangelists)
102n, 106, 214f, 295n.

Index of Names

Names italicized are those of modern writers mentioned or discussed.
* indicates a participant in the Assembly.
[*] indicates members or Commissioners who did not attend.
Letters in square brackets indicate alternative forms in which the names appear.